NATURAL RIGHTS LIBERALISM FROM LOCKE TO NOZICK

Edited by

**Ellen Frankel Paul, Fred D. Miller, Jr.,
and Jeffrey Paul**

CAMBRIDGE
UNIVERSITY PRESS

PUBLISHED BY THE PRESS SYNDICATE OF THE UNIVERSITY OF CAMBRIDGE
The Pitt Building, Trumpington Street, Cambridge, United Kingdom

CAMBRIDGE UNIVERSITY PRESS
The Edinburgh Building, Cambridge CB2 2RU, UK
40 West 20th Street, New York, NY 10011-4211, USA
477 Williamstown Road, Port Melbourne, VIC 3207, Australia
Ruiz de Alarcón 13, 28014 Madrid, Spain
Dock House, The Waterfront, Cape Town 8001, South Africa

http://www.cambridge.org

First published 2005

Printed in the United States of America

Typeface Palacio 10/12 pt.

A catalog record for this book is available from the British Library

Library of Congress Cataloging-in-Publication Data
Natural rights liberalism from Locke to Nozick / edited by Ellen Frankel Paul,
Fred D. Miller, Jr., and Jeffrey Paul.   p.   cm.
Includes bibliographical references and index.
ISBN 0-521-61514-3
1. Human rights–Philosophy.   2. Liberalism–Philosophy.   3. Natural law.
I. Paul, Ellen Frankel.   II. Miller, Fred Dycus, 1944-   III. Paul, Jeffrey.
JC571.N3327   2005
323'.01–dc22   2004056934
CIP

The essays in this book have also been published,
without introduction and index, in the semiannual journal
Social Philosophy & Policy, Volume 22, Number 1,
which is available by subscription.

CONTENTS

INTRODUCTION

Natural rights theory holds that individuals have certain rights—such as the rights to life, liberty, and property—in virtue of their human nature rather than on account of prevailing laws or conventions. The idea of natural rights reaches far back in the history of philosophy and legal thought. Arguably, it was already recognized in nascent form by ancient Greek thinkers such as Aristotle in the fourth century b.c., who argued that citizens who are equal by nature have the same natural right (that is, just claim) to political office (*Politics* III.16.1287a8–14). During the Middle Ages the concept of natural rights began to emerge in a more recognizably modern form. Medieval canon lawyers, philosophers, and theologians entered into heated debate over the status of individual property rights, with some contending that the right to property was natural and others that it was merely conventional.

In the early modern era, theories of natural rights were advanced by seminal thinkers, including Hugo Grotius, Thomas Hobbes, and Samuel Pufendorf. The most influential of these was the English philosopher John Locke, especially in his *Second Treatise of Government* published in the late seventeenth century. Locke contended that prior to the political state there had existed a state of nature, in which human beings possessed rights to "life, liberty, and estate." "The *State of Nature* has a Law of Nature to govern it," he wrote, "which obliges every one: And Reason, which is that Law, teaches all Mankind, who will but consult it, that being all equal and independent, no one ought to harm another in his Life, Health, Liberty, or Possessions."[1] Locke argued that every human being has a natural right to self-ownership: "every Man has a *Property* in his own *Person*. This no Body has any Right to but himself. The *Labour* of his Body, and the *Work* of his Hands, we may say, are properly his."[2] By extension individuals also have a right to acquire and possess private property: "Whatsoever then he removes out of the State that Nature hath provided, and left it in, he hath mixed his *Labour* with, and joyned to it something that is his own, and thereby makes it his *Property*."[3] Individuals may leave the state of nature to form governments, according to Locke, in order to preserve their rights, but the positive laws of political society "are only so far right as they are founded on the Law of Nature,

---

[1] John Locke, *Two Treatises of Government*, ed. Peter Laslett, rev. ed. (New York: Cambridge University Press, 1963), 311.
[2] Ibid., 328–29.
[3] Ibid., 329.

by which they are to be regulated and interpreted."[4] A ruler who flouts the law of nature and the natural rights of his subjects may be removed.

The revolutionary implications of natural rights liberalism are evident in the American Declaration of Independence of 1776: "We hold these truths to be self-evident, that all men are created equal, that they are endowed by their Creator with certain unalienable Rights, that among these are Life, Liberty and the pursuit of Happiness.—That to secure these rights, Governments are instituted among Men, deriving their just powers from the consent of the governed,—That whenever any Form of Government becomes destructive of these ends, it is the Right of the People to alter or to abolish it, and to institute new Government. . . ."

During the nineteenth century, natural rights liberalism was eclipsed by the rise of utilitarianism, having suffered nearly mortal wounds at the hands of David Hume and Jeremy Bentham in the latter half of the eighteenth century. Hume disparaged previous attempts by Locke to demonstrate the existence of natural rights, while Bentham's remark in "Anarchical Fallacies," his critique of the French Declaration of Rights of 1789, that natural rights were "nonsense upon stilts" mocked natural rights liberalism. As the nineteenth century unfolded, more blistering attacks would follow, rendering natural rights liberalism intellectually passé. Similar mockery occurred at the turn of the twentieth century in the United States with the rise of Progressivism, and had a similar effect.

It took the publication in 1974 of a shrewd and cleverly argued book, *Anarchy, State, and Utopia*, by Harvard philosopher Robert Nozick to rekindle interest in natural rights liberalism and make it an acceptable subject for intellectual discourse. The book begins with a ringing declaration: "Individuals have rights, and there are things no person or group may do to them (without violating their rights)." The political implications of this simple declaration were stunning to the modern ear. In contrast to collectivist theories that had dominated twentieth-century political discourse, Nozick declared that "a minimal state, limited to the narrow functions of protection against force, theft, fraud, enforcement of contracts, and so on, is justified; that any more extensive state will violate persons' rights not to be forced to do certain things, and is unjustified; and that the minimal state is inspiring as well as right."

Anarchy, State, and Utopia breeched the obscurity of academic publishing and became something of a cause célèbre. In the *New York Review of Books*, Peter Singer described Nozick's book as "a major event in contemporary political philosophy." It was widely discussed in the mainstream press and received the prestigious National Book Award. In Great Britain, it was anointed by the *Times Literary Supplement* as one of "The Hundred Most Influential Books Since the (Second World) War." A flood of reviews and journal articles ensued, some sympathetic, most critical.

---

[4] Ibid., 316.

Anarchy, State, and Utopia, Nozick's first book, remains his best known and most widely regarded. In the years that followed, he published widely, but with the exception of a handful of pages, never again in political philosophy. *Philosophical Explanations* (1981), *The Examined Life* (1989), *The Nature of Rationality* (1995), *Socratic Puzzles* (1997), and *Invariances* (2001) all received scholarly attention, but none achieved the breakout success of *Anarchy, State, and Utopia*.

Nozick once whimsically wrote, "I did not want to spend the rest of my life writing 'The Son of Anarchy, State, and Utopia,' 'The Return of the Son of. . . .' " [5] Nonetheless, *Anarchy, State, and Utopia* is undoubtedly his best known and most influential work and will likely remain the principal achievement for which he is remembered by future generations of philosophers.

This collection is dedicated to the memory of Robert Nozick, who died in 2002 at the age of sixty-three. Born in 1938, he received his undergraduate degree from Columbia University and his Ph.D. from Princeton, and at the remarkably young age of thirty he was appointed full professor of philosophy at Harvard University. Nozick was a charter member of the editorial board of *Social Philosophy & Policy*, and his sage guidance and friendship are sorely missed. It is, then, with great pleasure, tinged with sadness, that we publish these essays in his honor. Academics honor the best among them by subjecting their views to relentless criticism, and using their arguments as a springboard for creativity. Some of our contributors examine Robert Nozick's political philosophy in this spirit, offering a diverse set of critiques that Nozick himself would have thoroughly enjoyed. Other contributors examine earlier figures in the liberal tradition, including Locke and the American founders. The remaining authors analyze natural rights liberalism's central doctrines.

The first two essays in this collection examine the natural rights tradition of the American founders and the provenance of this tradition in the political philosophy of John Locke. In his essay, "The Political Needs of a Toolmaking Animal: Madison, Hamilton, Locke, and the Question of Property," Paul A. Rahe writes that when Benjamin Franklin suggested that man is by nature a toolmaking animal, he summed up what was for his fellow Americans the common sense of the matter. It is not surprising, then, that when Britain's colonists broke with the mother country over the issue of an unrepresentative parliament's right to tax and govern the colonies, Americans defended their right to the property they owned on the ground that it was, in a most thoroughgoing sense, an extension of themselves—the fruits of their own labor. This understanding came from Locke, who based the argument of his *Two Treatises of Government* (1689) on the unorthodox account of providence and of man's place in the natural world that Sir Francis Bacon had first articulated. All of this helps to

---

[5] Robert Nozick, *Socratic Puzzles* (Cambridge, MA: Harvard University Press, 1997), 2.

explain why the framers of the United States Constitution included within it a clause giving sanction to property in ideas of practical use, that is, to patents for inventions and copyright for authors.

The Lockean tradition of political philosophy, of which Nozick is the most prominent contemporary exponent, resonates deeply within the American political culture, writes Michael Zuckert in his essay "Natural Rights and Imperial Constitutionalism: The American Revolution and the Development of the American Amalgam." Zuckert explores the formative moments of the American political culture and, at the same time, attempts to clarify the role of Lockean philosophy in the American Revolution. One of the currently dominant approaches to the revolution emphasizes the colonists' commitment to their rights, but identifies the relevant rights as "the rights of Englishmen," not natural rights in the Lockean mode. However, this approach misses the way the Americans construed their positive or constitutional rights in the light of a Lockean background theory. In actuality, the Americans created an amalgam of traditional constitutional principles and Lockean philosophy, an amalgam that nearly guaranteed that they and the British would speak past each other. The ambiguities and uncertainties of the British constitution as extended to the colonies provided an incentive to the Americans (but not the British) to look to Locke as a guide to their rights, thereby placing Lockean theory at the heart of American political thinking for generations.

The next three essays in this volume focus on the connection between Locke and Nozick. Critics of Robert Nozick's libertarian political theory often allege that the theory in general and its account of property rights in particular lack sufficient foundations. Edward Feser's "There Is No Such Thing as an Unjust Initial Acquisition" takes them to task. A key difficulty is thought to lie in Nozick's account of how portions of the world that no one yet owns can justly come to be initially acquired. But the difficulty is illusory, because (contrary to what both Nozick and his critics assume) the concept of justice does not meaningfully apply to initial acquisition at all. Moreover, the principle of self-ownership provides a solid foundation for Nozick's libertarianism, and when seen in the light of this principle and its full implications, the standard examples of purported injustice in acquisition are revealed to be nothing of the kind.

In "Nozick and Locke: Filling the Space of Rights," Jeremy Waldron addresses the question: Do property entitlements define the moral environment in which rights to well-being are defined, or do rights to well-being define the moral environment in which property entitlements are defined? Nozick argued for the former alternative, and he denied that any serious attempt had been made to state the latter case, which he called the "reverse" theory. Waldron argues that in actuality Locke's approach to property can be seen as an instance of the "reverse" theory, and that Nozick's can, too, inasmuch as it shares a number of features with the Lockean approach. Waldron notes, however, that his essay is not intended as a criticism of Nozick. On the contrary, Waldron acknowledges the integrity and the importance of Nozick's insistence that welfare, property, and justice be integrated into a single theory with clearly established priorities.

In his essay "Toward a Theory of Empirical Natural Rights," John Hasnas remarks that since Lockean and Nozickian arguments for limited government are grounded on the individual's possession of natural rights to life, liberty, and property, their arguments can be no more persuasive than the underlying arguments for the existence of natural rights. The problem is that such arguments are notoriously weak. Hasnas offers an alternative conception of natural rights: "empirical natural rights" that are not beset by the objections that are typically raised against traditional natural rights. Hasnas's empirical natural rights are rights that *evolve* in the state of nature rather than rights that individuals are antecedently *endowed with*. He argues that empirical natural rights are true natural rights, that is, pre-political rights with natural grounds that can be possessed in the state of nature, and, when taken together, form a close approximation to the Lockean rights to life, liberty, and property. Furthermore, empirical natural rights are normatively well grounded because respecting them is conducive to social peace, which possesses instrumental moral value regardless of one's conception of inherent value. Hasnas conceives of empirical natural rights as *solved problems*, and he contends that these rights are an attractive alternative and a potentially more secure footing for limited government than the natural rights of Locke and Nozick.

The next three essays discuss Nozick in combination with other prominent American political theorists of the twentieth century. In "History and Pattern," David Schmidtz compares Nozick on justice to his Harvard colleague, John Rawls. In *Anarchy, State, and Utopia*, Nozick argues that patterned principles of justice are false, and he offers a historical alternative. Along the way, Nozick accepts Rawls's claim, which Rawls had put forward in *A Theory of Justice* (1971), that the natural distribution of talent is morally arbitrary, but Nozick denies that there is any short step from this premise to the conclusion that the natural distribution is unjust. Nozick also agrees with Rawls on the core idea of natural rights liberalism; namely, that we are separate persons. However, Rawls and Nozick interpret this idea in different ways—momentously different ways. The tension between their interpretations is among the forces shaping political philosophy to this day.

In "Libertarianism at Twin Harvard," Loren E. Lomasky wryly proposes that the views of Rawls and Nozick might not be as radically divergent as is conventionally supposed. To demonstrate this proposition, Lomasky invents "Twin Harvard" counterparts of Rawls and Nozick. The twist is that Twin Rawls turns out to be a leading libertarian theorist while Twin Nozick endorses a regime of sweeping redistribution. In each case the position follows from familiar elements in the theories of their respective, real-world counterparts. Lomasky concludes that Twin Rawls actually makes better use of familiar Rawlsian themes—such as the veil of ignorance, strains of commitment, and the priority of liberty—than does Rawls himself. Moreover, Rawls's own attempts at combating libertarianism are seen to be weak, sometimes embarrassingly so. Libertarianism is a specter that he devoutly wishes to exorcise, but cannot. Conversely, the rejection of libertarianism by Twin Nozick (and Nozick?) is striking but shallow.

John Patrick Diggins, in his essay "Sidney Hook, Robert Nozick, and the Paradoxes of Freedom," observes that, while Nozick and Hook shared a passion for freedom and for understanding liberty in all its complexities, the two philosophers, one a libertarian and the other a democratic socialist, occupied different worlds when it came to how they viewed property and power. Nozick believed that freedom and justice depended upon a minimal state that would be severely restricted in its exercise of power. Sidney Hook never renounced his conviction, born of his early attraction to Marxism, that truly dangerous power is wielded not principally by government but by private individuals of great material wealth: by industrialists. Diggins examines the divergent views of these two seminal thinkers on such issues as human rights, private property, democracy, and judicial review. Their differences are profound, yet they shared a common interest in the life of the mind and in exploring such hoary philosophical topics as free will versus determinism and the grounding of moral values.

The remaining six essays in this volume offer lively critiques of various aspects of Nozick's political philosophy and of libertarianism. In "Begging the Question with Style: *Anarchy, State, and Utopia* at Thirty Years," Barbara H. Fried writes that Nozick's book has achieved the status of a classic. Not only is it the central text for all contemporary academic discussions of libertarianism, but together with Rawls's *A Theory of Justice*, it also arguably framed the landscape of academic political philosophy in the last third of the twentieth century. Many factors account for the enduring influence of Nozick's book. Fried considers one factor that has received relatively slight attention: Nozick's use of rhetoric to charm and disarm his readers. His clever rhetoric simultaneously established his credibility with readers, turned them on his ideological opponents, and helped his arguments over some of their serious substantive difficulties.

In chapter four of *Anarchy, State, and Utopia*, observes Richard J. Arneson, Nozick raises intriguing questions about whether or not it is ever morally acceptable to act against what are agreed to be an individual's natural moral rights. The examination of these questions opens up issues concerning the specific content of these individual rights, issues that Arneson addresses in his essay "The Shape of Lockean Rights: Fairness, Pareto, Moderation, and Consent." Arneson explores Nozick's questions by posing a number of thought experiments and using considered responses to them in order to specify the shape of individual rights. Arneson provisionally concludes that a conception of individual moral rights quite different from Nozick's is attractive, and suggests that this alternative conception merits further development.

In *Anarchy, State, and Utopia*, Nozick seeks to demonstrate that principles of justice in acquisition and transfer can be applied to justify the minimal state, and no state greater than the minimal state. This approach, argues Richard A. Epstein in his essay "One Step Beyond Nozick's Minimal State: The Role of Forced Exchanges in Political Theory," fails to acknowledge the critical role that *forced exchanges* play in overcoming a range of public-goods and coordination problems. These problems can be overcome by taking property and compensating the owners in cash or in kind in an amount that leaves them better off (by their own lights) than before the transaction. Forced exchanges use coercion to form the state, Epstein explains, but the just compensation requirement guards against state-imposed redistribution for collateral purposes. Once forced exchanges are allowed to form a state, they may be used by the state thereafter to justify the powers of taxation and eminent domain, which can be legitimately used to support infrastructure (e.g., roads, sewers, and public utilities) that neither the minimal state nor private markets can supply.

In his essay "Natural Rights and Political Legitimacy," Christopher W. Morris explores the relationship between natural rights and the legitimacy, or lack thereof, of the state. While Nozick's theory allows for a minimal state without the express consent of the governed, Morris finds the absence of consent, on a natural rights foundation, problematic. If we have a natural right to liberty, he writes, it is hard to see how a state could be legitimate without first obtaining the (genuine) consent of the governed. In considering the threat that natural rights pose to state legitimacy, he distinguishes minimal from full legitimacy and explores different understandings of the nature of our natural rights. Even though he concludes that natural rights do threaten the full legitimacy of states, he suggests that understanding our natural right to liberty to be grounded in our interest might not commit us to requiring consent for minimal legitimacy. Thus, even if natural rights effectively block the full legitimacy of states—on the assumption that rarely, if ever, will the requisite consent be forthcoming—they may allow minimal state legitimacy.

In "Consent Theory for Libertarians," A. John Simmons, like Morris, is concerned with the legitimacy of the state in natural rights theories. Simmons contends that libertarian political philosophers, including Nozick, have erred in neglecting the problem of political obligation and that they ought to embrace an actual consent theory of political obligation and state legitimacy. If libertarians followed this recommendation, their position on the subject would be not only internally consistent but correct. Simmons identifies the tension that exists in libertarian thought (and especially in Nozick's) between its minimalist and its consensualist strains, and argues that, on libertarianism's own terms, the consensualist strain ought to prevail. He then describes the form of the consent theory that he recommends to libertarians. The essay concludes with an extended defense of his preferred form of consent theory against contemporary liberal-egalitarian critiques of it (both explicit and implicit), including those of Ronald Dworkin, John Rawls, and their followers.

In "Prerogatives, Restrictions, and Rights," Eric Mack offers a defense of the moral side constraints to which Nozick appeals in *Anarchy, State, and Utopia,* but for which Mack believes Nozick fails to provide a sustained justification. Mack identifies a line of anticonsequentialist argumentation that is present in Nozick's work and that, in the terminology of Samuel Scheffler, moves, first, to affirm a personal *prerogative* that allows the individual not to sacrifice himself for the sake of the best overall outcome and, then, affirms *restrictions* (i.e., moral side constraints) that prohibit the individual from suppressing others' exercise of *their* personal prerogatives, even if such suppression would serve the overall good. Mack argues that one ought to follow this line of anticonsequentialist argumentation all the way to the affirmation of restrictions by showing that the rationale for the adoption of the personal prerogative is not satisfied unless the accompanying restrictions are adopted as well.

As the essays in this volume remind us, Robert Nozick came to the views articulated in *Anarchy, State, and Utopia* through a process of critical inquiry and reflection. What better way to honor Nozick than by continuing to reflect on the novel and controversial arguments that he framed three decades ago, and that resonate to this day not only among political philosophers, but also in the larger arena of public life.

ACKNOWLEDGMENTS

The editors gratefully acknowledge the generous support of the Pierre F. and Enid Goodrich Foundation, which made possible this special volume in honor of Robert Nozick.

We also wish to recognize several individuals at the Social Philosophy and Policy Center, Bowling Green State University, for their diligent assistance in the preparation of this volume. They include Mary Dilsaver, Terrie Weaver, and Assistant Director Travis Cook.

We thank Assistant Managing Editor Tamara Sharp for her assiduous attention to the details of the production process, and Managing Editors Harry Dolan and Teresa Donovan for their painstaking editorial assistance.

CONTRIBUTORS

Paul A. Rahe is Jay P. Walker Professor of History at the University of Tulsa. He has published widely in scholarly journals and essay collections in the field of ancient, early modern, and American political thought, and is the author of *Republics Ancient and Modern: Classical Republicanism and the American Revolution* (1992). He is an editor of *Montesquieu's Science of Politics: Essays on the Spirit of the Laws* (with David W. Carrithers and Michael A. Mosher, 2001). He has been awarded research fellowships by the Center for Hellenic Study, Washington University's Center for the History of Freedom, the National Endowment for the Humanities, the Woodrow Wilson International Center for Scholars, and Clare Hall at Cambridge University, among others. He has served on and chaired the board of trustees of the Institute of Current World Affairs and is currently a member of the executive board of the Historical Society.

Michael Zuckert is Nancy Reeves Dreux Professor of Political Science at the University of Notre Dame. He is the author of numerous articles and books in early modern political philosophy and the American political tradition, including *Natural Rights and the New Republicanism* (1994), *The Natural Rights Republic* (1996), and *Launching Liberalism* (2002).

Edward Feser is Visiting Assistant Professor of Philosophy at Loyola Marymount University in Los Angeles. He is the author of numerous articles in political philosophy, philosophy of mind, and philosophy of religion, and in 2002 was a visiting scholar at the Social Philosophy and Policy Center, Bowling Green State University. He is the author of *On Nozick* (2003) and *Philosophy of Mind: An Introduction* (forthcoming).

Jeremy Waldron is Maurice and Hilda Friedman Professor of Law and Director of the Center for Law and Philosophy at Columbia University in New York. He is the author of more than one hundred articles on the history of political thought, legal philosophy, and theory of politics (including articles on rights, justice, property, culture, constitutionalism, and toleration). He is the author of *The Right to Private Property* (1988), *Law and Disagreement* (1999), and *God, Locke, and Equality: Christian Foundations in John Locke's Political Thought* (2002). He has lectured throughout the world and is a member of the American Academy of Arts and Sciences.

John Hasnas is Associate Professor of Law at George Mason University. He has been a visiting professor at the Washington College of Law at American University as well as a visiting scholar at the Kennedy Institute of Ethics in Washington, DC, and the Social Philosophy and Policy Center, Bowling Green State University. His research concerns jurisprudence and political philosophy, and he has published widely in both law reviews and philosophy journals on topics such as rights theory, antidiscrimination law, criminal jurisprudence, legal indeterminacy, political obligation, and corporate ethics. He presents a theory of nonpolitical, legal regulation of human interaction in a new book, *Common Law Liberalism* (forthcoming).

David Schmidtz is Professor of Philosophy and joint Professor of Economics at the University of Arizona. He is the author of *Rational Choice and Moral Agency* (1995) and *Social Welfare and Individual Responsibility* (with Robert E. Goodin, 1998). He is the editor of *Robert Nozick* (2002) and *Environmental Ethics: What Really Matters, What Really Works* (with Elizabeth Willott, 2002). His articles have appeared in the *Journal of Philosophy*, *Ethics*, and *Political Theory*, and his current projects include two books, presently titled *The Purpose of Moral Theory* (forthcoming) and *Elements of Justice* (forthcoming).

Loren E. Lomasky is Professor of Philosophy and Chair of the Philosophy, Politics, and Law program at the University of Virginia. He has published numerous articles in moral and political philosophy, and is the author of *Persons, Rights, and the Moral Community* (1987) and *Democracy and Decision: The Pure Theory of Electoral Preference* (with Geoffrey Brennan, 1993). He has also held research appointments sponsored by the National Endowment for the Humanities, the Center for the Study of Public Choice, the Australian National University, and the Social Philosophy and Policy Center, Bowling Green State University.

John Patrick Diggins is Distinguished Professor of History at the Graduate Center, the City University of New York. He is the editor of *The Liberal Persuasion: Arthur Schlesinger, Jr., and the Challenge of the American Past* (1997); and he is the author of *Max Weber: Politics and the Spirit of Tragedy* (1996); *On Hallowed Ground: Abraham Lincoln and the Foundations of American History* (2000); *John Adams* (2003); and *O'Neill's America: The Playwright as Historian* (forthcoming).

Barbara H. Fried is William W. and Gertrude H. Saunders Professor of Law at Stanford Law School. She has written extensively in tax policy, property theory, and political theory, and is the author of *The Progressive Assault on Laissez Faire: Robert Hale and the First Law and Economics Movement* (1998).

Richard J. Arneson is Professor of Philosophy at the University of California at San Diego, where he has taught since 1973 and served as department chair from 1992 to 1996. He has published numerous essays on moral and political theory, with emphasis on the theory of justice. Some of his recent work defends act consequentialism, and some of it explores moderate versions of deontology or right-based views. He is currently writing on traditional ethical doctrines of just war and warfare.

Richard A. Epstein is James Parker Hall Distinguished Service Professor of Law at the University of Chicago and Peter and Kirsten Bedford Senior Fellow at the Hoover Institution. He is a member of the American Academy of Arts and Sciences, a Senior Fellow of the Center for Clinical Medical Ethics at the University of Chicago Medical School, and a director of the John M. Olin Program in Law and Economics, University of Chicago. He has served as editor of the *Journal of Legal Studies* and the *Journal of Law and Economics*. He is the author of numerous books including *Takings: Private Property and the Power of Eminent Domain* (1985); *Bargaining with the State* (1993); *Moral Peril: Our Inalienable Right to Health Care?* (1997); *Torts* (1999); *Skepticism and Freedom: A Modern Case for Classical Liberalism* (2003); and *Cases and Materials on Torts* (2004).

Christopher W. Morris is Professor of Philosophy at the University of Maryland, College Park. He is the author of *An Essay on the Modern State* (1998), and the editor of *Violence, Terrorism, and Justice* (with R. G. Frey, 1991) and *Practical Rationality and Preference: Essays for David Gauthier* (with Arthur Ripstein, 2001).

A. John Simmons is Commonwealth Professor of Philosophy and Professor of Law at the University of Virginia. He has been an editor of *Philosophy and Public Affairs* since 1982 and has edited *International Ethics* (1985) and *Punishment* (1995). He is the author of *Moral Principles and Political Obligations* (1979); *The Lockean Theory of Rights* (1992); *On the Edge of Anarchy: Locke, Consent, and the Limits of Society* (1993); and *Justification and Legitimacy: Essays on Rights and Obligations* (2000). He has published more than four dozen essays in scholarly journals, and his current work includes a text in political philosophy (forthcoming); a *For & Against* volume (with Kit Wellman, forthcoming) on the duty to obey the law; and articles on early modern theories of the state and states' territorial claims.

Eric Mack is Professor of Philosophy at Tulane University, where he is also a faculty member of the Murphy Institute of Political Economy. He has published numerous articles in moral, political, and legal philosophy. His recent publications include "The State of Nature Has a Law of Nature to Govern It," in *Individual Rights Reconsidered* (2001); "Self-Ownership, Taxation, and Democracy: A Philosophical-Constitutional Perspective," in *Politics, Taxation, and the Rule of Law* (2002); "Self-Ownership, Marxism, and Equality," in *Politics, Philosophy, and Economics* (2002); and "Libertarianism and Classical Liberalism" (with Gerald Gaus), in *Handbook of Political Theory* (2004).

THE POLITICAL NEEDS OF A TOOLMAKING ANIMAL: MADISON, HAMILTON, LOCKE, AND THE QUESTION OF PROPERTY

By Paul A. Rahe

Aristotle's definition is really this—that man is by nature the citizen of a city (*Stadtbürger*). This definition is just as characteristic for classical antiquity as is Franklin's definition for Yankee civilization (*das Yankeetum*)—that man is by nature a maker of instruments.[1]

—Karl Marx

I. Introduction

Karl Marx was arguably right in contending that Aristotle's claim that "man is by nature a political animal" was an accurate reflection of the spirit of classical civilization.[2] Was he similarly correct in singling out, as the distinguishing feature of *das Yankeetum*, the notion that man is really first and foremost a fabricator of tools? To sort out this question, one must consider what the American founders had in mind when they spoke of the right to property. One must trace their understanding to its roots, and one must ponder its consequences.

Property rights are the appropriate starting point because within the political ruminations of those whom our French cousins persist in calling *les Anglo-Saxons* property has long loomed large. "Abstract liberty," Edmund Burke observed, "like other mere abstractions, is not to be found."[3]

Liberty inheres in some sensible object; and every nation has formed to itself some favorite point, which by way of eminence becomes the criterion of their happiness. It happened . . . that the great contests for freedom in this country were from the earliest times chiefly upon the

---

[1] See Karl Marx, *Das Kapital: Kritik der politischen Ökonomie* (Frankfurt: Ullstein, 1969–71), 1:289 n. 13. Unless otherwise indicated, all translations are my own.

[2] Note Aristotle, *Politica*, ed. W. D. Ross (Oxford: Clarendon Press, 1957), 1252b27–1253a39; see also Paul A. Rahe, "The Primacy of Politics in Classical Greece," *The American Historical Review* 89, no. 2 (1984): 265–93; and Paul A. Rahe, *Republics Ancient and Modern: Classical Republicanism and the American Revolution* (Chapel Hill: University of North Carolina Press, 1992), 28–229.

[3] Edmund Burke, Speech on Moving Resolutions for Conciliation with the Colonies, March 22, 1775, in *The Writings and Speeches of the Right Honourable Edmund Burke* (Boston, MA: Little, Brown, and Co., 1901), 2:120.

1

question of taxing. Most of the contests in the ancient common-wealths turned primarily on the right of election of magistrates, or on the balance among the several orders of the state. The question of money was not with them so immediate. But in England it was otherwise.[4]

In England, as Burke claims, it was indeed otherwise, and it was so as well in England's colonies in North America. This, of course, was the point that Burke was attempting to bring home to his fellow members when he spoke these words on the floor of Parliament in March 1775, in a vain attempt to persuade his colleagues to seek a reconciliation with the American colonists whom they seemed so intent on driving into open rebellion.

Burke was, as always, perceptive in the extreme. The debates fore-shadowing and those occasioned by the American Revolution fully con-firm his claim. As early as 1764, for example, in what appears to have been the first highly influential pamphlet occasioned by the emerging colonial crisis, James Otis of Massachusetts anticipated the passage of the Stamp Act and the debate concerning the relationship between taxation and representation that it occasioned by sounding the very theme that Burke would subsequently identify as quintessentially English.[5] First, Otis pointed to "the great law of *self-preservation*" and identified "the *good* of mankind" as the "*end* of government." Then he argued that "above all things" government exists "to provide for the security, the quiet, and happy enjoyment of life, liberty, and property." Indeed, he contended, "there is no one act which a government can have a *right* to make that does not tend to the advancement of the security, tranquillity, and pros-perity of the people." "If life, liberty, and property could be enjoyed," he added, "in as great perfection in *solitude* as in *society* there would be no need of government."[6]

Samuel Adams was of a similar opinion. In February 1768, in a letter written on behalf of the Massachusetts House of Representatives, he traced the principle of representation to the fact that it "is acknowl-edged to be an unalterable law in nature that a man should have the free use and sole disposal of the fruit of his honest industry, subject to no controul."[7] New York's Alexander Hamilton agreed. In 1775, he blasted "the pretensions of parliament"—and not just on the grounds

---

[4] Ibid., 120–21.

[5] Parliament's attempt to tax the American colonists stirred up fierce opposition and effective resistance: see Edmund S. Morgan and Helen M. Morgan, *The Stamp Act Crisis: Prologue to Revolution* (Chapel Hill: University of North Carolina Press, 1953).

[6] James Otis, *The Rights of the British Colonies Asserted and Proved* (1764), in Bernard Bailyn, ed., *Pamphlets of the American Revolution, 1750–1776* (Cambridge, MA: Belknap Press of Harvard University Press, 1965–), 1:425–26.

[7] Samuel Adams, letter from the House of Representatives of Massachusetts to Henry Seymour Conway, February 13, 1768, in Harry Alonzo Cushing, ed., *The Writings of Samuel Adams* (New York: G. P. Putnam's Sons, 1904–8), 1:190–91.

that "they are subversive of our natural liberty, because an authority is assumed over us, which we by no means assent to." He placed even greater emphasis on the fact that such presumptions "divest us of that moral security, for our lives and properties, which we are intitled to, and which it is the primary end of society to bestow. For such security can never exist, while we have no part in making the laws, that are to bind us; and while it may be the interest of our uncontroled legislators to oppress us as much as possible."[8]

When George Mason drafted the Virginia Declaration of Rights in 1776, he gave vent to much the same opinion, claiming that "all men are by nature equally free and independent and have certain inherent rights, of which, when they enter into a state of society, they cannot by any compact, deprive or divest their posterity; namely, the enjoyment of life and liberty, with the means of acquiring and possessing property, and pursuing and obtaining happiness and safety."[9] John Adams echoed this opinion in the bill of rights that served as a preamble to the Massachusetts Constitution of 1780: "All men are born free and equal, and have certain natural, essential, and unalienable rights; among which may be reckoned the right of enjoying and defending their lives and liberties; that of acquiring, possessing, and protecting property; in fine, that of seeking and obtaining happiness."[10] Language to the same purpose was included in the bills of rights adopted in Pennsylvania, Vermont, and New Hampshire,[11] and articles in the constitutions of Maryland, North Carolina, and South Carolina reflect the same point of view.[12]

Language of a similar sort nearly made it into the United States Constitution. In 1789, when James Madison proposed a series of amendments to the recently ratified Constitution designed to placate all but the most irreconcilable of the Anti-Federalists, he at first included among the amendments a declaration, put forward by the ratifying conventions of Virginia and North Carolina and eventually supported by Rhode Island, to the effect that "government is instituted, and ought to be exercised for the benefit of the people; which consists in the enjoyment of life and liberty,

---

[8] Alexander Hamilton, *The Farmer Refuted, &c.*, February 23, 1775, in Harold C. Syrett, ed., *The Papers of Alexander Hamilton* (New York: Columbia University Press, 1961–79), 1:88.

[9] See Virginia (1776), in Francis Newton Thorpe, ed., *The Federal and State Constitutions, Colonial Charters, and Other Organic Laws of the States, Territories, and Colonies Now or Heretofore Forming the United States of America* (Washington, DC: Government Printing Office, 1909), 7:3813. For the various draft versions of this part of the declaration, see the Virginia Declaration of Rights, May 20–June 12, 1776, in Robert A. Rutland, ed., *The Papers of George Mason, 1725–1792* (Chapel Hill: University of North Carolina Press, 1970), 1:274–91, esp. 277, 283, and 287.

[10] See Massachusetts (1780), in Thorpe, ed., *The Federal and State Constitutions*, 3:1889.

[11] See Pennsylvania (1776, 1790), Vermont (1777, 1786, 1791), and New Hampshire (1784, 1792), in Thorpe, ed., *The Federal and State Constitutions*, 5:3082–83, 3099; 6:3739–41, 3751–53, 3762–63; 4:2453–54, 2457, 2471–72, 2474–75.

[12] See Maryland (1776), North Carolina (1776), and South Carolina (1790), in Thorpe, ed., *The Federal and State Constitutions*, 3:1688, 5:2788, 6:3264.

with the right of acquiring and using property, and generally of pursuing and obtaining happiness and safety."[13] Had this amendment been
approved by Congress and submitted to the states, it undoubtedly would
have been ratified, as was the Fifth Amendment, which, as a matter of
positive law, ruled out any person's being "deprived of life, liberty, or
property, without due process of law."[14] The adoption of the more abstract
claim regarding the fundamental purpose of the polity, however, would
not have altered in any way the substance of the governmental frame, for
its addition to the Constitution merely would have been a reassertion of
that instrument's spirit. In keeping with what was evidently then the
general opinion, in 1787 the delegates to the federal constitutional convention had shown a similar sensitivity to natural rights and the preservation of property.[15] Like the great majority of the leading figures in their
generation, they were aware that when human beings are deprived of
their right to the fruits of their labor, their liberties (both public and
private) and their lives are generally endangered as well.[16]

Prior to the framing of the Constitution, of course, there was the Declaration of Independence, drafted and signed in 1776. In it, Thomas Jefferson and the other members of the Continental Congress claimed on
their compatriots' behalf that "all men are created equal, that they are
endowed by their Creator with certain unalienable Rights, that among
these are Life, Liberty and the pursuit of Happiness," and that "to secure
these rights, Governments are instituted among Men, deriving their just

[13] Cf. proposed amendments to the Constitution, June 8, 1789, in William T. Hutchinson,
William M. E. Rachal, et al., eds., *The Papers of James Madison*, vol. 12, ed. Robert A. Rutland
et al. (Chicago, IL: University of Chicago Press, 1962–77; Charlottesville: University Press of
Virginia, 1977–), 196–211, esp. 200 and 203–4; with ratification by Rhode Island, May 29,
1790; Virginia Ratifying Convention, June 27, 1788; and North Carolina Ratifying Convention, August 1, 1788; in Jonathan Elliot, ed., *The Debates in the Several State Conventions*, 2d ed.
(Philadelphia, PA: J. B. Lippincott, 1896), 1:334, 3:657, 4:243. Note also James Madison, Notes
for a Speech in Congress, June 8, 1789, in Rutland et al., eds., *The Papers of James Madison*,
12:194. The amendment proposed by the three states reads as follows: "There are certain
natural rights of which men, when they form a social compact, cannot deprive or divest
their posterity; among which are the enjoyment of life and liberty, with the means of
acquiring, possessing, and protecting property, and pursuing and obtaining happiness and
safety."
[14] Edward Conrad Smith, ed., *The Constitution of the United States*, 11th ed. (New York:
Barnes and Noble Books, 1979), 49.
[15] Consider Max Farrand, ed., *The Records of the Federal Convention of 1787* (New Haven,
CT: Yale University Press, 1911–37), 1:147, 302, 402–3, 421–23, 428, 440, 469–70, 533–34,
541–42; 2:201–8 (June 6, 18, 25–27, and 29; July 5–6; and August 7, 1787), in light of Bernard
H. Siegan, "One People As to Commercial Objects," in Ellen Frankel Paul and Howard
Dickman, eds., *Liberty, Property, and the Foundations of the American Constitution* (Albany, NY:
State University of New York Press, 1989), 101–19. See also Marc F. Plattner, "American
Democracy and the Acquisitive Spirit," in Robert A. Goldwin and William A. Schambra,
eds., *How Capitalistic Is the Constitution?* (Washington, DC: American Enterprise Institute,
1982), 1–21.
[16] See Edward J. Erler, "The Great Fence to Liberty: The Right to Property in the American
Founding," in Paul and Dickman, eds., *Liberty, Property, and the Foundations of the American
Constitution*, 43–63.

powers from the consent of the governed" so that "whenever any Form of Government becomes destructive of these ends, it is the Right of the People to alter or to abolish it, and to institute a new Government, laying its foundation on such principles and organizing its powers in such form, as to them shall seem most likely to effect their Safety and Happiness."[17]

It has on occasion been suggested that, in substituting "the pursuit of happiness" for property, Jefferson intended to deny that property's acquisition and possession are among man's inalienable rights.[18] This is patently false. Some three years later, when revising Virginia's laws (as part of a committee appointed by the legislature of the commonwealth for that task), Jefferson took public note of the predilection of "wicked and dissolute men" for committing "violations on the lives, liberties and property of others," and then observed that what "principally induced men to enter into society" and what constitutes therefore government's "principal purpose" is their anxiety regarding "the secure enjoyment of these."[19] In adopting the Declaration of Independence in 1776, Jefferson's fellow delegates to the Continental Congress had simply redirected attention from property's possession to matters much more fundamental—to the fact that man's pursuit of happiness nearly always gives rise to a desire for "comfortable Preservation" (as Locke termed it), to the fact that its achievement requires and thereby justifies human acquisitiveness by means of labor, and to the fact that safeguarding labor demands the safeguarding of its fruits in property as well.[20]

In fact, no one spoke with greater force on this matter than Jefferson himself. In his Second Inaugural Address (1805), he put great emphasis on the protection of "that state of property, equal or unequal, which results to every man from his own industry, or that of his fathers."[21] Eleven years later, in his correspondence, he returned to the same theme, arguing that "to take from one, because it is thought his own industry and that of his fathers has acquired too much, in order to spare to others, who, or whose fathers have not exercised equal industry and skill, is to violate arbitrarily the first principle of association, 'the *guarantee* to everyone of

---

[17] Declaration of Independence, July 4, 1776, in Julian P. Boyd, ed., *The Papers of Thomas Jefferson* (Princeton, NJ: Princeton University Press, 1950-), 1:429.

[18] Cf. Richard K. Matthews, *The Radical Politics of Thomas Jefferson: A Revisionist View* (Lawrence: University Press of Kansas, 1984), with Jean Yarbrough, "Jefferson and Property Rights," in Paul and Dickman, eds., *Liberty, Property, and the Foundations of the American Constitution*, 65–83.

[19] See The Revisal of the Laws, June 18, 1779, Bill no. 64, A Bill for Proportioning Crimes and Punishments in Cases Heretofore Capital, in Boyd, ed., *The Papers of Thomas Jefferson*, 2:492–507, quotation at 492.

[20] See Jeffrey Barnouw, "The Pursuit of Happiness in Jefferson and Its Background in Bacon and Hobbes," *Interpretation* 11, no. 2 (1983): 225–48; Barnouw errs solely in drawing an untenable distinction between Bacon and Hobbes, on the one hand, and Locke, on the other.

[21] Thomas Jefferson, Second Inaugural Address, March 4, 1805, in James D. Richardson, ed., *A Compilation of the Messages and Papers of the Presidents, 1789-1897* (Washington, DC: Government Printing Office, 1896-99), 1:378–82, quotation at 382.

a free exercise of his industry, and the fruits acquired by it.' " [22] It was his firm belief, he subsequently explained to the French *philosophe* Pierre Samuel du Pont de Nemours, "that a right to property is founded in our natural wants, in the means with which we are endowed to satisfy these wants, and [in] the right to what we acquire by those means without violating the similar rights of other sensible beings." [23]

In much the same spirit, in his First Inaugural Address (1801), Jefferson had singled out as "the sum of good government" not just "a wise and frugal Government, which shall restrain men from injuring one another," but one which "shall leave them otherwise free to regulate their own pursuits of industry and improvement, and shall not take from the mouth of labor the bread it has earned." [24] Virtually no one in America thought it the responsibility of the government to specify the nature of human happiness and guarantee its achievement. But it was widely accepted that it is a proper task for government to protect and promote the pursuit of happiness, and few doubted that the freedom to acquire and use property was essential for that.

II. THE TOOLMAKING ANIMAL

Those who thought most deeply about the matter took the argument one step further. On July 13, 1787, at the federal constitutional convention in Philadelphia, Pennsylvania delegate James Wilson intervened in a debate concerning representation, denying "that property was the sole or the primary object of [government and] Society" and urging that population be the basis for representation. In his judgment, "cultivation [and] improvement of the human mind was the most noble object" pursued by man. "With respect to this object," he argued, "as well as to other *personal* rights, numbers were surely the natural [and] precise measure of Representation." [25]

Four months later, on November 22, 1787, when James Madison first published in the New York press what would eventually become the most famous number of *The Federalist,* he unpacked the logic underpinning Wilson's remarks in the course of advancing what, at first, might have seemed to some of his readers a hypothesis both novel and strange. "The rights of property" Madison traced to "the diversity in the faculties of men," and his defense of America's infant republican regime he

---

[22] Thomas Jefferson to Joseph Milligan, April 8, 1816, in Andrew A. Lipscomb and Albert Ellery Bergh, eds., *The Writings of Thomas Jefferson* (Washington, DC: Thomas Jefferson Memorial Association, 1903), 14:456–66, quotation at 466.

[23] Thomas Jefferson to Pierre Samuel du Pont de Nemours, April 24, 1816, in Paul Leicester Ford, ed., *The Works of Thomas Jefferson* (New York: G. P. Putnam's Sons, 1904–5), 11:519–25, quotation at 522–23.

[24] Thomas Jefferson, First Inaugural Address, March 4, 1801, in Richardson, ed. *A Compilation of the Messages and Papers of the Presidents,* 1:323.

[25] See Farrand, ed., *The Records of the Federal Convention of 1787,* 1:605 (July 13, 1787).

grounded on the premise that "the first object of Government" is "the protection" of the "different and unequal faculties of acquiring property."[26]

Alexander Hamilton further expanded on this argument in the *Report on the Subject of Manufactures* that, in his capacity as Secretary of the Treasury, he presented to Congress on December 5, 1791. Therein, he justified a policy of selective economic intervention on the part of the new American government not only on the grounds that promoting manufactures would strengthen the fledgling United States economically, tie its various regions more closely together, and make it more nearly self-sufficient with regard to the resources necessary for its own defense, but also because this particular branch of human endeavor would furnish "greater scope for the diversity of talents and dispositions, which discriminate men from each other."[27] "It is a just observation," he explained,

> that minds of the strongest and most active powers for their proper objects fall below mediocrity and labour without effect, if confined to uncongenial pursuits. And it is thence to be inferred that the results of human exertion may be immensely increased by diversifying its objects. When all the different kinds of industry obtain in a community, each individual can find his proper element, and can call into activity the whole vigour of his nature. And the community is benefited by the services of its respective members, in the manner, in which each can serve it with most effect.[28]

In Hamilton's opinion, it was one of the responsibilities of government to "cherish and stimulate the activity of the human mind, by multiplying the objects of enterprise." "Even things in themselves not positively advantageous," he contended, "sometimes become so, by their tendency to provoke exertion. Every new scene, which is opened to the busy nature of man to rouse and exert itself, is the addition of a new energy to the general stock of effort."[29]

---

[26] See *Federalist No. 10* (J. Madison), in Jacob E. Cooke, ed., *The Federalist* (Middletown, CT: Wesleyan University Press, 1961), 58.

[27] Alexander Hamilton, *Report on the Subject of Manufactures,* December 5, 1791, in Syrett, ed., *The Papers of Alexander Hamilton,* 10:254. That Hamilton favored a measure of economic intervention did not distinguish him from his fellow founders. No one opposed the Constitution's patent clause at the federal convention; no one objected to it during the ratification debates. There were, of course, subsequent disputes concerning Hamilton's program as Secretary of the Treasury, but these turned on the propriety of the particular proposals he advanced and on their constitutionality. At the state level, government intervention was much less controversial, and Madison, as president, proposed a constitutional amendment sanctioning a program of internal improvements on the part of the federal government. See Rahe, *Republics Ancient and Modern,* 573–747.

[28] Hamilton, *Report on the Subject of Manufactures,* in Syrett, ed., *The Papers of Alexander Hamilton,* 10:255.

[29] Ibid., 256.

What Hamilton, Madison, and Wilson had in common was an adherence to the opinion that James Boswell attributed to Benjamin Franklin one fine evening when, in the presence of Samuel Johnson, Franklin advanced the notion that man is by nature "a tool-making animal." [30] But if Franklin coined the famous phrase in which Marx took such inordinate delight,[31] it was far from the case that he was the first to think of man in this fashion. That honor is arguably due to Sir Francis Bacon (1561–1626), and the first to think through its significance for understanding property and its political imperatives was none other than John Locke (1632–1704).[32]

III. *Lógos* and *Téchnē*

To get a sense of what Bacon was up to, one need only attend to the manner in which he transformed familiar rhetorical tropes. Bacon was an unabashed admirer of the author of *The Prince* (1513). "We are much beholden," he wrote, "to Machiavelli and others, that write what men do, and not what they ought to do." With this statement, Bacon endorsed the Florentine's repudiation of the classical and Christian understanding of virtue and his substitution of a view that defined human excellence strictly in terms of its contribution to "security and well-being." [33] Bacon differed with his mentor in only one fundamental respect. In his *Discourses on Livy* (1517), Machiavelli had suggested that there are three types of human beings who are especially deserving of praise: above all others, the authors and founders of religions; then, those who have established republics or kingdoms; and, finally, commanders of armies who have increased the possessions of their kingdom or country.[34] Bacon addressed the same issue in his *Novum Organum* (1620), but ignored entirely those who had first established the world's religions. The admiration that Machiavelli had reserved for these men and for the "founders of cities and empires, legislators, saviors of their country from long endured evils, quellers of tyrannies, and the like" Bacon bestowed solely on "the authors of inventions"—men whose discoveries had conferred "benefits" on "the whole race of man." It was, he contended, better in all respects for human

---

[30] James Boswell, journal entry, April 7, 1778, in George Birkbeck Hill, ed., *Boswell's Life of Johnson* (Oxford: Clarendon Press, 1887), 3:245.

[31] See Marx, *Das Kapital*, 1:150, 289 n. 13.

[32] For Locke's acknowledgment of his debt to Bacon, see John Locke, *Of the Conduct of the Understanding*, sec. 1, which I cite from *The Works of John Locke* (London: Thomas Tegg, 1823), 3:203–89. See also John Locke, *An Essay Concerning Human Understanding*, ed. Peter H. Nidditch (Oxford: Clarendon Press, 1979), bk. 4, chap. 12, sec. 12.

[33] Cf. Sir Francis Bacon, *Of the Advancement of Learning*, bk. 2, chap. 21, sec. 9, in James Spedding, Robert Leslie Ellis, and Douglas Denon Heath, eds., *The Works of Francis Bacon* (London: Longman, 1857–74), 3:430, and Bacon, *De dignitate et augmentis scientiarum*, bk. 7, chap. 2, ibid., 1:729 (translated at 5:17), with Niccolò Machiavelli, *Il principe*, chap. 15, in Machiavelli, *Tutte le opere*, ed. Mario Martelli (Florence: G. C. Sansoni, 1971), 280.

[34] Machiavelli, *Discorsi sopra la prima deca di Tito Livio*, bk. 1, chap. 10, in Martelli, ed., *Tutte le opere*, 91–93. Cf. Aristotle, *Politica*, 1253a29–39.

beings to exert themselves in order "to establish and extend the power and dominion of the human race itself over the universe" than for them to labor merely "to extend the power of their country and its dominion among men."[35]

This was, to say the least, a highly controversial opinion. In the first half of the seventeenth century, as the English antiquarian and writer John Aubrey soon thereafter remarked,

> 'Twas held a strange presumption for a Man to attempt an Innovation in Learnings; and not to be good Manners, to be more knowing than his Neighbours and Forefathers; even to attempt an improvement in Husbandry (though it succeeded with profit) was look'd upon with an ill Eie. Their Neighbours did scorne to follow it, though not to doe it, was to their own Detriment.[36]

More to the point, Aubrey added, " 'Twas held a Sin to make a Scrutinie into the Waies of Nature," for those who were taught that it was "a profound part of Religion to glorify God in his Workes" were inclined to think also that an attempt to conquer nature had to be predicated on doubts as to the bounty of Providence, on ingratitude for God's benevolence, and on an impious pride in the capacities left to fallen man.[37]

Thus it was that Bacon found it necessary to turn the Book of Genesis on its head, arguing that it was an appropriate and even a righteous task for the practitioners of the "arts and sciences" to pursue progress in the arts and improvements in the sciences for the purpose of conferring on human beings once again that "dominion over creation" that they had supposedly lost as a consequence of the Fall. Lest the titanic ambition underpinning so formidable a project be judged a grave sin, Bacon looked to God's judgment in search of religious sanction for science's liberation of mankind from the supposed consequences of that very same judgment of God. "[C]reation was not by the curse made altogether and for ever a rebel," Bacon insisted, "but in virtue of that charter 'In the sweat of thy face shalt thou eat bread,' it is now by various labors . . . at length and in some measure subdued . . . to the uses of human life."[38] In bringing his

---

[35] See Bacon, *Novum Organum*, bk. 1, aphorism 129, in Spedding, Ellis, and Heath, eds., *The Works of Francis Bacon*, 1:221–23 (translated at 4:113–15). See also Bacon, *Of the Advancement of Learning*, bk. 1, chap. 7, sec. 1, and Bacon, *De interpretatione naturae, proemium*, ibid., 3:301–2, and 518.

[36] Oliver Lawson Dick, ed., *Aubrey's Brief Lives* (Harmondsworth: Penguin, 1982), 27–28.

[37] Ibid., 28.

[38] Cf. Bacon, *De dignitate et augmentis scientiarum*, bk. 4, chap. 3, and Bacon *Of the Advancement of Learning*, bk. 2, chap. 11, sec. 3, in Spedding, Ellis, and Heath, eds., *The Works of Francis Bacon*, 1:608–9 (translated at 4:400–401), 3:381, with Gen. 1:28–30, 3:17–19, 9:1–3, and Ps. 115:16. See also Bacon, *Novum Organum*, bk. 2, aphorism 52, and "Valerius Terminus," chap. 1, in *The Works of Francis Bacon*, 1:365 (translated at 4:247–48) and 3:222–23, respectively; then, cf. *Of the Advancement of Learning*, bk. 1, chap. 6, sec. 8 (ibid., 3:297) with Gen.

Novum Organum to a conclusion with this hitherto unheard-of reading of Genesis 1:28, he paved the way for a profound reorientation of the Christian faith.[39]

To succeed in his quest—and succeed in time he did—Bacon had to discredit the view, universal among the classical philosophers, that contemplation is "the last or furthest end of knowledge," and he had to persuade future students of natural philosophy that learning is "a rich storehouse" not only "for the glory of the Creator" but also "for the relief of man's estate." Above all else, he had to convince them that improving the human condition "is that which will indeed dignify and exalt knowledge, if contemplation and action may be more nearly and straitly conjoined and united together than they have been."[40]

More than any other figure, Bacon was responsible for the subordination of theory to practice, which dictated applying reason (*lógos*) to the mechanical and industrial arts (*téchnai*) and thereby gave birth to what we know as modern technology.[41] It was with Bacon's great project in mind that Thomas Sprat, in his history of the Royal Society of London, wrote in 1667, "It was said of *Civil Government* by *Plato*, that then the World will be best rul'd, when either *Philosophers* shall be chosen *Kings*, or *Kings* shall have *Philosophical* minds. And I will affirm the like of *Philosophy*. It will then attain to perfection, when either the *Mechanic Laborers* shall have *Philosophical heads*; or the *Philosophers* shall have *Mechanical hands*."[42]

Two centuries later, when Lord Macaulay found an opportunity to express his judgment of Bacon's accomplishment, he remarked that "it was not by furnishing philosophers with rules for performing the inductive process well, but by furnishing them with a motive for performing it well, that he conferred so vast a benefit on society." As a consequence of this achievement, Macaulay added, the author of *The Advancement of Learning* should be regarded as one of the "few imperial spirits" to exercise "the rare prerogative" of conferring on "the human mind a direction which it shall retain for ages."[43]

4:17–24 and 11:6; and see Bacon, *De dignitate et augmentis scientiarum*, bk. 6, chap. 1, in *The Works of Francis Bacon*, 1:653 (translated at 4:440–41).

[39] For the earlier interpretations of the critical passage, see Jeremy Cohen, *"Be Fertile and Increase, Fill the Earth and Master It": The Ancient and Medieval Career of a Biblical Text* (Ithaca, NY: Cornell University Press, 1989).

[40] See Bacon, *Of the Advancement of Learning*, bk. 1, chap. 5, sec. 11, in Spedding, Ellis, and Heath, eds., *The Works of Francis Bacon*, 3:294–95. See also *Of the Advancement of Learning*, bk. 2, chap. 20, sec. 1 through bk. 2, chap. 21, sec. 11 (ibid., 3:417–32).

[41] For the close connection between Baconian science and the mechanical arts, see Bacon, *Novum Organum*, bk. 1, aphorisms 98–99, 110, 117, 129, and Bacon, *Cogitata et visa de interpretatione naturae*, ibid., 1:202–3, 208–9, 212–13, 221–23 (translated at 4:94–95, 100–101, 104–5, 113–15), and 3:612–17.

[42] Thomas Sprat, *The History of the Royal Society of London, For the Improving of Natural Knowledge* (London: J. Martyn, 1667), 397.

[43] Thomas Babington Macaulay, "Lord Bacon," in Macaulay, *Critical, Historical, and Miscellaneous Essays* (New York: Sheldon and Co., 1860), 3:336–495, esp. 458–59, 463–64, and 480.

It is no wonder, then, that Thomas Jefferson came to regard Bacon, along with Sir Isaac Newton and John Locke, as "the three greatest men that have ever lived, without any exception," men distinguished for having "laid the foundation of those superstructures which have been raised in the Physical and Moral sciences."[44] Nor is it any surprise that James Madison concurred, mentioning the same three individuals and singling out Bacon as a figure who "lifted the veil from the venerable errors which enslaved opinion, and pointed the way to those luminous truths of which he had but a glimpse himself." At the same time, Madison conferred even higher praise on Bacon's disciple John Locke.[45]

IV. PROPERTY

In his own lifetime and for a long time thereafter, as Madison's testimony suggests, Locke was best known as the author of *An Essay Concerning Human Understanding* (1689).[46] For this, Locke was to some degree responsible himself. Prior to his death, he kept his authorship of the *Two Treatises of Government* a secret, acknowledging his patrimony only in his will. The *Essay,* however, might not have encompassed the achievement that gave him the greatest satisfaction. Toward the end of his life, in a letter written to a young protégé, Locke remarked, "Propriety [by which he meant what we now call property], I have no where found more

---

[44] See Thomas Jefferson, letter to John Trumbull, February 15, 1788, in Boyd, ed., *Papers of Thomas Jefferson,* 14:561. See also Thomas Jefferson, letter to Benjamin Rush, January 16, 1811, in Paul Leicester Ford, ed., *The Writings of Thomas Jefferson* (New York: G. P. Putnam's Sons, 1892–99), 9:294–99. In the letter to Rush, Jefferson recalls a conversation with Alexander Hamilton and John Adams in which he referred to "Bacon, Newton, and Locke" as "my trinity of the three greatest men the world had ever produced." In this connection, see Silvio A. Bedini, *Thomas Jefferson: Statesman of Science* (New York: Macmillan, 1990). Cf. the praise bestowed on Bacon by "Poor Richard" in 1749, in Leonard W. Labaree et al., eds., *The Papers of Benjamin Franklin* (New Haven, CT: Yale University Press, 1959–), 3:339, with that subsequently accorded him by John Adams in a letter to Jonathan Sewall in February 1760, in Robert J. Taylor, ed., *Papers of John Adams* (Cambridge, MA: Belknap Press of Harvard University Press, 1977–), 1:41–45, at 42–43. When Hamilton, after his retirement from office, expressed an interest in conducting "a full investigation of the history and science of civil government, and the practical results of the various modifications of it upon the freedom and happiness of mankind," he stipulated that he wanted "to have the subject treated in reference to past experience, and upon the principles of Lord Bacon's inductive philosophy." See James Kent, letter to Mrs. Elizabeth Hamilton, December 10, 1832, in William Kent, ed., *Memoirs and Letters of James Kent* (Boston, MA: Little, Brown, and Co., 1898), 281–331, quotation at 327–28.

[45] See James Madison, "Spirit of Governments," for *The National Gazette,* February 18, 1792, in Rutland, et al., eds., *The Papers of James Madison,* 14:233–34.

[46] Cf. John Dunn, "The Politics of Locke in England and America in the Eighteenth Century," in John W. Yolton, ed., *John Locke: Problems and Perspectives: A Collection of New Essays* (Cambridge: Cambridge University Press, 1969), 45–80, who makes the point but overstates the case, with Steven M. Dworetz, *The Unvarnished Doctrine: Locke, Liberalism, and the American Revolution* (Durham, NC: Duke University Press, 1990), who gives a more balanced account.

clearly explain'd than in a Book intituled, *Two Treatises of Government*." [47]
He was so proud of the chapter on property in that work that he gave it
central place in his book.[48]

To understand Locke's intention, one must attend to his rhetoric and
strive to catch his drift.[49] As he depicts man's natural state in his *Second
Treatise*, it turns out in the end to be in all respects "an ill condition." [50] At
the outset, however, Locke depicts God's material provision for man as an
example of God's bounty. Nature he describes as "the common Mother of
all," [51] and God he dubs our "Father or Master." [52] Men appear as God's
"Children or Servants." [53] In justifying the appropriation of "Meat and
Drink" by human beings, Locke speaks of these as "things" which "Nature
affords for their Subsistence," [54] and he notes that "the Earth and all that
is therein, is given to Men for the Support and Comfort of their being." [55]
The "Fruits" and the "Beasts," which are "produced by the spontaneous
hand of Nature," [56] would appear to be more than enough to meet the
needs of human beings, for these "natural Provisions" are said to exist in
"plenty." [57] Locke even cites a letter written by St. Paul to Timothy claiming that "*God has given us all things richly . . . to enjoy*," calling the apostle's
assertion "the Voice of Reason confirmed by Inspiration." [58]

But in the course of Locke's argument, this reassuring depiction reveals
itself as a mirage, and God presents himself under another aspect as a
figure not unlike the absolute monarch whom Locke condemns in his
First Treatise, a figure "likelier by want and the dependance of a scanty
Fortune, to tye them to hard Service, than by liberal Allowance of the
Conveniencies of Life, to promote the great Design . . . *Increase* and *Multiply*." [59] Nowhere does Locke suggest that men are like "the ravens" who

[47] John Locke to Richard King, August 25, 1703, in Esmond S. de Beer, ed., *The Correspondence of John Locke* (Oxford: Clarendon Press, 1976–89), 8:56–59, esp. 58.

[48] See John Locke, *Two Treatises of Government: A Critical Edition with an Introduction and
Apparatus Criticus*, 2d ed., ed. Peter Laslett (Cambridge: Cambridge University Press, 1970),
Second Treatise, chaps. 4–5, which constitute the fifteenth and sixteenth chapters of the thirty
contained in the work as a whole. Chapter 5, "Of Property," in the *Second Treatise* thus stands
as the centerpiece of the work. In citing the *Two Treatises of Government*, I have used this
Laslett edition, adopting the corrections suggested by Nathan Tarcov, *Locke's Education for
Liberty* (Chicago, IL: University of Chicago Press, 1984), 229–30 n. 324, and 253–54 n. 187.

[49] For a defense of this approach, see Paul A. Rahe, "John Locke's Philosophical Partisanship," *The Political Science Reviewer* 20 (1991): 1–43. For a more elaborate discussion, see
Michael P. Zuckert, *Launching Liberalism: On Lockean Political Philosophy* (Lawrence: University Press of Kansas, 2002), 25–126.

[50] See Locke, *Two Treatises of Government, Second Treatise*, chap. 9, sec. 127.

[51] Ibid., chap. 5, sec. 28.

[52] Ibid., sec. 29.

[53] Ibid.

[54] Ibid., sec. 25.

[55] Ibid., sec. 26.

[56] Ibid.

[57] Ibid., sec. 31.

[58] Cf. ibid. with 1 Tim. 6:1–18.

[59] Consider *Two Treatises of Government, First Treatise*, chap. 4, sec. 41, in light of a later
passage in chap. 5, secs. 45–46. It may not be fortuitous that Locke begins the *First Treatise*

"neither sow nor reap." He nowhere mentions "the lilies" that "toil not" and "spin not." He nowhere tries to persuade men to be "content" with the "food and raiment" they have received from God. And he nowhere exhorts them against a "trust in uncertain riches." For the most part, in fact, he sidesteps what is to be found in the Gospel of Luke and the Epistles of Paul, and he asserts, instead, that when "God . . . gave the World in common to all Mankind," he "commanded Man also to labour, and the penury of his Condition required it of him."[60]

Thus, in spite of all that God has given man richly to enjoy, man's neediness turns out to be his defining quality. That which is on offer from "un-assisted Nature" is "of so little value, *without labour*" that Locke judges it "but a very modest Computation to say, that of the *Products* of the Earth useful to the Life of Man 9/10 are the *effects of labour*." Then, without a pause, he corrects himself, saying, "Nay, if we will rightly estimate things as they come to our use, and cast up the several Expenses about them, what in them is purely owing to *Nature*, and what to *labour*, we shall find, that in most of them 99/100 are wholly to be put on the account of *labour*." By the time Locke has once again reviewed his estimates, not one thousandth of the value of the useful things we draw from cultivating the earth is credited to nature and nature's God, for "Nature and the Earth furnished only the almost worthless Materials."[61] Lockean man does not come into property in the fashion in which he might enter a theater and temporarily occupy a seat, as Cicero, Seneca, and Grotius had once thought; for there is no theater, and there is no seat—at least not until Lockean man has fashioned one for himself.[62]

By the time he drafted his *Two Treatises of Government*—during the crisis, in the period stretching from 1679 to 1683, occasioned by the attempt to exclude the Catholic heir apparent, James, the duke of York, from succession to the English throne—Locke had been thinking along these lines for a while.[63] In 1677, he had written in his journal the following:

with the word "Slavery" and ends it with "Adam" and that the central chapters of his tract as a whole deal with slavery and property: see *First Treatise*, chap. 1, sec. 1; chap. 11, sec. 169; and *Second Treatise*, chaps. 4–5. The *First Treatise* deserves more attention than it has been accorded: see, for a start, Zuckert, *Launching Liberalism*, 129–46; and Thomas L. Pangle, *The Spirit of Modern Republicanism: The Moral Vision of the American Founders and the Philosophy of Locke* (Chicago, IL: University of Chicago Press, 1988), 131–275.

[60] Cf. 1 Tim. 6:1–18 and Luke 12:15–34 with Locke, *Two Treatises of Government, Second Treatise*, chap. 5, secs. 32 and 35.

[61] Locke, *Two Treatises of Government, Second Treatise*, chap. 5, secs. 36–37 and 40–45.

[62] Cf. Marcus Tullius Cicero, *De finibus bonorum et malorum libri quinque*, ed. L. D. Reynolds (Oxford: Clarendon Press, 1998), 3.20.67; Lucius Annaeus Seneca, *De beneficiis* (Pisa: Giardini, 1982), 7.12.3–6; Hugo Grotius, *De iure belli ac pacis libri tres*, ed. P. C. Molhuysen (Lugduni Batavorum: A. W. Sijthoff, 1919), II.ii.2; and John Locke, *Questions Concerning the Law of Nature*, ed. and trans. Robert Horwitz, Jenny Strauss Clay, and Diskin Clay (Ithaca, NY: Cornell University Press, 1990), question XI, folio 112, ln. 7, through folio 113, ln. 11; and consider Lev. 3:16–17 and 17:10–14 in light of Lev. 25:23 and Num. 11.

[63] The precise date of composition remains and is likely to remain in dispute. The arguments for dating Locke's completion of the original draft to the period immediately follow-

If we consider our selves in the condition we are in this world, we cannot but observe that we are in an estate the necessitys whereof call for a constant supply of meat drinke cloathing and defence from the weather and very often physick; and our conveniences demand yet a great deale more. To provide these things nature furnish[es] us only with the materials for the most part rough and unfitted to our uses[;] it requires labour art and thought to suit them to our occasions, and if the knowledg of men had not found out ways to shorten the labour and improve severall things which seeme not at first sight to be of any use to us we should spend all our time to make a scanty provision for a poore and miserable life. . . .

Had man kinde noe concernments but in this world [and] noe apprehension of any being after this life[,] they need trouble their heads with noe thing but the history of nature and an enquiry into the qualitys of the things in this mansion of the universe which hath fallen to their lott, and [with] being well skild in the knowledg of materiall causes and effects of things in their power[,] directing their thoughts to the improvement of such arts and inventions, engins and utinsils as might best contribute to their continuation in it with conveniency and delight.[64]

In his *Two Treatises of Government*, Locke goes even further, intimating that a lack of provision is God's only provision for man, and concluding that human neediness justifies and even sanctifies a liberation of man's acquisitive instincts. The fact that "unassisted Nature" is for all intents and purposes "*wast[e]*," that "the benefit of it amounts to little more than nothing," that what nature provides is "scarcely . . . worth any thing," that the "Materials" furnished by "Nature and the Earth" are "almost worthless," and that they are unable to meet man's innumerable "Wants"

---

ing the first publication of Robert Filmer's *Patriarcha* in 1680 were advanced by Peter Laslett in "The English Revolution and Locke's *Two Treatises of Government,*" *Cambridge Historical Journal* 12, no. 1 (1956): 40–55, and then further developed in Laslett's introduction to Locke, *Two Treatises of Government*, 45–66. The arguments were further refined and given a new twist by Richard Ashcraft, in Ashcraft, "Revolutionary Politics and Locke's *Two Treatises of Government:* Radicalism and Lockean Political Theory," *Political Theory* 8, no. 4 (1980): 429–86, and Richard Ashcraft, *Locke's Two Treatises of Government* (London: Allen and Unwin, 1987), 286–97. Laslett was not persuaded by all of Ashcraft's refinements: see Peter Laslett, addendum to introduction, 1987, in John Locke, *Two Treatises of Government*, student edition, ed. Peter Laslett (Cambridge: Cambridge University Press, 1988), 123–26. Since that time, other authors have entered the fray: see Mark Goldie, introduction to John Locke, *Two Treatises of Government*, ed. Mark Goldie (London: J. M. Dent, 1993), xix–xxi; David Wootton, introduction to John Locke, *Political Writings of John Locke*, ed. David Wootton (New York: Mentor, 1993), 7–122, esp. 49–64; and John Marshall, *John Locke: Resistance, Religion, and Responsibility* (Cambridge: Cambridge University Press, 1994), 205–91, esp. 222–65. In no way does this ongoing dispute affect my argument.

[64] See Locke's journal, February 8, 1677, "Understanding," in R. I. Aaron and Jocelyn Gibb, eds., *An Early Draft of Locke's Essay Together with Excerpts from His Journals* (Oxford: Clarendon Press, 1936), 84–86.

renders personal appropriation through human labor not only necessary but just. In order to endure, much less to increase and multiply, men must "subdue" the earth; and to accomplish this and secure for themselves both "Food and Rayment," they must "sow" and "reap," "toil" and "spin," and place their "trust in" the "uncertain riches" that St. Paul had exhorted them never to trust.[65]

In providing for himself, man reveals his true nature. Men have many failings, but they have an astonishing capacity to contrive their future preservation, and they are set off from the other animals by their ability to labor methodically toward that end. The one and only quality that is uniquely human, Locke suggests in his *Second Treatise,* is the fact that "every man has a *Property* in his own *Person*" that "no Body has any Right to but himself."[66] First and foremost, man is "Master of himself." He is *"Proprietor of his own Person,* and the actions or *Labour* of it." As a result, "the *Labour* of his Body, and the *Work* of his Hands, we may say, are properly his." The very act of laying hold of an object "from the common state Nature placed it in" makes it, no less than an acorn or apple consumed, "a part of him."[67]

Locke argues that because the fruits of the soil rot, there was, early in human history, a natural limit to the land that a man in the state of nature could profitably and justly lay hold of for his own purposes. In consequence, there would always be "enough, and as good left" for others who might present themselves, and no one could have grounds to object to anyone's appropriation of the land.[68] At a later time, however, the invention of money rendered it sensible for human beings, eager to make provision for their own preservation and long-term comfort, to farm more extensive tracts of land, to sell on the market what they harvested, and to safeguard the precious metals and gems given to them in recompense. Then, there ceased to be land "enough, and as good left" to be labored on by others. Even in this circumstance, Locke argues, the appropriator of the land committed no crime: for in consenting to take *"a little piece of yellow Metal"* of no real value in return for things useful in themselves, men made their peace with the fact that "different degrees of Industry were apt to give Men Possessions in different Proportions." Nor can such an appropriator be accused of lacking decency, for he is best characterized

---

[65] Cf. Locke, *Two Treatises of Government, Second Treatise,* chap. 5, secs. 32 and 42–45, with 1 Tim. 6:1–18 and Luke 12:15–34.

[66] Locke, *Two Treatises of Government, Second Treatise,* chap. 5, sec. 27.

[67] Ibid., secs. 26–28, 32, 35–37, 41–42, and 44–45. See Harvey C. Mansfield, Jr., "On the Political Character of Property in Locke," in Alkis Kontos, ed., *Powers, Possessions, and Freedom: Essays in Honour of C. B. Macpherson* (Toronto: University of Toronto Press, 1979), 23–38. In his notebooks, Locke wrote, "We ought to look on it as a mark of goodness in god that he has put us in this life under a necessity of labor." See Locke, *Commonplace Book, 1661* (p. 310, manuscript in the collection of Arthur J. Houghton, Jr.), quoted in John Dunn, *The Political Thought of John Locke: An Historical Account of the Argument of the 'Two Treatises of Government'* (Cambridge: Cambridge University Press, 1969), 232 n. 3.

[68] Locke, *Two Treatises of Government, Second Treatise,* chap. 5, secs. 33, 36–37, and 46.

as a benefactor of mankind—liberal, humane, and generous in a fashion suggested by the praise that Sir Francis Bacon lavished on inventors. As Locke observes, "He who appropriates land to himself by his labour, does not lessen . . . the common stock of mankind." He increases it.[69]

Technological progress is Locke's theme—chiefly in agriculture, but also in the industrial arts.[70] In his opinion,

> the provisions serving to the support of humane life, produced by one acre of inclosed and cultivated land, are (to speak much within compasse) ten times more, than those, which are yeilded by an acre of Land, of an equal richnesse, lyeing wast[e] in common. And therefor he, that incloses Land and has a greater plenty of the conveniencys of life from ten acres, than he could have from an hundred left to Nature, may truly be said, to give ninety acres to Mankind. For his labour now supplys him with provisions out of ten acres, which were but the product of an hundred lying in common. I have here rated the improved land very low in making its product but as ten to one, when it is much nearer an hundred to one. For I aske whether in the wild woods and uncultivated wast[e] of America left to Nature, without any improvement, tillage or husbandry, a thousand acres will yeild the needy and wretched inhabitants as many conveniencies of life as ten acres of equally fertile land doe in Devonshire where they are well cultivated?[71]

Where trade is constrained by the absence of a medium of exchange and ingenuity is denied inspiration, men are fated to be poor. But where there is money and ingenuity receives its reward, though there will be an unequal distribution of the land and of the other means of production, and some men will be constrained to work for others, all concerned will come out ahead. Locke was aware of the relationship between supply and demand, and he understood why it was that the "King of a large fruitful Territory" in America "feeds, lodges, and is clad worse than a day Labourer in *England*."[72]

---

[69] Ibid., secs. 36–37 and 46–50.

[70] For the relationship between Locke's thinking and that of the agricultural improvers inspired by Bacon, see Neal Wood, *John Locke and Agrarian Capitalism* (Berkeley: University of California Press, 1984), 15–114. It would be a mistake, however, to suppose that Locke's program of improvement was strictly agricultural: see J. E. Parsons, Jr., "Locke's Doctrine of Property," in Parsons, *Essays in Political Philosophy* (Washington, DC: University Press of America, 1982), 127–54. See also Patrick Kelly, "All Things Richly to Enjoy": Economics and Politics in Locke's *Two Treatises of Government*," *Political Studies* 36, no. 2 (1988): 273–93.

[71] Locke, *Two Treatises of Government, Second Treatise*, chap. 5, sec. 37.

[72] Ibid., sec. 41. Consider ibid., secs. 33, 36–37, 40–43, and 46–50, in light of John Locke, *Some Considerations of the Consequences of Lowering the Interest and Raising the Value of Money*, in *The Works of John Locke*, 5:40; note Bacon, *Novum Organum*, bk. 1, aphorism 129, in Spedding, Ellis, and Heath, eds., *The Works of Francis Bacon*, 1:221–22 (translated at 4:114); and see Leo Strauss, *Natural Right and History* (Chicago, IL: University of Chicago Press,

An account that starts out as a hypothetical history of the origins of property is quickly transformed into a celebration of the "Invention and Arts" that in the course of the ages have so much "improved the conveniencies of Life." Locke repeatedly contends that the transformation that labor works on objects and even land gives to them virtually all of the value that they in the end possess: "Whatever *Bread* is worth more than Acorns, *Wine* than Water, and *Cloth* or *Silk* than Leaves, Skins, or Moss, that is wholly *owing to labour* and industry." It would be almost beyond human capacity, he suggests, to list everything that labor contributes toward the production of a single loaf of bread: "For 'tis not barely the Plough-man's Pains, the Reaper's and Thresher's Toil, and the Bakers Sweat, is to be counted into the *Bread* we eat; the Labour of those who broke the Oxen, who digged and wrought the Iron and Stones, who felled and framed the Timber imployed about the Plough, Mill, Oven, or any other Utensils, which are a vast Number, requisite to this Corn, from its being seed to be sown to its being made Bread, must all be *charged on* the account of *Labour,* and received as an effect of that." To put together a simple *"Catalogue of things, that Industry provided and made use of, about every Loaf of Bread"* would be "almost impossible, at least too long, to reckon up."[73]

The focus of Locke's entire argument is his claim that "God gave the World . . . to the use of the Industrious and Rational, (and *Labour* was to be *his* Title to it;) not to the Fancy or Covetousness of the Quarrelsom and Contentious."[74] If man is "an intellectual Creature, and so capable of *Dominion* . . . over the inferiour Creatures," it is because he possesses the very industrious rationality that Locke attributes to the "All-wise Contriver" in whose image and likeness man is said to have been made.[75] It is, as we shall see, by depicting man as a toolmaking animal on the Baconian model that Locke seeks to make sense of the emergence and development of civil society.

V. A Society for Toolmaking Animals

"In the beginning," Locke observes, "all the World was *America,* and more so than that is now; for no such thing as *Money* was any where

---

1974), 234–51. C. B. Macpherson's otherwise admirable exposition of the fifth chapter of the *Second Treatise* is marred by his inability to distinguish labor at subsistence wages from slavery: cf. C. B. Macpherson, *The Political Theory of Possessive Individualism: Hobbes to Locke* (Oxford: Clarendon Press, 1962), 203–14, with Locke, *An Essay Concerning Human Understanding,* bk. 2, chap. 21, secs. 45–50; and see Locke, *Two Treatises of Government, First Treatise,* chap. 5, secs. 42–43.

[73] Locke, *Two Treatises of Government, Second Treatise,* chap. 5, secs. 40–44. Cf. Adam Smith, *An Inquiry into the Nature and Causes of the Wealth of Nations,* bk. 1, chap. 1, sec. 11, in *The Glasgow Edition of the Works and Correspondence of Adam Smith* (Oxford: Clarendon Press, 1976).

[74] Locke, *Two Treatises of Government, Second Treatise,* chap. 5, sec. 34.

[75] Ibid., *First Treatise,* chap. 4, sec. 30, and chap. 6, sec. 53. Cf. ibid., *Second Treatise,* chap. 5, secs. 34, 37, 40, and 42–43, with *First Treatise,* chap. 6, sec. 53, and *Second Treatise,* chap. 2, sec. 6, and chap. 6, sec. 56. See also Locke, *An Essay Concerning Human Understanding,* bk. 1, chap. 1, sec. 1, and bk. 4, chap. 17, sec. 1.

known."[76] Prior to money's invention, human beings were able to secure their livelihood by hunting and gathering, by animal husbandry, and even by planting and reaping in a fashion consistent with semi-nomadic life, as the aboriginal peoples in the neighborhood of Britain's colonies in North America were known to do. Barter took place as well. But in the absence of the money required to drive trade, men in the natural state must have been "needy and wretched," and quite possibly even more so than those who in Locke's day were eking out a living in the wilds of the New World.[77] There was, however, recompense—or so we are at first encouraged to assume.

In the *First Treatise,* when Locke takes note of "the busie mind of Man" and criticizes "the Practices which are in use and credit amongst Men," he proclaims that "the Woods and Forests, where the irrational untaught Inhabitants keep right by following Nature, are fitter to give us Rules, than Cities and Palaces, where those that call themselves Civil and Rational, go out of their way, by the Authority of Example."[78] In the *Second Treatise,* he sounds the same themes, deploying language borrowed from Ovid to describe man's natural state as a *"Golden Age"* prior to the time when "vain Ambition, and *amor sceleratus habendi,* evil Concupiscence had corrupted Mens minds into a Mistake of true Power and Honour." This Golden Age, he insists, "had more Virtue, and consequently better Governours, as well as less vicious Subjects."[79] Its patriarchal chieftains actually earned the description "nursing Fathers" accorded them in the Bible. From this perspective, the invention of money presents itself as a secular fall from grace, bringing to a conclusion a "poor but vertuous Age" in which human beings subsisted in a condition of "Innocence and Sincerity."[80]

When closely reexamined, however, "the first ages of the World" turn out not to have been virtuous at all—unless one thinks virtue consistent with a mere dearth of temptation. If there was then "little room for Quarrels or Contentions about Property," it was simply because "Men were more in danger to be lost, by wandering from their Company, in the then vast Wilderness of the Earth, than to be straitned for want of room to plant in."[81] In those distant times, human beings possessed "little Properties" and for that reason displayed even "less Covetousness."[82] There

---

[76] Locke, *Two Treatises of Government, Second Treatise,* chap. 5, sec. 49.

[77] Ibid. Consider sec. 49 in light of secs. 36, 41, 43, 46, and 48 in the same chapter, as well as chap. 6, sec. 65, and chap. 8, secs. 106–8. For the travel literature in Locke's library dealing with the New World, see William G. Batz, "The Historical Anthropology of John Locke," *Journal of the History of Ideas* 35, no. 4 (1974): 663–70.

[78] Locke, *Two Treatises of Government, First Treatise,* chap. 6, sec. 58.

[79] Cf. ibid., *Second Treatise,* chap. 8, sec. 111, with Publius Ovidius Naso, *Metamorphoses,* ed. William S. Anderson (Leipzig: Teubner, 1982), 1.131.

[80] Locke, *Two Treatises of Government, Second Treatise,* chap. 8, sec. 110.

[81] Ibid., chap. 5, secs. 31 and 36.

[82] Ibid., chap. 6, sec. 75.

were "few controversies," and there were "few Trespasses, and few Offenders"—but only because "the Fashion of the Age," "their Possessions," and the "way of living" they adopted "afforded little matter for Covetousness or Ambition." To a considerable degree, the "equality of a simple poor way of liveing" restricted "their desires within the narrow bounds of each mans smal propertie."[83] The invention of money served solely to liberate human desire from its circumstantial restraints. In the end, it was "the desire of having more than Man needed" that gave rise to the tacit agreement that "altered the intrinsick value of things, which depends only on their usefulness to the Life of Man," and this rendered it possible for *a little piece of yellow Metal*" to be "worth a great piece of Flesh, or a whole heap of Corn."[84]

This liberation of the passions at the same time inspired the "Ambition and Luxury" that "taught Princes to have distinct and separate Interests from their People."[85] To what Locke speaks of in *Some Thoughts Concerning Education* (1693) as "the Desire of having in our Possession, and under our Dominion, more than we have need of,"[86] one can similarly trace the restless imagination, the busy mind, and the profound spiritual uneasiness that sometimes elicit from man, as described in the *Two Treatises,* "a Brutality below the level of Beasts."[87] In the former book, Locke tells us that "Covetousness" is "the Root of all Evil."[88] In the latter, he insists that the comparatively innocent "Inhabitants" of the "Woods and Forests" really are "irrational" and "untaught."[89] Nowhere, however, does he suggest that what he describes in the *Two Treatises* as "the desire of having more than Man needed" is reducible to what he calls in *Some Thoughts Concerning Education* the "love of Dominion."[90] The former is, he makes clear, first and foremost a desire to provide for one's own future comfort and security. As such, although it needs to be restrained in light of the dictates of humanity and long-term self-interest, this desire deserves greater consideration and respect than are ordinarily deemed its due: for "foresight and an Ability to lay up for the future, as well as to supply the present necessity" are the capacities that separate human beings from the other "Beasts of Prey" and make it possible for human beings to become both "Civil and Rational."[91]

---

[83] Ibid., chap. 8, sec. 107.

[84] Ibid., chap. 5, sec. 37, where I see no reason to accept Laslett's emendation.

[85] Ibid., chap. 8, sec. 111.

[86] John Locke, *Some Thoughts Concerning Education,* ed. John W. and Jean S. Yolton (Oxford: Clarendon Press, 1989), sec. 110.

[87] Locke, *Two Treatises of Government, First Treatise,* chap. 6, sec. 58.

[88] Locke, *Some Thoughts Concerning Education,* sec. 110.

[89] Locke, *Two Treatises of Government, First Treatise,* chap. 6, sec. 58.

[90] Consider Locke, *Two Treatises of Government, Second Treatise,* chap. 5, sec. 37, and Locke, *Some Thoughts Concerning Education,* sec. 105, in conjunction with ibid., secs. 103–4 and 110.

[91] Note Locke, *Two Treatises of Government, Second Treatise,* chap. 7, secs. 79–80, and cf. ibid., *First Treatise,* chap. 6, sec. 58, with ibid., *Second Treatise,* chap. 3, sec. 26; then see Locke, *Some Thoughts Concerning Education,* secs. 103–5 and 110. Note the central example in *Two Treatises of Government, Second Treatise,* chap. 7, sec. 79.

Locke was impressed by the "busie Humour" evidenced by children, and in *Some Thoughts Concerning Education* he takes note of the inability of adults to remain "perfectly idle."[92] But he nowhere asserts that human beings really like to labor. Most men, he concedes in *An Essay Concerning Human Understanding*, are "lazy and inconsiderate,"[93] and children, he adds in *Some Thoughts Concerning Education*, delight far less in "Industry and Application" than in "Novelty" and in "Change and Variety."[94] To entice the young to study, he notes, one must trick them into thinking it play, while adults, for their part, tend to be energetic in pursuing recreation alone.[95] As he puts it in *Of the Conduct of the Understanding*, "Labour for labour-sake is against nature."[96]

In *Some Thoughts Concerning Education*, Locke attempts to come to grips with this fact by identifying "*Foresight* and *Desire*" as man's "two great Springs of Action." Where "there is no Desire," he observes, "there will be no Industry."[97] In *An Essay Concerning Human Understanding*, he speaks in the same fashion of "uneasiness," describing it as "the chief if not only spur to humane Industry and Action."[98] Thus, while from one perspective the invention of money might seem to occasion man's fall from grace, from another it is seen to make possible his ascent to the calculating, industrious rationality that constitutes, in Locke's judgment, not just "the highest Perfection, that a Man can attain to in this Life" but also "the dignity of his nature."[99]

From this latter perspective, human beings would appear closely to resemble "un-assisted Nature" itself. The intelligence and the character that they possess at birth is "of so little value, *without labour*," Locke tells us in *Some Thoughts Concerning Education*, that it would be "a very modest Computation to say" that "of all the Men we meet with, Nine Parts of Ten are what they are, Good or Evil, useful or not, by their Education."[100] As Locke observes in *Of the Conduct of the Understanding*, we may suppose ourselves "reasonable creatures, but it is use and exercise only that makes us so," for "nature gives us but the seeds" of reason, and we become rational "no farther than industry and application has carried us."[101] If

---

[92] Locke, *Some Thoughts Concerning Education*, secs. 129, 152, and 207.

[93] Locke, *An Essay Concerning Human Understanding*, bk. 1, chap. 4, sec. 15.

[94] Locke, *Some Thoughts Concerning Education*, secs. 72, 74, 167, and 207.

[95] Ibid., secs. 72–76, 128–29, 148–55, 167, and 206–9.

[96] Locke, *Of the Conduct of the Understanding*, sec. 16.

[97] Locke, *Some Thoughts Concerning Education*, sec. 126. See ibid., secs. 46 and 51.

[98] Locke, *An Essay Concerning Human Understanding*, bk. 2, chap. 20, sec. 6.

[99] Consider Locke, *Some Thoughts Concerning Education*, sec. 122, in conjunction with Locke, *An Essay Concerning Human Understanding*, bk. 2, chap. 21, sec. 51; Locke, *Of the Conduct of the Understanding*, sec. 6; and John Locke, "An Essay Concerning Toleration," in *Scritti editi e inediti sulla toleranza*, ed. Carlo Augusto Viano (Turin: Taylor, 1961), 98. See also Locke, *Two Treatises of Government, Second Treatise*, chap. 5, secs. 48–49.

[100] Cf. Locke, *Some Thoughts Concerning Education*, sec. 1, with Locke, *Two Treatises of Government, Second Treatise*, chap. 5, secs. 37, 40, 42–43, and 45. See also Locke, *Of the Conduct of the Understanding*, sec. 38.

[101] Locke, *Of the Conduct of the Understanding*, sec. 6. See also ibid., secs. 2–3.

the first "Americans" failed to make any real progress in "the arts and sciences," [102] it is not hard to see why. "Letters seldome come in amongst a People," Locke observes in his *Second Treatise*, "till a long continuation of Civil Society has, by other more necessary Arts provided for their Safety, Ease, and Plenty." [103]

Almost everything that Locke asserts regarding childhood and the authority of parents applies in similar fashion to early man. "We are *born Free*," he writes in the *Two Treatises*, but only "as we are born Rational; not that we have actually the Exercise of either." [104] Accordingly, the first human being could no more be "presumed" and "supposed capable of knowing the Law" of reason than a child, an idiot, or a lunatic, and "to turn him loose to an unrestrain'd Liberty, before he has Reason to guide him," would not be "the allowing him the privilege of his Nature, to be free." On the contrary, it would be "but to thrust him out amongst Brutes, and abandon him to a state as wretched, and as much beneath that of a Man, as theirs." [105] The infantile character of primitive man explains why, in "the first Ages of the World," human beings drew "no distinction betwixt Minority, and full Age," and government by patriarchs was the norm. It was "easie, and almost natural," Locke concedes, for "Children to make way for the *Father's Authority and Government*." What might appear to be a great alteration was, in fact, "an insensible change." And that minuscule change opened the way not only for the rule of clan chiefs but, he hints, for the rule of priests as well, "since 'tis as certain, that in the Beginning, *The Father of the Family was Priest, as that he was Ruler in his own Houshold*." [106]

In Locke's opinion, this *"Frame of Government"* was both "obvious and simple," and it was quite well "suited to their present State and Condition," [107] ceasing to be so only when the discovery of money gave rise to man's political coming of age. The tacit agreement to take gold and silver in exchange for goods that are perishable liberated the human imagina-

---

[102] Ibid., sec. 6.

[103] Locke, *Two Treatises of Government, Second Treatise*, chap. 8, sec. 101. Consider Locke, *Essay Concerning Human Understanding*, bk. 2, secs. 6–8; and bk. 4, chap. 12, sec. 11; and Locke, *Two Treatises of Government, Second Treatise*, chap. 5, secs. 37 and 41; in light of secs. 43, 46, and 48–49 (in the same chapter); chap. 6, sec. 65; chap. 7, sec. 92; and chap. 8, secs. 102, 105, and 108. The fact that thinking is a species of making or construction and that it is therefore painful and laborious is yet another indication of nature's niggardliness: see Locke, *An Essay Concerning Human Understanding*, bk. 1, chap. 1, sec. 1; chap. 2, secs. 8–10; chap. 4, secs. 15–16 and 22; bk. 2, chap. 13, sec. 27; bk. 3, chap. 6, sec. 30; and bk. 4, chap. 2, sec. 4; chap. 3, sec. 6; chap. 12, secs. 7–9; and chap. 20, sec. 6; and Locke, *Of the Conduct of the Understanding*, secs. 4, 7, 16–17, 20, 23–25, 28, 30, 37–39, and 45. Cf. Locke, *Two Treatises of Government, Second Treatise*, chap. 6, sec. 56, with Locke, *An Essay Concerning Human Understanding*, bk. 3, chap. 1, sec. 1, through chap. 2, sec. 8, esp. chap. 1, sec. 5.

[104] See Locke, *Two Treatises of Government, Second Treatise*, chap. 6, sec. 61, which should be read in light of secs. 55 and 59.

[105] Ibid., secs. 59–60 and 63.

[106] Ibid., secs. 74–76. See ibid., chap. 8, secs. 105–11, esp. 107.

[107] Ibid., chap. 8, secs. 105–11, esp. 107.

tion, and it inspired in man the "temptation to labour for more than he could make use of"; it gave rise to foresight and calculation, and in due course, it made it possible for him to sever the "Bonds of this Subjection" and throw off "the Swadling clothes" that he was "wrapt in" so that he could be "at his own free Disposal."[108]

Initially, the invention of money gave birth to inequality, and this stirred up disputes and gave rise to conflicts. As men came to require an impartial umpire for the settling of their quarrels, the loose, patriarchal dominion of tribal chieftains and holy men gave way to the de facto rule of absolute monarchs. Adhering closely to his rhetorical purpose, Locke asserts that man's circumstances under absolute monarchy are far worse than they ever were when he was in his natural state. At the same time, however, Locke enables us to discern that human beings are, overall, less wretched and needy under arbitrary government than when left entirely ungoverned. Absolute monarchy is a halfway house between man's original condition and what Locke has in mind when he speaks of civil society. Because an absolute monarch has an interest in the peace and in the well-being of his kingdom, often enough he will be inclined to act as an impartial judge when arbitrating the disputes of his subjects. To this degree, his subjects will have escaped the ill condition into which mankind was at first born. But those whom the monarch governs have no comparable umpire to whom to appeal when their dispute is with him; and in this undoubtedly important respect, they remain "perfectly," as Locke puts it, in the state of nature. It is only natural that a ruler who is unchecked will take advantage of the power he wields when the interests at stake are his own. To this, one can add that rulers are prey to flattery— especially to the flattery of crafty, greedy, and ambitious priests—and they are for this reason exceedingly vulnerable to "Ambition, Revenge, Covetousness," and many another "irregular Passion."[109]

In the end, then, under absolute monarchies, "the Industrious and Rational" are but rarely provided in full measure with the protection that they seek when they submit themselves and their property to government. In breaching its trust, such a polity forfeits all claim to loyalty: it not only can but it should be replaced. For, according to Locke, government arises from consent, and it cannot seriously be supposed that anyone would consent to his own destruction. No one who lived in the age of

---

[108] Consider ibid., chap. 5, sec. 51 in light of ibid., chap. 6, sec. 55; then see Locke, *An Essay Concerning Human Understanding*, bk. 1, chap. 2, secs. 5–27.

[109] Consider Locke, *Two Treatises of Government, Second Treatise*, chap. 7, secs. 87–94; chap. 8, secs. 105–12; chap. 11, secs. 134–39; chap. 14, sec. 162; and chap. 18, sec. 199; in light of chap. 5, sec. 45. Note that, in reaching judgments and in enforcing them, patriarchs exercise "the executive power of the Law of Nature" and that alone: ibid., chap. 6, sec. 74. There is no sign that they are authorized and have the "Authority" to do so on behalf of anyone but themselves: ibid., chap. 7, sec. 89. In this connection, see Richard Ashcraft, "Locke's State of Nature: Historical Fact or Moral Fiction?" *American Political Science Review* 62, no. 3 (1968): 898–915, esp. 908–14, and Ashcraft, *Locke's Two Treatises of Government*, 152–66.

Charles II, James II, and Louis XIV, and no one who lived through the English Civil War (1642–51) or considered the similar struggles taking place on the European continent in the mid-seventeenth century could fail to discern that Locke had both kings and priests in mind when he denounced "the Fancy" and "Covetousness of the Quarrelsome and Contentious."[110]

The history of human association that Locke adumbrates in his *Two Treatises* reaches its denouement when he gives an account of the manner in which industriously rational men not only fabricate a species of political society that is genuinely civil but also doff the allegiance they once pledged to these putative viceroys of God and render man for the first time fully "Master of himself, and *Proprietor of his own Person*" by removing him and fencing him off, to the greatest extent that they can, "from the common state Nature placed" him in.[111] This they can achieve with Locke's aid by tending the "seeds" of reason within them and by examining "more carefully *the Original* and Rights of *Government*" and discovering "ways to *restrain the Exorbitances,* and *prevent the Abuses* of that Power which they" have "intrusted in another's hands only for their own good."[112]

Locke's tract has two purposes, which correspond to the two parts of politics: first, and above all else, he desires to convince his readers that consent is the sole foundation of government and that safeguarding and encouraging industry is government's only legitimate aim; second, he aspires to reveal how men may confine the prerogative of princes and establish political institutions guaranteeing impartial judgment and rendering safe and secure the property each man holds in his life, his liberty, and his estates. Ultimately, it is the expectation that man can liberate himself from fatherly rule both human and divine that accounts for the revolutionary call to arms that Locke passes off as an *"appeal to Heaven."*[113] When he exhorts men to emulate the "Omnipotent, and infinitely wise Maker" envisaged in the Bible, Locke encourages them in the discovery

[110] Locke, *Two Treatises of Government, Second Treatise,* chap. 5, sec. 34.

[111] Consider ibid., secs. 26–28 and 44, in light of sec. 34.

[112] Consider Locke, *Two Treatises of Government, Second Treatise,* chap. 7, secs. 87 and 93, through chap. 8, sec. 112 (esp. chap. 7, sec. 94, and chap. 8, sec. 111); chap. 9, secs. 123–31; chap. 11, sec. 134, through chap. 12, sec. 148; chap. 14, sec. 162; chap. 15, secs. 171 and 173; in light of Locke, *Of the Conduct of the Understanding,* sec. 6.

[113] Consider Locke, *Two Treatises of Government, Second Treatise,* chap. 13, sec. 149; chap. 14, sec. 168; chap. 16, secs. 176, 192, and 196; chap. 18, secs. 204, 208–10; and chap. 19, secs. 220–43; in light of chap. 3, secs. 20–21. In making Jephtha's appeal to heaven his model (ibid., chap. 3, sec. 21; chap. 14, sec. 168; chap. 16, sec. 176; and chap. 19, sec. 241), Locke ignores the more pertinent example of self-restraint under tyrannical provocation evident in David's similarly worded appeal and lights upon what he knows (ibid., chap. 8, sec. 109) to have been an ordinary case of war: cf. Judg. 11:1–40 (esp. 27, 30–40) with 1 Sam. 24:6, 12, 15, 26:9–11, 23. Note John Locke, *A Letter Concerning Toleration,* ed. Mario Montuori (The Hague: Martinus Nijhoff, 1963), 86–89. As Tarcov, *Locke's Education for Liberty,* 66, points out, Locke nowhere suggests that God will intervene to see that justice is done. See *Two Treatises of Government, Second Treatise,* chap. 16, sec. 176.

that, by and large, they are their own "Workmanship"—and not, as he so vigorously asserts early on, that of almighty God.[114]

Such would appear to be the aim of Locke's argument.[115] Such is certainly its drift.[116] Subtly, by means of a refined, philosophical rhetoric, without ever explicitly repudiating the doctrine of Providence or denying the existence of the Christian God, and while expressly reaffirming and obliquely subverting the faith of his fathers, Locke carried his readers from where John Aubrey had found them toward a posture of radical autonomy. Had they ever realized where they were tending, had they fully caught his drift, most of his early readers in the seventeenth and eighteenth centuries no doubt would have recoiled in horror, which is presumably why Locke never openly divulged what he was about.[117]

---

[114] In keeping with this fact, except where politically salutary (*Two Treatises of Government, Second Treatise,* chap. 4, sec. 23; chap. 11, sec. 135; chap. 13, sec. 149; chap. 14, sec. 168; and chap. 15, sec. 172), Locke silently abandons his initial claim (ibid., chap. 2, sec. 6) that man is God's "Property" and asserts, instead, that he is "absolute Lord of his own Person" (ibid., chap. 5, secs. 27 and 44; and chap. 9, sec. 123). His inconsistent treatment of the question of suicide is explicable in similar terms: cf. ibid., chap. 2, sec. 6 with chap. 4, sec. 23; note Locke, *An Essay Concerning Human Understanding,* bk. 2, chap. 21, secs. 53 and 57; and see George Windstrup, "Locke on Suicide," *Political Theory* 8, no. 2 (1980): 169–82.

[115] It is possible, of course, that Locke badly missed his aim—but then one must question his sanity, for the contradictions in his argument are too glaring; the inconsistencies, too obvious. They cannot have escaped the notice of a man with his wits about him. It can hardly be an accident that the figure that emerges from the most exacting attempt ever mounted to make sense of Locke as a pious Christian in the Puritan mold is a "profoundly and exotically incoherent" thinker guilty of nearly every intellectual failing that one finds excoriated in his epistemological writings. Locke was "brought up in a Calvinist family"; and though the logic of his new way of ideas clearly pointed away from the doctrines he had imbibed in the nursery, we are told that he never managed to fully liberate himself from a posture of blind credulity. On this reading, his oft-revised *Two Treatises of Government* turns out to be an "incoherent and carelessly written work"; and, as a consequence of the tension between his faith and the dictates of his reason, both it and his *Essay Concerning Human Understanding* are "in so many ways patently inconsistent and absurd" that one can render the arguments there presented explicable only by supposing their author a victim of "intellectual akrasia"—profoundly insecure, ridden by anguish, and "very neurotic." See Dunn, *The Political Thought of John Locke,* passim, esp. 13, 29, 80–82, 92–93, 164, 187–99, and 256–60. For further elaboration of the view that Locke was a victim of "intellectual akrasia," see John Dunn, "Individuality and Clientage in the Formation of Locke's Social Imagination," "'Trust' in the Politics of John Locke," and "From Applied Theology to Social Analysis: The Break between Locke and the Scottish Enlightenment," in John Dunn, *Rethinking Modern Political Theory: Essays, 1979–83* (Cambridge: Cambridge University Press, 1985), 13–67. Note also Dunn, "Consent in the Political Theory of John Locke," in John Dunn, *Political Obligation in Its Historical Context: Essays in Political Theory* (Cambridge: Cambridge University Press, 1980), 29–52.

[116] One cannot paper over the difficulties: Locke was either sane and devious, as his contemporaries tended to suppose—see Maurice Cranston, *John Locke: A Biography* (New York: Macmillan, 1957); Richard Ashcraft, *Revolutionary Politics and Locke's Two Treatises of Government* (Princeton, NJ: Princeton University Press, 1986); and Rahe, "John Locke's Philosophical Partisanship," 1–43—or he was deeply troubled and intellectually at odds with himself, as Dunn, *The Political Thought of John Locke,* contends. There really is no alternative. Cf., however, A. John Simmons, *The Lockean Theory of Rights* (Princeton, NJ: Princeton University Press, 1992).

[117] Whether any argument for natural rights and the natural equality of man can ultimately be sustained in the absence of the Christian God is, of course, another matter

VI. Conclusion

As should by now be clear, when James Wilson declared that the "primary object of [government and] Society" is the "cultivation [and] improvement of the human mind," when James Madison asserted that "the first object of Government" is "the protection" of the "different and unequal faculties of acquiring property," and when Alexander Hamilton argued for selective economic intervention on the part of the new American government in such a way as to furnish "greater scope for the diversity of talents and dispositions, which discriminate men from each other," they were tracing the logic of the argument that Locke presented in his *Two Treatises of Government*. That they were not alone among their compatriots in thinking that there was more to the protection of property rights than a prudential provision for self-preservation and commodious living is evident from the fact that those in attendance at the federal convention in Philadelphia voted unanimously and without adverse comment to adopt the suggestion advanced by Madison and South Carolina delegate Charles Pinckney that the new federal Constitution provide for the establishment of the world's first permanently organized patent office—an institution designed for the protection of the rights of inventors and for the encouragement of their activity.[118]

The patent was, of course, nothing new. The practice of granting a temporary monopoly to those who had imported or invented new products and techniques of use had a long history in England and had been promoted in the sixteenth century by Queen Elizabeth I's chief minister William Cecil, Lord Burghley, and his young nephew Francis Bacon. This was, however, a matter of royal indulgence and had no standing per se as a legal right.[119] It was left to the Americans to create a new species of

---

entirely: see Jeremy Waldron, *God, Locke, and Equality: Christian Foundations in Locke's Political Thought* (Cambridge: Cambridge University Press, 2002). For Locke, the natural-rights argument—which is difficult, if not impossible, to square with the account of nature that he provides in *An Essay Concerning Human Understanding*—may be entirely rhetorical, a public teaching crafted to suit his immediate ends. The same concerns may explain Locke's undoubted interest in Socinian argumentation: see Marshall, *John Locke*, passim, esp. 327–451.

[118] See Farrand, ed., *Records of the Federal Convention*, 2:324–26, 505–6 (August 18 and September 5, 1787). Originally, Madison argued that the government should have the power "to encourage by premiums [and] provisions, the advancement of useful knowledge and discoveries"; Pinckney explicitly called for the government to have the power "to grant patents for useful inventions." See George W. Evans, "The Birth and Growth of the Patent Office," *Records of the Columbia Historical Society* 22 (1919): 105–24. Madison revealed an interest in patent law well before the convention. See Bill for Granting James Rumsey a Patent for Ship Construction, November 11, 1784, in Hutchinson, Rachal, et al., eds., *The Papers of James Madison*, 8:131–33. See also Irving Brant, *James Madison* (Indianapolis: Bobbs-Merrill, 1941–61), 2:370. Because the patent clause was uncontroversial, the Constitution's most eloquent defenders and exponents deemed it unnecessary to speak of it at length, but they did manage to hint at its importance by giving its discussion central place: see *Federalist No. 43* (J. Madison), in Cooke, ed., *The Federalist*, 288.

[119] For a comprehensive discussion of the origins of the patent, see Harold G. Fox, *Monopolies and Patents: A Study of the History and Future of the Patent Monopoly* (Toronto: University

property, honoring man's capacity as a toolmaking animal, and to give it not just legal but constitutional sanction.

In the aftermath of the American Revolution, when Major Pierre-Charles L'Enfant developed his grand plan for the city of Washington in the District of Columbia, he deliberately left space midway between the White House and the Capitol for a national church. In the *Observations Explanatory of the Plan* that accompanied his plans, he proposed that "this Church" be "assigned to the special use of no particular Sect or denomination" and that it be "equally open to all." L'Enfant envisaged this great ecclesiastical edifice as a temple suited to rituals "such as public prayer, thanksgivings, funeral orations," and the like; and it was to serve also as "a proper shelter for such monuments as were voted by the late Continental Congress for those heroes who fell in the cause of liberty, and for such others as may hereafter be decreed by the voice of a grateful Nation." [120]

The church planned by L'Enfant was never built. In its place, a monument was constructed with a tellingly different purpose. In 1836, during the presidency of Andrew Jackson, Congress approved plans submitted by William Parker Elliot for an ambitious and impressive Greek revival structure—a neoclassical "temple of the useful arts"—to house the Patent Office and to provide showrooms for the display of the models submitted by the nation's inventors.[121] Though no longer used for its original purpose, the building still stands as a fitting reminder of the central place of honor reserved within the American regime for the useful arts whose cultivation constituted, in the opinions of Sir Francis Bacon and John Locke, and in those of James Wilson, James Madison, Alexander Hamilton, and a great many other Americans, both "the highest Perfection, that a Man can attain to in this Life" and "the dignity of his nature."

History, University of Tulsa

---

of Toronto, 1947), 3–189. See also William Hyde Price, *The English Patents of Monopoly* (Cambridge, MA: Harvard University Press, 1913), 3–46; and Arthur Allan Gomme, *Patents of Invention: Origin and Growth of the Patent System in Britain* (London: Longmans Green and Co., 1946), 5–12. See also E. Wyndham Hulme, "The History of the Patent System under the Prerogative and at Common Law," *Law Quarterly Review*, vol. 12, no. 46 (1896): 141–54, and vol. 16, no. 61 (1900): 44–56.

[120] See Elizabeth S. Kite, *L'Enfant and Washington* (Baltimore, MD: Johns Hopkins Press, 1929), 61–66, where the plan and L'Enfant's observations are reprinted. See also Report of June 22, 1791, in ibid., 54–55. L'Enfant's purpose in developing his plan was to reinforce or at least imitate the separation of powers by setting the White House, the Congress, and the Supreme Court at a sufficient distance from each other that three separate communities would grow up within the District of Columbia. The nondenominational church was to be the central point at which the three converged. See James Sterling Young, *The Washington Community, 1800–1828* (New York: Columbia University Press, 1966), 1–10.

[121] See Louise Hall, "New Threat to Washington Landmark: The Design of the Old Patent Office," *Journal of the Society of Architectural Historians* 15, no. 1 (1956): 27–30; and Jane B. Davies, "A. J. Davis' Projects for a Patent Office Building, 1832–1834," *Journal of the Society of Architectural Historians* 24, no. 3 (1965): 229–51. The phrase used to describe the structure was coined by Elliot's older brother Jonathan.

NATURAL RIGHTS AND IMPERIAL CONSTITUTIONALISM: THE AMERICAN REVOLUTION AND THE DEVELOPMENT OF THE AMERICAN AMALGAM

By Michael Zuckert

I. Introduction

Robert Nozick surely went where few men have gone before: he won a National Book Award and a great deal of public acclaim for writing an admittedly witty and clever, but nonetheless difficult and often technical book of philosophy. When *Anarchy, State, and Utopia* appeared in 1974, it stood next to John Rawls's *A Theory of Justice* (1971) as the second political philosophy "blockbuster" of the decade, convincing most observers that the obituaries for political philosophy regularly pronounced in the 1950s and 1960s were greatly premature. Rawls and Nozick—in those days regularly pronounced almost as one word—had not only revived political philosophy, but they had revived a specific tradition: Lockean liberal theory. Both made explicit appeal to Locke; neither was an orthodox Lockean. Nozick appealed to Lockean rights, but explicitly eschewed the Lockean social contract. Rawls appealed to a version of the contract, but eschewed Lockean natural rights. Each, in a sense, took in one half of the Lockean political philosophy, in both cases generously leavened with Kant and various other non-Lockean elements. Prior to Rawls and Nozick, Lockean theory certainly may have been in eclipse, but it remains a striking fact that our two revivalists burst onto the scene as (partial) legatees of Locke, the thinker known as "America's philosopher" for the great role he had in shaping American political culture. It is noteworthy that Rawls and Nozick not only struck so many resonant chords in Locke-land, but failed to have quite that kind of impact elsewhere. Might it not be the case that the reception Rawls and Nozick received, the plausibility and persuasiveness either or both of them had, stemmed in some large part from their Lockean tonalities in a deeply Lockean political culture? Rawls's later turn to a "political conception," admittedly rooted in the American political culture, would seem to be one piece of evidence for this.

I am, in any case, taking that hypothesis as a means to segue to my theme: the formation of America's Lockean political culture (or at least one element of it) in the eighteenth century. I wish to examine one particular moment in the development of this American Lockean tradition. My inquiry is meant, at the same time, to make a contribution to understanding the American Revolution—its cause and its meaning. Indeed, I mean to explore two themes in particular: first, the American Lockean political culture (what I call the "American amalgam" or the "natural rights amalgam") as a cause of the American Revolution, and then the Revolution as a cause of the natural rights amalgam. I hope in the course of my argument to clarify and make plausible the chicken-and-egg paradox contained in my two themes.

In Section II below, I will briefly review the state of the historiographical argument on the causes of the American Revolution in order to clarify where I am picking up the question. Section III traces the development of the "natural rights amalgam"—the synthesis of natural rights thinking and Whig constitutional theory—as a cause of the Revolution. Section IV traces the historical contingencies in the political struggles leading up to the Revolution, which made the Lockean rights philosophy appear so attractive to the Americans, and which produced the amalgam.

II. The State of the Argument on the Causes of the American Revolution

On the fiftieth anniversary of the Declaration of Independence, the mayor of Washington, DC, Roger Weightman, read to the assembled celebrants a letter from Thomas Jefferson, who that day lay dying at his estate outside Charlottesville, Virginia, not far from Washington. In the letter, Jefferson attempted to capture for his fellow Americans, and for the entire world, the meaning of the American Revolution: it signaled that "all eyes are opened or opening, to the rights of man." Since the Declaration of Independence, the document being celebrated that very day, gave prominent place to the "unalienable rights" for whose sake "governments are instituted among men," Jefferson's identification of the meaning of July 4, 1776, has prima facie plausibility.[1]

Yet the experts in such matters have not been so sure. Progressive historians, most famously represented by Charles Beard and dominant in American historiography during most of the first half of the twentieth century, thought that the Revolution and founding were much more about economics and class interests than the rights of man. Consider the outspoken judgment of economic historian Louis M. Hacker:

> The [revolutionary] struggle was not over high-sounding political and constitutional concepts; over the power of taxation or even, in the final analysis, over natural rights. It was over colonial manufacturing, wild lands and furs, sugar, wine, tea, and currency, all of

---

[1] Thomas Jefferson to Roger Weightman, June 24, 1826, in Thomas Jefferson, *Writings*, ed. Merrill D. Peterson (New York: The Library of America, 1984), 1516–17.

which meant, simply, the survival or collapse of English mercantile capitalism within the imperial-colonial framework of the mercantilist system.[2]

The economic interpretation of the Revolution led historians to judge statements like Jefferson's as largely superficial ideological statements, masking the more fundamental economic and social roots of the conflict. As the eminent colonial historian Edmund S. Morgan summarized the views of the Progressive historians, "The social and economic interpretation . . . shows [the revolutionary leaders] as hypocrites pursuing selfish interests while they mouth platitudes about democracy and freedom. . . . [T]heir insistence on freedom and equality is shown to be insincere."[3]

Morgan himself, with his book *The Stamp Act Crisis* (1953), and after him Bernard Bailyn, with his *The Ideological Origins of the American Revolution* (1967), fostered the reorientation of thinking away from the economic approach and toward an understanding of the revolution that gave far more weight to the opinions, theories, and principles of the actors in those events.[4] Neither Morgan nor Bailyn nor most of their followers quite revived Jefferson's view of the meaning of 1776, however. Morgan's very valuable research focused attention on the constitutional dimension of the struggle. Colonial constitutional arguments had been discounted in the era of Progressive historiographical domination, because, it was said, the colonists in fact did not take a consistent position on the constitution, but instead engaged in a series of ad hoc adjustments to each shift in British imperial policy intended to appease the formerly pressed colonial objections and concerns. In other words, it did not appear to progressive historians that the Americans had a consistent constitutional theory or that their constitutional arguments were sincere statements of their views, but rather special pleadings gotten up for changing occasions, largely having the character of rationalizations for positions adopted for other reasons. Thus Carl Becker concluded his survey of colonial constitutional argumentation: "[S]tep by step, from 1764 to 1776, the colonists modified their theory to suit their needs."[5] Moreover, it was said by most of the

---

[2] Louis M. Hacker, *The Triumph of American Capitalism* (New York: Simon and Schuster, 1940), quoted in *The Causes of the American Revolution*, 3d ed., ed. John C. Wahlke (Lexington, MA: D. C. Heath and Co., 1973), x.

[3] Edmund S. Morgan, "The American Revolution: Revisions in Need of Revising" (1957), reprinted in Edmund S. Morgan, *The Challenge of the American Revolution* (New York: W. W. Norton and Co., 1976), 45.

[4] Edmund S. Morgan and Helen M. Morgan, *The Stamp Act Crisis: Prologue to Revolution* (Chapel Hill: University of North Carolina Press, 1953); Bernard Bailyn, *The Ideological Origins of the American Revolution* (Cambridge, MA: Harvard University Press, 1967). See also Bernard Bailyn, "Political Experience and Enlightenment Ideas in Eighteenth-Century America," *American Historical Review* 67, no. 2 (1962): 339–51.

[5] Carl Becker, *The Declaration of Independence* (New York: Random House, 1942), 133.

Progressive historians, the colonists' constitutional arguments, as constitutional arguments, were not very solid.[6]

Morgan demonstrated, to the contrary, that from the time of the protest
against the Stamp Act onward the colonists put forward a consistent
constitutional position, possessing all the earmarks of a theory in which
they truly believed and in terms of which they acted. Admittedly, this
constitutional theory underwent a process of refinement and development, but on the main point—whether Parliament could tax the colonies
in any way—the Americans from the outset were agreed that Parliament
could not do so. They therefore did not, as charged, slyly shift their
grounds as Britain attempted to accommodate them. For the most part,
Morgan attended to the constitutional arguments and the rights the colonists claimed as Englishmen, not those they claimed as men. He does
note from time to time how colonial spokesmen such as James Otis ran
these two kinds of rights together, but on the whole Morgan did not give
us a picture of the Revolution quite like Jefferson's.

Bailyn, writing in 1967, about a decade after Morgan, had an even
larger impact on thinking about the Revolution. He embraced the term
"ideology," but meant by it something different from the epiphenom-
enal set of beliefs that para-Marxist Progressive historians had in mind.
Like Morgan, he wanted to call attention to the causal importance of
the colonists' beliefs and opinions—their ideologies. He did not look to
their constitutional thinking so much, however, as to a system of thought
he identified with the English Whig opposition, that is, with those
Whigs who stood in opposition to the Whig administration of Robert
Walpole during the early eighteenth century. This was much less a
legal/constitutional style of thought and much more political in character. The main theme that Bailyn presented as an almost paranoid
approach to politics was the notion of power against liberty: liberty is
always endangered by the depredations of those in power, who, as
often as not, conspire against the liberty of those they rule. The colonists, Bailyn argued, viewed the events of the 1760s and 1770s through
lenses of this sort, and thus were quick to see evil intent in the policies
of the British administrations. Bailyn's approach to the revolution quickly
joined with other strands to produce the now well-known "republican
synthesis." As sponsored by scholars such as Gordon Wood and J. G. A.
Pocock, this "republican synthesis" emphasizes themes of classical republicanism, tracing back to Aristotle and Machiavelli, rather than the themes
of Lockean liberalism more frequently noted in American thinking before

---

[6] For a discussion of Progressive views on American constitutional argumentation, see
Jack P. Greene, *Peripheries and Center: Constitutional Development in the Extended Polities of the
British Empire and the United States, 1607–1788* (Athens: University of Georgia Press, 1986),
144–50.

the emergence of the new republican historiography.[7] As with Morgan, the "rights of man" play a role in Bailyn's account, but by no means so central a role as they do in Jefferson's assessment of the Revolution. They play even less of a role in the republican synthesis, which identifies political ideologies of an anti-rights orientation: not individualistic and modernist natural rights, but communitarianism and classical republicanism—the duties of man—form the core of the republican synthesis.[8]

Both the Morgan- and the Bailyn-inspired lines of interpretation have thrived in the decades since these two scholars put forward their main theses. In my book *The Natural Rights Republic* (1996), I have reconsidered at some length the republican synthesis and made a case for taking Enlightenment natural rights commitments more seriously than the synthesizers do, and for seeing the commitment to republicanism of the American founding generation not as a classically inspired alternative to the natural rights/social contract philosophy, but as an implicate of it. The same is true, I will argue, of the constitutional arguments of the Americans; they, too, are implicates of the natural rights/social contract philosophy.

Many fine scholars have followed along Morgan's general line and have extended his argument in important directions. Two are particularly worth mention here, for they form the immediate backdrop for my argument in this essay. Jack P. Greene, a political historian, and John Phillip Reid, a legal historian, are the two who have most energetically carried forward inquiries into the constitutional issues of the American Revolution. Both Greene and Reid retain Morgan's emphasis on the seriousness and sincerity of the Americans' constitutional commitments. Thus Greene titled one of his essays "The Ostensible Cause Was . . . the True One: The Salience of Rights in the Origin of the American Revolution."[9] (The rights he has in mind are the "rights of Englishmen" rather than natural rights.)

Greene and Reid go beyond Morgan in a number of ways, however. First, they do not limit themselves to the constitutional issues surrounding the Stamp Act; both cover the full range of events and issues culminating in the Revolution. Second, more than Morgan, they validate the colonists' position as constitutionally correct, or at least as constitutionally defensible. Third, they have a more fully worked out notion of wherein constitutional correctness lies. Greene, Reid, and a handful of other scholars argue to the second point that the imperial constitution was not as settled as the Progressive historians who dismissed the colonists' position

---

[7] Gordon S. Wood, *The Creation of the American Republic* (Chapel Hill: University of North Carolina Press, 1968); J. G. A. Pocock, *The Machiavellian Moment* (Princeton, NJ: Princeton University Press, 1975).

[8] The literature on the republican synthesis is immense. For a fuller account of it, see Michael P. Zuckert, *Natural Rights and the New Republicanism* (Princeton, NJ: Princeton University Press, 1994), chap. 6; and Michael P. Zuckert, *The Natural Rights Republic* (Notre Dame, IN: University of Notre Dame Press, 1996), chap. 7.

[9] *Reviews in American History* 16, no. 2 (1988): 198–203.

as patently untenable would have us believe. Although the British were operating with an evolving theory of the constitution that emphasized parliamentary sovereignty, this new constitutionalism was an innovation and was by no means so well established that it ruled out of court older constitutional ideas such as those the Americans asserted. The legitimacy of the American position was especially defensible in light of what Greene and Reid identify as the prevailing criterion for establishing constitutional legitimacy: "[T]he source of the authority underlying both the seventeenth century English constitution, and the contemporary American constitutions was custom." [10] In general, Anglo-American constitutionalism was one of usage and custom, ultimately bespeaking a form of consent by the parties affected by the constitutional arrangements. The colonists had a strong case that custom and usage favored their claims regarding the limited or nonexistent powers of Parliament in America and, more importantly perhaps, their "claim that rights established through custom 'were beyond modification by Parliament' as well as by the king." [11]

Despite Greene's and Reid's very friendly assessment of the colonists' case, this recent wave of scholarship still remains distant from Jefferson's assessment of the Revolution. The scholars affirm that the Revolution was about rights, of course, but the "rights of Englishmen," not the rights of man. Reid is quite dogmatic, in fact, in depreciating the Jeffersonian reading of the Revolution: he once published an article titled "The Irrelevance of the Declaration [of Independence]." [12] Reid does not literally mean that the Declaration was "irrelevant" (although he identifies other documents as more authoritative and significant), but he means that its natural rights philosophy was irrelevant. That is, he thoroughly contests Jefferson's assessment. According to Reid, "the British Constitution, not Locke [and the natural rights philosophy] supplied the American Whigs with their theoretical motivation." [13] Greene, to the same effect, affirms that the Anglo-American dispute was "essentially a constitutional one pitting opposing interpretations of the colonial position in the imperial order." [14]

---

[10] Reid, quoted in Greene's *Peripheries*, 146. See also, John Phillip Reid, "In Accordance with Usage: The Authority of Custom, the Stamp Act Debate, and the Coming of the American Revolution," *Fordham Law Review* 45 (1976).

[11] Greene, *Peripheries*, 146. The internal quotation is from Barbara A. Black, "The Constitution of the Empire: The Case for the Colonists," *University of Pennsylvania Law Review* 124 (1976), 1203.

[12] John Phillip Reid, "The Irrelevance of the Declaration," in *Law in the American Revolution and the Revolution in Law: A Collection of Review Essays in American Legal History*, ed. Hendrik Hartog (New York: New York University Press, 1981).

[13] John Phillip Reid, *Constitutional History of the American Revolution: The Authority to Legislate* (Madison: University of Wisconsin Press, 1991), 5.

[14] Jack P. Greene, "Origins of the American Revolution: A Constitutional Interpretation," in *The Framing and Ratification of the Constitution*, ed. Leonard W. Levy and Dennis J. Mahoney (New York: Macmillan, 1987), 40.

More important than their disagreement with Jefferson's retrospective (1826) interpretation of the meaning of the Revolution is the fact that the Greene/Reid view fails to take sufficient account of what the patriots were actually saying before and during the Revolution itself. It thus fails to capture the true theory of the colonists and is of little help in understanding the natural rights amalgam, which got so firmly planted in the soil of the American political culture at this formative moment. I do not mean to contest the Greene/Reid emphasis on the constitutional dimension of the revolutionary conflict, but I do plan to challenge the way they develop their argument and many of their chief conclusions. In doing so, I mean to take as a point of departure the important set of distinctions that Greene has made more clearly than any previous writer on the subject. On Greene's account, there were "three sets of operative constitutions in the British empire: the British constitution, the specific constitutions of individual colonies, and the emerging imperial constitution."[15] I will focus my attention on the third—the imperial constitution itself. My claims are these: First, the American theory of the imperial constitution is more questionable from a traditional or customary perspective than Greene and Reid allow, a point that the Americans themselves concede with some regularity. Second, the natural rights philosophy figures decisively in shaping and validating the American version of the imperial constitution; it is true that the debate between the Americans and the British was in essence a debate about the constitution and not about natural rights, but the fact that the Americans read the constitution through natural rights/social contract colored glasses produced the version of the constitution to which they adhered. Third, the suitability of the natural rights theory to undergirding the American constitutional position was a central factor in the planting in America of the Lockean political culture to which, two centuries later, Rawls and Nozick appealed.

It is fairly widely agreed that there were three particularly good formulations of the American theory of the empire: Thomas Jefferson's *A Summary View of the Rights of British America,* dating from July 1774; James Wilson's *Considerations on the Nature and Extent of the Legislative Authority of the British Parliament,* dating from August 1774; and John Adams's *Novanglus* essays, running in the Boston press from January to April 1775. All three contain remarkably similar theories of the imperial constitution, and all three defend their theories in broadly similar ways.

III. The Natural Rights Amalgam as a Cause of the Revolution

The conflict leading up to the Revolution was indeed a battle over the true character of the constitution of the British empire. The British view

---

[15] Greene, *Peripheries,* xi; also see 65.

was put with unusual perspicuousness in the Declaratory Act passed by Parliament in 1766, along with Parliament's repeal of the 1765 Stamp Act, which had attempted to lay a tax on various items of colonial commerce. The Declaratory Act stated unequivocally that Parliament "had, hath, and of right ought to have, full power and authority to make laws and statutes of sufficient force and validity to bind the colonies and people of America, subjects of the crown of Great Britain, in all cases whatsoever." The power to legislate "in all cases whatsoever" derives from the status of the colonies in America; they are "his Majesty's dominions in America," and as such "have been, are, and of right ought to be, subordinate unto, and dependent on the imperial crown and Parliament of Great Britain." [16]

The American theory of empire was almost the complete negation of the parliamentary theory: according to the American colonists, Parliament has the right to legislate for them *in no cases whatsoever*.[17] Other than ties of blood and affection, the only legal link to Britain is through the King. The American colonies are connected to Britain and to each other, for that matter, only by virtue of having a common monarch. Parliament is no part of this link. The King enters into the constitutions of the separate American colonies just as he does into the British constitution. Just as the King-in-Parliament can legislate and tax in Britain, so the King-in-the-New-York-Assembly can legislate and tax in New York. The American doctrine led to the startling conclusion that George III was not only King of Great Britain, but also, individually and independently of Parliament, King of New York, Rhode Island, Virginia, Barbados, and so on. Likewise, the doctrine implied that the legislative assemblies of those entities were exactly on a par with the great British Parliament itself.

Although Americans today are familiar with constitutional indeterminacy from our own experience, we might still wonder how it could be possible that eighteenth-century British and American views diverged so markedly. The answer lies in three facts about the imperial constitution of the eighteenth century. We must recall, first, that neither Britain itself nor the empire had a constitution of the sort we normally think of, a written document with a designated body to interpret it authoritatively. There were written documents with constitutional status—for example, the

---

[16] *Declaratory Act*, 6 George III, c. 12; reprinted in Henry Steele Commager, *Documents in American History* (New York: Appleton-Century-Crofts, 1963), 1: 60–361.

[17] Knowledgeable readers will discern that I have somewhat simplified the colonial position in order to make its contrast with the British as stark as it was in principle. Some of the colonists did in fact recognize the right of Parliament to regulate the external commerce of the colonies, but they said this was not an inherent power of Parliament but a power the Americans specially consented to because of its convenience for coordinating trade within the broader Anglo-American world. Thus, Adams frames the issue as follows: "The question is not . . . whether the authority of Parliament extends to the colonies in *any* case, for it is admitted by the Whigs that it does in that of commerce; but whether it extends in *all* cases" (emphasis added). John Adams, *Novanglus* VIII, in vol. 4 of *The Works of John Adams*, ed. Charles Francis Adams (Boston, MA: Little and Brown, 1851), 100.

Magna Carta (1215) or the Bill of Rights adopted in the wake of the Glorious Revolution (1688–89)—but there was a great open-endedness as to what documents counted as constitutional and how much unwritten customs and understandings counted; above all, perhaps, there was no clear process in place for effecting constitutional change and authoritatively pronouncing constitutional meaning.

The second fact of great importance was that the constitutional issues that arose in the course of the eighteenth century overreached whatever consensus on constitutional principles had been achieved at the end of the seventeenth century. That century had been, in effect, one long constitutional crisis that reached a political settlement in the Glorious Revolution and a constitutional settlement in the Bill of Rights. That settlement established the unquestioned presence of Parliament in the governance of the nation. The Bill of Rights established (or reestablished) that the King may not legislate, tax, dispense with or suspend the laws, or raise or quarter armies without the consent of Parliament. To properly appreciate the settlement of 1689, one must realize that the King was also part of Parliament, for his assent was needed for legislation. The constitutional order of 1689 mandates that governance is not to be by King alone, but by King and Parliament. Sharing of power between crown and Parliament is the keynote of the constitution. The Bill of Rights is thus very clear in establishing limitations on the power of the King acting alone, but says nothing whatsoever about limitations on the powers of King-in-Parliament. But the constitutional issues of the eighteenth century were precisely about that question: Were there limits to what the King and Parliament could do together?

Likewise, the settlement of 1689 concerned the governance of Great Britain itself, that is, the political entity over which the King reigned and which had representation in the British Parliament. The settlement was silent about the principles of governance of entities, especially colonial entities, outside that sphere. As John Adams said in a *Novanglus* essay, "[T]here is no provision in the common law, in English precedents, in the English government or constitution, made for the case of the colonies." [18] How the principles of the constitution were to apply to these entities, that is, to the question of the imperial, rather than the domestic constitution, is precisely what was at issue in the eighteenth century and precisely that about which the constitutional consensus as captured in the Bill of Rights had nothing to say.

The third key fact was that the colonies had been settled, and the terms of their relationship with the motherland had been originally undertaken before the Glorious Revolution. Indeed, in the early parts of the seventeenth century, the actual character of the domestic constitution was beset

---

[18] Adams, *Novanglus* XII, in ibid., 170. See also *Novanglus* VIII: "*[C]olonization* is *casus omissus* at common law" (ibid., 121).

with great and fundamental unclarities, especially regarding the powers of the King and of Parliament. Many of these constitutional uncertainties were clarified over the course of the century, culminating in the constitutional settlement after the Glorious Revolution. But one question that was propelled into the eighteenth century was whether those changes effected in 1689 affected the relations with the colonies or not. The Americans tended to say no: they had not been consulted nor had they consented to those changes. The British tended to say yes. The entire governance of Great Britain was put on such a footing that the sovereignty of King-in-Parliament was now established. The King had no claims to independence of Parliament such as was implicit in the pre-1689 relations between King and colonies and in many of the documents, such as the colonial charters, on which the colonies rested.[19] In brief, then, the three factors that made such deep constitutional conflict possible were the inherent character of the constitution, the uncertainty over how the domestic constitution should be extended beyond the traditional boundaries of Great Britain, and the historical change in the character of the constitution that occurred between the seventeenth-century settlement and the eighteenth-century conflict.

By far the longest of the three main defenses of the American constitutional position was Adams's *Novanglus* essays. Adams went longest not only because of his legendary volubility—his book *A Defense of the Constitutions of Government of the United States of America* was a three-volume affair written in response to a two-page letter by the French philosophe and political economist Anne-Robert-Jacques Turgot. Like his *Defense*, Adams's *Novanglus* was written as a response to another's writing, in this case a series defending the British constitutional position by a writer using the pseudonym "Massachusettensis," now known to be Boston politician and lawyer Daniel Leonard. Some of Adams's great prolixity was due to his obsessive desire to address in one way or another every word of his opponents' texts, but more followed from his effort to supply a thorough consideration of the legal constitutional issues in their own terms, that is, in the terms of common law, custom, and usage that Greene and Reid would much later maintain were the sole constitutional methodology for discerning and construing the British constitution.

Adams attempted to demonstrate two propositions above all else in his long, thorough, and (it must be said) somewhat rambling and disorderly disquisition. First, he attempted to show that the constitutional status the British were claiming for America—a part of the British empire, subject to the sovereignty and control of the ruling British authority, Parliament— had no standing in the British constitution; that is, there was no such status in the constitution and, a fortiori, no such status could characterize the American colonies. Second, he attempted to show that the constitu-

---

[19] Greene, *Peripheries*, 58.

tional status he and his fellow Americans claimed for themselves (viewing the colonies as, in effect, parallel political communities attached to Britain and each other via a common King, but not through Parliament) was indeed a recognized status within the constitution.

Given their heavy emphasis on custom, usage, common law, and practice, the *Novanglus* essays are a good test case to demonstrate the strengths — and the weaknesses—of the Greene/Reid view of the nature of the prerevolutionary conflict. Just as they say, Adams put great weight on precedent; as a trained lawyer he put much weight also on legal technicalities, in which I will not follow him here.[20] The core of Adams's first argument is the claim that the common law, the repository of English law, recognizes no such entity as the "British empire": "British empire" is "the language of newspapers and political pamphlets," not of the law.[21] The law recognizes no imperial powers in the British state either. According to Adams, there are, under the constitution, no "subject" entities, that is, no political bodies ruled by but not represented in Parliament. The core of Adams's second argument affirming the constitutional status the Americans claimed for themselves is the observation that there was a universally recognized period in the seventeenth century from the ascension of James as King of both England (as James I) and Scotland (as James VI), when he governed England with the English Parliament and Scotland with the Scottish Parliament. Thus, during this period, the kind of "imperial" entity Adams claims the empire to be was clearly known to the constitution. James was King of both countries and the two parliaments were separate and parallel institutions. The colonies, Adams argues, were settled on these very terms, and the colonists had never consented to any change in terms that would grant Parliament authority over them, in contrast to the change in Britain itself when England and Scotland united under one King and one Parliament in 1707.

As the scholarship of Charles McIlwain and John Phillip Reid shows, Adams's constitutional arguments are not incompetent or obviously incorrect, but Adams himself concedes that as thus far stated they are problematical. Indeed, I would maintain that they are more problematical than these scholars see them to be. With regard to Adams's first line of argument, the one denying the constitutionality of empire, it turns out there are unrepresented political entities subject to parliamentary authority. Ireland is the chief example, but the English Channel islands of Jersey and Guernsey also qualify. Arguably, so do the American colonies, and in

---

[20] As a legal historian, Reid explores many of these technical issues in great depth. See Reid's *Constitutional History of the American Revolution* (Madison: University of Wisconsin Press, 1986–93). An older but still valuable legalistic account can be found in Charles H. McIlwain, *The American Revolution: A Constitutional Interpretation* (1923; reprint, Ithaca, NY: Cornell University Press, 1958). A good account that blends legal and broader theoretical themes is C. Bradley Thompson, *John Adams and the Spirit of Liberty* (Lawrence: University Press of Kansas, 1998), 66–87. See also Black, "The Constitution of the Empire."

[21] Adams, *Novanglus* III, in vol. 4 of *The Works of John Adams*, 37.

particular, Adams's native Massachusetts. As he concedes, Parliament legislated for the colonies in the Navigation Acts of the seventeenth century. Moreover, and more unsettling to his precedential argument, he notes in one of his essays that "[i]t has been twice acknowledged by our [Massachusetts] house of representatives, that parliament was the supreme legislative [body]." [22] As he insists in the very same passage, these acknowledgments were by no means the steady consensus of the colony, but they surely count for something as evidence of general understandings, or perhaps, as evidence of consent to parliamentary authority.

As to the cases of Jersey and Guernsey, Adams concedes he does not understand how it can be that they are subject to Parliament: there must be some special circumstances, or, as he seems to think more likely, "it is an usurpation. If it is an usurpation, it ought not to be a precedent for the colonies; but it ought to be reformed, and they ought to be incorporated into the realm by an act of parliament and their own act." [23] Adams is certain that this precedent or this practice is not properly normative, nor can it have achieved a properly constitutional status. Contrary to what Greene and Reid and others claim, Adams does not in fact consider precedent by itself authoritative. In the words of contemporary legal philosophy, he brings to his efforts at constitutional interpretation a background theory, which provides him a standard or criterion by which to identify valid constitutional precedent and reject invalid precedent. He knows prior to the empirical evidence on usage and custom what the parameters of the constitution must—and must not—be.

Just what the background theory is begins to come to light in his treatment of the difficult case of Ireland. The Declaratory Act of 1766, the act to which Adams and the other American patriots so much objected in principle, was modeled on, indeed reproduced, the language of a similar act passed a half-century earlier regarding Ireland. It was, moreover, an accepted constitutional principle that when specifically named in an act of Parliament, Ireland was subject to that act.[24] Adams brings to bear three responses of increasing force and radicalness to the case of Ireland. First, he claims that "although [the members of Parliament] claim a power to bind Ireland by statutes, [they] have never laid one farthing of tax upon it." [25] This is important, but only in a limited way in the context. If the issue were still what it appeared to be at the time of the Stamp Act—whether Parliament could tax the colonies—this would be an important precedent. If the power to tax is a different and somehow more constrained power than the power to legislate, then the failures to tax Ireland

[22] Adams, *Novanglus* VIII, ibid., 113.
[23] Adams, *Novanglus* XII, ibid., 169–70. The Channel Islands had come to be part of England when William of Normandy, to whose kingdom they had belonged since 933, conquered England in 1066.
[24] Adams, *Novanglus* X, ibid., 151–59.
[25] Ibid., 151.

could be taken as a precedent against Parliament's authority to tax Americans. But by 1774, neither Adams nor other patriots were making that distinction; the power to tax and the power to legislate were on the same footing.

Adams's second reply to the precedent of Ireland is to claim that "the authority of parliament to bind Ireland at all, if it has any, is founded upon entirely a different principle from any that takes place in the case of America."[26] That principle is consent, explicit consent in a specific act, not the implicit consent perhaps inferable from custom and usage.[27] The explicit act of consent was "Poynings' law" (1494), a series of laws made by the Irish Parliament during the reign of Henry VII under the guidance of an agent of Henry, Sir Edward Poynings (1459–1521). These laws provided that "all the former laws of England were made of force in Ireland ... and by a construction, if not by the express words, of these laws, Ireland is still said to be bound by English statutes in which it is specifically named."[28] We have here, says Adams, a "voluntary act, the free consent of the Irish nation, and an act of the Irish Parliament."[29] Adams's ostensible point is that no American legislature had passed a "Poynings' law," but the deeper background point is that this is what it would take to gain legitimacy for parliamentary rule.

Third, Adams is not convinced that this act of consent goes as far as Daniel Leonard or the British think it does. "These are the principles upon which the dependence and subordination of Ireland are founded. Whether they are just or not is not necessary for us to inquire."[30] Of course, by saying this Adams is implicitly raising the question of their justice—and implicitly giving his answer as well. Behind Poynings' law stands the English conquest of Ireland, a token of which is the fact that these laws, so favorable to the claims of England, are named for the English King's military agent in Ireland. While Adams does not pursue the matter further here, he hints quite broadly that consent given under such circumstances is no consent, and perhaps, that such consent is irrational and therefore not to be taken seriously. Behind Adams's construal of the constitution, then, stands a political philosophy of consent. It should already be apparent that it is not a matter of his having, on the one hand, a certain theory or reading or interpretation of the constitution, and on the other, a certain political philosophy to which he adheres. No, the reading of the constitution is shaped by the political philosophy. As Adams says quite

---

[26] Ibid.
[27] Both Reid and Greene emphasize consent implicit in usage. For a discussion of Blackstone's effort to bring the common law (based on custom) into a conjunction with Lockean political philosophy (based on consent), see Michael P. Zuckert, *Launching Liberalism* (Lawrence: University of Kansas Press, 2002), chap. 9. On the role of consent in Adams, see Thompson, *John Adams,* 80.
[28] Adams, *Novanglus* X, in vol. 4 of *The Works of John Adams*, 157.
[29] Ibid.
[30] Ibid., 158.

explicitly in opposition to a position like the one Reid and Greene attribute to the Americans: "[T]he sense and practice of nations is not enough. Their practice must be reasonable, just, and right." [31] The measure of what is "reasonable, just, and right" is the background political philosophy in terms of which he is interpreting the constitution.

The foregoing three responses to the precedent of Ireland illuminate the background theory that Adams brought to his first line of constitutional argument. His second line of constitutional argument was to the effect that the status he claimed for the Americans was a recognized status within the constitution. The chief pieces of evidences he cited for this dated from before the Glorious Revolution and the constitutional settlement it ushered in. The British replied to Adams's argument that the revolution changed (or settled) the constitution in such a way that the earlier kind of monarchical independence was no longer possible. This position is as plausible as Adams's, and it is not clear whether the British constitution has the resources to settle this squabble rationally and with any definitiveness. All three of the factors making for constitutional indeterminacy are in play here, especially the temporal difficulty of figuring out what changes subsequent events can make in prior relationships, and the spatial difficulty of projecting relationships reasonably well understood within the British Isles onto political entities far away and somehow different.[32]

Adams recognizes the limits to practice, usage, and even explicit consent as interpretive guides to the imperial constitution because the Americans at the time of the settlement (and subsequently) were "confused" by "two ideas," both erroneous, that they held: "[O]ne derived from the feudal, the other from the canon law. By the former of these systems, the prince, the general, was supposed to be sovereign lord of all the lands conquered by the soldiers in his army; and upon this principle the King of England was considered in law as sovereign lord of all the land within the realm." [33] From the canon law came the idea that the pope, as head of Christendom, had a claim over all the land in the world, a claim that somehow transferred to the King when England broke with Rome. The upshot of both was that the colonists mistakenly came to believe themselves to hold their titles from the King and to owe him natural allegiance thereby.[34] That belief, in turn, made them vulnerable to parliamentary claims of authority when the constitution shifted toward parliamentary supremacy; that is, they were subject to British governing authorities and

---

[31] Adams, *Novanglus* VII, ibid., 105.

[32] Thompson, *John Adams*, 80: Adams was "caught in a constitutional time warp. . . . [T]he imperial English constitution consented to by the Americans was that which existed before 1688." On the three dimensions of constitutional indeterminacy, see Section III above.

[33] Adams, *Novanglus* VIII, in vol. 4 of *The Works of John Adams*, 125.

[34] Ibid., 124–25.

to King-in-Parliament in the new post-1688 order, which succeeded the quasi-feudal order they initially believed themselves to be subject to.

Adams denies that Parliament had any right to "succeed to" the feudal authority of the King, but more importantly, Adams rejects the whole quasi-feudal theory of the constitution as mistaken from the outset. The colonists may have understood themselves and their situation in those terms, but they misconstrued their actual situation. Adams believes that he knows better than they themselves what their status was. The colonists' true status at the time of settlement (and thereafter) was established not by the common law, or by any existing constitutional law of Britain, but by natural law. When an emigrant left England, "he carried with him, as a man, all the rights of nature." He had a claim to protection from the King so long as he stayed within the realm, and the King had a reciprocal claim on him of allegiance. But once he left the kingdom, he was, in effect, in a state of nature, in full possession of his primal natural rights.[35]

"How then," Adams asks, "do we New Englandmen derive our laws? I say not from parliament, not from common law, but from the law of nature, and the compact made with the King in our charters." The emigrants were freed from the common law, but they were free to accept "just so much of it as they pleased to adopt, and no more. They were not bound or obliged to submit to it, unless they chose it."[36]

The background theory to which Adams appeals here should be easy to identify: it is the Lockean natural rights/social contract philosophy. From these raw materials Adams constructs his view of the imperial constitution. The latter can be discerned in its true shape only on the basis of the Lockean philosophy. The constitution Adams limns is that interpretation of the imperial relationship that makes the most coherent sense of the historical record as interpreted in terms of the principle of political legitimacy expressed in the Lockean theory. Certain parts of the historical record are rejected as inconsistent with the background political philosophy, for example, the quasi-feudal self-understanding of the parties to the original settlement. Adams as a constitutionalist is a sort of Dworkinian, in that he affirms the need to interpret specific constitutional questions in the light of a background political theory. He is far from the positive law patron of custom and usage only, portrayed by Reid and Greene.

Adams, in other words, developed a constitutional theory of the sort I have elsewhere called an amalgam.[37] It was a composite of the Lockean natural rights philosophy and English Whig constitutional theory as expressed in the Bill of Rights. All ambiguities or uncertainties in Whig constitutionalism, especially when required to produce answers to con-

---

[35] Ibid., 121–22.
[36] Ibid.
[37] See Zuckert, *The Natural Rights Republic*, chap. 4.

stitutional questions prompted by the temporal and spatial extensions represented by the attempt to apply the constitution to the American colonies, were filled in by reference to the natural rights philosophy. More to the point, perhaps, the entire constitution was reinterpreted in terms of the background political philosophy, so that the Americans came to a view of the constitution that found it importantly illegitimate even as applied within Britain, for the British constitution did not provide the kind of representation the Americans concluded was needed. Large numbers of Britons, including many of the wealthiest ones, lacked representation in Parliament.

Despite the fact that Adams wrote by far the longest of the colonial expositions of the American theory of the imperial constitution, his was not in all ways the best version, especially not for bringing out clearly how the background theory acted within the theory to reshape it. Substantially better on that score is James Wilson's relatively brief 1774 essay on parliamentary authority.[38]

Wilson, writing almost six months before Adams published his *Novanglus* essays, defended almost the same version of the imperial constitution the Bostonian soon would. "[A]ll the different members of the British empire are distinct states, independent of each other, but connected together under the same sovereign right of the same crown." [39] The tie through the King is sufficient to maintain the bonds among the English and the colonists in the new world.

> [T]he inhabitants of Great Britain and those of America . . . are fellow subjects; they are under allegiance to the same prince; and this union of allegiance naturally produces a union of hearts. It is also productive of a union of measures through the whole British dominions. To the king is intrusted the direction and management of the great machine of government. He therefore is fittest to adjust the different wheels, and to regulate their motions in such a manner as to cooperate in the same general designs.[40]

Wilson, it will be noticed, strikes out for an even greater independence of the parts of the empire than Adams, denying even the consent-based authority in Parliament to regulate trade that Adams concedes. Wilson explicitly looks to the King to carry on that task, so far as it needs to be done. He thus breaks even more emphatically with usage, custom, and precedent than Adams does, for he rejects all the years of generally accepted

---

[38] James Wilson, *Considerations on the Nature and Extent of the Legislative Authority of the British Parliament,* in *The Works of James Wilson,* ed. Robert G. McCloskey (Cambridge, MA: Harvard University Press, 1967), 2: 721–46.

[39] Ibid., 745.

[40] Ibid.

trade regulation through the Navigation Acts. In this, Wilson takes the most radical position of any pre-independence American. It is very clear, moreover, that the Greene/Reid description of colonial constitutional reasoning does not fit Wilson, for precedent and usage per se have little weight with him.

Accordingly, Wilson is more open about the difficulties with the precedents for parliamentary authority, or nonauthority, than Adams is. Although he asserts (like Adams) that the legal precedents support his claim "that it is repugnant . . . to the genius of the British constitution . . . that they [the colonies] should be bound by the legislative authority of the parliament of Great Britain," he concedes that the most important legal decisions affirm that, where named explicitly, Ireland, Jamaica, and Virginia have all been held to be so bound.[41] He rejects these legal contentions, however, on a dual ground: first, and most importantly, "it is repugnant to the essential maxims of jurisprudence, to the ultimate end of all governments, . . . and to the liberty and happiness of the colonies" that they should be subject to parliamentary authority.[42] Armed with this knowledge, he is able to see that the pronouncements to the contrary in the legal cases he considers are mere dicta, that is, pronouncements of no legal authority because not directly involved in settling the cases in which they were propounded.[43] But, secondly, Wilson is yet more certain that the principle that the colonies when named are under parliamentary authority could never be acceptable as valid constitutional law. "These positions are too absurd to be alleged; and a thousand judicial determinations in their favour would never induce one man to subscribe his assent to them."[44] On this last point Wilson cites Blackstone as an authority for the proposition: "Where a decision is manifestly absurd and wrong, such a sentence is not law."[45]

Wilson is, like Adams, a trained lawyer, yet he proceeds differently from his fellow patriot. Rather than beginning with details of the common law and moving from there to the natural law principles that supply the underpinnings and interpretive guidance to the true imperial constitution, Wilson begins straight off with the natural principles and builds his version of the imperial constitution on them. He thus presents a clearer and more thorough account of those natural law foundations.

His beginning point is the claim to sovereignty raised on behalf of parliamentary authority: "[T]here is and must be in every state a supreme, irresistible, absolute, uncontrolled authority, in which the *jura summi imperii*, or the rights of sovereignty reside." That is, he begins with the theoretical claim raised by the British, and responds by observing that as necessary

---

[41] Ibid., 735–38.
[42] Ibid., 735.
[43] Ibid., 738–39.
[44] Ibid., 739.
[45] Ibid., 739n.

as sovereignty is, it is not the first fact about political life, but is itself "founded" on something: "its tendency to promote the ultimate end of government." If alleged possession of sovereignty in some body or other "would . . . destroy, instead of promoting, that end, it ought, in that instance, to be rejected."[46] The correct understanding of the constitution, Wilson thus makes clear at the outset, is the one, and only the one, that conforms with and serves "the ultimate end of all government."

In order to understand that end, Wilson rehearses the rudiments of Lockean natural rights/social contract philosophy. He begins with the affirmation of a state of nature, that is, the claim that by nature all are "equal and free: no one has a right to any authority over another without his consent." All lawful government is founded on the consent of those who are subject to it: such consent was given with a view "to ensure and to increase the happiness of the governed, above what they could enjoy in an independent and unconnected state of nature."[47]

Wilson interprets the consent requirement not so much as actual or historical consent but as rational consent: his question about consent is not ultimately to be answered by digging around in law cases or in the records of history, but by thinking in terms of the rationality of imputing consent to one or another political arrangement. Thus, he asks his readers to consider the differences between the situations of the British and the American peoples relative to the British Parliament. For the British, Parliament is a fit instrument to which to entrust sovereign power, for it is constructed in such a way as "to ensure and to increase the happiness of the governed." Members of the House of Commons are directly responsible to the people of Britain, and there are other institutional arrangements to encourage them to know, sympathize with, and serve the interests and protect the rights of those they govern.[48]

The same cannot be said for the Parliament relative to the Americans. The structural features of that relationship have almost the opposite incentive and effect. Given the disconnect between authority and responsibility, "[a] candidate [for Parliament] may recommend himself at his election by recounting the many successful instances, in which he has sacrificed the interests of America to those of Great Britain. A member of the House of Commons may plume himself upon his ingenuity in inventing schemes to serve the mother country at the expense of the colonies."[49] Given the insusceptibility of the British imperial model to serve the ends of government for the colonies, Wilson concludes that the Americans cannot be considered to have consented to parliamentary sovereignty over them.

The only alternative is that somehow the people of Great Britain have some original "uncontrolled authority" over the Americans, which they

[46] Ibid., 723.
[47] Ibid.
[48] Ibid., 723–30.
[49] Ibid., 734.

then transfer to their representatives in Parliament. Wilson finds this idea simply incredible. "Have they," he thunders, "a natural right to make laws, by which we may be deprived of our properties, of our liberties, of our lives?"[50] This notion cannot be correct, not because Wilson shows that custom, usage, and precedent fail to support it, but because it conflicts with the first principle of political philosophy: "All men are by nature, equal and free." It is the truths of political philosophy, then, that guarantee that the imperial constitution cannot be what the Declaratory Act says it is, and that leaves connection via the King to be the only alternative to complete and absolute independence. Since the historical record and precedent do bespeak a connection, the imperial constitution must be as Wilson depicts it. Like Adams, Wilson derives a theory of the constitution that is an amalgam of Lockean rights philosophy and the historical constitution, combined in such a way that the amalgam satisfies the requirements of legitimacy (first and foremost) as laid out in Lockean theory and encompasses as much of the historical constitution, interpreted in terms supplied by Lockean theory, as can cohere with the background philosophy.

While Wilson betters Adams's lengthy exposition of constitutional theory, Thomas Jefferson's *A Summary View of the Rights of British America* (1774) is probably the finest of the statements of the colonial theory of the imperial constitution. Like the later Declaration of Independence, it combines an exposition of theory with a concrete list of grievances, both of which are forcefully, even uncompromisingly, put. Like Wilson, Jefferson leaves the reader in no doubt as to the ultimate source of the colonists' claims: "[T]hese are our grievances which we have thus laid before his majesty with that freedom of language and sentiment which becomes a free people, claiming their rights as derived from the laws of nature, and not as the gift of their chief magistrate. . . . [We] are asserting the rights of human nature."[51]

Jefferson's statement of American rights needs to be put into the context of a frequently voiced thesis about the positions taken by the colonials in the prerevolutionary conflict over parliamentary authority. According to this thesis, the Americans began with appeals to positive rights—constitutional and charter rights—and, unsuccessful with this appeal, radicalized their position over time, ending up with the appeal to natural law and natural rights by the time of the Declaration of Independence. This thesis captures something of the movement of American argumentation in that appeals to natural standards did indeed grow in prominence as the conflict wore on, but it is positively misleading so far as it suggests that the appeal to natural standards replaces the constitutional

---

[50] Ibid., 732.

[51] Thomas Jefferson, *A Summary View of the Rights of British America*, in vol. 1 of *The Papers of Thomas Jefferson*, ed. Julian P. Boyd (Princeton, NJ: Princeton University Press, 1950), 134.

argumentation. For Jefferson, as for Adams and Wilson, the appeal to natural rights and natural law is accompanied by a continuing appeal to, and promulgation of, a theory of the constitution. The two kinds of appeals do not appear as alternatives, but in the later phases of the conflict the colonists refine and strengthen their constitutional argument by grounding it in and harmonizing it with their natural rights argument.

So in the case of A Summary View, written before either Wilson's or Adams's essays, Jefferson gives us a theory of the imperial constitution that is in the decisive respects the same as theirs. Parliament has no authority in America, and indeed is spoken of as "a body of men foreign to our constitutions, and unacknowledged by our laws." [52] The King is the one tie the Americans have to the British, and Jefferson specifies that tie more concretely than the others do: "his majesty . . . [holds] the executive powers of the laws of these states." [53] The King is the executive head of government in each of the American states just as he is in Great Britain. He is to execute the laws of each political body in that political body, and in none of them (e.g., Virginia) the laws of another (e.g., Britain).

Jefferson concedes that custom, usage, and precedent do not fully agree with the true constitution. "Our ancestors . . . who migrated hither were laborers, not lawyers." They were, accordingly, "persuaded to believe" things about their status that were false, for instance, that they held their land from the King. Along the same lines that Adams will argue, Jefferson admits that the original colonists greatly misunderstood their situation and, therefore, some precedents speak against the truth. The truth is not to be inferred merely from precedent, custom, and usage.

The truth is that the colonists came to America in exercise of their natural right to withdraw from England. When they did that, they were in effect in a state of nature, free and equal with one another, capable of contracting into a new political society. They acted conservatively in some ways, for they again accepted the King as part of their government and they adopted much of the English common law as their law. The legislative authority is quite another thing from the executive role of the King, however. Just as the English could not reasonably place their legislative power in an irresponsible officer like the hereditary monarch, so the Americans could not reasonably be construed to have placed their legislative power in the hands of a distant and unrepresentative parliament. "From the nature of things, every society must at all times possess within itself the sovereign power of legislation." [54] The Americans have placed this power in their own legislatures, a placement confirmed by the fact that the colonial assemblies have been unchallenged in making law for the colonies from the beginning.

[52] Ibid., 129.
[53] Ibid.
[54] Ibid., 132.

Although there may be differences of nuance among the writings of Jefferson, Wilson, and Adams, all three of these American statements of the nature of the constitution agree on the important matters: (1) that the imperial constitution includes no role for parliamentary authority over the colonies, except for what they might specifically agree to for regulation of commerce; and (2) that the British theory of parliamentary sovereignty within the empire is unacceptable, in part because it is innovative and contrary to (most of) the prior understandings of the relationship between colonies and motherland, but far more decisively because that reading makes the constitution theoretically illegitimate and practically dangerous. The power of the American position, then, derives neither from a pure appeal to the constitution (for that was ambiguous and contestable), nor from an appeal to natural law and rights in themselves, but from the appeal to the amalgam of the two that the Americans constructed. It was the amalgam that persuaded them that the British were nefariously innovating and that the colonists had every right, as loyal subjects, to resist those innovations. The amalgam, in other words, was the real cause of the American Revolution.

IV. The American Revolution as a Cause of the Amalgam

Not only was the American amalgam—Locke plus the constitution, or the constitution Lockeanized—a cause of the American Revolution, it was also the case, paradoxically, that the conflict culminating in the Revolution was a cause of the amalgam, and thus in some part responsible for ensconcing in the nascent American political culture a fundamentally Lockean orientation.

In order to see how the Americans came to the amalgam, it is necessary to move well back from 1774, to the Glorious Revolution itself and the Bill of Rights of 1689, a document that best captured the nature of the British constitution according to those who successfully made that revolution.[55] We must, first, set aside all presuppositions we might have of the similarity of this constitution and its underlying theory to the modern constitution and modern (eighteenth-century) political philosophy, as expressed, say, in the Declaration of Independence or in the three documents analyzed in Section III. I have written on this topic at length elsewhere, so here I will only very briefly summarize arguments better made

---

[55] The Glorious Revolution, so-called because there was no bloodshed to speak of, was the momentous event of 1688–89 when William of Orange marched into England with the support of a large part of the English nation and expelled King James II. The settlement after the revolution, captured in the Bill of Rights, not only established the right of William and his wife Mary as the new monarchs in place of James II, but also affirmed prerevolutionary Whig conceptions of the constitution, in particular the role of Parliament in the governance of the nation. The revolution put a decisive end to the perceived efforts by the Stuart monarchs, James and his predecessors, to turn England into an absolutist monarchy on the model of France.

in other places.[56] The Bill of Rights of 1689 contains a theory of rights
completely different from that in the Declaration of Independence. We
can see this difference by referring to a set of five "rights variables" that
together make up what we might call a "rights regime."

Source of Rights. According to the Declaration of Independence, the
source of rights is "the creator," that is, God or nature. In the English
document, on the other hand, "the rights and liberties asserted and claimed
are the true, ancient and indubitable rights of the people of this kingdom." These are "ancient rights and liberties"; the English document is
nowhere near as explicit as the American document, but it pointedly does
not find the source of rights in nature or nature's God. If anything, rights
derive their authority, their very being perhaps, from their antiquity—not
from nature or divinity, but from history and prescription.

Possessors of Rights. The American Declaration declares rights to be the
endowment of "all men." This accords with finding the origin of rights in
a universal source. The English document, on the contrary, declares rights
that belong only to "the people of this kingdom," not to "all men." Most
of the rights, moreover, do not apply to Englishmen as individuals, but to
political bodies such as Parliament. For instance, it is declared to be a
right that the King not levy taxes or make (or ignore) laws without the
consent of Parliament. The core is the sharing of power: these major
powers of the community can be exercised only by joint action of King
and Parliament, or by King-in-Parliament.

Duty Bearers. Every right in the full sense implies a corresponding
duty in someone. In the case of the American document, the rights belong
to "all men" in a condition prior to and independent of political life. The
corresponding duty bearers would thus seem also to be "all men." The
duty bearers corresponding to the rights in the English Bill of Rights are
not so easy to identify, largely because the rights listed are so various. So
far as they are mostly affirmations of limitations on the power of the King,
or, conversely, affirmations of parliamentary powers, the duty bearer seems
mostly to be the King. Thus, it is the King who is explicitly identified as
the one who is not to "suspend the laws ... without the consent of
Parliament." Likewise, the prohibition against "the raising or keeping [of]
a standing army within the kingdom in time of peace, unless it be with
the consent of Parliament" seems to impose a duty on the King.

Substance of Rights. The American Declaration lists a series of rights,
but it specifies that these are only some "among" those with which "all
men" are "endowed." There is nonetheless a kind of coherence to the list
supplied, as there is to the more common list of "life, liberty, and property." The first right, the right to life, is a right to what is most one's own:

---

[56] See my "Natural Rights in the American Revolution: The American Amalgam," in
Zuckert, *Launching Liberalism*, 274–84.

one's life. Given the nature of a human life, it is difficult to see how it could be anything other than one's own, how it could in any sense belong to others. Given the dependence (or base) of life in or on the body, the right to life must contain a right to bodily immunity, the right not to have one's body seized, invaded, harmed, or controlled by others. The right to liberty extends the right to life: one has bodily immunities from others, but one has also a right to the use of one's body. The natural right to liberty proclaims the prima facie rightfulness of active use of the body. The right to property involves an extension of rights from the spheres of one's own life, body, and actions to the external world. The three basic rights together amount to an affirmation of a kind of personal sovereignty, a rightful control over one's person, actions, and possessions in the service of one's interests and purposes. As an integrated system of immunities and warrants, the specific rights add up to a comprehensive right to the pursuit of happiness, that is, the right to procure or shape a way of life self-chosen.

The rights affirmed in the American Declaration thus do form a kind of system; they are coherent, complementary, and intelligibly related to each other. This quality differentiates them from the rights in the English Bill of Rights. The latter lists thirteen rights, ranging from the rights that the King not suspend or dispense with laws, not levy taxes, and not keep a standing army without the consent of Parliament, to the rights of subjects "to petition the King" and not be subjected to excessive bail. These rights are part of a commitment to constitutional government, but they hardly form a system of inherently interrelated parts. Although obviously important, the rights here do not reach the level of fundamentality or universality visible in the list of rights enumerated in the Declaration of Independence.

Function of Rights. According to the American document, the securing of natural rights is the sole legitimate end of government. Rights not only function as standards for the conduct of good and legitimate government, but also serve as the standards for the invocation of one of the most important rights: the right to alter or abolish governments that are not conducive to their proper end (that is, the securing of rights). It is this right that the Americans invoked in 1776 when they announced their severing of all political ties with the British nation.

Most striking, by contrast, about the English Bill of Rights, is its silence on the ends of government. It contains nothing corresponding to the Americans' firm announcement of the ends of political life. The rights in the English document do not function as a justification or triggering condition for invocation of the right of revolution, either, for the document nowhere invokes or affirms such a right or describes the action taken in 1688 as a revolution. The King is said to have "abdicated," not to have been deposed or overthrown. The historical actors might be perplexed to hear that their deed has come to be called the "Glorious

Revolution."[57] The rights announced have far more the character of constitutional powers and arrangements than what we ordinarily think of as individual rights; they thus seem to be means of political life rather than ends. The English remain silent about the ends these means serve.

The rights regimes in the English Bill of Rights and America's Declaration of Independence are thus completely different from each other. They seem to arise from two different universes of political thought. The key to the theory of the English document perhaps appears most clearly from the fact that it is neither issued in the name of, nor does it speak of, "all men." It nowhere affirms that "all men are created equal," which in the American document is meant as an affirmation of the original—that is, pre-political—equality of all men. As James Wilson made clear, this original equality means that by nature no one has rightful authority over another: politically speaking, men start out in a state of nature. All political authority must derive, therefore, from "the consent of the governed," and must always be mindful (how was a much-debated question) of the original equality.

The English issued their document in the name of "the Lords Spiritual and Temporal and Commons." Together with the King, these are the "estates of the realm" who together constitute Parliament. The English begin from the constitution of their polity, not from some pre-political situation of equality. That polity is emphatically not one of equality in the Lockean sense, for "the Lords Spiritual and Temporal," as well as the King, have a call on political authority by virtue of who they are. The English document affirms, above all, the constitutional mandate that power must be shared between King and Parliament, but it actually bespeaks a deeper kind of sharing: the joint possession of authority by the different estates or classes of the realm. The constitutionalism of the Bill of Rights, at bottom, is this sharing or participation in rule among these elements of the community and the monarch. This notion of constitutionalism harks back at least to Aristotle and Polybius and their theory of the mixed regime, or, as it was often called in England in the seventeenth century, the Mixed Monarchy.[58]

The mixed-regime analysis underlying the Bill of Rights is nicely restated by Daniel Leonard writing as Massachusettensis:

> The security of the people from internal rapacity and violence and from foreign invasion is the end and design of government. The simple forms of government are monarchy, aristocracy, and democ-

[57] For discussion of the labeling of the displacement of James II as an abdication rather than a revolution, see Zuckert, *Natural Rights and the New Republicanism*, 6–7.

[58] Even though Locke published his *Two Treatises of Government* as a defense of the Glorious Revolution, his philosophy was not what inspired the actors of 1688–89. Thus, even though Locke was a supporter of the 1688 events, his political philosophy finds expression in the American Revolution, not in the Glorious Revolution.

racy. . . . Each of these species of government has advantages peculiar to itself and would answer the ends of government were the persons entrusted with the authority of the state always guided, themselves, by unerring wisdom and public virtue, but rulers are not always exempt from the meanness and depravity which makes government necessary to society.[59]

As was typical of the theorists of the mixed regime, Leonard proceeds to enumerate the ways in which each simple regime can go wrong. The solution to the problem that each tends to degenerate into a monster of injustice when alone is the mixture of the simple regimes:

> A government formed on these three principles in due proportion is the best calculated to answer the ends of government and to endure. Such a government is the British constitution, consisting of King, lords, and commons, which at once includes the principal excellences and excludes the principal defects of the other kinds of government. It is allowed by both Englishmen and foreigners to be the most perfect system that the wisdom of the ages has produced.[60]

Armed with this analysis, we are now prepared to understand the evolution of the other line of interpretation of the imperial constitution—the British line. The Americans claimed from the outset and always that they were due "the rights of Englishmen." Their charters said as much. But what were "the rights of Englishmen"? Taking the Bill of Rights as the most authoritative written statement on that subject that could be consulted, we find—on the topic of greatest contention in the colonial conflict—"that levying money for or to the use of the crown by pretense of prerogative, without a grant of Parliament, for longer time, or in other manner than the same is or shall be granted, is illegal."[61] The right of Englishmen, hence, is the right to have taxes levied not by the King, but by Parliament. And that is exactly what the Stamp Act and other measures were—taxes levied by Parliament. The colonists claimed to be entitled to the rights of Englishmen, and that is precisely what the British thought they enjoyed.

Of course, here is a place where the extension of the constitution from the homeland to the imperial context introduced a great uncertainty into constitutional reasoning. The Bill of Rights was written with the homeland in mind, and the people of Britain were indeed represented in the Parliament whose power to tax and legislate was affirmed in the docu-

---

[59] Massachusettensis, January 9, 1775, reprinted in *The Political Writings of John Adams*, ed. George A. Peek (Indianapolis, IN: Bobbs-Merrill, 1954), 33–34.

[60] Ibid., 34.

[61] Greene, *Peripheries*.

ment. That the people were represented in Parliament was the reason that justified parliamentary, and not monarchical, prerogative power. Do the same powers extend over peoples not represented in Parliament? The constitution did not say in direct terms, and two traditions of interpreting the proper extension arose.

If one takes the Bill of Rights quite literally, as the British tended to do, then the extension of parliamentary powers to the colonies seems legitimate. If one takes the overall context in which the authorization of parliamentary taxation occurs, then the extension is less clearly justifiable. In the absence of a body with constitutional interpretive authority (other than Parliament itself, in this case acting as judge of its own powers), there is no clear-cut way to settle the uncertainty.

Each side naturally tended to favor the interpretation of the constitution that gave it more control over the situation. This was only to be expected in the face of the uncertainty of the constitution itself. But neither side left matters at a mere assertion of its own interest. The British made two sorts of arguments to justify their version of the imperial constitution, or their way of extending the domestic constitution to the empire. First, they appealed to the doctrine of sovereignty. If the empire ultimately was comprised of one people, then there must be one highest and supreme (sovereign) power within it. In the nature of things, that could only be Parliament.[62]

Furthermore, the British never admitted that the Americans, even if subject to the authority of Parliament, were being denied the rights of Englishmen. This, and not sovereignty, is what the dispute was really about, for the Americans believed that without representation in Parliament they were being denied one of their essential rights as Englishmen if Parliament taxed them or passed internal regulations for them. It is at this juncture that the theory of the constitution underlying the Bill of Rights becomes particularly relevant. The main point of the constitution is not representation of individuals, but of estates. The institutional arrangement that makes the constitution both legitimate and beneficent is not representation and electoral control per se, but the mixed character of the regime: the co-presence of the monarchic, aristocratic, and democratic elements. As Leonard had said, any one of the pure regimes can suit in principle; the problem is that all of them are subject to abuse, corruption, and decay. The mixture is beneficial largely because it prevents the regime from undergoing the decay that is the fate of the pure regimes.

According to the mixed-regime theory of the constitution, it does not matter whether each and every individual is represented. It does not

---

[62] For an account of the debate in Parliament, see the letter from Jared Ingersoll to Governor Thomas Fitch of Connecticut, February 11, 1765, reprinted in John Braeman, *The Road to Independence: A Documentary History of the Causes of the American Revolution* (New York: Capricorn Books, 1963), 61–64.

matter that the suffrage was extremely limited (to perhaps 10 percent of the commons), nor that large and populous areas of Britain lacked representation altogether. What mattered was that there be a real presence of elements of each of the simple regimes in the complex mix. The British constitution, even with imperfect representation, more than adequately did that. This theory of the mixed regime was the ultimate basis for the most sophisticated response by the partisans of parliamentary authority to the American complaints: the theory of virtual representation. This theory was put forth forcefully by Thomas Whately, the secretary to the British treasury.[63] Whately admitted the "Privilege, which is common to all *British* subjects, of being taxed only with their own Consent, given by their Representatives." The Americans laid claim to that privilege, and he wished they "may . . . ever enjoy the Privilege to all its extent: may this Pledge of Liberty be presumed inviolate to the utmost Verge of our Dominion, and to the latest Page of our History!!"[64] Unbidden, Whately extended the principle even beyond the immediate question at stake in the Stamp Act: "let us not limit the legislative rights of the British people to subjects of taxation only: no new law whatever can bind us that is made without the concurrence of our representatives."[65]

Having conceded so much, having so strongly affirmed Whig constitutional principles, Whately also insisted that the colonists were represented in Parliament, despite the fact that "they [did] not indeed choose the members of that Assembly." This paradox was not limited to the colonists alone, for "nine tenths of the people of Britain" were in the same situation! Whately listed all those in Britain who did not vote for members of Parliament, and yet were thought to be represented there. It was a long list indeed. The class of the enfranchised, Whately wrote, "comprehends only a very small part of the Land, the Property, and the People of this Island." Excluded from the franchise was "all landed property . . . that is not freehold and all monied property whatsoever." The very wealthy merchants of London, the inhabitants of several large cities, the East India Company, which had nearly sovereign power in India, had no vote at home.[66] The Americans, Whately argued, must be misconstruing the right to be represented if their theory of representation would lead to the conclusion that so many of the most affluent and powerful in Britain are "subject to taxes without their consent," and "arbitrarily bound by laws to which they have not agreed." The American error is precisely the claim that to be represented in Parliament one must personally have a hand in selection of representatives. This is unnecessary because "every Member

---

[63] Thomas Whately, "The Regulations Lately Made Concerning the Colonies and the Taxes Imposed upon Them, Considered," London, 1765, reprinted in Braeman, *Road to Independence*, 55.

[64] Ibid.

[65] Ibid., 57.

[66] Ibid., 57–58.

of Parliament sits in the House, not as representative of his own Constituents, but as one of that august Assembly by which all the Commons of
Great Britain are represented." It is the estate of the commons that is
present in the constitution, and not merely these particular persons who
happen to be electors.

The Americans were "a part, and an important part of the Commons of
Great Britain." Accordingly, Whately wrote:

> They are represented in Parliament, in the same Manner as these
> Inhabitants of Britain are, who have not Voices in elections; and they
> enjoy, with the Rest of their fellow-subjects, the inestimable Privilege
> of not being bound by any laws, or subject to any taxes to which the
> Majority of the Representatives of the Commons have not consented.[67]

Although the Americans greeted the theory of virtual representation with
scorn, it is in fact an extremely plausible application of the underlying
theory of the constitution, as contained in the Bill of Rights, to the situation of the colonists, to whom the "rights of Englishmen" had been
promised. In order to favor their preferred mode of extending the constitution to their own case (as requiring their actual involvement in the
selection of their representatives), the colonists required a competing political theory. The Lockean theory filled the bill admirably, for here it was
clear that the rights that eventuated in the claim to representation were
individual rights, and not rights of estates or classes. The principle of
mixing regime elements was less important than that recognition of the
citizens as individuals possessing personal rights of liberty and property,
individuals whose consent was needed in order to tax them or legislate
for them. That is to say, the Lockean natural rights/social contract philosophy brought with it an entirely different form of constitutionalism, a
form that happened to cohere extremely well with the Americans' constitutional imperatives.

From the perspective of Lockean political philosophy, the Whately rendition of the constitution could not be the correct one—a good reason,
then, for the Americans to see in the Lockean political philosophy the true
grounds of political legitimacy. From a Lockean perspective, parliamentary constitutionalism was not merely an instance of historical or legal
interpretation gone awry, but was an attempt to fasten on the Americans
a form of political authority that failed to respect them as rights-bearers
and free men. Slaves are those who are systematically denied their status
as rights-bearers, and it was to a state of slavery that the Americans came
to believe the British were attempting to consign them.

[67] Ibid., 59.

V. Conclusion

I certainly do not mean to claim that the colonists' perception of Lockean rights theory as a solid basis for their preferred constitutional model was the only factor leading to the embrace of Locke and the construction of the American amalgam. Locke was a presence in America long before these conflicts over the nature of the constitution, and there were other lines of development in the colonies that turned them toward Locke.[68] Nonetheless, Locke filled a very definite function for the American colonists at a critical moment in history, and there can be little doubt that he was so attractive to them because he did so.

Political Science, University of Notre Dame

---

[68] See Zuckert, *Natural Rights Republic,* chap. 6.

THERE IS NO SUCH THING AS AN UNJUST INITIAL ACQUISITION*

By Edward Feser

I. Introduction

The notion that Robert Nozick's political philosophy amounts, in Thomas Nagel's words, to a "libertarianism without foundations"[1] has become something of a cliché, and like most clichés it is at best an oversimplification. Although he is not explicit about it, Nozick does seem to assume that most of the rights he ascribes to individuals follow from the thesis of self-ownership—the claim that each person has full property rights in his body and its parts, in his talents and abilities, in his labor and energies, and so forth—and this thesis surely is as plausible a moral first principle as any to which Nozick's opponents typically appeal. G. A. Cohen, who is perhaps Nozick's most perceptive interpreter and critic, not only grants that Nozick more or less *does* have an ostensible foundation for his system in the thesis of self-ownership, but even concedes that Nozick's anti-egalitarian and anti-redistributionist conclusions *really do follow* from the thesis, that the thesis is intuitively highly plausible, and that it cannot be refuted.[2] Critics of Nozick thus have no choice, in Cohen's view, but to try to find some way of avoiding commitment to this thesis. They cannot prove it false, and must rest content with trying to show that however attractive and reasonable it is, it has not been proven true. If Cohen is right, then it is hard to see how Nozick's political philosophy is in worse shape than any other. (Indeed, if Cohen is right, then it seems to be, if anything, in much *better* shape than other political philosophies.)[3]

* The original draft of this paper was written in the summer of 2002 while I was a Visiting Scholar at the Social Philosophy and Policy Center, Bowling Green State University. I thank the directors of the Center, Fred D. Miller, Jr., Ellen Frankel Paul, and Jeffrey Paul, for hosting me. I also thank colloquium audience members at Bowling Green State University for comments on that draft.

[1] Thomas Nagel, "Libertarianism without Foundations," in Jeffrey Paul, ed., *Reading Nozick: Essays on Anarchy, State, and Utopia* (Totowa, NJ: Rowman and Littlefield, 1981).

[2] G. A. Cohen, *Self-Ownership, Freedom, and Equality* (New York: Cambridge University Press, 1995).

[3] Given these concessions, one might say that with enemies like Cohen, Nozick doesn't need friends. That Cohen is correct in his generous interpretation of Nozick's position, but incorrect in his ultimate rejection of that position (and, in particular, in his rejection of self-ownership) is something I try to show in Edward Feser, "Taxation, Forced Labor, and Theft," *The Independent Review* 5, no. 2 (2000), and in Edward Feser, *On Nozick* (Belmont, CA: Wadsworth, 2004), chap. 3.

56   © 2005 Social Philosophy & Policy Foundation. Printed in the USA.

Cohen's views aside, a weak link in Nozick's case might nevertheless be thought to reside in his theory of property rights—rights, that is, to resources *external* to oneself. Self-ownership may well rule out taxation of earnings from labor, as Nozick insists and as Cohen allows; it may thus doom any scheme of eliminating inequalities in wealth and income arising from prior inequalities in labor-enhancing personal endowments. Still, insofar as there are also inequalities in wealth and income that derive from inequalities in initial holdings in external resources, the egalitarian may be thought to have a toehold, for even if it is granted that you own yourself and your talents, labor, and the like, it is another question whether you own anything else. If it can be shown that you do not own, or at least do not fully own, those external resources that you have utilized in exercising your self-owned powers to acquire the wealth you possess, then the question of the redistribution of some of that wealth via taxation would appear to be reopened.

Nozick's theory of property rights has three components: the principle of justice in *acquisition,* which concerns the way in which previously unowned resources can justly come to be owned; the principle of justice in *transfer,* which concerns the way in which one might justly come to own a holding previously owned by someone else; and the principle of justice in *rectification,* which concerns the way in which past injustices in acquisition and transfer are to be corrected.[4] Famously (or notoriously), Nozick does little more than provide a sketch of these principles; and the first principle, on which the other two rest (since you cannot transfer property or return it to its rightful owner until it comes to be owned by someone or other in the first place), is usually taken to be the most problematic. If, as nearly all of Nozick's commentators, friendly and unfriendly, agree, Nozick fails to give an adequate theory of justice in acquisition, then his libertarianism appears to have at most *partial* foundations, and this may be enough to undermine it. For if, contrary to what Nozick implies, existing inequalities in holdings reflect significant injustices in the initial acquisition of resources, then redistributive taxation of a sort incompatible with Nozick's libertarianism may be justified. This, in any case, is what certain egalitarian opponents of Nozick suggest,[5] as do his so-called left-libertarian critics, who accept the thesis of self-ownership but also insist on equal ownership of external resources.[6]

---

[4] Robert Nozick, *Anarchy, State, and Utopia* (New York: Basic Books, 1974), 150–53. Note that "acquisition" is used here in a technical sense, not in the ordinary sense in which one might come to acquire something previously held by someone else; in Nozick's terminology, the latter case would be a case of "transfer."

[5] See, e.g., Will Kymlicka, *Contemporary Political Philosophy: An Introduction* (New York: Oxford University Press, 1990), 117; and Jonathan Wolff, *Robert Nozick: Property, Justice, and the Minimal State* (Stanford, CA: Stanford University Press, 1991), 111.

[6] See, e.g., Peter Vallentyne and Hillel Steiner, eds., *Left-Libertarianism and Its Critics: The Contemporary Debate* (New York: Palgrave, 2000).

There is a serious difficulty with this criticism of Nozick, however. It is just this: There is *no such thing* as an unjust initial acquisition of resources; therefore, there is no case to be made for redistributive taxation on the basis of alleged injustices in initial acquisition.

This is, to be sure, a bold claim. Moreover, in making it, I contradict not only Nozick's critics, but Nozick himself, who clearly thinks it is at least possible for there to be injustices in acquisition, whether or not there have in fact been any (or, more realistically, whether or not there have been enough such injustices to justify continual redistributive taxation for the purposes of rectifying them). But here is a case where Nozick has, I think, been too generous to the other side. Rather than attempt—unsatisfactorily, in the view of his critics—to meet the challenge to show that initial acquisition has not in general been unjust, he ought instead to have insisted that there is no such challenge to be met in the first place.

Giving what I shall call "the basic argument" for this audacious claim will be the task of Section II of this essay. The argument is, I think, compelling, but by itself it leaves unexplained some widespread intuitions to the effect that certain specific instances of initial acquisition are unjust and call forth as their remedy the application of a Lockean proviso, or are otherwise problematic. (A "Lockean proviso," of course, is one that forbids initial acquisitions of resources when these acquisitions do not leave "enough and as good" in common for others.) Thus, Section III focuses on various considerations that tend to show how those intuitions are best explained in a way consistent with the argument of Section II. Section IV completes the task of accounting for the intuitions in question by considering how the thesis of self-ownership itself bears on the acquisition and use of property. Section V shows how the results of the previous sections add up to a more satisfying defense of Nozickian property rights than the one given by Nozick himself, and considers some of the implications of this revised conception of initial acquisition for our understanding of Nozick's principles of transfer and rectification.

II. The Basic Argument

The reason there is no such thing as an unjust initial acquisition of resources is that there is no such thing as *either* a just *or* an unjust initial acquisition of resources. The concept of justice, that is to say, simply does not apply to initial acquisition. It applies only after initial acquisition has already taken place. In particular, it applies only to *transfers* of property (and derivatively, to the rectification of injustices in transfer).

This, it seems to me, is a clear implication of the assumption (rightly) made by Nozick that external resources are initially unowned. Consider the following example. Suppose an individual A seeks to acquire some previously unowned resource R. For it to be the case that A commits an injustice in acquiring R, it would also have to be the case that there is some individual B (or perhaps a group of individuals) against whom A commits the injustice. But for B to have been wronged by A's acquisition of R, B would have to have had a rightful claim over R, a *right* to R. By hypothesis, however, B did *not* have a right to R, because *no one* had a right to it—it was unowned, after all. So B was not wronged and could not have been. In fact, the very first person who could conceivably be wronged by anyone's use of R would be, not B, but *A himself*, since A is the first one to own R. Such a wrong would in the nature of the case be an injustice in *transfer*—in unjustly taking from A what is rightfully his—not in initial acquisition. The same thing, by extension, will be true of all unowned resources: it is only *after* someone has initially acquired them that anyone could unjustly come to possess them, via unjust transfer. It is impossible, then, for there to be any injustices in initial acquisition.[7]

Now someone might object that if resources are in fact initially *commonly* owned, this argument would not work. But this objection fails for two reasons. First, the argument *would* in fact still work even if resources are initially commonly owned; second, resources are in any case *not* initially commonly owned.

The first point is actually a fairly trivial one. If resources start out *commonly* owned, then for this very reason they do not start out *unowned*, in which case there is no *initial* acquisition of *any* sort to speak of, unjust or otherwise. We all (somehow) *just own* everything. Thus, anyone who takes R without the consent of the rest of us would be committing (if he is committing an injustice at all) an injustice in transfer rather than acquisition. This is perfectly in line with my claim that injustices in holdings can take place only after someone already has ownership of resources, either through initially acquiring them from their unowned state or because the resources are "just owned" from the start; it has no tendency to show that initial acquisition itself can be just or unjust.

Of course, this raises the question of *how* exactly we come collectively to own all resources, which leads us to the second point. Those who object

---

[7] This argument (earlier versions of which appear in Feser, "Taxation, Forced Labor, and Theft," 231, and in chapter 5 of Feser, *On Nozick*) first occurred to me as a natural extension to the case of initial acquisition of property in the state of nature of what F. A. Hayek has argued concerning the inapplicability of the concept of justice to the results of impersonal processes like that of the market. See F. A. Hayek, *Law, Legislation, and Liberty*, vol. 2, *The Mirage of Social Justice* (Chicago, IL: University of Chicago Press, 1976); see also Edward Feser "Hayek on Social Justice: Reply to Lukes and Johnston," *Critical Review* 11, no. 4 (1997): 581–606; and Edward Feser, "Hayek, Social Justice, and the Market: Reply to Johnston," *Critical Review* 12, no. 3 (1998): 269–81. Anthony de Jasay has argued along similar lines in de Jasay, *Against Politics: On Government, Anarchy, and Order* (London: Routledge, 1997), 171–76; his argument is lucidly summarized in N. Stephan Kinsella's review of *Against Politics* in *The Quarterly Journal of Austrian Economics* 1, no. 3 (1998): 85–92. And, of course, related ideas have been expressed by Hume.

to Nozick's assumption that resources start out unowned[8] typically rest content with noting that there are alternative possibilities, especially the possibility that resources start out commonly owned, as if the mere existence of this alternative casts doubt on Nozick's assumption—indeed, as if merely noting the possibility of common ownership were enough to establish its actuality. But why is the assumption of common ownership of resources any less in need of justification than the assumption that resources are unowned? Why should we regard the former assumption, and not the latter, as the default assumption to make?

Surely the reverse is true: the claim that we all own everything is *more* in need of justification than the claim that no one initially owns anything. Surely such a claim is not merely unjustified, but counterintuitive, even mysterious. Consider the following: a pebble resting uneasily on the surface of the asteroid Eros as it orbits the sun, a cubic foot of molten lava churning a mile below the surface of the earth, one of the polar icecaps on Mars, an ant floating on a leaf somewhere in the mid-Pacific, or the Andromeda galaxy. It would seem odd in the extreme to claim that any particular individual owns any of these things: In what sense could Smith, for example, who like most of the rest of us has never left the surface of the earth or even sent a robotic spacecraft to Eros, be said to *own* the pebble resting on its surface? But is it any less odd to claim we *all* own the pebble or these other things? Yet the entire universe of external resources is like these things, or at least (in the case of resources that are now owned) started out like them—started out, that is to say, as just a bunch of *stuff* that no human being had ever had any impact on. So what transforms it into stuff we all commonly own? Our mere *existence*? How so? Are we to suppose that it *was* all initially unowned, but only until a group of *Homo sapiens* finally evolved on our planet, at which point the entire universe suddenly became our collective property? (How exactly did *that* process work?) Or was it just the earth that became our collective property? Why only *that*? Does something become collective property only when we are capable of directly affecting it? But why does *everyone* share in ownership in that case—why not only those *specific individuals* who are capable of affecting it: for example, explorers, astronauts, or entrepreneurs? It is, after all, never literally "we" collectively who discover Antarctica, strike oil, or go to the moon, but only particular individuals, together perhaps with technical assistance and financial backing provided by other particular individuals. Smith's being the first to reach some distant island and build a hut on it at least makes it comprehensible how he might claim—plausibly or implausibly—to own it. This fact about Smith gives some *meaning* to the claim that he has come to own it. But it is not at all clear how this fact would give meaning to the claim that *Jones,*

---

[8] See, e.g., Cohen, *Self-Ownership, Freedom, and Equality,* chaps. 3 and 4; and Kymlicka, *Contemporary Political Philosophy,* 117–18.

whom Smith has never met or even heard of, who has had no involvement in or influence on Smith's journey and homesteading, and who lives thousands of miles away (or even years in the future), has *also* now come to own it. Still less intelligible is the claim that Smith's act has given all of us—the human race collectively, throughout all generations—a claim to the island.

Whatever objections one might raise against Locke's "labor-mixing" theory of property,[9] it at least provides the beginnings of a story that makes it clear how anyone can come to own something. Locke's initial acquirer does, after all, *do* something to a *specific* resource, and does it *with* something he already owns (his labor), so that it is at least not *mysterious* why one might suppose he comes to own the resource, whether or not one thinks that this supposition is ultimately defensible. The common-ownership assumption, by contrast, appears to suppose that we can, all together, simply and peremptorily come to own *everything* without having to lift a finger— or worse, that we don't *come* to own it at all, but just *do* own it—the pebble on Eros, Andromeda, and all the rest. Surely it is the common-ownership advocate who has the greater burden of proof!

There is another problem with the common-ownership assumption besides its lack of support, namely, that it seems irremediably indeterminate. Indeed, at first sight it appears vacuous. If everyone has an equal right to every part of the world, how does this differ exactly from Nozick's assumption that everything is initially unowned—an assumption on which, too, everyone has an equal right to everything (since no one, at the start anyway, has *any* right to anything in particular at all)? Ownership, that is to say, seems to imply exclusion. *Your* (or even *our*) owning something implies that there are others who *do not* own it; thus, it appears that we cannot intelligibly *all* own something, much less everything. This is no doubt (part of) why Locke, though he held that God initially gave the world to mankind in common, also held that individuals can acquire portions of it for their exclusive use. Initial common "ownership" in the Lockean sense entails only that the various resources constituting the world are initially "up for grabs"; for these resources truly to become anyone's property in any meaningful sense, specific individuals actually have to go out and do something with them.

The problem, then, is that if everyone owns everything, no one owns anything. This remains true if we take not a Lockean construal of common ownership, but a construal on which one must get the permission of every other human being, as co-owners of the world, to use any part of the world—what Cohen calls the "joint ownership" interpretation of common ownership.[10] In what sense do you own something if *no one* is in

[9] John Locke, *Two Treatises of Government* (1690), ed. Peter Laslett (Cambridge: Cambridge University Press, 1967), *Second Treatise*, sec. 26.

[10] Cohen, *Self-Ownership, Freedom, and Equality,* 94.

principle excluded from it, if *everyone* has a say over everything and anything you seek to do with it?[11] One's "ownership" becomes purely formal and practically useless. This joint-ownership construal also has the difficulty that it is incompatible with any substantial (as opposed to formal) form of *self*-ownership, since, given that I cannot so much as *move* without using parts of the external world, it entails that I cannot do anything with my self-owned powers without the permission of everyone else.[12] And it is, of course, for this reason *wildly* impractical. These considerations would seem to tell decisively against the assumption that resources are initially commonly owned (in the joint-ownership sense at least), even if there were *some* reason to believe this assumption, which (as I have suggested) there is not.

Another, and at first sight more promising, interpretation of common ownership is to suppose that we do not "collectively own everything" so much as we each own our own individual and equally divided portions of external resources, a construal Cohen calls "equal division" ownership.[13] But *which* portions exactly does each person own, and why *those*? Do we all get equal amounts of zinc and copper, for instance, or does one person get the copper, another the zinc, and so forth? And how are "resources" individuated in the first place? Is my backyard one resource or many, since it might include not only a lawn and a couple of trees, but also hidden oil and mineral deposits? For that matter, is a can of oil itself one resource or many, since I could use part of it for fuel, another part for lubrication, a third to make paint, etc.? (And why a *can* of oil, rather than a barrel or a thimbleful?) Do resources get gathered up again and redivided every time a new person is born, so as to maintain equality in distribution? Do we move people's homes periodically so that we can carve up the land again every so often to guarantee equal plots for newborns? (Why *land*, anyway? What if I want to live on a houseboat? Do we all get equal portions of the surface of the oceans, so as to leave this option open for everyone?) To avoid these problems, do we simply divvy up the "cash value" of all resources? How do we know what that value is independently of a system of market prices, which presupposes *private* ownership and the *inequalities* that go along with it? And since, given changing needs and circumstances, that value is itself perpetually changing, do we need constantly to re-collect and redistribute wealth so as to reflect the "current" economic value of resources? Yet if a demand for equal outcomes is what motivates the equal-division model in the first place, even such periodic "resetting" of the system would not be enough to satisfy such a demand; for as Cohen observes, given inequalities in

---

[11] This sort of problem seems endemic to egalitarianism. Rawlsians famously seek to guarantee equal self-esteem for all; yet, clearly, to quote Gilbert and Sullivan's *The Gondoliers*, "when everyone is somebody, then no one's anybody."

[12] Cohen, *Self-Ownership, Freedom, and Equality*, 98.

[13] Ibid., 103.

persons' (self-owned) natural endowments, even an initial equal distribution of basic *resources* will still result in significant inequalities of *wealth*.[14] In this case, what is the point of insisting on initial equal-division common ownership?[15] (There seems to be little point, at any rate, if one grants the thesis of self-ownership, or at least grants that the thesis is plausible enough that the critic of Nozick is best advised to look elsewhere for a way of undermining his anti-egalitarian and anti-redistributive conclusions.)[16]

These questions seem unanswerable, perhaps even *in principle* unanswerable. But even if one insists otherwise, the issue here is not (or is not primarily) whether some scheme of common ownership can after all be made coherent and practicable. Rather, the issue is that given the difficulty of seeing how this can be done—given the *work*, intellectual and physical, required to institute a common-ownership scheme—it is counterintuitive in the extreme to suggest that the world just *starts out* commonly owned, to suggest that the assumption of common ownership is the natural default assumption to make. Nor are taking resources as initially unowned and taking them as initially commonly owned even on a par as starting points in the theory of property. Nozick's opponents accuse him of being "blithe" in his assumption that resources are initially unowned,[17] but their assumptions are, if anything, more glib. Nozick, however, has good reason for his facile assumption: We clearly need to *do* something to get ownership started, and the "we" who do it are typically *specific individuals* acting on *specific and isolated bits* of the extra-personal world. The natural conclusion to draw from this is that the world starts out unowned, and that it is precisely and only the people who actually do something to change this fact who come to own the particular parts of the world on which they act.[18] At the very least, *this*, I suggest, is the natural default position to take, with the common-ownership advocate being the one who needs to justify his moving off of it. But then, as I have argued,

---

[14] Ibid., 102–5.

[15] Differences in natural *needs* as well as in natural endowments also cast doubt on the point, and the justice, of insisting on an equal distribution of resources. Consider Giganto, a one-thousand-foot-tall mutant, who needs to acquire a *massive* amount of water, food, and land just in order to survive. While leaving, we can stipulate, enough for others to support themselves, he nevertheless uses *much* more of these resources than anyone else. Is this inequality *unjust*, however? Surely not. But then, how can *any* inequality, *just by virtue of being an inequality*, be unjust?

[16] By the same token, the common-ownership advocate also has to face the difficulty that "resources" by themselves are pretty useless; one has to *do* something to make them usable (digging, collecting, refining, etc.). Therefore, in forcibly redistributing those resources, one is inevitably forcibly redistributing the value produced by people's labor, thus violating self-ownership.

[17] Cohen, *Self-Ownership, Freedom, and Equality*, 94.

[18] Thus, it won't do for the egalitarian to respond that perhaps the world *starts out* unowned, but then immediately becomes commonly owned—for now the question is: *When* and *how* exactly did this happen? Obviously, the human race as a whole never collectively "mixed its labor" with all external resources, in one great act of communal initial acquisition!

the natural default position to take on initial acquisition is also that it is never unjust.[19]

III. Labor-Mixing and the Lockean Proviso

Even many of those who are inclined to grant that there is *something* to the argument of the above section might find their confidence shaken when recalling Nozick's own discussion of Locke's theory of property. Doesn't Nozick show the whole notion of labor-mixing to be dubious as a means of acquiring property? Doesn't he show that others are dealt an injustice if one acquires unowned resources in a way that violates the Lockean proviso? I answer: no, and no.

Nozick famously asks:

> Why does mixing one's labor with something make one the owner of it? . . . [W]hy isn't mixing what I own with what I don't own a way of losing what I own rather than a way of gaining what I don't? If I own a can of tomato juice and spill it in the sea so that its molecules (made radioactive, so I can check this) mingle evenly throughout the sea, do I thereby come to own the sea, or have I foolishly dissipated my tomato juice?[20]

The answer to this question is obviously (and obviously intended to be) that the tomato juice has been dissipated foolishly. But how does this cast doubt on the idea that one can come to own something by mixing his labor with it? If the example had instead involved my dumping my tomato juice into a *puddle* of (unowned) water, the plausible conclusion to draw would be that I *have* come to own that water. Of course, there are going to be cases that are intermediate between the puddle and sea examples, where we are not sure whether to say I have come to own the water or have simply lost the tomato juice within it. Nevertheless this is no special problem for the notion of acquiring property by labor-mixing. What we have here is just one more example of the sort of vagueness classically illustrated by the paradox of the heap. A million grains of sand

---

[19] We also should keep in mind that one of the benefits of the market—which purportedly comes into existence only *after* property titles have already been established—is that it best allows individuals to make use of localized knowledge of needs, circumstances, and the like. (See F. A. Hayek, *Individualism and Economic Order* [Chicago, IL: University of Chicago Press, 1948].) Surely, then, one of the benefits of allowing people individually initially to acquire resources and thus establish the property titles the market depends on—as opposed to having a central authority divide the titles up equally—is that it would allow these initial acquirers to make use of analogously localized knowledge: for example, knowledge of what unowned resources are *worth the bother* of acquiring in the first place (given local needs and circumstances). The suggestion, in short, is that the market principle applies just as much in *initially acquiring* property as it does (less controversially) in transferring it.

[20] Nozick, *Anarchy, State, and Utopia*, 174–75.

constitute a heap of sand, and ten grains do not, but at what precise point in removing grains from a heap are we no longer left with a heap? There is no principled way to answer this question, but that fact casts no doubt on the existence of heaps of sand. We can make do with paradigm cases of heaps. Similarly with labor-mixing: there are paradigm cases where mixing one's labor (or tomato juice, or whatever) plausibly results in ownership, and there are paradigm cases where one has merely frittered away one's labor (or juice) to no effect. Whittling a piece of driftwood that has washed up on the beach seems a good example of the former; gently blowing in the direction of the driftwood as it floats by fifty yards off shore seems a good example of the latter. That there are intermediate cases where it is unclear how to apply the labor-mixing principle does not cast doubt on the principle itself.

Furthermore, if I had dumped in the sea, not an ordinary can of tomato juice, but a *lake*-sized can of it, or a lake-sized can of soda pop, or nuclear waste that makes the sea glow green, it seems it would *not* be implausible in such cases to say that I have come to acquire the sea. This suggests that the key idea behind the labor-mixing principle is that of *significantly altering* a resource, at least by coming to *control* that resource, hence the intuition that by building a house on a plot of land, I have plausibly come to own that plot, but not the valley, mountain range, or continent in which the plot is situated. To acquire *those* (unowned) things, I would have to do something dramatically to affect them, too, or to bring them under my control—for example, by sending out herds of my cattle to graze on an expanse of unowned land, or by building a fence around it, or by sending an army out to secure the borders of the territory I want to claim. To take a real-world example, it would not be *absurd* for the United States government (whether or not one would *approve* of this) to claim ownership of the area of the moon's surface on which Apollo 11 landed, where part of the spacecraft remains to this day and is accessible to astronauts who could be sent there again with relative ease. It would, however, be dubious for the government to claim ownership of the entire moon, and absurd for it to claim ownership of the surface of Pluto, to which the government has never sent a spacecraft. Less easy to settle is the question of whether the government could claim ownership of a distant asteroid on which it lands a probe, but which is traveling in such an orbit that it could not within the next few hundred years be reached again by a spacecraft. The difference in the intuitive plausibility of claims to ownership in these cases clearly reflects a difference in how much *effect* or *control* we have had or could have on these various extraterrestrial regions. Thus, Locke's labor-mixing criterion seems to capture a deep and widespread intuition about how ownership comes to be established, embodied in a set of paradigm cases that form the conceptual starting point for thinking about less clear cases (such as the ownership of patents). The basic idea is that the first person to come across a previously unowned item and *do something significant with it* has a rightful claim over it. And not only does this *in fact* serve as our working model of property acquisition (Locke hardly took his labor-mixing principle from thin air), it is hard to imagine what an alternative model would even look like.

It must be remembered that the claim is *not* that one's having a significant effect on or exerting control over a resource makes one's initial acquisition of it *just*, for I claim that initial acquisitions are neither just nor unjust; the claim is, rather, that such effort or control makes it an *acquisition*, period. Still, one might wonder how such effect or control can give rise to a claim of *justice* against others who might seek unjustly to transfer the resource once initial acquisition has occurred. "You just happen to have been the one who got there first. Why should you have a right to it?" But this ought not to be mysterious to anyone who accepts the thesis of self-ownership or at least takes this thesis to be coherent (as even Cohen, who rejects it, does). For in owning my body parts, I also "just happen" to be the one to own them. I just "got there first," as it were—I did not *do* anything particularly *special* to get the body parts—yet I still clearly *own* them (perhaps, to appeal again to the notion of having a significant effect or degree of control, because I have as much control over and effect on them as one could possibly have). I certainly have, at the very least, *more* of a claim to them than anyone else does, as even someone who rejects the thesis of self-ownership would presumably acknowledge. But why can't the same be said for the initial acquirer of an external resource? "Why *shouldn't* I have the right to it?" he can plausibly retort. "After all, who *else* has a better claim to it? *I'm* the first to do anything with it!" Why is the burden of proof on the initial acquirer of an external resource to justify his claim, any more than it is on the initial "acquirer" of your arm (i.e., *you*) to justify the claim to the arm? Why isn't the burden instead on the person who wants to deny such a claim—a person who himself didn't do *anything at all* to acquire the resource, not even show up first?[21]

These considerations suggest that the notion of rights to external resources may be a conceptual extension of (and parasitic upon) the idea that one has a right to one's body parts, talents, abilities, labor, and the like. In both cases, one *establishes* such rights by just "showing up" and being the first to "take possession"—in the latter case by simply being born with certain things, and in the former case by incorporating into what is unowned part of what one is born with. One transfers one's sense of what is "mine" from one's body to the things one's body significantly

---

[21] That we do in fact, in everyday life, put the burden of proof on the denier of claims to property is evidenced by the *presumption* that exists in law that the possessor of a holding is the rightful owner of it. This reflects our intuitive sense of justice in holdings. It is only (egalitarian) philosophers who—bizarrely—put the burden on the *possessor* to prove that we shouldn't expropriate his holdings. Such philosophers are reminiscent of the epistemological skeptic who challenges you to *prove* you're not dreaming, or are not a brain in a vat, or whatever—as if it were such strange logical possibilities, rather than the commonsense belief in the external world, that had the presumption in *their* favor!

interacts with. This would certainly account for the intuitive sense of the justice of the "finders keepers" principle even among children, and also for the sense of personal violation one feels when his property is taken from him without his consent. It accounts as well for why egalitarians such as John Rawls and Ronald Dworkin, seeing, as Cohen notes,[22] that personal endowments are just as "arbitrary" as the initial distribution of external resources, conclude that (the fruits of) these personal endowments are as ripe for redistribution as (they claim) the external resources are. The fact that who initially gets to acquire which external resources depends largely on chance is, in the final analysis, no more noteworthy than the fact that who gets born with which personal endowments is also a matter of chance. Thus, self-ownership and (some form of) Nozickian property ownership appear ultimately to stand or fall together. The "arbitrariness" of the former is really no different in principle from the arbitrariness of the latter, so that if one wants to eliminate the "arbitrariness" in the one case, he ought to have no scruples about doing so in the other as well. Rawls and Dworkin thus opt to do away with self-ownership, and do so rather casually; Cohen (to his credit) does so only with reluctance. To understand his reluctance, however, is to understand why Nozick takes the violation of property rights to be of a piece with the violation of rights to one's own person.[23]

I will return to these themes (in Sections IV and V). Before doing so, however, I need to consider the claim that violations of the Lockean proviso constitute clear examples of injustices in initial acquisition. This is, I suggest, only half right. Such violations do (very often, at least) embody injustices; they are not, however, injustices in initial acquisition.

Locke's proviso on the initial acquisition of resources was that the acquirer had to leave "enough and as good . . . in common for others" to acquire,[24] and Nozick's gloss on this proviso is that it "is meant to ensure that the situation of others is not worsened." [25] The standard example of a purported violation of the proviso involves someone appropriating for himself a resource that others had previously held in common—a water

---

[22] Cohen, *Self-Ownership, Freedom, and Equality*, 93.

[23] Left-libertarians are egalitarians who try to combine a commitment to self-ownership with an egalitarian distribution of external resources (e.g., Vallentyne and Steiner, *Left-Libertarianism and Its Critics*, cited in note 6). This is a position that, if I am right, is inherently unstable. For although self-ownership and equal resource ownership are *in principle* compatible, the considerations that lead egalitarians of any sort to advocate the latter would also justify rejecting the former. Some left-libertarians are keen, for example, on redistributing *inherited* wealth, which the inheritor did nothing to earn or acquire; but none of us did anything to earn or acquire our natural talents and abilities either, or even our body parts—we just "inherit" them from our parents. Therefore, if the former can be redistributed, why not the latter? If it is objected that redistribution of the latter would involve too serious an interference with people's lives, then (as with Cohen, who rejects self-ownership) it would seem that it is a moral principle of noninterference of some sort that is really what the left-libertarian is committed to, and not self-ownership per se.

[24] Locke, *Second Treatise*, sec. 27.

[25] Nozick, *Anarchy, State, and Utopia*, 175.

hole in the midst of a desert, say, which is the only source of water for those living in the surrounding area. Doesn't the person who appropriates this water hole commit a clear injustice against those who had been using it (since he now, say, charges them for water that they previously took for free, or even forbids them to use the water, in either case clearly leaving them worse off)? Doesn't such an example serve as a counterexample to the claim that there are no unjust initial acquisitions? Yes and no: yes, this person's behavior is an injustice; no, it is not a counterexample, because the person who takes possession of the water hole is *not* an initial acquirer, but a *thief*.

The correct interpretation of this sort of case is, I suggest, as follows: The water hole is not unowned in the first place when the person in question tries to acquire it. After all, other people had been using it, and their use (especially since it is presumably regular, continuous use) *itself* amounted to initial acquisition of the water hole. Their use counts as a kind of labor-mixing, a bringing of the resource under their control. Thus, they have every right to object to what the would-be acquirer tries to do, precisely because *they* have already acquired it. His act amounts to what Nozick would call an "unjust transfer" of the resource, an attempt to take it from its rightful owners without their consent.[26]

One might object that in this case we are dealing with a *community* of users of the water hole, not a single individual who came across an unowned resource; doesn't this conflict with what I said earlier about individuals, rather than "all of us collectively," being the ones who come to own resources? It does not, because nothing in what I said above rules out cases where a number of people together initially acquire a resource. Indeed, historically, this probably has happened quite often, as families and tribes moved into virgin territory. What I denied above was that "all of us collectively," that is, the human race *as a whole,* ever appropriated all unowned resources *as a whole* in a way that gave rise to common ownership of them. It is quite easy to see how a (relatively) small group of individuals might together acquire, say, a discrete tract of land, so that they all come to have common ownership of it, perhaps because they all know one another and are consciously devoted to a common purpose, and because their efforts are intertwined in such a way that it is hard to sort out exactly who has done what. This is very different from claiming that some much larger group (of perhaps thousands or hundreds of thousands of people or more) has "collectively" initially acquired a continent, where the "group" is *not* consciously working together as a whole, where its members largely do not know each other and are separated by geographical and communal boundaries, and where it is easy to demarcate

---

[26] Accordingly, Kymlicka's description of this sort of case as an "initial acquisition" involving "the use of force" (*Contemporary Political Philosophy,* 108) is incoherent, for if *force* is used it can't be an *initial* acquisition at all; it must be an (unjust) *transfer*.

which bits of territory have been worked by which individuals and/or subgroups. It is not plausible to say in this sort of case, much less in the case of the human race as a whole, that "all of us collectively" have acquired resources. Rather, it is a matter of many discrete individuals and groups engaging in many discrete acts of initial acquisition.

Another objection to my interpretation of the water-hole case would be that those who were previously using the water hole might not *claim* it as their property; they might claim only the right to use it for certain purposes. As many property theorists have pointed out, however, any "property right" to something is really a bundle of rights: the right to use something (perhaps in certain ways but not others, perhaps for a certain period of time), the right to sell it or lease it, the right to exclude others from it, the right to destroy it, and so forth. *Full* ownership of something entails having all of these rights to it; having only some of these rights entails having (one of a number of degrees of) *partial* ownership. Since the right to use the water hole just is one among the bundle of rights constituting ownership of it, anyone who claims the right to use thereby claims partial ownership. The correct thing to say about the water-hole example, then, is that the users are not claiming *full* ownership of it, but they are, whether they realize it or not, claiming *partial* ownership (even, at least, temporary ownership) of it. The violation of their property rights by the newcomer thus consists in his taking over the water hole in such a way that they are no longer able to use it as they once did. If he treated it in some other way, however—acquiring *other* rights over it that the previous users neither claimed nor wanted to claim, in a way that would allow them to continue using it as they always had—then he could presumably become a partial owner of the hole as well, "initially acquiring" those aspects of it that no one had yet claimed.

This raises the question of whether our paradigmatic individual initial acquirer of an unowned resource *fully* owns what he has acquired. The right answer seems to be that he does if (unlike the water-hole users) he claims he does after mixing his labor with it in such a way that he has had a significant effect on or taken control of it in all the ways relevant to all the various rights one could claim over it. If he comes across a water hole that *no one* has ever used, and if he only bathes in it from time to time, perhaps he has only acquired in effect the right to use it; if instead he builds a fence around it, posts guard dogs, and so forth, he has acquired full ownership. The situation is really, in essence, no different from what it was when we were considering initial acquisition as acquisition of a single amorphous "property right." Whether it is one right or a bundle of them, if an individual mixes his labor with a resource in such a way that he takes control of or significantly affects a resource in ways covered by all the relevant rights in question, then he has acquired that resource. His acquisition is neither just nor unjust; it is those who would seek without his consent to deprive him of the rights he has so acquired who are the first who could be said to act unjustly. And if he has (by having a *very* significant effect on the resource) indeed so acquired *all* the rights that one could acquire to the resource, then his ownership of it is full ownership.

IV. Self-Ownership and the Self-Ownership Proviso

Even one who grants that what has been said so far explains away *some* of the intuition that initial acquisitions can be unjust might suspect that the last example above raises a more formidable problem for my thesis. I have said that if someone comes across and mixes his labor with a water hole that *no one* has ever used—so that there is no question of any *previous* users being made worse off (by having their partial property rights violated)—then he comes *fully* to own it. But where does this leave *future* potential users of the water hole? What if some lost and thirsty traveler stumbles across the desert and comes across the water hole, and it is the *only* water hole within hundreds of miles? What if all other sources of water on earth dry up, leaving the owner of the water hole with a monopoly on water? Wouldn't my thesis imply that he has the right to charge whatever he wants for the water, or even to exclude anyone else, however close to death's door that person might be as a result of thirst? And wouldn't this be a case of leaving others worse off by his initial acquisition, even if these others had no previous claim to the hole?

There are two possible responses that an advocate of my position could take, one a hard-line approach and the other a soft-line approach. The first involves holding that this is the place where the advocate must simply bite the bullet and argue that however selfish, cruel, or wicked the initial acquirer would be to exploit his water hole for personal gain, or even to refuse (from sheer misanthropy) to let anyone drink from it, he still commits no *injustice* in doing so, much less in initially acquiring the resource.[27] He has a *right* to act that way, even if there are other moral considerations that ought to move him not to use his right in that way. The hard-liner could then insist that moral pressure (rather than government expropriation) will usually be enough to get monopolists in this sort of situation to do the right thing, and that such situations are so rare, in any case, that the worry is a merely academic one, unlikely to crop up in

---

[27] Eric Mack, "The Self-Ownership Proviso: A New and Improved Lockean Proviso," *Social Philosophy and Policy* 12, no. 1 (1995): 189, draws a related distinction between hard-line Lockean-Nozickian property theorists and their softer compatriots. His distinction is between theorists who accept the need for a Lockean proviso and those (the hard-liners) who do not. Mine is between those (the hard-liners) who reject a Lockean proviso, full stop, because initial acquisition is neither just nor unjust, and those who also reject it, and for the same reason, but would nevertheless go on to endorse some other principle that, while not pertaining to initial acquisition, still does something similar to the job the Lockean proviso was intended to do. As we will see below in the text, Mack's own view lends itself to this last, softer interpretation (which I will endorse), but unlike me, Mack does not seem to reject the notion that initial acquisitions can, as such, meaningfully be said to be just or unjust.

the real world. *Any* philosophically coherent moral view, precisely because it makes consistent and systematic intuitions that are usually ill defined and haphazardly applied in everyday life, is likely to have *some* odd consequences under certain rare circumstances. But as long as these circumstances are primarily hypothetical, and are likely to remain so, the odd consequences by themselves are not enough to justify rejecting the theory. This sort of problem is not a *special* problem for the view under discussion.

There is, I think, much merit in this hard-line reply. In any case, egalitarians, some of whose favored theories *in practice* have led to mass poverty and even mass murder (witness the Communist regimes of the twentieth century), ought to think twice about chiding their opponents for leaving the door open to unsavory consequences that are, and promise to continue to be, highly speculative. (A monopoly on water is surely a *much* less likely prospect than an egalitarian regime's tending toward totalitarianism and economic incompetence.) Still, it is always preferable to avoid having to bite bullets, if one can manage it. Is there a way to do so in this case?

There is. An alternative, soft-line approach could acknowledge that the initial acquirer who abuses a monopoly over a water hole (or any similar crucial resource) does commit an injustice against those who are disadvantaged, but such an approach could still hold that the acquirer nevertheless has not committed an injustice in acquisition—his acquisition was, as I have said, neither just nor unjust. Nor does he fail to own what he has acquired; he still cannot be said to have *stolen* the water from anyone. Rather, his injustice is an unjust *use* of what he owns, on a par with the unjust use I make of my self-owned fist when I wield it, unprovoked, to bop you on your self-owned nose. In what sense does the water-hole owner use his water unjustly, though? He doesn't try to *drown* anyone in it, after all—indeed, the whole problem is that he won't let anybody near it!

Eric Mack gives us the answer we need in what he has put forward as the "self-ownership proviso" (SOP).[28] This is a proviso not (as the Lockean proviso is) on the *initial acquisition* of property, but rather on how one can *use* his property in a way that respects others' self-ownership rights. It is motivated by consideration of the fact that the talents, abilities, capacities, energies, etc., that a person rightfully possesses as a self-owner are inherently "world-interactive"; that is, it is of their very *essence* that they are directed toward the extra-personal environment.[29] Your capacity to use your hand, for instance, is just a capacity to grasp and manipulate external objects; thus, what you own in owning your hand is something essentially grasping and manipulating.[30] Now if someone were to cut off

---

[28] Ibid., passim.

[29] Ibid., 186.

[30] In case there are implications of this example that Mack would not want to commit himself to, I should note that the example is mine, not his. In particular, the example might

your hand or invasively keep you from using it (by tying your arm against your body or holding it behind your back), he would obviously be violating your self-ownership rights. But there are, Mack suggests, other, noninvasive ways in which those rights might be violated. If, to use an example of Mack's, I effectively nullify your ability to use your hand by creating a device that causes anything you reach for to be propelled beyond your grasp, making it impossible for you ever to grasp or manipulate anything, I have violated your right to your hand as much as if I had cut it off or tied it down. I have, in any case, prevented your right to your hand from being anything more than a *formal* right, one that is practically useless. In the interests of guaranteeing respect for *substantive, robust* rights of self-ownership, then, "[t]he SOP requires that persons not deploy their legitimate holdings, i.e., their extra-personal property, in ways that severely, albeit noninvasively, disable any person's world-interactive powers." [31]

The SOP follows, in Mack's view, from the thesis of self-ownership itself; or, at any rate, the considerations that would lead anyone to accept that thesis should also, in his view, lead one to accept the proviso. [32] A brief summary of a few of Mack's thought experiments should suffice to give a sense of why this is so. [33] In what Mack calls the *Adam's Island* example, Adam acquires a previously uninhabited island and later refuses a shipwrecked Zelda permission to come ashore, as a result of which she remains struggling at sea (and presumably drowns). In the *Paternalist Caging* example, instead of drowning, Zelda becomes caught offshore in a cage Adam has constructed for catching large sea mammals, and, rather than releasing her, Adam keeps her in the cage and feeds her regularly. In the *Knuckle-Scraper Barrier* example, Zelda falls asleep on some unowned ground, whereupon a gang of oafish louts encircles her and, using their bodies and arms as barriers, refuses to let her out of the circle (accusing her of assault if she touches them in order to climb over or break through). In the *Disabling Property Barrier* example, instead of a human barrier, Adam constructs a plastic shield over and around the unowned plot of ground upon which Zelda sleeps, accusing her of trespassing upon his property when she awakens and tries to escape by breaking through the plastic. And in the (similarly named) *Disabling Property Barriers* example,

---

seem to suggest an Aristotelian-Thomistic conception of natural function, and though this by no means troubles me, it might not be what Mack himself has in mind (nor, of course, is it something every philosopher is going to sympathize with). Mack's view nevertheless seems to require *something* like this conception. And something like it—enough like it to do the job Mack needs to be done, anyway—is arguably to be found in Larry Wright's well-known reconstruction, in modern Darwinian terms, of the traditional notion of natural function. See Larry Wright, "Functions," *Philosophical Review* 82, no. 2 (1973): 139–68.

[31] Mack, "The Self-Ownership Proviso," 187.

[32] See Feser, *On Nozick*, chapter 3, for an overview of the various sorts of arguments that can be and have been given in defense of the thesis of self-ownership.

[33] Mack, "The Self-Ownership Proviso," passim.

Adam, instead of enclosing Zelda in a plastic barrier, encloses in plastic barriers *every* external object that Zelda would otherwise be able to use—thus, in effect, enclosing her in a larger, all-encompassing plastic barrier of a more eccentric shape. In all of these cases, Mack says, although Zelda's *formal* rights of self-ownership have not been violated—no one has invaded the area enclosed by the surface of her skin—her rights over her self-owned powers, and in particular her ability to exercise those powers, have nevertheless been nullified. But a plausible self-ownership-based theory surely cannot allow for this. It cannot, for instance, allow the innocent Zelda justly to be *imprisoned* in any of the ways described!

If Mack is right, then it seems we have, in the SOP, grounds for holding that a water-hole monopolist would indeed be committing an injustice against anyone he refuses water to, or to whom he charges exorbitant prices for access. The injustice would be a straightforward violation of a person's rights to self-ownership, a case of nullifying a person's self-owned powers in a way analogous to Adam's or the knuckle-scrapers' nullification of Zelda's self-owned powers. It would *not* be an injustice in initial acquisition, however. The water-hole monopolist *still* owns the water hole as much as he ever did; he just cannot use it in a way that violates other individuals' self-ownership rights (either by drowning them in it or by nullifying their self-owned powers by denying them access to it when there is *no* alternative way for them to gain access to the water necessary for the use of their self-owned powers).

Is Mack right? The hard-liner might dig in his heels and insist that none of Mack's examples amount to self-ownership-violating injustices; instead, they are merely subtle but straightforward property rights violations or cases of moral failings of various other sorts (cruelty, selfishness, etc.). The *Adam's Island* case, for starters, is roughly analogous to the example of the water-hole monopolist, so that it arguably cannot give any non-question-begging support to the SOP, if the SOP is then supposed to show that the water-hole example involves an injustice. The *Disabling Property Barriers* case might also be viewed as unable to provide any non-question-begging support, since Adam's encasing everything in plastic might plausibly be interpreted as his *acquiring* everything, in which case we are back to a water-hole-type monopoly example. The *Knuckle-Scraper Barrier* and *Disabling Property Barrier* examples might be explained by saying that in falling asleep on the unowned plot of land, Zelda in effect has come (at least temporarily) to acquire it, and (by virtue of walking) to acquire also the path she took to get to it, so that the knuckle-scrapers and Adam violate her *property* rights (not her self-ownership rights) in not allowing her to escape. The *Paternalist Caging* example can perhaps be explained by arguing that in building the cage, Adam has acquired the water route leading to it, so that in swimming this route (and thus getting caught in the cage) Zelda has violated his property rights and, therefore, can justly be caged. Accordingly, the hard-liner might insist, we can explain all of these examples in a hard-line way and thus avoid commitment to the SOP.

Such a hard-line response would be ingenious (well, maybe), but still, I think, ultimately doomed to failure. Can the *Paternalist Caging* example, to start with, plausibly be explained away in the manner that I have suggested? Does Adam commit *no* injustice against Zelda even if he *never* lets her out? It will not do to write this off merely as a case of excessive punishment (explaining the injustice of which would presumably not require commitment to the SOP). For suppose Adam says, after a mere five minutes of confinement, "I'm no longer punishing you; you've paid your debt and are free to go, as far as I'm concerned. But *I'm* not going to bother exerting the effort to let you out. I never *forced* you to get in the cage, after all—you did it on your own—and you have no right to the use of my self-owned cage-opening powers to fix *your* mistake! So *teleport* out, if you can. Or get someone *else*—if you can find someone—to let you out." Adam would be neither violating Zelda's rights to external property nor excessively punishing her in this case; nor would he be invasively violating her self-ownership rights. But wouldn't he still be committing an injustice, however *non*invasively? Don't we need something like the SOP to explain why this is so?

The barrier examples, for their part, do not require Zelda's walking and falling asleep on virgin territory, which thus (arguably) becomes her property. We can, to appeal to the sort of science-fiction scenario beloved of philosophers, imagine instead a bizarre chance disruption of the structure of space-time that teleports Zelda into Adam's plastic shell or into the midst of the knuckle-scrapers. There is no question now of their violating her property rights; yet don't they still commit an injustice by nullifying her self-owned powers in refusing to allow her to exit? Consider a parallel example concerning property ownership itself. If your prized $50,000 copy of *Captain America Comics* number 1, due to another rupture in space-time or just to a particularly strong wind that blows it out of your hands and through my window, suddenly appears on the floor of my living room, do I have the right to refuse to bring it back out to you or to allow you to come in and get it? Suppose I attempt to justify my refusal by saying, "I won't touch it, and you're free to have it back if you can arrange another space-time rupture or gust of wind. But I refuse to exert my self-owned powers to bring it out to you, or to allow you on my property to get it. *I* never *asked* for it to appear in my living room, after all!" Would anyone accept this justification? Doesn't your property right in the comic book *require* me to give it back to you?

The hard-liner might suggest that this example transports the SOP advocate out of the frying pan and into the fire. For if the SOP is true, wouldn't we also have to commit ourselves to a "property-ownership proviso" (POP) that requires us not to nullify anyone's ability to use his *external* private property in a way consistent with *its* "world-interactive powers"? If I build a miniature submarine in my garage, and you have the only swimming pool within one thousand miles, must you allow me the use of your pool lest you nullify my ability to use the sub? If (to take an example of Cohen's cited by Mack) I own a corkscrew, must I be provided with wine bottles to open lest the corkscrew sadly fail to fulfill its full potential?[34]

Mack's response to this line of thought seems basically to amount to a bit of backpedaling on the claim that his proviso really follows from the notion of self-*ownership* per se—so as to avoid the conclusion that a (rather unlibertarian and presumably redistributionist) POP would also, in parallel fashion, follow from the concept of *property* ownership. His response seems, instead, to emphasize the idea that the considerations favoring self-ownership also favor, via an *independent* line of reasoning, the SOP.[35] In my view, however, a better response would be one that took note of some relevant disanalogies between property in oneself and property in external things.

Note first that the self-owned world-interactive powers, the possible use of which the SOP is intended to guarantee, are possessed by a *living* being who is undergoing development, which involves passing through various stages; therefore, these powers are ones that *flourish* with use and *atrophy* or even *disappear* with disuse.[36] To nullify these powers even for a limited time, then, is (very often at least) not merely temporarily to inconvenience their owner, but, rather, to bring about a permanent reduction or even disablement of these powers. By contrast, a submarine (or a corkscrew) retains its powers even when left indefinitely in a garage (or a drawer). This difference in the effect that nullification has on self-owned powers versus extra-personal property plausibly justifies a difference in our judgments concerning the acceptability, from the point of view of justice, of such nullification in the two cases; that is, it justifies adoption of the SOP but not of the POP.[37]

Second, there is an element of *choice* (and in particular, of *voluntary acquisition*) where extra-personal property is concerned that is morally

---

[34] Ibid., 201.

[35] Ibid., 202.

[36] Here, again, we see the possible relevance to the SOP of an Aristotelian-Thomistic understanding of human nature.

[37] Would this justify adoption of a POP when the property in question is an *animal*, which also is a living being having powers subject to atrophy, etc.? I think not, for an animal is analogous to a corkscrew or submarine at least in the sense that if left alone—if *left in the wild*, that is—*it too* doesn't lose its natural powers. Indeed, it is taking an animal *out* of the wild that is likely to cause those powers to atrophy. It is the *owner* of the animal who takes the creature from the wild and then finds he lacks the wherewithal to keep it alive and active who is responsible for its atrophying powers, *not* those who would refuse to give him food for the animal and a yard for it to run around in—just as the owner of a corkscrew who broke it while using it to hammer nails could blame no one but himself for nullifying its powers. Thus, an animal owner would not have a legitimate claim against others, based on appeal to a POP, that they should furnish him with food, etc., for the animal.

relevant here. One's self-owned powers, along with the SOP-guaranteed right to the non-nullification of those powers, are not something one chooses or acquires; one *just has* them—indeed, to a great degree one *just is* the constellation of those powers, abilities, etc.—and owns them *fully*. By contrast, extra-personal property is something one chooses to acquire or not to acquire, and as we have seen, one always acquires property rights in various *degrees,* from partial to full ownership—*and this would include the rights guaranteed by a POP.* If one *chooses* to acquire a corkscrew under conditions where wine bottles are unavailable, or are even likely at some point to become unavailable, one can hardly blame others if one finds oneself bottle-less. To fail to acquire POP-like rights regarding the corkscrew (by, say, contracting with someone else to provide one with wine bottles in perpetuity) is not the same thing as to have those rights and then have them violated. Someone who buys a corkscrew and then finds that he cannot use it is like the person who acquires only partial property rights in a water hole that others have already acquired partial use rights over. *He* cannot complain that his co-owners have violated his rights; he *never acquired* those other rights in the first place. Similarly, the corkscrew owner cannot complain that he has no bottles to open; he *never acquired* the right to those bottles, only to the corkscrew. If *full* ownership of a corkscrew requires POP-like rights over it, then all that follows is that corkscrew owners who lack bottles are not full owners of their corkscrews.

Altogether, then, the SOP seems intuitively plausible and well able to withstand even the strongest objections. It allows us to defend a very strongly libertarian (Lockean-Nozickian, anti-egalitarian, anti-redistributionist) conception of property rights, while at the same time slightly softening the hard edge that critics of libertarianism object to in this conception. In particular, the SOP allows me to defend my central thesis in this paper without having to take on board what I have called the "hard-line thesis." And it does all this without drawing us into the briar patch of the Lockean proviso, understood as a constraint on initial acquisition, with all the redistributionist hay that critics of libertarianism have tried to make of it. Thus, I am inclined to endorse the SOP, with gratitude to Mack for developing what seems to be a major contribution to the theory of self-ownership (and to libertarian theory in general).[38]

V. Some Implications

If what I have argued so far is correct, then the way is opened to the following revised case for strongly libertarian Lockean-Nozickian prop-

---

[38] Another benefit the SOP brings to libertarian theory is that it arguably affords a way of explaining why the mere *threat* or *risk* of harm to oneself counts as a rights violation no less than the actual infliction of the harm does. For your property rights in yourself seem *strictly* to have been violated only when you have *actually* been harmed, but if the fear imposed by a threat or risk keeps you from using your self-owned powers, then that would seem to violate the SOP, and thus itself count as an injustice.

erty rights: We are self-owners, having full property rights to our body parts, powers, talents, energies, etc. As self-owners, we also have a right, given the SOP, not to have our self-owned powers nullified—we have the right, that is, to act within the extra-personal world and thus to acquire rights to extra-personal objects that the use of our self-owned powers requires.[39] This might involve the buying or leasing of certain rights or bundles of rights and, correspondingly, the acquiring of lesser or greater degrees of ownership of parts of the external world, but as long as one is able to exercise one's powers to *some* degree and is not rendered *incapable* of acting within that world, the SOP is satisfied. In any case, such rights can only be *traded* after they are first *established* by initial acquisition. In initially acquiring a resource, an agent does no one an injustice (it was *unowned*, after all). Furthermore, he has mixed *his* labor with the resource, significantly altering it and/or bringing it under *his* control, and is *himself* solely responsible for whatever value or utility the resource has come to have. Thus, *he* has a presumptive right to it, and, if his control and/or alteration (and thus acquisition) of it is (more or less) complete, his ownership is accordingly (more or less) full. The system of strong private property rights that follows from the acts of initial acquisition performed by countless such agents results, as a matter of empirical fact, in a market economy that inevitably and dramatically *increases* the number of resources available for use by individuals, and these benefited individuals include those who come along long after initial acquisition has taken place. (Indeed, it *especially* includes these latecomers, given that they were able to avoid the hard work of being the first to "tame the land" and draw out the value of raw materials.)[40] The SOP is thus, in fact, rarely, if ever, violated. The upshot is that a system of Lockean-Nozickian private property rights is morally justified, with a strong presumption against tampering with existing property titles in general. In any case, there is a strong presumption against any general *egalitarian* redistribution of wealth, and *no case whatsoever* to be made for such redistribution from the general theory of property just sketched, purged as it is of the Lockean proviso, with all the egalitarian mischief-making the proviso has made possible.

Even with Nozick's original Lockean proviso, however, the grounds for making such mischief were greatly exaggerated. It is true that Nozick

---

[39] It might be objected that at most, the SOP requires *liberties to use* extra-personal resources rather than rights over them. But when we keep in mind that property rights come in bundles of component rights, it is clear that a *liberty* to use is just a *right* to use, a right that may be only partial (i.e., a right to use only under certain conditions, at certain times, and so forth). *Full* ownership is just the possession of *all* the relevant liberties.

[40] Mack, "The Self-Ownership Proviso," 207–8, 212–16; see also David Schmidtz, "The Institution of Property," *Social Philosophy and Policy* 11, no. 2 (1994): 42–62. Incidentally, Schmidtz argues that given the benefits of initial acquisition, there are times when the Lockean proviso not only allows but *requires* such acquisition. (But requires it of *whom* exactly? That this question has no clear answer seems to me another reason for abandoning the Lockean proviso.)

spoke of a "historical shadow" cast over the principle of justice in transfer by the proviso,[41] and even contemplated the notion that a one-time redistribution of wealth along the lines of some egalitarian or other patterned principle of justice might be a way of rectifying past injustices in acquisition and transfer.[42] But this never sat well with the individualism that permeates Nozick's overall philosophy. "We as a society," as any good Nozickian knows, never commit injustices against anyone, past or present; it is only *specific individuals* and *groups* of individuals who can commit them. And this would include injustices in acquisition, if only there were any. The rectification of such injustices *could not* be achieved by taxing *everyone* in accordance with some egalitarian reading of the Lockean proviso. Indeed, this would only result in new injustices against those whose current holdings were *not* a result of past injustices in acquisition (or even against those whose holdings partly resulted from such injustices, but not to an extent that would justify the inevitably arbitrarily-set level of taxes they would be forced to pay in restitution). Such rectification could only be achieved, consistent with Nozickian principles, by dealing with *specific* claims of *specific* past injustices filed by *specific* individuals against other *specific* individuals, and treated by the state on a case-by-case basis rather than as a matter of general social policy. Fortunately, since there are no injustices in acquisition, all of this becomes moot.

What about past unjust transfers—among which we can, as we have seen, now classify at least some injustices previously thought of as injustices in acquisition? The same individualistic, case-by-case approach applies here. The case made on behalf of black Americans descended from slaves, and on behalf of American Indians, for "reparations" owed to them by the U.S. federal government is thus revealed to be simplistic at best, unfounded at worst, and in any case liable to compound past injustices by inflicting new ones on innocent (and already, from a Nozickian point of view, massively overburdened) taxpayers. This fact is obscured by the sloppy and collectivist manner in which these issues are usually discussed: as a matter of what "whites" owe to "blacks," or of what "we" (American citizens in general) owe to "the Indians."

As a matter of historical fact, of course, there was never any such thing as "the white man" doing anything to "the Indians." There were instead a multitude of different Indian individuals and groups (often in conflict with, and inflicting injustices upon, *each other*, and often in *alliance* with certain whites) who had various interactions with various groups of whites (English, Spaniards, French, etc., and various subgroups and individuals within these groups). Some of these interactions were unjust; some were dubiously moral but not strictly unjust; and some were perfectly just. Similarly, in the case of American slavery, specific individual blacks were

---

[41] Nozick, *Anarchy, State, and Utopia*, 180.
[42] Ibid., 231.

dealt injustices by specific whites and groups of whites (and sometimes also by blacks who took *other* blacks as slaves or sold them into slavery, even *within* the United States). "Blacks in general" were not taken as slaves by "whites in general." Rectifying such injustices must therefore take account of all of this complexity, as well as the question of *exactly which* whites here and now owe *exactly how much* of what they have to *exactly which* past injustices committed by *exactly which* ancestors. Furthermore, it must carefully disentangle the extent to which government (and which *level* of government in which cases) was responsible for a given injustice from the extent to which certain private individuals were.[43]

Taking account of all this complexity is, I say, on a Nozickian account a necessary condition of rectifying past injustices in transfer, but merely to note this fact is to make plain that the injustices in question *cannot* for the most part be rectified, for the questions raised by these complexities are at this late date simply unanswerable.[44] (This is no doubt partly why political activists agitating on behalf of slavery reparations and similar causes simply *ignore* these complexities.) Thus, in the American context at least, past injustices in transfer have no tendency significantly to call into question existing property titles. (I make an exception to this claim in cases where injustices committed against citizens *by the government* in the wake of, say, the New Deal, are concerned, since who did what to whom is, in such cases, presumably much easier to establish. Hence, the revised Nozickian position I am advocating is, insofar as it entails a repeal of the welfarist measures of the twentieth century, not *entirely* a defense of the status quo.)

In fact, I believe that in most cases, *rectifiable* injustices in transfer are just going to be those already handled by existing legal concepts and practices (e.g., those covering criminal offenses and breach of contract) that apply to injustices that are easily identifiable because they are relatively recent; and in light of this, there seems little need for any interesting, separate "principle of justice in rectification" at all.[45] And since, as

[43] Does the role of government in slavery imply that there is, after all, a kind of collective guilt on the part of whites despite the points I've made? Not if we keep in mind that talk about "government" is shorthand for a complex of institutions, individuals, and individual actions existing over a very long period of time, and that culpability for the "actions" of "the government" as a whole (to the extent that we can cash out this figurative way of talking in literal terms) clearly does not attach equally (or, in most cases, at all) to every private citizen or official of that government who has ever lived. The problem with appeals to what "the government" has done, like the problem with appeals to what "whites" have done, is that these appeals too often ignore such complexities.

[44] For more detailed discussion of this and other difficulties with reparations schemes, see Edward Feser, "Injustice Compounded," *Liberty* 15, no. 10 (2001): 28–29 and 41.

[45] What about an extreme case, such as that of the Soviet Union, in which the officials of a government commit injustices in transfer on an enormous and systematic scale and for decades, after which the government suddenly collapses? Wouldn't those setting up a replacement government need a principle of justice in rectification? It seems to me that when the complexities involved in this sort of case are taken into account, it will look much like the American Indian and slavery cases discussed above in the text and in note 43, and

what I have argued implies, there is no need either for a "principle of justice in acquisition," Nozick's principle of justice in transfer—on which, as Jonathan Wolff has put it, "a transfer is just if and only if it is voluntary"[46]—turns out to constitute virtually the entirety of Nozick's entitlement theory of justice in holdings. Nothing more, though also nothing less, is needed. (This is not to say that there is no need for a theory of acquisition, i.e., a theory of how things come to be acquired, which I have only sketched; it is just that this will not be a theory of *justice* in acquisition.)

VI. Conclusion

This outcome has the virtue of restoring to Nozick's system the theoretical simplicity and elegance that his (rather unsystematically articulated) commitment to the Lockean proviso threatened to distort. At the same time, replacement of the Lockean proviso with the self-ownership proviso allows us to sidestep the (arguably) counterintuitive consequences of rejecting the former. Still, since there is no such thing as an unjust initial acquisition, very strong property rights to unowned external objects come to be quite easy to obtain; and they, together with the thesis of self-ownership, give us Nozick's principle of justice in transfer, with all its highly anti-egalitarian and anti-redistributionist consequences. The picture that results is very much a libertarianism *with foundations*.

Philosophy, Loyola Marymount University

---

thus will reduce to a collection of individual injustices in transfer; most of these injustices will not be susceptible to rectification in practice, and those that can be rectified will need to be dealt with on a case-by-case basis. So while those setting up a replacement government would certainly need a guiding principle of *some* sort, I'm not sure that it would be a Nozickian principle of justice in *rectification* per se, or even a *fundamental* principle of justice at all (as opposed to a second-order pragmatic principle governing the application of fundamental principles—such as the principle of justice in transfer—in untidy real-world circumstances).

[46] Wolff, *Robert Nozick*, 83.

NOZICK AND LOCKE: FILLING THE SPACE OF RIGHTS

By Jeremy Waldron

I. The "Reverse" Theory

There is a passage in *Anarchy, State, and Utopia* (1974) where Robert Nozick voices the following general misgiving about the claim that people have affirmative rights *to* various things, such as social assistance or welfare:

> The major objection to speaking of everyone's having a right *to* various things such as equality of opportunity, life, and so on, and enforcing this right, is that these "rights" require a substructure of things and materials and actions; and *other* people may have rights and entitlements over these. No one has a right to something whose realization requires certain uses of things and activities that other people have rights and entitlements over. Other people's rights and entitlements to *particular things* (*that* pencil, *their* body, and so on) and how they choose to exercise these rights and entitlements fix the external environment of any given individual and the means that will be available to him. . . .
>
> There are particular rights over particular things held by particular persons, and particular rights to reach agreements with others, *if* you and they together can acquire the means to reach an agreement. . . . No rights exist in conflict with this substructure of particular rights. Since no neatly contoured right to achieve a goal will avoid incompatibility with this substructure, no such rights exist. The particular rights over things fill the space of rights, leaving no room for general rights to be in a certain material condition. The reverse theory would place only such universally held general "rights to" achieve goals or to be in a certain material condition into its substructure so as to determine all else; to my knowledge no serious attempt has been made to state this "reverse" theory. (*ASU*, 238)[1]

It may seem a nice idea to base some human rights on material needs, but Nozick is saying that, in the real world, the resources that would have to be used to satisfy these needs may already be owned by private individuals. And if all the relevant resources are privately owned, there is simply

---

[1] Here, and in what follows, "*ASU*" refers to Robert Nozick, *Anarchy, State, and Utopia* (New York: Basic Books, 1974). Accordingly, "*ASU*, 238" refers to page 238 of that work.

nothing to be done: the property rights that particular individuals have over particular things "fill the space of rights, leaving no room for general rights to be in a certain material condition."

Nozick's argument here assumes that claims based on need occupy a relatively superficial role in a general theory of economic entitlement. It is as though we first figure out who owns what, applying the principles that determine property rights, and *then* figure out whose needs are left unsatisfied and what is to be done about them. On this approach, welfare rights (if there are any) live only in the interstices of property. Some of what Nozick says suggests that this subordination of welfare to property is more or less unavoidable: "Things come into the world already attached to people having entitlements over them" (*ASU*, 160). He thinks this is clearest in the case of body parts: you may need these kidneys or this retina, but my entitlement to them is necessarily prior to yours, for we cannot even grasp my status as a person without comprising in that status a rightful claim to the limbs, cells, and organs that make me who I am (*ASU*, 206). Nozick thinks that the subordination of welfare to property holds for some external objects as well: "Isn't it implausible that how holdings are produced and come to exist has no effect at all on who should hold what?" (*ASU*, 155). The trouble with welfare rights, on this account, is that they "treat objects as if they appeared from nowhere, out of nothing" (*ASU*, 160). "[I]s *this* the appropriate model," he asks, "for thinking about how the things people produce are to be distributed?" (*ASU*, 198).

The virtue of the passage that I quoted at the beginning of this essay (*ASU*, 238) is that it forces us to confront issues of moral priority in the economic sphere. All sides to the debate can benefit from this. Often in philosophical discussions about welfare, we assume that it is already known who owns what and that the question is simply whether people can be forced to contribute out of their own wealth to relieve the needs of the poor. Nozick observes correctly that this way of arguing underestimates the challenge of welfare rights. The idea that a person's right to use or receive resources might be based generally on need, rather than on some proprietorial relation between *this* person and *this* thing, poses a threat to the conventional understanding of property. Property entitlements will never be secure if they are subject to challenge on this basis. So, he thinks, we have to choose: Either particular people have acquired property entitlements in particular things, in which case others cannot have welfare rights that can be enforced against them, or people in general have welfare rights to material and economic security, and others cannot have property rights that can be used to resist the demands of these welfare rights. One or the other of these statements can be true, but not both. We do not have to accept Nozick's resolution of this conflict in order to agree with him about the importance of confronting it honestly and explicitly.

Nozick's position is that "particular rights over things fill the space of rights, leaving no room for general rights to be in a certain material condition." He maintains that the alternative is to stipulate the general rights first, and then try to fit property entitlements around them. "[T]o my knowledge," he says, "no serious attempt has been made to state this 'reverse' theory" (*ASU*, 238). Is this right? Has no one made a serious attempt to use welfare rights to define the environment in which property rights operate? Has no one made a serious attempt to construct the mirror image of Nozick's view—that is, a conception in which welfare rights fill up most of the space of rights in respect of material things, leaving little room (or less room than one would intuitively think) for rights to private property?

In the "reverse" approach, rights based on needs would be *fundamental* in our theory of human access to and use of resources. And instead of making these rights the basis of a duty of charity incumbent upon existing property-holders, we would take them as a basis for calling property arrangements into question, so that the existence of unsatisfied need would become an objection not just to the way property rights are being exercised (e.g., selfishly, thoughtlessly, etc.) but to their very shape and distribution. In proclaiming welfare rights, we would not be begging property-holders to be a little more generous. Rather, we would be asking this question: By what right do they claim to hold something as exclusively their own in the face of others' needs? We would insist that property answer at the tribunal of need, not the other way round.

Philosophers have toyed with versions of such a "reverse" approach as part of the reaction to *Anarchy, State, and Utopia*. In "Property Rights and Interests" (1979), Virginia Held compares acquisitive economic activity to a game, "where winners and losers compete on friendly terms as if engaged in a sporting event." The idea is that winners are allowed to keep their winnings and "losers may prefer having had a chance to play the game and especially having a chance to play again and win, than to ... be assured all along of an even apportionment of all proceeds."[2] But Held did not think that this game-playing could possibly trump the serious business of securing welfare rights:

> Economic justice is a serious matter. While those with moral rights to decent lives are deprived of these rights, playing games is not only frivolous but immoral. However, if such rights *were* respected ... , and if, on utilitarian grounds, playing economic games could be justified in terms of the maximization of interests, well then there might be nothing wrong with capitalist games between consenting adults. But first, the children ought to be fed.[3]

[2] Virginia Held, "Property Rights and Interests," *Social Research* 46 (1979): 577.
[3] Ibid., 579.

Elsewhere she suggests, provocatively, that welfare rights are really the only property rights there are. People are entitled to what is needed for a decent life and adequate self-development. "Beyond this there are no moral rights to property." Held concedes that people do have property interests that go beyond this, but she denies that there is anything wrong (as there would be in the case of rights) with dealing with these in a utilitarian way.[4] This seems to me a fine example of what Nozick would call the "reverse" theory.

More notoriously, John Rawls's argument in *A Theory of Justice* (1971) has more or less exactly the structure that is required for the "reverse" theory. This should not be a surprise. Despite the "no serious attempt" rhetoric, Nozick criticizes Rawls's book on exactly this score, for relegating property entitlements to relatively superficial levels (*ASU*, 206):

> The nature of the decision problem facing persons deciding upon principles in an original position behind a veil of ignorance limits them to end-state principles of distribution. The self-interested person evaluates any non-end-state principle on the basis of how it works out for him; his calculations about any principle focus on how he ends up under the principle. . . . Rawls's procedure assumes that no fundamental entitlement view is correct, that . . . there is some level so deep that no entitlements operate that far down. (*ASU*, 201–2, 206)

Any attempt to generate anything like property entitlements based on original position premises would lead, says Nozick, to approximations at best: "It is difficult to see how such attempts could derive . . . the *particular convolution* of historical entitlement principles" (*ASU*, 202). This is what Rawls says too. Rawls's remarks on property are very sparse, but they indicate that property rights are relegated to an entirely derivative status in what is otherwise a well-developed theory of human claims in respect of material resources. It is true that Rawls's first principle of equal liberty comprises the right to hold personal property.[5] But like many such rights, this right to hold property has nothing to do with the existence-conditions for property entitlements. It is simply a right not to be excluded from the list of those who may hold property if there are any property rights to be held (as women and slaves sometimes have been excluded in the past).[6] Whether there are to be private property rights in significant resources is for Rawls an open question depending on how his principles of justice bear on the circumstances of a particular society. Though "[c]ertain insti-

---

[4] Virginia Held, *Rights and Goods: Justifying Social Action* (New York: Free Press, 1984), 190.
[5] John Rawls, *A Theory of Justice* (Cambridge, MA: Harvard University Press, 1971), 61.
[6] See Jeremy Waldron, *The Right to Private Property* (Oxford: Clarendon Press, 1988), chap. 1.

tutional forms are embedded within the conception of justice,"[7] private property is not one of them. Rawls does work with an example of "a property-owning democracy."[8] But this is just an illustration; it "is not intended to prejudge the choice of regime in particular cases."[9] A just society might be capitalist or socialist:

> Which of these systems and the many intermediate forms most fully answers to the requirements of justice cannot, I think, be determined in advance. There is presumably no general answer to this question, since it depends in large part upon the traditions, institutions, and social forces of each country, and its particular economic circumstances. The theory of justice does not include these matters. . . . The political judgment in any given case will then turn on which variation is most likely to work out best in practice. A conception of justice is a necessary part of any such political assessment, but it is not sufficient.[10]

The parameters of this assessment are the principles of justice, which include rights of exactly the sort that Nozick classified as general rights *to* various things (*ASU*, 238), such as equality of opportunity and the rights defined by the difference principle. Now, the difference principle—the Rawlsian principle that permits social and economic inequalities provided that they are to the benefit of those who are worst off[11]—may not specifically define rights to welfare. But it is a principle governing the manner in which the basic structure generates social and economic inequalities, and it insists that the structure must be arranged in a way that maximizes the expectations of members of the worst-off group. As legal scholar Frank Michelman insists—in a fine essay that examines exactly the extent to which Rawls's work makes welfare rights fundamental—the difference principle mandates "an outcome-oriented appraisal of the pattern and makeup of distributive 'shares' precipitated by economic, political, and other societal processes."[12] I do not mean to deny the procedural aspect of Rawls's conception.[13] But in the illustration that Rawls provides of the operation of such a system, institutions to secure the provision of

---

[7] Rawls, *A Theory of Justice*, 262.

[8] Ibid., 274.

[9] Ibid. Rawls adds: "Nor . . . does it imply that actual societies which have private ownership of the means of production are not afflicted with grave injustices. Because there exists an ideal property-owning system that would be just does not imply that historical forms are just, or even tolerable. . . . [T]he same is true of socialism" (ibid.).

[10] Ibid.

[11] Ibid., 75–83.

[12] Frank I. Michelman, "In Pursuit of Constitutional Welfare Rights: One View of Rawls' Theory of Justice," *University of Pennsylvania Law Review* 121 (1973): 962–63.

[13] Rawls, *A Theory of Justice*, 88 and 274–75.

a social minimum feature prominently.[14] Welfare institutions can operate procedurally too;[15] procedural justice is not associated exclusively with the operations of the market. As Michelman puts it, in Rawls's illustration market procedures (if there are any) must be complemented by procedures designed to secure a social minimum, "which must be provided in order that the residual market determination of distributive shares may be considered just."[16]

So I think that, viewed in this way, Rawls's argument answers exactly to Nozick's specifications for the "reverse" theory. The basic structure of a Rawlsian society is not adjusted to secure the integrity of anything like property entitlements. Instead, it is adjusted to respect the elementary claims that people have in regard to the material wherewithal for basic survival, flourishing (under conditions of equality), and self-respect. Then, given principles of this kind as parameters, we examine what room there is in the circumstances of any actual society for private property rights in goods of various sorts. The basic rights associated with welfare and equality fill up the space of rights first, and then property rights, if there are any, have to contort themselves to fit this Rawlsian substructure.

Did Nozick forget this when he said "no serious attempt has been made to state this 'reverse' theory"? I do not know. He certainly regarded Rawls's conception as "serious":

> A Theory of Justice is a powerful, deep, subtle, wide-ranging systematic work in political and moral philosophy which has not seen its like since the writings of John Stuart Mill, if then. It is a fountain of illuminating ideas, integrated into a lovely whole. Political philosophers now must either work within Rawls' theory or explain why not. (ASU, 183)[17]

Nozick thought indeed it *was* possible to explain why one should not work within Rawls's conception. He said that before we go ahead with a

[14] For Rawls's discussion of the social minimum, see ibid., 276–77 and 285. There is, further, the question of the relation between the provision of a social minimum and the broader work that the difference principle has to do (in the tax system, for example) to secure equality. For Rawls's critique of any social minimum approach that is not pursued within that broader egalitarian context, see ibid., 316–17. Michelman's comments on this connection (Michelman, "In Pursuit of Constitutional Welfare Rights," 974–77) are very helpful. Michelman relies mainly on the welfarist rather than the egalitarian strand of Rawls's account of the difference principle.

[15] Cf. William Simon, "Legality, Bureaucracy, and Class in the Welfare System," Yale Law Journal 92 (1983): 1198–1269.

[16] Michelman, "In Pursuit of Constitutional Welfare Rights," 976.

[17] Cf. the suggestion in the New York Times obituary for Rawls, which informed readers that "[t]he conservative philosopher Robert Nozick . . . considered Dr. Rawls's argument egalitarian nonsense" (Douglas Martin, "John Rawls, Theorist on Justice, Is Dead at 82," New York Times, November 26, 2002, late edition–final, sec. C, p. 19, col. 1).

Rawlsian approach, we must be in possession of reasons for turning our backs on the concept of historical entitlement:

> [W]e do not need any *particular* developed historical entitlement theory as a basis from which to criticize Rawls' construction. If *any* such fundamental historical-entitlement view is correct, then Rawls' theory is not. . . . We would be ill advised to accept Rawls' theory and his construal of the problem as one of which principles would be chosen by rational self-interested individuals behind a veil of ignorance, unless we were sure that no adequate historical-entitlement theory was to be gotten. (*ASU*, 202–3)[18]

On the basis of the passage I cited at the beginning of this essay (*ASU*, 238), this seems right. Presumably, however, the epistemic burden is symmetrical. We would be ill advised to accept a Nozickian theory of historical entitlement (or to begin fleshing out principles that resonate with our proprietorial and libertarian intuitions) unless we were sure that no adequate theory of the Rawlsian kind—no adequate "reverse" theory—was to be gotten.

This last little exchange—"Don't go down the welfarist road until you are sure no entitlement theory is to be gotten," and "Don't go down the entitlement road until you are sure no welfarist theory is to be gotten"—suggests that it might be wise to develop a theory of entitlement and a theory of welfare hand in hand. We would try to ground property entitlements to vindicate our proprietorial intuitions, but we would do so in a way that also respected the impulse to assert welfare rights or rights to a social minimum. There would be no assumption that any one body of rights came into the arena first, to throw its weight around and fill up the space of rights, before the other was allowed to enter, to pick up the leavings. We would develop our property/welfare theory holistically.

Whether Nozick would regard this as a way of constructing the "reverse" theory, I do not know. It certainly has the characteristic of not permitting the construction or recognition of property rights to the extent that they conflict with certain imperatives of human welfare and survival. Whatever we call it, we do not need to look very far for instances of this kind of "reverse"/symmetrical approach. The first example I shall provide is the approach to property taken by John Locke. My second example is

---

[18] People sometimes attack Nozick for not having fleshed out his principle of justice in acquisition. The passage quoted above in the text provides an answer to that attack: "We are thus able to make this structural criticism of the type of theory Rawls presents and the type of principles it must yield, without having first formulated fully a particular historical-entitlement theory as an alternative to his" (*ASU*, 202–3). See also *ASU*, 230. Nozick is doing political *philosophy*, not setting out a political manifesto. I have discussed this further in Waldron, *The Right to Private Property*, 255–56, and in my article "What Plato Would Allow," in Ian Shapiro and Judith Wagner DeCew, eds., *Nomos XXXVII: Theory and Practice* (New York: New York University Press, 1995), 138–78.

Robert Nozick himself, in some of the features that his theory shares with Locke's.

Now citing these as examples might seem cheap or preposterous—preposterous because such imputations plainly contradict the tenor and the received understanding of these philosophers' works, and cheap if imputing this approach to Locke and Nozick were nothing but a provocation based on a throwaway line here and there. I am sensitive to these considerations. I shall try to show that the imputations are based on elements central to the arguments of Locke's *Two Treatises of Government* and Nozick's *Anarchy, State, and Utopia,* respectively. And I shall try to mitigate the outrageousness of these imputations by showing how they illustrate not only what I am calling the "reverse" position, but also the general importance of integrating claims about welfare rights with claims about property in the overall structure of a theory of justice.

II. John Locke on Charity

No one will deny that John Locke was a believer in property,[19] and his theory of the acquisition of property rights has something like the structure of what Nozick calls a historical entitlement approach. I will not go into the details, for they are very well known. It is sufficient to cite the locus classicus of Locke on justice in acquisition:

> Though the earth, and all inferior creatures, be common to all men, yet every man has a property in his own person: this no body has any right to but himself. The labour of his body, and the work of his hands, we may say, are properly his. Whatsoever then he removes out of the state that nature hath provided, and left it in, he hath mixed his labour with, and joined to it something that is his own, and thereby makes it his property. It being by him removed from the common state nature hath placed it in, it hath by this labour something annexed to it, that excludes the common right of other men: for this labour being the unquestionable property of the labourer, no man but he can have a right to what that is once joined to, at least where there is enough, and as good left in common for others.[20]

This argument is applied to land as well as to objects.[21] It is supposed to establish entitlements that are resilient against expropriation by the state,

---

[19] James Tully comes close in Tully, *A Discourse on Property: John Locke and His Adversaries* (Cambridge: Cambridge University Press, 1980).

[20] John Locke, *Two Treatises of Government,* ed. Peter Laslett (Cambridge: Cambridge University Press, 1988), 287–88 (*Second Treatise,* chap. 5, sec. 27).

[21] Ibid., 290–93 (secs. 32–36).

that form the basis for a market economy, and that probably generate considerable inequality under modern conditions.[22]

However, Locke's account of acquisition is not unconditional. He says that appropriation by labor is permissible "at least where there is enough, and as good left in common for others."[23] This is commonly referred to as "the sufficiency proviso," or even just "the Lockean proviso" (and that is what I shall call it).[24] The Lockean proviso is plainly relevant to our discussion. However, since Nozick adopts a version of it, I shall postpone my consideration of it until Section III, below, where I consider Nozick's conception of historical entitlement as an instance of the "reverse"/symmetrical theory.

Too much emphasis on the Lockean proviso belies a much more fundamental condition on his theory of property. This is what I shall call "the principle of charity."[25] The principle of charity requires property-owners in every economy to cede control of some of their surplus possessions, so they can be used to satisfy the pressing needs of the very poor when the latter have no way of surviving otherwise. I think the existence and importance of this condition shows that Locke held a version of the "reverse"/symmetrical theory: when considerations of desperate need are present, property rights must give way, because the fundamental definition of property rights is, in the last analysis, organized around the principle of satisfying need.

The principle of charity is not introduced in the *Second Treatise* chapter on property.[26] It is introduced in the course of Locke's argument against Sir Robert Filmer in the *First Treatise*. There Locke insists that anyone who is in desperate need has "a Title to so much out of another's Plenty, as will keep him from extream want where he has no means to subsist otherwise."[27] It is not an original doctrine: there are versions of it in Aquinas

---

[22] Ibid., 360–62 (secs. 138–40) and 299–302 (secs. 46–50).

[23] Ibid., 288 (sec. 27). Maybe this is not supposed to operate as a necessary condition on acquisition: Locke surely did not mean that no one should appropriate any resources if there is not enough for everyone. See Jeremy Waldron, "Enough and as Good Left for Others," *Philosophical Quarterly* 29, no. 117 (1979): 319–28. The proviso is better understood as a *sufficient* condition: Locke is saying that there is certainly no difficulty with unilateral acquisition (which satisfies the other provisos) in circumstances of plenty, but he is leaving open the possibility that some other basis might have to be found to regulate acquisition in circumstances of scarcity.

[24] The term "sufficiency proviso" was coined, I believe, by C. B. Macpherson in *The Political Theory of Possessive Individualism: Hobbes to Locke* (Oxford: Oxford University Press, 1962), 204 and 211. For "Lockean proviso," see *ASU*, 179.

[25] I am indebted to Virginia Held, "John Locke on Robert Nozick," *Social Research* 43 (1976): 169–82, and 171–75, for first bringing to my attention the significance of Locke's principle of charity in the context of an evaluation of Nozick's Lockean theory. See also Held, *Rights and Goods*, 132.

[26] What follows in the text is an abbreviated version of the discussion of the principle of charity in Jeremy Waldron, *God, Locke, and Equality: Christian Foundations in Locke's Political Thought* (Cambridge: Cambridge University Press, 2002), chap. 6.

[27] Locke, *Two Treatises*, 170 (*First Treatise*, chap. 4, sec. 42).

and in most natural law theories.[28] If it is taken at face value, it changes the complexion of Locke's theory of property quite significantly, mitigating the "disproportionate and unequal Possession of the Earth," which a market economy generates,[29] by providing in effect a right to a "safety net" for the poorest members of society.

The immediate context of Locke's introduction of the principle of charity is his attack on Filmer's claim that God gave the world and everything in it to Adam and his male heirs, and thus secured for them an entitlement to absolute political authority. Now Locke denied that there was in fact any such specific donation of resources by God to some humans at the expense of others.[30] But his strategy in the *First Treatise* is that of a lawyer—resisting each step in his opponent's argument by showing successively that even if the previous step is conceded, the next step does not follow, and so on.[31] So he insists that even if there was a donation, it was a donation of *property* not *sovereignty*. Property could become absolute power only if the proprietor of the world's resources were able to exploit his wealth to coerce political obedience. Locke dismisses this out of hand: "The most specious thing to be said, is, that he that is Proprietor of the whole World, may deny all the rest of Mankind Food, and so at his pleasure starve them, if they will not acknowledge his Soveraignty and Obey his Will."[32]

What are Locke's reasons for insisting that property rights cannot be exploited in this way? He offers a utilitarian argument,[33] but his main argument is based on elementary natural right:

---

[28] See, e.g., Aquinas, *Summa Theologiae,* ed. and trans. David Bourke and Arthur Littledale (New York: Blackfriars, 1969), II-II. q. 66, art. 7, concl.; Hugo Grotius, *The Rights of War and Peace* (New York: M. Walter Dunne, 1901), 92 (bk. 2, chap. 2, sec. 6). Again, see Held, "John Locke on Robert Nozick," 185. For a good general discussion, see Thomas A. Horne, *Property Rights and Poverty: Political Argument in Britain, 1605–1834* (Chapel Hill: University of North Carolina Press, 1990), chap. 1.

[29] Locke, *Two Treatises,* 302 (*Second Treatise,* chap. 5, sec. 50).

[30] Ibid., 161–62 (*First Treatise,* chap. 4, sec. 30).

[31] See ibid., 267 (*Second Treatise,* chap. 2, sec. 1) for a summary of his use of this strategy in the *First Treatise.*

[32] Ibid., 169–70 (*First Treatise,* chap. 4, sec. 41). Locke also argues that even if Adam *could* use his rights in this way, this would not show what Filmer wanted to show: "Should anyone make so perverse an use of God's Blessings poured on him with a liberal Hand; . . . yet all this would not prove that Propriety in Land, even in this Case, gave any Authority over the Persons of Men, but only that Compact might; since the Authority of the Rich Proprietor, and the Subjection of the Needy Beggar began not from the Possession of the Lord, but the Consent of the poor Man, who preferr'd being his Subject to starving" (ibid., sec. 43). Thus Filmer fails to dislodge political authority from its basis in the consent of the governed, and leaves as free as before the man who refuses (even suicidally) to be humbled by his needs in this way.

[33] Ibid. sec. 41. He argues that the inclusion of this power in the right of property would lead in practice to economic stagnation rather than "to promote the great Design of God, *Increase* and *Multiply.*" A man with this sort of dominion is likely to exploit it inefficiently with all men as his slaves, rather than promoting a liberal economy: "He that doubts this, let him look into the Absolute Monarchies of the World, and see what becomes of the Conveniences of Life and the Multitudes of People" (ibid).

God the Lord and Father of all, has given no one of his Children such a Property, in his peculiar Portion of the things of this World, but that he has given his needy Brother a Right to the Surplusage of his Goods; so that it cannot justly be denied him, when his pressing Wants call for it. . . . As *Justice* gives every Man a Title to the product of his honest Industry, and the fair Acquisitions of his Ancestors descended to him; so *Charity* gives every Man a Title to so much out of another's Plenty, as will keep him from extream want, where he has no means to subsist otherwise. . . .[34]

The language of this passage is interesting. In modern liberal theory, charity is not usually seen as a matter of right: to give of one's wealth to the poor is something one ought to do, but not something one owes to any assignable individual. It is often presented as a paradigm of a moral duty that ought not to be enforced.[35] Poor people should be grateful for charity, but they may not demand it or claim it or justify it as rightfully theirs. Some of what Locke says is suggestive of this tradition. He distinguishes the demands of charity from those of justice, drawing at least at a verbal level the distinction that modern liberals have made so much of. But, in order for his argument against Filmer to succeed, Locke needs to be able to show not only that it is wrong to withhold charitable assistance, but that *the rich man has no right to do so*, no right even to offer assistance subject to conditions such as political submission. For the most part, then, the Lockean language is emphatically stronger: though charity is contrasted with justice, still charity "cannot justly be denied." If it cannot justly be denied, then anyone who denies it cannot claim to be exercising his property rights. The sin of uncharitableness simply vitiates the exercise of the rights in question. A man in need has "a Right" to another's surplus goods: indeed, Locke talks of his having "a Title," in a way that suggests that this too is to be regarded as a property entitlement.

What about the fact that charity is regarded by Locke as a specifically Christian virtue? Shouldn't this be a reason for not enforcing it in a liberal theory? Apparently not, according to Locke. He does make a point of saying that many aspects of religion cannot be enforced by the state.[36] The clearest example is Christ's commandment to believe in him as the Mes-

---

[34] Ibid., 170 (*First Treatise*, chap. 4, sec. 42).

[35] I have discussed this view of charity in Jeremy Waldron, "Welfare and the Images of Charity," *Philosophical Quarterly* 36, no. 145 (1986): 463–82; reprinted in Jeremy Waldron, *Liberal Rights: Collected Papers 1981–1991* (Cambridge: Cambridge University Press, 1993), 225–49. I also have discussed this view in Jeremy Waldron, "On the Road: Good Samaritans and Compelling Duties," *Santa Clara Law Review* 40 (2000): 1062–88.

[36] John Locke, *A Letter Concerning Toleration*, ed. James Tully (Indianapolis, IN: Hackett Publishing, 1983), 18. (See also Jeremy Waldron, "Locke, Toleration, and the Rationality of Persecution," in Waldron, *Liberal Rights*, 88–114.)

siah,[37] which, as Locke argues in *A Letter Concerning Toleration* (1689), cannot and should not be enforced. For that case, however, we have specific reasons for nonenforcement: (1) belief is not subject to the will, and coercion works only through the will; and (2) what anyone believes (e.g., about Jesus being the Messiah) does not affect the well-being of anyone else.[38] Neither condition applies to the principle of charity. Indeed, it is noteworthy that when Locke writes in *The Reasonableness of Christianity* (1695) about the difference between what Christ requires us to *believe* (where uncoerced sincerity is of the essence) and what he requires us simply to *do*, it is charity Locke mentions as an illustration of the latter.[39] The matter is complicated by one passage in *The Reasonableness of Christianity* which suggests that charity may be a virtue that state power *could* be used to uphold but should not: Jesus' commandment to the rich young man to "sell all you have and give to the poor."[40] But Locke reads this as Christ's test to see whether the young man in question really would be willing to follow his commandments, not as an imperative addressed to all of us:[41]

> [O]ur Saviour, to try whether in earnest [the young man] believed him to be the Messiah, and resolved to take him to be his king, and to obey him as such; bids him give all that he has to the poor, and come and follow him; and he should have treasure in heaven. This I look on to be the meaning of the place; this, of selling all he had, and giving it to the poor, not being a standing law of his kingdom; but a probationary command to this young man; to try whether he truly believed him to be the Messiah, and was ready to obey his commands, and relinquish all to follow him, when he, his prince, required it.[42]

Selling all you have and giving it to the poor would be a form of what I want to call *radical* charity—giving away what you actually have a moral right to keep, giving away enough to impoverish yourself—and that is not what Locke is arguing for in the *First Treatise*. Radical charity may be a particular requirement imposed on particular people, but it is not intended as a general command. Radical charity is not required by the principle we

---

[37] Locke spends most of *The Reasonableness of Christianity*, 1695 (Bristol: Thoemmes Press, 1997), 17–112, arguing that nothing else is necessary for salvation.

[38] Locke, *A Letter Concerning Toleration*, 46.

[39] Locke, *The Reasonableness of Christianity*, 127. He cites the charitable requirements of the sheep and goats story in Matthew 25:31–46 (feed the hungry, give water to the thirsty, shelter the homeless, etc.) as his prime examples of what we are commanded to do as opposed to what we are expected to believe.

[40] Matthew 19:21.

[41] It seems the young man failed the test: "[W]hen the young man heard that saying, he went away sorrowful: for he had great possessions" (Matthew 19:22).

[42] Locke, *The Reasonableness of Christianity*, 120.

are discussing. The principle of charity from the *First Treatise* affects the rich man only in "the Surplusage of his Goods."[43]

The doctrine of charity is set out in Locke's *First Treatise,* but it is not mentioned explicitly in the *Second Treatise.*[44] We know that the two treatises were written at different times.[45] Is there any reason to believe that the author of the famous chapter on property in the *Second Treatise* (chapter 5) intended the theory he set out there to be qualified by the doctrine I have been discussing?

It is tempting for modern theorists who claim Lockean inspiration in their thinking about property but oppose the principle of charity to insist on a separation between the *Second Treatise* doctrine and the *First Treatise* doctrine in this regard. The *First Treatise* doctrine—which, contrary to what its title may suggest, was produced later by Locke—they might treat as an aberration, unwarranted by the premises of his original theory.[46] In general, I think this approach to textual exegesis is quite unsound, motivated as it is more or less entirely by a desire to find a theory of a certain shape in Locke and by an irritation at having to consider aspects of his thought on these matters that indicate a more complex view. For there is nothing actually in the text of the *Second Treatise* that precludes the principle of charity. The textual evidence for the independence of the two treatises in regard to charity is just Locke's silence on the issue in the *Second Treatise* chapter on property: there are several places where one would expect him to mention such a proviso (if he believed in it), and he does not, at least not in so many words. But this is quite inconclusive. We do not take Locke's silence on inheritance and bequest in the *Second Treatise* chapter on property to indicate a belief that property rights were not inheritable or subject to passage by bequest; instead, we see that the very extensive discussion of inheritance and bequest in the *First Treatise* naturally adds to and complements the discussion in the *Second Treatise.*[47] The fact is that there was no particular need to discuss inheritance and

---

[43] Locke, *Two Treatises,* 170 (*First Treatise,* chap. 4, sec. 42).

[44] There are hints of it, however, in the announcement with which Locke opens chapter 5 of the *Second Treatise:* "Men, being once born, have a right to their Preservation. . . ." Ibid., 285 (sec. 25).

[45] The *Second Treatise* was composed in 1679–80; the *First Treatise* was added a little later. (See Laslett's introduction to Locke, *Two Treatises of Government,* 61–66). But the two were published together by Locke (though anonymously) in 1689. For the view that the date of publication matters more than the date of authorship, see Waldron, *God, Locke, and Equality,* 7n. Had the dates of composition been reversed, with the *First Treatise* written much earlier, then there might have been a case for saying that its doctrine of property, packaged together with the principle of charity, was superseded by the more "modern" theory presented in the *Second Treatise.* But the fact that the *First Treatise* was added later really undermines this suggestion.

[46] This view was urged on me in discussion with several of my fellow contributors to this volume and by one of the editors.

[47] See Locke, *Two Treatises,* 204–10 (*First Treatise,* chap. 9, secs. 86–93); see also Jeremy Waldron, "Locke's Account of Inheritance and Bequest," *Journal of the History of Philosophy* 19, no. 1 (1981): 39–51; and Waldron, *The Right to Private Property,* 241–51.

bequest in chapter five of the *Second Treatise*, but argumentatively it is required for Locke's account of heritable political authority in chapter 9 of the *First Treatise*. And similarly, there was no particular need to discuss the principle of charity in chapter five of the *Second Treatise*, though it could be deployed for political advantage in the attack on absolutism in chapter 4 of the *First Treatise*. In any other context, the fact that different doctrines are mentioned in different chapters would not be adduced as grounds for separating them from one another. It is only the fact that the principle of charity is seen as an annoyance for a certain sort of "Lockean" theory that requires me to spend time defending the claim that two consistent sets of propositions written by the same author and published in different parts of the same book should be regarded as parts of the same theory (unless very good reason is shown why they should not be).

I used to think there *was* a substantial difficulty in accommodating the charity doctrine with the *Second Treatise* theory of property. The basis on which Locke argues for individual acquisition is the idea of mixing one's labor with resources or land: "joyn[ing] to it something that is his own, and thereby [making] it his *Property*."[48] On a literal interpretation of this argument, the laborer transfers to the object the inviolable right he has in his own person. Now, it is hard to see how that right can be overridden by the mere fact of another's need. Either the object contains the owner's labor or it does not: the other person's need cannot, as it were, drive the labor out. I used to think that what was going on here was that Locke was running two incompatible lines of argument to justify private property in the *Second Treatise*: one was entitlement-based, deriving from the exclusive right one has in one's person and one's labor,[49] and the other was based broadly on the notion of human need and what must happen in order for mankind to prosper.[50] The provisos and limitations seemed to make sense primarily in relation to the second of these lines of argument, and the same would be true of the principle of charity.

But I no longer think it makes sense to see the mixing of labor as a separate line of argument, less hospitable to modification by charity or the other provisos. I think the labor theory works only against a background of labor's significance in God's overall plan for the survival of the human beings he has created. Laboring is not just something we happen to do to resources, nor is being permitted to help oneself by labor just a divine indulgence of the self-interested inclinations of an acquisitive being. It is the naturally requisite next step following our creation, once we

[48] Locke, *Two Treatises*, 288 (*Second Treatise*, chap. 5, sec. 27).
[49] Ibid.
[50] Ibid., 285 (sec. 25): "Whether we consider natural Reason, which tells us, that Men, being once born, have a right to their Preservation, and consequently to Meat and Drink, and such other things, as Nature affords for their Subsistence: or Revelation, which gives us an account of those Grants God made of the World to Adam, and to Noah, and his Sons, 'tis very clear, that God, as King David says, Psal. CXV. xvi. has given the Earth to the Children of Men; given it to Mankind in common."

accept that we were created subservient to God's design "that Man should live and abide for sometime upon the Face of the Earth, and not that so curious and wonderful a piece of Workmanship by its own Negligence, or want of Necessaries, should perish again, presently after a few moments continuance."[51] If labor were not presented against this background, if it were just something I happen to own, there would be no answer to an embarrassing question that Nozick poses: "[W]hy isn't mixing what I own with what I don't own a way of losing what I own rather than a way of gaining what I don't?" (*ASU*, 174-75). Any account of the significance of labor rich enough to answer this question will have to hook up with the account based on need, and therefore will naturally be subject to the principle of charity.

Bearing this in mind, I think we can say that the substantive case for importing the *First Treatise* doctrine of charity into the *Second Treatise* theory of property revolves around the premises of Lockean natural law. The basic principle of the law of nature, said Locke, is the preservation of as many people as possible: "Everyone as he is *bound to preserve himself,* . . . so by the like reason when his own Preservation comes not in com-petition, ought he, as much as he can, *to preserve the rest of Mankind.*"[52] This sounds like a positive duty to do whatever will promote the pres-ervation of as many people as possible. Locke makes it clear that it goes far beyond mere nonaggression. It includes the power to pardon offend-ers; it even includes a duty to infringe property rights in an emergency, like "pull[ing] down an innocent Man's House to stop the Fire, when the next to it is burning. . . ."[53] Anyway, it has never been clear to me that the duty of charity—at least as Locke presents it—*is* a positive as opposed to a negative duty. Paragraph 42 of the *First Treatise* denies that property owners have the right to *withhold* their surplus goods from the poor. Thus, Locke seems to be committed not to a view about *giving* but to the view that neither the rich person nor civil society on his behalf is entitled to *resist* the poor when the poor attempt to seize his surplus goods. It is not a question of forcing the rich to *do* anything: it is enough that they be compelled simply to stand back and let the poor take what (on account of their "pressing Needs") is rightfully theirs.[54]

More specifically, at the beginning of the chapter on property, Locke tells us in very general terms that "[m]en, being once born, have a right to their Preservation, and consequently to Meat and Drink, and such other things, as Nature affords for their subsistence. . . ."[55] Now, this might be construed as mere rhetoric, except that Locke quickly puts it in

---

[51] Ibid., 204-5 (*First Treatise*, chap. 9, sec. 86).
[52] Ibid., 271 (*Second Treatise*, chap. 2, sec. 6).
[53] Ibid., 374-75 (*Second Treatise*, chap. 14, sec. 159).
[54] This is the point of my argument about "charity" in Waldron, "Welfare and the Images of Charity."
[55] Locke, *Two Treatises*, 285 (*Second Treatise*, chap. 5, sec. 25).

play to do some rather important work. For when he defends the legitimacy of unilateral appropriation, he raises the specter of starvation as a basis for his rebuttal of any consent requirement:

> [W]ill any one say [that a man] had no right to those Acorns or Apples he thus appropriated, because he had not the consent of all Mankind to make them his? . . . If such a consent as that was necessary, Man had starved, notwithstanding the Plenty God had given him.[56]

The prospect of starvation simply short-circuits any complaint based on the illegitimacy of appropriation without consent. Since the rights that are rebutted in this way are real rights—each person's right to partake in God's original donation—Locke is saying, in effect, that the right to withhold consent can be trumped by desperate need. He cannot consistently maintain that without also maintaining what I have called the principle of charity.

One last hurdle remains. Those who want to portray an uncharitable Locke are fond of telling us about the John Locke who was the author of an essay on the poor law—a draft of a representation concerning methods of employing the poor. That draft certainly seems devoid of the sort of compassion that one would associate with a generous spirit of charity. Locke talks about "begging drones" and "superfluous brandy shops," and he suggests that the idle poor should be whipped and mutilated if they go begging instead of doing the work assigned to them. Even little children should be given two or three hours of labor useful to the parish per day.[57]

I want to say two things about this. First, we should bear in mind that the paper on the poor law *does* assume that the poor have a right to subsistence. "[E]veryone must have meat, drink, clothing, and firing."[58] Secondly, Locke took very seriously the injunction to labor, and a poor man with an offer of gainful employment was not a person who had no means to subsist (within the meaning of the principle of charity). We have already seen that Locke is in favor of charity being enforced, but not *radical* charity.[59] Well, now we have a *second* form of radical charity that Locke is not prepared to enforce: this would be charity to someone who refuses to work when he *could* work, charity to someone who does not

---

[56] Ibid., 288 (sec. 28).

[57] John Locke, "An Essay on the Poor Law," in Mark Goldie, ed., *Locke: Political Essays* (Cambridge: Cambridge University Press, 1997), 184, 186–87, and 190–92.

[58] Ibid., 189. Locke also says that "if any person die for want of due relief in any parish in which he ought to be relieved, the said parish [must] be fined according to the circumstances of the fact and the heinousness of the crime" (ibid., 198).

[59] See above, text accompanying notes 40–43.

make any efforts to provide for himself or work to subsidize the cost of his provision.

I hope this textual and historical account of Locke's principle of charity has not been tedious. What I want to establish is that Locke believed very strongly that human survival and flourishing (and indeed the increase of a surviving and flourishing population) were the basic moral imperatives of economic life. In Section I of this essay, I discussed which moral considerations come on stage first and establish themselves as the substructure, which other rights and principles must then work around. Well, in Locke's theory, the substructure comprises the principle of preservation and increase. No rights exist in conflict with this substructure, and the whole argument in favor of property entitlement and acquisition is predicated on these first principles:

> God having made Man, and planted in him, as in all other Animals, a strong desire of Self-preservation, and furnished the World with things fit for Food and Rayment and other Necessaries of his Life, Subservient to his design, that Man should live and abide for some time upon the Face of the Earth, and not that so curious and wonderful a piece of Workmanship by its own Negligence, or want of Necessaries, should perish again, presently after a few moments continuance: God, I say, having made Man and the World thus, spoke to him, (that is) directed him by his Senses and Reason . . . to the use of those things, which were serviceable for his Subsistence, and given him as a means of his *Preservation*. And thus Man's *Property* in the Creatures, was founded upon the right he had, to make use of those things, that were necessary or useful to his Being.[60]

If this is the foundation of property, then property cannot be used to oppose other consequences that flow from these first principles. Elementary rights to material assistance in conditions of urgent need flow directly, and they must condition the property rights, not the other way round.

III. Nozick on Welfare

Now I want to return to the Lockean proviso and the work that it does in Robert Nozick's theory. Nozick is committed to the following proposition:

> A process normally giving rise to a permanent bequeathable property right in a previously unowned thing will not do so if the position

---

[60] Locke, *Two Treatises*, 204–5 (*First Treatise*, chap. 9, sec. 86).

of others no longer at liberty to use the thing is thereby worsened. (*ASU*, 178)[61]

What is this, if it is not a statement of what Nozick called the "reverse" theory (*ASU*, 238)? It gives priority to the right not to have one's material situation worsened, whether that situation consists in holding property rights or just in having access of some kind to the resources needed for a decent life. It gives these rights priority in exactly the sense that the "reverse" theory is supposed to give priority to welfare rights: property entitlements must work around them; no property entitlements are recognized if they are incompatible with these rights.

One can quibble with this—does the Lockean proviso really generate *rights?*—and I will explore the quibbles in a moment. For now, just observe how strongly this condition operates in Nozick's theory. It applies to acquisition: if I want to be the first to take a given resource into possession as a private holding, I may do so (by engaging in whatever the principle of justice in acquisition says: labor, occupancy, whatever), but only so long as the situation of others is not thereby worsened. The condition also applies to the exercise of one's property rights in whatever one has appropriated: "a person may not appropriate the only water hole in the desert and charge what he will" (*ASU*, 180), for previously the situation was that other people could come to the water hole and drink for free. And the condition renders one's property rights and their exercise vulnerable to revision in the light of changing circumstances: "[n]or may he charge what he will if he possesses one [water hole], and unfortunately it happens that all the water holes in the desert dry up, except for his" (*ASU*, 180).[62] It also affects justice in transfer:

A theory which includes this proviso in its principle of justice in acquisition must also contain a more complex principle of justice in transfer. Some reflection of the proviso about appropriation constrains later actions. If my appropriating all of a certain substance violates the Lockean proviso, then so does my appropriating some and purchasing all the rest from others who obtained it without otherwise violating the Lockean proviso. (*ASU*, 179)

Thus, the proviso affects property entitlements generally, even those at a great distance from the original acquisitions that got historical entitle-

---

[61] I follow Nozick in calling this "the Lockean proviso" (*ASU*, 179), though it differs somewhat from Locke's "enough, and as good left in common for others" proviso (Locke, *Two Treatises*, 288 (*Second Treatise*, chap. 5, sec. 27).

[62] Elsewhere I have argued that this affects not only acquisition, but also whatever we think we ought to do in the way of the rectification of injustice. See Jeremy Waldron, "Superseding Historic Injustice," *Ethics* 103, no. 1 (1992): 4–28; and Jeremy Waldron, "Redressing Historic Injustice," *University of Toronto Law Journal* 52 (2002): 135–60.

ment underway: "Each owner's title to his holding includes the historical shadow of the Lockean proviso on appropriation" (*ASU*, 180).

Despite this "shadow," Nozick believes that the Lockean proviso can be satisfied fairly easily. He argues against any interpretation of it that would limit acquisition to cases where there is no impact on other people's *acquisitive* opportunities (so that there is enough, and as good, left in common for others *to appropriate*).[63] If people are no worse off overall as a result of others' acquisitions, they have no ground for legitimate complaint (*ASU*, 176). This means we can appeal to "the various familiar social considerations favoring private property" on grounds of efficiency (*ASU*, 177)[64]—considerations that leave him confident "that the free operation of a market system will not actually run afoul of the Lockean proviso" (*ASU*, 182). I shall not quibble with this, though it is worth noting the honesty of Nozick's observation that the claim is an empirical matter and he may be wrong (*ASU*, 182). As we shall see, Nozick's objections to actually existing market economies have more to do with the brutal injustice associated with their establishment and with the particular property rights held by the rich than with any violation of the Lockean proviso (*ASU*, 230–31).

Does the ease with which the Lockean proviso can be satisfied in a market society based on property entitlements mean that we cannot use Nozick's embrace of the proviso as a ground for attributing to him what we have called the "reverse" theory? Not at all. A principle may be fundamental and it may define the substructure of rights, in Nozick's sense (*ASU*, 238), without being very demanding. All that is necessary to sustain the proposition that Nozick's theory is a "reverse" theory is to show that it is *not* the case that property rights fill up the space of rights leaving no room for rights such as a right not to have one's material condition worsened. The Lockean proviso shows this. Does it make any difference that the Lockean proviso is part and parcel of Nozick's conception of historical entitlement so that property rights (subject, admittedly, to that proviso) fill up the space of rights leaving no room for any

---

[63] See *ASU*, 176 and 178. Cf. Locke, *Two Treatises*, 288 (*Second Treatise*, chap. 5, sec 27).

[64] John Locke does something similar in his famous passage comparing the agricultural economy of England with subsistence economies of the Native Americans:

> There cannot be a clearer demonstration of any thing, than several Nations of the *Americans* are of this, who are rich in Land, and poor in all the Comforts of Life; whom Nature having furnished as liberally as any other people, with the materials of Plenty, *i.e.* a fruitful Soil, apt to produce in abundance, what might serve for food, rayment, and delight; yet for want of improving it by labour, have not one hundredth part of the Conveniencies we enjoy: and a King of a large and fruitful Territory there, feeds, lodges, and is clad worse than a day Labourer in *England*.

See Locke, *Two Treatises*, 296–97 (*Second Treatise*, chap. 5, sec. 41). This argument is based on maximin, though on a particularly strong version of it: Locke claims that the poorest participant in the English economy is better off than the *best*-off participant in the Native American economy.

other right to be in a given material condition? No, that is just being silly. At most it shows that Nozick is adopting what I referred to at the end of Section I as the "symmetrical" approach—developing his theory of historical entitlement hand in hand with a theory of people's rights to be in a certain material condition.

But does Nozick's version of the Lockean proviso actually enshrine *rights* to be in a certain material condition? There is certainly a difference between the proviso and Locke's principle of charity. The latter establishes that each person has a right to survive, and hence "a Title to so much out of another's Plenty, as will keep him from extream want, where he has no means to subsist otherwise...."[65] Nozick's version of the proviso respects only a claim not to be shifted from a certain baseline of well-being. It is a baseline defined (rather problematically—*ASU*, 177) as the condition one would be in but for the appropriation(s) or holding(s) whose legitimacy is now called into question. Moreover, it is not a claim to be and to remain at that level of well-being (however it is defined): it is only a claim not to be moved down from it by an appropriation (or the equivalent of an appropriation). If one's well-being declines for other reasons, the Lockean proviso does not generate a claim to have it restored. These are important points. But they do not affect the underlying argument about the shape of Nozick's approach. His theory begins with the assumption that the formation and justification of property entitlements must be responsive to concerns about well-being that are not embodied in property rights. In this sense, it is not true that on Nozick's account only property rights define the "substructure" of rights.

The Lockean proviso is not an incidental accretion to Nozick's conception that he could easily abandon. Without such a proviso, any principle of justice in acquisition (and anything founded on it, such as a system of ongoing property rights in a market economy) becomes morally very problematic, since it involves the unilateral imposition of duties (albeit negative duties) on people without their consent.[66] Few are willing to say that the imposition of such duties can be justified utterly without reference to the interests or needs of those whom they exclude from access to resources.[67]

That is very general. More specifically in Nozick's case, we see the importance of the Lockean proviso in assimilating the justification of initial acquisition to the kind of justification used for principles of justice

---

[65] Ibid., 170 (*First Treatise*, chap. 4, sec. 42).

[66] The point is made most forcefully by Immanuel Kant: "When I declare (by word or deed), I will that something external is to be mine, I thereby declare that everyone else is under obligation to refrain from using that object of my choice, an obligation no one would have were it not for this act of mine to establish a right." Immanuel Kant, *The Metaphysics of Morals*, ed. and trans. Mary Gregor (Cambridge: Cambridge University Press, 1991), pt. 1, sec. 8, 77 (VI, 255 in the Prussian Academy Edition). See also Jeremy Waldron, "Kant's Legal Positivism," *Harvard Law Review* 109 (1996): 1535–66.

[67] See also the discussion in Waldron, *The Right to Private Property*, 266–71.

in transfer. In the latter case, we justify transfers on grounds related to their representing Pareto improvements: because the transactions are voluntary, no one thinks that he loses in a market transfer. Therefore, so long as the parties are rational, a market transfer (barring externalities) makes at least some better off without making anyone worse off. In initial acquisition, by contrast, it looks as though there will be losers: I acquire this field as my property; and since you are excluded, you no longer have the access that you had before. The Lockean proviso ameliorates this problem. Now we say that an acquisition is legitimate only if it leaves no one worse off, that is, only if it is a Pareto improvement. Acquisition is thus assimilated to transfer so far as the principle of its justification is concerned.

By the way, it is interesting to note how Nozick's use of the idea of Pareto improvement differs from that of scholars involved in the Economic Analysis of Law (EAL).[68] When a change is justified as an improvement according to EAL, it is because it is thought that although some people benefit and some suffer from the change, the gains of those who benefit are sufficient to compensate the losses of those who suffer. This is the famous Kaldor-Hicks criterion of social improvement: a change that improves the situation of some by worsening the situation of others, is permitted if the winners win more than enough to compensate the losers.[69] For EAL, this gives the change in question the respectability of a Pareto improvement. But although a Kaldor-Hicks improvement is *like* a Pareto improvement in certain respects (e.g., in the amount of wealth-gain required), it is not *relevantly* like a Pareto improvement in the respects that ought to matter when we think about justice. True, in a Kaldor-Hicks improvement, we ensure that the winner gains enough to compensate the loser, so that no one *need* be worse off. But this assessment is not associated, in any way, with a practical determination actually to assign the loser any portion of what the winner gains. The preferences of the losing party are certainly taken into account in considering whether the change is an improvement: it must be the case that the loser would prefer a portion of the winner's gain to what he could secure in the absence of the change. But justice is not interested in facts about preferences *per se*. Justice is interested in facts about the satisfaction of preferences, and with a Kaldor-Hicks change there need be no actual satisfaction of this preference of the loser. Similarly, the legal imposition of a Kaldor-Hicks improvement has none of the consensual respectability of a Pareto improvement. When we impose a Kaldor-Hicks improvement, we are not in any way honoring the voluntary consent of the losing party. That the loser

---

[68] Exemplars of EAL include R. H. Coase, "The Problem of Social Cost," *Journal of Law and Economics* 3 (1960): 1–44; Guido Calabresi, "Some Thoughts on Risk Distribution and the Law of Torts," *Yale Law Journal* 70 (1961): 499–553; and Richard A. Posner, *The Economics of Justice* (Cambridge, MA: Harvard University Press, 1981).

[69] Cf. J. R. Hicks, "The Rehabilitation of Consumers' Surplus," *Review of Economic Studies* 8, no. 2 (1941): 108–116.

would consent (under condition C) adds nothing to the respectability of a change that involves no actual consent (because condition C is *not* satisfied).[70] To oppose a Kaldor-Hicks improvement in the name of justice is therefore not to oppose justice to human welfare, nor is it to oppose justice to people's revealed preferences, nor is it to oppose justice to a scheme that makes everyone better off. It is, rather, to insist on the importance of respecting actual individuals with their actual preferences in the actual world; and it is to oppose the imposition on individuals of actual losses for which nothing but hypothetical compensation is envisaged. Now Nozick will have none of this. He famously rejected the utilitarian idea that some people's gains can make up for other people's losses: what happens is that some people gain and others lose; nothing more (*ASU*, 33). And he is insistent on this point specifically in connection with the Lockean proviso:

> Someone whose appropriation otherwise would violate the proviso still may appropriate provided he compensates the others so that their situation is not thereby worsened; *unless he does compensate these others,* his appropriation will violate the proviso of the principle of justice in acquisition and will be an illegitimate one. (*ASU*, 178; emphasis added)

This is a striking difference between Nozick and the EAL: Nozick's account has integrity, theirs does not.

This is but one example of the integrity of Nozick's argumentation in *Anarchy, State, and Utopia*. When the book appeared, left-liberals were so shocked that many of them complained the book was written simply to promote a political agenda. Brian Barry's review was typical and a now-famous passage of it ran as follows:

> [T]he intellectual texture is of a sort of cuteness that would be wearing in a graduate student and seems to me quite indecent in someone who, from the lofty heights of a professorial chair, is proposing to starve or humiliate ten percent of his fellow citizens (if he recognizes the word) by eliminating all transfer payments through the state, leaving the sick, the old, the disabled, the mothers with young children and no breadwinner, and so on, to the tender mercies of private charity, given at the whim and pleasure of the donors and on any terms they choose to impose.[71]

---

[70] In some cases, we legitimate action on the basis of hypothetical consent, but not when the difference between the hypothetical and the real world is the presence of one of the conditions on which the hypothetical consent is predicated!

[71] Brian Barry, review of *Anarchy, State, and Utopia, Political Theory* 3, no. 3 (1975): 331–32.

I think this sort of abuse is quite unwarranted. If Nozick were standing for office and these were his policies, I guess there would be reason to vote for some other candidate. In fact, he was not in a position to starve or humiliate anyone or to eliminate any transfer payments through the state, nor was he was aspiring to any office where his "proposals" to this effect would be a matter of political concern. He was, as Barry reminds us, occupying a professorial chair in a philosophy department. He was not in fact *proposing* anything, or *calling for* anything, or indeed *urging* anything, except this: that we might try thinking about justice in a slightly different way. As Nozick pointed out in his preface to *Anarchy, State, and Utopia*:

> My emphasis upon the conclusions which diverge from what most readers believe may mislead one into thinking this book is some sort of political tract. It is not; it is a philosophical exploration of issues, many fascinating in their own right, which arise and interconnect when we consider individual rights and the state. (*ASU*, xii)

Nozick's integrity probably explains why his work has had more influence on the Left than on the Right. For those of us on the Left, it was Nozick (rather than, say, F. A. Hayek) who undermined our confidence in simple formulae of equality and who convinced us that "no end-state principle or distributional patterned principle of justice can be continuously realized without continuous interference with people's lives" (*ASU*, 163). Nozick laid down the challenge that we thought we needed to answer. (I am not saying we succeeded in answering it, but it was Nozick's challenge that sharpened our wits.) However, Nozick argued too honorably to be of much use to the triumphant Right in the 1980s and 1990s. He was never prepared to say that the historical-entitlement critique of equality and welfarism in his book amounted to a defense of actually existing market institutions, nor would he pretend that a Lockean defense of property could go any distance toward legitimizing contemporary disparities of wealth in (for example) the United States. On the contrary, he thought it undeniable that contemporary holdings would be condemned as unjust by any remotely plausible conception of historical entitlement. (The point of Nozick's argument in chapters 7 and 8 of *Anarchy, State, and Utopia* was that egalitarians were condemning the existing distribution for the wrong reason—that is, simply as unequal—rather than on account of the violence, fraud, expropriation, ethnic cleansing, state corruption, and so on, involved in the history of most holdings of property in America.) Once actual historical injustice was established, then the burden fell on the part of his conception dealing with the rectification of injustice. And for Nozick, it was an open question whether the actual operation of (say) Rawls's difference principle might approximate the operation of a plausible process for rectifying historical injustice. That, Nozick thought (quite rightly), would involve addressing some very difficult questions about time, counterfactuals, second-best principles, and so on:

> These issues are very complex and are best left to a full treatment of the principle of rectification. In the absence of such a treatment applied to a particular society, one *cannot* use the analysis and theory presented here to condemn any particular scheme of transfer payments, unless it is clear that no considerations of rectification of injustice could apply to justify it. (*ASU*, 231; Nozick's emphasis)

This was not what defenders of free markets and opponents of welfare wanted to hear in the 1980s and 1990s.

IV. Welfare and Justice

It is often said of welfare rights that they are impracticable or too expensive or too demanding. Some critics even argue that socioeconomic rights violate the logical principle "*Ought* implies *can*." Many nations, they say, do not have the resources to provide even minimal economic security for masses of their citizens, and since states differ considerably in this regard, it hardly makes sense to regard economic provision as a matter of universal human entitlement.[72]

In some cases, sheer scarcity will trigger the principle "*Ought* implies *can*." But the fact that this happens in some cases does not undermine the universalist thesis. The "ought" remains in the background, in all cases, commanding each country to do as much as it can in this regard, and its full force will be triggered for a given country whenever it acquires the ability to fulfill it. Moreover, in many cases, the alleged impossibility stems not from brute scarcity as such but from an assumption that the existing distribution of property is to remain largely undisturbed. When a conservative government in the West says in response to some plea for welfare provision, "The money simply isn't there," what is usually meant is that it would be either impolitic or improper to try and raise it from existing property-holders and income earners by taxation. On the one hand, if the objection is simply that raising the money would be impolitic, then really the "*ought*" of welfare rights is being frustrated, not by the "*can't*" of impracticability, but by the "*shan't*" of selfishness and political ambition. If, on the other hand, the objection is that the money is not the government's to distribute, then we are back where we began, with our question about the relative priority to be accorded to property rights as opposed to welfare rights. Either way, resting the matter simply on "*Ought*

---

[72] See, e.g., Maurice Cranston, "Human Rights, Real and Supposed," in D. D. Raphael, ed., *Political Theory and the Rights of Man* (London: Macmillan, 1967), 50–51.

implies *can*" underestimates the challenge posed by these rights to the underlying distribution of wealth and income.

Still, someone may press the question: Aren't these socioeconomic rights awfully demanding? They may say: The first generation of rights claims—civil and political rights—require only that we and our governments refrain from various acts of tyranny and oppression. They are "negative" rights correlative to duties of omission, whereas so-called second-generation rights—socioeconomic rights—are correlative to positive duties of assistance. An advantage of negative rights is that they never conflict with one another, for one can perform an infinite number of omissions at any given moment. With positive rights, by contrast, we inevitably have to consider the inherent scarcity of the resources and the services that are called for.

There are many things wrong with this argument. For one thing, the correlation of first- and second-generation rights with the distinction between negative and positive rights simply will not stand up. Many first-generation rights require the positive establishment and maintenance of certain frameworks, and all of them make costly claims upon scarce police and forensic resources. Even those first-generation rights that can be conceived in the first instance in terms of negative freedom— such as free speech and freedom of worship—still require more from a government than that it simply stay its hand. We set up a government to *protect* our rights, not simply to respect them. All serious political theorists recognize that protection is costly,[73] and that therefore first-generation rights as much as socioeconomic entitlements raise hard questions about priorities for us all.

It follows that where resources are scarce relative to human wants, *any* system of rights or entitlements will seem demanding to those who are constrained by it. If an economic system includes provision for welfare assistance, it may seem overly demanding to taxpayers. But if it does not include such provision, then the system of *property rights* in such an economy will seem overly demanding to the poor, requiring as it does that they refrain from making use of various resources that they may need. As usual, the question is not whether we are to have a system of demanding rights, but how the costs of the demands are to be distributed. That, of course, is why the question that Nozick raised in the passage cited at the outset of this essay is so important.[74]

Thinking about scarcity and practicability does have one important advantage: it forces proponents of second-generation rights to take seriously issues of distributive justice. It is an unhappy feature of the language of rights that it expresses demanding moral claims in a sort of

---

[73] See Henry Shue, *Basic Rights: Subsistence, Affluence, and U.S. Foreign Policy* (Princeton, NJ: Princeton University Press, 1980), 35–64.

[74] *ASU*, 238 (see above, text accompanying note 1).

"line-item" way, presenting each individual's case peremptorily, as though it brooked no denial, no balancing, no compromise. This feature of rights has always troubled those who are sensitive to the fact that individuals live in a social environment where the things that they may reasonably expect must be adjusted constantly to reflect similar claims and expectations on the part of others. If we want a framework that more adequately reflects the necessarily compromised character of rights claims (civil rights, property rights, welfare rights), we must turn instead to the modern discussion of justice. The theory of justice—not Rawls's theory necessarily, but theorizing about justice—is the proper matrix for reconciling conflicting claims of right. Modern theorists have not written nearly enough about the relation between liberal theories of rights and liberal theories of justice. Let me end with a gesture toward such an account.

Familiar claims of right will figure both as inputs and as outputs in our theorizing about justice. They function as *inputs* inasmuch as they help constitute our initial sense of the individual claims that need to be considered. That people are normally taken to have the right of freedom of worship, the right to participate in politics, and the right to work, helps us *frame* the problems of justice that a society of such persons gives rise to. We expect that many familiar claims of right will also figure among the *outputs* of an adequate theory of justice. We hope the institutional structure that is set up in this way is one that will be able to offer certain guarantees, though they may not be as strong or as unqualified as those we had in mind before we remembered the need to balance our own claims against those made by others. For example, we may go in with a sense that respecting a human being means respecting his freedom of worship, but come out (of the balancing process) with a religious guarantee that is perhaps somewhat modified by a recognition that children, for example, must be given an adequate education and not left at the mercy of their parents' convictions, and that certain aspects of religious practice must on occasion give way to independently grounded considerations of public administration.

The same is true in regard to socioeconomic claims. We go into the discussion of justice with the sense that people are not just the disembodied wraiths of liberal ideology, but needy individuals subject to vicissitudes of embodiment and materiality: we must have food and shelter, we must work, we get sick, we grow old, we are often dependent, and so on. A preliminary sense of the importance of all this—I mean its importance to each of us as individuals, not just its importance to society—is conveyed by provisions such as the second-generation rights we have been discussing.

However, things are less clear at the output end. Consider Rawls's theory, again, as an example. Rawls is anxious that the task of a theory of justice not be understood simply as an allocation of distributive shares: who gets what, when, and how? "We must not assume," he says, "that there is much similarity from the standpoint of justice between an administrative allotment of goods to specific persons and the appropriate design of society." [75] Thus, for example, the "difference principle" is not to be interpreted as dictating that the worst-off group be *given* a certain share of resources. The effect of the principle is that when we are designing or (more likely) evaluating and reforming the network of rules and procedures that constitute the institutional structure of society, we should do so in a way that is oriented toward the advantage of the worst-off group. The institutions should be designed to operate on the assumption that when the system is working, outcomes are evaluated purely procedurally. We are not to meddle with the outcomes of a just institutional structure even if we think that by doing so we could make the array of outcomes even *more* just from a distributive point of view.

Now, here is a curiosity. F. A. Hayek has taken the comments that I have just cited as grounds for claiming that the difference between Rawls's approach and his own approach is "more verbal than substantial." [76] Rawls's work, he says, has been "wrongly ... interpreted as lending support to socialist demands." [77] Hayek takes Rawls to agree with his own central claim that "[j]ustice is not concerned with those unintended consequences of a spontaneous order [such as a market] which have not been deliberately brought about by anybody." [78]

I think that Hayek is mistaken about this and that he exaggerates the implications of Rawls's refusal to consider the justice of particular allocations of goods. Rawls's position may be illuminated as follows. Suppose that, on one occasion, the institutions of our economy happen to yield a distribution of wealth, D_1, that is judged inferior in terms of the difference principle to another distribution, D_2. Should we immediately interfere and reallocate wealth so that we change D_1 into D_2? Rawls's answer, like Hayek's, is no. For Hayek the matter ends there. But for Rawls there is a further question to be addressed: Can we change the institutional structure (including the structure of property entitlements, if there are any) so as to render it more likely in the future that the normal operation of our economy will yield distributions like D_2 rather than D_1? The answer to this question may also be no, because the proposed change might be incompatible with institutional virtues such as publicity, stability, and the rule of law.[79] The new institutions that are being suggested may not, as it were, hold up, as institutions. Still—and this is what Hayek overlooks—the answer is not *necessarily* no. If change is possible and if the

---

[75] Rawls, *A Theory of Justice*, 64. See also ibid., 88: "If it is asked in the abstract whether one distribution of a given stock of things to definite individuals with known desires and preferences is better than another, then there is simply no answer to this question."

[76] Friedrich A. Hayek, *Law, Legislation, and Liberty*, vol. 2: *The Mirage of Social Justice* (London: Macmillan, 1976), xiii.

[77] Ibid., 100, and the footnote to that passage on 183.

[78] Ibid., 38, and the footnote to that passage on 166.

[79] See Rawls, *A Theory of Justice*, 54–60 and 235–43.

resulting institutional structure would be viable, stable, and so on, then we are *required* as a matter of justice to implement it, for the difference principle just *is* the requirement that we arrange (and, if necessary, rearrange) our institutions so that social and economic inequalities are to the greatest benefit of the least advantaged. So, for example, if we find ourselves in a market society that lacks basic welfare provision, we have to consider whether the institutional structure of a market economy would be wrecked qua institutional structure by the addition of what Rawls calls a "transfer branch," charged with administering a social minimum. Would that make it impossible for the economic structure as a whole to operate predictably, publicly, impersonally, and in accordance with other institutional virtues? Hayek has devoted a large part of his life to arguing that it would—that the modern regulated welfare state is incompatible with the rule of law.[80] It is pretty clear that Rawls disagrees with him about that. But the deeper disagreement is that Rawls thinks it is the job of a theory of justice to select principles for evaluating economic institutions along exactly these lines, whereas Hayek simply denies that this is a legitimate concern about justice.

I have taken this digression into the Hayek-Rawls misunderstanding because I want to stress that in a theory of justice such as Rawls's we cannot guarantee that socioeconomic rights will emerge in a familiar or predictable form. As an abstract matter we can say, with the drafters of Article 25 of the Universal Declaration of Human Rights, that everyone has "the right to a standard of living adequate for the health and well-being of himself and his family." But this may not necessarily emerge as a specific legal or constitutional guarantee: a just society may not have a *rule* to this effect, nor even any particular agency charged with administering this standard. There may be a variety of provisions and arrangements—tax breaks, educational opportunities, rent control (or its abolition), unemployment insurance schemes, etc.—all of which taken together may represent the best that can be done in an institutional framework to honor the underlying claim for the individuals in whose behalf it can be made.

This fact may upset welfarists who think it more important that a right be *proclaimed* than that it be secured. It may upset those who are uninterested in the viability of social institutions and in rule-of-law values. But people who strike these attitudes should reflect a little on the role that rights are supposed to play in our social and political evaluations. When we think about rights, we must do our thinking in political philosophy not just moral philosophy, and this means being willing to consider the embodiment of various moral concerns in the *institutional* arrangements of human society. Once we see this as the distinctive perspective of polit-

---

[80] See F. A. Hayek, *The Road to Serfdom* (Chicago, IL; University of Chicago Press, 1944); and F. A. Hayek, *The Constitution of Liberty* (London: Macmillan, 1960).

ical philosophy, we begin to see the inadequacy of the approach that leaves rights as simply programmatic claims, without considering how they fit together as a system and how the rights of one person might be made compatible (concretely, not just in theory) with the rights of another.

The approach I have suggested may upset those who want to maintain at all costs that each individual right is absolute, and who in consequence refuse to face issues of scarcity, conflict, and moral priority. (Some say this about property and some may say it about welfare rights.) This insistence is perhaps understandable: the modern preoccupation with rights is partly a response to the trade-offs that characterize utilitarian calculations; rights were supposed to express limits on what could be done to individuals for the sake of the greater benefit of others; but if rights themselves involve conflicts and balancing, it looks as though there is no getting away from the casuistry and complex moral calculations that were thought to be the hallmark of more blatantly consequentialist theories. I have some sympathy with this view. However, the insistence on absolutism does not make the conflicts go away; it does not make the situations that appear to call for trade-offs disappear. Those situations are not something that consequentialists and their fellow travelers have perversely *invented* in order to embarrass moral absolutists. There is a danger that, if we insist on the absoluteness of rights, we may end up with no rights at all—or no rights that embody the idea of real concern for the individuals whose rights they are.

The proper response to situations that pose conflicts and dilemmas is not to deny that they exist or to protect the term "rights" from being contaminated by them. It is to face up to the challenges they pose with the clearest sense we can get of the intrinsic worth of each individual's well-being and independence in a world that is also inhabited by others. Unless that sense becomes hopelessly attenuated, it is exactly what we should identify as our theory of rights. Rights are not to be thought of as moral absolutes, standing tragically unemployed, on the sidelines of a world riven by distasteful conflict and hard choices. On the contrary, they are supposed to be our best, most honest, and most respectful response to such a world.

Let me return, finally, to Robert Nozick. With his emphasis on rights as side constraints (*ASU*, 26 ff.), it is tempting to associate Nozick with the sort of absolutism I have just been attacking. And it is tempting to read his critical comments about welfare rights (*ASU*, 238) as an indirect consequence of this absolutism. I do not just mean that his absolutism about property leads him to reject welfare rights; I mean that he might be thought to reject welfare rights partly because of what they would have to amount to qua rights. In fact, I think Nozick has contributed immeasurably to our ability to think these things through carefully in a manner that is appropriate to justice and not merely to line-item claims of right. I hope I have been able to show in this essay that this is true of his discussion about "filling the space of rights" in *Anarchy, State, and Utopia* (238), and true also of his discussion of the Lockean proviso.

V. CONCLUSION

We began with Robert Nozick's challenge to come up with a moral theory—a "reverse" theory—that gives priority to welfare rights (or something like them) and recognizes claims to private property only to the extent that such welfare rights leave room for them. I have argued that the outlines of such a theory can be found in Nozick's own work—specifically in his insistence that historical entitlements to property must be conditioned on the operation of what he called the Lockean proviso. And I argued, too, that another version of the "reverse" theory can be found in the work of John Locke, not only in his own use of the Lockean proviso, but also in his insistence that property rights are qualified by an elemental principle of charity that entitles individuals to the surplus of goods that would otherwise belong to others, when they have no other means to survive. The point of adducing these two cases, in response to Nozick's challenge, is not to annoy or embarrass those who continue to develop the libertarian strands of the Lockean/Nozickian heritage. Rather, my aim has been to demonstrate the richness of that heritage and—particularly in Nozick's case—to highlight both the integrity of his view and the challenge that is posed by his theory of historical entitlement.

Law, Columbia University

TOWARD A THEORY OF EMPIRICAL NATURAL RIGHTS*

By John Hasnas

I. Introduction

With the publication of *Anarchy, State, and Utopia* in 1974, Robert Nozick breathed new life into the natural rights tradition of political philosophy. By opening his book with the statement "Individuals have rights, and there are things no person or group may do to them (without violating their rights),"[1] Nozick stimulated two distinct lines of philosophical investigation: a future-oriented inquiry into the implications that the existence of fundamental individual rights holds for morally acceptable public policy, and a backward-looking inquiry into the sources of and foundations for these rights. In this essay, I propose to pursue the latter line of inquiry.

To this end, I will begin with a brief overview of natural rights political philosophy in Section II. Because Nozick explicitly adopts John Locke's conception of natural rights as his own, I will first survey both Locke's and Nozick's rights-based arguments for limited government. I will then suggest that although both arguments are quite powerful, their persuasive force can be no greater than that of the underlying arguments for the existence of the natural rights upon which they rest. I will conclude Section II by suggesting that neither Locke nor Nozick has supplied an adequate version of the necessary underlying arguments.

Rather than attempting to supply this lack myself, I will offer in Section III an alternative conception of natural rights as rights that naturally evolve in the state of nature. I will then argue that these "empirical natural rights" form a good approximation of the negative rights to life, liberty, and property on which both Locke and Nozick rest their arguments and that such rights are normatively well grounded. I will conclude by suggesting that empirical natural rights can serve as an alternative grounding for rights-based arguments for limited government that would be more persuasive to those not already committed to a classical liberal position than the traditional conception of natural rights advanced by Locke and Nozick.

* I wish to thank my fellow contributors to this volume, Ellen Frankel Paul, and Ann C. Tunstall of SciLucent, LLC, for their exceedingly helpful comments on an earlier draft of this essay, and Annette Hasnas for the keen insight she provided into how human beings behave in the state of nature.

[1] Robert Nozick, *Anarchy, State, and Utopia* (New York: Basic Books, 1974), *ix*. (Hereinafter, *ASU*. Future references to this work will be identified by page number in parentheses in the text.)

II. The Natural Rights Tradition

A. Locke and Nozick

Natural rights political philosophy derives both the justification for and the limitations upon political authority from the natural rights of individual human beings. "Natural rights" are the pre-political rights individuals possess in the absence of established political authority, that is, in the state of nature. A natural rights–based argument for limited government has several familiar and easily identifiable features. It begins by identifying the rights individuals possess in the state of nature. It proceeds by presenting a list of the inconveniences inherent in life in that state and by arguing that to escape these inconveniences, individuals delegate some of the power derived from their natural rights to the exclusive use of a civil government. It then identifies the powers so delegated to conclude that a government that exercises these powers *and only these powers* is morally justified. Different versions of this argument can be generated by different lists of natural rights, different conceptions of the state of nature, different methods of delegation, and different lists of delegated powers.

In *Anarchy, State, and Utopia*, Robert Nozick advanced an argument for a severely limited form of government, his minimal state, that explicitly mirrored several of the features of John Locke's version of natural rights theory. Accordingly, it will be worthwhile to conduct a brief review of Locke's theory and to highlight its similarities to (and differences from) Nozick's. Doing so will also explain why both theories share the characteristic of being enormously influential to some and wholly unpersuasive to others.

Let us begin with a consideration of what Locke meant by the state of nature. This can best be done by contrasting Locke's account with the perhaps more familiar account of the state of nature given by Thomas Hobbes. Hobbes believed that human nature was such that in the absence of "a common power to keep them all in awe," human beings would behave so as to create a state of war "of every man against every man" in which "men live without other security than what their own strength and their own invention shall furnish them." [2] Hobbes's state of nature, therefore, was a world in which the utter want of personal security meant that there could be no industry, commerce, art, or learning—a world in which life was necessarily "solitary, poor, nasty, brutish, and short." [3] For Hobbes, the state of nature consisted not merely in the absence of an organized central authority, but in the absence of any mechanism of social control: the absence not merely of *government*, but of *governance*.

This is not Locke's conception of the state of nature. Political philosopher A. John Simmons argues persuasively that Locke's state of nature

---

[2] Thomas Hobbes, *Leviathan* (1651), ed. Herbert Schneider (Indianapolis, IN: Bobbs-Merrill, 1958), 106–7.
[3] Ibid., 107.

was not intended as an empirical description of human behavior, but as the specification of a normative condition: "the condition of men living together without *legitimate* government."[4] If this is the case, then the state of nature implies neither the absence of civil government, since one may be subject to an illegitimate one, nor the absence of governance, since human beings may make whatever interpersonal agreements or private arrangements they wish (within the law of nature) to provide for their personal security and comfort. And since Locke makes it clear that "men may make [promises and compacts] one with another, and yet still be in the state of nature,"[5] even if his state of nature is regarded as an empirical condition, it would be one that is consistent with a high degree of cooperative behavior.

The distinction between Hobbes's conception of the state of nature and Locke's is reflected in the different rights they ascribe to human beings in that condition. Hobbes's war of all against all is an entirely lawless state. Under such conditions, the only right of any relevance, and hence the only natural right human beings possess, is the right of self-preservation.[6] In contrast, Locke's state of nature, although it lacks a normatively binding human law, is not lawless. It is governed by the law of nature, which obligates human beings to act for the preservation of mankind: hence, no one may "take away, or impair the life, or what tends to the preservation of the life, the liberty, health, limb, or goods of another" (*STG* §6). Thus, the law of nature entails the existence of natural rights to life, liberty, and property: life, because the preservation of mankind requires individuals not to take their own or others' lives; liberty, because "all men are by nature equal," and hence possess the "equal right . . . to [their] natural freedom, without being subjected to the will or authority of any other man" (*STG* §54); and property, because "every man has a property in his own person" that entitles him to "[t]he labour of his body, and the work of his hands," such that whatever "he removes out of the state that nature hath provided, and left it in, he hath mixed his labour with, and joined to it something that is his own, and thereby makes it his property" (*STG* §27). In Locke's state of nature, human beings are invested with a panoply of rights.

Although human beings are obviously much better off in Locke's state of nature than in Hobbes's, their ability to enjoy the exercise of their

---

[4] A. John Simmons, "Locke's State of Nature," *Political Theory* 17, no. 3 (1989): 451.

[5] John Locke, *Second Treatise of Government* (1690), ed. C. B. Macpherson (Indianapolis, IN: Hackett Publishing, 1980), §14. (Hereinafter, *STG*. Future references to this work will be identified by section number in parentheses in the text.)

[6] See Thomas Hobbes, *Leviathan* (1651), ed. Herbert Schneider (Indianapolis, IN: Bobbs-Merrill, 1958), 109.

> The Right of Nature, which writers commonly call *jus naturale*, is the liberty each man has to use his own power, as he will himself, for the preservation of his own nature—that is to say, of his own life—and consequently of doing anything which, in his own judgement and reason, he shall conceive to be the aptest means thereunto.

natural rights is still far from secure. This is due to the absence of "an established, settled, known law" to serve as "the common measure to decide all controversies between [men]" (*STG* §124), "a known and indifferent judge, with authority to determine all differences according to the established law" (*STG* §125), and any organized "power to back and support the sentence when right, and to give it due execution" (*STG* §126). It is to escape these inconveniences and thereby secure the "mutual preservation of their lives, liberties and estates" (*STG* §123) that human beings delegate some of the power they derive from their natural rights to a civil government.

The method of delegation, for Locke, is clearly consent,[7] although the difficult question of what constitutes consent will not be addressed here. The amount of power delegated is that which is necessary to alleviate the inconveniences of the state of nature and to secure individuals' lives, liberties, and estates. This requires each individual to relinquish all of his right to punish those who transgress the law of nature (*STG* §130) and that portion of his right "to do whatsoever he thinks fit for the preservation of himself, and others within the permission of the law of nature" (*STG* §128) that is required for the preservation of civil society.

The consensual delegation of these powers establishes both the legitimate authority of civil government and the limits of that authority. The delegation of the right to punish gives the civil government the exclusive power to redress actions that violate the law of nature, that is, actions that "take away, or impair the life, . . . liberty, health, limb, or goods of another" (*STG* §6). The government is thus empowered to establish positive criminal laws in support of the law of nature and is vested with the exclusive authority to adjudicate and apply criminal punishment. The delegation of a portion of the right to liberty gives the civil government the power to establish general regulatory laws designed to achieve the common good. But because no individual possesses a right to act in contravention of the law of nature, no such power can be delegated to the government; hence, the government has no power to make any law, criminal or otherwise, that is contrary to the injunction to preserve mankind. Thus, the power of civil government, "in the utmost bounds of it, is limited to the public good of society" (*STG* §135). Further, because the delegation of power is consensual and "no rational creature can be supposed to change his condition with an intention to be worse," the government is obligated to use its delegated power "to secure everyone's property, by providing against those three defects above mentioned" (*STG* §131). Thus, civil government

is bound to govern by established *standing laws*, promulgated and known to the people, . . . by *indifferent* and upright *judges*, who are to

---

[7] "Men being, as has been said, by nature, all free, equal, and independent, no one can be put out of this estate, and subjected to the political power of another, without his own consent" (*STG* §95).

decide controversies by those laws; and to employ the force of the community at home, *only in the execution of such laws,* or abroad to prevent or redress foreign injuries, and secure the community from inroads and invasion. And all this to be directed to no other *end,* but the *peace, safety,* and *public good* of the people. (*STG* §131)

Turning now to Nozick's argument for the state, we find that it is virtually identical to Locke's with regard to its conception of the state of nature and the list of rights individuals possess therein. With regard to the state of nature, Nozick is seeking a conception that constitutes "the best anarchic situation one reasonably could hope for" because "if one could show that the state would be superior to even this most favored situation of anarchy, . . . it would justify the state" (*ASU,* 5). Nozick believes that Locke's conception, in which individuals who are free from legitimate political authority are both bound to behave morally and able to cooperate on the basis of contractual agreements and communal arrangements, meets this criterion. Accordingly, he explicitly adopts Locke's conception of the state of nature as one in which only government, not governance, is lacking (*ASU,* 9–10).

Further, although Nozick never explicitly identifies the rights individuals possess in the state of nature,[8] we may safely assume that the set of rights that Nozick ascribes to such individuals is either coextensive with or encompasses Locke's natural rights. In adopting Locke's conception of the state of nature, Nozick specifically cites Locke's characterization of it as being governed by the law of nature that requires "that 'no one ought to harm another in his life, health, liberty, or possessions'" (*ASU,* 10, citing *STG* §6). This, along with the substance of Nozick's extended discussion, strongly suggests that he believes that individuals in the state of nature possess the same substantive rights to life, liberty, and property for which Locke argues. If Nozick's list of rights differs from Locke's at all, it is by including an additional procedural right not to be punished for violating others' rights unless one's guilt has been established by a reliable and fair process.[9]

Nozick's argument begins to depart from Locke's when it comes to the method by which individuals delegate their power to the state and the specific powers that are delegated. Like Locke, Nozick recognizes that individuals' rights are not secure in the state of nature. Unlike Locke, however, he does not argue that individuals ever directly consent to the

---

[8] With the possible exception of the right to punish, Nozick deals with rights exclusively on the generic level. It is worth noting that Locke, too, fails to provide an exhaustive or authoritative list of individuals' natural rights, although he does discuss several specific rights (e.g., the right to preserve oneself and others by means within the law of nature, the right to execute the law of nature, and the right to pursue innocent delights), which I have subsumed in the traditional trilogy of life, liberty, and property.

[9] See *ASU,* 102. Nozick suggests but never explicitly affirms that such natural "due process" rights exist. See *ASU,* 101, 107.

authority of a civil government in order to secure them. Rather, Nozick contends that human beings in the state of nature will use their ability to contract with one another in order to hire private protective associations to secure their rights for them. He then makes the empirical claim that because of the special nature of the services that protective associations provide, market forces will result in the rise of one dominant protective association in any given geographical area.[10] To this he adds the normative assertion that the dominant association may legitimately prevent any competitor from taking action against its clients on the basis of any guilt-determination procedure of which the dominant association does not approve,[11] as long as it provides its competitors' clients with in-kind compensation in the form of its own protective services.[12] But once a dominant protective association thus suppresses its competitors and provides its services to all persons in a geographical area, it has all the necessary attributes of a civil government (*ASU*, 22–23). Therefore, Nozick concludes that a civil government can spontaneously arise through a series of morally legitimate steps, that is, steps that do not violate any of the rights individuals possess in the state of nature. For Nozick, then, individuals delegate their power to the state indirectly by consensually creating an entity that evolves into a state through unplanned but morally legitimate human interaction.

Nozick's method of delegation transfers less power and produces a more severely limited state than does Locke's. Like Locke, Nozick sees

---

[10] Nozick regards the provision of protective services as what economists call a "network industry," one in which the value of the good increases as the number of users increases. He argues that

> [t]he worth of the product purchased, protection against others, is *relative*: it depends upon how strong the others are. Yet unlike other goods that are comparatively evaluated, maximal competing protective services cannot coexist; the nature of the service brings different agencies not only into competition for customers' patronage, but also into violent conflict with each other. Also, since the worth of the less than maximal product declines disproportionately with the number who purchase the maximal product, customers will not stably settle for the lesser good, and competing companies are caught in a declining spiral. (*ASU*, 17)

Hence, "[o]ut of anarchy, pressed by spontaneous groupings, mutual-protection associations, division of labor, market pressures, economies of scale, and rational self-interest there arises something very much resembling a minimal state or a group of geographically distinct minimal states" (*ASU*, 16–17). For an interesting attempt to refute this argument, see Bryan Caplan and Ed Stringham, "Networks, Law, and the Paradox of Cooperation," *Review of Austrian Economics* 16 (2003): 309–26.

[11] It may do this either because its clients have a procedural right to have their guilt determined by a reliable and fair procedure that the dominant protective association is authorized to exercise for them or because nonclients do not have the right to punish the association's clients on the basis of guilt-determination procedures that the association deems unreliable or unfair (*ASU*, 107).

[12] This is because it is morally permissible to prohibit activities that impose risks on others only if "those who are *disadvantaged* by being forbidden to do actions that only *might* harm others [are] compensated for these disadvantages foisted upon them in order to provide security for the others" (*ASU*, 82–83).

individuals as delegating their right to punish rights-violators to what becomes the civil government, thus empowering it to establish (rights-protecting) criminal laws and to adjudicate and apply criminal punishment.[13] Unlike Locke, however, Nozick does not see individuals as delegating a portion of their right to liberty sufficient to empower the government to establish regulatory laws for the common good. Beyond relinquishing their right to punish, individuals delegate none of their right to liberty and only that portion of their right to property that is necessary for the state to supply protective services to those who are entitled to receive them as compensation.[14] The exceedingly spare nature of this delegation strictly limits the power of the state to that necessary to protect the rights of its citizens. Hence, Nozick's argument provides a justification for "the night-watchman state of classical liberal theory" (*ASU,* 25) that provides police, adjudicative, and national defense services, and nothing more.

B. *The arguments' persuasive force or lack thereof*

Natural rights arguments for limited government have a powerful but limited appeal. Their power comes from their argumentative structure. Their limitations come from the foundations on which this structure rests.

Natural rights arguments are structurally valid arguments. Given their assumptions about individuals' pre-political moral entitlements, they provide cogent justifications for both government power and its limitations. If individuals are truly vested with natural rights, then government can function morally and command obedience only to the extent that it does not violate them. Both Locke's and Nozick's arguments chart a well-reasoned course from Lockean natural rights to morally legitimate limited government. Locke's consent-based argument rests on the fundamental moral propositions that one who consents to what would otherwise be an invasion of a protected interest has not been wronged and that one is morally bound by one's freely undertaken agreements. These propositions imply that to the extent that one's obligation to obey political authority has been voluntarily assumed, no underlying right has been violated and one is morally bound to obey political authority. The intuitive appeal of these underlying propositions is so great that Lockean social contract theory has maintained a strong hold on popular imagination in the United States since the nation's inception. Nozick's argument, which rests par-

---

[13] Individuals also delegate their "due process" right to be tried by reliable and fair procedures, if they have such a right. See note 9 above.

[14] Nozick does not explicitly state that individuals delegate a portion of their right to property, but this is the clear implication of his claim that "the dominant protective agency must supply the independents—that is, everyone it prohibits from self-help enforcement against its clients on the grounds that their procedures of enforcement are unreliable or unfair—with protective services against its clients . . ." (*ASU,* 112. See generally, *ASU,* 110–13).

tially on the binding force of voluntary agreement and partially on a philosophically sophisticated account of morally legitimate human interaction, can exert a similar hold on the philosophical imagination. If Nozick's contentions regarding individuals' procedural entitlements and the conditions under which risky behavior may be restrained when compensation is paid are correct, then he, too, provides a cogent justification for moving from a Lockean state of nature to a limited civil government. Arguments such as these can be extremely persuasive to those who believe that individuals do, in fact, have pre-political Lockean rights.

This statement, however, indicates the limitations of the arguments' power as well. For as effective as they may be at deriving limited government from Lockean natural rights, their appeal to those who are not antecedently committed to the existence of such rights is only as powerful as the underlying arguments for the rights themselves. These underlying arguments, however, are much less compelling than those they support.

For Locke's or Nozick's argument to gain purchase, natural rights theorists must first establish not only that natural rights exist in a generic sense, but also that the set of legitimate natural rights is coextensive with Locke's rights to life, liberty, and property. Establishing the first of these propositions has presented a notoriously difficult challenge,[15] but even if it could be overcome, establishing the second may prove equally formidable. Even natural rights theorists do not agree about what natural rights exist, as the foregoing discussion of Hobbes and Locke illustrates. To establish that Lockean rights constitute *the* set of natural rights, a natural rights theorist would have to produce an argument robust enough to counter Hobbesian arguments that yield a more limited set of rights, yet not so robust that contemporary liberals can extend its logic to yield positive welfare rights to fundamental goods or services such as health care or a minimally decent standard of living. Whether natural rights theorists can ultimately meet these challenges remains an open question. It is clear, however, that neither Locke nor Nozick has done so.

---

[15] Loren Lomasky explains this difficulty as consisting in

those ills endemic to any account that attempts to base moral status and obligation on "nature": on some characteristic that all and only those beings who are moral claimants possess and which is sufficient to justify their moral claims. Natural rights theories are a subclass of such nature-based theories. They routinely are embarrassed by the absence of any characteristic *universally* shared by those beings they wish to single out as rights holders, possessed *only* by them, shared *equally* by them (else rights possession would be an analog function admitting of degree rather than all-or-nothing), and which can credibly be taken as *justifying* the preferred moral status that is ascribed to rights holders. All such attempts to ground rights—or morality in general—in nature fail because the class of moral claimants does not coincide with the class possessing property Φ, where Φ is the alleged natural basis of rights.

Loren E. Lomasky, *Persons, Rights, and the Moral Community* (New York: Oxford University Press, 1987), 37–38.

Locke's "disturbing paucity of foundational work in the *Second Treatise*" has been noted by Simmons, who points out that although "[t]he content of parts of the natural law and the rights defined by it receive considerable attention . . . very little is said about why these are our duties and rights."[16] Nozick himself explicitly recognizes both Locke's and his own failure to provide a firm grounding for natural rights when he declares at the beginning of *Anarchy, State, and Utopia* that the "task is so crucial, the gap left without its accomplishment so yawning, that it is only a minor comfort to note that we here are following the respectable tradition of Locke, who does not provide anything remotely resembling a satisfactory explanation of the status and basis of the law of nature in his *Second Treatise*" (*ASU*, 9). Nevertheless, the arguments that Locke and Nozick do provide are worth examining for what they reveal about the limitations on the persuasive force of natural rights theory.

Locke provides at least two lines of argument for the law of nature from which he derives his natural rights: one theological and one secular. The theological argument defines the law of nature as God's will with regard to human behavior, which human beings can discover by the powers of reason God impressed into their nature for that purpose.[17] When the law of nature is understood in this way, demonstrating its existence requires Locke to establish that God exists, that God created human beings as essentially rational creatures, that there is a normative duty to obey the commands of one's creator, and that reason allows human beings to derive the general principles of moral conduct from their knowledge of divine and human nature—none of which is an easy task.[18] The secular argument defines the law of nature as the law of reason commanding what is in the best interest of humanity. When it is understood in this way, Locke believes that the law of nature can be derived from the formal proposition that it is irrational to treat equals unequally and the substantive proposition that all human beings are of equal moral worth. This allows Locke to argue that the duty to preserve any human life logically entails the equal duty to preserve everyone's life, and hence the duty to preserve mankind by refraining from actions that impair the life, liberty, and property of others (*STG* §6).[19]

---

[16] A. John Simmons, *The Lockean Theory of Rights* (Princeton, NJ: Princeton University Press, 1992), 15.

[17] "[T]his law of nature can be described as being the decree of the divine will discernable by the light of nature and indicating what is and what is not in conformity with rational nature, and for this very reason commanding or prohibiting." John Locke, *Essays on the Law of Nature* (1676), ed. W. von Leyden (Oxford: Clarendon Press, 1988), 111.

[18] A good account of Locke's theological argument for the law of nature can be found in Simmons, *The Lockean Theory of Rights*, 23.

[19] The argument that Locke presents in §6 of the *Second Treatise* is not truly secular, since he supports his contentions that human life has value and that all human lives are equally valuable on the basis of the claim that they are all equally the workmanship of God. However, the argument itself is logically severable from its theological support. Any argument for the value of human life and for human moral equality can serve as well. Hence, it is not inappropriate to regard Locke as providing a secular grounding for his natural rights.

Nozick provides an argument that grounds rights not in the law of nature but directly on Kantian moral theory, identifying them as reflections of "the underlying Kantian principle that individuals are ends and not merely means" (*ASU*, 30–31). Nozick accepts the Kantian proposition that every human being possesses inherent moral value, that is, a dignity, that all others are required to respect. Rights, he argues, protect this dignity. By doing so, they "express the inviolability of other persons" (*ASU*, 32) and "reflect the fact of our separate existences. They reflect the fact that no moral balancing act can take place among us; there is no moral outweighing of one of our lives by others so as to lead to a greater overall social good. There is no justified sacrifice of some of us for others" (*ASU*, 33). Thus, Nozick believes that an individual's rights must be respected because the failure to do so "does not sufficiently respect and take account of the fact that he is a separate person, that his is the only life he has" (*ASU*, 33).

To the extent that Locke's or any natural rights argument has a theological basis, the limits of its appeal are patent. To begin with, establishing the existence of natural rights on this ground requires first establishing the existence of God, a proposition at least as difficult to substantiate as the one it is being offered to prove. Indeed, Locke does not even attempt to make such an argument, since he begins his *Essays on the Law of Nature* (1676) by simply assuming that God exists.[20] But even with this assumption, Locke must still prove that there is a duty to obey God's will. Although this may seem obvious at first, it is not. For, with Humean hindsight, we know that the *fact* that God commands something does not in itself imply that human beings *ought* to obey. What, then, is the source of this obligation? For Locke, the source of human moral obligation is the law of nature. But because the obligation to obey God is being offered to prove that the law of nature exists, the law of nature cannot serve as the source of the obligation without rendering the argument circular. And if Locke simply identifies divine commandment as the property that makes something morally obligatory, he runs directly into the naturalistic fallacy.[21] Finally, even if these problems could be surmounted, Locke would then face the task of establishing that his version of the law of nature correctly embodies God's will. Since he cannot rely on revelation, he can do this only by demonstrating that it is entailed by the respective natures of God

---

[20] "Since God shows Himself to us as present everywhere and, as it were, forces Himself upon the eyes of men as much in the fixed course of nature now as by the frequent evidence of miracles in time past, I assume there will be no one to deny the existence of God, provided he recognizes either the necessity for some rational account of our life, or that there is a thing that deserves to be called virtue or vice." Locke, *Essays on the Law of Nature*, 109.

[21] The naturalistic fallacy is the improper identification of a normative property with a natural property, or more precisely, "the fallacy that results from construing the 'is' of attribution as an 'is' of identity, and thus supposing, for example, that because pleasure is (attributive 'is') good, good is identical with pleasure." See George Edward Moore, *The Encyclopedia of Philosophy*, ed. Paul Edwards (New York: Macmillan, 1967), 5:379.

and human being. Given the obvious difficulty of providing a compelling account of God's nature and the philosophical debate not only about what constitutes human nature, but about whether there even is such a thing,[22] the prospects of Locke (or any natural rights theorist) providing a convincing demonstration of this point must be considered remote.

Locke's secular argument does not fare much better. In this case, however, the difficulty is not so much with the substance of the premises as with whether they lead to the desired conclusion. There will be little disagreement either with the formal proposition that equals should be treated equally or with the substantive claims that human life has value and that human beings are equal in some morally significant respect. The difficulty for Locke is to establish that the respect in which human beings are equal is one that gives rise to a duty to preserve mankind that entails all and only the rights to life, liberty, and property that he endorses. In this respect, Locke's argument is both too weak and too strong.

Locke's argument is strong enough to establish a duty to preserve every human life and this would seem to entail a duty not to kill others or deprive them of the things necessary to preserve their lives. Whether it is strong enough to establish Locke's extensive rights to liberty and property would depend on whether these rights are truly necessary for the preservation of life in society. Although Locke assumes that they are (*STG* §6), there appears to be little reason for this. Clearly a right to some freedom of action and a modest right to keep those things necessary to maintain life could be established, but this falls far short of rights to one's "natural freedom, without being subjected to the will or authority of any other man" (*STG* §54) and to keep whatever one "hath mixed his labor with" (*STG* §27). The life of all may be very well preserved consistently with great restrictions on personal liberty and severely limited rights to personal possessions. Hence, Locke's argument is too weak to persuade those not already committed to a classical liberal conception of rights.

The more serious problem with Locke's secular argument, however, is that it is much too strong. This is because the duty to preserve every human life that it entails can give rise to positive welfare rights as easily as it can the classical negative rights to life, liberty, and property. A duty to equally preserve everyone's life certainly generates a duty not to take others' lives or otherwise impair others' efforts to survive, but it also appears to generate a duty to act positively to maintain others' lives. Thus, to the extent that Locke's argument establishes the desired negative rights to life, liberty, and property, it also establishes positive welfare rights to benefits such as a minimal standard of living and life-preserving health care—again rendering it unpersuasive as an argument for the classical liberal configuration of rights.

---

[22] See Margaret MacDonald, "Natural Rights," in Jeremy Waldron, ed., *Theories of Rights* (Oxford: Oxford University Press, 1984), 29–30.

In some ways, it is not unreasonable to view Nozick as rehabilitating Locke's secular argument. By basing his argument on a Kantian foundation, Nozick can be seen as arguing not merely that every human life has equal moral value, as Locke did, but, more specifically, that every human being is equally possessed of a dignity that requires respect for his or her autonomy.[23] This is a much more promising basis for an argument for the existence of Lockean rights. On the one hand, it is strong enough to ground not only the right to life, but also broad negative rights to liberty and property. A duty to respect others' autonomy bars not only taking their lives, but also coercing their persons both generally and, more specifically, in order to deprive them of justly acquired possessions. On the other hand, it does not appear to be strong enough to ground positive rights, because a duty to respect others' autonomy does not entail a duty to sustain their lives or benefit them in other ways.

Unfortunately, Nozick's argument has its own set of drawbacks. To begin with, both its moral and its metaphysical foundations are far from securely established. To the extent that it is expressly tied to Kantian moral theory, it is subject to the conventional philosophical criticisms of this theory and will be convincing only to those who accept Kant's categorical imperative as the fundamental principle of morality.[24] Further, the argument's underlying metaphysical assumptions have been attacked by both feminists and communitarians. Nozick explicitly bases his argument on the contention that human beings are *essentially* separate entities: that rights "reflect the fact of our separate existences." Feminists explicitly reject what they call the "separation thesis,"[25] arguing that "women are 'essentially connected,' not 'essentially separate,' from the rest of human life, both materially, through pregnancy, intercourse, and breast-feeding, and existentially, through the moral and practical life."[26] Communitarians argue that because human identity is socially constructed, because the self is a product of one's social and political roles in one's community that

---

[23] Nozick can be seen as providing the secular supporting argument for human moral equality that Locke's actual argument based on divine creation lacked. See note 19 above.

[24] In its most familiar version, the categorical imperative enjoins us to "[a]ct so that you treat humanity, whether in your own person or that of another, always as an end and never as a means only." Immanuel Kant, *The Foundations of the Metaphysics of Morals*, trans. Lewis White Beck (Indianapolis, IN: Bobbs-Merrill, 1959), 9–10. Some of the more conventional objections to basing ethical theory on the categorical imperative are that it improperly discounts the moral significance of an action's consequences, that it cannot resolve conflicts among duties (e.g., whether one should lie to save an innocent life), and that it provides no ethical guidance in situations in which it is impossible to treat all as ends in themselves (e.g., an overcrowded lifeboat).

[25] The separation thesis consists in "the claim that human beings are, definitionally, distinct from one another, the claim that the referent of 'I' is singular and unambiguous, the claim that the word 'individual' has an uncontested biological meaning, namely that we are each physically individuated from every other, the claim that we are individuals 'first,' and the claim that what separates us is epistemologically and morally prior to what connects us. . . ." Robin West, "Jurisprudence and Gender," *University of Chicago Law Review* 55 (1988): 2.

[26] Ibid., 3.

"arises through the common understanding which underlies the practices of our society,"[27] the concept of a pre-social or pre-political separate self is nonsensical. They contend that the very capacities that Nozick identifies as the grounding for his pre-political rights—rationality, free will, moral agency, and the ability to live according to an overarching plan of life (*ASU*, 49)—are only possible because individuals are formed in an already existing political society, and, hence, that Nozick's argument is hopelessly circular.

The more serious problem with Nozick's argument, however, is that he does not make it. He supplies no account of the steps in reasoning that lead from either the categorical imperative or the recognition of human beings as essentially separate selves to their inherent possession of Lockean rights.[28] It may appear obvious that respect for individuals as ends in themselves requires a right to life and a right to a significant amount of control over one's existence, but it is not obvious that it requires the broad rights to liberty and property on which Nozick grounds his argument for the minimal state or that it necessarily excludes all positive rights. Unfortunately, all Nozick offers in support of his position is the claim that the possession of Lockean rights is necessary for individuals to have meaningful lives. But Nozick follows his assertion that "[a] person's shaping his life in accordance with some overall plan is his way of giving meaning to his life; only a being with the capacity to so shape his life can have or strive for a meaningful life" (*ASU*, 50) not with an argument showing why the possession of Lockean rights is necessary for this capacity, but with a list of ten questions that suggest that it may not be, followed by the declaration that he "hope[s] to grapple with these and related issues on another occasion" (*ASU*, 51). Because it seems obvious that one can have quite a meaningful life without rights guaranteeing that one remains *entirely* free from coercion by others (else no human being has ever had a meaningful life), Nozick's remarks have little prospect of convincing those who do not already agree with him.[29]

[27] Charles Taylor, "Atomism," in Alkis Kontos, ed., *Powers, Possessions, and Freedom: Essays in Honor of C. B. Macpherson* (Toronto: University of Toronto Press, 1979), 60.

[28] Judith Jarvis Thomson notes that Nozick's argument that individual rights are inviolable "rests entirely on the supposition that they are" (Judith Jarvis Thomson, "Some Ruminations on Rights," in Jeffrey Paul, ed., *Reading Nozick: Essays on Anarchy, State, and Utopia* [Totowa, NJ: Rowman & Littlefield, 1981], 137), while Thomas Nagel contends that "[t]o present a serious challenge to other views, [Nozick] would have to explore the foundations of individual rights and the reasons for and against different conceptions of the relation between those rights and other values that the state may be in a position to promote, . . . but no such arguments appear in the book" (Thomas Nagel, "Libertarianism without Foundations," in Paul, ed., *Reading Nozick*, 192–93).

[29] A charge frequently leveled against natural rights theories is that they violate the Humean proscription against deriving a normative conclusion from purely empirical premises. Jeremy Waldron, for example, states that "[t]he idea of *natural* rights is seen as a particularly glaring example of the 'Naturalistic Fallacy', purporting to derive certain norms or evaluations from descriptive premises about human nature." Jeremy Waldron, introduction to *Theories of Rights,* ed. Jeremy Waldron (Oxford: Oxford University Press, 1984), 3.

My critique of Locke's and Nozick's arguments does not, of course, suggest that natural rights theorists cannot supply a secure grounding for Lockean natural rights, merely that neither Locke nor Nozick (nor anyone else that I am aware of) has done so. Until that grounding is provided, arguments like Locke's and Nozick's, which are profoundly persuasive to those who are antecedently committed to Lockean natural rights, are likely to remain equally unpersuasive to those who are not.

III. An Alternative Conception of Natural Rights

A. "Empirical" natural rights

I make no pretense of being able to offer a satisfactory philosophical grounding for Lockean natural rights. Rather, I would like to sidestep the issue by offering an alternative conception of natural rights that is not beset by the foundational problems discussed in the previous section, but is nevertheless philosophically useful. In place of the traditional conception of natural rights as rights that human beings are inherently *endowed with* in the state of nature, I would like to offer a conception of natural rights as rights that *evolve in* the state of nature. For lack of a better term, I will refer to rights of this type as "empirical natural rights."

In offering this alternative, I am employing a conception of the state of nature that is similar to, but importantly different from, that employed by Locke and Nozick. Like both Locke and Nozick, I am interested in exploring human behavior in the absence of established government, not in the absence of any mechanism of interpersonal governance. Accordingly, my conception of the state of nature is one in which human beings are able to make interpersonal agreements or other private arrangements to ensure their personal security and enjoyment of life—that is, one that is consistent with both antagonistic and highly cooperative behavior. Thus, the conception of the state of nature that I am employing is much more like Locke's than Hobbes's. Unlike Locke and Nozick, however, I am advancing an empirical, rather than an essentially normative, conception of the state of nature.[30]

To the extent that a natural rights theory attempts to derive rights solely from a description of human nature, this charge may be well founded. However, neither Nozick's argument nor Locke's secular argument falls prey to this critique. Both philosophers ground their arguments on genuinely normative premises about the moral status of individual human beings. Hence, I have not addressed the Humean objection in this essay.

[30] See the discussions of Locke's and Nozick's conception of the state of nature in subsection II A.

Perhaps like most readers, I had always assumed that Locke's conception of the state of nature was a purely empirical one—that, like Hobbes, Locke was simply referring to a situation in which there was no organized civil government. Recently, however, I have been persuaded by A. John Simmons's argument referenced above in the text accompanying note 4 that this is not the case and that Locke is offering an essentially normative conception of the state of nature that "captures the distinctive moral component of that state" (Simmons,

In the previous section, I described both Locke and Nozick as making genuinely normative arguments, as drawing their normative conclusions from normative premises about the moral status of human beings. Accordingly, their conception of the state of nature is an essentially normative one. Both Locke and Nozick were interested in exploring the human condition in the absence of *morally legitimate* government. Thus, for Locke at least, a person subject to a repressive, morally illegitimate regime would still be in the state of nature with respect to that regime.

This normative conception of the state of nature is too broad for my purposes. I am interested in how human beings behave in the absence of any established political authority, morally legitimate or not. Thus, the conception of the state of nature that I intend to employ is one defined by the absence of civil government *simpliciter,* that is, of any entity claiming or generally recognized as possessing a monopoly over the legitimate use of force in a geographical area or otherwise vested with the traditional trappings of government, such as "finance through taxation, claim of sovereignty, ultimate decision-making authority, and prohibitions on competitive entry."[31] This conception sees the state of nature as an empirical state of affairs rather than a moral condition.

Once the state of nature has been specified, traditional natural rights theorists such as Locke and Nozick next ask what moral entitlements human beings possess therein. I intend to ask only what human beings do. This is an empirical question that can be answered only on the basis of empirical evidence.[32] Fortunately, there is a wealth of such evidence

---

"Locke's State of Nature," 451). This implies that Nozick, who adopts Locke's conception of the state of nature, is offering a normative conception of the state of nature as well. Thus, Locke and Nozick employ the state of nature to ask not how human beings *do* behave in the absence of civil government, but how they are *entitled* to behave in the absence of *morally legitimate* civil government.

Because in this essay I am interested in the former question, my remarks in the text accompanying and immediately following this note are intended to make it clear that I am adopting only Locke's and Nozick's *description* of the state of nature, not their normative characterization of it. Readers who naturally think, as I did, of the state of nature as a description of an empirical condition and who are unfamiliar, as I was, with its normative interpretation can probably avoid confusion by skipping the two paragraphs in the text immediately following this note.

[31] Tyler Cowen, "Law as a Public Good: The Economics of Anarchy," *Economics and Philosophy* 8 (1992): 250.

[32] Because there are relatively few historical examples of people living in a true state of nature, the question of how human beings behave in such a state is necessarily hypothetical. That is, I am forced by circumstance to ask how people *would* behave in the absence of civil government rather simply make empirical observations about how people living without civil government actually behave. Nevertheless, I intend to address this hypothetical question exclusively on the basis of observational data. That is, the evidence I will offer in support of my claim that people in the state of nature *would* behave as I describe is that, in the relevant historical cases that approximate the state of nature, people *did* behave in this way.

The counterfactual nature of the question being addressed does not imply that it cannot be adequately answered on the basis of empirical evidence. Indeed, I would argue that the best way to prove how people would behave under a counterfactual set of circumstances is

available both in the form of direct historical accounts of how those who found themselves in this situation behaved and in the form of analogies that can be drawn from situations in which existing governments failed to act with regard to particular avenues of human endeavor. Unfortunately, in the present context, space does not permit a thorough review of this evidence. Accordingly, I will have to make do with some broad generalizations accompanied by only a few illustrative supporting examples.[33]

First, the generalizations: Historical evidence suggests that life in the state of nature is indeed *originally* beset by the inconveniences Locke identifies. In the absence of civil government, most people engage in productive activity in peaceful cooperation with their fellows. Some do not. A minority engages in predation, attempting to use violence to expropriate the labor or output of others. The existence of this predatory element renders insecure the persons and possessions of those engaged in production. Further, even among the productive portion of the population, disputes arise concerning broken agreements, questions of rightful possession, and actions that inadvertently result in personal injuries for which there is no antecedently established mechanism for resolution. In the state of nature, interpersonal conflicts that can lead to violence often arise.

What happens when they do? The existence of the predatory minority causes those engaged in productive activities to band together to institute measures for their collective security. Various methods of providing for mutual protection and for apprehending or discouraging aggressors are tried. Methods that do not provide adequate levels of security or that prove too costly are abandoned. More successful methods continue to be used. Eventually, methods that effectively discourage aggression while simultaneously minimizing the amount of retaliatory violence necessary to do so become institutionalized. Simultaneously, nonviolent alternatives for resolving interpersonal disputes among the productive members of the community are sought. Various methods are tried. Those that leave the parties unsatisfied and likely to resort again to violence are abandoned. Those that effectively resolve the disputes with the least disturbance to the peace of the community continue to be used and are accompanied by ever-increasing social pressure for disputants to employ them.

Over time, security arrangements and dispute settlement procedures that are well-enough adapted to social and material circumstances to reduce violence to generally acceptable levels become regularized. Members of the community learn what level of participation in or support for

---

to show how they did behave when those circumstances or ones relevantly similar obtained. This, at any rate, is the approach I take in this essay.

[33] Hence, the essay is entitled "*Toward* a Theory of Empirical Natural Rights." The actual development of such a theory requires the hard work of providing the firm empirical grounding upon which the theory must rest. This, however, is the project of another day.

the security arrangements is required of them for the system to work and for them to receive its benefits. By rendering that level of participation or support, they come to feel entitled to the level of security the arrangements provide. After a time, they may come to speak in terms of their right to the protection of their persons and possessions against the type of depredation the security arrangements discourage, and eventually even of their rights to personal integrity and property. In addition, as the dispute settlement procedures resolve recurring forms of conflict in similar ways over time, knowledge of these resolutions becomes widely diffused and members of the community come to expect similar conflicts to be resolved in like manner. Accordingly, they alter their behavior toward other members of the community to conform to these expectations. In doing so, people begin to act in accordance with rules that identify when they must act in the interests of others (e.g., they may be required to use care to prevent their livestock from damaging their neighbors' possessions) and when they may act exclusively in their own interests (e.g., they may be free to totally exclude their neighbors from using their possessions). To the extent that these incipient rules entitle individuals to act entirely in their own interests, individuals may come to speak in terms of their right to do so (e.g., of their right to the quiet enjoyment of their property).

In short, the inconveniences of the state of nature represent problems that human beings must overcome to lead happy and meaningful lives. In the absence of an established civil government to resolve these problems for them, human beings must do so for themselves. They do this not through coordinated collective action, but through a process of trial and error in which the members of the community address these problems in any number of ways, unsuccessful attempts to resolve them are discarded, and successful ones are repeated, copied by others, and eventually become widespread practices. As the members of the community conform their behavior to these practices, they begin to behave according to rules that specify the extent of their obligations to others, and, by implication, the extent to which they are free to act at their pleasure. Over time, these rules become invested with normative significance and the members of the community come to regard the ways in which the rules permit them to act at their pleasure as their rights. Thus, in the state of nature, rights evolve out of human beings' efforts to address the inconveniences of that state. In the state of nature, rights are solved problems.

I turn now to the supporting examples. Two oft-cited examples of societies in which people lived for extended periods of time without a traditional civil government are ancient Israel in the time of the judges and medieval Iceland.[34] I prefer the example of Anglo-Saxon and early

---

[34] For a discussion of the latter, see William Ian Miller, *Bloodtaking and Peacemaking: Feud, Law, and Society in Saga Iceland* (Chicago, IL: University of Chicago Press, 1990); and David Friedman, "Private Creation and Enforcement of Law: A Historical Case," *Journal of Legal Studies* 8 (1979): 399–415.

Norman England because I believe it offers a wonderful test case of how human beings behave in the absence of central political authority. With the collapse of Roman rule in Britain at the beginning of the fifth century, civil government essentially disappeared from the island. As the literate Romans left, so did their law, and as the legions departed, so did its enforcement. This left the inhabitants living in kinship and tribal groupings exposed to outside aggression and with no authoritatively established mechanisms for dealing with internal disputes—truly a good approximation of the state of nature.

In such circumstances, people's most urgent need was for a method of deterring violence and theft. This was originally supplied in the form of the blood feud, which consisted in direct reprisal against aggressors. When someone was assaulted, killed, or otherwise wronged, the expected, socially accepted response was for the members of the aggrieved party's household or clan to wage private war against the wrongdoer.[35] Because the prospect of an immediate violent response from a victim's entire family or support group was sufficiently fearful to discourage attack, the blood feud was an effective deterrent. However, the risk to life and limb and the disruption of normal life that the blood feud entailed also rendered it highly inconvenient. The violence inherent in the blood feud created strong incentives for people to find alternatives to its prosecution. Hence, the practice developed of holding the feud in abeyance while attempts were made to reach a peaceful settlement through negotiation.

The forum for these negotiations was the moot, a public assembly that served as the chief instrument of social administration.[36] When both parties agreed, they could lay their dispute before the moot, whose members, much like present-day mediators, attempted to facilitate an accommodation that both parties found acceptable. The blood feud would be prosecuted only if no accommodation could be reached. Because such negotiated settlements avoided the strife and physical risk of the blood feud, community pressure gradually transformed the effort to reach them from an optional alternative to the feud to a necessary prerequisite for receiving the help of one's group in prosecuting it.[37]

Unsurprisingly, successful negotiations usually involved some form of compensatory payment. As repetition of this process taught the community what level of compensation would restore peace, "extraordinarily detailed schedules of tariffs ... for various injuries"[38] were established. Under the circumstances, requiring such payments constituted

---

[35] See Sir Frederick Pollock and Frederic William Maitland, *The History of English Law before the Time of Edward I*, 2d ed. (Cambridge: The University Press, 1898), 1:46.

[36] When the conflict was between members of households or tribes that did not participate in the same moot, the negotiations took place directly between the clans or tribes.

[37] Pollock and Maitland, *The History of English Law*, 46–47.

[38] Harold J. Berman, *Law and Revolution: The Formation of the Western Legal Tradition* (Cambridge, MA: Harvard University Press, 1983), 54.

a very sensible system. The threat of heavy financial burdens upon the wrongdoer and his kin is probably a more effective deterrent of crime than the threat of capital punishment or corporal mutilation . . . and at least equally as effective as the modern sanction of imprisonment; and it is surely less expensive for society. Moreover, in terms of retributive justice, not only is the wrongdoer made to suffer, but in addition—in contrast to today's more "civilized" penology—the victim is thereby made whole.[39]

The success of this method of securing peace caused it to spread throughout Britain (and all of Germanic Europe), with the result that "[t]he institution of fixed monetary sanctions payable by the kin of the wrongdoer to the kin of the victim was a prominent feature of the law of all the peoples of Europe prior to the twelfth century."[40]

The process of negotiating settlements of potentially violent conflicts and repeating and eventually institutionalizing successful resolutions gradually produced a broad body of customary law that served as the basis for the English common law. Having grown out of the resolution of actual conflicts by a process of trial and error, the rules that comprised this law were practical and remarkably subtle and nuanced. For example, no compensatory payment was due if one killed a thief, so long as one immediately publicized the killing[41]—a requirement apparently designed to prevent people from manufacturing evidence of a theft after the fact to legitimize murder. Further, actions that subjected others to humiliation, such as "binding a free man, or shaving his head in derision, or shaving off his beard,"[42] demanded larger compensatory payments than any but the most serious injuries. Why? Apparently because these were precisely the types of actions most likely to evoke a violent response and most in need of discouragement if peace were to be preserved.

By establishing a schedule of payments associated with various types of actions that damaged the interests of others, customary law (which was not distinguished from morality) established the obligations members of the community owed to their fellows. In doing so, it also established the restrictions on the behavior of their fellows that members of the community were entitled to enforce. That is, it established rights. These included, of course, rights not to be murdered, maimed, or physically assaulted that protected one's physical integrity. But they also included a right to be free of certain types of assaults on one's honor that protected one's psychic integrity, a right to the "peace" of one's home that gave one dominion over one's home and special protection against its invasion, and a

---

[39] Ibid., 55.
[40] Ibid.
[41] Pollock and Maitland, *The History of English Law*, 53.
[42] Ibid.

right to the enjoyment of possessions such as cattle when purchased before the proper number of witnesses or land when held by "folk-right."[43] In short, customary law established a set of personal rights that facilitated a peaceful existence in the society of others.

A second useful example, although not a territorial one, is supplied by the Law Merchant in medieval Europe. With the revival of long-distance trade in Europe during the eleventh and twelfth centuries, merchants found themselves conducting business across cultural and political boundaries. As foreigners, however, international merchants were vulnerable to expropriation by hostile local merchants and officials. In addition, linguistic and cultural differences, the need to transact business through third-party agents, and the plurality of local customs "gave rise to hostility toward foreign customs and ... ultimately led to mercantile confrontations"[44] for which there was no antecedently established method of resolution. Thus, *in their capacity as merchants*, medieval traders found themselves without civil government to provide security and resolve conflicts, a reasonable analog for the state of nature.

What happened? Local merchants wanted the benefits that could be reaped from long-distance trade, but foreign merchants would trade with them only if they had an assurance that their goods would not be expropriated and that they would be treated fairly. Accordingly, merchants sought arrangements that provided the needed assurance. Many such arrangements were tried. Those that worked best were widely copied and eventually institutionalized in the Law Merchant.

> The most viable mercantile practices were enforced in the Law Merchant so that local practices were undermined where they diverged from the Law Merchant. . . . Established custom lay at the foundation of the Law Merchant. The universal system of law thus sought out those customs which were "constant," those practices which were "established" and, in particular, those habits which were capable of sustaining a high level of commerce to the satisfaction of merchants, consumers and rulers alike.[45]

As a result, "[i]n twelfth-century Europe the transnational character of the law merchant was an important protection against the disabilities of aliens under local laws as well as against other vagaries of local laws and customs."[46]

---

[43] Ibid., 58–62.
[44] Leon E. Trakman, *The Law Merchant: The Evolution of Commercial Law* (Littleton, CO: F. B. Rothman, 1983), 11.
[45] Ibid.
[46] Berman, *Law and Revolution*, 342.

Medieval merchants also lacked an established system for resolving the disputes that arose among them. The court systems of the various nations and localities were not viable forums for mercantile disputes because they lacked expertise with regard to trade practices and worked too slowly for merchants who could not remain long in one place. In response, merchants began settling disputes among themselves on the basis of informal proceedings and highly streamlined decision-making procedures. To the extent that these procedures produced successful and rapid resolutions of mercantile disputes, they became regularized. The merchant courts that evolved in this way eventually grew into a European system of commercial courts in which merchant judges quickly applied the tenets of the Law Merchant to resolve commercial disputes.[47]

The process of applying the principles of the Law Merchant in these courts to resolve the actual disputes that arose among merchants established an extremely sophisticated body of customary commercial law that "supplied a great many if not most of the structural elements of the modern system of commercial law."[48] This law facilitated the creation of bills of exchange and promissory notes and recognized their negotiability, invented the chattel mortgage and other security interests, supported the development of deposit banking and bankruptcy law, and established the limited liability joint venture.[49] In doing so, the Law Merchant established the obligations that those engaged in commerce owed to each other, and hence the rights that each enjoyed as a participant in commerce. Thus, good-faith purchasers of goods gained the rights of holders in due course and the right to rely on an implied warranty of fitness and merchantability; creditors gained the preferential right to collect property on which they held a security interest; and entrepreneurs gained the right to enjoy limited liability in joint ventures and the protection of trademarks.[50] In short, in the absence of a European civil government, the inconveniences of the "mercantile state of nature" forced merchants to address the problems of security and dispute resolution themselves. The trial and error process by which they did so produced the Law Merchant and the system of merchant courts that eventually established a set of commercial rights that facilitated peaceful exchange and the flow of commerce.

Examples of situations in which civil government is entirely lacking will necessarily be rare. Evidence of how human beings behave in the absence of government is not limited to such examples, however, but may also be drawn from situations in which existing governments fail to act.

---

[47] See Trakman, *The Law Merchant*, 12–17. For a good synopsis of the development of the Law Merchant and merchant courts, see also Bruce L. Benson, *The Enterprise of Law: Justice without the State* (San Francisco, CA: Pacific Research Institute for Public Policy, 1990), 30–35.

[48] Berman, *Law and Revolution*, 350.

[49] Ibid., 349–50.

[50] Ibid.

My final two supporting examples will be of this type: one is drawn from the English common law and the other from the experience of sea horse fishermen in the Philippines.

In my opinion, the English system of common law offers valuable analogical evidence of how rights evolve in the state of nature, for although the English government provided a forum for resolving interpersonal disputes in its common law courts, until fairly recently it neither directly resolved the disputes nor provided substantive rules for doing so. Instead, the fundamental rules of social order were left to evolve out of the resolution of actual disputes in ways that seemed fair to the ordinary members of the community who served as jurors. And the rules that actually evolved through this process produced the much-vaunted "rights of Englishmen."[51]

Consider, for example, the common law of assault and battery. In modern terms, the law of battery forbids one from intentionally making "harmful or offensive contact" with another. This prohibits not only direct blows, but snatching a plate out of someone's hand or blowing smoke in his or her face. The law of assault forbids one from intentionally causing another to fear he or she is about to be battered, but it does not prohibit attempts at battery of which the victim is unaware or threats to batter someone in the future. These rules invest individuals with a fairly strong set of personal rights. They establish the right to be free not only from physically harmful contact, but from all offensive physical contact, as well as from fear that such contact will be immediately forthcoming. What accounts for this high level of protection for individuals' bodily and psychic integrity?

In earlier centuries, one of the most urgent social needs was to reduce the level of violence in society. This meant discouraging people from taking the kinds of actions that were likely to provoke an immediate violent response. Quite naturally, then, when suits arising out of violent clashes were litigated, juries tended to hold parties who had taken such actions liable. But what types of actions were these? Obviously, direct physical attacks on one's person were included, but affronts to one's dignity or other attacks on one's honor were equally if not more likely to provoke violence. Hence, the law of battery evolved to forbid not merely harmful contacts, but offensive ones as well. Furthermore, an attack that failed was just as likely to provoke violence as one that succeeded, and thus gave rise to liability. But if the intended victim was not aware of the attack, it could not provoke a violent response, and if the threat was not

---

[51] The advent of the English common law is usually dated to the reign of Henry II (1154–89), who provided a nascent form of trial by jury in royal courts. See Theodore F. T. Plucknett, *A Concise History of the Common Law*, 5th ed. (Boston, MA: Little, Brown, 1956), 19. The common law evolution of the rules of private law continued with relatively little interference from the political organs of the English government until well into the nineteenth century.

immediate, the threatened party had time to escape, enlist the aid of others, or otherwise respond in a nonviolent manner. Hence, the law of assault evolved to forbid only threats of immediate battery of which the target was aware.

In the absence of direct government intervention, people faced the problem of how to reduce public violence. They dealt with this problem in the entirely natural manner of holding those who took actions likely to provoke violence responsible for the injuries that resulted. As more and more cases were decided on this basis, people came to expect that future cases would be as well and adjusted their behavior to that expectation. Over time, these repeated decisions coalesced into the rules specifying what constitutes assault and battery. These rules define individuals' obligations to respect others' personal integrity, and hence their rights to be free from unwanted physical intrusions and threats. The strong personal rights protected by the law of assault and battery are the solution to the past problem of excessive social violence.

Finally, consider the modern example of the Philippine sea horse fishermen.[52] In one of the most impoverished regions of the Philippine Islands, the population survives by harvesting sea horses for export to Hong Kong and the Chinese mainland, where sea horses are prized for their supposed medicinal and aphrodisiacal properties. For most of the region's population, the sale of sea horses constitutes the only source of income beyond subsistence fishing. Until recently, the waters in this area were open to all and the fishermen simply went out and harvested as many sea horses as they could. By the mid-1990s, the population of sea horses in these waters was rapidly declining. One reason for this was the harvesting of pregnant sea horses, each of whom carried large numbers of young, before they could give birth. No fisherman was willing to forgo harvesting pregnant sea horses because doing so merely meant that another fisherman would take the sea horse and the first would have relinquished an immediate benefit for no resulting gain. The Philippine government had virtually no presence in this impoverished region and took no action to solve the fishermen's problem.

Sea horse fishermen in the village of Handumon were shown by a marine biologist how to construct netting with mesh small enough to contain adult sea horses, but large enough to allow newly born fish to escape. Armed with this knowledge, Handumon fishermen built their

---

[52] This example is taken from the PBS science show *Nova*, "The Kingdom of the Seahorse," broadcast on April 15, 1997. There is a large body of scholarly literature exploring how property rights evolve in the absence of government that, due to limitations of space, cannot be reviewed here. A good starting point for such a review is Harold Demsetz, "Toward a Theory of Property Rights," *American Economic Review* 57, no. 2 (Papers and Proceedings, 1967): 347–59. In addition, David Schmidtz provides a useful overview of some of the work in this field in David Schmidtz, "The Institution of Property," *Social Philosophy and Policy* 11, no. 2 (1994): 42–62, and recently, an entire issue of the *Journal of Legal Studies* has been devoted to the subject. See *Journal of Legal Studies* 31, part 2 (2002).

own floating cages in which they placed the pregnant sea horses that they found. They then allowed the sea horses to give birth before removing them from the water for sale. They also agreed to place a portion of the reef near their village off-limits to all fishing in an attempt to increase the sea horse population. These practices were successful at increasing the sea horse population, but as a result, fishermen from surrounding islands and villages began to "poach" sea horses from the waters around Handumon. In response, the Handumon villagers began patrolling these waters to keep the poachers out. Eventually, fishermen from surrounding areas came to Handumon to learn what the villagers were doing and copied their techniques. As a result, the sea horse population of the entire region is recovering.

In the absence of governmental action, the fishermen of the Philippines had to address the problem of the declining sea horse population themselves. The villagers of Handumon developed fishing practices and security arrangements that reversed the decline. The villagers' success stimulated others to inquire into their practices and copy them, thereby transforming them into widespread practices. These practices imposed new obligations on Philippine fishermen to respect each other's cages, to refrain from fishing in the preserve, and to participate in or support the security arrangements. Looked at from the fishermen's point of view, these obligations gave them property rights to the contents of their personal cages and to fish within the patrolled waters. The rights of the Philippine sea horse fishermen are the solution to the problem of the declining sea horse population.

These examples are offered as a temporary stand-in for more rigorous empirical evidence demonstrating that human beings in the state of nature act in ways that ultimately produce individual entitlements. What I am calling "empirical natural rights" are rights that evolve as a by-product of human efforts to address the inconveniences of the state of nature. Empirical natural rights are the solutions to the problems the state of nature presents.

B. The character of empirical natural rights

Are the rights I have labeled "empirical natural rights" truly natural rights? Traditionally, natural rights have consisted in moral entitlements that human beings possess simply by virtue of their humanity; rights that spring directly from human nature or fundamental principles of morality. Such rights are inherent in, not created by, human beings, and require no human interaction for their existence. The rights I have described clearly do not fit this model. They are not inherent in human beings and do not spring from human nature or fundamental moral principles. They are certainly not "natural" in the sense of not having been created by human action. Although not consciously created by any human mind, they depend on human interaction for their existence. Thus, although they are "the result of human action, but not the execution of any human design,"[53] they are indeed the creation of human beings.

Empirical natural rights are natural only in the sense that they are the rights that naturally evolve in the state of nature. Nevertheless, I want to claim that this is sufficient for them to be regarded as true natural rights. In my opinion, the essential element of a natural right is its pre-political character. Along with Simmons, I would argue that to qualify as a natural right, a right need only be one that "could be possessed independently of (and logically prior to) civil society, whose binding force is non-conventional"[54]—that is, one that has "natural grounds and could be possessed in the state of nature."[55] Empirical natural rights clearly meet this test. By definition, they are rights that human beings possess in the state of nature and that predate the formation of civil government. They depend on no conscious human convention (such as a social contract), but merely on the empirical fact (i.e., the natural ground) that human beings tend to act to relieve discomfort. A conception of rights as solved problems depends only upon a conception of human beings as natural problem-solvers.

Although empirical natural rights are true natural rights, they are quite different in character from traditional natural rights. Empirical natural rights are more flexible, more mutable, and less philosophically perfect entities than the rights usually advanced by natural rights theorists. Because traditional natural rights are logically derived from inherent features of human nature or fundamental principles of morality, they are typically seen as vesting individuals with conceptually complete, timeless moral entitlements. For example, the natural right to property is traditionally depicted as the right to the exclusive use and control of an object. In contrast, because empirical natural rights arise out of the uncoordinated efforts of human beings to resolve the problems they encounter in the state of nature, these rights rarely consist in such philosophically elegant entities. The empirical natural right to property can only be described in extremely inelegant terms as the right to a great amount of use and control of an object most of the time, with exclusive use and control at some times and no use or control at others.

If the natural right to property derives from one's moral entitlement to one's own person, as Locke would have it (*STG* §27), or from the Kantian injunction to treat all human beings as ends in themselves, as Nozick would have it (*ASU,* 30–31), then it is perfectly logical to see the right to property as consisting in the exclusive use and control of objects. Because

---

[53] Adam Ferguson, *An Essay on the History of Civil Society* (Edinburgh: Printed for A. Millar and T. Caddel in the Strand, London, and A. Kincaid and J. Bell, Edinburgh, 1767), part 3, § 2.
[54] Simmons, *The Lockean Theory of Rights,* 90.
[55] Ibid.

no one can have an ownership interest in another's person and no one is morally entitled to use another merely as a means, there is no ground for seeing individuals as vested with less than full control over their property. In contrast, the empirical natural right to property evolved to help human beings solve the problems of life in the state of nature, the most urgent of which was the need to peacefully resolve conflicts that would otherwise lead to violence. As the burgeoning literature on the evolution of property rights makes clear,[56] the recognition of individual property rights in what would otherwise be a commonly held resource is, in most cases, an excellent mechanism for accomplishing this end. But not in all cases. Consider, for example, the situation in which one person acquires all the real property surrounding the home of another and then denies the homeowner permission to cross his or her land in an effort to force the homeowner to sell at an extortionately low price. In this case, a property right that invests the acquisitive party with the exclusive use and control of his or her property is a prescription not for peace, but for violence. Not surprisingly then, property rights evolved to prevent the employment of this tactic by automatically granting enclosed property owners an easement of necessity that allows them to cross others' property. Consider, also, cases of emergency in which one person's life may depend on the use of another's property, such as when the captain of a ship caught in a deadly storm lashes the ship to another's dock. Once again, because a right to exclusive use and control that allowed property owners to deny others what they need to save their lives would be a prescription for violent confrontation, property rights evolved to permit the use of others' property in emergencies (although compensation must be paid for any damage done). Thus, in contrast to the more philosophically pleasing conception of the traditional right to property, the empirical right is a highly flexible, exception-laden one that invests individuals with the exclusive use and control of objects only to the extent that doing so facilitates a more peaceful life in society.

The same contrast can be seen in the context of individuals' personal rights. If natural human equality invests all human beings with the equal right to be free from subjection to the "will or authority" of others, as Locke would have it (STG §54), or if respect for human beings as ends in themselves demands respect for their autonomy, as Nozick would have it, then it is logical to see the natural right to liberty as consisting in the ability to act free from the direct application of coercion or its threat. In contrast, the empirical personal rights that actually evolved are both less and more extensive. As noted in the discussion of assault and battery, these rights are less extensive because they protect individuals not against the threat of coercion *per se*, but only against the threat of its *immediate* application. Yet they are more extensive because they protect individuals

---

[56] See, e.g., the journals cited in note 52 above.

against not only coercion, but also offense. The contours of these rights were determined not theoretically, but by what was necessary to reduce social violence to generally acceptable levels. Protection against the threat of future coercion was not necessary to achieve this end, so the rights did not include such protection. Protection against serious affronts to dignity was, so they did. Thus, whereas the traditional conception of the right to liberty consists in a conceptually neat sphere of protection against interference with one's activities, the empirical right to liberty consists in an oddly shaped, indented, and bulging bubble of personal protection that corresponds to precisely the amount of freedom necessary to solve the problem of excessive social violence.

Individual empirical natural rights, then, are theoretically imperfect, exception-laden, fuzzy-edged entities. Yet, taken together, they form a remarkably good approximation of Lockean natural rights. This is not coincidence, but is due to the empirical fact that Locke's set of broad negative rights to life, liberty, and property consists in precisely those rights that are most likely to produce peaceful relationships among human beings in the absence of civil government.[57]

Consider the right to life. Murder, as the least compensable of all injuries, calls forth the strongest desire for revenge and is more likely than anything else to provoke a violent response. The first priority of any community wishing to live in peace must be to discourage such intentional killings. As a result, the security arrangements that evolve invariably reserve their strongest disincentives for unjustified intentional killings. As these security arrangements give rise to patterns of behavior that become institutionalized into rules, the rules reflect the relatively greater seriousness of murder in comparison to other wrongs. Thus, the rules institutionalize a special level of protection for individuals against having their lives taken, a level of protection that is significant enough to cause the taking of life to be viewed as different in kind from other wrongs. In other words, the rules provide individuals with a distinct, especially important entitlement not to be unjustly killed by others—a right to life—that is identical to Locke's.

Next, consider the right to liberty. Besides murder, there are many other actions that provoke violent responses. Physical attacks on one's person or the immediate threat of such an attack will do so, as will physical restraints on one's freedom of movement and certain types of serious affronts to one's dignity. As a result, people in the state of nature establish security arrangements that discourage these actions and that eventually evolve into rules prohibiting assault, battery, and false imprisonment. Generally speaking, individuals respond violently only when others inter-

---

[57] Indeed, it is not unreasonable to view Locke and later natural rights theorists as providing a *post hoc* philosophical justification for a set of rights that had actually evolved, and in doing so, smoothing out their philosophically rough edges.

fere with the pursuit of their goals and desires in ways they cannot reasonably avoid. Otherwise, they nonviolently sidestep the interference. But unavoidable interferences are virtually always coercive ones. As a result, the rules that evolve in the state of nature are those that suppress coercion. When the rules prohibiting assault, battery, false imprisonment, and other forms of coercive interaction are taken together and viewed from the perspective of the individual member of the community, they look very much like a general right to be free from coercive interference with one's activities—that is, like a broad negative right to liberty. Although, as noted above, this empirical natural right is not identical to Locke's right to liberty, it does constitute a remarkably close approximation of it.

Now consider the right to property. Murder and the use of force against one's person are not the only actions that provoke violence. Depriving one of his or her possessions or attempting to do so will also elicit a violent response. In addition, violence frequently erupts when different people try to use objects held in common in incompatible ways. As a result, the security arrangements that people in the state of nature devise discourage the forcible dispossession of goods. As people conform their behavior to the incentives of these arrangements, rules evolve that protect possession and eventually give rise to a right of continued possession. Simultaneously, the members of the community search for peaceful resolutions to the disputes that arise over the use of common goods. As successful resolutions are found and repeated, rules governing the use of physical (and intangible) objects emerge. These rules specify procedures by which individuals can acquire control over an object and the extent to which they may exclude others from its use. As a matter of empirical fact, violent conflicts are usually best avoided by allowing those in proper possession of an object to exclude others from using it in most ways most of the time. Therefore, the rules that evolve tend to invest those in possession of an object with almost exclusive control over it.[58] However, because some ways of using objects and some forms of exclusion provoke rather than allay conflict, the rules do not permit those uses or those forms of exclusion. When taken together, the rules that protect possession, that prescribe the procedures by which individuals may acquire possession of objects, and that specify the ways in which those in proper possession may exclude others from using the objects create a set of individual entitlements that look very much like a negative right to private property. As previously noted, this empirical right to property is not

---

[58] But note that these rules do not result in everything being privately held. In certain cases, holding property in common does not produce conflict and may even facilitate peaceful interaction. This may be the case for roads and waterways that aid in commerce. See Carol Rose, "The Comedy of the Commons," in Carol Rose, *Property and Persuasion: Essays on the History, Theory, and Rhetoric of Ownership* (Boulder, CO: Westview Press, 1994), 105–62. Where there is no conflict, there are no resolutions, and hence no rules evolve that restrict the use of the commons.

a perfect match for Locke's right to property, but because the limitations on individuals' control over objects are relatively minor and infrequent, it is a reasonably close approximation of it.

Finally, note that there are no positive empirical rights. There is, of course, no reason why there cannot be. It is logically possible that people in the state of nature would respond to the insecurities and inconveniences of their condition in ways that produced rules imposing uncompensated obligations on individuals to supply others with particular goods or services. But, as a matter of fact, they do not.

Once practices that reduce the threat of violence to manageable levels have evolved, people in the state of nature may then confront the problems posed by the lack of assurance that they will have enough to eat, or will receive medical treatment when needed, or will obtain an education. They may try many different ways to address these problems. The evidence suggests that the arrangements that are most effective in doing so, and hence are repeated and become institutionalized, are those that involve reciprocal obligations to participate in mutual assurance schemes. That is, people agree to contribute their labor or some of their resources to a pool in return for the right to draw upon the pool when needed. In essence, people in the state of nature create self-insurance mechanisms.[59]

I suspect that the reason positive rights do not evolve in the state of nature is that they tend to give rise to rather than resolve interpersonal conflicts. The fundamental problem faced by people in the state of nature is to align individuals' incentives so that they pursue their personal interests in ways that facilitate rather than impede others in the pursuit of their interests. Eliminating the use of violence toward others as a means of pursuing one's interests is a major step in this direction. In contrast, imposing obligations on individuals to provide others with goods or services without compensation places the interests of individuals in con-

---

[59] And, of course, they encourage purely charitable activities on the basis of religious or cultural beliefs about what God requires or what will make one a good person.

A good source of analogical evidence of how people address these problems when government does not do so for them is historical research into the practices of Jewish communities in Christian Europe, immigrant communities in northern cities of the United States in the nineteenth and early twentieth centuries, and black communities in the southern United States during the segregation era. Although these groups existed within states with civil governments and thus were not, strictly speaking, in a state of nature, they were cut off from governmental provision of any welfare services and, as a result, were in a virtual state of nature with regard to such services. (Given the ubiquity of government in the modern world, isolated enclaves within modern states that are denied governmental services are perhaps the best modern proxies for the state of nature. Such enclaves supply real-world situations that allow empirical observation of how people behave in the absence of civil government.) David T. Beito, in his *From Mutual Aid to the Welfare State: Fraternal Societies and Social Services, 1890–1967* (Chapel Hill: University of North Carolina Press, 2000), demonstrates how the latter two groups were able to supply such services as poor relief, unemployment compensation, health care, old age annuities, and burial insurance through voluntary mutual assurance arrangements. See also Charles Murray, *In Pursuit of Happiness and Good Government* (San Francisco, CA: ICS Press, 1994), chap. 12.

flict. To the extent that individuals are required to serve others' interests, they are not free to serve their own. If individuals are required to give others some of their property or to labor for others without compensation, then they are in the position of those subject to forcible dispossession or coercive restrictions on their freedom of movement. As we have seen, these are situations that tend to provoke rather than resolve conflicts. Voluntary mutual assurance schemes in which everyone who participates receives a personal benefit do a much better job of aligning incentives, and hence would be selected for in the trial and error process by which people in the state of nature solve problems.

The absence of the evolution of positive rights in the state of nature can be usefully illustrated by the fact that no duty to rescue someone in danger ever evolved in either the customary or common law of England. Such a duty would create the fairly minimal positive right to the efforts of others to save one from danger when feasible. If any positive rights were to evolve, this would surely be one of the most likely candidates. The fact that it did not may be due to purely practical difficulties such as the inability to determine the level of risk a rescuer should be required to run, to judge whether a rescue would have succeeded, or to calculate what one person owes another for failing to save the other from a danger that the former did not create. But it may also be that holding individuals liable for failing to incur personal risks to render aid to others is simply a poor way of resolving disputes and promoting social peace. Indeed, it seems more like a recipe for drawing third parties into dangerous conflicts than for discouraging such conflicts. Whatever the reason, however, even this fairly minimal positive right failed to evolve.

In sum, then, empirical natural rights are true natural rights that evolve out of human interaction in the state of nature. They are theoretically imperfect, exception-laden entities that are the by-product of the efforts of human beings to learn how to live together peacefully in the absence of civil government. And yet, when taken together, they form a set of rights that corresponds fairly closely to Locke's negative rights to life, liberty, and property without also including any positive rights to fundamental goods or services. When we recall that the challenge that neither Locke nor Nozick could meet was to establish not only that natural rights exist, but that they consist in all and only the Lockean rights to life, liberty, and property, empirical natural rights begin to look like potentially useful philosophical entities.

C. The normative status of empirical natural rights

I have argued that empirical natural rights exist and form a fairly good approximation of the Lockean rights to life, liberty, and property. As yet, however, I have said nothing about why they are entitled to any respect. Empirical natural rights are merely the rights that evolve in the state of

nature. But the fact that they evolve is, in itself, without normative significance.[60] To argue from their mere existence to the conclusion that
individuals are morally entitled to have them respected would be to run
afoul of Hume's injunction against deriving normative conclusions from
purely empirical premises. What, then, is the normative basis for empirical natural rights?

I can offer no argument that empirical natural rights have any intrinsic
moral value. I cannot demonstrate that they capture any principles of
justice or embody any moral principles. I certainly cannot claim to know
which underlying moral theory is correct, or even whether to take a
deontological, consequentialist, or Aristotelian approach to ethics. I can,
however, argue that empirical natural rights have instrumental moral
value regardless of which moral theory and general approach to ethics
one adopts. This is because empirical natural rights facilitate peaceful
human interaction and peace is an important, if not preeminent, moral
value in virtually all moral theories.

To make this point, I would like to offer an analogue of the Rawlsian
concept of a "primary good" that might be called a "primary value."
Rawls defines primary goods as "things that every rational man is presumed to want [because t]hese goods normally have a use whatever a
person's rational plan of life."[61] Primary goods have universal instrumental value because "whatever one's system of ends, primary goods are
necessary means."[62] Thus, goods such as health, intelligence, liberty, and
wealth are all primary goods. Analogously, I would define a primary
value as something that every moral theory regards as valuable because
it normally advances the realization of the ultimate end of the (consequentialist or Aristotelian) theory or is entailed by the fundamental principles of the (deontological) theory. Primary values have universal
instrumental moral value because whatever a moral theory's ultimate
goals or requirements, primary values are means to their fulfillment.

Peace, I would argue, is a primary value. Whatever the end (or ends) of
a consequentialist moral theory, peace makes its realization more likely.
Whether the theory requires the maximization of one or the optimal
increase in each of many human goods such as pleasure, happiness, the
satisfaction of rational desires, social wealth, knowledge, friendship, etc.,
peace is a necessary prerequisite to the achievement of the theory's goal.
Further, whatever an Aristotelian moral theorist may mean by human
flourishing, a peaceful social environment is necessary for its realization.
It is much more difficult for one to live well or reach one's potential when

---

[60] This is the cost of adopting a purely empirical definition of the state of nature. See the
beginning of subsection III A. By rejecting a normative definition of the state of nature of the
type employed by Locke and Nozick, I have forgone the opportunity to claim any normative
significance for results of human behavior within it.
[61] John Rawls, *A Theory of Justice* (Cambridge, MA: Harvard University Press, 1971), 62.
[62] Ibid., 93.

surrounded by strife. Finally, it is difficult to imagine a deontological moral standard that does not either explicitly prescribe peaceful behavior or implicitly require a peaceful environment in order for human beings to behave as it prescribes.

Peace, then, is morally valuable because it is a prerequisite for or facilitates the realization of all other moral values. Empirical natural rights are rights that exist precisely because they facilitate peaceful interaction among human beings. Hence, empirical natural rights are entitled to respect because they are instrumental in promoting the primary value of peace. They are entitled to respect not merely because they *evolve* in the state of nature, but because they *are productive of peace* in the state of nature. Therefore, empirical natural rights have genuine, if instrumental, moral value.

D. The philosophical value of empirical natural rights

In Section II, I argued that the weakness of natural rights political philosophy lies not in its derivation of limited government from the existence of Lockean natural rights, but in its inability to supply a firm normative foundation for Lockean natural rights. I now want to suggest that empirical natural rights can supply such a foundation.

Let me begin by reviewing the essential role that natural rights play in political philosophy. Natural rights serve as a basis on which to determine whether political authority is morally justified. To be morally legitimate, political authority must come into existence in ways that are consistent with the natural rights of those subject to it. To retain its legitimacy, political authority must not be exercised in ways that violate those natural rights. Thus, the essential philosophical purpose of natural rights is to serve as a ground upon which to morally evaluate both the existence and the actions of civil government. To serve this purpose, natural rights must be morally well-grounded entities whose existence in no way depends upon civil government. That is, natural rights must be morally legitimate, logically pre-political entities; they must be rights that can exist in the state of nature.

As previously discussed, empirical natural rights are neither direct grants from God, logically deducible from inherent features of human nature, nor directly entailed by fundamental moral principles. Further, they are artificial entities in the sense that they are the creation of human action. They are natural only in the sense that they naturally evolve in the state of nature and are logically independent of the existence of civil government. Yet, if they are normatively well grounded, this is all that is required for them to perform philosophically as natural rights; for as long as they supply a ground outside of the political realm on which to base evaluative judgments about political arrangements, a sort of normative Archimedean point from which to move the political world, they need possess no particular ontological, metaphysical, or normative pedigree to function as true natural rights.

Further, empirical natural rights are normatively well grounded. They exist only because they have been proven to facilitate peaceful social relationships among human beings. Empirical natural rights are, by their nature, productive of peace. And peace is a primary value, one that is morally valuable, if not in itself, then instrumentally because it facilitates the realization of virtually all other moral values. Empirical natural rights help produce the good or help ensure that human beings act rightly regardless of how the good and the right are defined. They therefore possess genuine moral value.

Finally, when taken together, empirical natural rights comprise a set of rights that corresponds closely, although not perfectly, to Locke's negative rights to life, liberty, and property. Because murder, coercive interference with others' persons and freedom of movement, forcible dispossession of goods, and conflicts over the use of resources are the activities most likely to produce violence in the state of nature, these are the activities that people in the state of nature most urgently seek to discourage. Hence, the rules that evolve out of these efforts vest individuals with rights that protect their lives, persons, freedom, and goods against invasion by others. These rights may be conveniently and reasonably grouped together under the rubric of the rights to life, liberty, and property to produce a set of rights almost as extensive as Locke's. However, because giving some people claims over the labor or possessions of others tends to promote rather than reduce interpersonal conflict, no positive rights evolve. As a result, empirical natural rights consist in almost everything that constitutes Lockean rights and nothing else.

Once natural rights theorists such as Locke and Nozick complete their demonstrations that Lockean natural rights entail that only limited government can be morally justified, they face the skeptical question of why one should believe that Lockean natural rights and only Lockean natural rights exist and should be respected. The philosophical value of the concept of empirical natural rights is that it can supply an answer to this question: Lockean natural rights and only Lockean natural rights exist because Lockean rights and only Lockean rights evolve in the state of nature. And Lockean natural rights should be respected because doing so promotes social peace, which is necessary to realize any and all other moral values.

The fact that (Lockean) empirical natural rights exist and are normatively well grounded tells us nothing, in itself, about the contours of a morally justified civil government. Those contours are determined by the method by which individuals delegate the power conferred by these rights to the government and the amount of power so delegated. Thus, empirical natural rights will not by themselves settle any of the substantive questions concerning the morally proper extent of government power.

They will, however, get the natural rights project off the ground by providing the normative grounding for natural rights that Locke and Nozick could not.

Grounding one's argument for limited government on empirical rather than traditional natural rights has both advantages and disadvantages. The main advantage is the potentially greater persuasive force of arguments grounded on empirical natural rights. Because accepting the existence and normative force of empirical natural rights requires no prior theological, metaphysical, or normative commitments, arguments based on these rights can have a very broad appeal. One need not believe in the existence of God, or that certain substantive propositions are self-evident, or that human beings are essentially equal or essentially separate or have any essential non-socially-constructed nature at all to believe that empirical natural rights exist. One need only observe the behavior of people in the state of nature.[63] Therefore, arguments based on empirical natural rights should have the power to persuade not only those who do not subscribe to a Lockean or Nozickian theological or metaphysical position, but also those who do not engage in theological or metaphysical reflection at all. Answering the question of why one should believe that natural rights exist by pointing at the way the world works is a much more promising way of persuading those of primarily empirical intellectual orientation than is presenting a complex theological or metaphysical disquisition. Further, one need not subscribe to any particular moral theory to recognize the normative force of empirical natural rights. One need only appreciate that empirical natural rights are productive of peace and that peace is a primary value. Therefore, arguments based on empirical natural rights have the potential to persuade not only those who do not subscribe to Kantian moral theory, but all those who perceive the normative value of peace. Thus, empirical natural rights can allow natural rights–based arguments for limited government to avoid the metaphysical and normative cul-de-sacs in which they have become trapped in the past.

The main disadvantage of basing arguments for limited government on empirical natural rights is that the grounding is less certain than that aspired to by those who base their arguments on traditional natural rights. God's commands, the essential features of human nature, and the inviolability of individuals all represent morally fundamental considerations. If natural rights really derive from one of these sources, then they have an absolute moral force that is not subject to being overridden or abridged for the sake of other moral concerns. There really can be no stronger grounds upon which natural rights can rest. The normative force of empirical natural rights, in contrast, derives from their capacity to promote

---

[63] Or, more accurately, one need only review the available historical evidence of how people behaved when living either in societies without civil government or in situations in which extant governments did not provide basic security or welfare services.

social peace. But peace is an instrumental moral value and, as such, retains its value only so long as it promotes more ultimate moral values. This implies that empirical natural rights may be overridden or abridged when doing so would better promote such ultimate moral values. And this apparently opens the door to arguments that there are conditions under which civil government may legitimately abridge empirical natural rights.

I believe, however, that this does not constitute as serious a drawback as it may initially appear. In the first place, peace is a primary value. Therefore, although peace may possess only instrumental value, it is a particularly strong form of instrumental value. Because peace facilitates the realization of all other moral values, cases in which social peace must be sacrificed to attain a more ultimate moral value are exceptionally rare.[64] Indeed, it is difficult to imagine a situation in which sacrificing a peaceful social environment would truly help to realize a more significant moral end. This suggests that the conditions under which civil government would be justified in abridging an empirical natural right would be equally rare. But secondly and more significantly, there is, at present, no alternative to employing empirical natural rights. It would indeed be better to ground arguments for limited government on natural rights derived from morally fundamental values that cannot be overridden. As we saw in Section II, however, neither Locke nor Nozick was able to provide an effective argument demonstrating that Lockean natural rights can be derived from such values. This, of course, does not mean that such arguments may not be found, and, indeed, such arguments constitute the holy grail of natural rights theory. But while the quest for them continues, empirical natural rights represent the best available ground for natural rights–based arguments for limited government. The fact that arguments based on empirical natural rights cannot provide a guarantee that there are no situations in which one's natural rights can be legitimately overridden is no reason not to make such arguments, if empirical natural rights are the only well-grounded natural rights one has. I conclude, therefore, that the advantages of empirical natural rights outweigh their disadvantages sufficiently to render them a philosophically promising foundation for arguments for limited government.

IV. Conclusion

Shorn of all metaphysical and normative presuppositions and viewed from a purely empirical perspective, rights are solved problems. When

---

[64] This claim must be read in context. It is, of course, true that nations are often forced to go to war to realize values more important than maintaining international peace. But this is not the sense in which the term "peace" is being used at present. The peace protected by empirical natural rights is "social peace," i.e., the peace internal to a society that consists in the maintenance of nonviolent relationships among the members of a community.

human beings with their various and often incompatible personal interests live together in a world of scarcity, conflicts invariably arise. Given all that human beings have in common, certain types of conflicts regularly and widely recur. The discomfort and disruption these conflicts produce give rise to a widely shared desire to resolve or avoid them.

In a society with civil government, this desire frequently expresses itself in a call for action by government to address the problem. For example, in a society beset by racial antipathy, citizens may exert sufficient pressure to cause the government to enact a law prohibiting employers from making any employment-related decisions on the basis of race. Imposing such an obligation on employers simultaneously vests citizens with a right to be free from racial discrimination in the workplace. Thus, the right to be free from discrimination is the solution to the problem of widespread racial antipathy. In a society with civil government, rights are often the solutions to social problems *that are produced by politically effective forces.*

In the state of nature, there is no civil government for people to call on to resolve widely recurring conflicts for them. Hence, they must find ways to resolve such conflicts for themselves. They could do this through explicit collective action. The members of the community could meet together to create a set of rules to regulate their future behavior toward one another. They do not. Rather, they pursue many uncoordinated efforts to address the problems caused by the conflicts; they repeat successful resolutions and discard unsuccessful ones; and they observe, learn from, and copy the successful resolutions of others. In doing so, they create widespread practices to which the members of the community conform their behavior, practices that eventually evolve into rules imposing obligations on community members and, hence, simultaneously endowing them with rights. For example, the need to reduce public brawling causes members of the community to bring pressure on their fellows not to engage in the actions most likely to give rise to it. This evolves into the obligation to refrain from making harmful or offensive physical contact with others, which vests each member of the community with the right not to be battered. Thus, the right not to be battered is the solution to the problem of excessive public violence. In the state of nature, rights are the solutions to social problems—*solutions that have been proven by experience to produce a predominantly peaceful social environment.*

From a purely empirical standpoint, the difference between the rights one enjoys due to membership in a society with civil government and one's natural rights is the problem-solving mechanism employed in their creation. To the extent that societies with civil government employ the political process to resolve social problems, citizens' rights reflect, for good or ill, the dominant political influences within their society. In contrast, because people in the state of nature are forced to employ a trial and error process of learning through experience to resolve their social problems, their rights reflect the practical demands of maintaining life in society with others. Accordingly, what I have been calling empirical natural rights encapsulate the wisdom of centuries of human experience concerning how human beings can best live with each other in peace. Because a peaceful social environment is a prerequisite to the attainment of almost everything that makes life worthwhile, this is a wisdom that should not be lightly disregarded. I believe that it is also a good basis from which to make moral judgments about the quality of civil government and its actions. Accordingly, I offer empirical natural rights as an alternative foundation for the classical liberal arguments for limited government advanced by John Locke and Robert Nozick.

Law, George Mason University

HISTORY AND PATTERN*

By David Schmidtz

I. Introduction

The agenda for current philosophical work on justice was set in the 1970s by John Rawls and Robert Nozick. Nozick said, "Political philosophers now must either work within Rawls's theory or explain why not."[1] There is truth in Nozick's compliment, yet when it came to explaining why not, no one did more than Nozick.

Rawls spent the next three decades responding first to Nozick, then to a barrage of criticism from all directions. In part because of this, no short treatment can capture every nuance of Rawls's evolving theory.[2] However, Section II of this essay offers a brief overview of Rawls, and the next four sections reflect on several facets of Nozick's response. Section III explains why Nozick thinks patterned principles of justice are false, and what a historical alternative might look like. Section IV concerns Nozick's skepticism about the very idea that justice is essentially a distributive notion. Section V explains the difference between being arbitrary and being unjust. Nozick accepts Rawls's premise that the natural distribution of talent is arbitrary, but denies that there is any short step from this to a conclusion that the natural distribution is unjust. Section VI notes that Nozick also agrees with Rawls on the core idea of natural rights liberalism: namely, that we are separate persons. However, Rawls and Nozick interpret that idea in different ways—momentously different ways. The tension between their interpretations is among the forces shaping political philosophy to this day.

The remaining sections of this essay are more speculative. Section VII explains how Nozick's tale of the "experience machine" can be seen to

* For comments, I thank Alyssa Bernstein, Geoffrey Brennan, Jason Brennan, Tom Christiano, Andrew I. Cohen, Andrew Jason Cohen, Tyler Cowen, Teresa Donovan, David Estlund, Jerry Gaus, Allen Habib, Alex Kaufman, Mark LeBar, Loren Lomasky (especially Loren, for insight and inspiration over a period of many years), Cara Nine, Ellen Frankel Paul, Guido Pincione, Thomas Pogge, Dan Russell, Michael Smith, Horacio Spector, and Matt Zwolinski. I thank the Earhart Foundation for financial support in the fall of 2002 and Australian National University's Research School of Social Sciences for its wonderful hospitality during a ten week stay in 2002. The support of the folks at Liberty Fund in Indianapolis during the final stages of this project goes beyond anything I will ever be able properly to thank them for.

[1] Robert Nozick, *Anarchy, State, and Utopia* (New York: Basic Books, 1974), 183.
[2] A recent book on liberalism by Jon Mandle offers an "overview" of Rawls spanning 133 pages, indicating how hard it would be to summarize Rawls in a few paragraphs. Jon Mandle, *What's Left of Liberalism?* (Lanham, MD: Lexington Books, 2000).

illustrate a particular way, Rawls's way, of failing to be serious about the separateness of persons. Section VIII revisits the Rawlsian original position, asking how we would design the thought experiment if our objective were to articulate a genuinely procedural conception of justice. I conjecture that it might end up amounting to a prescription for Nozickian utopia.

II. RAWLS

A. An alternative to utilitarianism

According to Rawls, we should think of society as a cooperative venture for mutual advantage. Cooperation enables us all to flourish, but we each want a larger share of cooperation's fruits, so cooperation inevitably involves conflict. One way to resolve the conflict is to distribute the fruits so as to maximize overall utility. Yet this proposal fails to acknowledge that people entering into cooperative ventures are separate persons, contributing to those ventures in pursuit of their own legitimate hopes and dreams. Failing to respect their separate projects and separate contributions is unjust.[3] It may even be the paradigm of injustice.

Utilitarianism in its standard form treats character and talent as if they matter only insofar as they affect aggregate well-being. Rawls, though, says that, contra utilitarians, when one person's gain comes at another person's expense, we hardly begin to justify trade-offs merely by making sure winners win more than losers lose. To Rawls, justice is less like an outcome of utilitarian calculation and more like an outcome of a bargaining process in which bargainers have a right to walk away from any proposal they find unacceptable. Rational contractors, meeting to negotiate an institutional structure to govern their future interactions, will want a system that promises to be good for all—a system that sacrifices no one for the greater good.

Accordingly, Rawls asks us to imagine contractors meeting to arrange institutions that will distribute fruits of cooperation in a mutually agreeable way. And if we imagine contractors distributing fruits of cooperation, we may as well imagine contractors distributing inequalities. This is quite a shift on Rawls's part. There is no easy way to explain what would make the shift legitimate, but it occurs quietly over a span of fifteen pages in *A Theory of Justice* (1971). First, Rawls says that "persons are not indifferent as to how the greater benefits produced by their collaboration are distributed, for in order to pursue their ends they each prefer a larger share to a lesser share. A set of principles is required for choosing among

---

[3] How separate are persons, exactly? Does Rawls presume that individuals are self-contained Robinson Crusoes, as he is sometimes accused of doing by communitarians and feminists? See Andrew Jason Cohen, "Communitarianism, 'Social Constitution', and Autonomy," *Pacific Philosophical Quarterly* 80, no. 2 (1999): 121–35.

the various social arrangements which determine this division of advantages." [4] Here, "advantages" refers to benefits of collaboration. Four pages later, Rawls says that a concept of justice applies "whenever there is an *allotment* of something rationally regarded as advantageous or disadvantageous." [5] Not everything regarded as advantageous is a product of collaboration, though, so there is a problem in connecting this sense of advantage to the previous one. [6]

Finally, a few pages later, Rawls speaks of circumstances of justice as those where "none are known to be advantaged or disadvantaged by social and natural contingencies." [7] So, by the end of this discussion, advantages have become not fruits of cooperation in particular, or even goods more generally. They have become *competitive* advantages—the kind of thing we can contrast with disadvantages.

This shift puts Rawls in a position to ask what he wants to ask: Why should anyone have a competitive advantage? Suppose, then, that we treat advantages as if they were fruits of cooperation, and suppose also that we treat inequalities as if their existence requires our agreement. These suppositions imply a startling result: that unless we agree to permit inequalities and on how to distribute them, we have a right, as separate persons, to leave the table not with whatever advantages we brought to it, but with equal shares of the value of the group's pooled advantages.

B. Two principles

We now can say what Rawls is arguing for: the two principles that form the core of his theory of justice.

1. Each person affected by an institution is equally entitled to the most extensive sphere of liberty compatible with a like liberty for all.

[4] John Rawls, *A Theory of Justice* (Cambridge, MA: Belknap Press of Harvard University Press, 1971), 4.

[5] Ibid., 8 (emphasis added).

[6] In passing, what is an "allotment"? Does the sun have an allotment of planets, or are we reserving "allotment" to refer to (potentially blameworthy) allocation *decisions*? On the one hand, if we use the term's broader sense—allotment as simply the fact of how things are distributed—it becomes true that there is an allotment of advantages, just as there is an allotment of planets, but it becomes false that the concept of justice applies whenever there is an allotment. (It does not apply to the allotment of planets.) On the other hand, if we use the term's narrower sense—allotting as deliberately assigning—it becomes at least arguably true that the concept of justice applies, but then it becomes false that the natural lottery of talent is an allotment, and it is this natural lottery that Rawls wants his theory of justice to cover.

[7] Rawls, *A Theory of Justice*, 19. In passing, is it enough that none are *known* to be advantaged or disadvantaged? What if some of us have disadvantages none of us know about? Does not knowing about a disadvantage suffice to make it fair?

2. An inequality is allowed only if the institution that allows it thereby works to the greatest advantage of the least advantaged.[8]

There has been relatively little discussion of the first principle. Despite appearances, the principle does not call literally for a "most extensive system of liberty" but for a modest package of constitutional rights to free speech, to a fair trial, and so on.[9] We may think the principle should be interpreted more expansively, or we may question Rawls's stipulation that the first principle always takes priority over the second. (In a little-noticed passage, Rawls quietly retracts the idea that his first principle has lexical priority: "While it seems clear that, in general, a lexical order cannot be strictly correct, it may be an illuminating approximation under certain special though significant conditions.")[10] However, few reject the first principle as such. The controversy surrounds the second principle, not the first.

Rawls refers to the second principle as the "difference principle." What does this principle say? The intuitive idea is this. Contractors initially assume they are entitled to an equal share of the pie, but realize they can make the pie bigger by encouraging each other to work harder. They encourage each other by rewarding people who make the pie bigger: offering a larger share of the pie to those who do a larger share of the work. In effect, we allow inequalities when inequalities make us all better off. This leads to a precursor of the difference principle.

The precursor:

An inequality is allowed only if the institution allowing it thereby works to the advantage of everyone affected, that is, only if everyone receives more than what *would have been* an equal share in a more equal but less productive scheme.

Rawls went on to say that the precursor "is at best an incomplete principle for ordering distributions."[11] It says departures from equal shares must make everyone better off. However, "there are indefinitely many

---

[8] Ibid., 302. The full statement of the principle is: Social and economic inequalities are to be arranged so that they are (a) to the greatest advantage of the least advantaged, and (b) attached to offices and positions open to all under conditions of fair equality of opportunity. Part (a) is the notorious "difference principle."

[9] One frustrating thing about reading Rawls is that he systematically takes initially bold, clear, inspiring, unambiguous positions, then later reworks and retracts these statements so as to make them consistent with (or in technical terms, in reflective equilibrium with) his second principle.

[10] Rawls, *A Theory of Justice*, 45.

[11] John Rawls, "Distributive Justice," in *Philosophy, Politics, and Society*, ed. Peter Laslett and W. G. Runciman (Oxford: Blackwell, 1967), 58–82. Reprinted in John Rawls, *Collected Papers*, ed. Samuel Freeman (Cambridge, MA: Harvard University Press, 1999), 135. Page citations are to the latter.

ways in which all may be advantaged when the initial arrangement of equality is taken as a benchmark. How then are we to choose among these possibilities?"[12] A complete theory specifies how to divide the gains.

There are two ways of proceeding from here. First and most obviously, we may doubt we need a theory that is "complete" in this sense. All we need is a theory telling us what is unjust, and the precursor is complete enough for that. It rules out sacrificing some people for the general good. Therefore, it rules out arrangements that fail to respect the separateness of persons. Indeed, we may conclude we do not *want* a "complete" theory. When we ask what we want from a basic structure, we realize we *need* incompleteness. Rawls sketches four ways of completing a theory and says his difference principle is what self-interested bargainers would choose, but he never discusses the possibility that choosing among the four is not a theory's job, and indeed is not a basic structure's job. Perhaps any of the four, if freely chosen by people to be governed by it, would qualify as just.

A basic structure's job is to get a political community off the ground, enabling voters and legislators to define and refine their community's norms as they go. Communities whose basic structure evolves toward completion in ways that are good for everyone, as broadly specified by the precursor, will be just. The final sentence of Jon Mandle's summary of Rawls says that when "the design of the basic structure is at stake," citizens rely "on principles that all reasonable people can share."[13] Because the precursor is more open-ended than the difference principle, it is closer to being what reasonable people can be presumed to share, thereby getting a political community off the ground but deferring ongoing elaboration to voters and legislators. In any case, getting from the precursor to a full-blown difference principle is not easy. We easily can imagine the precursor being part of an overlapping consensus among real-world reasonable people. We cannot say the same of the difference principle.

Rawls sometimes says that all we do at the level of theory is pick a framework; societies work out details. This is the right thing to say. Basic structure is merely that; most of what makes a society liberal cannot be guaranteed by the basic structure but is instead in the hands of people and communities working out their own destinies within institutional structures.[14] In a thought experiment, I imagine *myself* picking something as specific as the difference principle, but if I ask what *everyone I know* could agree on, an honest answer will be more general, specifying that whatever we pick must be in everyone's interest, as much as possible. No

---

[12] Rawls, *A Theory of Justice*, 65.

[13] Mandle, *What's Left of Liberalism?* 151.

[14] See John Tomasi, *Liberalism Beyond Justice: Citizens, Society, and the Boundaries of Political Theory* (Princeton, NJ: Princeton University Press, 2001), for the most developed version of this idea.

matter how badly I personally wanted the principle to say more, it could not say more without being rejected.[15]

A second way to proceed, Rawls's way, is to assume that we need a complete theory. We then choose a way of completing the precursor. One way to complete the precursor would be to target one social position and maximize the prospects of persons in that position.[16] Which position should be so favored? One option is the position of those who otherwise are least favored—the group to which life has otherwise been least kind. Roughly, we make the smallest share as large as it can be. We thus arrive at the difference principle: an inequality is allowed only if the institution allowing it thereby works to the greatest advantage of the least advantaged.

Who is Rawls talking about when he speaks of the least advantaged? First, Rawls says the "least advantaged" refers not to the least advantaged person but to the least advantaged economic class. Second, the class is defined by wealth and income, not by any other demographic. In Rawls's theory, "least advantaged" refers in practice to typical representatives of the lowest income class, no more, no less.[17] Their natural and social disadvantages, and their needs, are not unusual but are instead stipulated to be "within the normal range."[18]

Why does Rawls use a term like "least advantaged" to refer to people who are not literally the least advantaged? Rawls takes a contractarian approach for a reason: justice is supposed to embody an ideal of reciprocity, unlike utilitarianism. "The first problem of justice concerns the relations among those who in the everyday course of things are full and active participants in society."[19] Rawls envisions a bargaining situation where there is no such thing as a class that other classes do not need. He says, "since everyone's well-being depends upon a scheme of cooperation without which no one could have a satisfactory life, the division of advantages should be such as to draw forth the willing cooperation of everyone

---

[15] Rawls acknowledges that we do not need a "complete" theory in the international arena. In fact, in that arena, we do not want a complete theory; we want instead to recognize that "peoples" have a right to self-determination. Interestingly, Rawls shows more willingness in the international arena to compromise liberties protected by the first principle than to compromise the economic protections of the difference principle. (The Rawlsian right to life that any minimally decent society has to respect includes a right to economic security.) See John Rawls, *The Law of Peoples* (Cambridge, MA: Harvard University Press, 1999), 65.

[16] When we are targeting one particular group as the group whose prospects are to be maximized, it will be hard to characterize the process or the result as an implication of any principle of reciprocity. Reciprocity is a two-way street, not aimed at any particular group, not even the group we think ought to be most favored. It would seem reasonable to give up on saying that this theory has anything to do with reciprocity, but Rawls always insisted there was a connection. For example, see John Rawls, *Justice as Fairness: A Restatement*, ed. Erin Kelly (Cambridge, MA: Harvard University Press, 2001), 123–24.

[17] Rawls, *Justice as Fairness: A Restatement*, 59 n. 26.

[18] Rawls, *A Theory of Justice*, rev. ed. (Cambridge, MA: Belknap Press of Harvard University Press, 1999), 83.

[19] Ibid., 84.

taking part in it, including those less well situated."[20] The less well situated, then, are contributors: they are least advantaged *workers*, not least
advantaged *people*. Thus, what Rawls calls least advantaged is the class
with the least amount of bargaining strength compatible with still having
a lot. The least advantaged, as Rawls defines the class, have a claim to a
share of the social product based not on their needs but on the fact that
they contribute to it.[21] The difference principle is meant to acknowledge
their contributions, not their needs.

C. Strains of commitment

But is the greatest advantage of the least advantaged the *only* result to
look for? Officially, the answer is yes. Taken at face value, the difference
principle says that if we can make the least advantaged better off in the
amount of one penny, justice requires us to do so even when the cost to
the more advantaged is a billion dollars. As Rawls admits, this "seems
extraordinary."[22] So, what does Rawls conclude?

He says, "The difference principle is not intended to apply to such
abstract possibilities."[23] Obviously, though, level of abstraction is not the
issue. And whether a principle applies does not depend on whether
Rawls intended it to apply. (Suppose Joe says, "There are no two-digit
prime numbers." Jane, well-trained in the art of the clever counterexample, asks, "What about eleven?" Joe responds, "The principle is not meant
to apply to such abstract possibilities.")

As it happens, Rawls is right about the principle not applying to such
possibilities, but for a different reason: namely, the principle applies not
to redistributive decisions case by case, but to the choice of society's basic
structure.

Rawls could have noted that he did not intend to impose excessive
"strains of commitment."[24] Principles must not ask so much as to make
it unrealistic to expect people to comply. Rawls mainly has in mind not
asking too much of the least advantaged, but as critics have noted, it is at
least as urgent that the system not ask too much of people whose productivity sustains the system. Pushing them so hard that they revolt, or
emigrate, would be bad for all, especially the least advantaged.

D. Indeterminacy

What Rawls calls the "veil of ignorance" is supposed to deprive bargainers of information that otherwise might lead them to seek an agree-

---

[20] Rawls, *A Theory of Justice* (1971), 15.
[21] See Cynthia A. Stark, "How to Include the Severely Disabled in a Contractarian Theory
of Justice" (unpublished manuscript, 2004).
[22] Rawls, *A Theory of Justice* (1971), 157.
[23] Ibid.
[24] Rawls, *Justice as Fairness: A Restatement*, 104.

ment biased in their favor. In particular, bargainers are supposed not to know what position they personally will occupy in the final distribution.[25] Rawls thinks bargaining behind a veil of ignorance is a fair procedure for picking a basic structure; moreover, if the *procedure for picking* is fair, the structure picked must be fair. Does this follow? No. We design legal procedures to be fair, but fair procedures do not guarantee just results; fair juries sometimes deliver wrong verdicts. Likewise, fair bargaining procedures may lead self-interested bargainers to select just principles, but there is no guarantee.

There are two related problems here. First, there is no obvious reason to expect the bargaining process to be so determinate as to reach the same conclusion every time we run the experiment. Second, even if the experiment did have a single, robustly replicable result, it is hard to see why the result would be guaranteed to track justice.[26] If we were to run the experiment with *real people,* we would have some basis for holding people to whatever they actually agree to—after all, they agreed—but in the real world, different groups would choose different principles.

Less obviously, a similar indeterminacy of result afflicts hypothetical procedures too. In particular, consider the veil of ignorance. If bargainers do not know what position they will occupy, that makes the original position fair, but (as Rawls was aware) what suffices to make the situation fair is not enough to ensure that bargainers will choose the difference principle. Hence, we make more assumptions: bargainers not only do not know what position they occupy; they also do not know what skills they possess, or what skills are prized in their society. They do not know what they personally believe about morality and justice, and so have no basis for choice other than their calculation of what is in their interest. They do not know what probabilities to attach to prospects of being at the bottom, so they have no basis for discounting improbable risks.

Rawls says that if bargainers had to complete the precursor, the difference principle is what they would choose. Why? In *Justice as Fairness: A Restatement* (2001), Rawls refers to bargainers being "directed" by a maximin rule (according to which one would seek to make the worst possible outcome as good as possible). But why? If bargainers are not pathologically risk-averse, why do they choose as if they were? Why are they "directed" by maximin? Rawls's answer: They are directed by maximin

---

[25] Do we really need veils of ignorance as devices for controlling bias? I shall suggest an answer to this question shortly below in the text.

[26] There are two ways to view the procedure. Bargainers are either *deciding* what is right or *discovering* an independent moral reality. If our bargainers are merely hypothetical, we had better be able to show that there is an independent moral reality *we* are tracking when *we* decide to imagine bargainers agreeing to one thing rather than another. Otherwise, all we are doing is putting our own prejudices in the mouths of imaginary friends. If real bargainers actually agree to live by a principle, then that is altogether different. In that case, they actually gave their word to each other, and if their word does not count for something, they will not be able to live good lives together.

because they do not care what they gain above the minimum, so long as they know that (1) the minimum that would be provided under a maximin rule would be "completely satisfactory," and (2) the minimums of societies under alternatives to maximin are significantly below that level and may be altogether intolerable.[27]

Bargainers also know they are choosing principles for a closed society. The only way to enter is to be born into it. The only way to exit is to die. The more assumptions we add, though, the worse the strains of commitment when we lift the veil and rejoin this world. Can a thought experiment give us reason, here and now, to use the difference principle to assess basic structures? For example, if society would have to be closed for the difference principle to be a rational choice, and if in fact we live in an open society, subject to "brain drains," then where does that leave the difference principle? Rawls says bargainers "should not reason from false premises. The veil of ignorance does not violate this idea, since an absence of information is not misinformation."[28] There are two points here. First, the veil not only *deprives* people of knowledge they would have in the real world; it *endows* them with knowledge—for example, of conditions (1) and (2)—that no real bargainer has. Second, some of that endowed information—for example, that society is closed—is indeed misinformation.

E. "Least advantaged" is not a rigid category

Still, there is much to like about Rawls's theory. One attraction (and one reason to see the difference principle as less tilted than it may appear) is that the position of "least advantaged" is fluid. If Jack originally is least advantaged, then a system that works well on his behalf eventually lifts Jack into a better position than Jane, in which case, the system turns its attention to doing what it can for Jane, until she is sufficiently well off to make it someone else's turn, and so on.

Is this fluidity real? Yes, or at least it would be real in a society satisfying Rawls's difference principle. When Karl Marx was writing in the midnineteenth century, Europe was divided into somewhat rigid social classes, defined by birth. (The proper way to greet someone from a higher class was to bow, not shake hands.) When Rawls began writing in the midtwentieth century, academics still spoke as if things had not changed. (Marxism was prominent in intellectual circles. Incredible though it may seem today, the Soviet Union was held up as a model of justice *and* efficiency.)

---

[27] Rawls, *Justice as Fairness: A Restatement*, 98. I argued in "Rationality within Reason," *Journal of Philosophy* 89, no. 9 (1992): 445–66, that satisficing choice is genuinely a form of rational choice. In my *Rational Choice and Moral Agency* (Princeton, NJ: Princeton University Press, 1995), I argued that this opens up possibilities for reconciling elements of rationality with elements of morality. However, I never envisioned defending a suboptimal political regime on the grounds that I would prefer it to intolerable alternatives.

[28] Rawls, *A Theory of Justice* (1971), 153.

Thus, *if* we lived in a rigid society where sons of manual workers were fated to be manual workers (and daughters were fated to be wives of manual workers), then what would work to their greatest advantage would be to set a minimum wage as high as it could be without pricing employers out of business. Now suppose that a worker has an alternative: a fluid society where manual work pays less than it might, but where his sons and daughters can go to college and be upwardly mobile. Does he stay or does he go?

People born wealthy tend to prefer the more rigid world with high minimum wages, a world where manual workers are comfortable, secure, and stay in their place. Manual workers often prefer something more fluid, for themselves and for their children. What if people born wealthy want something for poor people that differs from what poor people want for themselves? Should what poor people want out of life affect our thinking about what is to their advantage?

Many people say they find it surprising and ironic that Rawls was a child of the comfortable middle class, whereas Nozick grew up poor. Upon reflection, though, it is not so surprising. If you are poor, the rich are like sports heroes—fantasy figures admired from a distance. It is people born to middle-class comfort who are close enough to the rich to resent the latter's additional advantages, and far enough from the poor to have a Dickens-like image of what being poor is like. Nozick often is accused of defending the rich, but in his own mind what Nozick was defending was the legitimacy of a poor person's dream of a better life.

In any case, an interesting feature of the less rigid world is that higher income classes will consist substantially of people who once were (or whose parents were) manual workers themselves. Higher-income classes, accordingly, will consist substantially of people who are better off because they grew up in a world where classes were fluid, and thus the chance to move up was real. They will be better off precisely because they grew up in a world where people born poor—people like they once were—had a chance to move up.

In a vertically mobile society, there will be a big difference between unskilled workers who have what it takes to move up and unskilled workers who, for whatever reason, do not. But this is a big difference *only* in vertically mobile societies. Behind the veil of ignorance, we have not yet chosen to create that kind of society, so these subgroups have similar prospects until we decide otherwise. Behind the veil, we are *deciding* whether to foster a society where talented young people are not held back by accidents of gender or social class.

This fluidity was not what Rawls had in mind. Rawls was not envisioning a world where working-class Jack can acquire skills that will make him wealthy later on. But if that world is best for Jack, then Rawls is right: what works for Jack works for every class, because in that world higher-income classes will contain substantial numbers of people who started (or whose parents started) as Jack did and made the most of the opportunity. If income mobility *is* to the benefit of younger people who earn less, then it *was* to the benefit of older people who once earned minimum wages themselves, then moved up.

In the end, there also is something to say on behalf of Rawls's insistence that we talk about classes, not individuals. There is a cliché: a rising tide lifts all boats. This cliché, as Rawls could see, is not literally true, but good societies make it roughly true. Realistically, the tide will never benefit literally every person, but good institutions can and in fact do make it true that the rising tide lifts all income *classes*. Even the least advantaged class will share in the tide of health benefits (life expectancy, safe water, immunizations, etc.) and wealth benefits (electric power, shoes, etc.) created by cooperation. If all goes well—that is, if Rawls's difference principle (or at least his precursor) is satisfied—then whole classes will not be left behind by the tide that people create when they contribute their talents to cooperative ventures in a free society.

Before we examine Robert Nozick's response to Rawls, we should note that Rawls's closest followers disagree over how Rawls is best interpreted and defended. There are hundreds of theories about how to pull together Rawls's arguments and about which to discard so that the remainder can be presented as an internally consistent whole. In later years, Rawls came to view his work not as a proof that his two principles are true, but instead as a way of articulating beliefs he considered implicit in contemporary Western democracies.[29]

Many of Rawls's followers were distressed by this seemingly colossal retreat. However, Rawls's later interpretation of his objective was exactly right. Rawls gave his readers a vision. It was a vision with grandeur, although it could not withstand scrutiny as the kind of philosophical deduction that some people wanted it to be. Rawls was claiming that, despite differences between their comprehensive moral views, there is an overlapping consensus implicit in how people live together in Western democracies. Rawls sought to identify the elements of that consensus and to explain, at an abstract level, why we believe in them.

Accordingly, our task is not to dwell on the argument's dubious details, but to reflect upon the degree to which we share this grand vision: (a) basic liberties come first, and (under normal circumstances) must not be sacrificed for anything; (b) we evaluate a society by looking at whether it is good for all and in particular by looking at the quality of life attainable by its nonprivileged members; and finally (c) we believe in (a) and (b) in part because they are fair, which in part means they are what we think we would choose if we were choosing impartially.

---

[29] This view begins to emerge most clearly in John Rawls, "Justice as Fairness: Political not Metaphysical," *Philosophy and Public Affairs* 14, no. 3 (1985): 223–51, reprinted in Rawls, *Collected Papers*, 388–414.

III. The Problem with Patterns

Nozick advanced the contemporary discussion with his fruitful distinction between historical and patterned principles of justice. The distinction is simple on the surface, but by the time we reach the end of Nozick's discussion, the two categories have become at least three, perhaps four, not as easily separated as we first thought. Some of Nozick's statements are hard to interpret, but the following definitions are roughly what Nozick intended.[30]

Current time-slice principles assess a distribution at a given moment. We look at an array of outcomes. It does not matter to whom those outcomes attach. For example, on an egalitarian time-slice principle, if the outcomes are unequal, that is all we need to know in order to know we have injustice. We do not need to know who got which outcome, or how they got it. History does not matter at all.

End-state principles say something similar, but without stipulating that the outcomes are time slices. So, for example, an egalitarian end-state principle could say that we look at lifetime income; if lifetime incomes are unequal, that is all we need to know. The difference between time-slice and end-state principles is this: Suppose the Smiths and the Joneses have the same jobs at the same factory, but the Joneses are three years older, started working three years earlier, and continually get pay raises in virtue of their seniority that the Smiths will not get for another three years. There is no time when wages are equal, yet lifetime income evens out in the end. We have injustice by an egalitarian time-slice principle, but an egalitarian end-state principle looks beyond the time slice to conclude that the kind of equality required by justice will be achieved in the end.

Patterned principles include both of the above as subsets or examples, but within the broader class are patterns that are neither time-slice nor end-state. They are patterned in virtue of attaching importance to how outcomes track traits of individuals. "Equal pay for equal work" is an example of an egalitarian principle that is patterned but neither end-state nor time-slice; it prescribes how outcomes should track labor inputs, but does not prescribe that outcomes be equal.

Historical principles say that what matters is the process by which outcomes arise. Historical principles are complicated because, notwithstanding Nozick's intended contrast, many patterned principles have a historical element, and vice versa. "Equal pay for equal work" is both patterned and historical; that is, it prescribes outcomes tracking a pattern of what people have done.

---

[30] I thank Mark LeBar and John Simmons for encouraging me to be clearer about these distinctions, and I especially thank Richard Arneson for a proposal about how best to draw the distinctions. I follow Arneson's proposal to a significant degree, but not enough to make him accountable for the result.

Nozick classifies Rawls's difference principle as patterned but not historical. (It prescribes a distribution while putting no weight on who produced the goods being distributed.) By contrast, what Nozick calls "entitlement theory" is historical but not patterned. Nozick says an entitlement theory's principles fall into three categories: (1) Principles of *initial acquisition* explain how a person or group legitimately could acquire something that had no previous owner. Previously unclaimed land is one example, as are inventions and other intellectual property. (2) Principles of *transfer* explain how ownership legitimately is transferred from one person (or group) to another. Finally, (3) principles of *rectification* specify what to do about instances of acquisition or transfer that were not legitimate.[31]

Nozick's preferred theory is a version of entitlement theory. Nozick says a distribution is just if it arises by just steps (the paradigm of which is voluntary exchange) from a just initial position.[32]

I am not sure Nozick should have said that. It sets the bar high: What can a historical theory say about a world where few titles have an unblemished history? Or perhaps that is simply how it is, and whether we like it or not, there is no way to get from here to a situation where distributions are just. Nevertheless, Nozick may have been mistaken to raise the topic of justice in distribution, since his theory seems to want to go in a different direction. That is, his theory seems to be about justice as how we treat each other, rather than justice as cleansing the world's distributions of original sin. In other words, the substantive core of Nozick's theory is not as previously stated. Nozick's is a theory of just transfer, not just distribution. His real claim is not that a distribution is just if it arises by just steps from a just initial position, but instead that a transfer from one person to another is genuinely just if genuinely voluntary. Nozick's theory ultimately is not so simple, but this is its essence.

Voluntary transfer cannot cleanse a tainted title of original sin, but any injustice in the result will have been preexisting, not created by the transfer. We are fated to live in a world of background injustice, all of us descended from both victims and victimizers, so it is a virtue of Nozick's theory that it does not pretend we might achieve perfect justice if only we could "even the score."[33] Still, Nozick thinks, it remains possible for

---

[31] Nozick, *Anarchy, State, and Utopia*, 150–53, 157–58, 173, and 208.

[32] Ibid., 150–53, 157–58, and 262–65.

[33] Richard Epstein, in as excellent a short discussion of Nozick as one will find, makes a related point: "Any system of property looks backward to determine the 'chain of title' that gives rise to present holdings. But this is not because of any fetish with the past but chiefly from the profound sense that stability in transactions is necessary for sensible forward-looking planning." See Epstein, *Skepticism and Freedom: A Modern Case for Classical Liberalism* (Chicago, IL: University of Chicago Press, 2003), 130. As Epstein would agree, though, dwelling too much on the past would be as problematic as ignoring the past, and for the same reason: it would reduce stability in transactions. A routine title search when selling a house is one thing; going back as many thousands of years as the land has been held is another.

moral agents, living ordinary lives, to abide by his principle of just transfer and, to that extent, to have clean hands. Presumably, Nozick would
have agreed that there is no future in evening the score.[34]

As an exemplar of the kind of society that would develop in accordance
with his own brand of entitlement theory, Nozick offers the ideal of a civil
libertarian, free-market society governed by a minimal state (roughly, a
government that restricts itself to defending the country's borders and
keeping the peace within its borders). In such a society, to the extent that
people trade by consent and on mutually agreeable terms, there will be
"strands" of patterns; people amass resources in proportion to their ability to offer goods at prices that make people around them better off.
Employees tend to be promoted when their talents and efforts merit
promotion, and so on. However, although society will be meritocratic to
that extent, the pattern will be only one among many. There will be
inheritance, gift-giving, and philanthropy too—all conferring goods on
recipients who may have done nothing to deserve such gifts.[35] Is that a
problem? Not to Nozick. Nozick joins Rawls in denying that merit is a
principle to which distributions (and transfers) must answer. The question, Nozick says, is whether people deal with each other in a peaceful,
consensual way.

The problem Nozick sees with patterned principles of justice such as
Rawls's difference principle is that, in Nozick's words, liberty upsets
patterns. "[N]o end-state principle or distributional patterned principle of
justice can be continuously realized without continuous interference with
people's lives." [36] Notice that Nozick neither argues nor presumes that
people can do whatever they want with their property. Nozick's point is,
if there is *anything* people can do—even if the only thing they are free to
do is give twenty-five cents to a basketball player—then that tiny liberty
will, over time, disturb the pattern.[37] It is a mistake, Nozick concludes,
to think end-state principles give people what entitlement principles do,
only better distributed. Entitlement principles recognize rights to choose
that end-state principles cannot recognize. None of the resources gov-

---

[34] Nozick endorses the undoing of wrongful transfers, but the point of undoing a wrongful transfer is simply that: to undo a wrongful transfer, not to make current holdings match
a favored pattern. Nozick has no solution (perhaps there is no solution) to the problem of
how to rectify injustice committed not by people now living but by their ancestors. There are
places where people have been evening the score for centuries, and it will not stop until
people learn to forget the past. For a state-of-the-art argument that successful rectification is
about victims and victimizers (or their descendants) getting together to repair damaged
relationships and set the stage for a peaceful future, see Linda Radzik, "Making Amends"
(*American Philosophical Quarterly*, forthcoming). I discuss Radzik and add my own thoughts
on rectification issues in David Schmidtz, *Elements of Justice* (New York: Cambridge University Press, 2005).
[35] Nozick, *Anarchy, State, and Utopia*, 158.
[36] Ibid., 163.
[37] I borrow the point from Edward Feser, *On Nozick* (Toronto: Wadsworth, 2004), 71.

erned by time-slice principles would ever simply be at a person's (or, for that matter, even a whole nation's) disposal.[38]

Although Nozick is right in seeing a huge problem with time-slice principles, not all patterned principles are prescriptions for time slices or even for end states. There are passages where Nozick seems to assume that by arguing against end-state or time-slice principles, he is clinching the case against patterned principles more generally. Not so. Not all patterns are the same, and not all require major interference. If we focus on time slices, we are focusing on isolated moments. We are taking such moments too seriously, when what matters is not the pattern of what people hold at a moment but the pattern of how people treat each other over time. Although even tiny liberties must upset the pattern of a static moment, there is no reason why liberty must upset an ongoing pattern of fair treatment.

A moral principle forbidding racial discrimination, for example, prescribes no particular end-state. Such a principle is what Nozick calls weakly patterned; it is sensitive to history as well as to pattern, and prescribes an ideal of how people should be treated without prescribing an end-state distribution.[39] It *affects* the pattern (as would a purely historical principle) without *prescribing* a pattern (or more precisely, without prescribing an end-state). And if a principle forbidding racial discrimination works its way into a society via cultural evolution rather than legal intervention, it need not involve any interference at all.

If we create a society where Martin Luther King's dream comes true, and his children are judged not by the color of their skin but by the content of their character, then what we achieve is a fluid, evolving pattern that tracks one dimension (merit) rather than another (skin color). In the process, society comes to require *less* intervention than the forcibly segregated society from which it evolved. Thus, although Nozick sometimes speaks as if his critique applies to all patterns, we should take seriously his concession that "weak" patterns are compatible with liberty. They may even promote liberty, depending on how they are introduced and maintained. So, the problem is not with patterned principles in

---

[38] Nozick, *Anarchy, State, and Utopia*, 167. Rawls's reply: "The objection that the difference principle enjoins continuous corrections of particular distributions and capricious interference with private transactions is based on a misunderstanding." On the next page, Rawls clarifies: "[E]ven if everyone acts fairly as defined by the rules that it is both reasonable and practicable to impose on individuals, the upshot of many separate transactions will eventually undermine background justice. This is obvious once we view society, as we must, as involving cooperation over generations. Thus, even in a well-ordered society, adjustments in the basic structure are always necessary." See John Rawls, *Political Liberalism* (New York: Columbia University Press, 1993), 283–84. Rawls's clarification makes it hard to see why Rawls thinks Nozick misunderstood him. (I thank Tom G. Palmer for this point.) In any case, this is a major challenge in constructing a well-ordered constitutional democracy: how to avoid "necessary adjustments" that tell citizens that ownership of their income is a political football, and they are, to that extent, governed by men, not law.

[39] Nozick, *Anarchy, State, and Utopia*, 164.

general but more particularly with end-state and especially time-slice principles.

A weakness in Nozick's critique of Rawls, then, is this: Nozick is right that time-slice principles license immense, constant, ludicrous interference with everyday interaction, but is Rawls defending such a view? In his first published article, Rawls said, "[W]e cannot determine the justness of a situation by examining it at a single moment." [40] Hence, we can doubt that Rawls ever entertained a time-slice conception. Rawls later said, "It is a mistake to focus attention on the varying relative positions of individuals and to require that every change, considered as a single transaction viewed in isolation, be in itself just. It is the arrangement of the basic structure which is to be judged, and judged from a general point of view." [41] Thus, to Rawls, a basic structure's job is not to make every transaction work to the working class's advantage, let alone to that of each *member* of the class. Instead, it is the trend of society as a whole over time that is supposed to benefit the working class. To be sure, Rawls was a kind of egalitarian, but he was not a time-slice or even an end-state egalitarian. The pattern Rawls meant to weave into the fabric of society's basic structure was a pattern of equal status, applying not so much to a distribution as to an ongoing relationship. [42]

The strength of Nozick's critique lies in how it drew attention to a prohibitive cost of any theory that *is* time-slice. Recent egalitarian work is an evolving response to Nozick's Wilt Chamberlain example and to the enormity of the flaw in time-slice principles that the example revealed. [43] Today's egalitarians are realizing that any equality worthy of aspiration will not be a static property of a distribution at a particular moment. It will instead concern how people are treated: how they are rewarded for their contributions and *enabled* over time to make contributions worth rewarding.

IV. THE VERY IDEA OF DISTRIBUTIVE JUSTICE

Nozick thought that a bias against respecting the separateness of persons lurks in the very idea of distributive justice. The idea leads people to think of goods as having been distributed by some mechanism for which we are responsible. Generally, Nozick believes, there is no such mechanism and no such responsibility. "There is no more a distributing or distribution of shares than there is a distributing of mates in a society in

---

[40] John Rawls, "Outline of a Decision Procedure for Ethics," in Rawls, *Collected Papers*, 14. The article was originally published in 1951.

[41] Rawls, *A Theory of Justice* (1971), 87–88.

[42] I thank Alyssa Bernstein for her help with this point.

[43] In this example, a million basketball fans choose to pay twenty-five cents each directly to Wilt Chamberlain in exchange for seeing him play—thus upsetting a previously existing pattern of distribution.

which persons choose whom they shall marry." [44] No one arranges a distribution of mates. Therefore, barring further argument, no one has a duty—indeed, *no one has any right*—to make sure the distribution of mates is fair.

Suppose for argument's sake that the fair way to redistribute whatever you have a right to redistribute is in accordance with the difference principle. We still face a prior question: What gives you any right to redistribute my income, or anything else? I may agree with Rawls that I do not *deserve* X, but so what? How does that give you a right to redistribute? [45] Does it beg the question to refer to X (my mate, say, or a wallet I found in a parking lot) as mine? Suppose we say yes, for argument's sake. Still, how do we get from there to a conclusion that you have a right to redistribute X?

Showing that I *don't* own my mate, or a wallet I found in a parking lot, is not enough; you have to show that you *do*. Barring more argument, you have no right to redistribute in accordance with the difference principle *even if the difference principle is the true principle of justice*. To establish that you have a right to distribute, what we need to show is not that what you want to do with the goods is *fair*. Rather, we need to show that the goods you want to distribute are yours to distribute.

Intuitively, we go some distance toward establishing that a government has a right to rearrange the natural distribution (or what people have done with it) if we can establish that the natural distribution is unjust. But is it? Here is what Rawls says: "The natural distribution is neither just nor unjust; nor is it unjust that persons are born into society at some particular position. These are simply natural facts. What is just and unjust is the way that institutions deal with these facts." [46]

What does Rawls have in mind? How should an institution deal with fact X? *When* should an institution deal with X? What if X is not otherwise unjust? If a distribution is not unjust, why would it need correcting? What exactly would count as *correcting* a distribution that is not unjust? (At the heart of a theory meant to show respect for the separateness of persons, why would justice mainly concern how institutions deal with facts about aggregate distribution—of talent or anything else?)

Earlier in the same passage, Rawls says, "[T]he difference principle gives some weight to considerations singled out by the principle of redress. This is the principle that undeserved inequalities call for redress." [47] But

[44] Nozick, *Anarchy, State, and Utopia*, 150.

[45] As Steven R. Smith (approvingly) summarizes, "individuals are seen by Rawls as not deserving their initial endowment packages. Consequently, talents are, to some degree, socially owned." *Consequently*? How would we get from the premise that talents are undeserved to the conclusion that talents are community property? Also, which community would we be talking about? Why not the United Nations, or the Church of Scientology? See Steven R. Smith, "The Social Construction of Talent," *Journal of Political Philosophy* 9, no. 1 (2001): 31.

[46] Rawls, *A Theory of Justice* (1971), 102.

[47] Ibid., 100.

if Rawls is right that the natural distribution is not unjust, unequal though it may be, and undeserved though it may be, then it does not call for *redress* either.

And why does Rawls say "undeserved"? Why not simply say that inequalities per se call for redress? Or if the notion of desert is doing work here that Rawls elsewhere seems committed to denying that the concept of desert can do, then why don't undeserved *equalities* likewise call for redress?

V. THE NATURAL LOTTERY: ARBITRARY BUT NOT UNJUST

Rawls says, "We are led to the difference principle if we wish to arrange the basic social structure so that no one gains (or loses) from his luck in the natural lottery of talent and ability, or from his initial place in society."[48] Why would anyone wish that? Rawls offers the following reason: "It may be expedient but it is not just that some should have less *in order* that others may prosper."[49] Here are three responses.

First, Nozick *agrees* that it is unjust if some have less so that others may prosper. Where Rawls and Nozick disagree is over the question, "less than what?" Rawls rejects the idea of some having less than an *equal share* (not of the actual social product, but of what the social product would have been in a regime of strict equality) so that others may prosper. Nozick rejects the idea of some being deprived of their *earnings* so that others may prosper. Can we know which baseline is more respectful of separate persons? Can we even know which is more generous? How? (To judge from history, the equal shares baseline in a regime of strict equality would never amount to much.)

Second, in the real world, no human being fixes the natural lottery, assigning hardworking characters to some and lazy characters to others. Is there a difference between a lottery Jane wins by luck of the draw and a lottery rigged to make sure Jane wins? Is there a difference between Jack turning out to be less skilled than Jane and a situation where Jack deliberately is held back so as to make sure Jane will be more skilled than Jack? Rawls says, "Once we decide to look for a conception of justice that *nullifies* the accidents of natural endowment and the contingencies of social circumstance . . . we are led to these principles. They express the result of leaving aside those aspects of the social world that seem arbitrary."[50] But "arbitrary" has two meanings. Natural distributions can be arbitrary, meaning *random*. Or human choices can be arbitrary, meaning

---

[48] Rawls, "Distributive Justice," 140. Strictly speaking, this consideration leads only to a precursor form of the difference principle, which specifies that arrangements ought to be mutually advantageous.

[49] Rawls, *A Theory of Justice* (1971), 15 (emphasis added).

[50] Ibid. (emphasis added).

capricious.[51] In one case, no choice is made. In the second, an unjustified choice is made, unjustified in virtue of being literally unprincipled.[52]

The two are not equivalent. Fair lotteries are lotteries where winners are chosen at random. A *rigged* lottery is unfair because it *fails* to be arbitrary in the benign sense. It is by *failing* to be arbitrary in the benign sense that it *counts* as arbitrary in the bad sense. What of the natural lottery, then? The natural lottery is arbitrary in the benign sense, but how does that connect to being unfair in the way that capricious choice is unfair?

Rawls says, "Intuitively, the most obvious injustice of the system of natural liberty is that it permits distributive shares to be improperly influenced by these factors so arbitrary from a moral point of view."[53] However, when "arbitrary" means random, as it does here, there is nothing obvious about any connection between being arbitrary and being improper. Capricious choice wears impropriety on its sleeve; the natural lottery does not. Had Jack's mother assigned Jane all the talent, deliberately leaving Jack with none, we might at very least wonder why. In fact, though, Jack's mother did not assign him less talent. It just happened. It was chance, not caprice.

A Rawlsian might respond that everything is deliberately assigned. When we deliberately fail to correct a natural distribution, we deliberately fail to correct what is otherwise unjust; when we deliberately fail to correct what is otherwise unjust, we deliberately commit injustice. Before any such argument can get started, though, we need to show that what we are declining to correct is otherwise unjust. The difference principle may correct a natural distribution, but Rawls understands that before this can seem like justice, we need to show that the distribution being corrected is otherwise unjust. Is it? Rawl himself (as discussed in the previous section) says no.

The third response is this: If we *did* assign Jack less talent, the reason would not be "so others may prosper." Making Jack *untalented* would not help others. If we sought to assign Jack a talent level that would make people around Jack better off, we would assign Jack *more* talent, not less. What would give us reason to compensate Jack would be to make Jack a talented provider of high-quality services.[54]

---

[51] Cara Nine argues that arbitrariness is an essentially theory-laden concept, so that X is arbitrary only if X is wrong by the lights of a given moral theory. In that case, if we want to argue for a theory, and want to start with premises about what is arbitrary, the argument is likely to be question-begging. See Nine, "Moral Arbitrariness" (Ph.D. dissertation, University of Arizona, 2005).

[52] When we call a choice arbitrary, we are implying not only that it is unjustified, and not only that it is wrong, but also that it exhibits a certain arrogance: there is nothing a person could say, or would even be inclined to say, to justify his or her choice. A person might say, "I can do whatever I want."

[53] Rawls, *A Theory of Justice* (1971), 72.

[54] In any system, the main way in which the talented *share* their talent is precisely by going as far as their talent can take them. What people pay in taxes normally will be trivial

Ironically, if we did assign Jack his place in a distribution of talent "so that others may prosper," it is Rawls, not Nozick, who would hesitate to compensate Jack. The worry: we would be compensating Jack not for disadvantages but for services rendered. Rawls allows compensation for services rendered as a way of manipulating incentives on behalf of the least advantaged, but the only compensation Rawls treats as required by justice per se is compensation for disadvantages.

One way to rationalize the idea that Jane's being a more talented worker entitles *Jack* to compensation is to say that if Jane is more talented, Jane captures more of the pie; therefore, Jack and others necessarily get less. However, it is Rawls's point, after all, that the pie's size is a variable. Society can, if all goes well, be a mutually advantageous venture. Almost everyone can have a better life than they could have had on their own, and the reason is simple: Talented bakers don't capture pie. They *make* it.[55] Thus, it is an anomaly when Rawls says, "We are led to the difference principle if we wish to arrange the basic structure so that no one *gains* (or loses) from his luck in the natural lottery. . . ." Gaining is good, not bad, so why prevent it? There is a problem with gaining only if people gain at someone else's expense, and in that case the problem is still with the losing, not the gaining.

No one reasonably thinks we live in a zero-sum world.[56] When a baby is born with a damaged spinal cord, it is not so that healthy babies prosper. When the next baby is born healthy, needing no special care, this baby's health does not come at the first baby's expense. The natural lottery is not zero-sum. Wanting to make sure that no one *gains*, thereby treating features that individuate us as persons as things to *nullify*, is, in Nozick's words, "a risky line to take for a theory that otherwise wishes to buttress the dignity and self-respect of autonomous beings."[57]

From Rawls's perspective as well as Nozick's, any argument for taxing what Jack pays to hear Jane play piano has to come from a different direction. We can and should give up the idea that there is something wrong, crying out for correction, when Jack and Jane reap mutual benefits from the sharing of her talent. To justify taxing what Jack pays Jane, we will have to argue, more simply and more honestly, that what the government will do with the money (helping the least advantaged, say) is important enough to justify taking the money. In truth, however, when we tax income, we are trying to raise revenue, not correct injustice. Why pretend otherwise?

---

by comparison. To take an obvious case, how much did Thomas Edison pay in taxes? The answer is that we do not need to know, because we know that no matter how many millions Edison might have paid, the good done by his taxes was *nothing* compared to the good done by his inventions.

[55] Even the most self-reliant bakers, of course, cooperate.

[56] This is not to deny that the assumption is at some level intuitively compelling, or that it tacitly informs a lot of political theorizing.

[57] Nozick, *Anarchy, State, and Utopia*, 214.

If we think a government needs to tax what Jane pays Jack for services rendered, as a way of financing programs, then we should honestly say so, and reject the premise that the only way to justify a tax is to prove that it is rectifying an injustice. And once we reject that premise, we no longer need to posit that the natural distribution is unjust (or worse, to posit that while the natural distribution is not unjust, it still needs to be redressed). The distribution of talent per se is a moral nonissue. People often lack the money to solve otherwise solvable problems. That may not be a problem of justice, but it is, in any case, the real issue. The problem is not that Jane and Jack have unpaid debts to society, but that society really needs their money.

Let me put the point in a different way. Even if, as Rawls says, there is no *injustice* in a natural distribution, there may yet be a problem. Being born with a cleft palate is a problem. The problem is not that a cleft palate is unjust but that it is bad. Its badness gives us some reason to intervene so as to fix the problem, assuming we can fix the problem without violating rights or otherwise doing more harm than good.

Note the nature of the real issue: We are not trying to fix an improper distribution of cleft palates. We are trying to fix cleft palates.

VI. The Separateness of Persons

Nozick sometimes is accused of having no foundation, of merely assuming what he needs to prove. Needless to say, it is hard to develop a solid foundation for a theory of justice. No philosopher is widely regarded as having succeeded in doing so. Still, Nozick could have replied that, rightly or wrongly, he was borrowing Rawls's foundation. (And if any philosopher were regarded as having developed a solid foundation, it would be Rawls.) For the sake of argument, Nozick accepted Rawls's premises about the separateness and inviolability of individual persons. Thus, Nozick says, the "root idea, namely, that there are different individuals with separate lives and so no one may be sacrificed for others, underlies the existence of moral side constraints."[58] If this premise is not a foundation, then Rawls does not have a foundation either. Nozick's departure from Rawls was to treat such premises not as imaginary devices designed, defined, then discarded on the road to Rawls's two principles; instead, Nozick asked, when we pay homage to personal inviolability, what if we meant it? When we say people are entitled to the most extensive sphere of liberty compatible with a like liberty for all and that this principle, the first principle of justice, takes priority over all other considerations, what if we actually meant it?[59]

[58] Ibid., 33. See also A. R. Lacey, *Robert Nozick* (Princeton, NJ: Princeton University Press, 2001), 25ff.
[59] For a cogent critique of the retreat from the first principle's original maximalist formulation, see Loren Lomasky, "Libertarianism at Twin Harvard," in this volume.

Rawls says, "[W]hen society is conceived as a system of cooperation designed to advance the good of its members, it seems quite incredible that some citizens should be expected, on the basis of political principles, to accept lower prospects of life for the sake of others."[60] Rawls is complaining about the principle of utility, but as Thomas Nagel notes, the same complaint applies to the difference principle.[61]

Some critics think it is worse than that. At least under the principle of utility, everyone counts as one. Peter Singer says:

> Nozick is able to make the telling point that the fundamental flaw Rawls finds in utilitarianism—the failure to rule out "even the tendency to regard men as means to one another's welfare"—can be found in Rawls's own principle. The maximin rule treats the better-off as a means to the welfare of the worst-off. Indeed, one could say (though Nozick does not) that the tendency to treat people as a means to another's ends is greater under the maximin rule than under utilitarianism, since a utilitarian would give *equal* consideration to everyone's interests, whereas the maximin rule forbids giving *any* consideration to the interests of the better-off, allotting them goods *solely* in so far as doing so assists the worst-off.[62]

Routinely, people sacrifice in the name of their overall best interest. Jane sometimes gives up a night at the movies to study for an exam. According to utilitarianism, it is no better and no worse, other things equal, if Jane sacrifices *someone else* in the name of her overall best interest.[63] Matt Zwolinski summarizes: "It is because utilitarianism sees no morally relevant difference between tradeoffs within a life and tradeoffs between lives, that it is said to fail to take seriously the separateness of persons." Zwolinski finds it curious that Rawls and Nozick could end up in such different places, having seemingly started with the same concern.[64]

---

[60] Rawls, *A Theory of Justice* (1971), 178.

[61] Thomas Nagel, "Rawls on Justice," in *Reading Rawls*, ed. Norman Daniels (Stanford, CA: Stanford University Press, 1989), 13.

[62] Peter Singer, "The Right to Be Rich or Poor," in *Reading Nozick*, ed. Jeffrey Paul (Oxford: Blackwell, 1981), 48. Rawls likely would reply that utilitarianism is cavalier in its willingness to benefit some at the expense of others, so long as total utility thereby increases. Rawls's theory requires that transfers be justified to each individual. Singer probably would say that if that means the well-off have a veto, then Rawls's theory has all the problems of Nozick's; if not, the distinction between Rawls's theory and utilitarianism has not yet been made.

[63] For excellent discussions of how the separateness of persons issue relates to issues of personal autonomy and agent-relative values, see chap. 5 of Horacio Spector's *Autonomy and Rights: The Moral Foundations of Liberalism* (Oxford: Oxford University Press, 1992); Eric Mack, "Moral Individualism: Agent-Relativity and Deontic Restraints," *Social Philosophy and Policy* 7, no. 1 (1989): 81–111; and Eric Mack, "Self-Ownership, Marxism, and Egalitarianism," *Politics, Philosophy, and Economics* 1 (2002): 75–108.

[64] One difference, explored by Matt Zwolinski in his "The Separateness of Persons" (American Philosophical Association, 2003), is that while Nozick thinks of separateness as implying restrictions on how people may be treated, Rawls thinks of separateness as a

My hypothesis is this: there are two "separateness" issues. (1) Rawls cares about our separateness as *consumers* and says we cannot make up for one consumer having less by enabling others to have more. More precisely, Rawls *does* think we can make up for one person having less by enabling others to have more. For example, we can make up for the more advantaged having less (than they otherwise would) by enabling the less advantaged to have more, so long as we do not plunge the more advantaged below a baseline of equal shares.[65] Only then do we use people as mere means. To deem people separate in any other way is to assign undue weight to factors "so arbitrary from a moral point of view." (2) Nozick respects our separateness as *producers*. To Nozick, dismissing what we *do* as arbitrary is disrespectful. Nozick wants to buttress our dignity as producers of goods we bring *to* the table, not merely as consumers of goods we take *from* the table.

One factor separating Nozickians from Rawlsians is that Nozickians tend to see rewards (i.e., products) as created by workers, and thus as presumptively belonging to workers (meaning that workers normally are within their rights to sell their products to willing customers on mutually agreeable terms). Rawlsians tend to see rewards as created by society and as society's responsibility to distribute according to principles of justice. Implicit in the latter view: there is no fundamentally real category of separate producers; society has productive components, and produces or fails to produce according to its success in arranging the reward structures of its components.

Rawls does not say why what separates us as consumers (we have separate stomachs, and so on) is less arbitrary than what separates us as producers. Not only is this a difference between Rawls and Nozick; it divides theorists of justice in general. The question is, should we treat production as external to the topic of justice? Is it true that when we think about justice, we need not and maybe should not think about which arrangements empower human beings to undertake the productive activities on which welfare and progress depend? Robert Paul Wolff says that Nozick's criticism is on target: "The veil of ignorance has the effect of making all considerations on the production side so thoroughly hypothetical, so *abstract* in the bad sense, that inevitably the difference princi-

---

meta-level desideratum. It does not restrict what we can do to people; instead, it restricts what we can offer as a justification for what we do.

[65] Rawls in effect holds that the sole implication of separateness is to require a basic structure to justify *to each person* the assigning of a consumption bundle to that person. See Zwolinski, "The Separateness of Persons," for more on the distinction between respecting separateness in the sense that rules out involuntary transfers from one to another and respecting separateness in the sense of involuntary transfers having to be justified to each individual. (But I note here that Rawls and his followers are not saying each individual has to agree that the transfers are justified; it is enough that "reasonable" people agree.)

ple comes to be construed as a pure distribution principle, with the distributable goods and services exogenously given."[66]

The problem of cooperation, for Rawls, is a problem of how to distribute what people contribute, which translates into a question of how to distribute inequalities. The Nozickian worry is: Isn't contributing the essence of cooperating? Can we truly have a problem of *cooperation* that is not centrally a problem of how to *respect* what people contribute? What if normal people reject the idea that a basic structure's job is to distribute inequalities, and instead say a basic structure's job is to respect the fact that people are separate as producers, not only as consumers?

For Rawls, we reject utilitarianism and undertake a contractarian thought experiment, partly because the latter does not lump us together as utilitarianism does. Rawls acknowledges and even stresses the separateness of persons in his opening statements, but as the theory takes shape, it increasingly reflects an attitude that separateness is regrettable. Having begun with contractarianism, Rawls's subsequent moves seem aimed at mitigating the separateness with which contractarian thought begins. Nozick, by contrast, not only acknowledges our separateness as producers; he celebrates it. Nozick denies that we are obliged to benefit each other per se. Our obligation is simply to deal with each other only on mutually acceptable terms.

If the goods Rawls wants to distribute had no history, that would be different:

> If things fell like manna from heaven, and no one had any special entitlement to any portion of it, and no manna would fall unless all agreed to a particular distribution, and somehow the quantity varied depending on the distribution, then it is plausible to claim that persons . . . would agree to the difference principle rule of distribution. But is *this* the appropriate model for thinking about how the things people produce are to be distributed?[67]

This shows that Nozick's complaint is not that Rawls has a bad idea about how to distribute manna so much as that Rawls has a bad idea about what counts as manna. To Nozick, advantages are not what bargainers *find* on the table; advantages are what bargainers *bring* to the table. And respecting what people bring to the table is the exact essence of respecting them as separate persons.

Does Rawls treats advantages as manna? That is how Nozick reads him. Many read Rawls the same way. Moreover, there is no consensus that this reading is unkind; many embrace Rawls because they *like* the

---

[66] See Robert Paul Wolff, *Understanding Rawls* (Princeton, NJ: Princeton University Press, 1977), 201.

[67] Nozick, *Anarchy, State, and Utopia*, 198.

idea of treating advantages as manna. Rawls, trying to soften earlier statements, said, "[T]he difference principle represents an agreement to regard the distribution of native endowments as a common asset and to share in the benefits of this distribution whatever it may be. It is not said that this distribution *is* a common asset. . . ."[68] But if we cannot say the distribution *is* a common asset, what gives us a right to agree (or worse, treat people as if they had agreed) to regard it as if it were?

Nozick concedes that the difference principle applies to manna from heaven, but adds that what we *achieve* is not manna. Treating achievement as manna fails to respect the separateness of achievers, and, consequently, fails to elicit their willing participation. Rawls accepts the latter, the incentive issue, as a concern. For Nozick, though, the issue is about respect, not incentives. Respecting people's histories, Nozick believes, is a crucial part of respecting their separateness.

VII. THE ORIGINAL POSITION AS EXPERIENCE MACHINE

Nozick's story of the "experience machine" illustrates his concern for the separateness of persons as productive agents capable of making their world better. The experience machine lets us plug our brains into a computer programmed to make us think we are living whatever we take to be the best possible life. The life we think we are living is a computer-induced dream, but we do not know that. Whatever experience would be part of the best possible life for us—anything at all—will in fact be part of our felt experience. Nozick asks, "Would you plug in? *What else can matter to us, other than how our lives feel from the inside?*"[69]

Nozick's story is among the most talked-about puzzles in contemporary philosophy. Nozick does not present the story as connecting to his critique of Rawls, and I have no evidence that Nozick himself saw a connection, but there is a connection nonetheless. Nozick's idea is that a person is not merely a location of experience. What makes us agents is what we do, what we strive to do, and what we accomplish. The experience machine robs us of moral agency. What about Rawls's original position? Does it do something similar?

If what makes us agents is not experiencing but striving, there could be a problem. Rawls insists that agency in the sense of striving is morally arbitrary, at least when the topic is what we can claim from the basic structure as a matter of justice. Rawls's thought experiment, the veil of ignorance, assumes that what matters—what we focus on when choosing principles—is the sort of bundle we could be given by an experience

---

[68] Rawls, *Justice as Fairness: A Restatement*, 75 (emphasis added).
[69] Nozick, *Anarchy, State, and Utopia*, 43 (emphasis in original). See also David Schmidtz, "The Meanings of Life," in *Robert Nozick*, ed. David Schmidtz (New York: Cambridge University Press, 2002), 199–216.

machine. Rawls says a person behind the veil "has a conception of the good such that he cares very little, if anything, for what he might gain above the minimum."[70] To critics, this looks far-fetched, but it becomes plausible when we see Rawls as using the phrase "a conception of the good" to mean a conception of the good we can *have* rather than a conception of the good we can *do*.

What if our conception of the good has to do with what we achieve in life? Is it true that we don't care what we *achieve* above the minimum? Is it true that we shouldn't care, or that behind the veil, we wouldn't care? Should we suppose that, behind the veil, Michelangelo and Edison do not care what they achieve above the minimum, or that the rest of us would not care? Even if that were imaginable, what difference would it make once the veil is lifted and people find out who they are? Once the veil is lifted, what is to stop someone like Michelangelo from saying, "I'm sorry. You designed the veil to prevent me from knowing what really matters. It wrongly required me not to think beyond my own advantage in material terms. It required me to deliberate as if my talent were not a sacred calling. Given what I have inside me, I have no *right* not to care what I achieve above the minimum."

Since a few of us will in fact turn out to be Edisons and Michelangelos, have we any right not to care what we *collectively* achieve above the minimum? If some groups of bargainers decide they do care, would they be mistaken? Suppose this leads some groups to favor the position of the *most* talented? Would they be wrong?[71]

Nozick's ideal basic structure would give us a chance to *live* a life, not just experience it. Real life contains danger and failure and episodes of deprivation that a risk-averse person would avoid, but those things go with really living. Rawls wants us to live a life too, of course, yet when selecting principles, we are supposed not to know or care about the life we so far have lived. Until the veil is lifted, we are to focus solely on how much we get, untainted by morally arbitrary questions about who we are and whether we did anything to deserve that much.[72] What we thereby

---

[70] Rawls, *A Theory of Justice* (1971), 154.

[71] Nozick asks us, how would Rawlsian bargainers assign grades? Nozick says Rawlsian bargainers cannot even consider letting grades track performance. Bargainers want to make the lowest grade as high as possible. They do not care (or do not know they care) about the difference between giving the best grade to the best student and giving the best grade to the worst.

It would be easy to overstate Nozick's point. In a zero-sum game, as where an average grade is fixed, Nozick would be right, but when we speak of positive-sum games, as in real market societies, everything changes. In a positive-sum game, Rawls can rule out giving the best grade to the worst student on *strategic* grounds, allowing that rewards can be used to manipulate the talented into performing in a way that enlarges the pie (maximizing the smallest slice). Nozick's complaint is not that such rewards would be too small, but rather that their rationale is brutally disrespectful.

[72] For an argument that we can deserve X in virtue of what we do after receiving X, see David Schmidtz, "How to Deserve," *Political Theory* 30, no. 6 (2002): 774–99. I thank Dan Russell for reminding me of this argument's relevance.

set aside as arbitrary is *doing*—precisely what is missing from the experience machine.

It must seem obvious that nothing is stopping Rawls from making room in his theory for less advantaged people to have opportunities to do things, and deserve things, not just experience them. However, if Rawls were to do that, it would have an awkward consequence. If we say bargainers would choose principles that explicitly express respect for what less advantaged people do, perhaps letting respect for their welfare be merely implicit, as in Nozick, we will be agreeing not merely to respect what less advantaged people do *from now on*, on the grounds that such respect is in their interest. We will also be choosing to respect what they have been doing all along. And if we are to give them the respect that is in their interest, we will also have to regard ourselves as giving them what they deserve and have deserved all along. Otherwise, our attitude toward them is a paternalistic simulation of respect, not the real thing.

If we acknowledge that people command respect in virtue of what they have been doing all along, we are acknowledging that respect is not a matter of us deciding what they reasonably would accept on the assumption that their history does not matter. Nor is respect compatible with insisting that we care about history and about what people deserve, then proceeding to pick principles of justice as if such things did not matter (or as if they begin to matter only after, and only if, we pick principles that underwrite them). If such things matter, then the moment when such things have to be taken into account is the moment when we are picking principles of justice.

VIII. The Original Position as Utopia

Nozick accuses Rawls of devising a procedure guaranteeing that end-state and not historical principles will be chosen. Far from denying it, Rawls goes further, saying his intent was to guarantee that not only patterned principles in general but the difference principle in particular will be chosen. Rawls repeatedly stresses, "We want to define the original position so that we get the desired solution."[73]

The conclusion is not that Rawls's project is illegitimate but, rather, that it has to be understood as Rawls later came to understand it. That is, the project is to articulate what "we" implicitly believe, not to force us to a conclusion we would rather reject. Thus, Rawls's admitting why he designed the original position as he did, disconcerting though it may be, does not prove that his principles are wrong, or even that his argument is bad. Perhaps the original position is, after all, a fair test of competing conceptions, and perhaps Rawls's two principles are uniquely capable of passing that test.

[73] Rawls, *A Theory of Justice* (1971), 141.

How would we decide whether the original position is a fair test? Rawls says, "The idea of the original position is to set up a fair procedure so that any principles agreed to will be just."[74] Yet, needless to say, our imagining a jury reaching a guilty verdict is no substitute for a fair trial. To set up a fair procedure, we first must set up a procedure. What goes on in our imagination is not a procedure, let alone a fair one.

One reason to see the original position as fair is that it would, if it were real, put bargainers in a position of not being able to bias the negotiation in their own favor. Not knowing what position they will occupy forces real bargainers to negotiate in a more impartial way. But if *this* feature is what marks the original position as fair—as I believe—then the other features (e.g., the assumption that society is closed) are dispensable. Or at least, the other features are dispensable if the objective is to "set up a fair procedure so that any principles agreed to will be just." The other features are required only insofar as the objective is instead "to get the desired conclusion."

A. Suppose we do not know what conclusion we desire

Suppose there is no "desired conclusion" and our only goal is to set up a fair procedure and then let people get whatever conclusion *they* desire. That is, suppose we theorists could set aside our preconceptions regarding what conclusion is "desired." If we simply wanted to preserve the impartiality (thus the fairness) of the original position, and had no other agenda, what procedure might we set up?

Here is a suggestion. Suppose we theorists put *ourselves* behind a veil of ignorance. Imagine us trying to construct a fair bargaining game *without knowing anything about our own conception of justice*. Suppose we do not *know* what solution we desire, and thus, unlike Rawls, cannot "define the original position so as to get the desired solution." What would we do? Would we posit that bargainers do not care who brought what to the table; they care only about what they get, yet care little for what they might get above the minimum?[75] Would we posit grave risks in seeking gains above the minimum? Would we assume severely handicapped people are not represented at the bargaining table? Would we imagine ourselves picking rules for a closed society? Would we assume bargainers start with equal claims to (the distribution of) each other's advantages, conceived as a collective asset?

---

[74] Ibid., 136.

[75] As Thomas Nagel worries, "Keeping in mind that the parties in the original position do not know the stage of development of their society, and therefore do not know what minimum will be guaranteed by a maximin strategy, it is difficult to understand how an individual can know that he 'cares very little, if anything, for what he might gain above the minimum'." See Nagel, "Rawls on Justice," 12.

Presumably, we would do none of the above. We might assume bargainers do not know their position in the distribution, since intuitively
that has something to do with impartiality, which intuitively has something to do with fairness. But if we did not know our conception of
justice—if we had no idea whether we were egalitarians or elitists, no
idea which conception we endorsed—then we would not be designing
the situation so as to converge on any particular conception. In that
setting, we would expect bargainers to try to choose principles that were
good for all. We would have no reason to predict anything more specific
than that. We would *expect* different sets of bargainers to converge on
different conclusions.

Moreover, that would not trouble us, insofar as we took seriously the
idea of procedural justice: the idea that justice is about following a given
procedure rather than reaching a given conclusion. On a procedural conception, we conclude that if, after fair deliberation, people agree to bind
themselves to each other in a particular way, then by that very fact they
are bound to each other in that way. If other people, after similarly fair
deliberation, agree to bind themselves on different terms, then they *are*
bound on those different terms. By the lights of procedural justice, the fact
that groups of people are bound in different ways is not a problem.

B. *Suppose we do not know whether equal shares is the default*

Consider another modification of the Rawlsian experiment: Instead of
assuming that bargainers begin from a position of strict equality, assume—
more abstractly but less controversially—that bargainers begin from a
situation where nothing needs rectifying. No one complains about how
anyone acquired current holdings. (Some are satisfied that holdings are
sufficiently equal. Some are satisfied that no one is in possession of stolen
property. Others realize they have not yet picked principles of justice, and
therefore lack standards for judging current holdings. Anyway, no one is
complaining.) We assume *nothing* about how things are distributed in this
situation, and thus avoid building our preference for egalitarian (or non-
egalitarian, as the case may be) principles into the situation's starting
point. Such a procedure would have advantages over Rawls's. To mention only one, by not specifying any particular distribution, we avoid
giving that specified distribution a position of unearned privilege in the
debate about what the distribution ought to be.

Is this thought experiment relevant to a real world where people *do*
have complaints about existing holdings? Maybe not, and maybe that is
a good objection. But in that case, we must conclude not that we should
reject *this* thought experiment but that we should reject *all* such thought
experiments, including Rawls's. All such experiments, including Rawls's,
assume that we need not return goods to their rightful owners, and that
we can focus on distributing goods as if goods were presenting them-

selves to us in an unowned state. If that assumption is wrong, then all such thought experiments are wrong.

IX. Conclusion: What We Can Learn

We live in a world where goods have histories, and where people care not only about the goods; they care about the histories too. To respect people—to give them their due—is to respect their history, not merely to assign them goods. Nozick argues that no theory of justice is plausible unless it takes history seriously. A theory takes seriously our separate personhood only if it takes seriously our separate histories. For example, as Rawls would have agreed, sometimes justice is about returning a stolen wallet to the person from whom it was stolen. Why return the wallet to that person? Not to restore a previously fair pattern but to restore the wallet to the person from whom it was stolen. We know justice is about *returning* the wallet, not *distributing* it. The wallet's history morally trumps any thoughts about how it might best be distributed.

At the same time, taking our histories seriously—taking them every bit as seriously as Nozick takes them—does not rule out taking certain patterns seriously. The larger project of which this essay is a part explains how a theory may integrate patterned and historical principles together to form a pluralistic theory that makes room for principles of desert, equality, reciprocity, and need.[76]

Philosophy, University of Arizona

---

[76] Schmidtz, *Elements of Justice* (see note 34).

LIBERTARIANISM AT TWIN HARVARD*

By Loren E. Lomasky

I. Introduction

On Twin Earth, where soaring elms and beeches are nourished by the gentle rain of XYZ, there is a town called Cambridge, Massachusetts, in which can be found one of the planet's premiere universities, Harvard by name. The institution was favored during the final quarter of the twentieth century by the presence of a pair of innovative philosophers who, between them, revived what had become the rather stiff and staid discipline of political philosophy. Coincidentally, they went by the names John Rawls and Robert Nozick. Rawls was renowned for his model of a veil of ignorance behind which are chosen fundamental principles of justice for a well-ordered society's basic structure. Nozick was less inclined to plumb foundations, but with dazzling ingenuity and craftsmanship he explored implications of the assumption that individuals are inviolate self-owners who are at liberty to transact with willing others so as to advance the various ends to which they are drawn.

Attentive readers will have noticed a striking parallel to the Rawls and Nozick of our own planet. At this point, however, the parallels end. For (Twin) Rawls, despite some inclinations to the contrary, came to espouse a robust libertarianism and ended up reviving a classical liberalism that the advanced thinkers of Twin Earth had, for the preceding century, declared defunct. (Twin) Nozick, however, although taking off from a vantage point that appeared even more rigorously libertarian than that of his colleague, established the permissibility of sweeping redistribution under state aegis in the name of justice.

The question I pose in this essay is: Which of the philosopher-pairs has landed on more suitable ground—the familiar Harvard pair or their counterparts at Twin Harvard? I come down in favor of the latter duo, not only because the contrary assessment would make for an exceedingly flat conclusion, but also because there are prominent themes running through the arguments of our familiar Rawls and Nozick that push them in the direction of their Twin Harvard counterparts. Most of the succeeding discussion will concern itself with Rawls. That is because there are several

* A draft of this essay was prepared while I was enjoying a residential fellowship from the Centre for Applied Philosophy and Public Ethics, Charles Sturt University, in Canberra, Australia. I have benefited from discussions following talks at the Social and Political Theory program seminar at the Australian National University and the Harvard College Department of Government.

strands running through his writings that need to be untangled and then brought together again to weave the libertarian fabric worn by his Twin Harvard counterpart. Nozick's anti-libertarianism is simpler, and is essentially confined to one aspect of his entitlement theory of justice in property holdings. Once that is set out, alternatives become clear-cut: either bite the bullet and join forces with Twin Nozick's intrusive state or else redesign the entitlement theory so as to domesticate it for cohabitation with a minimal state.

Section II finds in both Rawls and Twin Rawls three motifs strongly supportive of libertarianism. Of course, only Twin Rawls actually takes that route, so Section III examines Rawls's explicit arguments against libertarianism. What may be most revealing about these critiques is how uncharacteristically lame they are. Section IV introduces the entitlement theory of Twin Nozick and its striking divergence from libertarianism. Section V is given over to speculation and summing up.

II. THREE LIBERTARIAN MOTIFS

A. The priority of liberty

Any examination of Rawls's central political views must commence with *A Theory of Justice* (1971),[1] and at the center of that center are his two principles of justice. The second principle and, especially, its subsidiary component, the difference principle, has received disproportionate attention in the literature, not least by Rawls himself. However, it bears emphasizing that throughout the development of Rawlsian justice, an unvarying feature is the lexical priority of individual liberty. The initial statement of this principle (and its priority) is:

> First: each person is to have an equal right to the most extensive basic liberty compatible with a similar liberty for others. (*TJ*, 60)

It is followed by the second principle, in which economic inequalities are countenanced just so long as they work to the advantage of all.

Noteworthy is the *maximalism* of the initial statement of the first principle along the three dimensions of person, quantity, and kind. To the question, For which citizens is liberty to be secured? the answer is: *All of them*. To the question, How much liberty are they to enjoy? the answer is:

---

[1] John Rawls, *A Theory of Justice* (Cambridge, MA: Harvard University Press, 1971); hereafter cited as *TJ*. Citations to other books by Rawls will be abbreviated as follows: *TJ2* for *A Theory of Justice: Revised Edition* (Cambridge, MA: Harvard University Press, 1999); *PL* for *Political Liberalism* (New York: Columbia University Press, 1993); and *LP* for *The Law of Peoples* (Cambridge, MA: Harvard University Press, 1999). Further below I shall use the abbreviation *ASU* for Robert Nozick, *Anarchy, State, and Utopia* (New York: Basic Books, 1974).

As much as can be achieved. And to the question, Which liberties matter? the suggested answer is: *They all do.* These maximalisms display Rawls as the legitimate heir to the classical liberal tradition running from John Locke and, especially, Immanuel Kant,[2] for which the defining feature is the primacy of liberty among political goods. Rawls observes at the outset of his book that "Justice is the first virtue of social institutions" (*TJ*, 3); here he seems to indicate that the first virtue of justice is commitment to the overriding importance of liberty. Is it possible to deny the fundamentally libertarian flavor of a theory in which this principle enjoys lexical priority?

It cannot be denied on Twin Earth, where, as will be exhibited below, the first principle serves as the centerpiece of Twin Rawls's libertarianism.[3] On our planet, though, things are different. Almost immediately Rawls inserts qualifiers to limit the scope of the principle, and then in *A Theory of Justice* and follow-up works, he continually backs away from giving full force to a liberty requirement. It is not possible in this context to offer a detailed tour of the unwinding of the first principle, but a few selected highlights will indicate the direction of the process. Almost immediately after stating the first principle, Rawls offers an initial specification:

> The basic liberties of citizens are, roughly speaking, political liberty (the right to vote and be eligible for public office) together with freedom of speech and assembly; liberty of conscience and freedom of thought; freedom of the person along with the right to hold (personal) property; and freedom from arbitrary arrest and seizure as defined by the concept of the rule of law. (*TJ*, 61)

Conspicuously absent from this catalog are economic liberties, including freedom of contract to buy and sell, to employ and be employed, or to accumulate and invest.[4] A right to hold property is included, but it is

---

[2] Ancestral to the first principle of justice is Kant's formulation of the categorical imperative as applied to the basic structure of civil society: "The universal law of right is as follows: let your external actions be such that the free application of your will can co-exist with the freedom of everyone in accordance with a universal law." Immanuel Kant, "Introduction to the Theory of Right," *The Metaphysics of Morals*, in Hans Reiss, ed., *Kant's Political Writings* (Cambridge: Cambridge University Press, 1970), 133. In the *Critique of Pure Reason* he maintains, "A constitution providing for the *greatest human freedom* according to laws that permit *the freedom of each to exist together with that of others* . . . is at least a necessary idea, which one must make the ground not merely of the primary plan of a state's constitution but of all the laws too." Immanuel Kant, *Critique of Pure Reason*, ed. and trans. Paul Guyer and Allen W. Wood (Cambridge: Cambridge University Press, 1998), 397 (A316/B373), emphases in the original.

[3] A complementary argument along lines that Twin Rawls would approve is offered by James M. Buchanan and Loren E. Lomasky, "The Matrix of Contractarian Justice," *Social Philosophy and Policy* 2, no. 1 (1984): 12–32.

[4] It is not only liberties favored by would-be capitalists that are absent. Rights to educate one's children in a preferred manner, to engage in sexual relations with members of whichever sex one favors, to participate in risky recreational activities, to shut one's door to census takers, and a hundred other liberties great and small also are omitted.

explicitly limited to personal property, although no explication of what this includes/excludes is supplied.

When Rawls turns (in Section 42 of *A Theory of Justice*) to comparison of economic systems, he observes that market-based economies possess several advantages over command systems. Markets are less administratively cumbersome for distribution of consumption goods, and they more efficiently respond to the preferences of households (*TJ*, 270). Markets afford scope for individuals to move between jobs in response to changes in relative wage levels; they also decentralize economic power (*TJ*, 272). But if this should seem to provide a strong rationale for endorsing private property regimes, Rawls demurs. "It is evident . . . that there is no essential tie between the use of free markets and private ownership of the instruments of production" (*TJ*, 271), he affirms, adding that "[w]hich of these systems and the many intermediate forms most fully answers to the requirements of justice cannot, I think, be determined in advance" (*TJ*, 274). That is because the appropriateness for a given society of a set of economic institutions will depend on particular facts about its history and circumstances. The theory of justice is neutral between socialist and individual ownership of productive resources.

When some two decades later Rawls rethinks these matters for the revised edition of *A Theory of Justice* (1999), the conclusion is unchanged:

> [J]ustice as fairness leaves open the question whether its principles are best realized by some form of property-owning democracy or by a liberal socialist regime. This question is left to be settled by historical conditions and the traditions, institutions, and social forces of each country. As a political conception, then, justice as fairness includes no natural right of private property in the means of production. (*TJ2*, xv–xvi)

In another respect, though, Rawls's ideas about the priority of liberty have shifted significantly. Under the influence of H. L. A. Hart's critique,[5] he concedes Hart's point that the notion of a "most extensive total system of equal basic liberties" is not well-defined; whether one set of liberties is more extensive than another will often depend on prior contestable judgments concerning which among competing activities is more or less valuable.[6] Thus, the first principle is either without content or question-begging. To avoid this dilemma, Rawls abandons the maximization of basic liberties, instead redrafting the first principle to read:

---

[5] H. L. A. Hart, "Rawls on Liberty and Its Priority," *University of Chicago Law Review* 40 (1973): 534–55.

[6] If one set of liberties is a superset of another, then it is the more extensive. This seems uncontroversial. Whether there are similarly uncontroversial comparisons to be made among systems neither of which is a subset of the other is a further and more difficult issue.

Each person has an equal right to a *fully adequate* scheme of equal basic liberties which is compatible with a similar scheme of liberties for all. (*PL*, 291, emphasis added)

These liberties are specified by a list that is then defended against the charge of being makeshift via an argument attempting to show that these are the sort of things that contractors in the original position might opt for so as to give full effect to their two moral powers of cleaving to a conception of the good and exercising a sense of justice.[7] The retreat from maximization is presented as a virtue of the new formulation,[8] and Rawls notes that this reformulated first principle, like its predecessors, is neutral between private ownership of capital goods and socialist production.[9]

Throughout the evolution of the theory of justice as fairness, Rawls maintains the priority of a liberty principle, yet, as the preceding sketch indicates, the content of protected liberties becomes increasingly modest in successive iterations. Rawls deems this a theoretical improvement, but Twin Rawls draws the opposite conclusion. To understand the crux of their disagreement it will be useful to turn to the rationales given for the priority of liberty (either in a maximalist sense or through a list of specified liberties) over other goods that can be advanced via political means.

One rationale is the importance to individuals of standing one to another in a relationship of equal citizenship. In a well-ordered society, self-respect endures disparities in wealth because these are justified by reference to the position of the least well-off member. To be subordinate to others as a participating member of a social union is, however, demeaning. It is to possess less than a full share of the social bases of self-respect. That is why inequality of basic liberties, as opposed to inequalities of wealth, would be rejected by contractors in the original position.[10] Under this interpretation of the priority of liberty, it is clear that what is required above all is *equality* of basic liberties with one's fellows so as to be able to look them in the eye from a position of parity. Moreover, the liberties that

[7] The list reads as follows: "[F]reedom of thought and liberty of conscience; the political liberties and freedom of association, as well as the freedoms specified by the liberty and integrity of the person; and finally, the rights and liberties covered by the rule of law" (*PL*, 291). Much of the remainder of this lecture, "The Basic Liberties and Their Priority," is given over to rendering this itemization less vague.

[8] Rawls writes, "It is wise, I think, to limit the basic liberties to those that are truly essential in the expectation that the liberties which are not basic are satisfactorily allowed for by the general presumption when the discharge of the burden of proof is decided by the other requirements of the two principles of justice" (*PL*, 296). The point of this difficult statement seems to be that nonbasic liberties will be afforded recognition at a lower level when and only when they do not interfere either with the application of these list-specified basic liberties or with the melioration of social and economic inequalities via the second principle.

[9] See *PL*, 298.

[10] See *TJ*, 546–47.

are most crucial to citizenly self-respect are those requisite for full participation in the political activities of the country, as opposed to those liberties that take as their object essentially private activities, of which wealth creation and accumulation are paradigmatic. Taking account of this rationale alone, Rawls has judged well to distance himself from a rhetoric of maximizing a generalized stock of liberty and instead to privilege a delimited collection of politically salient liberties.

There is, however, a second rationale for the priority of liberty, one directly responsive to persons' capacity to formulate and pursue particular conceptions of the good. What citizens can be presumed to possess in common is a commitment to acting justly toward each other, where the duties of justice bear alike on everyone. But no such commonality characterizes the ends to which they direct themselves, the advancement of which confers meaning on their lives and which contribute no less importantly than does equal citizenship to their enjoyment of self-respect. A just order is one in which individuals, motivated by goods that they take to be of compelling, even transcendent value, nonetheless respect the rights of others to show themselves indifferent to these goods while instead pursuing other ends that may seem to be of negligible worth.[11]

Rawls observes that under favorable conditions in which necessities of survival are reliably satisfied, "the obstacles to the exercise of the equal liberties decline and a growing insistence upon the right to pursue our spiritual and cultural interests asserts itself. Increasingly it becomes more important to secure the free internal life of the various communities of interests in which persons and groups seek to achieve, in modes of social union consistent with equal liberty, the ends and excellences to which they are drawn" (TJ, 543). With regard to these ends and excellences, the specifically political liberties enjoy no distinctive pride of place—or, rather, they do not for those individuals whose pursuit of the good life is primarily conducted in venues outside the public arena. What those individuals need from others is generalized noninterference, and because in the original position they do not know which particular ends will command their allegiance, they have reason to value a wider rather than narrower scope of liberty. Thus, they will regard the latter versions of the first principle as insufficiently responsive to whatever interests they will find themselves to have that lie beyond the practice of citizenship as such. Instead, they will resist shrinkage of the original guarantee of maximal equal liberty. They will understand this liberty in a wide sense, even if they do not arrive at one definitive account of where it is at its most expansive. That is, Hart's critique may lead them to agree that no maximizing function for liberties is derivable a priori. They will, however,

---

[11] See the example of the grass counter (TJ, 432). Its point is, among other things, that even bizarrely idiosyncratic pursuits are to be afforded due deference. The counting of blades of grass lacks, if anything does, defining political features. It is a fundamentally private undertaking that, despite its oddity, is to be afforded full protection in a free society.

nonetheless insist that we often have good reason between competing alternatives to judge that one is more favorable than the other to the exercise of unimpeded self-determination. In particular, they are very likely to hold that both theory and historical practice amply demonstrate that liberty is enhanced by an order of private ownership of productive assets rather than collective control by state bureaucracies. If so, they will be in accord with Twin Rawls, who shares with our Rawls a commitment to the priority of liberty, but who understands that principle to commend an order of generalized noninterference rather than one in which political freedoms are privileged.

B. Strains of commitment

Deliberators in the original position decline to adopt the principle of (maximizing expected) average utility, preferring instead the maximin strategy (of securing the best possible minimum) incorporated in the difference principle. The choice is overdetermined. It is stimulated in part by difficulties of ascertaining behind the veil of ignorance any probabilities concerning which social position they will occupy, and in part by an aversion to gambles that put them at risk of falling below a satisfactory minimum. Both of these prongs of the Rawlsian argument are controversial and have generated numerous responses. They will not be examined further here.

There is, however, a third prong of the argument that is substantially independent of the other two and that carries considerable conviction in its own right. Unless individuals will be regularly and reliably motivated to act in accord with chosen principles, at least under favorable conditions, those principles are unsatisfactory as the framework for a society's basic structure. The problem with utilitarianism is, simply put, that it demands too much of individuals. It requires them to acquiesce in the sacrifice of much, perhaps all, of that which they value for the sake of maximizing a putative social good. One who assents to a utilitarian strategy because it holds forth the prospect of a greater expected return for self than does any of its competitors is apt to find himself unable or unwilling to accede to its demands should he turn out to be unfortunate in the lottery of life's events. And even if one should prove to be among the fortunate beneficiaries of the utility principle, this good luck could be undone by the defections of less fortunate others. Thus, a rational individual alive to the risks of instability will be dissuaded from endorsing in the original position the principle of average utility. The integrity of society is unnecessarily imperiled by erecting its institutions on foundations from which individuals will predictably tend to defect. By way of contrast, justice as fairness rejects extreme sacrifice. It guarantees to each a decent minimum, indeed the most favorable minimum that can be secured by any social design. For that reason, invoking the Rawlsian idiom, it is burdened by lesser "strains of commitment" than is utilitarianism.[12]

Although Rawls does not explicitly draw the connection, concern for keeping the strains of commitment low for all parties supports the priority of the liberty principle. To be left alone to serve those ends that hold out surpassing value for oneself, rather than being required to drop them for the sake of what is proclaimed to be a superior social product, is mandatory for those whose personal projects hold out great significance. Such individuals could not rationally accede to a system in which it is likely that they will be forcibly separated from that which they hold dear. The strains of commitment counsel against endorsement of such potentially onerous demands.

One must ask, though, *which* liberty principle will find favor with contractors intent to specify a basic structure that they will subsequently find congenial to their moral powers? The Rawlsian "fully adequate scheme" of civil freedoms answers in some measure to the concern that one will not be involuntarily divorced from one's ends. To be in possession of a full range of political freedoms renders one well-provisioned in a democratic environment to campaign actively on their behalf. However, the assurance thereby provided is slim. One's potential opponents are equally graced with democratic freedoms, and if at the end of the contest they should command a majority, then it will not necessarily be much consolation to have had one's day at the polls. If the subjectively measured costs of the required sacrifice are high, then even those who possess a firm sense of justice may find themselves reluctant to go along. So the same considerations that lead Rawls to endorse the two principles over average utilitarianism support construing the liberty principle broadly, as broadly as it presents itself in its initial maximizing formulation.

There are further reasons to believe that strains of commitment cut against the official Rawlsian statement of justice as fairness. Rawls has argued that the difference principle meliorates those strains (against the utilitarian alternative) by rendering the losers in life's lottery as well-off as they can be. That may be true, but it leaves open questions about the impact of those strains on other strata of the population. Because individuals are represented as not only rational but also reasonable, they are motivated by a concern for reciprocity (see *PL*, 17–18). They are prepared to forgo some measure of advantage in order to ensure gains for their fellows. They are not, then, purely rational egoists. Neither, though, are they perfect impartialists. Between their own preferred ends and those of others, they are not neutral. The more they are required to forgo the former so as to advance the latter, the greater the strains of commitment under which they labor. It would seem, then, that the same sort of concern for social stability that spoke against utilitarianism will also pronounce

---

[12] See the discussions in *TJ*, 176–78 and *PL*, 17.

against unchecked requirements of redistribution. A theorist has done only half the job by ascertaining the view from the bottom; it is requisite also to see how things present themselves from a top-down perspective. From that vantage, the nature of the impositions potentially placed on the more well-off are arguably more than they will be prepared to bear.

The strict logic of the difference principle entails that for the sake of even very small enhancements to the least well-off, their better-advantaged fellows must be prepared to bear enormous costs, limited only by the crossover point at which they would themselves assume the position of society's least well-off. "[I]t seems extraordinary that the justice of increasing the expectations of the better placed by a billion dollars, say, should turn on whether the prospects of the least favored increase or decrease by a penny" (*TJ*, 57). Can the demands of justice impose so stringently on the more advantaged, and if they do, will not the rigor of the system generate strains of commitment that only moral saints and heroes will find themselves able to abide?

Rawls's immediate answer is that "the difference principle is not intended to apply to such abstract possibilities" (*TJ*, 157). Rather, it is incorporated in a basic structure designed for the most part to create a tide that raises and lowers boats together.[13] But even if that response suffices to rule out the most extreme imagined counterexamples, it nonetheless remains true that the elevation of the craft in which the better-off sail is strictly constrained by the course of the other boat. There is no presumption that the degree of interconnection is minimal. Rather, the presumption goes in the other direction. Rawlsian egalitarianism is limited only by a Paretian criterion of mutual advantage. For all that can be said in advance, that might dictate a high degree of equality and concomitantly great sacrifices on the part of the more favored groups. It is not clear why those who are required to earn and keep less will rationally accede to that demand.

Rawls's most revealing and candid response to this worry is supplied in Section 17, "The Tendency to Equality." In response to the fact that people come into society with vastly different abilities and vastly different prospects flowing therefrom, he observes:

> The natural distribution is neither just nor unjust; nor is it unjust that persons are born into society at some particular position. These are simply natural facts. What is just and unjust is the way that institutions deal with these facts. . . . The social system is not an unchangeable order beyond human control but a pattern of human action. In justice as fairness men agree to share one another's fate. (*TJ*, 102)

To this the indicated response is: *Exactly!* Bonds uniting citizens in the Rawlsian conception reveal themselves to be extraordinarily tight. It is no

---

[13] See Rawls's discussion of "chain connection" and "close-knitness" in *TJ*, 81–83.

small thing to agree to share one's fate with another. That is the sort of undertaking embarked on within a family, by friends or lovers determined to pursue the good life together, partners in a far-reaching enterprise, a platoon's soldiers guarding each other's backs, congregants joined in common worship, or devotees of a mutually adored good. In such settings, the success of one constitutes in no small measure the success of all, and an individual who is not prepared to sacrifice some of her own quota of the good, indeed sacrifice liberally, is an anomalous partner in the pursuit. And of course it is not uncommon for the strains of commitment inherent in such intimate relations to rupture the bonds that formerly held the parties close.[14]

It is quite otherwise when the tie among persons is nothing more than a citizenship held in common. Here intimacy is very much the exception rather than the rule. The comprehensive theories of one's compatriots will often incorporate commitments and ideas of the good that leave one unmoved—or worse. In such cases one is obliged to respect their liberty to follow their own fervid musings or strange gods, but it is to demand too much to add to the standing order of noninterference the further requirement that positive assistance be afforded—that, in a word, one join one's fate to theirs. The two principles of justice are seen in such instances to be in direct tension with each other. The liberty principle allows individuals to devote themselves to their own preferred conceptions of the good and thus to distance themselves from others who acknowledge ends that are indifferent or antithetical to their own. (Or rather, such permission is afforded by a liberty principle that extends beyond a basketful of privileges confined to the political arena.) The difference principle binds individuals together. Something has to give.

And so it does. Rawls has second thoughts concerning the intensity of social bonds under a justice as fairness regime. In the revised edition of *A Theory of Justice*, the striking passage about individuals sharing each other's fate disappears.[15] Most likely, during the interval between the two editions Rawls had come to believe that he had expressed himself more forcefully than was felicitous. Perhaps some friendly critics had asked him whether he really wished to hitch to the theoretical structure of *A*

---

[14] Daniel McDermott suggested in conversation that Rawls may mean by the sharing of fate simply the fact that generation of the cooperative surplus depends on the adherence by each to society's rules and procedures. I do not think that this can be what Rawls intended here. Under any cooperative scheme, the output will be a function of the various inputs, but Rawls explicitly says that the willingness to share one another's fate is distinctive of justice as fairness. Indeed, if he is not making such a claim, then the character of this section of *TJ* as a defense of the difference principle evaporates.

[15] The corresponding passage reads, "The social system is not an unchangeable order beyond human control but a pattern of human action. In justice as fairness men agree to avail themselves of the accidents of nature and social circumstance only when doing so is for the common benefit. The two principles are a fair way of meeting the arbitrariness of fortune; and while no doubt imperfect in other ways, the institutions which satisfy these principles are just" (*TJ2*, 88).

Theory of Justice so weighty a wagon of social solidarity. Whatever the impetus behind the revision, the text of the second edition has become anodyne. Citizens are still to share in society's assets but not each other's fates.

It is not clear that such revision by omission is satisfactory. The reader may suspect that it camouflages rather than eliminates a fundamental problem with the project. The Rawls of 1971 must have believed that the bonds of social solidarity to be imputed to citizens in a well-ordered regime based on the two principles of justice are substantial enough to make it sensible, if perhaps edging toward the far end of the metaphorically appropriate, to use the language of sharing one another's fate. Either he had misjudged then concerning how much can legitimately be spun out from contractors' posited sense of justice, or by the time he prepared the revised edition he had devised a different strategy to explain why the strains of commitment embedded in the difference principle are not too onerous for individuals reliably to bear. Unfortunately, no explanation of the transition is offered in the 1999 edition. An author may, of course, admit to prior missteps. Such frankness is commendable. Indeed, in this spirit of generosity Rawls has often acknowledged the force of his critics' remarks and revised accordingly. The problem here, however, is that the withdrawn passage is, arguably, no misstatement at all. Rather, it serves to explain an otherwise puzzling feature of the Rawlsian account. There is no mystery why the *least well-off* individuals find justice as fairness agreeable; under no alternative basic structure for society will they do better. The more recalcitrant problem is to explain why the *more well-off* accede to a system in which they demonstrably are less well-served than they would be under other social arrangements. Will they not be inclined to regard themselves as unjustifiably exploited? The answer that immediately suggests itself is this: Not if they take themselves in some very strong sense to be implicated in the fate of their less favored brethren. Absent this understanding, it is doubtful that justice as fairness can survive the strains of commitment.

Exactly this line of reasoning can be seen in the celebrated works of Twin Rawls. He, too, determines that the difference principle expresses a profound depth of social solidarity. But for Twin Rawls, this amounts to an utterly convincing reductio ad absurdum of the so-called second principle of justice. In large and diverse liberal societies where persons are spatially spread out from each other, espouse markedly different religious and philosophical comprehensive theories, and differ no less substantially with regard to their personal affections than in their various conceptions of the good, it is outlandish to suppose that they can regard their own success or failure as tightly bound up with the achievements of distant others. Because they have a sense of justice, they will forswear aggressive interference against others for whom friendly regard may be limited or altogether lacking. And because they are prudent, they will insist on reciprocal noninterference from others. That is not quite all that Twin Rawls includes in his theory of justice (see Section III below), but it is the dominant strand. It is what makes him Twin Harvard's most illustrious libertarian.

That Twin Rawls zigs where Rawls zags does not constitute disproof of the latter's theory. Perhaps it is our Rawls who has gotten things (more nearly) right. It is impossible decisively to defend one Rawls over the other without performing a more thorough excavation of the theory of justice than is possible here. Instead, I offer an ad hominem argument against our Rawls's understanding. Although arguments ad hominem normally carry a somewhat unsavory flavor, in this case that may be mitigated by the fact that the one arguing against Rawls's understanding is Rawls himself. That argument is initiated in *Political Liberalism* (1993), where he does not abandon his support of the difference principle but concedes that it is one among several ways of reasonably distributing the benefits and burdens of social cooperation. But in *The Law of Peoples* (1999), Rawls distances himself further from the difference principle by denying, against the urging of his own disciples,[16] that it is a suitable basis for interaction among the world's peoples.[17] The reasoning and illustrative examples Rawls provides in the latter book are somewhat opaque, but the upshot is that there is no general requirement of economic redistribution from the world's wealthier countries to those less well-off. Only for peoples in considerable distress, what Rawls calls "burdened societies" (meaning thereby essentially the same as the more familiar locution "failed states"), is there a duty of positive assistance, and then only to the "point at which a people's basic needs (estimated in primary goods) are fulfilled and a people can stand on its own" (*LP*, 119). This is because the world's peoples have reason primarily to value their own autonomy and preferred national culture rather than subscription to an egalitarian cosmopolitanism. Beyond contingent temporary provision to address episodes of distress, duties owed by the wealthy to the less well-off are modes of noninterference (e.g., observance of treaties, nonintervention, and adherence to human rights and rules of war; see *LP*, 37), and they are returned in kind: one is struck by the sweepingness on the international level of an equal liberty principle, and by the rejection of egalitarianism as inconsistent with each society's overriding interest in devoting its energies to its own distinctive interests. Although Rawls does not quite put it this way, a fair reading of his text is that attention to diminishing strains of commitment commends a system of global justice in which each people is only minimally implicated in the doings of others.

---

[16] Especially Charles Beitz, *Political Theory and International Relations* (Princeton, NJ: Princeton University Press, 1979); and Thomas W. Pogge, *Realizing Rawls* (Ithaca, NY; Cornell University Press, 1989).

[17] For reasons that need not be explored here, Rawls prefers to speak of the benefits and requirements of international justice as primarily attaching to *peoples* rather than *states*.

If the argument is persuasive—Twin Rawls finds it so—then it is no less persuasive when recast as an argument safeguarding the nonimplication of individuals within a given society in the projects of others.

C. *Choice behind the veil of ignorance*

Perhaps the most distinctive aspect of Rawls's methodology is his casting the problem of eliciting basic principles of justice as a choice-theoretic determination behind a suitably specified veil of ignorance. People are stripped of individuating knowledge that would allow them to tailor principles to suit their own particular situations. Deprived of such data, they rationally direct themselves toward principles under which they will do comparatively well, regardless of who they turn out to be or how favorable the circumstances they confront. Thus, they legislate to safeguard their basic liberties—the first principle—and to ensure an economic status that is at least minimally satisfactory for enabling them to live as ends-pursuers—the second principle. I argued in Section IIA that Rawls backs away from a rendering of the liberty principle that adequately serves the former aim. To that result can now be added equally cogent reasons to maintain that the second principle's invitation to engineer a massively redistributivist welfare apparatus will be declined in the original position. Rather, strong property rights, including robust freedom of contract, will be endorsed, modified only by guaranteed provision of a minimally decent floor beneath which individuals will not be allowed to fall: a "social safety net." [18]

Although contractors in the original position are screened from individuating knowledge, they have access to general facts, including those of social theory (*TJ*, 142). That theory is not, of course, a completed science: oases of relative clarity are surrounded by expanses of obscurity, and despite a generally progressive course, the theory dead-ends into occasional cul-de-sacs and regressions. Nonetheless, intelligent design of social institutions, not least a society's basic structure, entails judicious use of the best approximations to knowledge that we have while simultaneously guarding against being impaled on unacknowledged spikes of ignorance. So, for example, any tolerably fair and efficient design will build in a recognition that "the point of the institution of property is that, unless a definite agent is given responsibility for maintaining an asset and bears the loss for not doing so, that asset tends to deteriorate." This was well known already by the contemporaries of Adam Smith, although this statement in fact comes from Rawls (*LP*, 39). I believe that by the time of the original drafting of *A Theory of Justice*, enough was known about the equity and efficiency properties of collective ownership of the means of

---

[18] As noted below in the text, allowance is also to be made for political provision of public goods, but insofar as these are truly public, only incidental redistribution is thereby occasioned.

production to decisively rule out socialism as a feature of a society's basic structure. Three decades on and counting, this is beyond serious dispute. Any contemporary invocation of the original position will, therefore, make quick work of dispatching Marxist fancies to the dustbin of defunct social theories.

Are there other propositions about the working of economic/political systems that were not brought behind Rawls's original veil of ignorance but that now are well-attested presumptions without which the practice of intelligent social design cannot be conducted? One plausible candidate is this: There is no amount of self-seeking battening on the public fisc, of blithely robbing Peter to pay Paul, that cannot be given a semi-plausible justification suitable for thirty-second sound bites. Or, to phrase it more soberly, "[W]hether the aims of the principles covering social and economic inequalities are realized is . . . difficult to ascertain. These matters are nearly always open to wide differences of reasonable opinion; they rest on complicated inferences and intuitive judgments that require us to assess complex social and economic information about topics poorly understood" (*PL*, 229). If the rules of the political game allow for taking and then redistributing property just so long as a majority can be assembled to testify that they are acting for the sake of some lofty ideal of social justice—perhaps one that goes by the name of "justice as fairness"—then it is predictable that those rules will be frequently and extravagantly bent in the service of interests that are neither impartial nor likely to advance the positions of the least well-off. Knowing this, contractors in the original position will be loath to afford carte blanche to the proliferation of allegedly welfarist measures. They will realize that the point of the institution of property as noted above will be imperiled by such a loosening of rights to the continued possession of that which has been acquired through voluntary transactions. It is eminently knowable behind the veil of ignorance that rent-seeking, the investment of resources in the attempt to secure windfall returns through political subventions, is a negative-sum game. Moreover, it is a game that society's already well-advantaged are likely to be especially good at. The upshot is that even if the veiled deliberators are motivated by a strong concern for the least well-off (make that *especially* if they are motivated by a strong concern for the least well-off), the deliberators will erect constraints on the ability of political actors to redefine property rights in the service of some ostensible ideal.

Suppose that we judge it a good thing, all else being equal, that resources flow to their most economically valued use. One way this desideratum could be pursued is via a process of hearings and speeches by all parties who take an interest in the subject, followed by votes in the legislature on competing allocative proposals. Another way in which the desideratum can be pursued is to allow trades of rights assignments until an outcome is reached in which no parties are willing to exchange their holdings for some other set on offer (i.e., they have landed on some point on the Pareto frontier). It is a simplification but not an oversimplification to say that the most important conclusion of the first century of post–Adam Smith economics is that the second strategy pays off better than the first. Indirection triumphs over direct pursuit of the desideratum. The most important finding of its second century may be that the aims of social justice also are better pursued by an indirect strategy. This remains true even if one believes that how the upper strata of society fares is irrelevant to concerns of justice and that exclusive focus is to be directed to the least well-off. It is not paradoxical hyperbole to maintain that the prospects of the poor are enhanced by disallowing all special pleading in legislatures and regulatory bodies on behalf of the poor. Impartial enforcement of a regime of strong property rights and binding contracts almost certainly will better serve them.[19]

Admittedly, this is a first approximation. Before pulling back the veil and entering into the full light of political day, allowance will be made for collective provision of genuinely public goods, those for which features of nonexcludability and nonrivalry of consumption render market provision awkward. Additionally, it is appropriate to legislate a safety net for those who find themselves in exigent straits and who are unable to extricate themselves therefrom, either through their own actions or through the voluntary subventions of others. This latter condition is responsive to strains of commitment that otherwise might render the precepts of justice too onerous for the poor to embrace, while the positive-sum character of the remainder of economic transacting will lessen those strains on all. Twin Rawls, who enjoyed the benefits of a thorough grounding in the central insights of twentieth-century social theory, drew precisely this conclusion. It was not beyond the reach of the other Rawls. Therefore, it is worth considering why he, too, did not gravitate toward libertarianism.

III. Rawls on Libertarianism

A. Moral arbitrariness

Rawls uses the term "system of natural liberty" to characterize a social order in which individuals enjoy full and equal liberty, and in which they are free to capitalize on their talents and fortune so far as they are able (*TJ*, 59–60). This interpretation of the second principle of justice's requirement of mutual advantage treats all persons impartially by ensuring their rights to transact with willing others in their pursuit of advancement. It does not, however, take notice of their various starting points. But because those who have been well-favored by a lucky turn of the natural lottery's

---

[19] Richard A. Epstein offers a substantially identical construal of the original position in "Rawls Remembered," available online at http://nationalreview.com/comment/comment-epstein112702.asp [posted November 27, 2002; accessed April 14, 2004].

wheel (or in subsequent social engagements) will tend to capture more of society's goods than do those who have been less well-favored, consequent shares of the good things of life will not accurately reflect any antecedent merit. "Intuitively, the most obvious injustice of the system of natural liberty is that it permits distributive shares to be improperly influenced by these factors so arbitrary from a moral point of view" (*TJ*, 72).

This essentially completes the critique of libertarianism in *A Theory of Justice*. Little more could have been expected. The term "libertarian" was then barely recognizable in a political context, and the classical liberalism from which contemporary libertarianism springs had been sharply out of favor for more than a century. In an already very large book, it may have seemed excessive to devote more ink to what seemed a mere historical footnote. Accordingly, Rawls turns forthwith to other, more viable interpretations of the second principle of justice. Had he been conversant with the writings of Twin Rawls, however, he would have realized that this is to give too short shrift to the libertarian alternative. Even if it is granted that one's place in the natural lottery of talents and initial social position is morally arbitrary, it does not follow that a structure mostly dedicated to safeguarding the rights of individuals to act from those starting places is also morally arbitrary. The point from which one begins is neither here nor there, morally speaking, but that one proceeds therefrom to freely exercise one's two moral powers so as to advance favored ends while simultaneously affording due recognition and respect to other agents is laden with moral significance. Recall Rawls's remark: "The natural distribution is neither just nor unjust. . . . What is just and unjust is the way that institutions deal with these facts" (*TJ*, 102). There are two broadly contrasting ways in which the political institutions of a society can deal with these facts. One is through the adoption of policies and procedures contrived so as directly to bring about some favored distributive configuration. The other is through a system of law that reinforces the capacity of self-directing individuals to generate valued outcomes.[20] The first of these is exemplified by the Rawlsian difference principle, the second by the Twin Rawlsian maximum equal liberty principle. Neither of these represents a simple surrender to moral arbitrariness. If there is a case to be made in favor of the first against the second, it must be *made*, not simply assumed by default.

B. Libertarianism is not political

In lecture 7 of *Political Liberalism*, "The Basic Structure as Subject," Rawls contrasts justice as fairness with Robert Nozick's libertarianism.

---

[20] This is to invoke Nozick's distinction between "patterned" principles of distribution and those, such as his entitlement theory, that are historical or otherwise unpatterned. See *ASU*, 155–60.

There is, Rawls claims, no special role for the basic structure within libertarian theory. The state is on a par with private associations insofar as it emerges from a historical series of voluntary transactions with willing clients who are at liberty either to purchase the package of services the state offers at its stipulated selling price or to decline to deal. "By viewing the state as a private association the libertarian doctrine rejects the fundamental ideas of the contract theory, and so quite naturally it has no place for a special theory of justice for the basic structure" (PL, 265).

This critique is multiply problematic. First, it's not clear that it is a critique, rather than simply a characterization. What's wrong with applying principles of justice that hold for private transactions to the evolution of a minimal state? Isn't that a gain from the point of view of theoretical parsimony? Does it not make the birth of political structures seem a bit less ad hoc? Even if Nozickian transactors are removed from social contract understood as deliberation behind a suitably defined veil of ignorance, why should we take that to be a theoretical defect? It is not obvious that the *actually* agreeable carries less weight than the hypothetically agreeable.

Second, even if Rawls does nail Nozick dead to rights, that is not equivalent to having dispatched libertarianism. Perhaps the flaws exhibited in Nozick's theory—assuming that they are in fact flaws—are idiosyncratic. If something more than victory in a one-on-one skirmish is to be achieved, then Rawls must train his sights more broadly on the gamut of exponents of the "system of natural liberty."

Third, Rawls grossly mischaracterizes Nozick's argument. Contra Rawls, it is not Nozick's view of the transition to the minimal state that "[n]o one can be compelled to enter into such an agreement and everyone always has the option of becoming an independent" (PL, 265). This is a remarkable inversion of the extended Nozickian argument for the permissibility of *disallowing independent status* and instead compelling individuals to enter into a civil order.[21] Whether or not that argument carries plausibility,[22] any useful critique/characterization of the progression of Nozick's *Anarchy, State, and Utopia* must minimally get it straight.

C. Libertarianism is illiberal

Rawls maintains that reasonably just constitutional democratic societies assure "sufficient all-purpose means to enable all citizens to make

[21] "An independent might be prohibited from privately exacting justice because his procedure is known to be too risky and dangerous" (ASU, 88). So begins the first sentence of chapter 5, "The State," in which Nozick argues for a transition to a minimal state such that all inhabitants of a territory are mandatorily enrolled as citizens subject to and protected by its structure of law. It is preceded by the chapter "Prohibition, Compensation, and Risk," in which the theoretical machinery for justifiable prohibitions and associated compensations is developed. A reading of Nozick in which this protracted argument is omitted, indeed reversed, is very much a *Hamlet* minus the Prince of Denmark.

[22] My own view is that it misfires. See Loren E. Lomasky, *Persons, Rights, and the Moral Community* (New York: Oxford University Press, 1987), 143.

intelligent and effective use of their freedoms." Otherwise impeccable systems of formal liberties that fail to incorporate such a guarantee, he adds, "are an impoverished form of liberalism—indeed not liberalism at all but libertarianism. The latter does not combine liberty and equality in the way liberalism does; it lacks the criterion of reciprocity and allows excessive social and economic inequalities" (*LP*, 49).

It is not immediately evident why Rawls says that libertarianism fails the criterion of reciprocity. A libertarian order more than any other rejects forced transactions and the exploitation consequent thereon. Instead, it privileges voluntary exchange, the paradigm instance of mutual benefit and reciprocity. To make sense of Rawls's denial of libertarian reciprocity, he must be understood as maintaining that the freedom of transactors separated by large disparities of wealth and power is not genuine. Someone perched on the edge of exigency is obliged to take whatever bargains she can get, no matter how hard, no matter how divorced from her conception of the good life.

So interpreted, this becomes a variation on the strains-of-commitment theme. The least well-off individuals in a libertarian order will find the meager share they receive from the cooperative surplus scant return for their adherence to the rules of that order. They will regard its formal equality as imposing on them a far greater burdens-to-benefits ratio than is borne by the more well-off. Unlike the high-flyers of laissez faire, the least well-off have scant rational stake in the order's sustenance. It will be unreasonable to expect them to agree to adhere to a regime of rights in which their own rights are of little value.[23] Thus, compliance will have to be secured more by threat of *force majeure* than through the proper functioning of a sense of justice. This appears to be what Rawls means when he says, "A libertarian regime would not have stability for the right reasons, which is always lacking in a purely formal constitutional regime" (*LP*, 49–50).

If strains-of-commitment arguments are to be taken seriously—as Section IIB above argues they must be—then this is Rawls's most formidable anti-libertarian thrust. A libertarian order that allows individuals to fall through the cracks is not one to which all can reasonably commit their allegiance. But rather than constituting a decisive objection to libertarianism, this argument instead amounts to a criterion for choosing among libertarian programs. The decided majority of prominent libertarian proponents have maintained that the central principle of maximum equal liberty is to be accompanied by a contingent and secondary principle of publicly provided subventions for those who are unable through their own voluntary undertakings or the assistance of willing others to elevate

---

[23] Rawls returns repeatedly in his writings to issues surrounding the *value* of liberty. See, for example, *TJ*, 204–5 and 224–27; and *PL*, 324–31.

themselves above the floor of exigency.[24] Among those who fall into this camp are Locke, Kant, Mill, Hayek, and, of course, Twin Rawls;[25] Nozick is the most conspicuous holdout.[26] The presence of a social safety net, albeit one that will only infrequently be invoked in a society in which the state is not an active encroacher on people's freedom to advance their own interests,[27] ensures that a vigorous reciprocity will be preserved. For reasons previously adduced while discussing the scope of the liberty principle, such a regime will lessen strains of commitment by affording maximum scope for the pursuit of those ends that really matter to individuals. There do not, therefore, seem to be any compelling reasons why Rawls need have rejected libertarianism. He could have marched shoulder to philosophical shoulder with his Twin Harvard counterpart.

IV. NOZICKIAN REDISTRIBUTION

I now turn briefly to the curious case of Twin Nozick. This discussion is included because symmetry is aesthetically engaging. One reason for brevity is because no journey to Twin Harvard is needed to discover a Nozick who arguably has rejected libertarianism.[28] Another is that once it is first set out, the idea unfolds itself.

[24] I decline to enter into a debate here concerning whether the term "libertarian" ought to be reserved only for those who disallow all claims to positive provision that issue in welfare rights. Those who feel the need for more scrupulosity in this regard may read these passages as a characterization of *classical liberals* or proponents of a *system of natural liberty*.

[25] I also have supported this position. See, for example, Lomasky, *Persons, Rights, and the Moral Community*, 125–29.

[26] Assuming that his invocation of the Lockean proviso does not indeed join him with these predecessors. See *ASU*, 175–82. Nozick suggests there that the need for forced redistribution to achieve a decent welfare floor would, in the absence of prior illegitimate state actions, be academic.

[27] Examples of state encroachment include occupational licensure, minimum wage laws, restrictive zoning ordinances, cartelization of an education industry that disastrously underserves the poor, victimless crime laws, etc.

[28] Nozick's so-called recantation from libertarianism has occasioned more excited reactions, especially from libertarians who had been inspired and energized by *Anarchy, State, and Utopia,* than its meager dimensions can support:

> The libertarian position I once propounded now seems to me seriously inadequate, in part because it did not knit the humane considerations and joint cooperative activities it left room for more closely into its fabric. It neglected the symbolic importance of an official political concern with issues or problems, as a way of marking their importance or urgency, and hence of expressing, intensifying, channeling, encouraging, and validating our private actions and concerns toward them. . . . There are some things we choose to do together through government in solemn marking of our human solidarity, served by the fact that we do them together in this official fashion.

Robert Nozick, *The Examined Life: Philosophical Meditations* (New York: Simon and Schuster, 1989), 286–87. An even more cursory statement along these lines is repeated in Robert Nozick, *The Nature of Rationality* (Princeton, NJ: Princeton University Press, 1993), 32. For what it may be worth, my view is that Nozick never seriously challenged the libertarianism of *Anarchy, State, and Utopia*. (Had he desired to do so, the result certainly would have been a good bit more impressive than the negligible reflection offered above!) Rather, he simply wished to move on with his philosophical life, and so he offered a modest gesture by way of unhitching himself from a yoke of libertarian political theory.

Twin Nozick embarks from a (Twin?) Lockean foundation of basic rights to life, liberty, and property, arriving at what he dubs the "entitlement theory" (of justice in holdings). According to the entitlement theory, one has justifiable title to some item so long as one has come to possess it either through just original acquisition, just voluntary transfer, or just compensation by way of rectifying a prior injustice. No other criteria are needed. (See *ASU*, 150–53.)

It is important to observe that a situation is not rendered just because it could have been produced via justice-observing means. "The fact that a thief's victims voluntarily *could* have presented him with gifts does not entitle the thief to his ill-gotten gains. Justice in holdings is historical; it depends upon what actually has happened" (*ASU*, 151–52; emphasis in the original). All I need to know to establish that the landed property or chattel in my possession is rightfully owned by me is that I have acquired it from a party who has rightfully acquired it from someone who has rightfully acquired it from someone who has . . . rightfully appropriated it from an unowned condition. That, however, is the rub. Even very new things are mostly made from not-so-new things that were in turn made from yet older things. The chain goes back a very long way, and land goes back further still. How often will one be able to determine with any assurance that a chain of title is unsullied by any episode of injustice? The question is not a merely theoretical one; history is awash with episodes of rapine, murder, enslavement, plunder, and dispossession. The hope for achieving pristine title is a will-o'-the-wisp.[29]

Twin Nozick begins and ends by espousing libertarianism—for a world of perfect compliance. That, most assuredly, is not our actual world. (Nor is the history of Twin Earth a much cheerier tale.) There can be no hope of unraveling the tangled skein of injustices so as to place things in the hands where they properly belong. Not only do we lack an adequate historical knowledge taking us back with no gaps to Adam and Eve/Lucy, but even if the record were complete we would not know what to do. Those who suffered wrongs in the distant past are beyond human ability to render whole; those who suffer contemporary rights violations would not even exist had their conception not been brought about through causal sequences involving yet other rights violations. In so convoluted a moral realm there is nothing for the entitlement theorist to do other than throw up her hands and admit that Humpty Dumpty is not to be put back together again. Instead, the best that can be achieved is to start over from a Day One in which people will be allowed to transact howsoever they choose from a starting point of equality. That requires in turn a Day Zero given over to radically equalizing holdings and other natural assets so that all will be equally placed on the social starting line.

---

[29] Even if some previously undiscovered object is extracted from the state of nature, its acquirer was in a position to lay hands on it because of a causal chain along which at least some of the links incorporate rights violations.

Twin Earth critics objected that this prior equalization was unjustified because there can be no presumption that, in the absence of prior injustices, all would be equally situated. Twin Nozick agreed with the premise, but he argued that if there is absolutely no reason to hold that A deserves more than B, and no reason to hold that B deserves more than A, then the only morally nonarbitrary conclusion to draw is that neither is to have more than the other. Equality wins by default. Thus Twin Nozick regretfully concluded that the libertarian consummation, although devoutly to be wished, will have to be preceded by redistributive shock treatment. First the time of Tribulations, and only then the Millennium.

This planet's Nozick draws no such conclusion. Neither, though, does he reject it. Instead, he hedges:

> How, if at all, do things change if the beneficiaries and those made worse off are not the direct parties in the act of injustice, but, for example, their descendants? Is an injustice done to someone whose holding was itself based upon an unrectified injustice? How far back must one go in wiping clean the historical slate of injustices? What may victims of injustice permissibly do in order to rectify the injustices being done to them, including the many injustices done by persons acting through their government? I do not know of a thorough or theoretically sophisticated treatment of such issues. (*ASU*, 152).[30]

Could it be that Nozick's inability to come up with a thoroughly satisfying account of how to understand entitlements in a morally checkered world contributed to leading him away from political philosophy in general and libertarianism in particular? Possibly. To be sure, he does not react with the extreme pendulum swings of Twin Nozick. But neither does he avail himself of the insights of Twin Rawls so as to spell out a plausible libertarianism for a world of very imperfect compliance.

V. Conclusion

It is time to sum up—or rather, to "fess up." There is no such institution as Twin Harvard. However, there could be. More importantly, there is a possible world in which the Rawls and Nozick of the actual Harvard theorize very much as do their Twin Harvard counterparts. The interesting question to consider is how distant that possible world might be. My hunch is that it is rather far. No small modal alterations would be likely to thrust Rawls into the libertarian camp of Twin Rawls. However, that is not because Rawls's theoretical underpinnings are fundamentally hostile

---

[30] I make a start at addressing some of these issues from a libertarian vantage point in Lomasky, *Persons, Rights, and the Moral Community*, 141–46.

to libertarian propositions. The bulk of this essay has been given over to showing that they are in fact hardly more than a hair's breadth away from yielding a recognizably libertarian position. Rather, the reason Rawls is not libertarian in any close-in possible world is because he is more committed to his egalitarian redistributionist conclusions than he is to the premises that generate those results. Whenever he enters into wide reflective equilibrium, opposition to libertarianism is one of those relatively fixed points unlikely to be dislodged.

This assessment does not stem from amateur psychophilosophy but rather from the plain evidence of the texts. What I mean is this: Rawls is one of the most gifted moral philosophers of our time, perhaps any time. Yet whenever he verges into a territory that might prove congenial to libertarian conclusions, he conducts himself awkwardly. The devolution of the first principle of justice from a stirringly Kantian clarion call to a restricted listing of an assortment of political freedoms does not display Rawls at his most impressive. The first-you-see-it-now-you-don't assessment of justice as fairness as a willingness to share one another's fate is similarly unprepossessing. Strains of commitment are exacerbated by Rawls's defenses of the difference principle, and he fails to take adequate account of the sorts of social science precepts that deliberators behind a veil of ignorance will invoke in order to make an intelligent choice among competing institutional structures. Finally, when he explicitly undertakes to criticize libertarianism, his remarks are perfunctory and ill aimed, sometimes embarrassingly so. I do not mean in any way to demean Rawls when I suggest that his continued inability to come to terms successfully with libertarianism is due to an internal tension between his methodology and his convictions. One or the other has to give; invariably it is the former. It is too late to attempt to convince him to go over to the other side (the dark side?), but it remains timely to suggest that libertarian theorists regard Rawls not so much as an antagonist but rather as a potential ally.

As for Twin Nozick, he reminds us that the entitlement theory retains lots of untapped potential, some for pushing further along in a libertarian direction, some for speeding off in reverse. The final quarter of the twentieth century was graced by two political philosophers of exceptional power and ingenuity. Whatever else it may prove to feature, philosophy in the twenty-first century will continue to draw on their extraordinary legacies.

Philosophy, University of Virginia

SIDNEY HOOK, ROBERT NOZICK, AND THE PARADOXES OF FREEDOM

By John Patrick Diggins

What cannot be tested in action is dogma.[1]

—Sidney Hook, 1933

[W]e strongly feel that the causal determination of action threatens responsibility and is undesirable. It is puzzling that what is desirable for belief, perhaps even necessary for knowledge, is threatening for action. Might not there be a way for action to parallel belief, to be so connected to the world, even causally, in a way that is desirable? At the least, it would be instructive to see where and why the parallel fails. If it did not fail, causality of action would be rendered harmless— determinism would be defanged.[2]

—Robert Nozick, 1981

I. Pragmatism, Marxism, and Libertarian Humanism

"Freedom is a fighting word," declared Sidney Hook in the late 1950s, at the height of the Cold War.[3] As a philosopher who found himself inescapably drawn into the strident world of contemporary politics, Hook was forced to think about human freedom far removed from its expressions in the seventeenth- and eighteenth-century Enlightenment. He recognized that the term "freedom" was as ambiguous as any abstract concept such as justice or truth or love. He also recognized that as an idea freedom was shot through with ironies, antinomies, and paradoxes. A fighting word, its many meanings would not easily be recollected in tranquility.

The character of freedom cannot be fully grasped by referring only to older notions of natural law and natural right, as though the imperatives of duty and the capacity to pursue happiness as a self-determining agent draw their inspiration from "Nature and Nature's God," to use the terms of Thomas Jefferson. Hook regarded himself as a Jeffersonian, but he was

---

[1] Sidney Hook, *Towards the Understanding of Karl Marx: A Revolutionary Interpretation*, ed. Ernest B. Hook (1933; reprint, Amherst, NY: Prometheus Books, 2002), 178.

[2] Robert Nozick, *Philosophical Explanations* (Cambridge, MA: Harvard University Press, 1981), 170–71.

[3] Sidney Hook, *Political Power and Personal Freedom: Critical Studies in Democracy, Communism, and Civil Rights* (New York: Collier Books, 1962), 377.

also an ardent pragmatist and naturalist, one who believed that all reliable knowledge derived from experience illuminated by the assistance of scientific explanation. The study of nature itself may tell us little about the norms and ends that should guide our ethical life, but historical experience shows that the idea of freedom arose when people became conscious that a human need had run up against a constraint—some hindrance or obstacle that John Dewey liked to call a "problematic situation." Freedom becomes one of the responses of the mind to such a situation, a political technique for overcoming problems that restrict human development, a legal method for resolving conflicting interests—not an end in itself but a means of settling issues that divide the human race.

Sidney Hook was a Marxist as well as a pragmatist, and he spent the major part of his intellectual life trying to separate the original ideas of Karl Marx from their totalitarian perversions under Lenin and Stalin. Marx believed in freedom as much as Dewey did, and both men shared a common premise that philosophy's task is not to interpret the world but to change it. Marx's eleventh thesis on the German philosopher Ludwig Feuerbach (1845) was as historically significant as the American philosopher Charles S. Peirce's essay "The Fixation of Belief" (1887). Both documents sought to demonstrate that philosophy turns to science in showing the way to knowledge by means of experimental naturalism, where practice rather than theory is the ultimate verification of an idea whose properties cannot be known unless we can observe the "effects" brought about by the deliberate introduction of change into life. As to freedom, Hook said of Marx that "the original inspiration of his thought was humanistic and libertarian. Property for him was a source of power, not so much to use as to exclude others from use. Consequently private property in the means of life carries with it power over those who must live by their use."[4]

Sidney Hook and Robert Nozick occupy two different worlds when it comes to property as power, on the one hand, and property as liberty, on the other. One philosopher saw property as a potential instrument of oppression, the other as the natural right that guarantees freedom. The untimely death of Nozick in 2002 deprived the world of a voice of reason on the Right that was just as important as Hook's voice once was on the Left. Both Hook and Nozick were Jews of eastern European ancestry; both were born and raised in New York City and went on to become famous academic philosophers in their early years; and each served as an exemplary public intellectual, a critical thinker who sought to relate his discipline to contemporary issues of social policy.

Nozick first made his reputation with *Anarchy, State, and Utopia* (1974), a treatise that takes us back to John Locke in order to argue that the state comes into existence to protect life, liberty, and property and has no

---

[4] Ibid., 380.

purpose in reorganizing society for reasons of justice or equality. Years earlier, Hook made his reputation with *From Hegel to Marx* (1936), a treatise that takes us back to the mid-nineteenth century and the origins of socialist ideas in the thoughts of the young Hegelians and even anarchists such as Max Stirner.

But Hook also delved into a matter that drew the attention of Karl Marx as a young reporter. It dealt with a legal dispute involving German peasants who were being denied their traditional right to gather dead wood for fuel for their cottages. In the early part of the nineteenth century in Germany, many intellectuals had looked to the state as the expression of the common interests and ideals of society. The philosopher G. W. F. Hegel had helped to create the illusion that the state must be regarded as a transcendental force apart from the daily operations of government. But Marx followed closely the debate in the Rhenish Provincial Assembly regarding a proposed wood-theft law that would make the appropriation of dead wood from privately owned forest lands a crime. Small landowners had little interest in the legislation, for their fields had too few trees to make the matter of any consequence, and they lived in the neighborhood and could keep watch on their property. But the large land-proprietor could only have his wardens effectively defend his land if a law making wood-gathering a penal offense were passed and enforced. The matter was hotly disputed in the assembly, where it was concluded that both large and small property owners were entitled to equal rights of protection. "Marx seized this principle," writes Hook, "and hurled it at the heads of the representatives, barbed with the following question: what protection was the state giving to the poor, the paupered wood-stealers themselves, who were also citizens of the political community? The poor were not stealing wood in order to sell it. They merely made sporadic raids on private forests in their vicinity in order to gather fuel for their cottages. The stringency of the winter and the high price of wood had intensified the abuse." In fact, Hook continues, "the poor had always enjoyed the immemorial right (forgotten conveniently by the historical school of law) of carting off dead wood." But now, on the pretext that such activity endangered the living trees, the poor were told to cease wood-gathering as the state stepped forward to defend the property of one class against the welfare of others. "The organs of the state," wrote the young Marx in the *Rheinische Zeitung,* "have now become the ears, eyes, arms, legs, with which the interest of the forest owners hears, spies, appraises, defends, seizes, and runs."[5]

Such harsh episodes in history drove Marx toward socialism, as it did his twentieth-century exponent, Sidney Hook. But Robert Nozick viewed property as an absolute right and the state as a minimal institution. In

---

[5] Sidney Hook, *From Hegel to Marx: Studies in the Intellectual Development of Karl Marx* (1936; reprint, Ann Arbor: University of Michigan, 1962), 158–60.

Hook's attitude toward history, the state was no more minimal than property was moral. Had Hook pondered Nozick's thesis, he might have thought of Max Stirner, the nineteenth-century anarchist who made the ego and its desire the supreme definition of life, and property and interests an exclusive possession.[6] The pragmatist, as well as the Marxist, sees human nature as social, the fully autonomous individual as a conceit, and the opposition between private interest and the general good as a genuine conflict that must be acknowledged in various historical situations.

In *Anarchy, State, and Utopia,* Nozick offers a telling critique of the Marxian theory of socialism, especially the labor theory of value.[7] But the scene Hook describes in *From Hegel to Marx* does not imply the theory of Marxist exploitation in the strict sense of the term, for the wood was not produced but simply had rotted and died; hence, no labor and its presumed "surplus value" are implied. Historically, in England, as opposed to Germany, an earth covered with dead wood might have been regarded as the commons, a resource that the community shared, and the German law prohibiting wood-gathering would resemble the move to the enclosure of common lands that took place in eighteenth-century England. The plight of the German paupers may have had more to do with Locke than with Marx, since any access to nature was perhaps more vital than the activity of labor itself. Many of the subjects Nozick deals with in his critique of Marxism are handled astutely, but they may be irrelevant to the ways of law and the power of the state in the nineteenth-century Germany that Hook describes. Nozick judges Marxism defective in many respects. Labor (in particular, organized, union-led workers), Nozick argues, refrains from undertaking the risks of capitalist investment. He also holds that value has much to do with the productive effort of work and not the vicissitudes of the market and consumer demands. And he contends that the origins of private property came into existence as much from seizing the land as from tilling the soil. Nozick insists that property justly acquired can be legitimately held, whereas Hook the pragmatist is less interested in the origins of an institution than in its consequences as they relate to social justice. A possessiveness about private property that deprives poor people of access to fuel as a means of sustaining life and health may have been too much for even Locke. Hook turned toward socialism because he wanted to see the desperate, stooped-over, wood-gathering peasants liberated from the whip of necessity.

And Nozick? He, too, would have wished to see peasants liberated. Nozick believed that no one could be truly free under conditions of total deprivation, where the simplest needs of existence go unmet. Life must offer choices to be made and acted upon, and Nozick would hardly

---

[6] Professor Stephen Cahn informed me that at one of the meetings of the eastern branch of the American Philosophical Association, Hook did deliver a commentary on part three of Nozick's *Anarchy, State, and Utopia.*

[7] Robert Nozick, *Anarchy, State, and Utopia* (New York: Basic Books, 1974), 253–62.

countenance an act of appropriation that worsened the condition of others. The case of the dead wood in the German forests may have had more to do with possession than appropriation, with simply owning land rather than expropriating the labor-value of those who work upon it. Nonetheless, the decision of the Rhenish Provincial Assembly in nineteenth-century Germany could very well have violated what Nozick calls the Lockean proviso:

> A process normally giving rise to a permanent bequeathable property right in a previously unowned thing will not do so if the position of others no longer at liberty to use the thing is thereby worsened. It is important to specify *this* particular mode of worsening the situation of others, for the proviso does not encompass other modes. It does not include the worsening due to more limited opportunities to appropriate ... and it does not include how I "worsen" a seller's position if I appropriate materials to make some of what he is selling, and then enter into competition with him. Someone whose appropriation otherwise would violate the proviso still may appropriate provided he compensates the others so that their situation is not thereby worsened; unless he does compensate these others, his appropriation will violate the proviso of the principle of justice in acquisition and will be an illegitimate one.[8]

It seems that in Nozick's formulation of the proviso, Locke might well have come to the rescue of the German peasants just as Marx did. The differences between Nozick and Hook on the subjects of property and political economy are as wide as those separating the libertarian from the socialist. Less apparent are the many philosophical issues they shared in common. "Over the years," wrote Nozick in *Philosophical Explanations* (1981), "I have spent more time thinking about the problem of free will—it felt like banging my head against it—than any other philosophical topic except perhaps the foundation of ethics."[9] The question of free will and the sources of morality and ethics were also uppermost to Hook, who likewise believed that the answer to such issues lies less in institutions and authoritative doctrines than in the life of the mind. The libertarian anarchist Nozick and the democratic socialist Hook shared many concerns. Hook had a deep passion for freedom, and both he and Nozick believed that to enjoy the blessings of freedom one must undertake the task of understanding it in all its complexity. Since Nozick's views on freedom are better known than those of Hook, this essay will focus on the writings of the latter, with periodic side glances at Nozick's thoughts to

---

[8] Ibid., 178.
[9] Nozick, *Philosophical Explanations*, 293.

register a possible caveat, a whispered demur, or perhaps a loudly spoken, steadfast counterconviction.

II. Free Will and Moral Responsibility

Nozick's thoughts on free will were almost purely philosophical to the extent that he remained convinced that its absence would stunt human stature and undermine all value considerations. Nozick believed that the possibility of free will enhanced personal dignity as well as moral responsibility, an issue that Hook took up in his 1958 essay "Moral Freedom in a Determined World." Nozick also felt deeply that the world of action, to the extent that it could be explained as causally determined (meaning that events and actions can be traced to prior conditions), precludes the idea that choices are freely made. Nozick seems close to Friedrich Nietzsche and the German sociologist Max Weber in insisting that we freely choose our values or else we live by ingrained habit, and that we are responsible for our choices. If I understand Nozick correctly, his view is that morality is not something that resides beyond us in religion or metaphysical principles. On the contrary, it originates within us and is self-determined. So much for theory, but Hook, good pragmatist that he was, always related theory to practice, and he applied the quandary of moral determinism to the court of law.

Hook's essay, published in *Commentary* in 1958, presages issues in constitutional law that would emerge decades later, issues such as the "diminished capacity" of the accused criminal that supposedly renders him unresponsible for his actions, or the "victim" status of a cancer patient who sues tobacco companies for billions of dollars because a cigarette culture of nicotine is, so goes the reasoning, as irresistible as catnip. Locke defined freedom as one's capacity to act according to one's will, and libertarians believe that a free act results from the conscious volition of an agent rather than from some condition or emotion such as desire or passion. In the courtroom, however, the prosecuting lawyer replaces Locke and the attorney for the defense replaces the libertarian, as the one standing trial is depicted as more sinned against than sinning, one who is not the cause of his own actions. Appropriately, Hook's target was the great trial lawyer Clarence Darrow, who in 1924 had defended Nathan Leopold and Richard Loeb in the murder of fourteen-year-old Bobby Frank. The case outraged the public when it was discovered that Leopold and Loeb, two highly educated University of Chicago students, had decided to prove their Nietzschean "overcoming" of weakness and to will their own lives by taking the life of a young student. After quoting a poem by A. E. Housman, a soliloquy of a boy about to be hanged, Darrow in his closing remarks to the jury stated: "I do not know what it was that made these boys do this mad act, but I know there is a reason for it. I know they did not beget themselves, I know that any one of an infinite number of causes reaching back to the beginning might be working out in these boys' minds, whom you are asked to hang in malice and in hatred and injustice, because someone in the past has sinned against them." [10]

Such reasoning, Hook protested, had little to do with moral freedom and responsibility. Suppose we have been affected by causes not of our own choosing, by original sin, for example, or suppose we choose to do what we do, and hence are not sinned against, are we then to be credited for our actions even if they produce evil results? That all choices may be determined is no more grounds for their excusability than if all choices are freely willed, and it is obvious that if we cannot condemn actions that are predictable or unavoidable, neither can we praise them. Hook questioned the thesis that because human beings are determined they are not to be morally responsible; for whenever it is possible to alter the determining conditions by awareness of alternatives, by intelligent reflection and informed action, no specific act can be regarded as unavoidable.

Bringing intelligence to bear upon human actions constituted Hook's theory of ethics, and it derived from Dewey's philosophy of pragmatism. Nozick tells us that the issue of ethics banged against his head as much as that of free will, and of course the two are closely related. Nozick dealt with ethics as a relation of the self with others, with the Kantian injunction against using another person for one's own ends, and Nozick's idea of morality involved awareness, responsibility, and sensitivity—an "ethical pull" that compels our responsiveness to others. Both Nozick and Hook believed that ethics could be a matter of rational demonstration; both were aware of the tensions between deontology and teleology, between knowing what is right apart from the good, on the one hand, and undertaking actions whose consequences promise to realize the good, on the other. Each philosopher, moreover, saw the mind as a value-seeking self, and while Nozick believed that we benefit from our moral actions by virtue of a growth and self-development that serves the needs of others, Hook remained convinced that we cannot know the implications of our actions for others until we know how to choose what course of action to take. Neither philosopher had much use for Nietzsche's notion that religion concocted the doctrine of free will so as to punish us with "the hangman's metaphysics."

In his 1949 essay "The Ethical Theory of John Dewey," Hook observes that an action that simply satisfies needs and fulfills wants is inadequate, for when such an action is questioned it "becomes necessary to give adequate or relevant grounds for regarding what is desired as desirable and what is enjoyed as enjoyable." Ancient classical philosophers, although rarely addressing the issue of free will, did see creatures of desire remain-

---

[10] Clarence Darrow, closing arguments in *Illinois v. Nathan Leopold and Richard Loeb* (1924), as cited in Sidney Hook, "Moral Freedom in a Determined World," in Hook, *The Quest for Being* (New York: Dell Publishing, 1963), 30.

ing in a state of ignorance beyond reason and moral responsibility. Closer to our time, Max Weber saw the conflict of different values as insoluble as "a war of the gods." Hook, in contrast, saw no grounds for pessimism even when modern science had superseded older moral categories, when an empirical concentration on the factual had relegated the ethical to the margins of inquiry, when the "is" could be verified but the "ought" only pondered.

In his essay on Dewey, and in "A Critique of Ethical Realism" (1929) and elsewhere, Hook challenges the view that moral values and principles have an objective status independently of the human subject and his or her situation and emotions. The ethical realist is aware that knowledge of our changing moral attitudes over time need not threaten the conviction that supreme ethical values, notions of good and bad, may remain invariant. But the idea of good as an object of desire involves choice often based upon needs, interests, and even passions, a process of deliberation between conflicting impulses in which critical reflection serves the role of comprehending and clarifying. It was Hook's conviction that between the immediately desired and the ultimately desirable comes the role of intelligence, which compels us to consider both the causes of why we want to do what we have an urge to do and also the consequences of so thinking and acting. Only then can human conduct be elevated from the descriptive to the normative, from the "is" to the "ought," giving the desired the quality of the desirable.[11]

One wonders how this Hook-Dewey formulation might work out in applied social policy in a court of law. An attorney for a tobacco company could try to convince the jury that a cancer-stricken complainant had the freedom to consider both the causes prompting him or her to smoke and the consequences of consuming two packs a day. The attorney for the complainant, in contrast, would no doubt claim that cigarette advertising is designed to keep smokers in a state of primitive desire, with its visual imagery promising pleasure, relaxation, beauty, elegance, erotic innuendo, and other spurious delights that feed on the fables of fulfillment, a feeding frenzy in which reflective intelligence is helpless to control desire and its passions and obsessions.

As an aside, one might add an observation. Contemporary French poststructuralists claim that human desire was about to break into the realm of freedom until capitalist society brought its mechanisms of repression to bear on the mind. Do not they need to reconsider their premises?[12]

---

[11] Sidney Hook, "The Ethical Theory of John Dewey," in *The Quest for Being*, 49–70; and Sidney Hook, "A Critique of Ethical Realism," in Hook, *Pragmatism and the Tragic Sense of Life* (New York: Basic Books, 1974), 136–61.

[12] I have in mind the adherents to the thesis of *Anti-Oedipus*, by Giles Deleuze and Felix Guattari, and the philosophical investigation into the problem of desire: see Constantin V. Boundas, ed., *The Deleuze Reader* (New York: Columbia University Press, 1993); and Hugh J. Silverman, ed., *Philosophy and Desire* (New York: Routledge, 2000).

Unreflective, unadulterated desire is precisely what consumer capitalism feeds upon. The more the desire, the more the dividends. For the Madison Avenue advertising agency, the best appeal is to the helpless, offering an image that projects desire onto things, what Marx called the "fetishism of commodities." For sales purposes, the best consumer may be the addict. But Hook the Marxist, as one who believed in free will, would have to defend corporate capitalism against the complaints of the addicted.

It may be that contemporary French poststructuralists are preoccupied with power, domination, and manipulation because they would like to see political philosophy serve the emancipatory purposes of life. Sidney Hook had the same goal. Many philosophers had placed ethical teaching within the domain of authority, some theory of being that is independent of human experience or some doctrine unrelated to needs and interests. As a pragmatic naturalist, Hook sought to relate value to freedom, to the choice of what one ought or should do when confronting a problematic situation. Decision and action became central to the philosophy of pragmatism, and freedom finds its expression in the possibility of alternatives and in the agony of choice. Such a description may tell us how freedom is exercised. The question that haunted Hook's generation was of another magnitude. Historically, the struggle toward freedom meant breaking the bonds of the past. In recent history, freedom's antagonist became the future itself.

III. Friedrich von Hayek and Leon Trotsky

Locke may have laid the foundations for freedom in the seventeenth century, and in the nineteenth century Marx may have demonstrated how freedom cannot fulfill itself without collective ownership and democratic control. But in the mid-twentieth century, the question was not how freedom was won but how it came to be lost. With Mussolini's Italy, Hitler's Germany, and Stalin's Russia having crushed the spirit of liberalism, the heritage of Western civilization seemed to be in peril. In 1940, as America was debating whether to enter World War II, even fiercer debates broke out among philosophers, and articles appeared in *The New Republic* and elsewhere with titles such as "Our Guilt in Fascism." [13] Pragmatism seemed to be on trial, for while Dewey and Hook had offered a philosophy that would make intelligence responsive to problematic situations, neither thinker had any policy advice to give America when confronting European totalitarianism. How to interpret fascism and Stalinism became an obsession to the New York intellectuals of the late 1930s, for neither phenomenon had any premonition in orthodox Marxist theory or in classical liberalism, where tyranny was assumed to belong to the past and to have been overcome by the march of progress. But the return of tyranny

---

[13] Waldo Frank, "Our Guilt in Fascism," *The New Republic*, May 6, 1940, 603–8.

in modern times perplexed the intellectual, and Dewey and Hook feared that if the United States went to war against Hitler, American democracy at home would be at risk.

The one thinker on the scene who appeared to have the answer to totalitarianism was the then rather obscure Austrian economist Friedrich A. von Hayek. His little book *The Road to Serfdom* (1944) became a bestseller right after the war and convinced many, the public at large as well as the philosophical community, that he was telling America what, for a long time, it did not want to hear. Years later, Hayek's writings would also be taken seriously by Robert Nozick—particularly the Austrian's criticisms of theories of distributive justice. Hayek claimed that human intelligence is too limited to enable governments to know enough about each person's situation in order to distribute economic benefits according to meritorious categories. With England's socialist state in mind, and with a side glance at America's New Deal, Hayek feared that both countries could well be traveling along the road to serfdom. Hayek held that freedom from government intervention is the first principle of political freedom, and he argued that in European dictatorial regimes this principle was violated when the state took over private enterprise. The political regimentation of the economy, Hayek told his readers, paved the way for fascism and communism, and in America, with the regulations imposed by Franklin D. Roosevelt's administration, one could witness what came to be called "creeping socialism," a sure sign that liberty is succumbing to servitude. What made Hayek's thesis so appealing to the public was his conviction that socialism was the "disease" of the intellectual class.[14]

In a brilliant debate between Hook and Max Eastman, appearing in 1945 in *The New Leader* and later reprinted in Hook's *Political Power and Personal Freedom* (1959), Hayek's thesis was expounded with wit and undeniable conviction, on the one side, and scrutinized with logic and irrefutable demonstration, on the other.[15]

Eastman was one of the most charismatic figures in twentieth-century intellectual history. Once an editor of *The Masses* (from 1912 to 1918) of the Greenwich Village era, a poet who wrote paeans to the Bolshevik Revolution, a translator and champion of Trotsky who smuggled out of Russia Lenin's last will and testament given to him by his widow, Krupskaya, a document that warned against Stalin coming to power, Eastman was also one of the first to turn against the Soviet Union. Preceding other disillusioned intellectuals of the left, he became an early anticommunist whom Stalin himself called "a gangster of the pen."[16] At the end of World War II,

[14] Friedrich A. von Hayek, "Les intellectuels et le socialisme," *Commentaire* 25, no. 99 (2002), 673–83.

[15] Sidney Hook, "Freedom and Socialism," *The New Leader*, March 3, 1945, 4–6; and Sidney Hook, *Political Power and Personal Freedom* (New York: Criterion Books, 1959).

[16] Stalin and the American Stalinists dubbed Eastman the "notorious crook" who was part of the "Trotskyist conspiracy." See Daniel Aaron, *Writers on the Left: Episodes in American*

Eastman challenged Hook's socialist conviction that a planned economy can be democratic. He reiterated Hayek's thesis that such notions as "public welfare" and "common interests" have no sufficiently defined meaning to prescribe a specific course of action, and, hence, the idea of the collective good may simply be a mystique for the augmentation of state power.

Hook responded that Hayek's case had yet to be proven in America's democratic society; the results were not in about the New Deal. But in Europe, according to Hook, Hayek got the scenario backward. Neither in Mussolini's Italy, nor in Hitler's Germany, nor in Stalin's Russia did a state-managed, planned economy precede the death of democracy. On the contrary, fascism and communism alike were antidemocratic, and each movement first seized the power of the state to destroy any possibility for political democracy to develop.[17] In Hayek's scenario, a collectivized economy is the first step toward totalitarian power, whereas in the communist scenario a privatized economy guarantees the domination of capitalism. Both perspectives seem to partake of economic determinism, with the mode of production decisive, whether it be collectivist or privatist. But Hook had already questioned determinism as a principle of explanation. A few years prior to his debate with Eastman, Hook began to reconsider his socialist assumptions and his Marxist education, and he came to recognize that, in history, political action may be more decisive than economic development, that history is made not by the processes of production but by the paradoxes of mutation, by the appearance of leaders who break the genetic chain of history and bring forth fundamental change and, hence, make freedom possible. With this observation I come to the thesis of one of Hook's most profound texts, *Reason, Social Myths, and Democracy* (1940).

This book, which revealed again Hook's passion for freedom and his awareness of all its complexities, and which scrutinized the concept of the dialectic and left it in shambles, failed to receive the attention it deserved, as did his *The Hero in History* (1943). One reason for this failure, perhaps, was that to write about history as the story of heroes invoked Thomas Carlyle and the alleged fascist mystique of great men as the dynamic element in history, a point of view that the drama critic Eric Bentley warned against in his *Heroes and Hero-Worship* (1944). But Hook's *Reason, Social Myths, and Democracy* appeared in 1940, the same year that saw the publication of James Burnham's *The Managerial Revolution* and Edmund Wilson's *To the Finland Station*. Both of these latter texts surpassed Hook's in sales and favorable receptions, and the message of both was, curiously,

---

Literary Communism (New York: Harcourt, Brace, and World, 1961), 315. For Eastman's debates with Hook, see John P. Diggins, *Up from Communism: Conservative Odysseys in American Intellectual History* (New York: Harper and Row, 1975).

[17] Sidney Hook, "Socialism without Utopia: A Rejoinder to Max Eastman," in Hook, *Political Power and Personal Freedom* (1962 Collier ed.), 424–37.

deeply deterministic. The ex-Trotskyist Burnham argued that history would be determined not by the mode of production but by the shift of power from owners to managers, from property and money to bureaucracy and technology, and the "new class" would be the basis of new ruling elites. Wilson believed that Lenin's arrival at the Finland Station in 1917, after the Czarist regime had fallen and the Bolsheviks had yet to seize power, was the culmination of the Italian philosopher G. B. Vico's conviction that the social world is the work of man, not of God, and that history can be made by acting upon it. Wilson praised Lenin as the political philosopher who showed the world how to carry out thought in the world of action. But while Wilson was working on his book, the Moscow show trials were taking place in 1937–38, and writers could only wonder about a regime that would have former Bolshevik leaders publicly confess their "crimes" before facing the firing squad, a ghastly spectacle later captured in Arthur Koestler's 1941 novel *Darkness at Noon*. One can notice a quiver of doubt in Wilson's text about the future of the Soviet Union, but he regarded Lenin almost as an inevitable force of nature. Yet Hook, who had been a friend of Wilson, a fellow writer who also contributed to the *Partisan Review,* saw things entirely differently. Hook raised a simple but telling question: What if Lenin, in crossing the Gulf of Finland, had fallen through the ice and drowned? To contemplate the October Revolution without Lenin is like contemplating the American Civil War without Abraham Lincoln.

It is by reading Hook's *Reason, Social Myths, and Democracy* and *The Hero in History,* both of which came out during the years of the Second World War, that one fully senses Hook's impatience with determinism and its perversions, and his passion for freedom and its possibilities. In a way, his quarrel was not so much with Marx as with the Marxists. For Marx himself had always emphasized the agency of human activity as much as the inexorability of history. But thinkers such as George Plekhanov (1857–1918), the Russian philosopher of historical materialism, insisted that the individual, no matter how great, is dispensable in historical understanding. Had Lenin slipped under the ice, another leader would have stepped forward to take his place, for history remains the domain of economic necessity and moves by its own logic. Similarly, the geniuses of culture, figures like Shakespeare and Goethe, are less the creators than the products of their times and can hardly be said to change the course of history. Hook made short shrift of such arguments, as he did of those of the English philosopher Herbert Spencer (1820–1903), who insisted that the leader can make changes in society only to the extent that society has made changes in the leader, and those of Hegel, who believed that the "cunning of reason" demonstrated not that people make history but that history works itself out through their actions, even behind the back of their intentions.

The figure Hook focuses upon, however, is Leon Trotsky, the intellectual hero, at least for a while, of the New York intellectuals, the brilliant writer who would show up at meetings and cause the crowd to gasp, "The pen (*Pero*) has arrived!" Edmund Wilson, noting all the calumny heaped upon Trotsky by the Stalinists, summed up his glowing estimate in 1940: "And as the fires of the Revolution have died down in the Soviet Union at a time when the systems of thought in the West were already in an advanced state of decadence, he has shown forth like a veritable pharos, rotating a long shaft of light on the seas and the reefs all around."[18] Hook examined the mystique of Trotsky as beacon in two places: "Reflections on the Russian Revolution" (a chapter in *Reason, Social Myths, and Democracy*) and "The Russian Revolution: A Test Case" (a chapter in *The Hero in History*). After Hook's critique, the "veritable pharos" no longer shone so brightly.

Hook used the rise of Soviet Communism as evidence that history is not determined but instead may well turn on the appearance of the purposeful, event-making leader. The hero in history is a man or woman (Hook cited Cleopatra, Theodora, and Catherine II of Russia) whose decisive actions have a preponderant influence in determining an issue or happening whose consequences would have been profoundly different had such action not been taken. In the course of modern Russian history, that phenomenon was Lenin. It is unfortunate that Hook, who died in early 1989, did not live to see the fall of Soviet Communism. For Mikhail Gorbachev was the event-making leader whose actions set in motion the train of events leading to Communism's unexpected and sudden collapse. Urged by President Ronald Reagan, at a summit in May of 1988, to join him in beginning nuclear disarmament, Gorbachev also announced that the Soviet Union would no longer send in tanks to put down uprisings in its satellite regimes, and in late 1989, the regimes began to crumble like a house of cards. But one wonders if Gorbachev qualifies as a hero or a great man in history. After all, he did not intend to bring down Communism but to save it by reforming it. What, then, did Lenin intend when he seized power in the name of Karl Marx?

Trotsky would have had no trouble answering the question. History moves with "inexorable necessity," he claimed; hence, the October Revolution had "a deep natural inevitability" regardless of who the leaders were. Hook conceded that the fall of the Czarist system may have been unavoidable, especially in the tumult of World War I, but it did not follow that the Bolsheviks should have swept into power not as a possibility but as an actuality, particularly since the Bolsheviks were a minority party nowhere as representative as the peasant-based Social Revolutionaries or the party's real majority faction, the Mensheviks, and nowhere as committed to democracy as the liberal Constitutional Democrats (Kadets). Hook showed the inconsistency in Trotsky's claim that Lenin was "needed" to make the October Revolution and, at the same time, that his existence

---

[18] Edmund Wilson, *To the Finland Station: A Study in the Writing and Acting of History* (1940; reprint, New York: Farrar, Strauss, and Giroux, 1972), 505.

was "a product of the whole past of Russian history." In truth, Lenin was needed because Marx scarcely prophesized revolution in backward Russia, and Lenin himself acknowledged that workers on their own could not make a revolution; it had to be forced upon the country by a vanguard. Trotsky was in an even more difficult situation with his book *The Revolution Betrayed* (1937), in which he claimed that "the tendencies of bureaucratism" that made possible Stalin's totalitarian reign resulted from the "iron necessity" of a development that gave birth to a privileged minority, and "it is perfectly obvious that the poorer the society which issues from a revolution, the sterner and more naked would be the expression of this 'law.'"[19] Trotsky, Lenin's revolutionary comrade, faced a double fallacy: the Bolsheviks took power in a poor, undeveloped country, precisely where Marx deemed successful democratic revolution highly improbable, and then blamed the conditions of poverty for producing the bureaucracy that gave Russia despotism instead of democracy. In Trotsky's thinking, everything had to have happened as it had happened, both the revolution and its degeneration. But how, Hook asked, can an idea like revolutionary socialism be betrayed unless it "presupposes the grounded possibility of another type of action"?[20]

Had Robert Nozick been part of Hook's older generation, he may have refined the question even further. Nozick expressed bemusement when he considered that some philosophical schools of thought have "held that freedom is knowledge of necessity." Why are you free when you do what you've got to do? "The puzzle is why knowledge of what one is stuck with should constitute freedom rather than, say, knowledge of unfreedom." Does knowledge of necessity, the awareness of the "causal conditions" behind a development, mean that such knowledge will not result in an action's "not being done or wanted"?[21] To feel the force of necessity is to accept a life of submission and obedience when, in fact, freedom may be born in resistance and disobedience.

Where Hook addressed the philosophy of history to challenge determinism, Nozick did so to challenge contextualism. In a long footnote in *The Nature of Rationality* (1993), Nozick questions whether the history of science or the history of ideas can be reduced to a contextual situation in which the thinker is wrestling with a specific problem or intervening in a particular controversy. Both of these possibilities imply that there are no universal issues or timeless topics in the world of thought but only immediate responses to concrete circumstances. Cannot the political theorist be

[19] Leon Trotsky, *The Revolution Betrayed* (Garden City, NY: Doubleday, Doran, and Co., 1937), as cited in Sidney Hook, "Reflections on the Russian Revolution," in Hook, *Reason, Social Myths, and Democracy* (New York: Humanities Press, 1940), 150.

[20] Hook, "Reflections on the Russian Revolution," 152; and Sidney Hook, "The Russian Revolution: A Test Case," in Hook, *The Hero in History: A Study in Limitation and Possibility* (1943; reprint, Boston, MA: Beacon Press, 1955), 184–228.

[21] Nozick, *Philosophical Explanations*, 349–50.

trying to uncover timeless truths that apply to various situations? Must Machiavelli be valid only for sixteenth-century Florence and Madison only for eighteenth-century Philadelphia? Both Hook and Nozick resisted the assumption that freedom is compromised by the necessity of circumstance or context.[22]

However philosophers wrestle with this issue, in politics the sense of necessity in the face of momentous events seems irresistible. Lincoln felt it during the Civil War, and indeed the very beginning of the American Republic had as much a sense of fate as of freedom. The opening line of Jefferson's *Declaration of Independence* announces: "When in the course of human events, it becomes necessary. . . ." This is one paradox of American freedom: Americans declared their independence from England by claiming that they had no choice but to do so. The Jeffersonian tradition left America with many more paradoxes, and Hook explored them in the spirit of a true philosopher, the thinker who enables us to see problems without claiming to have solved them.

IV. Human Rights, Democracy, and Judicial Review

Hook arrived at his study of freedom by way of prior Marxist and pragmatist convictions. Although the writings of Karl Marx came to be associated with radicalism and those of John Dewey with liberalism, the *oeuvres* of both men express little patience with the classical tradition of liberal political philosophy, a tradition arising from Hobbes and Locke and resting on the social contract theory of natural rights. Marx saw formal political freedom as meaningless until private property is abolished and the worker and citizen become one. Dewey believed that the doctrine of natural rights brought about the atomization of society and the eclipse of the public. One philosopher looked to the proletariat to usher in the economic transformation of industrial society; the other looked to scholars and students to usher in a new "beloved community" in which education, not revolution, would be the vehicle of liberation. But when Hook wrote on freedom he had to address ideas and institutions neglected in Marxism and pragmatism, especially the nature of human rights, the role of the state, and the legitimacy of judicial review. In a liberal America where Marxism had failed to establish its roots and pragmatism had failed to transform the national character, Hook had to think anew.

Hook's *The Paradoxes of Freedom* was delivered as the Jefferson Memorial Lectures at the University of California, Berkeley, in the spring of 1961. The ironies are rich. Berkeley would soon be the scene of campus uprisings demonstrating angrily against the Vietnam War—a politics of

---

[22] Robert Nozick, *The Nature of Rationality* (Princeton, NJ: Princeton University Press, 1993), 211–14.

protest spirited philosophically, to a certain extent, by thinkers of the Hegelian-soaked Frankfurt School, whose idea of "Critical Theory" brought back to life the mystique of dialectical reason that Hook, Eastman, and Wilson thought they had buried once and for all in their writings of the late 1930s.[23] Another irony is even more telling. Although Hook's lectures were presented in honor of Jefferson, the topics that Hook addressed—the Constitution, the Supreme Court, and racial desegregation—were topics that had left Jefferson uneasy as an advocate of states rights over national sovereignty. The anarcho-libertarianism of Nozick would perhaps be closer to the spirit of Jefferson than would the democratic socialism of Hook, who said that he had once thought of himself as a Jeffersonian until he met others who also did so, and he intended *The Paradoxes of Freedom* to be an examination, not an incantation. Dewey once observed, in his introduction to the selected writings of Jefferson, that the liberal American political philosopher had the right values but used the wrong language. Dewey avoided elaborating the point, but in some ways his most notable student, Hook, did it for him in his Berkeley lectures.[24]

The first incantation that Hook examines is the Jeffersonian conviction of unalienable rights. Hook regarded freedom as a "fighting word" because the human rights that make political freedom possible are in conflict, and the values that sustain freedom may be plural, ambiguous, and contestable. In the area of law, he saw nothing absolute or essentialist in the U.S. Constitution or Bill of Rights, nothing metaphysical and universal, nothing predicated on a definition alone or on a sense of necessity rather than contingency. One of Hook's targets was Alexander Meiklejohn, the legal scholar who had declared: "No one who reads with care the text of the First Amendment can fail to be startled by the absoluteness. The phrase 'Congress shall make no law . . . abridging the freedom of speech,' is unqualified. It admits of no exception . . . under any circumstance."[25] Hook cites Jefferson from his First Inaugural, where the president emphasized that for a right to be "rightful" it must be "reasonable," and, Hook notes, "to be reasonable is to be absolute about nothing except about being reasonable." The imperative to be reasonable is a value preference, and Hook asks: "In morals is there any concrete value or right which one can define as unconditionally or absolutely valid in all circumstances?"[26] Conflicts are inevitable in relations between, for example, the right to free speech and the right to personal safety, the right to liberty and property and the right to life and self-preservation, the citizen's right to habeas

---

[23] Sidney Hook, "Reflections on the Frankfurt School," in Sidney Hook, *Marxism and Beyond* (Totowa, NJ: Rowman and Littlefield, 1983), 120–29.

[24] Sidney Hook, *The Paradoxes of Freedom* (Berkeley: University of California Press, 1962).

[25] Alexander Meiklejohn, *Political Freedom* (New York: Harpers, 1960), 20; as cited in Hook, *The Paradoxes of Freedom*, 15.

[26] Hook, *The Paradoxes of Freedom*, 15.

corpus and the government's right to suspend it "when in cases of rebellion or invasion the public safety may require it," as the Constitution reads. All rights are conditional and relative to circumstance, and "no matter how the conflict between rights be resolved, one or the other right must be alienable."[27]

Hook agreed with David Hume that the needs that brought government into existence establish the criteria for determining whether or not government should be continued, revised, or overthrown. He also agreed with Jeremy Bentham that the assertion of one's rights could be the "retrenchment of liberty" on the part of another and that every law presupposes the constriction of someone's freedom.[28] Although Hook had reservations about the "egoistic hedonism" in utilitarianism,[29] as a pragmatist he insisted that the quality of an act cannot be assessed independently of its consequences for society. Thus, he took on Justice Hugo Black's contention that the language of the Constitution "is composed of plain words easily understood," words that are "'positive,' 'absolute,' 'emphatic.'" That the Supreme Court could be locked in a *"prolonged* conflict" over the First Amendment suggests that the Constitution is far from being transparent or immediately comprehensible.[30] The Constitution itself lays down a set of liberties that may be in conflict, for example, the right to bear arms and the right to public safety, the right of an owner to his property, and the right of government to restrict the misuse of said property. The Constitution itself offers no guidance as to which right has priority, and Hook suggests in *The Paradoxes of Freedom* that the best way to understand law is not by defining what it is but by observing what it does and judging it according to the values of a democratic society.

But here Hook the socialist had to contend with Jefferson the individualist. During Hook's era, the opposition to Franklin Roosevelt's New Deal came from Republicans who identified themselves as Jeffersonians, even though FDR himself hailed Jefferson as his predecessor. Hook notes that in Jefferson's time the doctrine of rights provided the means by which the authority of the state could be resisted in a society that had yet to feel the full fruits of democratic self-government. Hook acknowledges that Jefferson saw no significant role for the nation-state (and Joseph J. Ellis, in his 1998 book *The American Sphinx,* suggests that if we want to know what government should do about education, crime, pollution, unemployment, drugs and AIDS, malfeasance in the corporate world, and the rule of money in the political, we shall find no answer in the thought and life of Thomas Jefferson). And Jefferson himself, Hook notes, presents America's political culture with a series of paradoxes in his

---

[27] Ibid., 14.
[28] Ibid., 10.
[29] Ibid., 6.
[30] Ibid., 25.

conviction, one held even more strongly today, that men and women are free only to the extent that the state is not free to interfere with their lives. In rebutting this position, Hook reasons somewhat as Alexander Hamilton reasoned in *The Federalist* (1787–88) and as John Adams did in his three-volume *Defence of the Constitution* (1787), when they observed that power and liberty are not necessarily in all instances incompatible and that the state as an instrument of power may serve human needs and not always pose a threat to human freedom. "By way of summary," Hook notes, "I can point to at least three crucial truths which this interpretation [the state as enemy] underplays, and sometimes overlooks":

> First, the paradoxical fact that a man can be free only because other men are not free to prevent him, and that, in consequence, unless the state is free to forestall this prevention and enforce a man's freedom, no man can be free. Second, the empirical fact that, in our world of modern science, technology, and industry, men can use their political freedom most effectively to further the values of an open society only when the state is also free to help create the social and economic conditions of a free culture. Third, the paradoxical fact that in the inescapable conflict of rights and duties, obligations and responsibilities, there can be no absolute obligation except ... the moral obligation to be intelligent.[31]

One way to be intelligent is to recognize what Jefferson himself taught, that the past has no binding authority over the present and that the dead should not be allowed to control the living. Although Hook did not invoke Jefferson's dictum of the "sovereignty of the present generation," he could well have done so in the following passage, in which he quotes Jefferson saying: "Were we directed from Washington when to sow and when to reap, we should soon want bread." In light of the state of communications in Jefferson's day, Hook adds, "this would very probably have been true."

> Today when farmers are directed from Washington what to sow and when to reap, we suffer from no want of bread. Thirty years ago when farmers sowed and reaped what and when they pleased, many of them went without bread. It would be difficult to convince American workers that the government or state which gave them the legal rights to organize and bargain collectively—something many of them could not win for themselves by their own power—which gave them the multiple, even if still inadequate, protections of present-day social welfare—that this state was an enemy whose inherent tendency to get out of hand must be kept in automatic check. Eternal vigilance

[31] Ibid., 61–62.

against the state—as against every other aggregation of power—
must still be retained lest the state diminish men as it seeks to improve
their lives. But eternal vigilance as a slogan, as a set of attitudes
which views all government controls as a set of manacles upon the
mind and body—is not the price of freedom but the guarantee of
social stagnation and reaction.[32]

Hook's statement reads like a peroration to the New Deal. The case he
made for democracy as the expression of freedom had broad support
during the 1930s and 40s, when the popular Franklin Roosevelt had won
four straight elections to the presidency and the New Deal's developing
welfare state had enjoyed legitimacy. By the time Hook wrote *The Paradoxes of Freedom* in 1961, however, much of the public had turned against
a strong executive, the New Deal and the welfare state had reached their
limits, and another branch of government began to assert itself—the
Supreme Court. It was the decisions of the Court that now made possible
the rights of minorities that Jefferson's democratic majority had denied.
Knowing full well that Jefferson despised judicial usurpation, what he
called "the tendencies of judges to enlarge their jurisdiction," the challenge Hook faced was to see if judicial review could be reconciled with
democracy.

It would be less than honest to claim that Hook succeeded in reconciling the two, one expressing authority, the other freedom. He recognized
that in the past the Court often took the side of big business against the
rights of labor, but even in more recent times, in regard to civil rights,
when the Court upheld cases of minorities, he remained unimpressed
even though he supported school desegregation. He had no use for the
decision of *Brown v. Board of Education* (1954). Here the Court "sought to
make amends, and reversed itself with pitifully inadequate and illogical
arguments which suffer from comparison with the eloquent and logical
dissent of Justice Harlan in 1883 in which he sought in vain to uphold
Congress's right 'to destroy the branches of slavery after its roots had
been destroyed.' "[33] The issue of race was the major issue that Hook's
faith in democracy failed to resolve. Of Jefferson's faith in the people,
Hook claimed it may or may not be justified. "But a genuine democracy
can rest on no principle which contradicts it. That is why the modern
defenders of judicial supremacy—since we are all democrats now!—
strain themselves by heroic feats of semantic reinterpretation to acknowledge this faith too. But in vain!"[34] In the debate over repealing the Judiciary
Act of 1801, Hook observed, Hamilton, in the caustic words of Gouverneur
Morris, did not wax rhapsodic about democracy but instead "blurted out

[32] Ibid., 60–61.
[33] Ibid., 93.
[34] Ibid., 96–97.

the truth about his faith and those of his fellow Federalists: 'Why are we here? To save the people from their most dangerous enemy: to save them from themselves.' "[35]

Curiously, when Hook writes of freedom he is open to its paradoxes. But when he writes of democracy he will not allow it to rest on any contradictory principle. When he wrote of the contradiction between natural right and popular sovereignty, or between the liberty of the individual and the tyranny of the majority, or between those who would use the ballot to preserve democracy and those who would use it to welcome a dictatorship (the tragic scenario of the Weimar Republic), Hook sensed the presence of such conflicts in American history and the modern world. But, like Dewey, he had no answer to them other than to call for more democracy and more intelligence. Pragmatism promised to help us get through life by showing how to confront a "problematic situation." But when it came to the problem of democracy, the pragmatists shunned looking into Alexis de Tocqueville's text for much the same reason the Jesuits once shunned peering into Galileo's telescope.

That African Americans, women, and ethnic and other minorities had to turn to the courts to assert their rights suggests a cruel irony of democracy, if not a paradox or contradiction, and the post–World War II Nuremberg trials indicate that if justice is to be done, the people are not to be allowed to be judges in their own cause. The democratic people so precious to Hook and Dewey may not have needed to be saved from themselves, but certainly others did have to be saved from those who did not feel the need to be saved. In the course of American history, the egalitarian values that Jefferson espoused had to be realized in the very political institutions he opposed: a strong executive and an activist judiciary. The values of democracy would be made possible only by the government's mechanism of control and the rulings of judicial fiat. The pragmatists always believed that the human mind could get along without authority; not once did Dewey or Hook consider that freedom based on rights might have to be realized through it.

V. Conclusion

One can imagine Sidney Hook and Robert Nozick "up there" in the heavenly afterlife, not finding God but perhaps meeting Socrates, and occupying themselves with debates that have always made philosophy matter. No doubt both thinkers would be happier knowing that the issues that had agitated the life of the mind during their time on earth remain arguments without end. Machiavelli preferred being in hell with the politicians to being in heaven with the priests. And Hook? On his hospital death bed, the philosopher quipped that the only point of going on living

[35] Ibid., 97.

would be if there were one more great cause to argue and fight for. Nozick also lived for the clash of ideas and concepts. In the view of these men, to be with the saints instead of the sinners is to be without the impassioned controversies of political philosophy—a boredom worse than death.

But wherever our two philosophers may be, one can imagine them claiming that decisions about their afterlife must have the same status as decisions had in their respective earthly lives. All choices would be up to them as free, self-determining agents. So would the answers to perennial questions. Is freedom synonymous with property, as the libertarian Nozick insisted? Or, as the socialist Hook argued, may property be not only a source of freedom but also a species of power that has the potential for hindering another's freedom? Nozick regarded security of property as the prerequisite of liberty; Hook viewed collective social control as the prerequisite of democracy. If our two philosophers were to argue these contradictory positions, I would think that Hook would be amused to hear Nozick say that "there is something wrong with knockdown arguments, for the knockdown argument to end all knockdown arguing." The philosopher, Nozick advised, should avoid serving as an indoctrinator. "Why are philosophers intent on forcing others to believe things?" asked Nozick. "Is that a nice way to behave toward someone?"[36] No one ever knocked Hook out of the philosophical ring; hence, the Jake LaMotta of American thought had no need to worry about knockdown arguments.

History, The Graduate Center, City University of New York

---

[36] Nozick, *Philosophical Explanations*, 5.

BEGGING THE QUESTION WITH STYLE: *ANARCHY, STATE, AND UTOPIA* AT THIRTY YEARS*

By Barbara H. Fried

I. Introduction

With thirty years' distance on its publication, one can safely assert that Robert Nozick's *Anarchy, State, and Utopia* (1974) has achieved the status of a classic. It is not only the central text for all contemporary academic discussions of libertarianism; together with John Rawls's *A Theory of Justice* (1971), it also arguably framed the landscape of academic political philosophy in the last decades of the twentieth century. This is perhaps an appropriate moment to reflect on the book and ask, why? Why exactly has this book been so influential?[1]

I start with the conviction—reinforced by a recent close rereading of the book—that the answer cannot be found in the cogency of its affirmative argument. Many of the critical observations in the book—chiefly of Rawls, but also (in passing) of Bernard Williams, H. L. A. Hart, Marxian eco-

* I am grateful to Joe Bankman, Tom Grey, Pam Karlan, Ellen Frankel Paul, Seana Shiffrin, and Bob Weisberg for their very helpful comments on previous drafts of this essay. I am also grateful to my fellow contributors to this volume and to the participants in the Berkeley GALA and the UCLA Law and Philosophy Workshop, at which earlier versions of this essay were presented. All errors and indiscretions are mine alone.

[1] It has been suggested to me that while *Anarchy, State, and Utopia* has been very influential within the academy, its influence (along with the entire Lockean tradition) on "rank-and-file" libertarians outside the academic mainstream has been slight, as compared to the influence of works by Ayn Rand, Ludwig von Mises, Murray Rothbard, Robert LeFevre, Leonard Read, and a number of others who are marginal (or completely invisible) figures in the academic philosophical community. I quote: "Rank-and-file libertarians always regarded him as someone who was fun to have around, mostly because of the hand-wringing and tooth-gnashing that he caused among establishment academics who had to watch one of their own say these awful things, but he was never regarded by libertarians as a serious theorist. He was seen as someone who liked to watch his own mind at work (and whose mind was indeed enjoyable to watch at work), and who asked good questions that serious theorists needed to work on, but he was not a positive contributor to libertarian thought. . . . I've met Objectivists, neo-Objectivists, Randians, neo-Randians, Rothbardians, Lefevrians, Austrians, neo-Hobbesians, Galambossians, Konkinians, religionists, and utilitarians, but I have never met someone who could fairly be described as Nozickian, in the sense of treating Nozick as a serious contributor to his/her world view. Nozick is important because academic philosophers talk about him, and libertarians talk about him because he is important to academic philosophers. But he is not important to modern libertarianism." E-mail correspondence from Gary Lawson, March 25, 2002. This account of the split between academic and rank-and-file libertarianism is intriguing, and well worth pursuing in its own right, but not one I am competent to assess. For purposes of this essay, I confine my focus to how Nozick has been absorbed by his primary audience.

nomics, and egalitarian theory in general—remain important, fresh, and illuminating thirty years later. By contrast, the affirmative argument for the minimal state that makes up the bulk of the book is so thin and undefended as to read, often, as nothing more than a placeholder for an argument yet to be supplied.[2] The book's central intuition ("Individuals have rights, and there are things no person or group may do to them") continues to resonate thirty years later, precisely because, articulated at that level of generality, it will provoke dissent only among hard-core utilitarians. (Indeed, even utilitarians will blanch more at the rhetoric of rights than at anything that follows from it.) The problem is defending the particular version of rights that make up libertarianism. Where Nozick has not simply begged the question, the answers he provides are often internally contradictory or seemingly random with respect to any coherent moral vision.

In true Nozickian fashion, I am going to leave a proper defense of that bald assertion for another day, in order to pursue another topic entirely: the role of rhetoric in *Anarchy, State, and Utopia*. But by way of down payment on the substantive claim, I offer a (partial) list of the substantive questions begged or dodged in Nozick's book, and one example on which I shall elaborate.

First the list (moving through the book roughly in order). Nozick fails to: establish the moral relevance of hypothetical accounts of how a minimal state *could* come into being; explain why invisible-hand mechanisms for producing the state are morally more appealing than processes (like Locke's social compact theory) that choose the state intentionally; deal with even the most elementary challenges posed by a Coasian analysis to his conception of rights and rights violations ("boundary crossings"); defend the huge exceptions he has created, where expeditious, to the "no boundary crossing" rule, and explain how these exceptions differ from the utilitarian solution; defend the analytically incoherent but argumentatively crucial distinction drawn between acts that harm others with 100 percent certainty and those that pose a risk of harm; give content to the three principles of justice that make up his scheme of distributive justice; justify even the sketchy version of justice in acquisition and justice in transfer that he gives us; and defend the hodgepodge of nonredistributionist conclusions he has pulled out of those principles—and in particular, the assumption that they would jointly bar the taxation of exchange value.

Many of these problems have been discussed extensively in the critical literature on *Anarchy, State, and Utopia* over the past thirty years. Here is one that has not: the peculiar (indeed, radically subversive) relationship of Part III of the book (on Utopia) to the two parts that precede it. Nozick's

---

[2] No doubt, there is a more general lesson here about the vulnerability of all comprehensive schemes of political philosophy, giving the critic the (always) easier hand to play.

basic argument in Part III is that the only plausible utopian vision is a meta-utopian one, in which each person is allowed to choose his own version of an ideal community from a broad menu of possibilities, assuming that such a community can plausibly be created given the preferences of others. Since it is implausible to think that everyone's tastes in utopias will be the same, Nozick argues, it is implausible to think that the best of all possible worlds would produce only one kind of utopia. Here is Nozick's own list of the range of "utopian" communities that might well flourish in a meta-utopian world:

> Visionaries and crackpots, maniacs and saints, monks and libertines, capitalists and communists and participatory democrats, proponents of phalanxes (Fourier), palaces of labor (Flora Tristan), villages of unity and cooperation (Owen), mutualist communities (Proudhon), time stores (Josiah Warren), Bruderhof, kibbutzim, kundalini yoga ashrams, and so forth, may all have their try at building their vision and setting an alluring example.[3]

At first crack, this meta-utopian, free-market vision of utopia seems perfectly consistent with Nozick's libertarian impulses. Why not let a hundred flowers bloom at the level of social organization, just as libertarians would have us do at the level of individual choice? But a moment's reflection surfaces the problem here. Unlike choice operating at the individual level, the outcome of social choice binds all community members. As Nozick concedes, many of the potential utopias included in his list above—indeed, virtually all—would, as part of their collective identity, regulate the behavior of their members in ways that are "unjustifiable on libertarian grounds," including by "paternalistic intervention into people's [private] lives" and by requiring that individuals pool income on egalitarian grounds. Individual members would be prohibited from opting out of many of these regulations as long as they remained in the community. How could such a situation be tolerated from a libertarian perspective? Why is this not exactly the sort of coercion that Nozick has spent the preceding three hundred pages arguing against?

Because, answers Nozick, in his meta-utopia, individual members of any community are always free to exit a given community entirely. As long as they have that choice—as long as it is, in Nozick's terms, a voluntary "association" and not "East Berlin" (*ASU*, 299)—then they can meaningfully be said to have chosen whatever rules they are subjected to within that community, by virtue of choosing to remain in the community itself. That they would have preferred, in the best of all possible worlds,

---

[3] Robert Nozick, *Anarchy, State, and Utopia* (New York: Basic Books, 1974), 316. Subsequent references to the book will appear parenthetically in the text, abbreviated as *ASU*, with page numbers following.

to have the same community but stripped of certain coercive features is hardly reason to question the voluntariness of their choice to take the package deal when presented on a "take it or leave it" basis. After all, says Nozick, people are daily required to "swallow the imperfections of a package P (which may be a protective arrangement, a consumer good, a community) that is desirable on the whole ... when no more desirable attainable different package is worth to [them] its greater costs over P, including the costs of inducing enough others to participate in making the alternative package" (*ASU*, 321).

At this juncture, the alert reader will begin to realize the trouble that the Nozick of Parts I and II is in. For if it is morally sufficient to say to any member of a community who does not like the particular rules and regulations under which he must live, "If you don't like it, leave it," —if the mere possibility of exit is enough, that is, to establish the moral acceptability of any compulsory rules to which those who remain are subject— then why has Nozick bothered with the preceding three hundred pages of *Anarchy, State, and Utopia* at all? Why does it not follow from the justificatory role of exit at the community level that *any* state, with *any* compulsory package of rights/restrictions/prohibitions, developed by *any* procedure whatsoever, is morally justified, as long as dissenters who do not like that particular package are permitted to exit? And why then didn't Nozick limit his ambitions in Parts I and II merely to proposing his libertarian version of utopia to compete, in the marketplace of state-ideas, with all those mildly redistributive, social-welfarist, democratic states out there, in the hope that he could drum up enough takers to get it up and running on some utopian island somewhere? Why waste one second tearing down the legitimacy of those mildly redistributive, democratic regimes when (in the view of the Nozick of Part III) those regimes have proved their legitimacy simply by their survival in the face of competing ideas about the ideal state, given the option of exit?

The potential for his free-market vision of communities (in which the option of exit justifies whatever occurs within the community) to moot all that precedes it in *Anarchy, State, and Utopia* is not entirely lost on Nozick. To parry that threat, Nozick suggests that collective compulsion is morally permissible at the level of subnational communities but not at the level of nation-states, because of the differing harms that such compulsion is countering. Because we live face-to-face with comembers of our immediate communities, Nozick suggests, we "cannot avoid being directly confronted with what [we find] to be offensive" in their nonconforming choices. Being forced to see others do things that offend us, Nozick invites us to conclude, is a cognizable harm in a Lockean scheme, along with the classic harms of force and fraud, and therefore a sufficient basis for compelling others to live as we want them to live. ("Must the vast majority cloister themselves against the offensive minority?" asks Nozick, seemingly incredulous the answer could be yes [*ASU*, 323].) At the level of nation-states, by contrast, since we "need not be directly confronted by these individuals or by the fact of their nonconformity," we cannot claim harm to ourselves from their nonconformity adequate to justify compulsion (*ASU*, 322).

This is pretty amazing stuff to issue from libertarian quarters, and it is worth a moment's reflection. Start first with Nozick's (astonishing) concession that offense at others' behavior might actually constitute a cognizable harm in the Lockean sense. Many people with far less attachment to libertarian principles than Nozick have argued that the sort of third-party, "nosy" preferences (over what others do) that Nozick is describing here ought not to count at all in social policy. Why should I have a right to veto my neighbor's choice of mates just because it offends my sensibilities?[4] Lest one think that Nozick's deference to nosy preferences extends only to classic "morals" offenses, consider the following: "If the majority may determine the limits on detectable behavior in public, may they, in addition to requiring that no one appear in public without wearing clothing, also require that no one appear in public without wearing a badge certifying that he has contributed *n* percent of his income to the needy during the year, on the grounds that they find it offensive to look at someone not wearing this badge (not having contributed)? . . . Since I do not see my way clearly through these issues, I raise them here only to leave them" (*ASU*, 323). If Nozick cannot see his way clear to explaining why offense at others' unwillingness to aid the poor is not an adequate basis for compelling them to do so, then I think we have found a form of libertarianism that Rawlsians can make their peace with (and most libertarians, one presumes, cannot).

Now consider the grounds on which Nozick has sought to contain this concession to local communities. He has walled off the local case from the national one only by the slender empirical claim that we are not, *as a matter of fact*, offended by our far-removed fellow-citizens' refusal to aid the poor, because we are not, *as a matter of fact*, generally confronted with their refusal. What, then, if the nightly news starts carrying regular features on polygamists in Utah, nonredistributionists in Montana, atheists in New York, and homeschoolers in Texas? Is that enough to give the majority, offended by all four practices, a harm-based reason to mandate a monogamist, socialist, Christian state with compulsory state education for all children? If it is—and it is hard to see what in Nozick's argument would permit us to say no—then the Nozick of Parts I and II might as well pack it up and go home, turning in his libertarian union card on his way out the door.[5]

---

[4] A standard liberal argument against counting external (nosy) preferences is given in Ronald Dworkin, *Taking Rights Seriously* (Cambridge, MA: Harvard University Press, 1977), 234–38.

[5] There are other grounds that Nozick might more profitably have seized on to differentiate the local from the national case here. One that comes to mind is the practical difficulty

The foregoing problem may not be the most serious one with the book. After all, the Nozick of Parts I and II could rescue himself from this problem just by excising the third part. But it is illustrative, I think, of the many crucial junctures at which, rather than elaborating his libertarian precepts and defending them against obvious criticisms, Nozick begs or dodges the question. If the enduring prominence of *Anarchy, State, and Utopia* cannot be explained (or explained adequately) by the cogency of Nozick's argument, then what explains it? One important factor at play, I suspect—which I will not pursue directly here—is the ad hominem one. Nozick, by virtue of his academic position at Harvard and his academic reputation, lent respectability to a set of arguments that has had few champions within the mainstream academy, and none of his stature. Arguments that were easy for the academic establishment to marginalize when they came from the likes of Murray Rothbard and Ayn Rand suddenly demanded to be taken seriously simply by virtue of the fact that they came from Robert Nozick. Nozick was hardly unaware of the strategic value of his endorsement—a fact that he played on in *Anarchy, State, and Utopia* in ways I will return to below.

Other explanations for the book's canonical status come to mind as well. One is that, because so few mainstream academics have been willing to speak up for libertarianism, someone looking (for pedagogical or other purposes) for a defense of the libertarian state as a counterpoint to liberal egalitarianism, utilitarianism, etc., did not have many other places to go. *Anarchy, State, and Utopia* may be best in class, if for no other reason than it is almost the only in class. Yet another explanation—somewhat less flattering to the book's critics—is that the book's argumentative weaknesses are precisely what has made it an attractive candidate for canonical status among the liberal egalitarians, who were all too happy to build up the book's importance in order to tear it (and, a fortiori, all of libertarianism) down.

All of these explanations no doubt have some force. I want to focus attention on yet another factor at play: the role that rhetoric has played in the popularity of the book. For purposes of this essay, I mean by "rhetoric," roughly, its standard, lay definition: "The art of using language so as to persuade or influence others."[6] *Anarchy, State, and Utopia* is, in this sense, in many respects a rhetorical tour de force. Much of its charm

---

(costliness) of exit from both communities and the practical availability of meaningful alternatives. As I have suggested elsewhere, it is no easy matter to defend the proposition that *any* particular baseline of exit options is required by libertarian principles in order to validate the "choice" to stay put. See Barbara H. Fried, "If You Don't Like It, Leave It: The Problem of Exit in Social Contractarian Arguments," *Philosophy and Public Affairs* 31, no. 1 (2003): 40–64. But at least the end to which such an inquiry gestures—to give individuals meaningful choice over the arrangements they are living in—seems to be in tune with broad, libertarian values. One cannot say the same of the ground that Nozick has chosen here (whether we are in fact offended by our neighbors' chosen lifestyles).

[6] Shorter Oxford English Dictionary (1773), s.v. "rhetoric."

comes from its discursive playfulness, which is a far cry rhetorically from the earnest, dense, and often ponderous character of much of political philosophy. My colleagues who teach the book regularly in courses on political philosophy report that their students—even the vast majority who disagree vehemently with the book's politics—love to read it, because it is just plain fun.

The captivating playfulness of the book draws the reader in; once hooked, the reader confronts a variety of other rhetorical devices designed to nudge, cajole, seduce, or otherwise persuade her to Nozick's programmatic conclusions. Let us start with the matter of tone. The brash, insouciant, dressed-down, *je ne regret rien* tone that Nozick strikes in *Anarchy, State, and Utopia* mirrors the substantive agenda of the book: it shrugs off stern duty as instantiated in the conventional, ponderous academic style, just as Ayn Rand's Atlas invites all of us to shrug off stern duty instantiated in the substantive burdens of egalitarianism.[7] The rhetorically liberated "I" of Nozick's book anticipated—and quite possibly hastened—the moment at which libertarians would not only come out of the closet, but indeed take center stage in the political arena. Like Adam Bellow's recently published defense of nepotism,[8] it cleared the air of shame for the self-regarding practices we are all wont to engage in, declaring itself proud to stand up for the freedom to pursue one's self-interest, for the view that every man is, after all, an island. The book's sympathetic readers (then and now) no doubt experienced this manifesto, not without reason, as a liberating release from the stifling left-liberal orthodoxy of academic political philosophy circles, in which most disputes turn out to be nothing more than friendly family quarrels. There is some suggestion in the book that Nozick may have experienced a different, more personal, sort of release as well. I am thinking here of Nozick's reference to "the not wholly admirable pleasure of irritating or dumbfounding people by producing strong reasons to support positions they dislike or even detest"—a pleasure that Nozick declares himself (not wholly convincingly, to this reader's ear) to have outgrown by the time he wrote the book (*ASU*, x). Even without such a guilty pleasure as inducement, Nozick could well have regarded it as a public service to throw a bomb into the middle of this clubby party, and see what was left standing at the end of the day.

The brash, insouciant tone of much of the book is only one of the many rhetorical devices that Nozick deploys to charm and disarm his audience, simultaneously establishing his own credibility with readers, turning them on his ideological opponents, and deflecting attention from some of the more serious gaps in his affirmative argument. In the balance of this essay, I want to take a look at these various devices at work. Some are

---

[7] I thank Gillian Lester for this shrewd observation about the parallels in the book's rhetorical and substantive performances.

[8] Adam Bellow, *In Praise of Nepotism: A Natural History* (New York: Doubleday 2003).

clearly more successful than others in enhancing the persuasiveness of the various substantive claims in the book. Whether any ultimately succeeds in winning converts to an argument that could not have compelled their allegiance on the merits is a harder question.

Many of these rhetorical devices, although they have the potential for mischief, are not inconsistent with the possibility that Nozick's substantive argument holds water. Others seem to be deployed solely to deal with the (to my mind) justifiable anxiety that it does not. (The reader will discern a difference on this score between the rhetorical devices discussed in Sections II and III below, and those discussed in Section IV, which clearly fall more in the latter camp.) Of course, it is hard to separate rhetoric from substance, particularly where rhetorical devices are employed to dodge substantive problems. At various points below, the discussion undoubtedly veers from observations about rhetoric to quarrels about substance. But for the most part, I want to detach from what I regard as the substantive problems with Nozick's argument. I also mean to make no claims about Nozick's intent with respect to the rhetorical maneuvers in the book. I assume that the rhetorical choices here are not accidental (how could they be?), but I have no basis to conjecture about the extent to which Nozick was conscious of, and motivated by, the strategic role such choices might play in winning over his audience.

Finally, I do not mean to imply that there is something inherently suspect or unusual about the use of rhetoric to enhance the persuasiveness of a substantive argument or the credibility of the author. After all, that is its function. It is the writer's job to do the best he can by his argument. It is our job as readers to discern whether the rhetorical stratagems being deployed to that end are in service of good arguments or bad ones. To the extent it is the latter here, well—"use every man after his desert, and who shall 'scape whipping?"[9] I would wager there is no academic who has not, at one time or another, deployed numerous rhetorical devices, some of which are catalogued here, to slide the reader past inconsistencies or gaps in an argument. To name just a few of the more popular devices: the fatal concession to the counterargument phrased as a minor qualification and buried in a parenthetical or a footnote; the preemptive self-accusation; the feigned modesty to win the reader's trust; the go-for-it strategy of brash overstatement; the strategy of offering up the only example we can think of that proves our point as if it stands for hundreds of others we simply don't have time to report on; and the strategy of skewering the opposition for its minor vices while ignoring its possibly more substantial virtues. The fact is, we are all guilty of begging, dodging, or otherwise underhandedly dispatching the question with style. To that extent, I hope the balance of this essay will be read, not as singling out a class of one, but as an exemplum of a much larger class to which all

---

[9] William Shakespeare, *Hamlet*, 2.2.528–29. References are to act, scene, and line.

of us, to differing degrees, belong. I hope it will be read in part as well as an implicit (if, one might sometimes feel, too grudging) tribute to someone who was in his own way a master stylist.

II. Behold, Diogenes, the Only Honest Man

One of the book's recurring tropes to pry readers loose from their habitual attachment to Nozick's chief targets (egalitarianism in its various guises and utilitarianism) is to suggest that Nozick alone, on the contemporary political philosophy scene, can be trusted to go wherever the truth leads him. The message is conveyed through a kind of rhetorical Mutt and Jeff routine, in which Nozick alternately portrays himself as a humble toiler in the vineyards of truth, and portrays his antagonists as intellectual con men or sentimental fools. These two approaches clearly work in tandem to establish Nozick's claim to (unique?) credibility. I take up the first one here, and the second in Section III below.

A. Witness for the prosecution

Probably the strategically most important rhetorical device Nozick employs to establish his own credibility is to cast himself in the preface as the unwilling convert (the "Witness for the Prosecution" move). Noting his long-standing attachment to more conventional, nonlibertarian views, Nozick assures the reader that no one could have been more surprised than he to discover that libertarianism was the answer to which honest inquiry (when he was finally willing to undertake it) led him:

> [M]any persons will reject our conclusions [that the only aid to the poor that is morally permissible is voluntary charity] instantly, knowing they don't *want* to believe anything so apparently callous towards the needs and suffering of others. I know that reaction; it was mine when I first began to consider such views. With reluctance, I found myself becoming convinced of (as they are now often called) libertarian views. . . . My earlier reluctance is not present in this volume, because it has disappeared. (*ASU*, ix–x)

Whatever the truth of the claim here asserted (that Nozick came to libertarianism only reluctantly),[10] its strategic value is obvious. Like Glenn

---

[10] I have no basis to judge the truth of the claim myself. But one person who does has vouched for it: "I knew [Nozick] before *ASU* was a gleam in his eye, and he really had been a leftist, having been a member, and if I recall correctly the ring leader, of the YPSL (the Young People's Socialist League) at Columbia. The chapter eventually became the SDS, with all of the tumult that ensued at Columbia, but that was after Nozick's time. He really was a convert to libertarianism; [I] knew his fellow graduate student who accomplished the deed." Correspondence with Ellen Frankel Paul, 2003.

Loury coming out in the end for affirmative action after all, David Brock turning on the Right, or Colin Powell defending the U.S.-led invasion of Iraq, the reluctant convert who comes to see the truth only slowly and painfully, and at great personal cost (my views simultaneously "[put] me in some bad company" and at odds with "most people I know and respect" [*ASU*, x]), is the most valuable front man any movement can put forward. Who can doubt the man who has paid so dearly for the truth? This is not to deny that the costs of conversion—paid in hard self-examination as well as admissions against material interest—are very real in many cases. That they *are* is (after all) the underlying social reality from which the figure of the convert derives its rhetorical power. But the decision to call attention to one's status as a convert, and thereby lay claim to the enhanced credibility bestowed by that status, is a rhetorical choice and not a substantive one, and it carries the same strategic advantages in any case whether the conversion was in fact hard-earned or not. (That is to say, the rhetoric of the reluctant convert free-rides in any given case on the reality in the general case.)

Closely related to the figure of the reluctant convert (establishing his bona fides by contrast to past beliefs) is the believer who, even once converted, is unafraid to acknowledge the weaknesses of his own convictions—indeed, insists on doing so as a matter of intellectual integrity—and stands ready to modify them, or indeed abandon them entirely, whenever truth requires it. Who could distrust a fellow such as that? The balance of Section II looks at some of the rhetorical devices deployed in *Anarchy, State, and Utopia* to create and sustain that persona.

B. The artless artist

"*I am no orator. . . .*"[11] Nozick announces his allegiance to the truth up front, in the guise of a methodological commitment. Simultaneously exposing and disavowing the pretentions to completeness that characterize many contemporary works of political philosophy ("There is room for words on subjects other than the last words"), Nozick declares that he, alone, is going to tell it like it is, warts and all (*ASU*, xii). Here is his charming description of the usual deceptive arts practiced by his profession:

> Indeed, the usual manner of presenting philosophical work puzzles me. Works of philosophy are written as though their authors believe them to be the absolutely final word on their subject. . . . One form of philosophical activity feels like pushing and shoving things into some fixed perimeter of specified shape. All those things are lying out there, and they must be fit in. You push and shove the material into the rigid area getting it into the boundary on one side, and it bulges

[11] William Shakespeare, *Julius Caesar*, 3.2.219–20.

out on another. You run around and press in the protruding bulge, producing yet another in another place. So you push and shove and clip off corners from the things so they'll fit and you press in until finally almost everything sits unstably more or less in there; what doesn't gets heaved *far* away so that it won't be noticed. . . . *Quickly,* you find an angle from which it looks like an exact fit and take a snapshot; at a fast shutter speed before something else bulges out too noticeably. Then, back to the darkroom to touch up the rents, rips, and tears in the fabric of the perimeter. All that remains is to publish the photograph as a representation of exactly how things are, and to note how nothing fits properly into any other shape. (*ASU*, xii–xiii)

This is great stuff. Who would not be disarmed by the candor of a master magician laying bare all the sleights of hand and other tricks of his trade, thereby simultaneously establishing his mastery (I know how all this is done, and could do it again at any time, if I wanted) and turning state's evidence on himself and all the fellow members of his guild? And who could resist the artfully artless promise that follows to abjure those arts himself in favor of the unvarnished truth—a promise made all the more credible by his having just told us how it is done. (Now, of course, thanks to his forthcomingness, we'd catch him out if he ever tried it again himself, wouldn't we?) We philosophers, confides Nozick, "are all actually much more modest than [our method would suggest]. Having thought long and hard about the view he proposes, a philosopher has a reasonably good idea about its weak points; the places where great intellectual weight is placed upon something perhaps too fragile to bear it, the places where the unravelling of the view might begin, the unprobed assumptions he feels uneasy about" (*ASU*, xii). And so, declares Nozick, in a Prospero-like renunciation of the tricks of his trade: "I propose to give it all to you: the doubts and worries and uncertainties as well as the beliefs, convictions, and arguments" (*ASU*, xiv).[12]

The classic model here for the self-described plainspoken, honest man is the conclusion of Mark Antony's famous funeral oration in *Julius Caesar*:

> I come not, friends, to steal away your hearts.
> I am no orator, as Brutus is;
> But (as you know me all) a plain blunt man
> That love my friend . . .
> For I have neither wit, nor words, nor worth,
> Action nor utterance, nor the power of speech
> To stir men's blood; I only speak right on.
> I tell you that which you yourselves do know,

---

[12] "But this rough magic / I here abjure . . . I'll break my staff, / Bury it certain fathoms in the earth, / And deeper than did ever plummet sound / I'll drown my book" (*The Tempest*, 5.1.50–57).

Show you sweet Caesar's wounds, poor poor dumb mouths,
And bid them speak for me.[13]

In Nozick's case, like Mark Antony's, what makes this a rhetorical
device rather than a truly artless description of method is the distance
between those professions of intellectual modesty and the speaker's true
imperial ambitions. Managing this tension is a tricky business, to which
I will return in Section IV. (It is fair to say that Nozick is no Mark Antony
in this regard, but then, who is?) First, however, I want to take a closer
look at the various rhetorical devices used to sustain the claims of intellectual modesty and self-doubt throughout the book.

All of these devices convey in different ways (earnest, tongue-in-cheek,
playful) the sense that Nozick can be counted on to be his own harshest
critic. That impression serves several aims simultaneously. It reassures
skeptical readers that they can relax: if there are hard questions to be
asked, Nozick will ask them. It invites readers to infer that if, at any point,
no hard questions are asked, it is because there are no hard questions *to*
ask. (After all, if there were, can't we trust the author to have asked
them?) And, finally, it invites readers to conclude that if any portion of his
affirmative argument resurfaces after being subjected to such intense scrutiny, it is because the doubts expressed turned out not to be fatal after
all.[14]

C. The self-accuser

The most frequent device delivering on the promise to give it all—the
"doubts and worries and uncertainties"—is (a) the unadorned proposition put on the table, followed by (b) a barrage of unanswered (and often
unanswerable) questions. Exhibit A here is Nozick's famous discussion of
Locke's labor theory of ownership. After coyly producing Locke's theory
as a stand-in for his own unspecified theory of justice in acquisition,
Nozick acknowledges that Locke's theory "gives rise to many questions."
Two paragraphs of probing questions duly follow, touching on the moral
basis for Locke's claim, the scope of ownership thereby established, and
the problem of satisfying Locke's proviso that "enough and as good [be]
left in common for others" (*ASU*, 174–75). Most of the time, Nozick
allows the sheer volume of his skeptical questions to attest to his honor-
ableness as an author. But on occasion he cannot resist calling attention to
it, lest anyone should have missed it. Here is one such example: "While
feeling the power of the questions of the previous two paragraphs (it is *I*

[13] *Julius Caesar*, 3.2.218–25.
[14] I use the word "resurfaces" advisedly, as typically Nozick does not try to resurrect the
affirmative case hard on the heels of his own (unanswered) assault on it. Rather, he typically
reintroduces it several pages or even chapters later, without any acknowledgment of the
criticisms and abuses that he himself heaped on it. For further discussion, see Section IV
below.

who ask them), I do not believe that they overturn a thoroughgoing entitlement conception" (*ASU*, 237). To my ear, at least, the parenthetical here is a rhetorical misstep, the condescension so palpable as to risk (indeed, almost court) insubordination from the reader.

D. Giving the devil his due

"*But Brutus is an honorable man.*" By going out of his way to give the devil his due on small matters, Nozick demonstrates his continued willingness to change course on large matters as well, should truth compel it. (Happily, in the end, it doesn't, but we know he would have told us if it did.)

Consider one of the more overt rhetorical plays along these lines, in which Nozick invites the reader along as he recreates one of the moments in which he himself is stunned to discover the implications of his own argument. After establishing that the just libertarian state might, under some circumstances, be required to purchase liability insurance for individuals engaged in risky activities, Nozick concludes: "Thus we see how . . . another *apparent* redistributive aspect of the state would enter by solid libertarian moral principles! (The exclamation point stands for *my* surprise.)" (*ASU*, 115). Well, maybe it does, but then again, maybe it doesn't. It is no small feat, in the intellectual realm as much as the physical one, to sneak up on one's self, unawares (the self being snuck up on being the unaware one, that is, not the sneaking self). A more plausible account of what Nozick's exclamation point stands for, along with the italicized *my*, is something like this, I think: Behold, you see before you a man whose intellectual integrity is so uncompromised that he will go wherever his principles take him, even if doing so compromises the political ends that cynics might mistakenly have taken to be his true motive.

Most of the time, Nozick eschews overt self-congratulation of this sort, in favor of more indirect plays for the reader's confidence. Sometimes this takes the form of earnest frettings out loud about exactly how far it is fair to push his claims. Consider here Nozick's fussing over how best to put the thought (central to his argument against the redistributive state) that taxation is a form of slavery. He first tests the water with the slightly equivocal "Taxation of earnings from labor is on a par with forced labor . . ." (*ASU*, 169), but follows it up immediately with confessions of doubt as to whether even this equivocal claim is sustainable: "I am unsure as to whether the arguments I present below show that such taxation merely *is* forced labor; so that 'is on a par with' means 'is one kind of.' Or alternatively, whether the arguments emphasize the great similarities between such taxation and forced labor, to show it is plausible and illuminating to view such taxation in the light of forced labor" (*ASU*, 169 n. *).

Other times, Nozick simply acknowledges matter-of-factly the limits of his argument—the parts of his argument that he is not even going to try to prove, the conditions that must hold true for his argument to go through, etc. Consider, for example, Nozick's list in Part III of only some of the still-to-be-resolved details about his utopian state: how the central authority will be selected, how it will be policed, whether there could be toll charges on exit to compensate for benefits an individual has gotten from the community, and what rights children have to learn about exit options (*ASU*, 329–30). Consider as well his concession that much work remains to be done to figure out when to prohibit involuntary boundary crossings through a "property" rule and when to permit them, provided ex post compensation is paid: "To say that [boundary crossings] should be allowed if and only if their benefits are 'great enough' is of little help in the absence of some social mechanism to decide this." And the various considerations he himself has put on the table, Nozick concedes, "do not yet triangulate a solution in all its detail" (*ASU*, 73). Or finally, consider Nozick's confession at the end of his discussion of the principle of rectification: "These issues are very complex and are best left to a full treatment of the principle of rectification. In the absence of such a treatment . . . , one *cannot* use the analysis and theory presented here to condemn any particular [distributive] scheme . . ." (*ASU*, 231). The rhetorical (as contrasted with substantive) function of all of these concessions is to reassure the reader that because Nozick has told the truth here, when it is manifestly not to his argumentative advantage, he can be trusted to tell it elsewhere as well.

E. The abject penitent

"Alas, why would you heap this care on me? / I am unfit for state or majesty." [15] Not infrequently, Nozick's effusions of self-doubt are concluded with an abject confession of inadequacy and a plea for the reader's indulgence as he reluctantly sets these doubts aside for another day. The confession of inadequacy serves to convey to the reader that he (the reader) cannot possibly think worse of Nozick's argument at this juncture than Nozick thinks of it himself. This ritualized form of self-debasement is, of course, designed to provoke protestations to the contrary in his readers, who find themselves thinking that Nozick—modest fellow that he is—is really much too hard on himself; that, really, if you think about it, few could have done better than he has here.

An apt model here is the passage from *Richard III* quoted at the outset of this section.[16] Richard offers first a fake demurral when the crown is offered to him (through prearrangement) by one of his henchmen: "Alas, why would you heap this care on me? / I am unfit for state or majesty." To Richard's protestations of unworthiness, the rhetorically compelled response is, of course, to insist, to the contrary, on his inestimable worth, and to press the crown on him once more, with redoubled zeal ("Call him

---

[15] *Richard III*, 3.7.204–5.
[16] Ibid., 204–26.

again, sweet prince. Accept their suit. / If you deny them, all the land will rue it"). This is followed by Richard's inevitable capitulation to the hench-man's pleas, couched in false humility:

Will you enforce me to a world of cares?
Call them again, I am not made of stones,
but penetrable to your kind entreaties,
Albeit against my conscience and my soul.

Typically, Nozick's protestations of inadequacy are delivered with flat earnestness—the careful philosopher flagging for us (in case we have missed it) the serious gaps in his argument that remain to be filled. At other times, the rhetorical self-flagellation is so extravagant, verging on burlesqued, as to raise suspicions that Nozick is having a little fun at the expense of his anxious readers. Consider here Nozick's treatment of his decision (in Part I) to derive the minimal state from a Lockean (moralized) state of nature. Nozick tries first to defend that choice by stating that "since considerations both of political philosophy and of explanatory political theory converge upon Locke's state of nature, we shall begin with that" (*ASU*, 9). Anticipating that this may not seem an adequate defense of a stipulation on which the entire edifice of Part I is built, he preemptively makes the charge of inadequacy himself:

A completely accurate statement of the moral background ... is a task for another time. (A lifetime?) That task is so crucial, the gap left without its accomplishment so yawning, that it is only a minor com-fort to note that we here are following the respectable tradition of Locke, who does not provide anything remotely resembling a satis-factory explanation of the status and basis of the law of nature in his *Second Treatise*. (*ASU*, 9)

The extravagantly exaggerated diction of Nozick's confession here ("so crucial," "a gap so yawning," "only a minor comfort") undercuts the sincerity of his contrition while purporting to underscore it, communi-cating to us (with its mock gravity) that our anxieties in this department are more than a trifle ridiculous. At still other times, the conclusion that Nozick is having fun at our expense seems unavoidable—which brings us to the character of the charming rogue.

F. The charming rogue

This is a liminal figure, somewhere between the earnest penitent and the talk-radio belligerent denouncing his opponents as big, fat idiots (see Section IIIB below), who disarms the skeptics by conspiratorially telling them he's picking their pocket even as he does it. For a brief feint in this direction, consider Nozick's assertion that if a side constraint is violated, the transgressor is required to compensate the victim so as to leave him as well off as he would have been without the violation, which is followed by Nozick's confession: "Shamelessly, I ignore general problems about the counterfactual 'as well off . . . as X would have been if Y's action hadn't occurred'" (*ASU*, 57). Given the central role that compensation for boundary crossings plays throughout the book, a little (intellectual) shame might be in order here, if genuine. It is safe to say that it is not, and that readers who would prissily insist on real contrition are being mocked for their small-minded earnestness.

For a more striking example, consider Nozick's discussion (*ASU*, 84–97) of his principle that the state is required to pay compensation (to the would-be actor) whenever it prohibits productive activities that impose risks on others. After subjecting the principle to a barrage of skeptical challenges, Nozick concludes, in the voice of the earnest penitent, "I am not completely comfortable presenting and later using a principle whose details have not been worked out fully." But then Nozick the sly rogue takes over, mocking the very readers whose earnestness he has just aped. Maybe, says Nozick, it is okay to leave the principle in this "somewhat fuzzy state . . . [if] something like it will do. This claim, however, would meet a frosty reception from those many proponents of another principle [Rawls's] scrutinized in the next chapter, if they knew how much harder I shall be on their principle than I am here on mine. Fortunately, they don't know that yet" (*ASU*, 87).

Of course, all of these rhetorical devices, designed in different ways to give the devil his due, work to shore up the case for the angels only if the reader comes away with the impression that what the devil is due is, finally, trivial. For those (many) concessions in the book that are in fact trivial, this is easy to pull off. The classic how-to model here is provided by the daily corrections page of the *New York Times*. The sheer numerosity of the editors' corrections, coupled with their exquisite fussiness ("Due to a transmission error, the author of the recent biography of General Sherman was identified as Rufus G. Lighthouse rather than Rufus T. Lighthouse"), conspire simultaneously to impress on the reader that, as far as the *New York Times* is concerned, no error is too inconsequential to be worth correcting, while distracting attention from the fact that it is *only* inconsequential errors the editors have in fact confessed to.[17]

---

[17] I am indebted for this observation to Renata Adler, *Canaries in the Mineshaft: Essays on Politics and Media* (New York: St. Martin's Press, 2001). Some emendation is perhaps in order here, in light of the 2003 Jayson Blair scandal. To my ear, the *New York Times*'s paroxysms of front-page self-flagellation in the wake of disclosures that it had been "had" by a cub reporter, while in rhetorical demeanor miles apart from its bland, business-like daily corrections page, reflect a similar rhetorical strategy underneath. The comical excesses of this elaborate ritual of self-debasement, which chronicled, for days on end, every signpost on the road to the *Times*'s ruin, seem intended to communicate simultaneously the overwhelming social importance of the *Times*—why else would one possibly care?—and the unprecedented nature of its fall from grace.

For that not insignificant number of concessions that are not trivial, managing the fallout is a trickier business. Broadly speaking, Nozick proceeds on two rhetorical fronts here: he derides his opponents as infantile, in bad faith, etc., so as to suggest that whatever the problems with his own theory of distributive justice, it is the only intellectually respectable game in town; and he reasserts his affirmative argument unequivocally, as if those concessions had never been made, deploying a battery of rhetorical devices to protect it from any further attack. I take up both tacks in turn, in Sections III and IV respectively.

III. Fools and Knaves All

Partnered with his Mutt—Nozick the Humble, the earnest, patient toiler in the vineyards of truth—is the doppelganger Jeff—Nozick the Supercilious, writing off his intellectual antagonists as (variously) childish, grown intellectually soft from years of complacency induced by running the show, stupid, or in bad faith.[18] The attack on the opposition stands on its own as a rhetorical performance, but gains strength from playing off the confidence earned by Nozick the Humble.

Nozick sets the patronizing tone toward his antagonists right from the start, when he declares in the preface that "many people will reject our conclusions instantly, knowing they don't want to believe anything so apparently callous towards the needs and suffering of others," and he acknowledges that by being willing to face those hard truths, "I run the risk of offending doubly: for the position expounded, and for the fact that I produce reasons to support this position" (*ASU,* ix–x). The statement combines, with admirable economy, (a) the representation of the opposi-

---

[18] Most of Nozick's contempt in the book is reserved for egalitarians of various stripes. Utilitarianism comes in only for sporadic floggings. What accounts for this disproportionate allocation of critical attention is itself an interesting question, but one outside the scope of this essay. For what it's worth, I think it has a couple of possible explanations. One is simply occasion. The book was written partly as a response to Rawls's *A Theory of Justice,* which had been published just three years earlier, a motivation that leaves its imprint in the disproportionate attention given to egalitarian theories. Another explanation, I think, has to do with the close (and unacknowledged) kinship that Nozick's own theory has to utilitarianism. In particular, the basic intuition of utilitarianism that Nozick would like to reject (that the interests of the individual may sometimes be sacrificed for the general good) is essential to getting his own argument to go through at various critical junctures. That unacknowledged kinship would, I think, surface were Nozick to push hard on his criticisms of utilitarianism, and may partly explain his reticence to do so. In addition, one of the frequent criticisms of utilitarianism—the pragmatic problems with implementing it, given the difficulties of measuring welfare so as to make appropriate trade-offs—could be levied with as much force against Nozick's argument. Consider, for example, the difficulties entailed in ascertaining the counterfactual histories necessary to implement his principle of rectification, his particular interpretation of the Lockean proviso, and the requirement that "full market compensation" be paid for permissible boundary crossings. Some realization that his own argument might not fare much better than does utilitarianism against the charge of being held hostage to unresolvable empirical issues may explain Nozick's lack of enthusiasm for pushing this particular criticism hard.

tion (at least in the egalitarian wing) as weak-brained sentimentalists, who are offended even by the attempt to educate them out of their error through reason, and (b) the presentation of self as the weary but wise Wordsworthian realist, who (in contrast to his antagonists) has slowly come, with maturity, to assume the burdens of truth. The latter pose is struck more overtly in the succeeding paragraph: "Over time, I have grown accustomed to the views and their consequences, and I now see the political realm through them." But Nozick segues at the end into lofty, arch arrogance: "(Should I say that they enable me to see through the political realm?)" (*ASU*, x).[19] Nozick's tarring of the egalitarian camp alternates between a kind of patronizing sympathy for their pursuit of a utopian vision that they, in their childlike innocence, understandably yearn for, and imputations of intellectual laziness or plain bad faith.

A. Fools

Pity the poor children. . . . Mining the first vein, consider this Nozickian paraphrase of the egalitarian's case for equality: "Wouldn't it be *better* if the person with less opportunity had an equal opportunity? If one could so equip him without violating anyone else's entitlements (the magic wand?) shouldn't one do so? Wouldn't it be fairer?" (*ASU*, 236). So we might be tempted to think, suggests Nozick the Realist, until we are reminded of the cold, hard, grown-up truth that the only way to give more to those who have less is to seize holdings from those who have more to which they are "entitled," or to persuade those with more voluntarily to give it away to those with less (*ASU*, 235). It is worth pausing not just on Nozick's choice of the word "fairer" and even more unmistakably the term "magic wand" here to characterize the opposition as childlike moral simples, but (more subtly) on the use of the italicized "*better*." Quotation marks would have expressed straightforward dismissive contempt for the opposition's failure to define and defend "better." Italics are a much more inspired choice, expressing a subtler form of contempt—the condescending, if sympathetic, adult contemplating the touching plea of the wide-eyed, innocent child for world peace. ("Why can't we all just be friends?")

In the same vein, consider the following passage on the purported shortcomings of the minimal state: "But doesn't the idea, or ideal, of the minimal state lack luster? Can it thrill the heart or inspire people to struggle or sacrifice? Would anyone man barricades under its banner? It seems pale and feeble in comparison with, to pick the polar extreme, the hopes and dreams of utopian theorists" (*ASU*, 297). Obviously, the intent of this speech, like Mark Antony's somewhat subtler version ("I come to

---

[19] Probably not. This is another point at which I think Nozick is slightly tone-deaf and risks turning his audience against him by overplaying his hand rhetorically.

bury Caesar, not to praise him . . ."), is the opposite of the announced one: to drive the reader to conclude that the apparent vice of the minimal state—that it is not the stuff to set revolutionary hearts apatter—is its greatest virtue, and that critics' inability to see this point is merely a symptom of their greatest failing, which is their childish psychological attachment to utopianism.[20]

B. Knaves

The first half of Nozick's one-two punch (characterizing egalitarians as childlike utopians) is delivered in a voice tinged "more with sorrow than anger." The second (suggesting their intellectual complacency and/or bad faith) is delivered with straightforward, often snide, contempt. Again, Nozick sets the tone in the preface, when he suggests that those on the other side have grown complacent from their long domination of the academy, and that it falls to Nozick to remind them what a real defense of an argument entails:

> A codification of the received view or an explication of accepted principles need not use elaborate arguments. It is thought to be an objection to other views merely to point out that they conflict with the view which readers wish anyway to accept. But a view which differs from the readers' cannot argue for itself merely by pointing out that the received view conflicts with *it!* Instead, it will have to subject the received view to the greatest intellectual testing and strain, via counterarguments, scrutiny of its presuppositions, and presentation of a range of possible situations where even its proponents are uncomfortable with its consequences. (*ASU*, x)

By the end of this passage, the reader cannot help but be impressed with the Herculean labors that await the author in the balance of the book, by contrast to what his opponents have gotten away with. Segueing from imputations of laziness to imputations of bad faith, Nozick reminds his readers that "intellectual honesty demands that, occasionally, at least, we go out of our way to confront strong arguments opposed to our views" (read, the occasion is long overdue in this case), and that "[o]nly the refusal to listen guarantees one against being ensnared by the truth" (*ASU*, x and xi, respectively).

C. Are you still beating your wife?

The charges of bad faith sprinkled throughout the book are often explicit, as they are in the preface. So, for example, after stating that he is going to

---

[20] See also *ASU*, 328 and 330, on the same childish yearnings for a "sleek, simple utopian scheme" that everyone will accept, that is complete enough in theory "to cover all problems which actually will arise" (ibid., 330), and that will operate in practice exactly as predicted in theory (ibid., 328).

focus his critique on Bernard Williams's version of equality, Nozick concludes (with what one hears as an almost imperceptible sneer): "No doubt many readers will feel that all hangs on some other argument; I would like to see *that* argument precisely set out, in detail" (*ASU*, 233). The clear implication here, of course, is that egalitarians will resist doing so at all costs, so as to avoid the sort of withering (Nozickian) critique that inevitably awaits them if they do. In a similar vein, consider the not-too-subtle "intentionally" planted in the following defense of methodological individualism in political theory: "There are only individual people . . . with their own individual lives. . . . Talk of an overall social good covers this up. (Intentionally?)" (*ASU*, 33).[21]

At other times, Nozick conveys his antagonists' bad faith indirectly, through a careful choice of descriptors. Consider, for example, Nozick's deployment of the term "redistributionist" to describe end-state theorists, holding it out at arm's length for our inspection like three-day-old fish, his moral disgust at uttering the word barely contained: "[I]sn't it surprising that redistributionists choose to ignore the man whose pleasures are so easily attainable without extra labor, while adding yet another burden to the poor unfortunate who must work for his pleasures?" (*ASU*, 170). In addition to reducing his subjects to specimen-like objects, Nozick's choice to label them "redistributionists" rather than (say) egalitarians focuses attention on the means that end-state theorists might find it necessary to employ to achieve their desired end, rather than the desired end itself. This seems like an odd rhetorical choice on substantive grounds. (Would one describe libertarians as prison enthusiasts because they would throw in jail those who steal from their fellow citizens via redistributive taxation?) But it may well be a shrewd choice on strategic grounds, since it invites readers to confuse means with ends—to think that what really turns these people on is not the prospect of helping the poor, but the prospect of taking away *your* money in order to do it.[22]

---

[21] For yet another example, consider Nozick's insinuation that advocates of end-state distributive principles have deliberately sought out redistributive mechanisms that will obscure what they are up to: "Whether it is done through taxation on wages . . . or through seizure of profits or through there being a big *social pot* so it's not clear what's coming from where and what's going where, patterned principles of distributive justice involve appropriating the actions of other persons" (*ASU*, 172).

[22] There is some irony in Nozick's rhetorically loading the dice through this particular device, given the fuss he makes elsewhere in *ASU* about the use of the term "distributive justice." By using the word "distributive" in this context, argues Nozick, end-state theorists smuggle into the argument over who gets what the (undefended) presupposition that there is some "person or group entitled to control all the resources" to begin with, and by extension therefore to redistribute them at any time (*ASU*, 149). Instead, Nozick suggests, we should use the neutral word "holdings." As deployed by Nozick in the balance of the book, the word "holdings" comes to mean, roughly, "That which you, as a matter of fact, possess, which (in my view, for reasons I don't care to spell out or defend, though they have something to do with Lockean entitlement theory) it would violate your rights to take away from you."

The word "redistributionist" in Nozick's hands has a slight whiff of red-baiting about it—not substantively, but rhetorically, in the sense of describing one's enemies by a trait that is likely to elicit readers' reflexive, enflamed reactions. That tactic is more overt at various other points in the book, when (for example) Nozick matter-of-factly describes redistributive taxation as a form of slavery,[23] or treats egalitarianism as necessarily implying absurd conclusions that no egalitarian would embrace.

D. The parade of horribles

On the latter front, consider the conclusion to which Nozick pushes his observation that patterned principles will call into question intrafamily transfers (true enough in some situations): "Either families themselves become units to which distribution takes place . . . (on what rationale?)[24] or loving behavior is forbidden" (*ASU*, 167). Or consider the following: After implying that anyone who supports forced redistribution is logically compelled to bar dissidents to the program from exiting, Nozick concludes with this parenthetical: "(Would it also support, to some extent, the kidnapping of persons living in a place without compulsory social provision, who could be forced to make a contribution to the needy in your community?)" (*ASU*, 173–74). Well, no, it wouldn't, and no sane "redistributionist" would take it to do so (although some might take it to support international obligations of justice, which they will insist are not morally equivalent to kidnapping). But, obviously, the rhetorical point is scored just by posing the question.

Finally, there is Nozick's famous (and admittedly "slightly hysterical" sounding) suggestion that Rawls's difference principle implies forced eyeball transplants from the two-eyed to the blind: "On what grounds are

---

Consider, too, this passage, in which Nozick implies that ownership of others is not merely the by-product of end-state theories but their motivation: "End-state and most patterned principles of distributive justice institute (partial) ownership by others of people and their actions and labor. These principles involve a shift from the classical liberals' notion of self-ownership to a notion of (partial) property rights in *other* people" (*ASU*, 172). The slippery word "institute" here implies (without outright stating) that end-state principles are chosen in order to create partial ownership of others. This impression is underscored by the word "shift" here, which implies a parallelism in the intentions of "classical liberals" (undeniably to institute "self-ownership") and redistributionists.

[23] "This process whereby they take this decision from you makes them a *part-owner* of you; it gives them a property right in you. Just as having such partial control and power of decision, by right, over an animal or inanimate object would be to have a property right in it" (*ASU*, 172).

[24] There is an answer to this question, which Nozick treats as rhetorical. The rationale for treating families as the units to which distribution takes place is that families themselves tend to pool income and make consumption decisions jointly—the same rationale that explains why, since 1948, the U.S. income tax system has treated traditional families (married couples and their minor children), rather than each member of a family, as the taxpaying unit, and why the U.S. estate and gift tax system exempts from taxation all transfers of property between spouses.

such cases, whose detailed specifications I leave to the ghoulish reader, ruled inadmissible [in the Rawlsian scheme]?" challenges Nozick (*ASU*, 206–7). Again, there is no shortage of answers to this question, which Nozick treats (mistakenly) as a rhetorical one. But again, Nozick has probably gotten most of the rhetorical advantage he could hope for here just by posing the question and leaving it hanging there as a grim reminder of where egalitarianism might lead.

E. Are you still not beating your wife?

Sometimes Nozick's insinuation of intellectual laziness or dishonesty on the part of his opponents is simply perplexing, as when it catches out the opposition (gotcha!) doing (ostensibly nefarious) things that one assumes they would more than happily cop to in broad daylight.

Consider here Nozick's discussion of the failures of utilitarianism in the context of punishment theory. Nozick starts out as Reasonable Man here, acknowledging (as utilitarians would insist) that "[r]etributive theory seems to allow failures of deterrence," since its requirement that the punishment be proportionate to the crime does not take into account the probability (which is less than 1) of a boundary crosser's apprehension, conviction, and punishment (*ASU*, 60–61). This is, of course, a serious objection. It is really an instance of one of the principal objections that utilitarians have voiced against deontological theories: that the latter's fixation on the "rightness" of action at the individual level (focusing on the difference between nonfeasance and malfeasance, individual desert, etc.) prevents the state from acting so as to optimize interests that deontologists themselves hold paramount (protecting the innocent, etc.).[25] But, instead of engaging that complaint, Nozick the Reasonable Man gives way to Nozick the Contemptuous. Maybe deterrence theorists "would be in a position to gloat at retributivists' squirming over this," says Nozick, "if they themselves possessed another theory" (*ASU*, 61).

One would think that the one thing that utilitarians possess is another theory. Why don't they, in Nozick's view? Nozick's answer (*ASU*, 61–62) is a tour de force of slippery prose, which I leave to the reader to inspect up close for herself. Here is a rough (but I think fair) paraphrase: Well, actually, utilitarians do have another theory, but that theory says we should set punishment so as to maximize overall happiness. I consider this "bizarre" because it requires us to care as much about the happiness of the criminal as about that of the victim. ("Constructing counterexamples to this bizarre view is left as an exercise for the reader" [*ASU*, 62].) "Utilitarian deterrence 'theory'" (note the quotation marks, suggesting

---

[25] For an exhaustive catalogue of these arguments by two enthusiasts, see Louis Kaplow and Steven Shavell, *Fairness versus Welfare* (Cambridge, MA: Harvard University Press, 2002).

the author's disdain for the very prospect of dignifying this argument by that appellation) could avoid this result I consider bizarre only if utilitarians weighted happiness by reference to the virtue of different classes of individuals. But (aha!) that would make them desert theorists, and moreover, require them to figure out "proper" weights (let's see them do that!).[26] We retributivists don't have to do any of that because we don't give a damn about happiness to begin with.

Well, okay. But look at what has happened here: Nozick has parried utilitarians' weighty objection to retributivism by accusing utilitarians of being, well, utilitarians, which he points out that they could avoid only by becoming retributivists. But they can't do that, because they themselves forswore that possibility when they became utilitarians. To which utilitarians of the world could hardly be blamed for responding: Is this a joke? As to the rest of Nozick's audience, however, this barrage of arguments that carry themselves for all the world as if they were dispositive creates the general impression (reinforced by the dismissiveness of his tone) that, after two centuries of philosophers' phumphing around, Nozick has expeditiously dispatched utilitarianism in two pages.

IV. Nevertheless . . .

As I suggested at the outset, what makes Nozick's professions of intellectual modesty a rhetorical device rather than a straightforward description of method is the distance between those professions and what are, finally, the imperialist ambitions of the book. Those ambitions are put on the table right at the start, in Nozick's famous assertion that "Individuals have rights, and there are things no person or group may do to them. . . . So strong and far-reaching are these rights that they raise the question of what, if anything, the state and its officials may do" (*ASU,* ix). We encounter those ambitions again at the end, when Nozick declares them to have been met, planting the libertarian flag, as it were, on the entire realm of political philosophy:

> In this chapter and in the previous one we have canvassed the most important of the considerations that plausibly might be thought to justify a state more extensive than the minimal state. When scrutinized closely, none of these considerations succeeds in doing so (nor does their combination); the minimal state remains as the most extensive state that can be justified. . . . We have justified the minimal state, overcoming individualist anarchist objections, and have found all of

[26] "One would suppose that considerations of desert, which deterrence theorists had thought avoidable if not incoherent, would play a role here; one would suppose this if one weren't bewildered at how to proceed, even using such considerations, in assigning the 'proper' weight to different persons' (un)happiness" (*ASU,* 62).

the major moral arguments for a more extensive or powerful state inadequate. (*ASU*, 273–74, 276)

As I suggested earlier, sustaining these imperial claims in the face of the conceded (and very real) problems with his argument is a tricky rhetorical business. I turn now to the various strategies employed to accomplish it.

A. Pay no attention to the man behind the curtain

The most frequent strategy Nozick employs to neutralize his self-critique is simply to disregard it. This strategy has all the advantages of the heist in broad daylight in the public square. It seems so brazen, so certain not to work, that bystanders simply do not believe their eyes when all appearances suggest that that is precisely what is going on.

Sometimes problems are dispatched in this fashion by the flat-footed non sequitur, which, following hard upon some acknowledged difficulty, seems by virtue of its placement and rhetorical structure to respond to the difficulty, but in fact does no such thing.[27] At other times, problems are neutralized by being encapsulated as a minor qualification on an otherwise impregnable argument. For sheer economy, it is hard to beat the following example, trumpeting the efficacy of a dominant protective association's prohibitions on others' use of unfair or unreliable procedures of justice: "Leaving aside the chances of evading the system's operation, anyone violating this prohibition will be punished" (*ASU*, 103).

Most often, however, Nozick deals with the problems he has conceded to exist by waiting a discreet interval after his concession, and then pro-

---

[27] See, for example, Nozick's response to his (apt) concern that his attempt to justify the minimal state by showing that it *could* in theory come into being through a just (invisible-hand) process may be morally irrelevant: "[O]ne would feel more confidence if an explanation of how a state *would* arise from a state of nature [Nozick's emphasis] also specified reasons why an ultraminimal state *would* be transformed into a minimal one [my emphasis], in addition to moral reasons, if it specified incentives for [people doing what they ought, including providing compensation where required]." Instead of answering this objection, Nozick follows it up with this caveat: "We should note that even in the event that no nonmoral incentives or causes are found to be sufficient for the transition from an ultraminimal to a minimal state, and the explanation continues to lean heavily upon people's moral motivations, it does not specify people's objective as that of establishing a state. Instead, persons view themselves as providing other persons with compensation for particular prohibitions they have imposed upon them. The explanation remains an invisible-hand one" (*ASU*, 119). A fair paraphrase of this whole paragraph would go roughly as follows: I've shown how we could in theory get a just minimal state through an invisible-hand process. You might rightly object that I haven't shown we ever could in practice. But I'd like to point out that even if your objection is apt, the process I've shown you is an invisible-hand one.

I hesitate to include the "non sequitur" as a rhetorical device, as that description implies some subtlety and charm that maneuvers like this lack, at least to my ear. They are likely merely to irritate the close reader, raising the question whether Nozick is asleep at the switch here, or is simply counting on his readers to be so.

ceeding as if it had never been made, as if the very survival of his affirmative argument in the face of the prior onslaught testifies to its veracity. The typical life cycle of a Nozickian self-critique starts with the elaborate presentation of self-doubts (often accompanied by handwringing of various sorts, as we saw in Section II above), segues to equivocation, and then departs silently from the scene some pages later, leaving not a trace behind.

As an example of this technique, consider Nozick's argument in Part I of *Anarchy, State, and Utopia* as to how a dominant protective agency could establish a monopoly on coercive powers (thereby metamorphosing into the minimal state) without violating anyone's rights. Nozick the Reasonable takes the floor first, conceding at some length that it is very hard to come up with any natural rights theory of procedural justice (*ASU*, 96–101, 141). In particular, Nozick suggests, it is very hard to figure out what would be an optimal level of false positives and false negatives in conviction rates, and it is hard to come up with any other norms about required procedures. A little later, he acknowledges that reasonable people may disagree as well on questions of substantive justice—that is, which boundary crossings deserve punishment at all (*ASU*, 141–42).

But establishing the existence of some norms of procedural justice is critical to Nozick's argument that a dominant protective agency that complies with such norms thereby earns the right to extinguish other competing agencies (*ASU*, 140, 141). Here is how Nozick moves (silently) from skepticism about the possibility of establishing such principles, to equivocation, and finally, to the stipulation of such principles. First the equivocation:

> The natural-rights tradition offers little guidance on precisely what one's procedural rights are in a state of nature, on how principles specifying how one is to act have knowledge built into their various clauses, and so on. Yet persons within this tradition do not hold that there are *no* procedural rights; that is, that one may not defend oneself against being handled by unreliable or unfair procedures. (*ASU*, 101)

As a substantive matter, the last sentence would not seem to be any sort of rejoinder to the penultimate one. That natural-rights types mistakenly believe that there are such things as "procedural rights," such that one can justly defend oneself against others acting as though there are not, would hardly seem to be responsive to Nozick's prior arguments as to why they are wrong in thinking so. Yet, using this nonresponsive equivocation as a kind of rhetorical demilitarized zone, in the next section Nozick tentatively reasserts the claim that the dominant protective agency has a right to prohibit "unreliable or unfair" procedures, and implies we can take it as given that we all know what this category includes and can therefore evaluate whether a given protective agency has complied with the requirement.[28]

Finally, fifteen pages later, we have the Nozickian declaration of victory: "We have discharged our task of explaining how a state would arise from a state of nature without anyone's rights being violated. The moral objections of the individual anarchist to the minimal state are overcome. It is not an unjust imposition of a monopoly; the *de facto* monopoly grows by an invisible-hand process and *by morally permissible means*, without anyone's rights being violated and without any claims being made to a special right that others do not possess" (*ASU*, 114–15).[29]

The same maneuver is deployed at various critical junctures throughout the book. Probably the boldest and most important example is Nozick's treatment of the three principles on which his theory of just distribution is built: justice in acquisition, justice in transfer, and rectification. Nozick the Reasonable again takes the floor first, acknowledging that supplying defensible content to any of the three principles is a tricky matter, and one that he does not propose to undertake in the book. Justice in acquisition is sidestepped in a subsidiary clause/aside: "We shall refer to the complicated truth about this topic, *which we shall not formulate here*, as the principle of justice in acquisition" (*ASU*, 150; italics added). Justice in transfer is sidestepped in the concessionary adjective "complicated" and a parenthetical: "The complicated truth about this subject (with placeholders for conventional details) we shall call the principle of justice in transfer" (*ASU*, 150). The principle of rectification actually gets more than a half-dozen signature, probing, Nozickian questions, gesturing at the many difficulties that lay buried here, before we are invited to sidestep them as well: "Idealizing greatly, let us suppose theoretical investigation will produce a principle of rectification" (*ASU*, 152).

Well, suppose it doesn't? All moral arguments must take certain things as given. Nozick's matter-of-fact openness about doing that here borrows its presumptive respectability from that reality, while reinforcing his bona fides as an honest man (at least *he* is willing to acknowledge what every other philosopher does behind our backs). The problem, of course, is that without any content supplied for those three principles, Nozick's theory of just distribution rules out almost nothing, as virtually any substantive theory of distributive justice can be fit within its rhetorical structure. Nozick the Diffident concedes as much: "To turn these general outlines into a specific theory we would have to specify the details of each of the

---

[28] See Nozick's discussion of "How May the Dominant Agency Act?" (*ASU*, 101 ff.).
[29] For a similar declaration of triumph on this point, see *ASU*, 132–33: "[My invisible-hand argument] differs from views that '*de facto* might makes state (legal) right' in holding that ... the process of accumulating sole effective enforcement and overseeing power may take place without anyone's rights being violated; that a state may arise by a process in which no one's rights are violated."

three principles of justice in holdings. . . . I shall not attempt that task here" (*ASU*, 153).[30]

But in the very next sentence, Nozick the Diffident signals his imminent departure from the scene, ceding the floor to Nozick the Equivocator, who hints that he will draft Locke as a stand-in for himself until such time as he is ready to supply his own views: "(Locke's principle of justice in acquisition is discussed below.)" (*ASU*, 153). Less than ten pages later, the imperial Nozick has taken command, offering up a full-blown version of his theory of justice (sometimes coyly attributing it to his doppelganger Locke, sometimes taking responsibility himself). Without the slightest hint of self-doubt, Nozick pulls out of that theory a string of controversial, concrete policy conclusions: "On an entitlement view, . . . [w]hoever makes something, having bought or contracted for all other held resources used in the process . . . is entitled to it" (*ASU*, 160); "[e]ntitlements to holdings are rights to dispose of them" (*ASU*, 166); and taxation, which "violate[s] . . . a side constraint against aggression," amounts to "forced labor . . ." (*ASU*, 169). By the start of Part III, we confront the astonishing declaration of total victory: "No state more extensive than the minimal state can be justified" (*ASU*, 297). So much for Nozick the Diffident.

B. When in doubt, say it loud

Flat-footed, brash declarations pop up throughout the book, setting forth Nozick's major claims without elaboration or defense. ("Political philosophy is concerned only with *certain* ways that persons may not use others, primarily, physically aggressing against them" [*ASU*, 32]. Oh?) The function of this rhetorical posture seems to be to persuade the reader that the author's very confidence in his assertions dispenses with any need for argument.[31]

Where explanation would normally follow, one often instead gets paraphrase, acting for all the world like explanation but in fact amounting only to repetition.[32] Consider, for example, Nozick's elaboration of his famous assertion at the start that "Individuals have rights . . ." (*ASU*, ix):

[30] Indeed, when he makes a later appearance in his critique of Rawls, Nozick the Reasonable concedes that the principle of rectification could, in practice, demand adjustments that would swamp all other considerations of justice and in the end justify some system of distribution that looks a lot like the Rawlsian scheme (*ASU*, 231).

[31] The reigning muse for Nozick here might be E. B. White's Will Strunk. Strunk, said White, "scorned the vague, the tame, the colorless, the irresolute. He felt it was worse to be irresolute than to be wrong. I remember a day in class when he leaned far forward, in his characteristic pose—the pose of a man about to impart a secret—and croaked, 'If you don't know how to pronounce a word, say it loud! . . .' This comical piece of advice struck me as sound at the time, and I still respect it. Why compound ignorance with inaudibility? Why run and hide?" E. B. White, introduction to William Strunk, Jr. and E. B. White, *The Elements of Style* (New York: Macmillan, 1959), xi.

[32] Here, again, Nozick takes a page from White's Strunk. See White's charming description of Strunk's device for filling up the time he had created by following his own advice to "omit needless words": "In those days when I was sitting in his class, he omitted so many

> There are particular rights over particular things held by particular
> persons, and particular rights to reach agreements with others. . . .
> No rights exist in conflict with this substructure of rights. Since no
> neatly contoured right to achieve a goal will avoid incompatibility
> with this substructure, no such rights exist. The particular rights over
> things fill the space of rights, leaving no room for general rights to be
> in a certain material condition. (ASU, 238)

The thought here may be to exhaust the skeptic, or lull him into acqui-
escence, through sheer redundancy. Like many of the rhetorical strategies
employed in this book, repetition can backfire if not done with a deft
touch, since it always runs the risk of conveying, instead of self-confidence,
desperation. To my ear, the foregoing quote has a hint of such desperation. The hint is somewhat stronger in the following attack on equal
opportunity egalitarianism: "No centralized process judges peoples' use
of the opportunities they had; that is not what the processes of social
cooperation and exchange are *for*" (*ASU*, 236). The artless reiteration here,
topped off by the italicized "*for*," lends the statement a kind of plaintive
air, betraying rather than obscuring what one hears as Nozick's own
unease about the threadbareness of the argument.

C. The factitious (chimerical) world

The odd, pseudo-Lockean world in which Nozick's argument is lodged
belongs in the bestiary of Greek chimerae, half beast (the fabulist half)
and half man (grounded in reality). Every time we think we are happily
ensconced in the world of fable, some odd fact about how people actually
behave intrudes. Nozick is hardly alone in helping himself to the best of
both worlds—the ideal and the real—as needed to see the argument
through. But he is, as an absolute matter, a heavy user of the device,
routinely plucking out empirical claims to get him over some pretty
rough patches in his theoretical argument.

Examples of Nozick's factitious universe at work abound in *Anarchy,
State, and Utopia*. We already saw one at the start of this essay. When
Nozick realizes he has gotten himself into something of a jam by conceding that communities have a right to regulate the lives of their members
as long as their members are not formally prevented from exiting—
suggesting the obvious question, why not nation-states as well?—he bails

---

needless words, and omitted them so forcibly and with such eagerness and obvious relish,
that he often seemed in the position of having shortchanged himself—a man left with
nothing more to say yet with time to fill, a radio prophet who had outdistanced the clock.
Will Strunk got out of this predicament by a simple trick: he uttered every sentence three
times. When he delivered his oration on brevity to the class, he leaned forward over his
desk, grasped his coat lapels in his hands, and, in a husky, conspiratorial voice, said, 'Rule
Thirteen. Omit needless words! Omit needless words! Omit needless words!'" Strunk and
White, *The Elements of Style*, viii.

himself out by plucking out from the vast universe of possible social facts the following: people are annoyed by what others do if they meet them face to face, but not if they are far removed physically (*ASU,* 321–23).

Alternatively, consider Nozick's account in Part I of how the minimal state could (would?) evolve from a private protective agency through a just (invisible-hand) process. The entire fable is a confused amalgam of pure fantasy (how people in theory *could* behave), moralized fantasy (how they *would* behave if they behaved morally), psychological conditional reality (how they *are likely* to behave if placed in certain contexts), and prediction (how some actually existing protective agency will actually behave in the future).

Consider as well the following example, a variant on the exit problem. After stipulating to people's broad rights to extract, through voluntary contract, whatever concessions their legitimate bargaining power gives them, Nozick raises the possibility that a majority could justly coerce a minority into consenting to a more-than-minimal state by just such a process—that is, by threatening a boycott, which amounts to a collective agreement not to deal with others unless they accede to certain terms. How does Nozick contain this exception, which—like Nozick's harm-based justification for regulating nosy preferences—has the potential to swallow his entire libertarian worldview? He does so *not* by arguing that such a boycott would be morally impermissible. Indeed, he concedes that it does not violate any rights (*ASU,* 292). Instead, he contains it by offering reasons why, as a matter of empirical fact, "[i]t is highly unlikely that in a society containing many persons, an actual boycott such as the one described could be maintained successfully" (*ASU,* 292–93). Maybe, but maybe not. More importantly, it is not clear what moral relevance that empirical claim would have, even if right. In Part I, Nozick takes it as sufficient to justify the minimal state that one could imagine a just process by which it *might* have come into being. Why is it not sufficient to justify a more-than-minimal state that one could similarly imagine a just process by which it might have come into being? What's reality got to do with it?

Nozick's easy transit between the ideal and real worlds raises a substantive issue more than a rhetorical one. But at least one rhetorical aspect of his performance is worth noting. Nozick blurs the line between these two worlds, often making it impossible to decipher which world we are supposed to be in at any given moment, by casually slipping between the indicative and subjunctive moods, and by employing an indicative mood whose claims to facticity are ambiguous at best. Both moves serve to obscure (without outright denying) the counterfactual, speculative nature of his enterprise. The following passage from Nozick's account of how the minimal state could (would?) evolve is a perfect illustration of both devices:

> Will protective agencies *require* that their clients renounce exercising their right of private retaliation . . . ? Such retaliation may well lead

to counterretaliation by another agency or individual, and a protective agency would not wish *at that late stage* to get drawn into the
messy affair by having to defend its client against counterretaliation. . . . Initially, several different protective associations or companies will offer their services in the same geographical area. What will
occur when there is a conflict between clients of different agencies?
(*ASU*, 15)

After wobbling between the future-indicative "will" and the subjunctive "would," Nozick finally settles into the repeated use of "will" in a
fashion that invites us to imagine that the hypothetical is real, and that his
claims as to what "will" occur are themselves a factual refutation of all the
other, less salutary hypothetical scenarios one could dream up.[33] I take
up another example of the rhetorical blurring of fact and fiction in
subsection D.

D. The irresistible pull of the particular

Another of the recurring rhetorical features of Nozick's argument, often
employed in moving through the factitious universe, is the vertiginous
descent from broad general propositions to incredibly particularized examples and observations. Consider this description of what a good Lockean
protective association will (would?) do for its clients, to protect them
against independents' applying their own unfair legal procedures to punish acts the independents don't like:

> Th[e] dominant protective association will prohibit anyone from apply-
> ing to its members any procedure about which insufficient informa-
> tion is available as to its reliability and fairness. It also will prohibit
> anyone from applying to its members an [actually] unreliable or
> unfair procedure. . . . The protective association will publish a list of
> those procedures it deems fair and reliable (and perhaps of those it
> deems otherwise); and it would take a brave soul indeed to proceed
> to apply a known procedure not yet on its approved list. Since an
> association's clients will expect it to do all it can to discourage unreli-
> able procedures, the protective association will keep its list up-to-
> date, covering all publicly known procedures. (*ASU*, 102–3)

Now this is pretty hilarious stuff. First, there is the matter discussed
above: the seamless blend of the hypothetical and the supposedly real.
The "bravery" of the "brave" soul is real, I take it, along with the dom-

---

[33] Here, as elsewhere in this essay, I may be reading too much into something that reflects
nothing more than the sort of careless writing that we are all guilty of from time to time.
There isn't always providence in the fall of a sparrow.

inant protective association's willingness to punish deviations from its edicts in a fashion that would necessitate that bravery. In contrast, its willingness to confine the list of procedures it prohibits to those that are actually unfair (by unspecified criteria), rather than prohibiting all those it doesn't like because they materially disadvantage its members, is apparently not. The "chances of evading the system's operation" are real; the assertion that, notwithstanding those (real) chances, "anyone violating this prohibition will be punished" is not. There is as well the bizarre specificity of the portrait of what a hypothetical (good Lockean) dominant protective agency would do in such a situation: the "up-to-date" lists it would post; the inclusion not only of actually unfair or unreliable procedures, but also of those "about which insufficient information is available as to [their] reliability or fairness."

Often, the choice of particular examples to pose or worries to chase down seems so random with respect to the main argument, so improbable or insignificant as compared to other problems never raised, as to be inexplicable or downright loopy. Consider here Nozick's fretting over the problem of checkerboard rival private protective agencies that forbid outsiders to enter their territory: "But this would leave acute problems of relations with independents who had devices enabling them to retaliate across the boundaries, or who had helicopters to travel directly to wrongdoers without trespassing upon anyone else's land, and so on" (*ASU*, 55). *Helicopters?*[34] Why not spaceships? Or for that matter, why not independents who, hot to retaliate against their opponents, don't stand on ceremony when they encounter a "No Trespassing" sign decorously posted at the intervening border?

Consider, too, Nozick's discussion of the circumstances under which a dominant protective association is justified in refusing to give full faith and credit to an independent's legal judgment:

> If the agency deems the procedure unreliable or doesn't know how reliable it is, it need not presume its client guilty, and it may investigate the matter itself.... This protection of its client against the actual imposition of the penalty is relatively straightforward, except for the question of whether the agency must compensate the prospective punishers for any costs imposed upon them by having to delay while the protective agency determines to its satisfaction its own client's guilt. It would seem that the protective agency does have to pay compensation to users of relatively unreliable proce-

---

[34] I note, on behalf of the legal sticklers out there, that helicopter travel won't help Nozick's legally fastidious marauders much, since it—as much as foot-travel across a neighbor's land—constitutes trespass under the common-law definition of ownership rights in the Anglo-American legal tradition: "cuius est solum eius est usque ad coelum et ad inferos" (he who owns the land owns everything reaching up to the very heavens and down to the depths of the earth).

dures for any disadvantages caused by the enforced delay; and to the users of procedures of unknown reliability it must pay full compensation if the procedures are reliable, otherwise compensation for disadvantages. (*ASU*, 104)

Then comes the coup de grace: "(Who bears the burden of proof in the question of the reliability of the procedures?)" (*ASU*, 104).

This is a pretty odd tangent to find oneself out on. Nozick has not established that there is any such thing as procedural due process in the Lockean state of nature, let alone what it would require or whether a just state is required to give full faith and credit to another's fair determinations, and here we are worrying about whether the other side gets compensated for the delay in figuring out whether its judgment deserves full faith and credit, and who bears the burden of proof. Well, we are not worrying for long, because it turns out there are clear answers to the last two questions, even if there are not, by Nozick's admission, answers to any of the others.[35]

What on earth is going on here? Why these examples and worries, and not others? What is all this false particularity accomplishing?[36]

It is accomplishing a few things, I think. First, the meticulous attention to extraneous details distracts the reader from the threadbareness of the central proposition that Nozick is fleshing out.[37] The following is an unusually flagrant example. In his discussion of "Prohibition, Compensation, and Risk," after acknowledging that he is "shamelessly" (see Nozick the Charming Rogue) going to ignore the difficulty of answering the counterfactual question at the heart of his compensation scheme for involuntary border crossings—how well off would X have been without Y's action—Nozick states, "But one question must be discussed": whether X has an obligation to mitigate damage caused by Y's transgression (*ASU*, 57). A lengthy discussion ensues. This abrupt transition from the jugular

---

[35] For another example, see Nozick's discussion of why one can't leave to private contract the problem of coordinating among private protective agencies (*ASU*, 89–90).

[36] It has been suggested to me again that historical context may supply an answer that the text alone does not. I quote: "Much of this silly argument is a response to hotly debated issues between individualist anarchists and minimalists that went on at a furious pace in the early 1970s. That's where the whole business about protective agencies comes from: the Rothbardian anarchists. But since mainstream political philosophy didn't know anything about this tempestuous (and often pretty wacky) debate, Nozick's arguments just look preposterous and unique to him. They may be preposterous, but they occurred in a context, now pretty much lost to interpreters. The Rothbardian anarchists argued in this (often ludicrous) way, including all the minutiae [quoted above], and Nozick responded in kind." Correspondence with Ellen Frankel Paul, 2003.

[37] Just for the record, among the difficulties skipped over in the last example are the assumption that state-of-nature theory has a position on unfair procedures; that, notwithstanding Nozick's own concession that it is quite unclear what those unfair procedures are, all honorable dominant protective associations would know them when they see them (and see them in the same places); and that even a good Lockean dominant protective association would regard it as required, rather than merely optional, to defer to extraterritorial judgments arrived at by "fair" procedures.

to the capillary, introduced by the earnest and urgent "But one question must be discussed," seems designed to imply (contrary to what his "shamelessly" flamboyantly concedes) that what Nozick has chosen to explore in detail is in fact much more important than what he has "shamelessly" left by the wayside.

Second, like Nozick's fussy attention to small matters when giving the devil his due, the oddly concrete and specific nature of these details shores up his bona fides with respect to the central claims of his argument, reassuring us that we are dealing with someone who has really thought all this through. (If he hadn't, how would he ever have arrived at *this* obscure concern?) Finally, it aids in blurring the line between fact and fiction here. Even where Nozick does not overtly invite the reader to treat the hypothetical as real, the particularity of the tangents he chooses to run down invites that confusion. (Why is he telling us all this stuff about when and how lists will be posted, and whether they will be kept up-to-date, if it isn't real? Who could invent something like this, and who would bother?)

V. CONCLUSION

By this point, the reader will have detected more than a whiff of censoriousness in this essay's tone. Perhaps it is appropriate in closing to say something about the implicit ethical criticism that lies beneath it.

As I stated at the outset, I do not mean to suggest there is something inherently suspect about the use of rhetoric to enhance the persuasiveness of academic arguments. Since our arguments are communicated through the medium of words, we cannot avoid the rhetorical. Whether or not it is a virtue, it is a necessity. At the same time, it seems clear that rhetoric plays a different, and more problematic, role in academic arguments than in (say) literature. The difference, I think, largely has to do with the nature of truth content in the different enterprises. Upon reading the last stanza of Keats's "Ode on Melancholy," no one would think to take Keats to task for overstating the (empirical) claim that only those who know great pleasure can understand true sadness, or for confounding our judgment on the evidence by invoking an image so powerful that it overwhelms rational thought.[38] No one would think to say it, because it would so utterly misconceive the nature of truth in play in the poem.

---

[38] She dwells with Beauty—Beauty that must die;
    And Joy, whose hand is ever at his lips
Bidding adieu; and aching Pleasure nigh,
    Turning to poison while the bee-mouth sips:
Ay, in the very temple of Delight
    Veil'd Melancholy has her sovran shrine,
        Though seen of none save him whose strenuous tongue
    Can burst Joy's grape against his palate fine;
His soul shall taste the sadness of her might,
    And be among her cloudy trophies hung.

When one turns to the academic project, however, the truth content differs (or so it usually seems to me) in important ways that bear on the legitimate uses of rhetoric. The creation of affective states in readers still plays a legitimate role—maybe more so in political philosophy than, say, in tax policy, and maybe very little in the hard sciences, but a legitimate role nonetheless. When one is arguing over matters of (say) distributive justice, it is impossible not to cook the data in a deep sense—impossible, in Robert Lowell's great phrase, to just "say what happened."[39] Moreover, it is not clear that, even if we *could* just say what happened, we would want to. Overstatement, simplification, insistence on treating most moving parts of the argument as fixed, are all essential to make any argument comprehensible and hence usable. At the same time, truth in some nonsubjective, nonaffective sense seems to be at play here, and to make demands on us that it does not in literature—demands that may put off-limits some of the more engaging finds in any rhetorician's bag of tricks. Whatever irritation with Nozick one might detect on the surface of this essay undoubtedly reflects my own sense that he has not always adequately met those demands.

I recognize, however, that one could take an entirely different view of the matter—of whether there is such a thing as "the truth," even in the academic enterprise, and, assuming there is, what allegiance we owe to it. And so, let me end with a more charitable interpretation of the enterprise Nozick was engaged in in writing *Anarchy, State, and Utopia,* and the role that rhetoric plays in it. The book can be read, not as an inadvertent manifesto, but as a quite deliberate one, in which Nozick set out to provoke, enrage, excite, and otherwise arouse his audience to engaged response. In sustaining that very different enterprise, the free-ranging, loose, and occasionally irresponsible rhetorical style of the book was not merely excusable, but essential. In short, to reconnect people to politics as we live them, Nozick had to reconnect philosophy to the art of the manifesto.[40] Judging the book from this vantage point, the implicit criticism of this essay might be thought to rest on a simple category error, and be more than a little prissy to boot. Why should we force Nozick, or any other philosopher, to speak always in the voice of sweet reason? Why shouldn't he assume the role of prophet or gadfly if it serves his argumentative purposes? But then, it is a somewhat different canon to which this book belongs, and a different set of virtues by which it should be judged and remembered.

Law, Stanford University

---

[39] "Epilogue," in Robert Lowell, *Day by Day* (New York: Farrar, Straus, and Giroux, 1975).

[40] I am grateful to both Seana Shiffrin and Gary Lawson for pushing me on this point, each in a different way.

THE SHAPE OF LOCKEAN RIGHTS: FAIRNESS, PARETO, MODERATION, AND CONSENT*

By Richard J. Arneson

I. Introduction

The Lockean natural rights tradition—including its libertarian branch—is a work in progress. Thirty years after the publication of *Anarchy, State, and Utopia* (1974), Robert Nozick's classic work of political theory is still regarded by academic philosophers as the authoritative statement of right-wing libertarian Lockeanism in the Ayn Rand mold.[1] Despite the classic status of this great book, its tone is not at all magisterial, but improvisational, quirky, tentative, and exploratory. Its author has more questions than answers. On some central foundational questions, he refrains from taking a stand. There is spadework yet to be done on the project of developing the most plausible versions of Lockean and Lockean libertarian views. Prior to doing this work and articulating the sensible alternatives and what can be said for and against them, we are not yet in a position reasonably to opt for any particular version of Lockean theory, or for that matter to decide between the natural rights tradition and rival consequentialisms. This essay aims to explore hard and soft versions of Lockean theory. The exploration aims to persuade the reader to favor the soft versions.

Section II formulates four claims (all asserted by Nozick) and provisionally identifies the Lockean libertarian view with these claims. Section III notes that although Nozick in his 1974 book made scant progress toward providing a justification of his particular doctrine of rights, compared to advocates of rival doctrines, no rights theorist since then has made significant advances on that front, so Nozick's achievement has not been superseded. Section III also rehearses Nozick's view of rights as side constraints. Sections IV and V raise a question that Nozick first posed: Should rights be regarded as specifying ways individuals may not be treated, infringement of which is *never*, or *sometimes*, or *always* morally

* I thank Ellen Frankel Paul for helpful, constructive, and substantive comments on a prior draft of this essay. It goes without saying that her comments outstripped my ability to respond.

[1] Robert Nozick, *Anarchy, State, and Utopia* (New York: Basic Books, 1974). Further references to Nozick's book will take the form of parenthetical page citations in the text, using the abbreviation *ASU*. Nozick criticized arguments purporting to provide a moral foundation for capitalism that he located in Ayn Rand's writings. See Nozick, "On the Randian Argument," reprinted in Robert Nozick, *Socratic Puzzles* (Cambridge, MA: Harvard University Press, 1997), 249–64. This essay was first published in 1971.

acceptable, provided full compensation is paid to any victims? *Hard libertarianism* is defined as a version of Lockean libertarianism that replies "Never!" to this question along with offering strict interpretation and uncompromising affirmation of the four provisional claims detailed in Section II. Sections VI through VIII explore and criticize Nozick's own discussion of the question under review. An alternate phrasing of it is: Is every infringement of an individual natural right a violation of it? The discussion proceeds by raising several examples and interpreting them as counterexamples to hard libertarianism. Sections IX and X discuss examples that provide reasons to embrace a weak or soft interpretation of the Lockean norm of self-ownership. Sections XI and XII introduce further softening. Section XI proposes a Pareto constraint on the content of individual rights. Section XII proposes moderation, the idea that any natural moral right of any person should give way if the consequences for other people if one does not violate the right are sufficiently bad. Moderation says rights are side constraints that give way under pressure of consequences. In other words, people are inviolable, up to a point. Section XIII argues that the soft Lockean position at which we have arrived is not a repudiation but, rather, an intelligible development of the Lockean tradition, and in particular does not reject but only qualifies the claim of self-ownership. Section XIV summarizes the modifications to Nozick's version of libertarianism that this essay defends. Section XV notes that the considerations adduced in favor of soft as opposed to hard versions of Lockeanism consist entirely of descriptions of examples. But Nozick himself has rightly stressed that the evidence for a moral theory that consists in responses to puzzle cases is not to be sneered at.

II. Basics

The fundamental Lockean libertarian view comprises four claims:

1. Each person has a moral right to do whatever she chooses with whatever she legitimately owns unless her actions would harm nonconsenting others in certain ways that violate their rights.
2. Each person has the right not to be harmed by others, whether by physical assault, interference with her liberty by coercion or force, physical damage to her person or property, extortion, theft or fraud, breach of contract, libel, or threat of any of these things.
3. Each adult person legitimately owns herself.
4. All of these moral rights are forfeitable by misconduct, transferable from their holder to another by mutual consent, and waivable by voluntary consent of their holder.[2]

[2] Not all Lockean libertarians accept the claim that one's right to self-ownership is fully transferable and waivable. This claim implies that voluntary slavery contracts may be

An important derivative element in Lockean theory is that from the premises above, given a world in which material resources are initially unowned, it follows that individuals can acquire extensive private ownership rights over material resources.[3] The exact specification of this derivation, the characterization of its outcome, and the assessment of its success are crucial and tricky issues for Lockean theory, and are much debated.[4] For the purposes of this essay, I simply assume that some version of this derivation does succeed and that within Lockean theory strong rights of individual private ownership of material resources are justifiable.[5]

III. Why Side Constraints?

This bare-bones statement of the Lockean idea immediately prompts two closely related questions. The list of the ways in which people have a right not to be harmed is a motley set. One wonders, can ordering principles be found that explain and unify the items on the list and that justify each item's inclusion (or suggest revisions)? A second question is, what is the moral basis of individual rights so conceived? What are the

---

morally valid. Nozick takes this line, however, and it has the virtue of simplicity, so I include it in the statement of core Lockean libertarianism. See also John Simmons, "Inalienable Rights and Locke's Treatises," *Philosophy and Public Affairs* 12, no. 3 (1983): 175–204.

[3] Some readers may balk at my terminology here, on the ground that John Locke's initial premise is that the earth is communally owned. I believe my characterization in the text is correct as applied to Locke. Locke holds that initially the earth is unowned, and that all persons have provisional use rights, which can be supplanted by permanent bequeathable full private ownership rights, given certain conditions. See John Locke, *Second Treatise of Government* (1690), ed. C. B. Macpherson (Indianapolis, IN: Hackett Publishing Company, 1980), chap. 5. In this essay, I use the terms "Lockeanism," "Lockean theory," and "Lockean libertarianism" to refer to a family of views that develop doctrines of individual moral natural rights that are broadly similar to the basic position adumbrated by Locke. Although there are important libertarian strands in Locke's doctrines and arguments, his view is sufficiently different from the libertarianism of Rand and Nozick that it would be misleading to call Locke himself a libertarian. In this essay, "hard libertarianism" refers to an uncompromising version of libertarianism. Libertarianism also comes in softer versions. If one qualifies and weakens soft libertarianism sufficiently, eventually one arrives at the "soft Lockeanism" defended in this essay. To my mind, nothing essential hangs on the terminology, but the position I defend departs significantly from the doctrines standardly associated with libertarianism, so it is probably better to reserve the term "libertarian" for positions closer to the paradigm case. For the purposes of this essay, the paradigm libertarian is Nozick.

[4] For a recent discussion, see John T. Sanders, "Projects and Property," in David Schmidtz, ed., *Robert Nozick* (Cambridge: Cambridge University Press, 2002), 34–58. For skeptical discussions of the issue, see G. A. Cohen, *Self-Ownership, Freedom, and Equality* (Cambridge: Cambridge University Press, 1995). For discussions of John Locke's dealings with this issue, see A. John Simmons, *The Lockean Theory of Rights* (Princeton, NJ: Princeton University Press, 1992), chap. 5; and Jeremy Waldron, *The Right to Private Property* (Oxford: Oxford University Press, 1988). The literature on this topic is voluminous.

[5] I am assuming the correctness of the Lockean derivation of private property rights arguendo, in order to concentrate attention on other issues, and not because I believe the derivation is correct. For familiar reasons, I doubt it is correct.

reasons that should persuade reasonable persons to accept Lockean morality as correct?

In a review of *Anarchy, State, and Utopia*, Thomas Nagel reports with
some impatience that Nozick does not make much progress in answering
these questions:

> To present a serious challenge to other views, a discussion of liber-
> tarianism would have to explore the foundations of individual rights
> and the reasons for and against different conceptions of the relations
> between those rights and other values that the state may be in a
> position to promote. But Nozick's book is theoretically insubstantial:
> it does not take up the main problems. . . .[6]

I agree with Nagel that Nozick has not explored the foundations of individual rights, but I deny that this lack marks his book as theoretically
insubstantial. Decades later, moral philosophers have made only slight
advances in the understanding of the moral foundations of individual
rights. Nozick's modest achievement in exposing the beams above the
foundations looks more and more impressive with the passage of time.

At the most general level, a morality of individual rights denies that
moral principles postulate goals, which all persons equally have reason to
pursue, by whatever means would be most effective. Such goals might
be agent-relative, in the sense that what specific goal is set for a given
individual is relative to that individual. "Each person ought to seek to
maximize her own happiness" is an example of an agent-relative goal-
oriented principle. "Each person ought to seek to maximize aggregate
human happiness" is an example of an agent-neutral goal-oriented principle. An agent-neutral goal-oriented principle postulates the same goal
or goals for all persons.

In contrast, a morality of individual rights, as Nozick puts it, imposes
side constraints on choice of a course of conduct by an agent. Among the
available alternative actions a person might choose at a particular time,
rights rule out some options; that is, rights render these options ineligible.
The person who would respect rights confines her choice to the reduced
set of options, the ones that do not violate anyone's rights. From the
standpoint of an individual deciding what to do, rights are commands
addressed to her, and moreover addressed to her at this particular time:
"Do not now do anything that—now or later—violates anyone's rights!"[7]

---

[6] Thomas Nagel, "Libertarianism without Foundations," reprinted in Jeffrey Paul, ed.,
Reading Nozick (Totowa, NJ: Rowman and Littlefield, 1981), 191–93.

[7] The formulation in the text cannot be quite right as it stands. Suppose I wrongfully
launched a slow missile attack at you in the recent past, and now I can choose to launch a
countermissile that will prevent this attack from injuring you without violating anyone's
rights. A Lockean morality will hold that I must now launch the countermissile that will
block my previous attempted rights violation. Hence, against the statement in the text, it is

A right specifies a way that a person (or group of persons) should be treated or not treated—for example, not to be physically assaulted. Rights function not as goals to be promoted but as constraints to be respected. If A has a right not to be assaulted, that right does not tell me to act so as to minimize assaults on A. Rather, it tells me that I must not now choose any act that involves my assaulting A (or my inducing or assisting another to assault A). Rights belong to people, the right-holders. If A has a right not to be assaulted, this generates a duty on my part not to assault A, a duty that is owed to A, and one that is waivable by A and transferable by A to others.

As so far characterized, a morality of individual rights could consist entirely of agent-relative positive duties to help people in need and more generally to undertake specified sorts of actions toward specified other people.[8] The doctrine decisively does not go in that direction. The core content that fills the individual rights structure is the idea that the negative duty not to harm others in certain ways takes priority over any positive duties to give aid.[9] The libertarian versions of this moral theory are uncompromising in this regard: the moral rights that each adult person initially has are entirely negative—rights not to suffer interference or harm of certain sorts. No adult individual initially has any right to any sort of positive treatment or aid from others. No individual initially has any duty to provide such aid, though by voluntary acts such as binding oneself by contract or doing what brings about the birth of a child, or through inadvertence amounting to negligence, one may according to libertarianism come to have strict duties to provide others with aid, to which (under these circumstances) they have a right. This is the thesis

---

not enough that I choose actions that do not, now or in the future, violate anyone's rights. I must also choose actions that, to the greatest extent possible without introducing any new rights violations, undo the effects of past actions of mine that, left unchecked, will violate someone's rights in the future.

[8] This claim in the text might sound obviously false as a characterization of a morality of rights conceived as a morality of constraints, so some explanation is in order. A morality of goals postulates goals and directs the agent to undertake whatever means are necessary to reach the goals. A morality of constraints says the agent may pursue whatever goals she wishes provided that certain constraints on her choice of goals or courses of action to achieve the goals are respected. The constraints might either enjoin a positive act or direct the agent to refrain from a type of act. Thus, a morality of constraints might assert, "Don't harm your mother!" or "Whatever else you do, help your mother!" Just as the former, negative constraint does not say, "Do whatever is required to bring it about that your mother is not harmed (by another or by you)," the latter, positive constraint does not say, "Do whatever is required to bring it about that your mother is helped (by another or by you)." A positive constraint prescribes an action that must be done, not a goal that must be achieved. In a conciliatory spirit, I add that if the reader wants to insist that a morality of constraints can only consist of negative constraints, the reader is welcome to amend my text accordingly. Nothing I want to assert hangs on this point.

[9] This terminology of negative and positive duties is taken from Philippa Foot, "The Problem of Abortion and the Doctrine of Double Effect," reprinted in Philippa Foot, *Virtues and Vices and Other Essays in Moral Philosophy* (Berkeley: University of California Press, 1978), 27. This essay was first published in 1967. According to Foot, negative duties are duties not to harm, more generally to refrain from specified courses of action. Positive duties are duties to aid, to do something for somebody or other.

of self-ownership: Each adult person is the full rightful owner of herself, and possesses over herself the full rights to use and abuse that an owner of a piece of property has over that property. Since A owns herself, no other person B has any property rights in A, which would give B a right to dictate to some extent how A should use her own body (beyond the negative constraint not to harm others in certain ways).

Why should we accept that morality rightly construed has a side constraint structure, that it is constituted by side constraints? Also, why should we accept the further claim that the fundamental constraints are negative, not positive? Nozick tries to place this conception in an attractive light by clarifying some implications of one version of it and suggesting that these implications are plausible. In effect, Nozick tries to show that the Lockean structure is acceptable in reflective equilibrium.[10] Beyond that, he floats some suggestions about what the moral basis of Lockean rights theory might be, but I agree with Nagel that these suggestions do not advance the discussion very far.[11] However, this does not mean that Nozick's discussion has been superseded, since no one else has succeeded in advancing the discussion much further in the interim.[12]

This essay retreats from the large theoretical questions raised in the preceding paragraph. I shall instead follow Nozick's lead and explore variants of the particular side constraints and individual rights that Nozick espouses. The aim is to seek a position in the region of his version of libertarianism that, as it were, rounds off its sharp edges and brings us closer to a reflective equilibrium that considers and accommodates examples that tend to elicit nonlibertarian responses in many of us, even those of us who are initially sympathetic toward the spirit of Nozick's project.

---

[10] An individual is in a state of reflective equilibrium when she has critically examined pertinent arguments and affirms a set of general moral principles that explain and justify the moral judgments that she endorses about what to do in particular circumstances. The agent's particular and general moral judgments are in equilibrium. For this notion, see John Rawls, *A Theory of Justice*, rev. ed. (Cambridge, MA: Harvard University Press, 1999), 40–46.

[11] One suggestion that Nozick makes is that beings who have a capacity for rational long-term agency and meaningful life in virtue of those capacities acquire Lockean rights not to be harmed in specified ways, rightly deemed wrongful. See Nozick, *Anarchy, State, and Utopia*, 48–50. On its face, the suggestion is incomplete. Since persons whose Lockean rights are violated often succeed in leading meaningful lives, not suffering such violations cannot be a necessary condition for achieving a meaningful life. Anyway, why should possession of a capacity for meaningfulness bring it about that one is endowed with Lockean rights? Nozick recognizes this gap but does not hint at how one might fill it. For criticism of Nozick on this point, see Samuel Scheffler, "Natural Rights, Equality, and the Minimal State," reprinted in Paul, ed., *Reading Nozick*, 148–68.

[12] For the suggestion that rights confer the valuable status of inviolability (or at least limited violability) on every person and that this status is valuable, hence we have rights, see Frances Kamm, "Non-consequentialism, the Person as an End-in-Itself, and the Significance of Status," *Philosophy and Public Affairs* 21, no. 4 (1992): 354–89. Nagel seems to endorse Kamm's suggestion in Thomas Nagel, "Personal Rights and Public Space," *Philosophy and Public Affairs* 24, no. 2 (1995): 89–93. Kasper Lippert-Rasmussen refutes the suggestion in his "Moral Status and the Impermissibility of Minimizing Violations," *Philosophy and Public Affairs* 25, no. 4 (1996): 333–51.

One recurring suggestion is that within the side constraints framework, there are plausible candidates for the status of constraints other than those on which Nozick concentrated attention. Another is that perhaps morality has a hybrid structure that combines side constraints and goal promotion in some way. The most straightforward hybrid identifies moral goals that each person should pursue to some extent—the goals to be balanced off against constraints in deciding what to do in any case, with constraints having less than infinite weight (less than lexical priority). Another hybrid strategy suggests that for any right of any strength, if the consequences of abiding by it in any particular case would be sufficiently bad, one is morally permitted to do what the right, at the first level, prohibits.

IV. Nozick's Chapter Four Questions

One significant foundational question that Nozick leaves unresolved is the topic of chapter four of *Anarchy, State, and Utopia*. To introduce the topic, Nozick has us suppose we have some understanding of the content of the moral rights that we naturally possess. Nozick states, "Individuals have rights, and there are things no person or group may do to them (without violating their rights)" (*ASU*, ix). People have rights, moral claims not to be treated by other people in certain ways. An individual's right is partly constituted by the obligations of others to constrain their behavior by refraining from doing what the right forbids. Nozick suggests that we think of the right as drawing a boundary in moral space. The question then arises, *"Are others forbidden to perform actions that transgress the boundary or encroach upon the circumscribed area, or are they permitted to perform such actions provided that they compensate the person whose boundary has been crossed?"* (*ASU*, 57). In another terminology, we might say that actions that do what a person's right specifies one should not do *infringe* the right. Infringements that are, all things considered, morally wrong (at least partly on the ground that they are infringements) are *violations* of the right. The issue then arises whether all infringements of rights are violations. Nozick's question then can be rephrased: Are some or all infringements of rights coupled with full compensation to the injured right-bearer morally permissible?[13] Or are any and all infringements of rights morally forbidden (unless the right-bearer consents to what is done, in which case there is no real infringement)?

To make sense of what Nozick is up to in his chapter four discussion, we must suppose that we are thinking through questions about what

---

[13] Nozick identifies full compensation with compensation that leaves the recipient neither glad nor sad that the combination of the rights violation and the compensation for it occurred—a subjective view. An objective version would hold that the individual is fully compensated when she is rendered neither better off nor worse off by the combination of suffering the rights violation and receiving the compensation for it.

rights people have and what exactly rights require of people, without already having committed ourselves firmly to principles that entail particular answers to these questions. In Rawlsian terminology, we have not attained reflective equilibrium and we know it. Reflection on some examples and cases persuades some of us that Lockean accounts are on the right track, that some position in this neighborhood is correct, but much remains unsettled. If we take it for granted at the start of the discussion that all people are endowed initially with a particular set of moral rights, of known content and character, and that it is always morally wrong to act against anyone's rights without obtaining the individual's prior consent, Nozick's chapter four questions, which presuppose that the content and character of rights are to some degree unsettled, will appear either trivial or incoherent. Nozick will be read as asking, "Under what circumstances is it morally permissible to do what it is never morally permissible to do, namely, violate rights?"

This essay explores these questions. I shall endeavor to assess the adequacy of the responses and suggestions adduced by Nozick in his pathbreaking discussion and to follow some of his insights to see where they lead. I shall proceed by describing examples, considering possible responses, and formulating principles that would explain and justify the responses and that seem independently plausible.

V. Hard Libertarianism

The position I shall call "hard libertarianism" holds that Lockean natural rights (1) may never permissibly be infringed without the prior consent of the right-holder and (2) may always permissibly be infringed provided that the prior consent of the right-holder has been given. In addition, hard libertarianism affirms unequivocally and without any qualifications the four claims that make up the basics of Lockeanism as presented in Section II of this essay. Soft libertarian/Lockean positions substitute "sometimes" for "never" in (1) and "also" for "always" in (2), and in addition relax some or all of the four basic claims discussed in Section II. Beyond a certain point, substitution and relaxation of this sort renders the term "libertarianism" unapt.[14] Hard libertarianism is controversial both in what it allows and in what it prohibits. Consider some examples.

Whim. For no good reason A voluntarily requests that B saw off A's arm. B saws off A's arm. Provided that A is sufficiently morally competent to qualify as a right-bearer, he has the right to waive any right that he has and to set aside the protection to his interests (here, his intact arm) that his Lockean rights afford. If A is neither mentally retarded below an appropriate threshold nor so severely mentally ill that he is not reasonably

[14] See note 3 for my usage of the terms "Lockean" and "libertarian" and "soft."

deemed responsible for his choices, his moral rights include the right to waive any of his other rights.

Hiker. A is a hiker lost in a blizzard in the mountains. He stumbles upon a cabin that is privately owned by B and posted with "No Trespassing" signs. Although the door to the cabin is locked, A could break the lock, enter the cabin, build a fire using the cabin's furniture as fuel, eat the food from the larder, and save his life. Hard libertarianism holds that A is morally prohibited from taking B's property without B's permission even to save his life and even if he fully intends to provide full compensation for costs imposed on B by his taking.

In the face of these examples, the hard libertarian might stand fast by her position. If one were moved to alter hard libertarianism so that it yields a softer verdict on such cases, the next question would be, what sort of norms might be reasonable to embrace to give shape to the accommodations? In this connection it is helpful to pay attention to Nozick's insightful discussion that bears on these matters.

VI. Nozick on the Factors that Might Determine Permissible Boundary Crossing

Nozick mentions several considerations that militate against the proposal to allow any boundary crossing without prior consent provided full compensation is paid to any person whose right is infringed by the boundary crossing and who is injured thereby. I list all that Nozick mentions:

a. A system that allows boundary crossings with full compensation "embodies the use of persons as means" (*ASU*, 71).

b. "[K]nowing they are being so used, and that their plans and expectations are liable to being thwarted arbitrarily, is a cost to people" (*ASU*, 71).

c. "[S]ome injuries may not be compensable" (*ASU*, 71).

d. An agent may not know that she will have the means to pay compensation if injury occurs and compensation is called for (*ASU*, 71).

e. Some boundary crossings tend to produce widespread fear and anxiety not only in actual victims, but also in people who identify themselves as potential victims (*ASU*, 65–71).

f. A system that allows boundary crossings with full compensation licenses an unfair distribution of the benefits of what would be voluntary exchange scenarios except that the prospect of involuntary takings renders negotiation toward voluntary exchange a comparatively unattractive prospect. Suppose A owns a car, which B covets. Rather than negotiate with A and pay the price they agree on, B under a system that allows takings in the absence of voluntary consent can simply take the car and pay A the lowest amount of money that would induce A voluntarily to relinquish the car. Normally the price they would agree on would be somewhat higher than this, with the benefits that arise from the fact that B values the car more than A being split between A and B. Nozick points out that in this sort of case, permitting a taking rather than requiring B to negotiate to a voluntary agreement with A seems unfair (*ASU*, 63–65).

This list can be pared down. Regarding (c), one can just note that the principle that infringement of any right is allowed provided full compensation is paid to all injured victims does not on its face allow infringement of rights in any case when the infringement causes uncompensable injury. Also, the principle on its face forbids people from infringing a right and declining to pay full compensation because they lack the means to pay, so (d) on Nozick's list is otiose. The issue of compensation raises practical questions concerning what sorts of conditions on right infringement should be built into legal rules or social norms. But the theoretical question—what moral principles are correct?—is not touched by this sort of consideration. The proposal to allow all boundary crossings provided full compensation is forthcoming emerges unscathed from the worries about compensation expressed in (c) and (d).

The injunction in (a) against using people as means strikes me as not advancing the discussion and hence as eliminable from the list. Using people as means to one's ends cannot in itself be problematic. This occurs constantly in interactions we all would regard as innocuous. Kant's humanity formulation of the categorical imperative forbids using people (the humanity or rational agency in people) as *mere* means.[15] What is it to use a person *merely* as a means to one's ends? If I use you as a means to my ends, but only within limits prescribed by morality, I would say I am not using you *merely* as a means. Following this suggestion, let us say that the injunction against using people as means may be interpreted as the injunction never to use people as means to one's ends in ways that are unacceptable according to correct moral principles. Which principles are these? The slogan by itself does not say, and moreover, so far as I can see, does not point us toward any particular answer. So scratch entry (a) from the foregoing list of pertinent considerations.

Entry (b) should also be dropped. The worry that one's plans are liable to be interrupted by a boundary crossing is a cost to be compensated like any other. If the concern is that people who never actually suffer having their boundaries crossed might be troubled by anxiety that such things

---

[15] Immanuel Kant, *Groundwork of the Metaphysics of Morals*, ed. and trans. Mary Gregor, with an introduction by Christine Korsgaard (Cambridge: Cambridge University Press, 1998), 38. The principle states: "So act that you use humanity, whether in your own person or in the person of any other, always at the same time as an end, never merely as a means."

could happen to them, this anxiety is an aspect of the generalized fear consideration (to which I now turn).

Nozick makes the interesting suggestion (e) that certain harms such as assault tend to provoke generalized, widespread fear and anxiety, and that for this reason one should not treat the infliction of the harm along with full compensation as permissible. Of course, people's innocent activities that violate no one else's rights will sometimes cause harm to others, and people may fear suffering such harms. If it is permissible for A to inflict a harm on B, given that the infliction violates no right of B, then it can hardly be impermissible that A might also be inducing anxiety in C that a similar harm might befall him. For example, A might permissibly harm B by successfully wooing the person B ardently wants to marry, or by successfully applying for a job for which B, who is less well credentialed, also applied, and which he would have been granted but for A's application. But if one is inflicting harm by doing something that at the first level is forbidden by a moral right, the situation seems different.

One response that one might put in the mouth of the advocate of the proposal to allow boundary crossings with compensation is that the point about fear is not an objection to the proposal but, rather, indicates a complexity in the idea of paying full compensation. Suppose I assault B and as a consequence C, D, and E become fearful. We might hold that this sort of indirect harm is properly traceable to the infringer of the right, hence full compensation to victims should be understood broadly so that C, D, and E qualify as victims to be compensated. At this point, one might draw a line between reasonable and unreasonable fear responses. Suppose that C and D are in circumstances that are in relevant ways similar to B's, so that it is understandable and reasonable that they come to believe that there is some considerable probability they might be harmed in a way that is similar to what has happened to B. They become alarmed at this prospect. In contrast, E lives in Alaska, far away, or he has a moat with alligators around his house, or for some other reason the fact that I have assaulted B does not provide any grounds for E's altering upward his belief that he might be subject to assault (or provides grounds that reasonably raise the probability only below some threshold that should be tolerable). We might distinguish sharply between the reasonable fear experienced by C and D and the unreasonable fear experienced by E and require the boundary crosser to compensate fully the C's and D's of the world but not the E's. Alternatively, we might discount the cost of fear by the degree to which the person who experiences the fear of the boundary crossing should be held responsible for unreasonably becoming fearful and reduce the required compensation correspondingly. In any event, what Nozick seems to be calling attention to is a fact about appropriate compensation, not an objection to the proposal under review.

Nozick objects to this treatment of fear. He notes that it may in practice be very difficult to determine whether the vague anxiety E experiences is fear of assault or something else, and whether the fear is properly trace-able back to any particular boundary crossing or aggregate of boundary crossings. He also notes that even if no boundary crossings of a certain type in fact occur, the bare fact that the rules in play allow boundary crossings of that type provided compensation is forthcoming might elicit fear. Here I am inclined to draw the line. If no boundary crossings of type X have ever occurred, how can I reasonably fear such attacks? This anx-iety must be either de minimis or caused by my oversensitivity rather than by any actions of other persons. Or one might hold that B's fear of boundary crossing X in the absence of any instances of boundary cross-ings of type X, to the degree it is reasonable, must be caused by the fact that boundary crossings of other types occur, so that one should then hold the perpetrators of these other boundary crossings liable to pay for this extended but reasonable anxiety as well. The discussion in this and the two preceding paragraphs then leads to the conclusion that Nozick's consideration (e) also deserves to be eliminated from his list.

To recapitulate: Nozick cited six considerations, (a) through (f), as weigh-ing against the proposal to allow any boundary crossing without prior consent provided that full compensation is paid to any person whose right is infringed and who suffers injury. The foregoing discussion has suggested grounds for dropping all but (f) from his list.

VII. Fair Distribution of the Benefits of Exchange

I now turn to the sole remaining entry on Nozick's list, point (f), con-cerning the fair distribution of the benefits of voluntary exchange (versus unfair distribution in a system that allows boundary crossings with full compensation). Nozick's point is not that there is an independently deter-minable fair price for goods and services, which voluntary exchange tends to approximate. He disparages the medieval notion of "just price" as a possible basis for economic regulation. Nozick's point is that if one has full ownership rights in something, it is unfair that one is dispos-sessed of the something absent one's own voluntary choice to relinquish it. This is the norm that is directly challenged by the responses many of us have to the *Hiker* example introduced at the end of Section V above. There is more to be said about this example, but further examples may be useful. Consider the following.

Holdout. A proposes to use property he owns to start a widget-making factory, which would be profitable, and beneficial to many. The only feasible process for manufacturing widgets unfortunately spews a type of pollution that unavoidably inflicts small harm on a great many people, the millions of residents of a valley. Each resident suffers a one-dollar loss per year from this pollution. A proposes a scheme of compensation that involves establishing a park that will provide two dollars per year of benefit to each valley resident. Millions agree to this scheme, but one resident, B, refuses to relinquish his right not to be impinged on by harmful pollution unless virtually all of the profits of the factory's operation accrue to him.

Suppose the theorist responds that B has no right to gouge his cooperating and productive neighbors in this way. One might propose a "just price" intuition: If one's involvement in a productive activity amounts only to being slightly physically harmed by it, one has a moral right to be fully compensated for this inconvenience, no more and no less. But this principle sounds suspiciously ad hoc and tailored too specifically to the particular example to be very convincing.

One source of unease with the example might stem from concern that one's right not to be impinged on by others in ways that physically cause damage to one's person or property is not a full, tradable property right. After all, C should not be permitted to sell his right not to be harmed in specified ways in the future to D, who might wish to purchase such rights in the hope that their price might rise in the future. (Or should he? The hard libertarian might simply not blink in the face of any putative counterexample.) But the concern about gouging can arise when the rights at stake are ordinary property rights of an unproblematic sort, as in the following examples.

Spite. A installs a huge false chimney on the second story of his house. Its only point is to annoy his neighbor B by blocking B's view of the surrounding landscape. Or A might threaten to install such a chimney and agree to desist only if B pays A very close to B's reservation price, the maximum he would be willing to give to retain the unimpeded view.[16]

Easy Rescue. A is drowning. He is in a leaky boat that is slowly sinking, so there is ample time for negotiation. B happens to arrive on the scene in his boat, and offers to save A's life, a feat that can be accomplished at very small cost to B, if A agrees to transfer all of his financial assets to B in return for this easy rescue. (The example can be amplified with details such as that A is far wealthier than B or the reverse, or that A is far better off than B in aggregate lifetime well-being to this point or the reverse.)

Although Nozick does not discuss these two specific examples, it is clear that he would give no quarter to the position that B is under an enforceable duty to perform easy rescue and hence has no right to charge A whatever he is willing to pay for lifesaving service. However, Nozick discusses more sympathetically some pros and cons that might be applied to cases such as *Spite*. His thought is that the imperative of prohibiting boundary crossings without prior consent in order to ensure fair division of the benefits of exchange applies only to the category of productive

---

[16] This example is drawn from the 1855 French legal case *Keller v. Doerr*. I owe this reference to Gijs Van Donselaar, *The Benefit of Another's Pains: Parasitism, Scarcity, Basic Income* (Amsterdam: Department of Philosophy, University of Amsterdam, 1997), 2.

exchange. In the typical exchange, both parties benefit, and this sort of exchange is unproblematically productive. He defines an *unproductive exchange* as one that satisfies two conditions: (1) one party to the exchange is no better off as a result of it than if the other party did not exist at all, and (2) what this party who is no better off gets from the exchange is the other party's abstention from an activity she would not be motivated to engage in except for the possibility of selling abstention. Another test mentioned by Nozick is that one party to an unproductive exchange would be no worse off if the exchange were prohibited.[17] Where an exchange is in the offing that would be unproductive in this sense, morality does not insist on allowing the exchange to go forward. Depending on further circumstances, it might be right to forbid the activity by one party to the contemplated exchange that would become the object to be exchanged, and it might be right in some cases to require (and in others not to require) compensation accompanying the prohibition. If the first condition for unproductive exchange is satisfied but not the second, call the exchange *semiproductive*. Nozick suggests it may be morally acceptable to prohibit semiproductive exchange by prohibiting one of the parties from engaging in the activity, abstention from which is being exchanged, provided some compensation is given to the party whose favored activity is prohibited in this way.

Nozick applies this analysis to blackmail. In some cases, a blackmail exchange would be unproductive. In these cases, prohibition of blackmail with no compensation to the would-be blackmailer is appropriate. Other cases are mixed. Suppose A wants to publish secrets about B's life. Their inclusion in a book A is writing would improve the book. It is worth a thousand dollars to B to prevent the publication of these secrets. The value to A of his planned use of this information about B is $500. According to Nozick, A can legitimately charge at most $500 for declining to publish B's secrets. This latter case is one in which the first but not the second condition for unproductive exchange would be satisfied, but once B agrees to pay $500 to A, the latter's attempt to make a deal with B for further payment would be an attempt to bring about an unproductive exchange.

The problem with this line of analysis is that the hypotheticals it relies upon are unruly and cannot be tamed.[18] I would be better off if the party with whom I am negotiating an exchange did not exist at all in many circumstances in which this fact does not render the looming exchange in any way problematic or liable to special restriction or prohibition. I am being hired as a consultant to help write A's acceptance speech for the Nobel Prize in chemistry, but if A did not exist at all or had nothing at all

---

[17] Nozick, *Anarchy, State, and Utopia*, 84–87.
[18] In this connection, see the criticism of Nozick in Eric Mack, "Nozick on Unproductivity: The Unintended Consequences," in Paul, ed., *Reading Nozick*, 169–90.

to do with me, I would be better off, because I would then be next in line to receive the Nobel Prize for my chemistry achievements, which are good, but less good than A's. This fact does not render my exchange of my speechwriting services for A's cash on mutually agreeable terms a semiproductive exchange. The first condition as Nozick formulates it is satisfied, but this does not have the significance Nozick attributes to it. The same is true if I purchase A's abstention from entering a contest she is sure to win if she enters. My chances of winning are greater if A does not enter the contest, and better for that matter if A did not exist or had nothing at all to do with me.

For much the same reason, one cannot say that A wrongfully causes harm to B by physical interaction with B just in case A renders B worse off than would be the case if A did not exist. Nor can the condition be: just in case A renders B worse off than B would be if she had no interaction at all with A. Consider a case in which A has been B's trading partner for years. These interactions have brought a large profit to B. Today A viciously kicks B in the shin, seriously injuring his leg. B is still a net beneficiary of his interactions with A; nonetheless, A violates B's right not to be physically attacked when A kicks B in the shin.

Perhaps it is possible to revise Nozick's conditions on unproductive exchange while preserving the basic idea—or perhaps not. The judgment that in the *Spite* case A has no right to erect a false chimney on his own property and that it would not be wrong forcibly to prohibit A from harming B in this way need not wait upon the vicissitudes of further developments of Nozick's theory of unproductive exchange. In the example, A is being malicious. He is acting in a way he knows will harm B purely for the sake of harming B. (We can contrast *Spite* as specified in the text with an alternate version in which A is a lover of false chimneys and wants to erect this addition to the top of his house in order to improve its appearance by his lights. In the alternate version, A in some sense does the same thing as in the original version, but his intention and motivation are not spiteful, and this fact makes all the difference. In the alternate version, A has a moral right to act as he does and should not be prohibited from doing so.) A plausible interpretation of Lockean rights maintains that intention and motivation can affect the permissibility of what an agent does. An act might be permissible if done with a certain intention or with a certain motive, but the same act—the same physical movement leading to the same physical changes in the world—done with a different intention or motive might be impermissible.

One might object that *Spite* is a very odd case, from which no general normative implications flow.[19] In *Spite* there is no plausible motive except

---

[19] In this essay, I am concerned with what it is morally permissible and impermissible for people to do in various possible examples. I am not trying to devise a practical doctrine of laws and social norms, which might well be designed for ordinary cases, not extraordinary

malice that would likely explain the homeowner's desire to construct a false chimney on his house. But in the general case, it will not be possible to read off the agent's motive from his behavior. For this reason a regime of rights that rendered the limits of an agent's freedom sensitive to harmed-and-putatively-injured parties' hunches and guesses about the motives of the agent whose doings they find distressing would be an administrative chaos. So we should not understand the limits of people's moral rights in this way.

The objection makes a significant mistake. It fails to distinguish the theoretical question—"What rights do we have?"—from the practical question—"What sort of laws should be established in order to protect individual rights?" Epistemic and administrative difficulties will play a large role in answering the second question but not in answering the first. It will then sometimes make perfect sense for an advocate of individual rights to say, for example, that Smith has a perfect moral right to do X, but nonetheless it is morally correct that a just state should prohibit Smith from doing it, or that Smith has no moral right to do Y but nonetheless a just state should allow her to do it.[20]

VIII. WHY EVER ALLOW INFRINGEMENTS WITHOUT PRIOR CONSENT?

The flip side of the question, "Why not always allow any border crossing coupled with full compensation?" is "Why ever allow such border crossings not licensed by prior consent?" Discussing this issue, Nozick suggests that transaction costs—the costs of negotiating deals—play a key role. The costs of reaching a deal might be large because the number of parties whose agreement is needed may be large. It may be difficult to locate the agents from whom agreement must be obtained, and difficult or expensive to set in place the communications technology needed for negotiation. The process of making a deal may consume resources in many ways. At the limit, it may be physically impossible to negotiate with someone.

---

ones. That said, if a hard-libertarian reader is disposed to think that this and other cases I discuss are practically resolvable by writing careful contracts, I recommend consulting the theory of incomplete contracting on the economic importance of the impossibility of writing a complete contract that deals with all contingencies that might arise. See Oliver Hart, *Firms, Contracts, and Financial Structure* (Oxford: Clarendon Press, 1995), and the additional literature Hart cites.

[20] Here I presume that an adequate Lockean morality will integrate considerations of mandatory moral goals to be promoted and required side constraints to be respected, and will not go whole hog for either alternative. The fact that if we tried to establish rules that would require the state to enforce people's subtle right to X, the result would be that people's more important rights would be frustrated is then a relevant consideration for the question, what conception of rights should the state enforce?

When transaction costs are high, insistence on prior consent to any boundary crossing might leave all affected parties worse off than they would be if a more permissive rule were accepted. The transaction-cost consideration also introduces a reason of a quite different sort for sometimes allowing boundary crossing provided compensation is forthcoming. Consider an example in which at the time a choice has to be made, prior consent is impossible to obtain.

Coma. A has suffered a serious injury and needs immediate medical care, including surgery. Deliberately touching a person without her consent fits the technical definition of an assault, and imposing medical care on a person—which can significantly affect the patient's well-being for better or worse—without her consent is a serious breach of her rights. In this case, A is in a temporary coma and can neither give nor withhold consent to the surgery she needs to save her life.

It would violate the letter but not the spirit of hard libertarianism to allow the surgeon to provide medical care to A without first obtaining A's prior consent in situations of this sort. Three features of the situation favor this judgment: the infringement being proposed would be of great benefit to A; she is not capable of giving or withholding consent without delay that would dissipate this benefit; and she would consent if she were capable of giving or withholding consent. (The hard libertarian who is strict on this point would insist that A is out of luck if she has not previously contracted for care that encompasses this contingency or delegated to a specific agent the authority to choose in this contingency.)

The *Coma* case, from one perspective, is the tip of an iceberg. The underlying difficulty is that insistence on no impingement without consent only imperfectly safeguards an agent's liberty and vital interests. The giving and withholding of consent even under favorable conditions sometimes reflects the agent's distorted assessment or weakness of will. At such times, the agent voluntarily consents to what is bad for self and others.

Notice that some of the cases described previously either do not on their face appear to involve transaction-cost concerns or can be redescribed so it is clear that transaction costs are not driving the judgment that favors permitting infringement. Consider just one of these cases: *Easy Rescue* requires only a negotiation between two people; the negotiation concerns only the price to be paid by one for a simple service offered by the other, and there is plenty of time to negotiate. True, in any thin market setting like this, if the gap between the buyer's and seller's reservation prices is large, agreeing on a division of the gain from trade can be a challenge.

IX. CHIPPING AWAY AT SELF-OWNERSHIP

Easy rescue cases, interpreted as prompting the claim that people are under an enforceable duty to be minimally decent Samaritans, directly challenge the self-ownership thesis. Hard libertarians will resist this challenge, but so will others. To explore the moral basis of self-ownership, one should contrast easy rescue cases with another class of cases that they somewhat resemble. Nozick provides an example:

Accommodation. A is minding his business, harming no one. A allows B onto his property. A has no reason to be distrustful of B. However, B takes out a gun and shoots innocent people from A's window perch. Police arrive and attempt to apprehend B. A shouts to the police that he is simply going about his business and has a perfect right to be where he is, which happens to be in the way of the police as they seek to render B harmless.

Nozick raises the question, Does A in these circumstances have a duty to get out of the way of the police as they seek to incapacitate B, who is wrongfully threatening others?[21] One might hold that the police have the moral right forcibly to remove A from the premises so that he does not impede the urgent crime-fighting effort. One might also hold that if A has a duty to move out of the way of the police and does not, then it might be permissible, depending on further circumstances, for the police to shoot at B even if doing so risks harming A. Given that A is not accommodating in the way morality requires, it might be the case that the police, killing A foreseeably but unintentionally as they seek to stop B, do not violate any right that A possesses against them. We can perhaps simplify the complex issues the example raises by imagining a state of nature version of it.

State-of-Nature Accommodation. A is fleeing B, an evil aggressor who intends to kill A. Let us assume it would be morally acceptable for A to kill B in self-defense, but unfortunately A in the circumstances is unable to do anything that is likely to save his life by attacking B in self-defense. There is a small alcove in the rocks above, from which C is watching B's chase of A unfold. A can elude B and save his own life by jumping onto the alcove where C is standing. B, a heavy-set aggressor, will not be able to follow. C could move to the rear of the alcove to give A room to land safely. If C does not accommodate A in this way, A has no way to save his own life except by jumping to the alcove, landing where C now stands, and thereby killing him. In the circumstances, all the facts just described are mutual knowledge between A and C: A knows, C knows; A knows that C knows; C knows that A knows; and so on. C does not move to the rear of the alcove.

Consider the position that in these circumstances, C has a moral duty to accommodate by moving from the unowned land that he is currently using but which A now needs as a platform to land on, in order to save his life. If C does not make this accommodating move and A jumps to this

---

[21] Robert Nozick, "War, Terrorism, Reprisals—Drawing Some Moral Lines," reprinted in Nozick, *Socratic Puzzles,* 303. This chapter was initially a book review published in 1978.

spot, killing C, A is not violating any of C's rights. One might adhere to this position without rejecting the thesis of self-ownership. That is to say, each person fully owns herself, but this is of course compatible with there being limits on the rights anyone has to use unowned land. The moral basis for the requirement of accommodation is the proper understanding of the idea that in a state of nature any person is at liberty freely to use any unowned land. If one person wishes to use a particular piece of unowned land and this desired use is not in conflict with any use anyone else wishes to make of the land, the use is morally permissible. A limit on this right of free use is that if two or more individuals wish to use the same piece of land at the same time in conflicting ways, the one who begins using the land first has the right of way unless one would-be user has significantly greater need of it than the other. In the latter case, the person with the significantly greater need has the right to use. If A and B both wish to sunbathe on the same strip of unowned land, and A gets there first, A has the right to use the land in this way. But if C needs to lie down on this particular sunlit land in order to relieve her intense head-ache, A must give way to C. I suppose there is also a time-limit on the extent to which any individual can use and keep using any piece of unowned land. The longer one has used the land for one's own purposes, the stronger becomes the presumption that one must yield to give others a turn, if a queue of would-be users of the same land forms. I do not claim that free use rights so understood are clear and well defined: their inad-equacies, which perhaps warrant their supersession by private property rights, include their unclarity and vagueness. My claim is that our under-standing of the nature of free-use rights to unowned land, partial as it is, underwrites our understanding of the idea that in the example of *State-of-Nature Accommodation*, C's right to the unimpeded use of the alcove where she stands disappears when A arrives on the scene with a pressing need to use that same spot temporarily.

Seen in this light, the *Accommodation* case and the *State-of-Nature Accom-modation* case, which might look similar, in fact raise different issues. The latter raises questions about how to interpret rights to free use of unowned property and the limits of those rights. (These limits might continue in force after appropriation and cast a shadow on private ownership rights.) The former introduces a rights violator and other persons (the police) who are acting at risk to themselves to apprehend the rights violator, stop him from threatening others, and perhaps punish him in order to deter others from seeking to trample on people's rights. Those persons who act in this way act to preserve the system of rights that all of us are morally bound to uphold. In this sense they act for us, and we owe them coop-eration corresponding to the amount of cost and risk they incur in the efficient pursuit of this goal. Refraining from impeding their efforts when we can refrain at moderate cost and risk to ourselves is part of the fair return we owe to those who cooperate to uphold the system of human rights by preventing those who would violate rights to advance their own ends from succeeding in their efforts. Consider in this connection the following example:

Free Rider. A, B, C, D, and E cooperate to provide police protection in their neighborhood. These patrols significantly benefit everyone who lives in this area, including F, by deterring crime. Given the nature of this benefit, there is no question of accepting it or rejecting it; it falls on everyone in the area, willy-nilly. The cooperators demand that F pay one-sixth of the cost of the ongoing police patrols, but F refuses.

In these circumstances, F is dragooned into receiving the benefits of the cooperative scheme that supplies the public good of justice. Is it acceptable to dragoon F into paying his fair share of the costs? (The complication is that given that A, B, C, D, and E are going to provide the good, they have no choice but to provide it to F as well.) The hard libertarian answers "No." The hard libertarian holds that the individual should be left free to live as he chooses unless his actions harm nonconsenting other people in certain ways that violate their rights. Failing to reciprocate a benefit that another person has conferred on you, in the absence of any prior mutual agreement to reciprocate, does not constitute your harming the other, according to the hard libertarian, in any way that amounts to a violation of the other's rights.

One may appeal to two arguments, alone or in tandem, to support a "Yes" answer, that is, to hold that coercing F to pay his fair share of the scheme is acceptable. One is the Hart-Rawls principle of fairness.[22] When others cooperate to supply public goods that benefit a number of people, those who have cooperated have a right that the other beneficiaries pay their share of the costs—to refuse is to be a free rider, which one has no right to be.[23] I construe this principle to continue to apply when there is no voluntary acceptance of benefits received (because of the nature of the good, not because the cooperators have deliberately foisted the good on an unwilling recipient). The hard libertarian reply is that in the absence of some voluntary act that can plausibly be regarded as triggering an obligation, no duties or obligations beyond the negative duties not to harm ever arise for anyone.

---

[22] For a formulation of the Hart-Rawls principle of fairness, references to the relevant prior literature, and sharp skeptical discussion of the principle itself, see Nozick, *Anarchy, State, and Utopia,* 90–95; A. John Simmons, "The Principle of Fair Play," reprinted in Simmons, *Justification and Legitimacy: Essays on Rights and Obligations* (Cambridge: Cambridge University Press, 2001), 1–26; and A. John Simmons, "Fair Play and Political Obligation: Twenty Years Later," ibid., 27–42.

[23] The duty to refrain from being a free rider might be construed broadly, applying to any scheme that supplies significant public goods, or narrowly, applying only to public goods schemes that provide goods of justice (security of enjoyment of all people's natural rights). The rationale for holding to the narrow construal would be that one views the system of Lockean natural rights, properly understood, as of paramount moral importance, swamping other considerations in the determination of what we owe each other.

The second argument asserts straightaway that each person has a natural duty to promote justice—to do his part, when feasible and not excessively costly, to bring into existence and sustain schemes that protect people's moral rights. In the *Free Rider* case, the natural duty to promote justice applies to F and, in these circumstances, requires him to pay his fair share of the costs of police protection. The hard libertarian replies either by flatly denying the natural duty to promote justice or in a more subtle way by denying that the general duty to support justice anywhere and everywhere requires F (for example) to contribute to the particular local justice promotion enterprise that his neighbors have devised.[24]

In response one might argue that the natural duty to promote justice requires the individual to accept only modest risk and cost in the service of justice, but the contribution that is made must be an efficient use of his resources. Normally this efficiency requirement ties the general duty to promote justice to some local scheme that is operating or is on the horizon. One can more surely and easily promote justice nearby than from afar. This need not always be the case, so the natural duty of justice may allow some Oliver North's and Che Guevara's to be excused from local justice duties because they are contributing sufficiently to justice provision schemes elsewhere.[25] The important break from hard libertarianism occurs when one accepts the natural duty to promote justice along with the norm against free riding.

One issue is whether the individual has a moral duty to refrain from free riding in circumstances like the *Free Rider* case. A second issue is whether the duty is enforceable, whether it warrants coercive force. Hard libertarians tend to see coercion as a large evil. I disagree. Being coerced to refrain from acts one has a right to perform is morally odious, but coercion that prevents one from doing what one has no right to do is not so bad. If traffic laws are just, it is unfortunate if I am coerced to obey them, because it would be better if I willingly complied, so that I am not coerced (the state's threats directed at me being idle). But if I am disposed to disobey, and coerced not to do so by effective traffic law enforcement, the forcing of my will here is not a significant bad, and is definitely preferable to the state of affairs in which I am free of coercion and act wrongfully, violating significant rights of other people.

X. Self-Ownership Revisited

Construed in a libertarian spirit, self-ownership asserts that each person fully owns herself and may do with herself whatever she likes so long as

---

[24] For this argument, see A. John Simmons, "Associative Political Obligations," in Simmons, *Justification and Legitimacy*, 65–92.

[25] I am imagining that Oliver and Che, each in his own way, are deemed to be doing enough to advance the cause of justice in a distant country that the natural duty to promote justice cannot be interpreted as ruling out their disobeying some laws of their home country. This is a concession to the Simmons point cited in the previous footnote.

she does not thereby harm others. This entitlement includes the right of each person to destroy herself or waste her own life. As such, this same entitlement strictly forbids restriction of a person's freedom for her own good.[26]

One might instead hold that each individual has over herself the full rights that a private property owner has over whatever things he owns. These rights might not be unlimited, even setting aside the harm-to-others issue. Locke flirts with a stewardship conception of private ownership rights. He claims that one's ownership over a piece of land lapses if one lets the land go to waste.[27] Pressed to its logical limit, the no-waste condition would have it that if anyone else would use your land more productively and efficiently than you would, your right to own it gives way to the right of the more efficient would-be user. Suppose the idea is, rather, that one's uses must meet some acceptable threshold standard of productivity in order to satisfy the no-waste proviso.

By this line of thought, each person's self-ownership rights are also limited by a no-waste requirement. Owning oneself, one has a moral duty not to waste one's life but to make good use of it. A human life is (barring catastrophe) a precious opportunity for good, which ought not to be squandered. This norm leaves each individual vast realms of freedom to live as she chooses, because there are boundless varieties of ways to make something good of one's life. Still, there are limits. The no-waste condition is flagrantly violated by the agent who consents to be mangled for no good reason in the *Whim* case. Another example would be a self-indulgent, petulant suicide. An agent may violate the no-waste condition deliberately or by mistake. If self-ownership is understood by analogy with land ownership constrained by the no-waste requirement, paternalistic restrictions of an agent's liberty for her own good in extreme cases of mistake or folly are consistent with self-ownership, not wrongful violations of it.[28]

[26] Familiar qualifications to this formulation are needed. I might sign a contract that authorizes you to coerce me to stop eating when I try to indulge in rich desserts, and you might agree to this contract from concern for my good. When I lunge for the fancy chocolate cake and you restrain me, you are restricting my freedom for my own good, but in virtue of the contract, you are not violating any right of mine. The libertarian will also qualify the formulation to allow at least temporary paternalistic restriction of liberty in order to block egregiously nonvoluntary choices, as when I am about to drink poison in the false belief that the glass contains wine.

[27] Locke, *Second Treatise of Government*, chap. 5.

[28] Some readers will wonder to whom the duty not to waste one's life might conceivably be owed, and who would be entitled to decide that an individual is violating the duty and to intervene forcibly on the individual's behalf. On the first question, the duty not to waste one's life is owed to those—oneself and others—who stand to benefit if no waste occurs. This is a diffuse group. On the second question, in a Lockean theory, anyone is morally entitled to act to enforce people's natural rights. By the same token, anyone should be morally entitled to act to enforce the natural duty of each person not to waste his own life. Attempts at enforcement might spark umbrage on the part of the person who is being judged a life-waster, and quarrels may ensue, so here as in other cases of conflict around the enforcement of rights and duties, there is need for an impartial, reliable, judicious umpire, if one can be found.

XI. In Search of Principles: The Pareto Constraint

We need to search for principles that might unify some of the seemingly disparate responses to the various puzzle cases examined to this point. One possibility is that rights are subject to a Pareto constraint:

> *A state of affairs that can be improved by making someone better off without making anyone else worse off is morally unacceptable. The specification of individual rights should be adjusted (if possible) so that respecting everyone's individual rights does not produce such a state of affairs.*

This Pareto constraint varies in substance depending on the interpretation of "better off" and "worse off." On a subjective interpretation, one is better off just in case one's preferences are satisfied to a greater extent (with one's own ranking of preferences determining the priority of satisfying each of them). On an objective interpretation, one is better off if one's well-being, assessed by the correct standard, is greater. The objective interpretation obviously relies on controversial value-theory assumptions, but if it can be sustained, the Pareto constraint generates moral considerations of greater strength, and I adopt it here. The appeal of the Pareto constraint in the context of developing Lockean theory is evident in the following example:

Benign Trespasser. A is the absentee owner of a large estate with an orchard. B and C trespass on the land in the autumn, picking ripe fruit in the orchard that would otherwise rot. They do no damage. There is no feasible way to spread the benefits B and C receive to other people without dissipating them. A's absentee status renders it the case that no negotiation between A and B and C can occur that would fix a mutually agreeable price for this incursion on A's land. Here, the Pareto constraint on the interpretation of Lockean rights requires us to take the view that the right of private ownership allows benign trespassing.

Some of the examples discussed so far in this essay that suggest the need to qualify libertarian principles are not explained and justified by the Pareto constraint. Consider the *Easy Rescue* case. One might try to claim that some would be better off and none worse off in a society in which our conception of individual rights is adjusted so that all who find themselves in serious predicaments and need easy rescue have a right to easy rescue if anyone is in a position to provide it, and each person has a duty to provide easy rescue if he is in circumstances such that by easy rescue he can prevent a person's unwanted serious injury or premature death.

One might claim that from a suitable ex ante standpoint, before it is known who will be in the rescuer role and who will be potential beneficiaries of easy rescues, everyone gains by agreeing to a rule requiring easy rescue. But ex post, once it becomes evident who will in fact be playing what role on what occasions, it is no longer plausible to maintain that a rule mandating easy rescue renders everyone better off than he would be if the rules were not in place. Consider A, who is lucky enough never to need an easy rescue and unlucky enough to find herself sometimes in the rescuer role. She is ex post a net loser. Or consider B, who as it turns out finds himself in a position to extract a large monetary windfall by negotiating the terms of an easy rescue with Bill Gates, who happens to need this service and is extraordinarily flush with cash to pay for it. B is better off over the course of his life in a world in which Lockean natural rights are enforced and the rights are not adjusted by adding a duty of easy rescue. That way, he gains the windfall from Bill Gates, which he does not receive under the regime in which easy rescue is required.

So consider the proposal that initially Lockean rights should be adjusted in order to incorporate an ex ante Pareto requirement. The idea would be that the rules that specify the content of Lockean rights should be qualified as necessary to yield the result that, from an ex ante perspective (before it is known who will gain and who will lose from any rules alteration), one cannot alter the rules further in a way that would improve everyone's expected level of advantage from the operation of the system of rules.[29] To clarify the proposal, one would need to specify in a more determinate way the relevant ex ante standpoint. Even without clarification, it should be plain that the ex ante Pareto norm radically alters Lockean rights. This point becomes more vivid if attention is switched from *Easy Rescue* examples to examples that involve the forced utter sacrifice of some persons' interests to benefit others. Surely a Lockean rights perspective that retains its integrity must disallow killing one person when that would be a necessary means to saving two others. But from an ex ante perspective, not knowing whether one is the person to be sacrificed or one of the two to be saved, everyone's prospects are improved by acceptance of a policy that licenses an agency to kill one innocent whenever doing so saves more than one innocent. The ex ante Pareto norm, once accepted as qualifying a set of Lockean rights, transforms the "rights" perspective into something close to aggregative utilitarianism.

If the aim of the discussion in this essay is to explore the alternatives within the Lockean tradition rather than others that radically and brutally

---

[29] This example illustrates the ex ante Pareto norm: Suppose that 100,000 people live in an isolated valley and that each year each resident faces a 1 percent chance of suffering an automobile accident that will cost the individual, on the average, $20 if easy rescue is forthcoming and $100 if it is not. (Easy rescue will be forthcoming if and only if it is legally required.) If everyone in the valley is legally required to provide easy rescue if present at an automobile accident, each member faces a 1 percent chance per year of being required to perform this service at a cost to the rescuer, on the average, of $30. Money is linear with utility for valley residents and all have a neutral attitude toward risk. In these circumstances, the introduction of a legal requirement of providing easy rescue provides an ex ante Pareto improvement.

depart from it, we should interpret the Pareto norm as ex post rather than ex ante.

The ex post Pareto norm does not unequivocally ratify some of the judgments about examples that I am supposing soft Lockeans will want to ratify. *Easy Rescue* is one such case. *Hiker* is another. A rule allowing infringement in circumstances like those of *Hiker* could be devised that would improve everyone's welfare (compared to the hard-libertarian position that requires the hiker to perish), but if we vary the case by providing the lost hiker access to a pay telephone so negotiation with the cabin owner can occur prior to use of the mountain cabin, any rule that partially expropriates the property right to the cabin for the benefit of those who need emergency aid is worse for the cabin owner, who can benefit by selling temporary use of the cabin to those in need of it. If, given this amended version of the case, the judgment persists that the cabin owner's property right should give way in the face of the lost hiker's need, the basis of the judgment is not the Pareto constraint but a norm of fairness that prohibits gouging the needy in this sort of situation.

XII. Moderation

One possible nonlibertarian response to the *Easy Rescue* case denies that what warrants the limitation of self-ownership rights in this case has anything specifically to do with self-ownership. The idea would be that any moral right, however sacred, gives way if the consequences of upholding it in a particular case are sufficiently bad. Rights on this view are nonrigid, spongy side constraints.[30] For any individual deciding what to do and faced with a set of available courses of action that might be chosen, rights are side constraints that rule out certain courses of action and render them morally ineligible for choice, but if the consequences of abiding by these constraints would be sufficiently bad, they relax, and options that would otherwise be ineligible become eligible.

In an interesting footnote, Nozick sets aside the issue of whether rights are rigid or nonrigid side constraints. He comments, "The question of whether these side constraints are absolute, or whether they may be violated in order to avoid catastrophic moral horror, and if the latter, what the resulting structure might look like, is one I hope largely to avoid" (*ASU*, 30). Nozick does not declare a commitment one way or the other on this issue.

An alternative picture that contrasts with the rights-as-spongy-side-constraints metaphor represents rights as rigid but sometimes reconfigured under pressure of consequences. Sufficiently bad consequences can

---

[30] The term "spongy side constraint" is borrowed from Judith Jarvis Thomson, who uses it to describe a moderate position on the stringency of moral rights in her *The Realm of Rights* (Cambridge, MA: Harvard University Press, 1990), 154.

reshape the requirements that rights impose, the resultant rights being sometimes rigid again and sometimes nonrigid. For example, each person has a right of self-ownership, and no duty to use one's body to provide aid to the needy, but if the consequences of insistence on self-ownership would be sufficiently bad, the right dissolves, and may become a strict duty to aid, and correspondingly a right on the part of the needy to be assisted.

Judith Jarvis Thomson has suggested a useful way to characterize the stringency of a right: the degree to which it resists being overridden by counterconsiderations.[31] She proposes that a right is more stringent the greater the harm that would ensue for the right-holder if the right is not upheld. This formulation by itself explains the plausible thought that even though I have a right not to be violently assaulted and a right that my extra shirt button not be taken from me without my consent, the two rights are not on a par. They are not on a par in the sense that a greater weight of reasons is required to justify overriding the right against violent assault. A great harm is less easily offset than a small harm. Note also that if by some chance you would suffer grievous injury if your extra shirt button were stolen, the right to retain your extra shirt button would become correspondingly more stringent.

Thomson's formulation needs some tweaking.[32] Suppose that I would not be harmed at all if you stole from me the hard drugs I own and prize, because without your intervention I would use the drugs to my detriment. My right to the hard drugs I own then has zero stringency according to the formulation of the previous paragraph. However, the theft in these circumstances might be deemed an instance of wrongful paternalism, restriction of a person's liberty against his will for his own good. The individual has an interest in personal sovereignty, in not being subject to such paternalism, even if frustration of the interest does not harm him or reduce his welfare. Also, a person might have an interest in pursuing a valuable goal, the fulfillment of which would not enhance her own welfare. (Call such interests *agency interests*.) If A steals B's rowboat, which she was about to use to rescue someone in distress, the net effect may be no harm at all to B, who now is able to enjoy her picnic lunch in peace. But the significant loss to B's agency interest, we plausibly suppose, renders B's right to undisturbed possession of her rowboat a stringent right in the circumstances.

[31] Thomson, *The Realm of Rights*, chap. 6. An earlier discussion is in Judith Jarvis Thomson, "Some Ruminations on Rights," reprinted in Paul, ed., *Reading Nozick*, 130–47. This section of my essay is heavily indebted to Thomson's writings on the issue.

[32] In my essay "Moderate Deontology, Aggregation, and Rights" (typescript available from the author), I consider how one may aggregate goods and bads of various amounts that would accrue to the right-holder and others if one respects a right or not. Some doubt that failure to respect a person's serious right, such as a right not to be killed, could be offset by any aggregation of tiny benefits to others, however numerous these others. I argue against this plausible claim.

To accommodate these possibilities, I shall simply stipulate that a right is more stringent the greater the loss to the right-holder, in terms of the fulfillment of her interests (including welfare, personal sovereignty, and agency interests) if the right is not upheld.

According to the moderate view of moral rights, the stringency of a right depends on what is at stake for the right-holder. If the net effect on other people of infringing the right (acting against it), compared to what would happen to them if the right were not infringed, is positive and sufficiently large, the right is overridden. When a right is overridden, it is at least permissible, and may be mandatory, to infringe it. The ratio of the loss-to-the-right-holder-if-the-right-is-infringed to the net-loss-to-others-if-the-right-is-not-infringed determines whether or not infringement in a particular case is permissible. If the numerical value of the ratio is sufficiently large, the right may permissibly be breached. The simplest view would hold that there is one numerical value of this ratio that always marks the point of permissible infringement of any right. Another view would hold that this numerical value might vary depending on the type of right under consideration. For example, a one-to-three ratio might suffice for relatively inconsequential rights, so that it is morally permissible to steal my extra shirt button in order to prevent three similar thefts. The required ratio might shift for more consequential rights, so that it is not morally permissible to attack and kill one healthy, innocent person even in order to save three other healthy, innocent persons from a similar fate.

A further complication is that considerations of responsibility or deservingness might discount or amplify the value of the losses and gains of affected parties that determine whether a right in given circumstances may be overridden. A limiting case that illustrates this point is a lone individual defending herself against attack by evil aggressors. It's her life or theirs. Given the culpability of the agents who would suffer if the individual's right not to be attacked is upheld, their numbers do not matter. Even if the evil aggressors are legion, their cumulative loss if the individual defending her life manages to kill all of them would not morally outweigh her loss if she were wrongfully killed.

XIII. "Core" Self-Ownership: No Duty to Aid the Needy Per Se

None of the modifications to the Lockean individual rights doctrine that I have suggested contravenes the core of the libertarian self-ownership constraint, which I would formulate in this way: *The mere facts that one person is in a position to help another person who is in need of help and that the first person could provide assistance so that what she loses by providing aid is less than what the beneficiary gains are not sufficient to generate a duty to aid. Nor are matters changed if it is stipulated that nothing else the first person could do instead would help the needy to a greater extent (at lesser cost to herself than the gain to the beneficiaries). The mere fact that another is in need does not trigger an enforceable duty to aid.*[33]

This core self-ownership idea is consistent with the claim that one's ownership of things other than oneself is less than full. When the ratio of the good that one's possessions would do if used by others to the good those possessions would do if they remained entirely in one's own control exceeds a threshold, the right of ownership relaxes, as in the *Hiker* case.

Core self-ownership is also consistent with the claim that one has a natural duty to promote justice (the condition in which all people's natural rights are fully respected) to some extent. This duty can be understood so that it generates a duty to cooperate with citizens acting to uphold justice as in the *Accommodation* case. Core self-ownership is also compatible with the anti-free-rider norm suggested by the *Free Rider* case.

If core self-ownership is construed weakly as I have been suggesting, various other aspects of concern for fairness might be embraced without triggering conflict with this weak self-ownership constraint. One such aspect is that in thin market settings, where there are few buyers and sellers for a good or service, one does not have the right to charge whatever the traffic will bear. In particular, when the gap between the reservation prices of the would-be buyer and seller is very large, one does not have the right to force one party to an exchange at her reservation price even if one can do this by hard bargaining. This aspect of fairness colors the response to the *Holdout, Hiker,* and *Easy Rescue* cases. Notice that the rejection of the idea that in these examples the person in a strong bargaining position may legitimately charge whatever price she can negotiate does not rule out profit-taking in these settings by the person with the bargaining edge. Morality might accept profit-taking (beyond bare compensation for loss) but prohibit gouging or excessive profit-taking in such cases.

Objection: There is another element of self-ownership that equally merits designation as part of the core of the principle, and that straightforwardly conflicts with the judgments supposedly evoked (in my view) by *Holdout, Hiker, Free Rider,* and *Easy Rescue*. People are free to lead their lives as they choose (so long as they do not harm others) and may not be used against their will to advance the purposes of others.

Reply: It is wrong from the Lockean standpoint to force people against their will to advance other people's arbitrary ends, ends the coerced persons are not morally required to pursue anyway. The question then is, what ends are morally mandatory? The Lockean nonlibertarian holds that the promotion of justice for all—justice being identified with fulfillment of a Lockean set of rights—is an end that every person morally must

---

[33] Just for the record, I state that I do not myself endorse this statement of core self-ownership. In this essay I am exploring the natural rights tradition from within, not lobbing external criticisms at it.

adopt and pursue at least to a threshold reasonable extent. In like manner, the freedom to live as one chooses, within broad limits, is compatible with requiring individuals to comply with fairness norms in their dealings with one another.[34]

However, it should be noted that a problem is lurking in this neighborhood, one I shall not here attempt to resolve. Suppose one denies a duty to carry out easy rescues. Perhaps this is the point at which core self-ownership is thought to bite. With this denial in place, insistence on fairness conceived as ruling out charging whatever the traffic will bear in thin market settings will then be inconsistent with the Pareto constraint. To see this, note that A might be willing to rescue, but only if she profits by charging B his reservation price for this service, and B would prefer to pay this price rather than perish.

Even moderation (as introduced in Section XII), the norm that of those considered in this essay most radically alters the shape of natural rights theory, is strictly consistent with the core idea of self-ownership as I conceive it. The mere fact that a person is in need does not suffice to give the needy person a right to be assisted by anyone else, nor does it suffice to generate an enforceable duty to aid that falls on anyone else. But if someone is needy in the sense of being threatened with a loss that is excessive in relation to the cost that would have to be incurred by another individual who could avert the loss at least cost to herself, and if the threatened loss itself exceeds some threshold magnitude, then the moderation norm holds that a right to be aided and a corresponding duty to aid do arise.[35]

---

[34] For a contrary view, see Loren Lomasky, "Nozick's Libertarian Utopia," in Schmidtz, ed., *Robert Nozick*, 59–82. On p. 73, Lomasky writes, "Basic respect for autonomy enables pursuit of individual projects within a liberal order, but autonomy in any recognizable guise is the first casualty of a social arrangement in which everyone effectively owns a piece of everyone." To my ear this claim sounds wildly exaggerated. Consider a regime in which minimally decent Samaritanism is enforced: everyone has a minimal property right in everyone else that entitles each to command the aid of another in just those circumstances when (a) the aid will save a life well worth living, or bring about some comparably great benefit for its recipient, and (b) the aid can be provided at minimal cost to the giver. (If one likes, one can add a third condition: (c) the potential recipient of aid is not culpably responsible, beyond a certain threshold magnitude, for her dire predicament.) Whatever may be said for or against such a regime, it does not destroy autonomy in any recognizable guise (or in its most sensible guises). Much the same should be said of a regime in which each person has the following limited property right in the bodies of other persons: no one is permitted to be a free rider on cooperative schemes that provide important public goods of justice.

[35] There are two requirements here: the ratio between the benefit to the potential recipient of aid and its cost to the potential supplier must be sufficiently favorable, and the net magnitude of gain the recipient of aid would receive must be sufficiently large. One also wants the notion of "the person positioned to be able to supply aid at least cost to herself" to be sensitive to gains and losses over time. If Mother Teresa has already made huge sacrifices of her self-interest for the truly needy, whereas I have to this point in my life made nil sacrifices of this kind, and right now Mother Teresa could save a life at a cost of $10, whereas I could save the same life at the cost of $10.50 (suppose money here is linear with interpersonally comparable welfare), we want the moderate principle of Good Samaritanism to require me, not Mother Teresa, to provide the aid if anyone should in this instance.

XIV. THE PRINCIPLES CONSIDERED

Moderation expresses the idea that people are inviolable, up to a point. Individuals have rights that constrain what others may do to them, but the constraints give way when too much evil will ensue if those rights are upheld.

The other revisionary principles that I have invoked to support the judgments about puzzle cases that seem compelling modify the idea of inviolability, or individuals' fundamental entitlements. These principles can all be regarded as partial explications of the idea of fair dealing. It is not fair to begrudge anyone a benefit when allowing that whatever brings the benefit is costless to all others (including oneself). It is not fair to hold out for the maximum possible benefit for oneself when circumstances of thin markets give one a bargaining edge over those with whom one might contract on mutually beneficial terms. It is never fair to act maliciously toward others, aiming at nothing except harm or evil for them. There is also fairness toward oneself. One may not act with malice toward oneself. One has a duty to make something good of one's life—utterly squandering it is unfair to oneself. It is not fair to free ride on the cooperative behavior of others that provides one the public goods associated with secure enjoyment of the system of rights. A closely related point is that it is not fair to shirk one's duty to assume one's reasonable share of the costs of promoting justice (the system of natural rights, modified by these fairness requirements and by the principle of moderation itself). What is unfair in these ways one does not have a moral right to do.

These revisions to Lockean libertarianism all raise the Goldilocks problem.[36] In each case, fairness is identified with a proper or appropriate or reasonable weighing of conflicting principles, but nothing has been said in this essay to identify these optimal balance points. More needs to be said here. A sketch is not a moral theory.

"Fairness" here is just a term that encompasses various moral considerations. Ideally, one would like to have a theory of fairness rather than a collection of intuitions. But lack of a theory does not by itself impugn the intuitions about puzzle cases.

A serious concern that would need to be addressed in a satisfactory treatment is whether or not the revisions proposed in the libertarian position can coalesce into a stable doctrine. Is soft Lockeanism an unstable compromise of what further investigation would reveal to be incompatible elements? Can side constraints and entitlements cohere with outcome-oriented moral concerns? A full answer to these questions would

---

[36] In the fable "Goldilocks and the Three Bears," Goldilocks wanders into the bears' house, encounters three chairs, three beds, and three bowls of soup with different features, and for each of the triples ponders which one is "just right." Given multiple moral values, each one varying by degree, a moral theory sets their relative value and so determines, for any states of affairs that combine the values in different combinations, which state of affairs is best, which second-best, and so on.

require the development of a complete moral theory. But pending the construction of such a theory, I do not see a deep problem here. "People are inviolable, up to a point" sounds paradoxical, but the underlying idea is coherent: "You may do whatever you choose so long as you do not harm others in ways that violate their negative rights, unless (a) doing what you choose while violating no such right would allow excessively large losses to others' interests, in which case you must cater to their interests, or (b) failing to violate a right of another would lead to excessively large losses to others' interests, in which case you must violate the right." This is a consequence-constrained side constraint view.

XV. Conclusion

Throughout this essay, I have merely described examples and noted my own responses that take the form of judging the limits of people's rights in the situations as characterized. I have not advanced any argument supporting these responses except to note their inherent plausibility. The way is thus open for the hard libertarian to stand fast by her position and budge not. Against the assertion that the responses that contradict hard libertarianism are plausible, the hard libertarian can respond, "So what?" However, what Nozick says about the Randian position is relevant here:

> A large part of the attraction of the Randian view for people is the way it handles particular cases, the kind of considerations it brings to bear, its "sense of life." For many, the first time they encounter a libertarian view saying that a rational life (with individual rights) is possible and justified is in the writings of Miss Rand, and their finding such a view attractive, right, etc., can easily lead them to think that the particular *arguments* Miss Rand offers for the view are conclusive or adequate. Here it is not the argument which has led them to accept the view, but rather the way the view codifies, integrates, unifies, extends many of the judgments they want to make, feel are right, and supports their aspirations. If this is so, then one should hold the view so that it is open to challenge from just the sort of data that has provided its main support.[37]

I agree, and of course Nozick's own positive doctrine must answer to examples in just this same way. Libertarianism is open to challenge from the responses to cases that seem most compelling to us after scrutiny and reflection. On this basis my provisional conclusion is, "Down with hard libertarianism, up with soft Lockeanism."[38]

Philosophy, University of California at San Diego

---

[37] Robert Nozick, "On the Randian Argument," reprinted in Nozick, *Socratic Puzzles*, 249–64; see footnote 16 on p. 386.

[38] "Up with soft Lockeanism" means that this doctrine deserves to be regarded as a serious rival of the most plausible consequentialist morality. My own hunch is that consequentialism ultimately wins this competition.

ONE STEP BEYOND NOZICK'S MINIMAL STATE: THE ROLE OF FORCED EXCHANGES IN POLITICAL THEORY*

By Richard A. Epstein

I. Introduction

Like so many other scholars who work in the tradition of strong property rights and limited government, I owe a major intellectual debt to Robert Nozick for his 1974 masterpiece, *Anarchy, State, and Utopia*[1] —a debt that is now, sadly, beyond our ability to repay. The central points of his argument have been rehearsed often enough, so that a capsule summary should suffice here. As a political theorist, Nozick believed in two propositions. He believed, first, that the minimal state could be justified under the most exacting standards for political obligation, and, second, that—I choose my words carefully—any more extensive state violates the individual rights that the minimal state secures.[2] When these two propositions are united, it follows that the minimal state is the only permissible state. Anything less does not offer full protection to the rights that individuals have. Anything more than the minimal state violates those rights. In effect, the minimal state functions as both the lower and upper bound of a legitimate state, and hence as the only acceptable version thereof.

I think that these propositions are both wrong, and for the same reason; namely, they ignore, or at least understate, the critical role of *forced exchanges* at both stages of the argument. Perhaps the safest way to put this criticism is this: Nozick begins by developing a theory of the state, and only after that is completed does he develop his theory of individual entitlements in a chapter devoted to undercutting the case for redistribution.[3] By organizing his book in this way, he overlooks, or at least understates, the tension between his theory of political obligation, which gives a passing nod to the role of forced exchanges, and his theory of justice in acquisition

---

* I have benefited from comments at the workshop at the Social Sciences Division of the California Institute of Technology. My thanks to Justin Herring and Eric Murphy, The University of Chicago Law School, for their usual capable research assistance.

[1] Robert Nozick, *Anarchy, State, and Utopia* (New York: Basic Books, 1974). Hereinafter, *ASU*.

[2] For a nice summary of the argument, to which I shall revert later, see David Miller, "The Justification of Political Authority," in David Schmidtz, ed., *Robert Nozick* (Cambridge: Cambridge University Press, 2002), 10.

[3] *ASU*, chap. 7, "Distributive Justice," 149–231.

and transfer, which does not justify his conclusion. Contrary to Nozick's larger project, no state will form from any manipulation, however sophisticated, of what he terms the rules of justice in acquisition and justice in transfer. It is only when some individuals are *forced* to surrender their individual rights in exchange for the protection the state provides that the emergence of the state becomes possible. Nozick, of course, shows little willingness to move in that direction, writing as though all taxation is either a system of forced labor or, at least, "on a par with" one.[4] Yet once some willingness to tolerate forced exchanges is admitted into the political system, it is no longer possible or necessary to exhibit such doubts about taxation or to confine the state to the minimal functions that he posits for the night-watchman state. Rather, it is possible to organize government in such a way that it provides for conventional public goods without falling into the situation where it becomes a machine for the redistribution of wealth or opportunities from one group to another.

In order to make out this program, this essay is organized as follows. Section II examines the rights of individuals that Nozick claims should be recognized and protected in the minimal state. Section III elaborates on the definition of forced exchanges and shows how these fit into the overall structure of political theory. Section IV then shows how the elements of forced exchanges are embedded in the common law rules that adjust rights and duties between ordinary private individuals. Section V next explains how an explicit use of forced exchanges can fill in the gaps in Nozick's normative account of the original minimal state. Section VI then shows how this same justificatory apparatus allows some expansion of government beyond the bounds of the minimal state. Finally, Section VII shows that the acceptance of forced exchanges does not create an open season for the endless proliferation of state entitlements. A brief conclusion follows.

II. Individual Rights in the Minimal State

What, then, are the rights of individuals that the minimal state is bound to protect? I do not believe that Nozick had any direct engagement with the system of common law rules,[5] but his articulation of the minimal state draws heavily, in practice, from the ordinary system of common law rights and duties.[6] The initial building block of this system is individual autonomy, construed as the right of self-control free from the interference of others. Clearly, Nozick's mission would abort at the outset if the definition of autonomy were extended beyond self-rule to self-rule plus

---

[4] Ibid., 169.
[5] For my elaboration of these rules, see Richard A. Epstein, *Simple Rules for a Complex World* (Cambridge, MA: Harvard University Press, 1995).
[6] *ASU*, 149–82.

some minimum level of welfare guaranteed to all (although it is never clear *by whom*). The second building block or piece of the puzzle allows individuals to acquire ownership of property that is external to themselves, most notably land and chattels, or what Nozick terms "justice in acquisition." Nozick does not address any of the special problems raised by those resources, such as air and water, that have generally been regarded by legal systems as held in common. Further, he does not deal with the special problems raised by common carriers (e.g., railways, electricity, and power); nor does he address systematically the modern concerns with intellectual property, such as copyrights, trademarks, and patents.[7] A comprehensive theory of the minimal state would be required to explain whether and, if so, how these various common laws and statutory property-based institutions survive. Next, Nozick notes that the rules of transfer (contract and conveyancing) are critical to the overall operation of the system insofar as they allow for the constant recombination of initial rights, either to labor or services, by the individuals who hold them. This point is made clear when he notes that "[n]o one is entitled to a holding except by (repeated) applications of 1 [justice in acquisition] and 2 [transfer]."[8] Special attention has to be paid to the word "repeated," which does not play any role in the singular events that count as original acquisition, but does enormously expand the utility of justice in transfer. The repeated application of this one simple rule means that the inputs acquired in one transaction may, if not consumed, become, in whole or in part, the outputs of the next transaction. The constant repetition of this one strategy makes contract a tool of tremendous flexibility and introduces a versatility in transactions that counts as one of the prime ingredients of any social system. From individual rights can emerge a complex set of consensual arrangements through partnerships, leases, bailments, loans, and the like. All of these are created in ways that improve the utility of the parties to the agreements, without treading on the rights of third parties. Nozick clearly appeals to this repetitive feature of contractual life to explain how real voluntary agreements could solve the problem of creating a protective association, capable of defending its individual members (of full age and competence).

Finally, he defends what should be regarded as a variation on the law of tort. The individual's rights to one's person and to one's property (whether that property is acquired by initial acquisition or subsequent purchase) must be protected from the incursions of others, whether by force (including the threat thereof) or fraud. Nozick does not speak of this function as "protection" but as "rectification,"[9] where the difference in emphasis matters. Rectification, literally understood, means to make right

---

[7] Ibid., 141 and 182.
[8] Ibid., 151.
[9] Ibid., 152.

a (completed) wrong by supplying redress that restores the wronged party to the status quo ante, to the extent that the law can do so. Protection has a somewhat broader meaning, which includes the prevention of wrongs by allowing the interposition of relief before the fact either by state action or by private injunction. This broader meaning is in part a response to the long-standing debate over whether the primary function of the tort law is deterrence, compensation, or some mix of the two. Dealing solely with matters of rectification eliminates all levels of uncertainty in the picture; but the decision of whether or not to allow preventive relief necessarily requires a balance of two kinds of error: injunctions when they are not warranted, and no injunctions when they are clearly needed. That unavoidable uncertainty does not square well with a moral theory whose sole focus is the delineation of both right and wrong human actions, and Nozick does address these questions in the conventional terms, noting that any society, capitalist or socialist, *"should permit those polluting activities whose benefits are greater than their costs,"*[10] without noting the tension between his analysis and the stark theory of justification that he defends later. For these reasons, I shall use the broader term "protection" where Nozick would speak of "rectification." But even after these difficulties on terminology and remedies are duly noted, Nozick's basic position resonates quite closely with the general rules in Hume's *A Treatise of Human Nature* (1739).[11] In turn, Hume's position appealed quite consciously to the classification of legal rights articulated in Justinian's *Institutes,* and has remained, notwithstanding details in application, the mainstay of all common and civil law systems since that time.[12] Nozick cared little for any demonstration of how his own position tied in with the general conception of legal order as it developed down through the ages. But make no mistake, part of the appeal of his system is that it resonates with a set of legal rules, with small variations in detail, that are in common use in primitive and advanced cultures. Nozick's universalist argument benefits from the fact that there is much less variation in basic legal rules across time and space than is commonly acknowledged—at least before the rise of the modern regulatory state. He does not write in a void.

III. ENTER FORCED EXCHANGES

This close concordance between common practice and high philosophical theory is sufficient in my mind to show that Nozick is on to something that matters in his appeal to individual rights. But it is one thing to

[10] Ibid., 79 (italics in original).
[11] David Hume, *A Treatise of Human Nature* (1739), ed. L. A. Selby-Bigge (Oxford: Clarendon Press, 1888), 501–25.
[12] *Justinian's Institutes,* ed. and trans. Peter Birks and Grant McLeod (Ithaca, NY: Cornell University Press, 1987).

say that these rules of autonomy, acquisition, transfer, and protection (which includes both injunctions and rectification) are indispensable constituents of any legal order, and quite another thing to say that they alone offer the needed ingredients to constitute a full-fledged state, let alone one that uniquely satisfies the constraints of strong moral theory. As I have noted, I think that in the end Nozick is instructively and famously wrong on both counts. His austere account of the minimal state fails because it offers no credible explanation as to how the minimal state is formed. Yet once we add even one additional premise to the initial argument, it no longer follows that the minimal state is all that political morality allows. For example, Nozick's view would prevent the state from supplying what have been commonly termed public goods—namely, those goods (such as streetlights and national defense) that must be supplied to all members of a community if they are to be supplied to any individual member. This position can easily result in situations in which everyone is worse off in a world without taxation than they would be in a world with a well-designed system. In his classical exposition of the public goods issue, the economist Mancur Olson demonstrated that voluntary provision of these goods would result in their systematic underproduction, as no rational self-interested person would agree to shoulder the burdens of providing goods that he would receive even without his contribution. Instead, each member would want to "free ride" off the efforts of others. That strategy of nonsupport could be adopted by all individuals simultaneously, so that goods that everyone wanted no one would supply—a perfect rendition of the standard prisoner's dilemma game.[13] To be sure, this model is overdrawn since some individuals do act out of a sense of moral obligation even in collective situations.[14] But in large and anonymous settings, we can be confident that any level of compliance will, given individual self-interest, be far lower than optimal.

Nozick is aware of the difficulties of coordination, as he demonstrates in his discussion of the possibility of class action lawsuits against polluters,[15] but he overestimates the ability of clever voluntary solutions to overcome the standard public goods problem. The rules of property, contract, and tort, applied in combination, do not solve the problem. What then is the missing piece of the puzzle? Here my tack, as it has been for many years,[16] is to insist that the *one* missing piece of the puzzle is the

[13] See Mancur Olson, *The Logic of Collective Action* (Cambridge, MA: Harvard University Press, 1965).

[14] Note that the difficulty in providing public goods cannot be overcome by observing that individuals commonly make charitable contributions to strangers that seem impossible from the perspective of narrow self-interest. With charity, it is possible to target beneficiaries and to achieve one's aims without the cooperation of others. Contributions to public goods do not move in the direction of some preferred beneficiary and thus easily tend to break down.

[15] *ASU*, 80.

[16] See Richard A. Epstein, *Takings: Private Property and the Power of Eminent Domain* (Cambridge, MA: Harvard University Press, 1985): 334–38, criticizing Nozick on just these grounds.

practice of *forced exchanges,* initiated either by private parties or by the state. These are exchanges in which someone is required to surrender either liberty or (most commonly) property in exchange for compensation in cash or in kind. They are often described as the use of the state's power of eminent domain or condemnation, but in fact the issue goes far beyond the simple case where the government takes land for a road or a military installation. It also includes what are now termed "regulatory takings," which cover all government rules that limit the right of an owner to use or dispose of his property as he pleases, without dispossessing him from the land in question.[17] In some instances, these regulations are regarded as permissible without payment of compensation, but in others they are not. Deciding which forms of regulation are permissible without compensation and which are not presents some of the most devilishly difficult questions that arise in the operation of any mature legal system.

It is perhaps useful at the outset to give a simple catalogue of some of the common types of forced exchanges, as understood in opposition to an outright taking, where property is taken by the state which supplies nothing at all in exchange. The simplest version of a forced exchange is outright dispossession in which the state condemns a parcel of land for which it then pays the fair market value in cash. The taking of the land is forced on its owner, but it does not count as a form of theft because cash compensation is provided in exchange. The theory of the practice is that the landowner will be left (if compensation is calculated correctly) as well off as he was before the taking took place, while all the members of the society (including the individual whose property is taken) are left better off because the value to them of the land in its new use (say, as part of a road instead of a farm) is greater than the cash that they have been taxed to acquire it.

On this analysis, the taxes themselves are a form of taking (which is apparent to anyone whose property is seized if the taxes are not paid), which standing in isolation leaves all individuals who are taxed worse off than they were before. But if the benefits of good order or good roads acquired by taxes leave these taxpayers better off (by their own subjective lights) than before, this taking of cash is compensated *in kind* by the goods and services the government provides. In other takings situations, cash need not enter into the equation at all: the state could impose restrictions on how one person uses his land for the benefit of all his neighbors, and could impose *parallel restrictions* on the neighbors that give him benefits in exchange. In these regulatory takings, all persons could be required to suffer low-level nuisances (e.g., hearing voices from a neighbor's house) in exchange for being allowed to engage in similar activities that create similar low-level nuisances for others. If this live-and-let-live pattern is adopted generally, the alteration of the rule of strict liability for invasive behavior improves the situation of all against all.

---

[17] For a general discussion, see *Lucas v. South Carolina Coastal Council,* 505 U.S. 1003 (1992).

There are in fact many situations, both voluntary and coercive, where all the interests exchanged are property, not cash. The usual planned unit development (condominium or gated community) is organized by a set of (repeated) voluntary transactions that satisfy Nozick's most exacting tests for justice in acquisition and transfer, and yet no cash is involved; each purchaser of a unit is subject to restrictions that cost him, say, the equivalent of $100, for which he receives in exchange the benefit, worth perhaps $150, of like restrictions imposed on others. Various zoning ordinances, when properly constructed (which is usually not the case), could replicate that pattern of distribution when high transaction costs prevent people from being able to deal with these situations voluntarily.

Nozick touches on these complex situations in chapter nine of *Anarchy, State, and Utopia*, "Demoktesis," which asks how democratic institutions might justify more than the minimal state. But here his lack of legal knowledge leads him astray. At one point, he notes that it is possible for neighbors to buy the right to determine the color of a neighbor's house,[18] but he does so in the guise of an isolated transaction and not as a part of some comprehensive plan. Accordingly, he fails to see how these transactions typically govern all plots of land, reciprocally and simultaneously, and are often imposed by operation of law, and not by voluntary consent. He then carries the discussion further by speculating how it might be possible for each individual to acquire fractional interests in the labor of other persons. Such transactions do in fact take place in voluntary markets, as when a young golfer agrees to divide his future earnings with a set of backers who provide him with a stake that allows him to get established on the professional tour. But these arrangements are neither universal nor reciprocal. Everyone does not take a part-interest in the future earnings of all the others in the group. Nozick's effort to generalize on this theme is instructive, however, because it helps explain a scheme of general income taxation, whereby the state allows individuals to pursue whatever occupations they choose, and then taxes their earnings in accordance with a fixed (preferably flat) tax,[19] which is justified, as noted above, by the return benefits that individuals receive in a well-functioning state. But even here Nozick does not quite want to allow taxation into the system, even on a proportional basis,[20] which distinguishes his position from that of other classical thinkers such as John Locke,[21] Adam Smith,[22] and Friedrich von Hayek,[23] all of whom gravitate in that direction.

---

[18] *ASU*, 282.

[19] See Richard A. Epstein, "Can Anyone Beat the Flat Tax?" *Social Philosophy and Policy* 19, no. 1 (2002): 140–71.

[20] *ASU*, 169.

[21] John Locke, *Second Treatise of Government*, in *Two Treatises of Government*, ed. Peter Laslett (Cambridge: Cambridge University Press, 1989), 363.

[22] Adam Smith, *The Wealth of Nations* (New York: Modern Library, 1937), 777.

[23] Friedrich A. Hayek, *The Constitution of Liberty* (Chicago, IL: University of Chicago Press, 1960), 314.

Nozick is mistaken in his treatment of taxation, which looks solely at the cost and never at the benefit side. Here, and in other contexts, he fails to see how allowing forced exchanges introduces an extra degree of (analytical) freedom into the overall analysis, which requires close attention. It is now possible to have, as it were, justice in forced transactions so long as the party who is subject to coercion is left better off than before. This is not an effort to introduce into the law some Rousseauian notion that individuals may be forced to be free, for the use of forced exchanges is not designed to alter or override the preference structures that ordinary individuals hold. It is only intended to allow them to move to higher levels of utility (albeit with lower levels of political freedom) than they could achieve through voluntary transactions in light of the well-known coordination problems that arise in the provision of public goods. The full range of examples should make it clear how risky matters become once forced exchanges are allowed into the system. Clearly the permissible domain of forced exchanges should not be infinite, and one advantage of Nozick's more limited rules of acquisition, transfer, and protection is that they preclude petty and tyrannical abuses from the outset, abuses that often take place when the state uses its eminent domain power. But the price of his parsimonious assumptions is to block any coherent account for the legitimacy of the state at all. The key challenge, therefore, is to develop a set of rules that permit some forced exchanges while guarding against the potential for systematic abuses, including the forms of redistribution that were the subject of Nozick's attack. Within the American constitutional tradition (which speaks to concerns that transcend America's borders), this effort is dominated by two conditions that require some attention.[24] The forced exchanges in question should be made with "just compensation," and should only be allowed in those cases where they are for "public use." This formulation is suggestive of and consistent with the following set of conditions for allowing forced exchanges under the eminent domain power.

First, the transaction costs of voluntary arrangements must be high if not prohibitive. This condition alone suggests that it is not appropriate for me to take your watch while leaving its replacement cost in your mailbox. There are many individuals who can supply watches through ordinary market exchanges; why take the risk of abuse when the voluntarist solution is so attractive? It is clear that the public use requirement precludes

---

[24] See U.S. Constitution, Amendment V: "nor shall private property be taken for public use, without just compensation." For the moment at least, I put aside genuine questions associated with the reach of the "police power." That term, which appears nowhere in the Constitution, refers to the right of the state to pass regulations in order to advance "the safety, health, morals, and general welfare" of the public at large. Within the takings framework here, the police power sets out those conditions that justify the taking of property, without just compensation. For one discussion of the evolution of the police power, see William J. Novak, *The People's Welfare: Law and Regulation in Nineteenth Century America* (Chapel Hill, NC: University of North Carolina Press, 1996).

this transaction, even if it must allow many others. Rightly understood, the function of this requirement is to allow the state to supply public goods when the transaction costs of voluntary arrangements among multiple parties are prohibitive.

Second, the individual whom the state coerces must receive compensation that leaves him at least as well off by his own lights as he was before the forced exchange was undertaken. The point here is that coercion is justified not by some abstract appeal to the good of the community at large, but only by a specific showing that it causes no harm (or perhaps even works some net benefit) to the very individual who bears the brunt of that coercion. The requirement here raises obvious questions of valuation, but the reference to "his own lights" is intended to highlight the role of subjective value in the context of coerced transactions as another barrier against the abuse of state power. This requirement raises, in turn, some serious issues of measurement that cannot be escaped once any forced exchanges are allowed as legitimate.

Third, the transaction should work to the net benefit of those individuals who acquire the property in question. This condition will be easy to satisfy when ordinary individuals are able to use the coercive power of the state for their own advantage. They will only initiate transactions from which they hope to benefit. But the requirement is much more demanding in those cases when government agents act for the benefit of the community (against one of its members), using revenues that they have obtained through coercive means, for example, taxation. In one sense this position seems to be in tension with the view that all government coercion should be exercised for the benefit of those to whom it is directed. But in fact that condition is not violated here, because the willingness to provide full compensation means that the state power is only used to prevent a single individual or group from making a disproportionate exaction from the population as a whole. So understood, this third condition reveals the two-sided nature of the question of political legitimacy. Taken in connection with the second condition, it changes the view of the world from one of dominant reliance on the ideas of property and consent to reliance on the idea of making Pareto improvements, that is, bringing about new states of the world in which at least one person is better off and no one is worse off than before. This test is a "social" test insofar as it requires the welfare of each individual within the group to be taken into account before comparing two social states of affairs with each other. Voluntary transactions routinely generate Pareto improvements because no one will enter into them if they expect to be left worse off than before. Indeed, in virtually all voluntary, or win-win, situations, the transaction satisfies an even stronger condition in that all players regard themselves as better off with the deal than without it. Although the drafters of the Fifth Amendment adopted the "just compensation" standard before the formulation of the Pareto principle more than a century later, their views mirrored what that principle requires. We count as a social improvement any change that benefits each and every member of the society against whom coercion has been exercised. For these purposes, it does not matter whether that coercion has been exercised by general taxation and regulation or by the specific taking of particular pieces of property.

Fourth, in many cases it is desirable and feasible to have not only gains shared by all individuals in the group, but also a pro rata division of gain, so that no individual gains from public action more than any other. Stated otherwise, the ideal is that each person should get the same *rate* of return on his investment in collective activities as anyone else. Thus, in a simple three-person society in which A, B, and C are forced to contribute respectively (say by a tax on real property) 100, 200, and 300, then ideally, if A receives a 10 return (for a total of 110) on his contribution, B should receive 20 (for a total of 220), and C should receive 30 (for a total of 330). This is the same distribution that they would receive in any voluntary joint venture, and the coercive venture should follow the voluntary one in choosing this stable baseline in order to prevent a dissipation of surplus by factional intrigue. This fourth condition is needed because the simple just compensation requirement under conditions two and three is intended only to ensure that no individual *loses* from the use of state coercion. It does not speak about the distribution of the gain across other members of society. The Pareto test is satisfied if A ends up with property and public benefit worth 101 or more, B ends up with 201 or more, and C with 301 or more. The full 60 units of gain in the hypothetical example could be the focal point of factional struggles, or rent-seeking, that could wholly dissipate its amount. The highly stringent test of pro rata division is hard to satisfy in practice, but the point of this requirement is to prevent any two members of this three-party group from ganging up on the third in order to gobble up the lion's share of the surplus, even if the just compensation test has been met. The principles here, moreover, are easily expandable to any number of individuals. If the pro rata standard can be met, the level of political intrigue can be kept low. This is one argument for the flat or proportionate tax, whose form eliminates partisan battles over the steepness of any progressive tax. In making this argument, I do not mean to gloss over the serious measurement problems that are raised when voluntary transactions are not available to determine the value that each person attaches to some collective good such as law and order. There can be no doubt that these are highly variable in different contexts, and in practice we often assume that the benefit achieved from any given transaction is proportionate to the stake that individuals have in society, even when it is unlikely that this is the case in reality. Stated otherwise, there is nothing in this (or any other) model of governance that constrains public debate over whether to wage war or to make peace with foreign nations. But this is a problem that dogs any theory of collective action, even for the devotees of the minimal state.

The implications of this model are quite simple. No matter what his protestations to the contrary, Nozick, as I shall show, relies implicitly on this model of forced exchanges to justify the state. Yet once that assumption is laid bare, it is possible to identify extensions of state power that go beyond the minimal state without violating any of these same restrictive conditions. By the same token, these restrictions do argue strongly against, and thus limit if not preclude, the one form of government action that Nozick wished to ban: to wit, the forced redistribution of wealth through state coercion. Such forced redistribution flunks all four of the conditions set out above, and can be allowed, if at all, only if one introduces notions of diminishing utility of wealth that are so profound that they justify the very large administrative expenses needed to work a greater equalization of wealth with its consequent losses in productive capacity—a challenge that it is difficult to meet, to say the least.[25] Indeed, the last dollar lost would have to be worth nothing in order for this redistribution to work a Pareto improvement, a highly unlikely proposition.

IV. Forced Exchanges in Private Transactions

As I have noted, much of Nozick's account draws its intuitive force from its close connection to ordinary common law conceptions of right and wrong, as embodied in the law of property, contract, and tort. His rule of initial acquisition is like the first-possession rule of common law, which awards ownership of a thing to the party who captures it first. The law of contract is intended to secure voluntary transfer of human labor or the property acquired with it, and the rules of tort deal with the rectification of past wrongs and the prevention of future ones. The combination of contract and tort rules is of special importance because contract rules stress the role of consent in the creation of private obligations while tort rules emphasize the prohibition against the use of force and fraud to achieve private ends. But it would be a serious mistake to assume that the full range of common law rules shows any invariable preference for consent over coercion. Rather, the more complete statement of the applicable principles introduces a necessary note of complexity into the overall picture, which shows the irreducible role of coercion in private relations.

Looking at the rules for the acquisition of property, it is evident that they cannot rest on a system of universal consent, as that phrase is ordinarily understood. The individual who takes something from the commons necessarily reduces the amount that is available to others, which is said to give rise to the endless fretting over the famous Lockean proviso: leave enough and as good for others. Yet the moment the first person

---

[25] For my arguments on this point, see Richard A. Epstein, "Luck," *Social Philosophy and Policy* 6, no. 1 (1988): 17–38.

takes the best, then, by definition, this condition fails. The blunt truth is that the removal of things from the commons necessarily imposes losses on other individuals. It is only with the dubious kind of "implied" consent that we can assume that others have agreed to these losses, which is a desperate effort to make the stubborn facts fit a contractual analysis that simply cannot carry the day. In truth, however, consent does not explain the rule; only necessity does. Locke himself justified the right to remove resources from the commons by noting that we would all starve if we had to wait for uniform consent to act,[26] which was his way of noting that the coordination problem from unanimous consent was intractable: any one individual, and hence every individual, could hold out against a solution that is desired by everyone else in order to claim an ever-larger share of the pie. It was, therefore, preferable to have a legal order in which people could take unilaterally in order to avoid mass starvation. To that general position, the Lockean proviso offers only a crude guess at how we could prevent the first taker from consuming everything that is available; yet this proviso, too, operates as an external norm, not as the outgrowth of consent.

Locke's explanation of these arrangements is incorrect not only because he does not quite hit on the right rules, but also because he fails to couch the analysis in the language of forced exchanges. That language refers to discrete bundles of rights: each of us, without individual consent, gives up any right of blockade over others in exchange for the right to remove resources from the commons. The Lockean side constraint is stated too categorically when it insists that enough and as good be left behind. A better way to put the point is to note that privatization, without the consent of others, should be allowed only to the extent that its *marginal* benefits to the acquirers (and those who benefit through them) exceed the *marginal* costs to outsiders, taken over the society as a whole.

At this point, it is clear why Locke is correct to link the legal constraints on the removal of property from the commons to the existence of trade. So long as the trade of things is possible after they are taken from the commons, it is relatively unimportant who gets what: others can exchange property or labor in order to acquire those things that they value more greatly.[27] It is only when the possibility of trade is blocked that it becomes a social imperative to leave some resources of value behind for others who would starve if they were unable to provide for themselves. Without some such restraint, in a state of nature each individual in good Hobbesian fashion would take as much as he could, without regard to the welfare of others. The legal rules are intended to counteract the destructive consequences of that universal practice.

[26] John Locke, *Second Treatise of Government*, ed. C. B. Macpherson (Indianapolis, IN: Hackett Publishing Co., 1980), 18–30.

[27] See Ronald H. Coase, "The Problem of Social Cost," *Journal of Law and Economics* 3, no. 1 (1960): 1–44.

Yet even when trade is allowed, there may still be reasons to limit the ability to remove property from the commons. With water, some constraints are needed even (indeed especially) if trade is allowed. Trade expands the demand for water, and its excessive removal from a small river of the sort found in England destroys its "going concern" value for fishing, navigation, recreation, and the like.[28] Of course, valuation questions abound in this setting, but to treat them as insurmountable means that no one can remove any water from the river or, alternatively, that anyone and everyone acting in a noncooperative fashion can dam it or drain it dry. Limited use is what takes place, where the effort, however crude, is to allow those private uses whose value exceeds that of the collective uses that remain. One appropriate forced exchange, easily stated, limits the removal of water for use on the riparian property and prevents its resale, which might otherwise seem allowable by Nozick's rules of justice in transfer. That rule is not ideal because it does not allow for the comparisons of the utility that rival riparians receive from their water. But for my present purposes, the fine-tuning of a system of water rights is not to the point.

All that need be recognized here is that the creation of property rights in their multiple configurations does not involve some simple relationship of an individual to an object in the fashion that Nozick supposes. The creation of correlative duties that fall on nonowners is an indispensable feature of any regime of justice in acquisition for any and all forms of property rights. Look again at the four conditions enumerated in Section III and it seems clear that property arrangements (including resource-specific property arrangements that differ between land and water) satisfy these four constraints on the libertarian system. The coordination costs are high; there is a clear social improvement from the change in rights that is shared by all and all alike in common proportion. It is for just this reason that customary rules of this sort start to verge on contract and make sense from a consequentialist perspective in which they are not usually articulated.

It may be said, however, that these constraints on the removal of property from the commons depend on the choice of some pre-political or common law baseline, but in reality they do not. Let us assume a baseline of a state of nature in which the rule is that no one can take anything from the commons. At this point, an alternative rule that allows a free-for-all on possession is likely to do far better. The life expectancy of all individuals under the first rule is near zero, given the certainty of starvation. The second rule marks an improvement that is shared across the board, where it is difficult to figure out what restraints could guarantee equal access—the last and most stringent of our conditions. But the "free-for-all" rule

---

[28] See Richard A. Epstein, "On the Optimal Mix of Private and Common Property," *Social Philosophy and Policy* 11, no. 2 (1994), 17–41.

does not exhaust the gains with water, for example, so that the additional constraint that holds that each riparian (and only a riparian) can take water for reasonable personal uses marks an improvement over that rule. The key point is that the process of forced exchanges for social improvements shares this feature with voluntary contracts. Both create situations where *sequential* application of the same rule of forced exchanges can move the overall situation to a higher social level, even when judged by the exacting conditions set out above.

It is critical to note here that the process does *not* run in reverse. It is not the case that we could start (arbitrarily) with a rule that followed the customary system of water rights and justify a return to the state of nature. The losses suffered by all would block movement in that direction. The overall system, therefore, should be capable of reaching a unique equilibrium no matter what our original baseline. Where we start should make a difference solely in a high-transaction-costs environment when it might be less possible to shift across regimes. But conceptually, this analysis shows that Nozick's rules of acquisition through first possession are cut from a different cloth than the rules for contract (transfer) or for tort (protection/rectification) as he conceives them. The libertarian approach seeks to avoid consequentialist arguments, but in fact it only buries them out of view. Once individuals sense the justice of a certain practice, they choose to follow the practice even if they cannot articulate its reasons. Whatever the justificatory weaknesses of the categorical rule of acquisition through possession, that rule gives good and universal guidance to individuals who live within the legal framework—which is no small virtue if the effort is to develop a coherent approach that respects the rule of law.[29] Most people are happy if the instrumental logic of rules they accept is kept securely in the background.

The implicit breakdown of the libertarian approach is also evident when we press harder on the rules of contract and tort, which are not as categorical as Nozick would have them. Here two forms of correction are needed. First, there are many voluntary agreements that are not enforced because they are said to be against public policy. These include contracts to commit crimes or to fix prices. The argument for this nonenforcement is that the losses to third parties exceed the gains to the parties to the transactions, so that the refusal to enforce is a Pareto improvement over a rule that enforces all contractual undertakings indiscriminately. Once again, if we move back to a time before any contracts are formed, this rule also seems to provide social improvements in a high-transaction-costs environment. The moral intuition that promises are generally enforceable

---

[29] A philosopher might wish to stress that Locke at least seems to require that labor be "mixed" with possession in order to acquire ownership. This requirement strikes me as problematic if only because bare possession is needed in order to gain the right to mix the labor with the external thing. Locke seems to say as much when he notes that if picking the acorn does not establish ownership, no further act, such as boiling it, will.

is best explained by the observation that these produce gains for the parties involved and, in the ordinary case, also for strangers by increasing the opportunities for further transactions. The latter condition is false in criminal contract cases. The consequentialist approach gives a certain coherence to both the rule and the ordinary exceptions to it. No intuitive moral theory can do the same.

In like fashion, the entire law of restitution shows that forced exchanges are even allowed when initiated by private parties. The standard case of private necessity allows one person to take water from the well of another if that is the only way to prevent dying of thirst. The same rule has been applied in legal cases to permit one person to use the dock of another without permission in order to escape the ravages of a storm. Indeed, the legal system is so insistent on the maxim that "necessity suspends property rights" that it treats the owner of the dock as a wrongdoer if he seeks to use force to put the intruder off his premises. The argument in all these cases is that just compensation in the form of rental for the use of the dock or payment for damages caused is a preferred remedy to a voluntary situation in which the owner could hold out for a huge fraction of the wealth of the intruder if the usual rules of consent applied. Quite simply, consent becomes a viable requirement when lots of choices are available to a person in need. But it looks considerably less attractive in those cases where there is only one person who has the power of life and death, which is what the necessity rule is intended to forestall. Once again, the point here is that forced exchanges are part and parcel of the private law out of which Nozick attempts to construct his principles of justice in holdings. It remains to show how this paradigm is necessary to explain the emergence of the minimal state.

V. Toward the Minimal State

The previous discussion sets the stage for determining Nozick's error in thinking that voluntary transactions alone are sufficient to account for the creation of both the ultraminimal and the minimal state. The ultraminimal state arises when, within a given territory, one protective association emerges as the dominant market player. The minimal state arises in recognizable form when that dominant association becomes the only association within the community to which all persons, now citizens, subscribe. The simplest objection to this program is that it cannot happen on any realistic assumptions about individual self-interest.

Start with the formation of the ultraminimal state. Here it is clear that two or more people are entitled to band together for mutual aid and protection so long as their combined rights do not exceed the rights that they held separately. You and I can join together for self-defense, but not for attack. We can then admit additional members into our group so as to create ever-larger alliances. Other individuals have, of course, the same option to form or join groups in competition with our own, so the question arises: When entry is free, how can any organization assume a dominant position while hewing strictly to its mission of defense only, never aggression? One possible explanation of how dominance could be achieved comes from the creation of the kind of network externality that is common in telecommunications. Let us assume that the value of telephone service is directly proportional to the number of individuals who are connected to any given network. Here the network that gets a leg up on its rivals will be able, ceteris paribus, to offer the better service, and thus win over individuals who might otherwise choose to join some other network. This sequence confers a first-mover advantage, and opens up the prospect that all individuals will find themselves with a supplier that none of them really wants. Political philosopher David Miller, in his thoughtful critique of Nozick, identifies this as one weakness in the Nozickian system, because the protective association that comes first might not be the one that a majority of the individuals would choose to have.[30] The vagaries of path dependence could override the preference for majority rule.

There is good reason to question whether path dependence will, or should be, critical with either networks or political order. In practice, a first network may have an initial advantage, but several complications intrude. First, there is no clear delineation of territory before the fact that will allow anyone to decide which organization has the dominant territorial control. Only after a state is cobbled together can its territory be defined, and then it is too late for the analysis to work. Second, there is no clear lexical or temporal order in these cases. Over large populations, many different networks could overlap in the time of their formation or in the rate of their spread. The question here is a bit like asking which riparian is first to reach the river. In practice that question has proved so hard to answer that the first-possession rule used with respect to land has always given way to a proration rule among riparians with respect to water rights: no matter when you arrive, your use-rights are a function of the total frontage along the river, without any temporal priority. Third, even if one network did get a jump outside the starting gate, others may prefer to join a second network that better fits their personal needs, counting on some master agreement to link the two networks together. This often happens in telecommunications under "bill and keep" arrangements, where each side agrees to carry the traffic of the other while both keep the fees for those transactions that were initiated on their side of the network.[31] These deals involve no transfer payments, and they prove stable because they have a strong focal point due to their reciprocal nature. Fourth, the first mover always faces the risk of a mass switch of customers

---

[30] Miller, "The Justification of Political Authority," 16–17.
[31] See, for example, Telecommunications Act of 1996, 47 U.S.C. § 252 (2000).

to a rival association, brought on by an attractive group offer. Exactly how this works out in the end is dependent on the transaction costs needed to bring on any particular switch: in the limiting case, as transaction costs approach zero, the path advantages disappear as well. In the intermediate cases, all that one can say is that first-mover advantages would count for something if political institutions behaved like network industries, although it is uncertain by how much. But overall dominant positions should be hard to come by in light of the counterstrategies available to other parties.

Nor is it apparent that the analogy to network externalities applies to questions of political organization. On the unlikely assumption that each of these associations will respect the rights of other associations in their own activities, what motivation does anyone have to join any association except the one that promises the best mix of services and payments? No network externalities are at work so long as any assumption of mutual respect holds. Yet once that assumption is relaxed, membership in a small organization could easily confer advantages on groups that can hold out against their dominant rival. The apt analogy to these protective associations is not the network industry, but the small swing-party that holds the balance of power in forming coalition governments under a system of proportional representation. The new entrants enjoy powerful holdout potential disproportionate to their numbers, which should give them a comparative advantage against any larger established party.

Additional adjustments have to be made when members of a smaller association are brought as defendants before a larger one. Further modifications are required to deal with disputes in which, as often happens in cases of alleged self-defense, each party claims that the other is in the wrong. Still further adjustments are required in order to deal with situations that involve individuals from three or more groups, or with cases in which it is uncertain who is the wrongdoer or, for that matter, the victim. The transactional complexities will quickly outstrip the ability to have ad hoc voluntary arrangements, whether at the individual or associational level, to deal with the complexities across a myriad of protective associations. Indeed, the problem of enforcement against the various kinds of wrongdoers is a bit like the problem of autonomy and property in the first instance. The very reason why we start with an institution of property (which requires forbearance but not support from the world at large) is because we know (in a pretty strong sense) that the transaction costs of getting universal agreement on the rules against trespass and misappropriation are prohibitive. That same set of difficulties arises in the related context of enforcement agreements.

Once it is no longer possible to postulate one dominant agency, there is no way to see how any particular agency will be able to gain the total support of all individuals when the gains from holding out could prove so large. Nozick tries to deal with these possibilities by noting that in the intermediate stages it is possible (and necessary) to formulate rules that govern conflicts between individuals who have signed up with different protective organizations. Here the operative language is no longer consent. Rather, the leading trope is that the dominant association will allow its people to be hauled before another organization so long as it judges the procedures of that association to be as good as its own. But this requires some judgment as to the relative value of alternative regimes, which turns the inquiry back to the just-compensation rules associated with forced exchanges. Nozick himself recognizes the importance of the compensation element when he writes: "What is the explanation of how a *minimal* state arises? The dominant protective association with the monopoly element is morally required to compensate for the disadvantages it imposes upon those it prohibits from self-help activities against its clients." [32] In effect, the system does not operate by rules of justice in acquisition and transfer. His critical move necessarily represents an explicit deviation from the voluntaristic ideal. The introduction of compensation marks the move to a system of forced exchanges, which in international (and interstate) relations cashes out to a nondiscrimination requirement, whereby the outsiders have no grounds to protest if they are governed by the same rules that bind the locals.

At this point, it is only necessary to establish the strong link between a *nondiscrimination* rule and the system of forced exchanges mentioned above. This test plays out by noting that each person surrenders his right to be judged by his own sovereign in exchange for the right to be governed by rules that others apply to themselves. Using these standard-issue rules offers a powerful line of defense against abuse, bias, and favoritism that are everywhere the concerns of judicial proceedings. There is today a powerful need for a nondiscrimination provision for individuals who live or work outside their home territories. But this hardly establishes that it makes sense to have multiple authorities within any given territory. The rule of forced exchanges does not, indeed cannot, tell us *which* organization should have pride of place within a given territory, but it does say that whatever organization or group does emerge must apply its own rules to outsiders who are brought within the fold once territories are established. The use of this "like justice" requirement is meant to finesse strict proof of just compensation, which could not be established in any event in these highly specialized markets. The entire tale, therefore, speaks of a set of arrangements in which the nondiscrimination rule is an imperfect proxy for just compensation. In some cases the law relies on formal equality in the treatment of individuals as a proxy for nondiscriminatory treatment. That test works well in one direction, for explicit distinctions between individuals should be justified before they are tolerated. But the converse is less likely to hold. It is easy to envision rules that are formally equal that have a *disparate* impact on the regulated population. One illustration is a prohibition against all fur-

---

[32] *ASU*, 119.

ther development in a community when some landowners have already built while others have vacant land. At this point, the hard administrative question, of greater concern for lawyers than for philosophers, is whether the additional administrative costs (of figuring out whether the formal rule cloaks redistribution between neighboring landowners) are justified by the level of covert redistribution through regulation that they prevent.

In dealing with the philosophical issues, however, the exact form of the nondiscrimination rule is not the key point relevant to Nozick's voluntaristic claims. Rather, what matters the most is that the move from voluntary association to political organization takes place by means of forced exchanges and not by consensual transactions. The fact that the transactions follow this path should lead us to be cautious in defining the powers that are extended to the state precisely because its justificatory apparatus is of necessity suspect: our criterion for state power is weaker than actual consent, and the difficulties in measuring compensation are far greater. But once the method is understood, then oddly enough the need to posit intermediate protective associations disappears as well. Rather, it becomes possible to revert to the progression of social contracts that mark the evolution through Hobbes, Locke, and Hume. We start in the state of nature, a world in which anything goes. We realize that all individuals are better off if they mutually renounce the use of force and fraud, as Locke did with the rejection of license in favor of liberty. We then further realize that this renunciation will be written on the wind unless social institutions are established to secure the new prohibitions that are put in place. We next recognize that a system of taxation proportionate to property protected can be used to supply state services, including courts free from bias, to administer these rules. Nozick, like Hume, does not like the idea of "social contract." But in effect that is where the basic argument leads, so long as both words receive due emphasis. The word "contract" refers to the proposition that at each stage we are confident (but not positive) that the benefits conferred exceed the costs imposed, which is what happens in real contracts of hire and sale. We use the word "social" to connote the fact that these contracts are hypothetical, and we keep the four constraints on forced exchanges—high transaction costs, just compensation, net benefit, and proration of gain—to ensure that these hypothetical contracts do not run riot. The Nozickian effort to use voluntary sequential contracts to reach the minimal state thus fails. The effort to use forced exchanges with mutual benefits in high-transaction-costs environments succeeds, however imperfectly, in filling that gap. The question thus remains: How may that principle be used once the state is in formation?

VI. BEYOND THE MINIMAL STATE

We are now in a position to see the error in the second half of Nozick's argument, namely, that no state larger than the minimal state is permissible. We immediately should be suspicious of that position, insofar as it contravenes the common assumption that states routinely provide public goods for their citizens through the means of taxation, let alone a wide range of redistributive services, such as social security, that prove, on examination, to be far more controversial. That said, Nozick's conclusion would be correct if he could demonstrate that the voluntary approaches alone were sufficient to create the minimal state. But his argument loses all of its zip once it is recognized that forced exchanges are built into the foundations of any organized society. They are first built into society in the definitions of property and liberty and their correlative duties, and next in the creation of a single sovereign with monopoly power over all individuals within its territory. If, however, the method of forced exchanges is needed to explain and justify the creation of a principled state, there is no reason why the same methodology cannot be used to explain commonplace institutions that are developed once that state is established. Quite simply, the logic of forced exchanges is to allow for Pareto improvements that voluntary transactions cannot achieve. It is difficult to imagine, let alone identify, any moral theory that would sanction the use of this principle to account for the legitimate foundations of state authority only to turn around and reject the use of this principle once the state is created. The real test, therefore, is whether we can identify common institutions that satisfy this criterion. And we can.

In order to undertake this process, it is necessary to look at a set of midlevel institutions that are vital to the day-to-day operation of the system. These midlevel institutions often fly under the radar of philosophers and political theorists, but these institutions constitute key elements of any well-functioning state. I will begin with those that are not characteristic elements of the modern welfare state, but are considered to be elements of a sensible state devoted in large measure to the protection of liberty and property. Begin first with the security of transactions. To philosophers the important element about contract turns on the moral force of promises. Questions of proof and implementations are second-order questions that are best handled by lawyers with their superior technical skills. Three of the relevant devices of great note and importance are the statute of frauds, the various recordation statutes for real property (and some forms of personal property), and statutes of limitation. The statute of frauds identifies particular classes of contracts, such as those for the conveyance of land or the guarantees of personal contracts, that must be evidenced in writing.[33] Recordation statutes require that various deeds and liens (indicating a security interest for a loan or other debt) be recorded in order to be valid against subsequent purchasers of interests in the subject property. Statutes of limitations bar, upon the passage of time

---

[33] The original version of the statute dates from 1677 in England: 29 Charles II, c. 3 (1677). Variations of the statute are enforced in every state in the United States.

alone, claims that are otherwise valid. One key variation on the statute of limitations is the doctrine of adverse possession, which allows the unlawful possessor of land to trump the interest of the original landowner after the passage of time. All of these rules represent enormous areas of working law subject to many variations and exceptions. Their one common thread is that they show how no working legal system stops with the minimal state.

The initial point is that none of these well-nigh universal statutes is justified by reference to any basic moral principles of right conduct, including Nozick's. Quite the opposite: the statute of frauds denies the enforcement of serious oral promises solely for want of the formality. The recordation statutes for their part upset a central principle of justice in transfer, because first in time need not be higher in right. Let O first convey property to A, who does not record, after which O conveys the same property to B, who does record, and B will take priority over A, notwithstanding that at common law O had divested himself of all interest in the property by the initial conveyance. The statute of limitations blocks claims because of the staleness of evidence and the conviction that people should act to assert their rights within a reasonable period of time or forever hold their peace. I would be hard pressed to imagine any serious libertarian who would have an instinctive revulsion to statutes whose central purpose is to supply additional levels of security to property and contract even if they clashed with Nozick's rule of rectification, which does not explain how the passage of time purifies a legal wrong. Libertarians might, of course, seek to justify these statutes by some appeal to the common good. Although such an appeal gives these statutes safe passage, it spells the end of any constraint on government, for it is hard to see what legal doctrine, whether by statute or common law, could not pass muster under this test. That justification becomes an excuse factory for excessive state intervention unless it is tightly moored to the claims of the individuals within society. Indeed, just this loose test is used today in modern American constitutional law (where it travels under the name of the "rational basis" test), and it has had the (predictable) effect of fostering such intervention.[34] Under this test, so long as one group benefits from the passage of a statute, no court will look closely to see whether that benefit pales into insignificance in comparison with the harms that the statute imposes on others. Few statutes pass without some champions, so that in economic matters, the test has generally been interpreted as giving Congress and the states a free hand in the regulation of economic affairs.[35]

---

[34] See, for example, *Penn Central Transportation Co. v. New York City*, 438 U.S. 104 (1978), where a set of elusive rationales were used to justify the landmark preservation statutes that wiped out the air rights that the Penn Central Company had over Grand Central Station. For my critique of the test, see Richard A. Epstein, "The Ebbs and Flows in Takings Law: Reflections on the *Lake Tahoe* Case," Cato Supreme Court Review 1, no. 1 (2002): 5–30.

[35] See, for example, *Williamson v. Lee Optical of Oklahoma, Inc.*, 348 U.S. 483 (1955).

The basic constitutional guarantees of life, liberty, and property can easily be circumvented under a capacious police power test molded in these terms.

But what makes these rules (statutes of frauds, recordation, and limitation) interesting is that they also satisfy the more stringent tests set out above for deviations from the libertarian norms. Here, the best way to see the point is to press John Rawls's famous veil of ignorance test into service for a cause quite different from his own.[36] Behind the veil of ignorance, one does not know whether he would be a buyer or a seller, a claimant or a defendant. Any rule that increases the security of transactions reduces the costs of doing business, so that all individuals are left better off in all future transactions from the implementation of the rule. The compensation received in the ex ante position comes from your ability as a buyer who records to receive protection from the institutions that block your claim, for want of recording, on this occasion. It is, therefore, hard to find anyone who would prefer to operate in a world without these protections; nor is it possible typically to find anyone who seems to gain disproportionately from their implementation. These statutes come in the generic form as close to Pareto improvements as one could imagine, which is why they have always escaped controversy and condemnation.

There are, of course, cases in which sensible statutes or laws could be turned to more dubious ends. Certain individuals could be selectively exempted from these various rules so that it is no longer possible to say that the rules raise all people equally to a higher level of utility. Thus, serious issues would arise if a statute of limitations were lifted after it barred claims of a certain class, or if the allowable periods for adverse possession or recordation were so short that in practice no one could comply with them. But these ploys do nothing to undermine the strength of the general theory. Quite the opposite: they only confirm its use. Each and every one of these changes has to promise a fair chance of overall improvement in order to pass muster. The *selective* and *opportunistic* application of the rules counts as a form of bias that virtually ensures that these conditions are not satisfied. *Retroactive* changes in the law are yet another illustration of the same problem. As with all empirical applications of the general test, there are only strong presumptions that certain rules bring about illicit redistributions between persons. Nonetheless, there are clear warning signs when something is amiss, as with any rule that imposes *selective* burdens while generating *general* benefits, or the reverse. Thus, a rule that taxed the landowners in one part of a town to provide road improvements everywhere would be suspect, whereas one that imposed local taxes for local benefits would not be. In all cases, however, the ultimate question is whether the gains are pro rata with the exaction, so that the apparent mismatch of benefits and costs might be justified, for

---

[36] John Rawls, *A Theory of Justice* (Cambridge, MA: Belknap Press of Harvard University Press, 1971), 12 and 136–42.

example, if all the residents in one part of town made heavy, well-nigh exclusive, use of roads in the portion to which their special taxes were directed—an unlikely occurrence.

Thus far, I have discussed the use of forced exchanges only in connection with those legal rules whose purpose is to strengthen the system of property and contract rights that libertarians themselves would endorse. But the program here goes much further, for it often allows for sensible redefinitions of property rights when those redefinitions would work for the long-term advantage of all individuals in circumstances in which voluntary renegotiation is practically impossible. In an earlier essay, I discussed at length the various modifications of the boundary conditions associated with the law of trespass that work in this fashion.[37] The rules of live-and-let-live with respect to low-level invasions of noise and dust offer yet another example, as too do the rules that require individuals to provide lateral support for the land of their neighbors.[38] Indeed, regime changes in property rights also cover important restrictions on the ability of individuals to withdraw (in the manner that Locke had contemplated) common pool assets, such as oil and gas, or wildlife. Here the broad statement of "enough and as good" yields to very precise delineation of who can take how much and under what circumstances. The gains to all participants in the process can be quite startling. Overdrilling of oil and gas fields results in two forms of losses: the unnecessary reduction in output and the concomitant increase in the cost of removal. A sensible regime of well-spacing or unitization can reduce the number of wells and increase the total output of the field. If some surface owners are shut out from drilling altogether, then they could be given a fractional interest in the produce of other wells. So long as the net gains in production exceed the costs of running the cooperative scheme, it is possible to create a system that meets the basic criteria set out above. As with all such schemes, it is easy to envision variations that appear to be neutral on their face, but that in fact work prejudice to some participants in the system, at which point the proper judicial response is to block implementation of the system until the losers are compensated for their losses.[39]

The same approach accounts for much of intellectual property law, and helps explain why it is so difficult to fasten on the optimal rules for copyrights and patents, both of which are statutory creations. Here the ordinary theories of possession allow a person only to take hold of the thing that he has captured or occupied. These words do not capture

---

[37] Richard A. Epstein, "Deconstructing Privacy: And Putting It Back Together Again," *Social Philosophy and Policy* 17, no. 2 (2000): 1–24.

[38] For a more detailed discussion, see Richard A. Epstein, "Nuisance Law: Corrective Justice and Its Utilitarian Constraints," *Journal of Legal Studies* 8, no. 1 (1979): 49–102.

[39] For one such example, see *Ohio Oil Co. v. Indiana*, 177 U.S 190 (1899), which introduced a complex sharing arrangement between oil and gas producers that systematically favored the latter, who were in-state interests.

the situation with respect to those forms of property for which these physical modes of acquisition are inappropriate. Nonetheless, it is a commonplace argument that individuals will not invest in future writings or inventions unless they are secured a return for their labor, which cannot be achieved by exclusive control of a prototype or manuscript that anyone can build or reproduce at will. In essence, therefore, the great systems of intellectual property require all individuals to surrender their rights of imitation in exchange for the greater security that they receive for their own writings and inventions.[40] Even those who do not write or invent are beneficiaries of this system because they will be able to obtain access to things of value that would never be produced in the absence of these statutory schemes for intellectual property rights. The exact contours of these systems are by no means easy to define, either as to scope or as to duration, and the dangers of special pleading are evident here as everywhere else. The Copyright Term Extension Act of 1998, which tacked on twenty additional years to existing copyrights so as to delay the entrance of currently protected works into the public domain, is but one example of these dangers. The extension of the monopoly reduces the level of consumption—a social loss—without giving a new incentive to innovate, which is the functional justification for copyright in the first instance.[41]

For my present purposes, the ornate details of these property rights systems again are beside the point. What matters is how they tie in with Nozick's theory. In chapters 6 and 7 of *Anarchy, State, and Utopia*, Nozick makes some brief mention of these intellectual property rights,[42] but does not show in that brief compass how they fit in with his general views on justice in acquisition or transfer. Nor does he offer any account for these differences between different types of intellectual property. Rather, Nozick seems (his language is not clear) to make some elementary mistakes. Independent creation is a defense to an action for copyright infringement, but independence is not a defense, as he appears to suggest, to a suit for patent infringement. One reason is that copying is far easier to prove in the former case than in the latter. The compromises that are required in this area create important differences between the various subheads of intellectual property that can only be integrated into a general theory of property rights. Forced exchange from the common law baseline of property rights is the key tool that allows for understanding this area.

---

[40] For one exhaustive overview of the relevant trade-offs, see William M. Landes and Richard A. Posner, *The Economic Structure of Intellectual Property Law* (Cambridge, MA: Belknap Press of Harvard University Press, 2003); or see my account of how patents and copyrights should be understood in a world with forced exchanges, "Intellectual Property: Old Boundaries and New Frontiers," *Indiana Law Journal* 76, no. 4 (2001): 803–27.

[41] Sonny Bono Copyright Term Extension Act, Pub. L. No. 105-298, 112 Stat. 2827 (1998). The act was upheld by the United States Supreme Court in *Eldred v. Ashcroft*, 537 U.S. 186 (2003).

[42] *ASU*, 141 and 182.

VII. Prohibited Forced Exchanges

As I have noted, the conditions under which forced exchanges may be used to deviate from libertarian baselines are quite stringent. Even though these are satisfied in many of the cases noted above, it by no means follows that every invitation to invoke the theory of forced exchanges to alter the basic structure of individual rights to liberty and property will meet with similar success. It is important, therefore, to indicate those instances where the older, hard-edge common law rules continue to hold firm because the proposed forced exchanges do not represent any overall improvement to the status quo ante. One broad and important class of arrangements in which the common law rules hold firm are ordinary private contracts for matters such as sale, lease, and hire. In each of these situations, the creation of a competitive market tends to exhaust all the gains from trade. It is difficult to conceive of any move that trumps the competitive equilibrium that emerges from the interplay of voluntary forces. Hence, the classical principle of freedom of contract exerts a tenacious influence in this area. Thus, the usual array of wage and hour laws, the sort that were so contentious at the beginning of the last century, should all be rejected on the grounds that they cannot do better for workers than the workers could do for themselves. The same is true of efforts to impose wage, rent, and price controls on particular industries or on the economy as a whole.[43] Likewise under this model, it is not possible to make out a credible case for antidiscrimination laws with respect to employment, lending, and housing so long as ordinary individuals and firms have the full range of choices available in competitive markets. Ironically, in this area, the source of so much uneasiness rests in monopoly structures that government creates: when the state makes a given union the exclusive bargaining agent for all workers by majority vote, then some nondiscrimination principle may well be needed, especially in cases of discrimination by race, to counter potential abuses of that power.[44] Nor is there any case for either an antidiscrimination norm or usury laws in any segment of the lending market, for their effect is to freeze out high-risk customers who cannot compensate the lender in advance for the risk of default. To be sure, it is sometimes urged that these limits are needed to serve traditional libertarian ends, namely to block fraud or duress, but that remedy is wildly overinclusive when a simple disclosure requirement (e.g., the annual percentage rate on a loan) can negate any shortfall in information.

Stated generally, it is just these cases of contractual interference that give rise to the strongest passions of libertarians, and they are vindi-

---

[43] See ibid., 270–71, for Nozick's perceptive analysis of how rent control works an expropriation.

[44] See, for example, *Steele v. Louisville & Nashville Railroad Co.*, 323 U.S. 192 (1944) (new duty of fair representation to counter racial discrimination against black firemen).

cated twice over. Not only are the outcomes of these interferences consistent with the libertarians' limited theory of state power, but the case against these interventions remains every bit as strong even after we allow forced exchanges that generate social improvements. Nor does this outcome depend on some pre-political norm of pure competition. If someone looking forward from the state of nature thought that the baseline norm required wage, rent, or price controls, we could still insist on their removal on the grounds that such policies work for the long-run average disadvantage of all, especially when people have no knowledge of the roles that they will occupy once the veil of ignorance is removed.

The second area where the libertarian norms remain tenacious is on the question of state coercion for the redistribution of wealth from one person to another. Here the case is not so simple as a denunciation of theft. We do have state mechanisms that can determine conditions of eligibility for funds and trigger those according to need. But the hard question to ask is whether we can develop, in the style of Rawls, an argument that redistribution is justified as a system of social insurance that makes all better off in the state of nature than they would otherwise be. Here we find a complex trade-off between the inferior incentives that are created relative to the ability to even out the ups and downs in ways that provide gains across the board. The pervasive presence of health, life, and disability insurance in ordinary markets shows that there are demands for the smoothing of wealth across different states of the world, so the Rawlsian proposal here cannot be dismissed out of hand. But when one considers the voluntary mechanisms that have been devised to deal with questions of need, and the political risks that are associated with introducing social insurance programs of this sort, a credible case can be made that these programs do not work any kind of overall social improvement, and should be generally rejected on these grounds, notwithstanding their widespread adoption in modern times. The case for their severe limitation is, moreover, strengthened by the adoption of the rest of the program urged here, which promises a level of output and opportunity that should remove virtually all individuals from the conditions of poverty and want that could justify mandated assistance. Some modest program that deals with certain categorical disabilities (blindness, deafness, manifest incompetence, orphan status, etc.) and the like could still pass muster because such programs are relatively easy to monitor on the one hand, and give rise to little if any moral hazard from potential recipients on the other. Most generally then, the case for redistribution is far harder to make than the case for forced exchanges that produce ex post gains for all persons within the system. As a matter of political prudence, therefore, it is best to secure the programs of property rights and voluntary exchange *before* moving onto the treacherous shoals of forced redistribution of income or wealth. The guiding maxim is, redistribution *last*.

VIII. Conclusion

This essay has painted, in very broad strokes, an argument that tries to show, first, the core of good sense in the libertarian positions articulated by Nozick, and, second, their serious limitations. In so doing, I have deviated from Nozick in one particular: the willingness to allow forced exchanges to improve the state of affairs across the board from any distribution of rights that has enjoyed prior recognition. In so doing, I think that it is possible to achieve two goals simultaneously. The first is to change the criterion by which these legal arrangements are judged. The second is to show what kinds of institutions and practices should meet the tests of political legitimacy. The methodological bias in Nozick's writing is apparent from the opening sentence of *Anarchy, State, and, Utopia:* "Individuals have rights and there are things no person or group may do to them (without violating their rights)."[45] This statement aligns Nozick squarely in the deontological camp and exposes him to the relentless criticism that he cannot find any social justification for the rights that he posits but does not defend. The approach here, I believe, escapes that difficulty while preserving the best of his political instincts.

At all points, legal arrangements that protect those most private of institutions—autonomy and private property—are now rightly seen as social institutions adopted because of the overall convenience that they generate for the individuals who live subject to their rules. In each and every case the moral test has two components. The first one, which is based on the traditional criterion of a Pareto improvement, asks how anyone could prefer one legal arrangement if the second one leaves at least one person better off and no one worse off than before. The second component seeks to answer the question of how the gains from social improvements should be distributed by invoking the requirement of pro rata distribution of the gains in question. Once this approach is taken, the arguments over rights shed their deductive foundation. Each proposed claim of right has to be defended empirically for the consequences that it generates. This inquiry in turn requires that we make assumptions about how individuals act (i.e., the extent to which the rational self-interested model explains their behavior). It also introduces an element of genuine uncertainty about the resolution of difficult cases of institutional design, not only for the creation of property rights, but for the creation of the political institutions (separation of powers, checks and balances, etc.) that are used to secure them. But that is just the way it should be. Just as the libertarian cannot secure any deductive victories over his more collectivist adversaries, so too he does not suffer deductive defeats that rest on the

---

[45] *ASU,* ix.

supposed confusion of his conceptual universe.[46] The right solution depends on the knowledge that we can acquire of the world, and it is precisely because of our accumulated knowledge of various contractual and property rights regimes that I am willing to venture forth with this constrained form of libertarianism that builds on Nozick's work even as it deviates from it in many vital particulars of approach and outcome.

Law, University of Chicago; Hoover Institution

[46] For one famous attempt at inflicting such a defeat, see Robert L. Hale, "Coercion and Distribution in a Supposedly Non-Coercive State," *Political Science Quarterly* 38, no. 3 (1923): 470–94.

NATURAL RIGHTS AND POLITICAL LEGITIMACY*

By Christopher W. Morris

I. Introduction

"Individuals have rights, and there are things no person or group may do to them (without violating their rights). So strong and far-reaching are these rights that they raise the question of what, if anything, the state and its officials may do. How much room do individual rights leave for the state?"[1] As is well-known, Robert Nozick's reply to this question, in *Anarchy, State, and Utopia* (1974), is that any state more extensive than a minimal one will fail to be justified except under special circumstances (for instance, the rectification of serious wrongs). Some think that even minimal states will fail to be justified given the rights that we have. It may be that the constraints of justice leave no room for the state's exercise of its functions or even for its existence. If we possess (virtually) indefeasible natural rights to life, liberty, and possessions, then it is doubtful that the state may do very much, if anything, without violating our rights. This is Nozick's challenge.

The challenge would have passed unnoticed in the 1970s were it not for the quality of Nozick's argument. In much of the West—certainly in the political cultures influenced by the American and French revolutions—it was widely thought then, and perhaps now, that states are in large part justified to the extent to which they protect our fundamental rights. This might be thought to be the very purpose of the state. The French Declaration of the Rights of Man and of Citizen asserts: "Le but de toute association politique est la conservation des droits naturels et imprescriptibles de l'homme. Ces droits sont la liberté, la propriété, la sûreté et la résistance à l'oppression."[2] *The end of any political association is the conservation of the natural and imprescriptible rights of man. These rights are liberty, property, security, and resistance to oppression.* Americans learn at an early age that "to secure these rights"—the inalienable rights to life, liberty, and the pursuit of happiness enumerated in the Declaration of

* I am grateful to my fellow contributors to this volume and to other readers for helpful questions and comments on an earlier version of this essay and in particular to Fred Miller, David Schmidtz, and John Simmons for written comments. Ellen Paul's detailed comments have helped me, as always, to correct many confusions and errors, and Harry Dolan's excellent editing has discovered others that I have endeavored to address.

[1] Robert Nozick, *Anarchy, State, and Utopia* (New York: Basic Books, 1974), ix.

[2] Déclaration des Droits de L'Homme et du Citoyen, art. 2 (August 1789). Translation mine.

Independence—"governments are instituted among men." The thought seems to be that in the absence of just and effective government, individuals' fundamental rights are insecure. We turn to the state to secure them. Thus, we may evaluate states by how well they secure our rights and say that those that do well in this respect are justified or legitimate.

Nozick in effect challenged this conception of the justification of states, and this fact is not always appreciated. He argued that our rights are such that the state is not justified by how well it secures certain ends or meets certain goals (for instance, the respect of our rights). Rather, a state that fails to respect our rights (e.g., by instituting or maintaining certain unjust practices) fails to be justified or legitimate no matter how well it generally enforces or otherwise secures our rights (e.g., against violation by others). This would seem to be a consequence of the "historical" account of justice that Nozick sketches in Part II of *Anarchy, State, and Utopia*: "Whatever arises from a just situation by just steps is itself just."[3] Suppose that in order to secure our rights, a state violates some of them—for instance, it forbids us to enforce our own rights, or it seizes some of our assets without our permission. Then, even if a state were to prevent other violations of our rights, it would be unjust and presumably illegitimate. Nozick's attempt in Part I to show that a state *could* arise without violating anyone's rights does not show that a state that had violated people's rights would be legitimate.[4]

The authors of the Declaration of Independence may betray an awareness of this point, since the passage cited above goes on to note that governments "deriv[e] their just powers from the consent of the governed." In the absence of this consent, states presumably fail to be legitimate whatever their success in securing certain ends (for instance, the minimization of rights violations). But lack of clarity about the nature of consent, as well as many questions about state legitimacy, concealed the problems for a long time. After the publication of *Anarchy, State, and Utopia*, it was much harder to ignore them.

Suppose we have a fundamental right to liberty, one that is prior to and independent of government or the legal system. This right seems to entail that as long as one is not violating the rights of others or threatening others in ways that are unjust, others may not restrict one's liberty with-

---

[3] Nozick, *Anarchy, State, and Utopia*, 151.

[4] David Schmidtz's distinction between teleological and emergent justifications of institutions is helpful in this context. "The teleological approach seeks to justify institutions in terms of what they accomplish. The emergent approach takes justification to be an emergent property of the process by which institutions arise." David Schmidtz, "Justifying the State," *Ethics* 101, no. 1 (1990): 90. The account of justice that Nozick defends in Part II of *Anarchy, State, and Utopia* commits him to an emergent conception of justification. See also his critical discussion of "a utilitarianism of rights," the view that one may or must violate someone's rights whenever this would minimize the total quantity of rights violations in the world (*Anarchy, State, and Utopia*, 28). Someone who thought that a state's violation of people's rights would be permissible whenever it would make their rights more secure would not understand these rights, as Nozick does, as "side constraints."

out one's consent. States, however, restrict our liberty in numerous ways. So it would seem that to be justified, states must first obtain our consent. Recent discussions have made it clear that the consent in question must be genuine and that this requires that it be actual (explicit or implicit) rather than hypothetical.[5] I consent to something insofar as I actually agree, not insofar as I *would* agree if asked; consent is an *act* of the person. Earlier discussions often focused on the ways in which we might be said to consent (implicitly or tacitly) to government, perhaps by voting or merely by not moving to another country. It seems much clearer now that there is little that most people have done that could constitute the kind of actual consent, explicit or implicit, that would be required to justify a state. We cannot consent to something, at least in these contexts, unless we act voluntarily and knowing what we do. Voting and refraining from leaving the country are not acts that imply the consent needed to legitimate a state; we do not vote knowing or even believing that the act implies consent, and for the most part the choice "agree or move out" would be coercive. In general, merely accepting benefits or using resources does not constitute the requisite actual consent (explicit or implicit).

Consent is also to be distinguished from consensus or general agreement. Most forms of political organization depend to some degree on consensus or agreement. But the latter have to do largely with shared *beliefs* (or values). Sometimes terms like these are used to suggest more, but they essentially refer to agreement in belief or thought (or value). Consent, by contrast, involves the engagement of the *will* or commitment. Something counts as consent only if it is a deliberate undertaking. Ideally, an act is one of consent if it is the deliberate and effective communication of an intention to bring about a change in one's normative situation (i.e., one's rights or obligations).[6] It must be voluntary and, to some degree, informed. Consent can be explicit (express, direct), or it can be tacit or implicit (implied, indirect). Both are forms of *actual* consent. By contrast, (non-actual) hypothetical consent is not consent. If we believe that we have certain fundamental rights—for instance, rights to liberty—we may have to conclude that few if any existing states are justified or legitimate owing to lack of (actual) consent.[7]

---

[5] See especially A. John Simmons's writings, especially *Moral Principles and Political Obligations* (Princeton, NJ: Princeton University Press, 1979), chap. 3, and *On the Edge of Anarchy: Locke, Consent, and the Limits of Society* (Princeton, NJ: Princeton University Press, 1993), chaps. 3–4 and 7–8. See also Leslie Green, *The Authority of the State* (Oxford: Clarendon Press, 1988), chap. 6.

[6] What Jean Hampton calls "endorsement consent" might be interpreted as a form of genuine consent. "A regime that receives what I call *endorsement consent* gets from its subjects not just activity that maintains it but also activity that conveys their endorsement and approval of it." Jean Hampton, *Political Philosophy* (Boulder, CO: Westview Press, 1997), 96.

[7] See the works by Simmons and Green cited above in note 5. Discussions of consent are often less clear than they might be. Tacit consent is frequently confused with hypothetical consent (which is not a genuine species of consent), and agreement or consensus are often thought mistakenly to be forms of consent.

This implication of Nozick's argument may not have been apparent to most readers of *Anarchy, State, and Utopia* when the book first appeared, because of his attempt to argue in Part I that a state *could* emerge from the interactions of free persons in a "state of nature" without violating anyone's rights.[8] However, Nozick argued that more than a minimal state could not be justified: "Any state more extensive violates people's rights."[9] Yet a minimal state might also fail to be justified for lack of (actual) consent, as John Simmons rightly notes in his essay in this volume.[10] A consent theorist is normally understood to be someone who thinks that (genuine) consent is necessary to justify or legitimate a state. Nozick is not quite a consent theorist in this sense; he thinks that normally states are justified only if they obtain the consent of the governed, *except* in the circumstances described in Part I of *Anarchy, State, and Utopia*. The implications of Nozick's views, however, seem in the end virtually indistinguishable from those of most consent theorists.

A well-known reaction to the possibly anarchist implications of consent theory or of Nozick's account is to deny the premises that require consent for justification or legitimacy: since some states are justified, we do not have the rights that Nozick and others postulate. I imagine this is what many still believe. Others think that we do have these rights and that few, if any, states are justified or legitimate. I am not, however, certain that matters are quite as simple as this. Some states seem to have a kind of legitimacy, and yet they restrict our liberties in ways that seem to transgress the rights Nozick attributes to us. More needs to be said.

Consider the following possibility. Suppose there is a state that is as just as we could reasonably expect a state to be in our world. At first glance, it respects the constraints of justice and does not act unjustly. It also provides justice to those subject to its rule; it makes and enforces laws, adjudicates disputes, and provides mechanisms for collective decisions (e.g., contracts, corporate law, local governments, parliaments).[11] Some of the laws as well as a number of social programs seek to effect distributive justice. In general, government is responsive to the just interests or wishes of the governed. This state is also as efficient as we could reasonably hope. Not only do the trains run on time, but the schools instruct students to read and write and the Department of Homeland Security earns the

---

[8] Nozick's difficulty in establishing this—Part I takes up almost half of *Anarchy, State, and Utopia*—is an indication of the extent of the problem. I have argued that Nozick fails; see Christopher W. Morris, *An Essay on the Modern State* (Cambridge: Cambridge University Press, 1998), 166–71.

[9] Nozick, *Anarchy, State, and Utopia*, 149.

[10] See A. John Simmons, "Consent Theory for Libertarians," in this volume.

[11] Contracts are mechanisms for collective decisions, as they enable two or more individuals to act together. That the matter of state enforcement and adjudication of contracts is more problematic than most people think is defended in Morris, *An Essay on the Modern State*, 275–76.

respect of all. (Supporters of the privatization of transportation and education can substitute other examples.)

Suppose that this state "secures our rights" more effectively than any feasible alternative system of social organization, including anarchism. That is, our rights are less likely to be violated in a state such as this one than in other circumstances. However, this state necessarily restricts our liberty in certain important ways. Given that there are unjust and cruel people in the world, there is need for national defense and institutions for the administration of justice, and so the state forbids us from securing our own rights, except in prescribed circumstances of "self-defense." It does not allow groups of people to leave the state in order to form another state or political community (secession). To provide defense against the unjust and cruel, it appropriates a portion of our resources via taxation—something many consider "on a par with forced labor."[12] Under certain circumstances, the state requires most able-bodied citizens to serve in the military, as in the United States during World War II or in Israel today, and to participate in other collective ventures for the common good. Citizens are also compelled to serve on juries. Our hypothesized state may also make voting compulsory (with a line on the ballot for "none of the above"). We might in addition consider the possibility that we may not be permitted to do a number of things that are (genuinely) harmful to ourselves, though this adds a dimension to the thought experiment that is not, for the moment, essential. Let us at least suppose that this hypothetical state does not allow us permanently to alienate our liberty, for instance, by selling ourselves into slavery or by agreeing to onerous lifelong contracts (debt slavery, indentured servitude).

Suppose that most people in this hypothetical world live lives that are as good and as fulfilling as is typically possible in favorable circumstances. The state nevertheless appears to restrict people's liberties in a number of ways and thus to violate their right to be free, as well as their property rights. Suppose large numbers of people do not consent to these restrictions. Does the state (and its practices) fail to be justified?

Some will be tempted to deny the possibility of such a state. They may find the supposition that governments would not waste the time of jury members or the lives of conscripted soldiers too implausible to grant. This reaction is understandable, but I want to consider the question nevertheless. Suppose there were a just and relatively efficient state that secures our liberty but restricts it in a number of ways that appear to transgress our fundamental rights. Does it for that reason fail to be justified? Is it necessarily illegitimate?

---

[12] "Taxation of earnings from labor is on a par with forced labor." Nozick, *Anarchy, State, and Utopia*, 169.

II. Justification and Legitimacy

Until now I have talked rather casually about the justification and legitimacy of states, and I need to say something more. States in the sense I intend here are particular forms of political society, characteristically modern. Their jurisdiction is territorial; they claim to govern all who find themselves in their territory. The powers claimed by states are sweeping; they claim very extensive authority and typically back up these claims with considerable force.[13] States claim legitimacy. One of the central tasks of modern political philosophy is the assessment of this claim. I shall offer an account of what it means for a state to be legitimate and shall introduce a distinction between two kinds of legitimacy.

If a state is legitimate it has a certain status. At the least, its existence is permissible: it has a liberty to exist. It presumably also has a (claim-)right to exist. A state exists to the extent that a territory and its inhabitants are organized politically as I described above, when significant numbers of people comply with the laws and a good number believe the institutions to be legitimate. States are forms of governance, and they also claim certain powers, liberties, and rights related to governance. Legitimacy may also confer these. A legitimate state, we shall say, is minimally one that has a liberty, presumably a (claim-)right, to exist. It would presumably also possess the liberty or the right to establish laws and to adjudicate and to enforce these as necessary for the maintenance of order and other ends. Legitimacy in this minimal sense would be the right to exist and to rule.

The right to rule is often thought of as entailing obligations to obedience on the part of those who are ruled. Trivially, we have an obligation to obey any valid (obligation-creating) law.[14] If an obligation-creating law is valid and applies to us, then we are obligated. Often it is said that this obligation is merely "legal" and not necessarily moral; a more-than-minimal conception of legitimacy might construe the right to rule as entailing a moral obligation to obey the law and perhaps reasons to obey.[15] (Alternatively, instead of distinguishing moral and legal obligations, I prefer to say that subjects would have *genuine* obligations to a more-than-minimally legitimate state.) If a state is legitimate in this stronger sense, then it would be wrong or unjust for a citizen to violate a valid law (except in special circumstances).

---

[13] Details as well as some support for this account can be found elsewhere: for example, I have argued that states in modern times are distinctive territorial forms of political organization that claim sovereignty over their realms and independence from other states. See my *An Essay on the Modern State* (cited above in note 8); as well as my essay "The Modern State," in Gerald F. Gaus and Chandran Kukathas, eds., *The Handbook of Political Theory* (London: Sage Publications, 2004), 195–209; and my "Are States Necessarily Coercive?" (manuscript).

[14] My cumbersome formulation is due to the fact that many laws do not create or recognize obligations (e.g., power-creating laws).

[15] On reasons to obey, see my brief remarks at the conclusion of this essay.

It is useful explicitly to distinguish weaker and stronger conceptions of legitimacy. A legitimate state possesses a (claim-)right to exist and to rule. The right to exist entails obligations on the part of others not to threaten its existence in certain ways (e.g., not to attack or conquer it). We may now interpret the obligations correlative to the right to rule in different ways. A state is *minimally legitimate,* I shall say, if its right to rule entails that others are obligated not to undermine it, but are not necessarily obligated to obey it; I assume it is possible to disobey a state without undermining it. Someone would not undermine a state, for instance, by violating certain (valid) laws on occasion.[16]

By contrast, a state is *fully legitimate* if its right to rule entails an obligation of subjects, or at least citizens, to obey (each valid law).[17] This obligation may be thought of as a general obligation to obey the law, one that requires compliance with every law that applies to one except in circumstances licensed by law. The second, stronger understanding of legitimacy may be the most common one in contemporary discussions. "Justifying the state is normally thought to mean showing that there are universal obligations to obey the law. . . . [T]he goal of justification of the state is to show that, in principle, everyone within its territories is morally bound to follow its laws and edicts."[18] In addition, fully legitimate states have an *exclusive* right to exist and to rule that others may not challenge. This claim to exclusivity is captured in the popular (and in other respects misleading) Weberian characterization of the state as "a human community that (successfully) claims the *monopoly* of the legitimate use of physical force within a given territory."[19] As I have argued elsewhere, the right to use force is of minor significance compared to the state's other claimed powers. But the emphasis here on rights to monopolize is on target. John Simmons's characterization is helpful and captures my notion of full legitimacy:

---

[16] For instance, laws requiring drivers to come to a complete stop at stop signs, forbidding jaywalking, forbidding serving minors alcohol, or requiring the payment of local sales taxes on goods purchased out-of-state (in the U.S.). I pick examples of laws that most of us disobey with some frequency. Even noncompliance with more serious laws—e.g., military conscription laws and tax laws—may not undermine a state or threaten its existence. More could be said here as noncompliance with the law will undermine the state in some circumstances, but it is not essential to my point in the text.

[17] Someone is a subject in this sense if he or she is obligated by—subject to—the laws of a state. Citizens are a proper subset of the class of subjects; they are members of a state and enjoy a certain status and certain rights not extended to mere subjects.

[18] Jonathan Wolff, *An Introduction to Political Philosophy* (Oxford: Oxford University Press, 1996), 42.

[19] "[T]he right to use physical force is ascribed to other institutions or to individuals only to the extent to which the state permits it. The state is considered the sole source of the 'right' to use violence." Max Weber, "Politics as a Vocation" (1919), in *From Max Weber: Essays in Sociology,* ed. and trans. H. H. Gerth and C. Wright Mills (New York: Oxford University Press, 1946), 78 (emphases changed).

A state's (or government's) legitimacy is the complex moral right it possesses to be the exclusive imposer of binding duties on its subjects, to have its subjects comply with these duties, and to use coercion to enforce the duties. Accordingly, state legitimacy is the logical correlate of various obligations, including subjects' political obligations.[20]

But it will be helpful to invoke the weaker conception too.[21]

What establishes minimal legitimacy in my sense? Suppose a state to be just.[22] That is, suppose that it resembles the hypothetical state I described in Section I: It respects the constraints of justice and does not act unjustly. It provides justice to those subject to its rule; it makes and enforces laws, adjudicates disputes, and provides mechanisms for collective decisions (e.g., contracts, corporate law, local governments, parliaments). Some of the laws as well as a number of social programs seek to effect distributive justice. Government in general is responsive to the just interests or wishes of the governed. A state like this would be just. Suppose in addition that it is relatively efficient in its activities. Elsewhere I have argued that a relatively just and efficient state is one that is justified, and that justification confers minimal legitimacy.[23]

What is necessary or sufficient for full legitimacy? This is a matter of considerable controversy. I imagine that consent would suffice to legitimate fully a state that had certain properties, presumably those that also secure minimal legitimacy (e.g., justice).[24] If (virtually) everyone

---

[20] A. John Simmons, "Justification and Legitimacy," reprinted in Simmons, *Justification and Legitimacy: Essays on Rights and Obligations* (Cambridge: Cambridge University Press, 2001), 130.

[21] For those conversant with the literature, the distinction I am drawing between minimal and full legitimacy is not Simmons's important distinction between justification and legitimacy. The conception of minimal legitimacy that I am sketching is different both from many popular conceptions of legitimacy and from Simmons's notion of justification. Christopher Wellman employs a minimalist conception of legitimacy, albeit not mine: "[P]olitical legitimacy is distinct from political obligation; the former is about what a state is permitted to do, and the latter concerns what a citizen is obligated to do." Christopher H. Wellman, "Liberalism, Samaritanism, and Political Legitimacy," *Philosophy and Public Affairs* 25, no. 3 (1996): 212.

[22] "Without justice, what are kingdoms but great robber bands?" Augustine, *Political Writings*, ed. Ernest L. Fortin and Douglas Kries, trans. Michael W. Tkacz and Douglas Kries (Indianapolis, IN: Hackett Publishing, 1994), 30. "Justice is the first virtue of social institutions, as truth is of systems of thought." John Rawls, *A Theory of Justice* (Cambridge, MA: Harvard University Press, 1971), 3.

[23] Morris, *An Essay on the Modern State*, chaps. 4 and 6. In this book I do not explicitly draw the distinction between minimal and full legitimacy that I make here.

[24] Simmons reads Locke to say that a limited state's justification is "a necessary condition for the legitimation (by actual consent) of any particular limited state's rule. Consent is necessary—but not sufficient—for legitimacy and political obligation, (in part) because the justification of a type of state is necessary for consent to a token of that type to be binding. We cannot bind ourselves by consent to immoral arrangements.... A state must be on balance morally acceptable and a 'good bargain' for our consent to succeed in legitimating it." Simmons, "Justification and Legitimacy," 129 n. 18. See also Joseph Raz, *The Morality of Freedom* (Oxford: Clarendon Press, 1986), 88–94.

governed by a just state genuinely consents to its rule, then it is fully legitimate. Under these conditions, consent would suffice to confer full legitimacy. There may be less agreement, however, on the question of the necessity of consent.

Return to the hypothetical state described earlier. That state secured our rights in an efficient manner, more effectively, I hypothesized, than alternative arrangements. I should think that this state would be minimally legitimate. Its existence is permissible; indeed, I should think it has a right to exist and that its subjects (and others) are obligated not to threaten or undermine its continued existence. In addition, I should think that it possesses a right to establish laws, to adjudicate them, and to enforce them, and that others have an obligation not to prevent it from doing so. In general, given the considerable virtues of this state, I should think that others have an obligation not to interfere with it or to undermine its existence and governance. I make, however, no claims about this state's full legitimacy.

This hypothetical state's right to rule would not, however, be exclusive *de jure* as we normally would expect it to be. Rather, it would be exclusive only insofar as no competitor could better secure our rights. Suppose that this state is less efficient in securing our rights than I hypothesized: in certain respects it wastes resources and fails to do effectively all that it might. Suppose another set of agents and institutions could do better and succeeds in taking over the state without harming anyone. It would not have violated any right of the (prior) state.[25]

We should note something surprising here, namely, that the obligation not to interfere or to undermine is one that all persons would have, not merely citizens of the state or those otherwise subject to its laws (for instance, by virtue of residency). By contrast, the obligation to obey correlative to full legitimacy is normally understood to fall only to citizens and to other subjects of the law.

III. NATURAL RIGHTS

We must return to where we began, with the question of whether our rights leave any room for states to exercise their functions or even to exist. For instance, if we possess (virtually) indefeasible natural rights to life, liberty, and (some of our) possessions, then it is doubtful that states (absent our consent) may do very much, if anything, without violating our rights. The just and efficient state hypothesized earlier would be an incoherent fantasy.

Nozick is usually read as supposing that we have a number of natural rights. I do not want to determine whether this interpretation is correct or what are the best ways to understand traditional natural rights. My inter-

---

[25] Readers will recognize Hobbes's "sovereignty by acquisition" here.

est is in the rights we possess. I think that, in a number of senses, we have some natural rights. We seem to have a right to life and a right to liberty that are natural in the sense of being prior to and independent of convention and held by virtue of our being creatures of a certain kind (i.e., rational agents with interests often at variance with those of others). We may also have limited prior rights to property, but I am less certain about this. Rights of this kind necessarily do not depend for their existence on government and law, even if the state makes them more "secure." As rights that are prior to and independent of convention, they are also prior to and independent of any actual "social contract." In the metaphorical (and misleading) terms of seventeenth- and eighteenth-century philosophy, they are rights that are held in a "state of nature." Thomas Hobbes thinks that humans have no claim-rights prior to and independently of the state, so he denies that there are any natural rights in the sense relevant to my concerns. David Hume's account of justice is conventionalist, and thus he too appears to deny that there are any natural rights.[26]

Contemporary contractarians such as James Buchanan and David Gauthier argue that we can have rights prior to and independently of government.[27] Their accounts, however innovative, are nevertheless conventionalist, and under certain conditions a number of human agents may fail to have any rights. Gauthier is, of course, a hypothetical contractarian; on his view, actual conventions are not a necessary condition for the existence of rights. Nevertheless, neither he nor Buchanan attributes moral standing to all human agents by virtue of their natures, independently of certain interpersonal relations.[28] The conventional nature of our fundamental rights is an essential feature of the Hobbesian and Humean

---

[26] Note that rights can be natural in the ways described without committing one either to understanding them as indefeasible or to moral realism. Natural rights, much like natural duties, might be capable of being overridden by other considerations. And a projectivist or quasi-realist account of morals should be able to endorse such rights as well as natural duties.

[27] See James Buchanan, *The Limits of Liberty* (Chicago, IL: University of Chicago Press, 1975), chap. 2; and David Gauthier, *Morals by Agreement* (Oxford: Clarendon Press, 1986), chap. 7. See also Morris, *An Essay on the Modern State*, chap. 6.

[28] It is possible our natural rights may be *forfeited*, for instance, by committing serious injustices against others. (Locke suggests this possibility in his *Second Treatise of Government*, chap. 4, sec. 23. See A. John Simmons, *The Lockean Theory of Rights* [Princeton, NJ: Princeton University Press, 1992], especially 148–61.) But an important difference between the conventionalist rights defended by Gauthier and natural rights is that it is possible on the first view for some humans to lack rights even though they have not by any act forfeited them. For instance, agents who have little to offer others and in whom no one takes an interest may lack moral standing in Gauthier's theory. (Something has moral standing insofar as it is owed moral consideration—for instance, others are obligated to it.) Rights are held by virtue of conventions of various kinds, and it is possible that some agents, through no fault of their own, will fail to satisfy the conditions necessary for the attribution of moral standing. In some historical circumstances, it is possible that morals by agreement would not deem unjust a system of slavery or would not consider slavery an injustice to the slaves. See Christopher W. Morris, "Justice, Reasons, and Moral Standing," in *Rational Commitment and Social Justice: Essays for Gregory Kavka*, ed. Jules L. Coleman and Christopher W. Morris (Cambridge: Cambridge University Press, 1998), 186–207.

contractarian tradition to this day. By contrast, most neo-Kantian contractarians, including John Rawls, do not condition moral standing on the satisfaction of certain interpersonal conditions (such as the prospect of mutual gain). Aside from our basic moral standing—that accorded to all "free and equal persons" by neo-Kantian thinkers—most of justice for these theorists seems to be "constructed," so it is not clear that they admit the existence of natural rights in my sense of the term.

Most norms of justice require determination or specification, and this is typically customary—for instance, the implications of contract or property may differ from place to place, depending on custom or positive law. And some norms of justice seem to be largely conventional—for instance, norms governing fidelity, truth-telling, mutual aid or rescue, and assistance to strangers. But it is hard to believe that all of justice is conventional.[29]

Assume that we are right in thinking that parts of justice are natural and not conventional.[30] In order to determine the implications of our natural rights for the justification and legitimacy of states, we need to know more about the nature and bases of these rights. Contrast two conceptions of the purpose and nature of rights found in the literature. On one view, rights serve to protect the interests or well-being of the right-holder, who is the beneficiary of the correlative obligation(s). This is the interest or benefit conception of rights. By contrast, the choice or will conception of rights conceives their purpose to be the protection of people's choices. On this view, the freedom of agents to choose among alternatives is to be protected by duties imposed on others and owed to the agent.[31]

Rights as I have been understanding them in this essay are relations connecting a number of agents: the subject(s)—the right-holder(s)—and the object(s)—the agent(s) against whom the right is held, the bearer(s) of the correlative duty or duties. Rights have content: that which the right is a right *to* or that which the duty is a duty *to do* (or refrain from doing). It is customary to distinguish between rights in this sense—claim-rights—and (mere) liberties or Hohfeldian privileges. Someone has a liberty to do something if and only if he or she has no duty not to do that thing (i.e., is free from a duty to refrain from doing it). A claim-right to x is typically accompanied by a liberty to x. But such a claim-right may be conjoined with a duty not to refrain from x. For instance, the right to vote could be conjoined with a duty to vote (as in our hypothesized just state). More

---

[29] "One part of what is politically just is natural, and the other part legal." Aristotle, *Nicomachean Ethics*, trans. Terence Irwin (Indianapolis, IN: Hackett Publishing, 1985), 1134b19–20.

[30] Much more, of course, needs to be said about the distinction, and I am certain that many difficult questions are hidden by my quick characterizations.

[31] The origin of the distinction(s) between benefit and choice accounts is H. L. A. Hart's essay, "Bentham on Legal Rights" (1973), reprinted in H. L. A. Hart, *Essays on Bentham: Studies in Jurisprudence and Political Theory* (Oxford: Clarendon Press, 1982), 162–93. My way of drawing the familiar distinction will not necessarily correspond with others.

importantly, claim-rights can be accompanied by *powers*, the capacity to change one's normative relations. The right to *x* might be accompanied by the power to release others from their correlative obligations. For instance, someone may waive a right to be repaid a debt. To be able to alienate a right—for instance, to transfer it to another in exchange for something—is to possess a power. The (legal) right to vote is not alienable—we cannot transfer it to another—and some think that the right to life is similarly inalienable. This is to say that these claim-rights are not accompanied by certain powers.

Understanding fundamental rights as interest-protecting or choice-protecting may affect both the content of the rights and their accompanying elements. For instance, if the right to life is interest- or welfare-protecting, perhaps the right-holder will not be understood to possess the power to release others from their correlative duties (not to kill); by contrast, if our concern lies with the protection of choices, then we may understand the right to be alienable and the right-holder to possess the power to waive or to extinguish it.[32]

Nozick's well-known speculative remarks in *Anarchy, State, and Utopia* about the foundations of these rights suggest a choice-protecting conception. It is impermissible, Nozick suggests, to treat beings like ourselves as mere means to the ends of others. This may be because of the importance of our choices for the meaning of our lives: "A person's shaping his life in accordance with some overall plan is his way of giving meaning to his life. . . ."[33] Our fundamental rights may have something to do with the meaning of life for creatures such as ourselves. And there are other reasons for thinking that many fundamental rights are best understood as choice-protecting. Making choices is or can be good for us.

Now if our natural right to liberty is choice-protecting, then it would seem that consent is a necessary condition for the legitimacy (minimal or full) of states. If this is the case, then it is hard to imagine that any of our states, including the efficient and just one hypothesized earlier, are legitimate. Natural rights seem to constrain states by requiring them to secure the consent of the governed.

This is not an unreasonable interpretation of our natural rights.[34] But we should be careful and not be misled by the distinction between interest-

---

[32] But consider the matter broached above, the power to alienate one's right to be free and to sell oneself into slavery (for payment of debts or some other reason). Interest-protecting theorists may deny right-holders such a power. But it is not clear that choice-protecting theorists will necessarily be inclined to accord it to them; after all, once the agreement has been consummated, the voluntary slave no longer has any choices to make. But others will argue differently.

[33] Nozick, *Anarchy, State, and Utopia*, 50.

[34] I should note that some read Nozick's proviso on the appropriation of unowned resources as a basic interest-protecting right to the level of well-being one would have attained in the absence of appropriation. The interpretation of Nozick's account is more complicated than I have suggested. See Hillel Steiner, *An Essay on Rights* (Oxford: Blackwell, 1994), 236 n. 13.

protecting and choice-protecting conceptions of rights. These should be understood as alternative accounts of the immediate purpose or aim of rights: we have rights in order to protect interests or choices. The question is *what* is protected, interests or choices? Another question is *why* are they protected? It could be that a person's freedom, a sphere of choice, ought to be protected because it is in that person's interests to have that sphere of choice. The ground for the choice-protecting rights of people may be their interests.[35]

The right of liberty, we may think, is best understood as a choice-protecting right. We need, however, to inquire deeper into the grounds for this right. Nozick's speculative remarks about choice and the meaning of life do motivate a choice-protecting conception of the right of liberty. But so do other kinds of considerations. Choice-protecting rights may have their sources in their contribution to making our lives go well. Contrast people and nonhuman animals that lack the capacities necessary for rational agency of the kind we typically possess. The latter can have good lives—lives that are good for them, given their capabilities—without striving to do the sorts of things that agents such as ourselves typically do. John Stuart Mill views such lives as those of "a pig satisfied." He is right to think that such lives are less than what humans are capable of or should strive for, but he is wrong if his remark expresses contempt for such lives. A satisfied pig or turtle, which lives a long life, relatively free of suffering, and is able to reproduce, lives a good life—a good life for a pig or turtle. The lives we can live are different given our different capabilities; these affect what is good for us.

A good life for us will involve the exercise of our agency and of our capacities to choose. The exercise of these capacities contributes to our well-being both in itself and instrumentally. It contributes instrumentally to our lives going well simply because good choices will bring benefits and thus improve things for us. And it contributes intrinsically insofar as the exercise of our distinctive capacities is itself fulfilling or constitutive of our good. Given the sorts of creatures we are, exercise of our agency is important and should be protected by a choice-protecting right to liberty. Humans who lack the full capacities required for agency—young children, defective adults—do not need choice-protecting rights, at least insofar as they do not possess or can never acquire these capacities.

The intrinsic value of choice is especially important for the consideration of the right to liberty. Even if some choices fail to be instrumentally valuable, they may retain their intrinsic value. As some have argued, rights to choose allow the right-holder to choose wrongly.[36] Note, how-

---

[35] David Schmidtz's notes have helped me express this point more clearly.

[36] See Jeremy Waldron, "A Right to Do Wrong" (1981), reprinted in his *Liberal Rights: Collected Papers 1981–1991* (Cambridge: Cambridge University Press, 1993), 63–87. It is a property generally of (genuine) authority that it may bind even when in error. See Raz, *The Morality of Freedom*, 47–48, 60–62, and 159.

ever, that the intrinsic value of exercising one's agency by a mistaken decision to take one's own life (e.g., teenage suicide motivated by anger at one's parents) or a mistaken decision permanently to alienate one's liberty (e.g., by a lifelong contract of indentured servitude) would be outweighed by the consequent losses of one's life or liberty. So grounding a right to liberty (or a right to life) on the contribution of agency to our lives going well might not accord one the same powers as the line of thinking that Nozick sketches in *Anarchy, State, and Utopia*.

Suppose, then, that our right to liberty is choice-protecting and is grounded in the contribution of agency to our lives going well. Suppose in addition that a just and relatively efficient state, like the one hypothesized earlier, "secures these rights," that is, ensures that they are unlikely to be violated. Then might not such a state be minimally legitimate without obtaining our consent? Might we not say that "to secure these rights, governments are instituted among men" and that we may "alter or abolish" any government that "becomes destructive of these ends" (i.e., the security of our rights) without endorsing the principle that governments "deriv[e] their just powers from the consent of the governed"?

In *An Essay on the Modern State,* I supposed that a state that was just and relatively efficient would be legitimate in the sense I now dub minimal. It would have a right to exist and a right to rule, and we, citizens or not, would have an obligation not to undermine its rule or interfere with its rule. I then asked whether a state that is legitimate in this minimal sense would possess the full set of powers that states characteristically claim— most importantly, sovereignty. Something is sovereign insofar as it is the ultimate source of political authority in a realm, and I interpreted this authority to be comprehensive and supreme in Joseph Raz's sense: comprehensive in claiming the right to regulate any kind of behavior, and supreme in claiming the right to regulate all other sources of authority within its realm.[37] I concluded that minimally legitimate states typically would not possess the full powers of sovereignty. In effect, they would not be fully legitimate. I have been suggesting in this essay that even if natural rights block the full legitimacy of states, they need not block states' minimal legitimacy. To the extent that a state is just and relatively efficient, it will be minimally legitimate and we will have obligations not to undermine its existence or interfere with its governance.[38]

A state's minimal legitimacy need not imply more; that is, it need not imply that we will have an obligation to obey as this is traditionally understood. There is considerable skepticism in the contemporary literature that this more demanding obligation can be sustained. My skepti-

---

[37] See Joseph Raz, *Practical Reason and Norms* (1975; reprint, Princeton, NJ: Princeton University Press, 1990), 150–52, and Morris, *An Essay on the Modern State,* chap. 7.

[38] A comparison of this account to that defended by David Copp will have to await another occasion. See David Copp, "The Idea of a Legitimate State," *Philosophy and Public Affairs* 28, no. 1 (1999): 3–45.

cism may be stronger than that of many. A general obligation to obey the state requires compliance with every valid law or directive that applies to one except in circumstances prescribed by the state. It is commonly assumed that someone so obligated always has a reason (of a stringent or preemptive kind) to comply. But it is possible to deny this and to think that obligations, legal or moral, do not always entail reasons (of the right kind) to comply. In moral theory, the first position is labeled "internalism": an obligation to do x is always a reason (of a particular kind) to do x. (Technically, this is one kind of internalism. "Externalism" is the term for the family of anti-internalist positions.) If one rejects internalism, it will be possible to think that a state may be fully legitimate and that we nevertheless lack reasons to comply with its laws or directives in all instances. So one could admit an obligation to obey without conceding the question about reasons for action. In my view, it is the latter (reasons for action) that ought to be the focus of our attention, but I have followed the literature in formulating the questions in terms of obligation. Given that I do not think that states will possess full legitimacy, it does not matter very much for my concerns in this essay.

IV. CONCLUSION

The existence of natural rights appears to threaten the legitimacy of states. If we have a natural right to liberty, it is hard to see how a state could be legitimate without first obtaining the (genuine) consent of the governed. The "historical" account of justice Part II of *Anarchy, State, and Utopia* implies as much, but Nozick's attempt in Part I to show that a state could emerge from the just interactions of individuals without obtaining their consent may obscure the threat that natural rights pose to state legitimacy. The matter may not be as simple as it might first appear. We need to distinguish between minimal and full conceptions of legitimacy, and we need to be clearer about the kinds of natural rights that we possess.

A legitimate state has a right to exist and a right to rule. The right to exist entails obligations on the part of others not to threaten its existence in certain ways (e.g., not to attack or conquer it). A legitimate state also possesses the right to establish laws and to adjudicate and enforce these as necessary. A state is *minimally legitimate* if its right to rule entails that others are obligated not to undermine it but are not necessarily obligated to obey it. By contrast, a state is *fully legitimate* if its right to rule entails an obligation of subjects, or at least citizens, to obey (each valid law). This obligation may be thought of as the general obligation to obey the law, one that requires compliance with every law that applies to one except in circumstances licensed by law (e.g., justified or excused disobedience). In addition, fully legitimate states have an *exclusive* right to exist and to rule that others may not challenge, a right that is exclusive *de jure*.

It seems most plausible to understand our natural right to liberty as a choice-protecting right rather than an interest-protecting one. This would suggest that consent is necessary for the full legitimacy of states. However, a choice-protecting natural right to liberty might be grounded in our interests or welfare. I suggest that understanding the right to be free in this manner might not commit us to requiring consent for minimal legitimacy. Thus, even if natural rights effectively block the full legitimacy of states—on the assumption that rarely, if ever, will the requisite consent be forthcoming—they may allow minimal state legitimacy.

Well-behaved states may possess minimal legitimacy, and to this extent the skeptical implications of Nozick's framework may not be as great as expected. But he was right to be skeptical that states are fully legitimate.

Philosophy, University of Maryland

CONSENT THEORY FOR LIBERTARIANS*

By A. John Simmons

I. Introduction

It is curious that in libertarian political philosophy there is almost no discussion of the traditional problem of political obligation.[1] I call this "curious" not only because of my own belief that this problem is centrally important in political philosophy, but also because libertarians would seem to be oriented in political philosophy in a way that would make the problem of political obligation particularly central for *them*. After all, many libertarians regularly appeal to the insights of the so-called classical liberals, such as Locke, for whom the problem obviously occupied center stage. And many libertarians, like many of those classical liberals whose works they admire, both (a) insist on fundamental individual rights of personal liberty and property (and regard as uniformly unjustified self-interested or paternalistic or moralistic infringement of those rights) and (b) still accept (unlike the minority strain of libertarian anarchists) the possibility of morally legitimate political societies.[2] This seems to make the question of the source and nature of (and the limits on) our obligations to governments or fellow citizens absolutely basic and not at all easy, requiring a kind of delicate balancing act of affirming strong individual rights while still accepting justified political obligations. Finally, of course, libertarians' familiar emphasis on freedom of contract, and more

* Earlier versions of this essay were presented at the University of Michigan, Virginia Commonwealth University, and Brown University. For their lively discussions and helpful suggestions for the improvement of this essay, I am grateful to those audiences and to my fellow contributors to this volume. And for their careful reading and comments, I thank the editors of *Social Philosophy and Policy*.

[1] Libertarians do sometimes discuss purported justifications of the state and utilize the ideas of state (or governmental) legitimacy or authority, but they regularly do so without considering the related (on some theories correlative) notion of political obligation. It is one thing to give an account of what justifies the state or of what governments may and may not do to their citizens. It is another to give an account of what citizens or subjects are morally required to do (for instance, in the way of supporting government and obeying the law) and why they are required to do it. Libertarians have mostly appeared to presume certain positions on this latter issue, rather than explicitly stating and arguing for them. In what follows I will suggest that this approach is a mistake, that the issue is too complex to be dealt with by presumption.

[2] Exactly what kind of political society non-anarchist libertarians accept varies considerably, sometimes in substance and sometimes only in terminology. For instance, many libertarians reject the possibility of a legitimate *state* (usually meaning by this the distinctive contemporary form of the state) but accept the possibility of legitimate *government* or legitimate political *society*. Others accept the possibility of legitimate states, but only of more minimal states than the contemporary ones with which we are all most familiar.

generally on free consent as the most plainly legitimate basis for liberty-limiting arrangements (such as those involved in political societies), makes it seem natural for libertarians to centrally defend, with Locke, a consent theory of political obligation.

Strangely, though, libertarian political philosophers have not participated, by and large, in philosophical debates about political obligation, nor do libertarian political writings regularly even mention the problem in passing.[3] My objects in this essay will be several, beginning with an examination of *why* libertarians seem so uninterested in the problem. I will then try to argue that they are mistaken (on their own terms) in this neglect, and that, in fact, consistency with their most familiar claims about personal rights requires them to defend a theory of political obligation that grounds such obligations in actual, personal consent. Finally, and more importantly I think, I will maintain that if libertarians did defend such a theory, their view would be the *correct* account of political obligation and state legitimacy—despite the theory's current unpopularity—and I will argue that familiar contemporary objections to actual consent theories of political obligation and legitimacy are misguided. This is, to be sure, not really a defense of libertarianism, being only a carefully qualified defense of one aspect of the political philosophy that libertarians (along with the rest of us) *should* (but mostly seem not to) accept. As such, my arguments should be understood to bear at least as much on the concerns of *non*libertarian political philosophers as on those of libertarians.

I should note at this point my awareness that very little can be said about libertarianism that is both general and true. There are too many varieties of and purported foundations for libertarian thought for sound descriptive generalizations to be easy to find or for sound general critiques or evaluations to be confidently made. Libertarians who base their views in strong rights of self-ownership or strong rights to personal liberty will often diverge at important points, both from each other and from those of their libertarian comrades who begin with utilitarian or with contractual/mutual-advantage-style moral theories. And, of course, so-called left-libertarians depart from right-libertarians in numerous and

---

[3] Virtually none of the many books and articles specifically on political obligation (or on the duty to obey the law) produced during the past three decades has a libertarian author. The libertarian view that is most discussed in this literature is that of Robert Nozick. But even Nozick does not explicitly mention the problem of political obligation, despite the facts that two of his principal targets—H. L. A. Hart and John Rawls—are both centrally concerned with it (Hart in his account of "mutuality of restrictions" and Rawls in his defense of a natural duty of justice) and that Nozick's discussion of the principle of fairness has clear implications for debates about political obligation. As just a few of many possible further examples, none of the following substantial libertarian works appears to contain any explicit reference to the problem of political obligation: Tibor R. Machan, ed., *The Libertarian Reader* (Totowa, NJ: Rowman & Littlefield, 1982); Jan Narveson, *The Libertarian Idea* (Philadelphia, PA: Temple University Press, 1988); and David Boaz, *Libertarianism: A Primer* (New York: Free Press, 1997).

fundamental ways.[4] That said, however, I think the comments on libertarian political thought that I will make here apply at least quite widely across the range of possible libertarian political philosophies.

II. Consent vs. Minimalism

To begin, then, why this peculiar neglect by libertarians of the classical problem of political obligation? One possibility, of course, is that most libertarians simply never took seriously the claims of the state in the first place; another is that they have been too busy explaining and criticizing the excesses of bloated and tyrannical actual states to worry much about the more ideal conditions under which genuine political obligation and political legitimacy are possible. A third possibility is that many libertarians are simply *presuming* the truth of a consent theory of political obligation, without bothering to state this presumption (perhaps because they take it as too obvious to state). David Boaz of the Cato Institute, for instance, in his book *Libertarianism: A Primer*, without ever explicitly mentioning the problem of the source of our special obligations to governments or fellow citizens, at one point simply *defines* government as "the *consensual* organization by which we adjudicate disputes, defend our rights, and provide for certain common needs."[5] Here it is plain that Boaz really intends either to define only *legitimate* government or else by fiat to deny the title of "government" to apparent governments that are *non*consensual organizations. Either way, his remarks appear to simply presume consent theory standards for governmental legitimacy and political obligation.

What is striking about Boaz's pronouncement—aside from how much is left unsaid—is that it might seem to be in reasonably obvious tension with Boaz's earlier contention that the sole proper "role of government is

---

[4] On left-libertarianism, see Peter Vallentyne and Hillel Steiner, eds., *The Origins of Left-Libertarianism: An Anthology of Historical Writings* (Houndmills, UK: Palgrave, 2000); and Peter Vallentyne and Hillel Steiner, eds., *Left-Libertarianism and Its Critics: The Contemporary Debate* (Houndmills, UK: Palgrave, 2000). Vallentyne characterizes left-libertarianism as combining the familiar libertarian commitment to full self-ownership with the view that "natural resources . . . may be privately appropriated only with the permission of, or with a significant payment to, the members of society" (*Left-Libertarianism and Its Critics*, 1).

[5] David Boaz, *Libertarianism: A Primer*, 187 (my emphasis). Boaz contrasts government with the *state*, which is "a coercive organization asserting or enjoying a monopoly over the use of physical force in some geographic area and exercising power over its subjects" (187). Libertarians, like most theorists of the state, define the state in terms of its coercive powers, but libertarians tend to mean by coercion "*unjustified* coercion." For a dramatic example, consider Murray Rothbard's definition of the state as "an organization which possesses either or both (in actual fact, almost always both) of the following characteristics: (a) it acquires its revenue by physical coercion (taxation); and (b) it achieves a compulsory monopoly of force and of ultimate decision-making power over a given territorial area. Both of these essential activities of the State necessarily constitute criminal aggression and depredation of the just rights of property of its subjects (including self-ownership)." See Murray Rothbard, *The Ethics of Liberty* (Atlantic Highlands, NJ: Humanities Press, 1982), 171.

to protect people's rights."[6] If citizens unanimously consent to governmental institutions, of course, those citizens will have consensual rights against one another that the institutions not be undermined and that their rules be uniformly enforced (and they will also have obligations to comply with governmental rules). So there is nothing odd on its face about a libertarian asserting both that legitimate governments are confined to protecting rights and that their legitimate powers are consensual in origin. But the tension between these two theses is more apparent if one attends to *which* rights Boaz thinks it proper for governments to be protecting. Like any right-libertarian, Boaz has in mind a relatively limited role for government: the rights a legitimate government enforces are simply those implied by the "one fundamental human right"—that is, "the right to live your life as you choose so long as you don't infringe on the equal rights of others."[7] This fundamental right, he thinks, implies (or perhaps is identical to) a natural right of self-ownership, which in turn implies rights to be free of interference by others in one's performance of innocent actions, including one's making, keeping, and using property and one's making and having honored contracts with others.[8] Thus, there seem to be many rights that legitimate governments *must* not curtail, apparently even if such curtailments are *consented* to.

The tension to which I am pointing, then, is this: On the one hand, libertarians tend to believe that we enjoy virtually absolute freedom of contract, so that we can legitimate by our unanimous consent (and undertake obligations to uphold and comply with) virtually any kind of arrangement, organization, or institutional structure. This consensualist strain of libertarian thought thus appears to imply that virtually *any* kind of government or state can, in principle, be legitimate (and owed political obligations), including, say, socialist governments. On the other hand, the minimalist strain of libertarianism implies that only reasonably limited governmental arrangements can be legitimate—those that preserve and defend extensive rights of individual liberty and self-ownership, those that refrain from forced redistribution of property, those that do not limit freedom of contract by making morally alienable rights legally inalienable (and so on). But, of course, if all rights are alienable, then the right to enjoy minimal political arrangements is alienable as well. It may be *imprudent* for us to agree to surrender our right to be free of extensive government; but it must be morally possible for us to do so, since a person's imprudence does not, for libertarians, limit her right to alienate rights (provided only that this imprudence does not result from her having been, for example, reduced by illness or temporary incapacitation to a nonagent, coerced by others, or denied by them information to which she is entitled).

[6] Boaz, *Libertarianism: A Primer*, 127.
[7] Ibid., 59.
[8] Ibid., 64–82.

The observation that this tension exists in libertarian thought is not new or exciting.[9] But it does allow us to see, I think, why libertarians have tended to ignore the problem of political obligation. In their consensualist moments, libertarians can see consent theory standards of legitimacy and political obligation as no more than painfully obvious implications of the strong natural rights to freedom of contract and freedom from coercion that they embrace. As such, the implied theory of legitimacy and political obligation barely requires stating. And in their minimalist moments, a theory of political obligation may simply seem to libertarians to be altogether unnecessary. After all, if governments are in fact just performing their minimalist role of enforcing our basic natural rights, then it may seem that they are doing no more than requiring each of us to discharge obligations toward others (i.e., obligations not to violate their natural rights) that we had all along—obligations that are natural and that we would possess and could be legitimately required to discharge even if no political societies existed. No special theory of *political* obligation (owed to our government or to other persons qua fellow citizens) seems to be required to explain how we come to have enforceable obligations toward others when those obligations are logically *pre-political* and enforceable in nature. Government is simply taking on the enforcement task that private individuals would otherwise have to bear themselves.

III. PROBLEMS FOR MINIMALISTS

This tension between the consensualist and the minimalist strains of libertarian thought—along with the attendant obscuring of questions about political obligation—appears centrally in the most widely known and discussed of contemporary libertarian works in political philosophy: Robert Nozick's *Anarchy, State, and Utopia* (1974). The minimalist strain in Nozick's defense of libertarian political philosophy is obvious, especially in Part 2 of the book: "The minimal state is the most extensive state that can be justified. Any state more extensive violates people's rights." This minimal state is "the only morally legitimate state."[10]

The consensualist strain may not be quite so prominently displayed by Nozick, but it is equally present. Part 1 of his book is an attempt to show how a state could and (within limits) would arise from a state of nature without anyone's rights being violated in the process. One might think that an easy solution to Nozick's problem would be this: all of the people within a territory could simply come together and unanimously consent to the authority of a state, removing with their consent any concerns that

---

[9] Ellen Frankel Paul, for instance, points to a similar tension in her essay "The Time-Frame Theory of Governmental Legitimacy," in Jeffrey Paul, ed., *Reading Nozick* (Totowa, NJ: Rowman & Littlefield, 1981), 271–72.

[10] Robert Nozick, *Anarchy, State, and Utopia* (New York: Basic Books, 1974), 149 and 333.

the state might be violating their rights. Nozick could not, I think, deny that this *could* happen, and that the result would be a legitimate state. But in *Anarchy, State, and Utopia*, he is plainly concerned to explain how a state could arise under slightly less fanciful or idealized conditions. So the story Nozick actually tells involves the creation by individuals in the state of nature of numerous, small voluntary mutual-protective associations, aimed at addressing their lack of security and lack of power to enforce their own rights.[11] What makes the demands of such associations on their clients morally legitimate is simply that each client has freely consented to participate in (or to pay a share of the cost of) the defense of the rights of all of the association's clients. Similarly, when competition for clients among such associations eventually produces a dominant protective association within a territory,[12] the legitimacy of its demands will also be grounded in its clients' consent.

Only in the final stage of Nozick's story in Part 1—in which a genuine minimal state at last arises when nonclient "independents" in the territory are forced to accept membership and are compensated for their lost rights[13]—do legitimacy and obligation appear to turn on anything other than free personal consent. But, of course, the "principle of compensation"[14] by which Nozick attempts to justify this final move is probably the *least* libertarian-looking component of the entire book (as well as one of the least independently plausible basic principles defended in Part 1).[15] So, while Nozick is surely correct in denying that he is (like Locke) explaining the state in terms of a unanimous social compact,[16] the obligations of clients/citizens and the rights of associations/states are still in his story grounded for the most part in personal consent, even if this is consent

---

[11] Ibid., 12–13.

[12] Ibid., 15–17.

[13] Ibid., 101–119.

[14] Ibid., 82–83.

[15] What libertarian would argue that independents (i.e., those who have, at considerable cost, *resisted* incorporation into group protection schemes) can be legitimately coerced to join political society, so long as they are given *government* by way of compensation? It is hard to find a way to read Nozick's compensation arguments as anything other than a straightforward abandonment of his own (and libertarianism's) commitment to viewing rights as genuine "side constraints" on the actions of others—an abandonment motivated by Nozick's eagerness to defeat the individualist anarchist. Rights conceived as side constraints necessarily involve a sphere of protected choice (liberty, autonomy) for the rights-holder, not just a guaranteed level of well-being or personal utility. To use the moral analogue of the language most favored by legal theorists in their discussions of legal rights, Nozick appears in most of Part 1 of *Anarchy, State, and Utopia* to view entitlements as protected by *property* rules, but in his compensation arguments he appears to view entitlements as protected only by *liability* rules—this latter "protection" usually being regarded as no real protection at all by those influenced by classical liberal theories of rights. See, e.g., Guido Calabresi and A. Douglas Melamed, "Property Rules, Liability Rules, and Inalienability: One View of the Cathedral" (especially Parts 1–3) and Jules L. Coleman and Jody Kraus, "Rethinking the Theory of Legal Rights," both in Jules L. Coleman, ed., *Rights and Their Foundations* (New York: Garland Publishing, Inc., 1994).

[16] Nozick, *Anarchy, State, and Utopia*, 18 and 132.

given in stages and over a period of time. Nozick does not, of course, refer directly to the problem of political obligation, nor is his language the language of consent theory. But during that time (in Part 1) in which he keeps his argument within recognizably libertarian bounds, he reasons like a consent theorist.[17]

The minimal state of Part 2 of *Anarchy, State, and Utopia*, then, seems to be defended as the sole possible legitimate state in minimalist terms (i.e., as doing no more than enforcing our basic moral rights), while the minimal state of Part 1 gets its blessing from Nozick in consensualist terms. Yet we know that Nozick insists that we possess an unlimited moral power to alienate our rights and to undertake new obligations by free consent, such that even free contracts into slavery are morally binding.[18] How, then, can he avoid the tension noted above, in which unanimous free consent could in principle legitimate an extensive state that was declared illegitimate by Nozick's own minimalist standards? It is presumably insufficient to mumble something about this being a very unlikely development or about the imprudence of consensually empowering a modern redistributive state.

We might try the following. Perhaps Nozick means (in Part 2) that the minimal state is the only state that can be legitimate (and can be owed obligations of support and compliance) *without* unanimous consent from its citizens/subjects.[19] Since all such a minimal state does is enforce citizens' preexisting natural rights and obligations, there can be no moral objections to its operations or demands.[20] The minimalist standard of legitimacy defended in Part 2 could then be portrayed not as the sole such standard, but as the only standard of legitimacy applicable to *actual,* nonideal political societies, in which it is impossible to get unanimous consent to anything, no matter how reasonable it might seem. The consensualist standard of legitimacy and obligation, apparently defended in Part 1 of Nozick's book, could then be read as the correct (but in practice largely irrelevant) standard of legitimacy to apply to political arrangements more extensive than those of the minimal state.[21] Alterna-

---

[17] It is perhaps nowhere more apparent than in his brief attempt to demolish the consent theorist's rival: the fairness account of obligation and legitimacy (ibid., 90–95). The principle of fairness, Nozick argues, cannot be formulated so as "to obviate the need for other persons' *consenting* to cooperate and limit their own activities" (ibid., 95; emphasis in original).

[18] Ibid., 58, 283, and 331.

[19] See, for instance, Nozick's remarks concerning the possible outcome where "almost all in the society ... adhere to the ideal of the more-than-minimal state," as a result freely establishing "the analogue of the more-than-minimal state ... , under which each person retains the choice of whether to participate or not" (ibid., 293).

[20] Nozick appears to have a similar argument in mind in the following passage: "Since a structure that could arise by a just process which does not involve the consent of individuals will not involve limitations of their rights or embody rights which they do not possess, it will be closer, *insofar as rights are concerned,* to the starting point of individual rights specified by moral side constraints; and hence its structure of rights will be viewed as just" (ibid., 294; emphasis in original).

[21] "[I]n a free society people may contract into various restrictions which the government may not legitimately impose upon them" (ibid., 320). The problem, we can add, is that no

tively, consent theory's standards could be dismissed altogether as no part of Nozick's real strategy. Nozick is no consent theorist, we might argue. Indeed, the whole point of the way Nozick deals with independents in Part 1, we could claim, is precisely to show that so long as the state extends to persons its service of enforcing basic rights (and no more than this), their consent to its authority is irrelevant to its legitimacy. And consent can legitimate no state more extensive than the minimal state.

The problems with this latter reading of Nozick strike me as pointing to quite general problems for libertarian political philosophy. The first, most obvious problem is that this solution simply leaves hanging the libertarian's well-known commitment to the sanctity of contract. If free contract can legitimate any kind of nonpolitical arrangement, why should it be thought incapable of legitimating non-minimal *political* arrangements? The second, slightly less obvious problem faced by a libertarian trying to minimize the role of libertarianism's consensualist strain is this: there is no good reason, on libertarianism's own terms, to suppose that the minimal state *is* legitimate without the unanimous consent of its citizens/subjects.[22]

We have seen the likely libertarian argument on this point: since all the minimal state does is enforce preexisting, legitimately enforceable rights and obligations, no consent is required to legitimate its demands. But this position seems confused in a couple of ways, even ignoring all the ways in which it might seem confused if we helped ourselves to the resources of a nonlibertarian theory of rights or justice. For a minimal state, in fact, must do *more* than simply enforce preexisting rights and obligations; and the ways in which it must do more—by *limiting* the exercise of preexisting rights—would seem (from the libertarian perspective, at least) to require the consent of the rights-holders to legitimate them.

First, a minimal state must not only enforce rights and obligations—by threatening and (if necessary) using punishment to compel performance. If it is to function as a state, it must also deny to others the right of competitive enforcement of those rights and obligations. Nozick, of course, worries a great deal about this problem, but he addresses it only by the very nonlibertarian move mentioned earlier: by allowing others' rights of competitive enforcement to be legitimately infringed provided that compensation is made. Indeed, Nozick is really only able to argue for the minimal state's justifiably excluding "*dangerous* private enforcement" by competitor individuals or groups,[23] leaving it entirely unclear how anything but consent could legitimate the state's prohibiting private enforcement of rights by persons or groups that used procedures that were not

---

actual societies are "free" in the relevant sense—i.e., none enjoy the unanimous consent of their members.

[22] The arguments that follow, I believe, show why the "time-frame" theory of governmental legitimacy (as Ellen Frankel Paul calls it) is ultimately indefensible.

[23] Nozick, *Anarchy, State, and Utopia,* 133 (my emphasis).

dangerous, or procedures that were at least as reliable as the state's own. When push comes to shove, Nozick actually allows that "[a] dominant agency and another tiny one, or a dominant agency and an unaffiliated individual person, are on a par in the nature of their rights to enforce other rights."[24] Nozick's only real defense of the state's *special* claim to be the one that does the enforcing of rights flows from his very hesitant and enormously ad hoc speculation that perhaps the right to punish is "the only [natural] right" that is possessed not individually, but jointly—so that the dominant agency that becomes the state turns out (by definition) to hold (through the consent of its clients) a larger *share* of the collectively held right to punish than does any competitor agency or individual.[25] Since Nozick himself can barely advance the argument with a straight face, we can, I think, safely disregard it. But the result of doing so is that it is very hard to see how even a minimal state could legitimately perform its required functions *without* receiving the consent of those in its territory who possessed rival rights to perform those functions.

There is a second, similar problem for the libertarian, perhaps equally obvious, but certainly less widely discussed. Even the minimal state must do more than simply enforce preexisting rights and obligations (and exclude others' competitive efforts to do the same). As Nozick sees, in order to be a state, it must enforce these rights within a *geographical area*. But, as Nozick apparently fails to see, enforcing rights within a territory requires a state to place all sorts of limits on the property rights over land held by individuals within that territory. According to most libertarians, of course, natural property rights of the sort at issue here (preexisting, nonlegal [i.e., moral] property rights) are pretty full-bodied rights, with property holders being entitled to use their property more or less as they please, provided they do no direct harm to others in the process (or do not have obligations to others—for example, obligations of reparation of injury— that would otherwise limit their options). But in order to enforce rights within a territory, states (including, of course, *minimal* ones) must (among other things) control or prohibit movement across the borders of that territory. States also must prohibit property owners from giving, selling, or trading their land to alien nations or citizens (i.e., to those not bound by the state's laws), and must prohibit individual or group secession by landowners within the borders of the territory. But each of these restrictions, necessary as it may be to statehood and to the task of enforcing rights in the state's territories, constitutes a limitation on the rights of private landowners, a limitation that is *not* motivated by any direct harm to others that the landowner has done or threatened to do. States can acquire the rights to impose such restrictions on private landowners,

---

[24] Ibid., 134.
[25] Ibid., 139–40.

according to the libertarian's own position, only by obtaining the consent of those landowners.[26]

If this is correct, then the libertarian would be ill served by any attempt to jettison the consensualist aspect of libertarian political thought. Indeed, given that (as we have just seen) the libertarian's *minimalist* standard of legitimacy cannot be sustained by the libertarian independently of a reliance on consent-based rights and obligations, it is this minimalist standard that ought to be disposed of by libertarians. Libertarians, in short, should be consent theorists on the subjects of political legitimacy and political obligation. To those who observe that on the libertarian's own terms unanimous consent can justify almost anything—certainly including more-than-minimal political arrangements—the libertarian's response should be that this is correct, but that it is highly unlikely that anything like unanimous consent in a territory will ever be secured in order to legitimate such extensive, liberty-limiting arrangements. The more minimal the limitations of individual rights required by a state's institutions, the libertarian can argue, the more likely that state will be to enjoy something approaching unanimous consent (since all persons benefit, even if not equally, from enforcement of basic rights, but only some persons benefit from more extensive government). And since the best we can hope for in the real world is approximate political legitimacy, the argument continues, the minimal state is more likely than others to earn that consent which legitimates states. I do not myself find this line of argument persuasive, but it is at least one way in which a consent-based libertarian theory of political legitimacy can be reconciled with libertarianism's minimalist ambitions.

My arguments here suggest that libertarianism should be not only less minimalist in principle (if perhaps not in practice), but also slightly more *anarchist* in tone. Libertarianism has, of course, always been prepared—indeed, eager—to acknowledge with the anarchist the illegitimacy of most incarnations of the modern state. But while my arguments do not require libertarians to side with those "libertarian anarchists" who maintain that *no* state can possibly be morally legitimate, my arguments do, I believe,

---

[26] I should try to be perfectly clear about what I take the force of these arguments to be. I do not intend to maintain that a state *could not,* under any conceivable conditions, function as a state without denying these rights to residents. States *could* permit those within their territories to exercise competitive enforcement rights and full rights over their property in land while still *conceivably* functioning as states. For instance, it is certainly possible that some particular set of citizens would never (or would only very rarely) choose to exercise their rival enforcement rights, just as it could turn out that when citizens made their own decisions about the uses of their lands, this happened to result in no serious obstacles to their state's viability or effective functioning. My arguments are intended to suggest only that it is extremely unlikely (under anything resembling realistic conditions) that granting citizenries such full rights (to rival enforcement or to control over land) would be compatible with maintaining functioning states, and that states granting such rights in typical conditions could not *reliably* provide the kinds of services that we normally associate with functioning or stable states.

force the libertarian to acknowledge that only the actual consensual history of a state, not the nature of the functions it performs, can determine its legitimacy or illegitimacy. And in light of the apparent general scarcity of popular political consent in the real world, this means that merely downsizing or streamlining the state cannot have the legitimizing effects that libertarians often aver (though such downsizing might, of course, play a role in *encouraging* popular political consent).

None of this should sit too badly with libertarians. Given their preference for historical or process-oriented accounts of justice and property, a historical account of state legitimacy should seem reasonably natural. In fact, abandoning minimalism in favor of consensualism seems to me to make a political philosophy look more thoroughly libertarian, given libertarianism's traditional emphasis on the idea that we are free to choose anything, provided only that the choice does not wrong anyone else. If liberty is indeed the central concern of libertarianism, we might say, then libertarianism should be more concerned to defend freely chosen arrangements than to defend minimal ones; for however minimal arrangements may be, they may still be imposed contrary to the wills of those subjected to them, and so be apparent limitations of their basic right to liberty. Abandoning libertarianism's minimalism also seems to me to make libertarianism look more defensible; for it has always been difficult (for me, at least) to see how libertarians could hope to mount a compelling minimalist argument that appeals to strong basic rights of individual liberty and property without justifying these rights in a way that provides redistributionist or egalitarian liberals with material sufficient to defend at least modest rights to charity or welfare for those in genuine need. After all, poverty (and the superior economic power of others) often appears to be just as liberty-limiting as does state coercion. And if the moral possibility of private property is defended in terms of its necessity to true liberty (or self-government), so, it seems, must be a minimally decent standard of living. Thus, far from painting libertarianism into a corner, I am trying here to suggest for libertarianism a form that seems to me far less vulnerable to familiar counterarguments.

IV. CONSENT THEORY

Embracing a consent theory of legitimacy and political obligation will, of course, still leave the libertarian exposed to all of the numerous contemporary critiques of consent theory. And it is to those critiques that I will momentarily turn. One quick caveat first, however: I am aware that in claiming that libertarians should be consent theorists I have claimed something that may seem to be plainly false of some varieties of libertarianism. Utilitarian libertarians, for instance, might seem to be defending libertarian conclusions from foundations that are fundamentally opposed to consent theory. After all, the best-known of the classical utilitarians—Hume (whom for these purposes we can count as a utilitarian), Bentham, and Mill—are also among the best-known critics of consent theory. Hume argued against it so convincingly that the whole problem of political obligation in effect dropped off the philosophical radar screen for more than a century. Nonetheless, this much, I think, can be said in favor of the reasonably general truth of my claim that libertarians should be consent theorists: Any theorist, utilitarian or not, who thinks that his arguments entail the justice or moral legitimacy of free-market capitalism must be committed as well to a conception of personal property rights and personal rights to freedom of contract that makes these rights extremely strong and extensive. And anyone committed to such strong and extensive rights of property and contract should be moved by the arguments advanced above against minimalist libertarianism, arguments supporting the need for the libertarian to accept a consent theory of political legitimacy and political obligation.

Before I begin examining the arguments *against* such a consent theory, I should quickly make clear exactly what *kind* of consent theory I am arguing that libertarians (and the rest of us) should defend. According to any theory properly called a consent theory, person A's consent to government B's rule over A (or to membership in the political society governed by B) is a necessary condition for person A to have general political obligations (of obedience and support) to B (or to B's society) and for B to legitimately rule A. Typically, consent theorists hold that personal consent is not sufficient to bring about these results if consent is in important ways defective—for example, if it is nonvoluntary, unintentional, uninformed, or given to arrangements that violate others' rights. But consent that is free, informed, and non-rights-violating (etc.) is both necessary and sufficient for political obligation. Further, since no libertarian will subscribe to a theory that grounds obligations for one (competent) person in consent given by others (such as the consent of one's ancestors, the consent of the wise, or the consent of a majority of others in one's society or territory), I consider here only theories that ground obligation and legitimacy in *personal* consent.

The idea of binding personal consent can, of course, be understood in broader or narrower fashions. I do not have in mind here the familiar distinction between express and tacit consent. I take both to consist in the deliberate and effective performance of actions (or omissions) whose conventional or contextual point is to communicate to others the agent's intention to undertake new obligations toward and/or convey new rights to those others.[27] Thus understood, libertarians should have no concerns

---

[27] I defend this understanding of consent in A. John Simmons, *On the Edge of Anarchy: Locke, Consent, and the Limits of Society* (Princeton, NJ: Princeton University Press, 1993), 69–70, and 83–84; and in A. John Simmons, "'Denisons' and 'Aliens': Locke's Problem of

about consent being only tacit. The distinction I have in mind here is, rather, the distinction between conceptions of personal consent that iden- tify it only with certain *actual performances* (or series of actual perfor- mances) and those that expand the account of consent to identify it as well with certain dispositional, attitudinal, or related counterfactual fea- tures of persons—such as their attitudes of approval of or dedication toward something, their dispositions to consent, or the fact that they would have consented had they been able to do so, or been asked to do so, or had the occasion to do so arisen.

Libertarians seem unlikely to be sympathetic to such expansions of the concept of consent, and in that I agree with them. The facts that I approved of buying IBM stock at $48 per share, was disposed to do so, and would have done so had someone asked me to, unhappily do not establish that I did so. (As of this writing, the shares would now be worth more than twice that amount.) We do, of course, sometimes talk as if we think we can justify our treatment of others in terms of what they would have agreed to: if you are smashed by a bus in front of the hospital, and I drag you into the emergency room for treatment, I may say that it was per- missible for me to manipulate your body without your consent because you clearly *would* have consented to my doing so. When, however, further investigation reveals that you are a suicidal Christian Scientist who delib- erately walked in front of the bus—with the result that the medical treat- ment I procured for you not only frustrated your plans but violated one of your most cherished principles (your opposition to receiving any form of medical treatment)—I am likely to quickly abandon any consent-based justification for my action. But I am unlikely, I think, to believe that my action was therefore morally impermissible. My action was justified by the fact that I did what I had reasonable grounds to believe would be best for you, at a time when a critical choice about your well-being needed to be made and you were unable to make it for yourself. No appeal to your hypothetical consent is necessary to justify my actions, suggesting that even in cases where it is *true* that you would have consented to what I did (had you been able), the appeal to consent is probably really best under- stood as confused or as shorthand for some form of non-consent-based justification.[28]

Political Consent," in A. John Simmons, *Justification and Legitimacy: Essays on Rights and Obligations* (Cambridge: Cambridge University Press, 2001), 165–66.

[28] This is true as well, I think, of the justifications in consensual language that we some- times offer for our treatment of young children or persons who are insane. Our true concern is to do what we think is best for them in circumstances where they cannot choose for themselves, *not* to treat them as we imagine they would agree to be treated if only they had nondefective wills of their own—especially since, among other things, we could hardly claim to have very clear grounds for deciding what those wills would be like. Here I (apparently) disagree with Joel Feinberg, who uses an example like the one I use in the text above to argue that "dispositional consent" *does* perform like actual consent (in precluding "rightful grievances"), provided that there is very strong evidence of the disposition to

Of course, we need not settle here what counts as personal consent or which sorts of consent can actually ground personal obligations. For the purpose of the libertarian, *any* kind of consent that can be sufficient to undertake obligations and to alienate or renounce strong personal rights to liberty and property (including the right to enforce rights) will be an acceptable form of consent within libertarian consent theory. But libertarians do seem mostly to advocate *actual* personal consent as the only clearly binding form of consent. Actual personal consent theory is the strongest, most libertarian-looking form of consent theory, and it is the form of the theory advocated by many of the classical liberals to whom libertarians look for inspiration.[29] So I want to consider now the question of just how defensible such an actual personal consent theory of political legitimacy and political obligation really is.

V. CRITIQUES OF CONSENT THEORY

Consent theory has, of course, a reasonably respectable pedigree, having been defended in the works of major figures in the history of political philosophy and having played a prominent role in the political theory appealed to in the foundational political documents of a number of modern states.[30] But there has also long been a tradition of skepticism about consent theory that dates at least to Hume's famous essay "Of the Original Contract" (1748),[31] and this skeptical tradition is continued in the works of some of the most important contemporary social and political philosophers, such as Ronald Dworkin and John Rawls. Indeed, Dworkin's criticisms of consent theory amount to little more than a contemporary restatement of Hume's most famous objection: that nothing in the behavior of ordinary citizens of ordinary states (including their failure to emigrate) can be taken to count as binding consent to their governments' rule.[32] Even political behavior that might *look* consensual is in fact neither sufficiently deliberate (or intentional) nor sufficiently free (given the severely limited and extremely costly alternatives) for it to be properly understood as binding consent.

---

consent, no opportunity to actually solicit consent, and "serious loss or harm" at issue for the (dispositional) consenter. See Joel Feinberg, *Harm to Self* (New York: Oxford University Press, 1986), 173–74. While I agree with Feinberg that justifications for interfering with others' liberty are often available in the kinds of situations he describes, I think these justifications are mischaracterized when described as resting on the *consent* of the person who is interfered with.

[29] For a defense of this reading of Locke, see Simmons, *On the Edge of Anarchy*, 205–7.

[30] On the consent tradition, see A. John Simmons, *Moral Principles and Political Obligations* (Princeton, NJ: Princeton University Press, 1979), chap. 3.

[31] In David Hume, *Essays Moral, Political, and Literary*, ed. Eugene F. Miller (Indianapolis, IN: LibertyClassics, 1985), 465–87.

[32] Ronald Dworkin, *Law's Empire* (Cambridge, MA: Harvard University Press, 1986), 192–93.

Notice, however, that such arguments, even if convincing (as I believe they are),[33] are fatal only to a consent theory that is conjoined with perfectly inessential conservative ambitions regarding the legitimacy of contemporary states. That contemporary citizens have not authorized their states by free consent argues against consent theory only on the assumption that at least some contemporary states must turn out to be legitimate, according to any acceptable standard of legitimacy. Libertarians, of course, reject these conservative ambitions with respect to the modern state, so libertarian consent theorists are unlikely to find objections of the Hume/Dworkin sort very interesting. Nor *should* consent theorists, libertarian or not, be unnerved by such objections. The absence of legitimate contemporary states according to consent theory's standards argues no more strongly against those standards than the presence of extensive inequality in the world argues against liberal egalitarian standards of justice.

It would, perhaps, be a fair complaint against consent theory if its critics could show that it was practically *impossible* for a political community to satisfy its requirements for legitimacy. But it is, on the contrary, quite easy to imagine how legitimate societies (according to these requirements) could arise,[34] and even how they could sustain themselves in the face of newcomers and successive generations. Provided only that the society founded by its original members was able to acquire (via the consent of those members or others) appropriate rights of control over the land the society claimed as its territory, that society could legitimately exclude would-be immigrants, admit them only on the condition of their consent to existing arrangements, or charitably accept them as members of a different sort (not bound by the terms of the original charter). The same is true of the offspring of original members. Complications will abound, of course, if the opportunities of those excluded from the consensual society are in various ways severely limited by the conditions outside that society. But such complications are certainly not (for practical purposes) a *necessary* feature of the world.[35]

It might seem that offspring present special problems here, since they will only be capable of achieving the autonomy necessary for them to make meaningful choices if they are raised and socialized in certain ways. Accordingly, offspring might seem to have some claims against the consensual illiberal society, in particular, rights that it be structured at least liberally enough to facilitate their achievement of autonomy. (Perhaps the

---

[33] I defended an extension of Hume's argument in both *Moral Principles and Political Obligations*, 91–100, and *On the Edge of Anarchy*, 197–202, and 218–48.

[34] Like-minded persons could simply withdraw from their states and found such a society on unanimous, express consent, using as territory an island purchased from some sovereign power, or an independent reservation set aside for the purpose by a sovereign power persuaded of its utility, or (in the near future, perhaps) part of an extraterrestrial body taken by "right of first occupancy."

[35] Other objections to such consensual societies—based, for instance, on possible injustice—are addressed in the text below.

desired conclusion would then actually be disjunctive: either unanimous consent is insufficient to justify all kinds of illiberality in an enduring polity, or illiberal consensual polities may not extend beyond one generation.) In fact, such an argument ignores several obvious lines of defense available to the consent theorist. One is that the rights of offspring to conditions for the achievement of autonomy are held not against societies, but (principally) against parents, who may provide such conditions within the family (or in subsidiary groups) even in tremendously illiberal societies (just as these conditions have, of course, been regularly provided for children in actual illiberal societies, both historical and contemporary). Another possible line of defense against special worries about offspring is to argue that autonomy is not a good to be maximized but only a condition to be respected when it is present in a person. As such, there is no general moral responsibility (on society or on persons generally) to provide the conditions within which autonomy may (or may most easily) develop. Autonomous choices must be respected when made; but their frequency need not be maximized, nor need their possibility be guaranteed to all with the required capacities.

The mere fact that there are not now, and are unlikely to be in the foreseeable future, political societies in the world that are legitimate according to consent theory is no objection to that theory. It is simply a lamentable fact about the world, one to add to the other such facts lamented by libertarians. We need a deeper or more substantial attack than this on the consent theorist's account of legitimacy if we are to regard the libertarian's adoption of consent theory as a mistake. It might seem, perhaps, that we could mount just such an attack by relying on contemporary observations about various "deep" features of social life that were uniformly (and perhaps deliberately, self-servingly) ignored by the classical consent theorists. Feminist political theorists, for instance, have frequently charged that consent theorists ignore the fact that women are routinely denied opportunities for genuine political consent, and that in the case of women some form of *submission* is typically identified with binding consent.[36] Similarly, and more generally, it is often claimed that the conditions of actual political life are normally such that even apparently free consent given by many individuals will be "tainted" (and rendered nonbinding) by the unfair background conditions and unequal bargaining power in the context of which any agreements must be made.[37] Thus, Rawls writes:

[36] See, e.g., Carole Pateman, "Women and Consent," *Political Theory* 8, no. 2 (1980): 149–68.

[37] There is, of course, a familiar feminist argument that focuses more specifically, but slightly differently, on the background conditions for women's consent. If women live in conditions of sexist oppression, the preferences on which their choices and their consent are based are bound to be formed in ways that involve "tainted" internalizations of the expectations of their oppressors. As a result, women's consent cannot be viewed as nondefective, even where it appears to be given freely and informedly. For a general discussion of this line of argument, see John D. Walker, "Liberalism, Consent, and the Problem of Adaptive Preferences," *Social Theory and Practice* 21, no. 3 (1995): 457–71.

[T]he accumulated results of many separate and seemingly fair agree-ments entered into by individuals and associations are likely over an extended period to undermine the background conditions required for free and fair agreements. Very considerable wealth and property may accumulate in a few hands, and these concentrations are likely to undermine fair equality of opportunity, the fair value of the polit-ical liberties, and so on.[38]

If the apparent consent given in actual political societies is not sufficiently intentional or free to be binding, consent theorists' standards of legiti-macy may appear unrealistic.

But here again, these observations constitute objections to consent theory only if we begin by assuming that at least some actual political societies must satisfy defensible standards of legitimacy. And this is not something that libertarians (or we) ought simply to concede. Feminists surely do not want to argue that it would be impossible or undesirable for societies to include women as fully equal participants in the political community, or for societies to identify as women's binding political consent only those free, informed performances (or omissions) that should be so understood. If not, then the objection posed by feminists is not an objection to consent theory's standard of legitimacy, but only an objection to society's failure to take that standard seriously. As to Rawls's related but more general concerns, the same kind of response seems possible (though I will con-sider below a more potent aspect of the Rawlsian argument). Libertarian consent theorists will, of course, worry far less than Rawls does about the concentrations of wealth and power that may be produced by a history of free exchanges. But even those of us who *do* worry about the possibility that those concentrations will create unfair background conditions for political consent should be worrying principally about how to correct those conditions, not about the consent theory standard of legitimacy that condemns societies exhibiting the conditions. Only if it were impossible or wrong to correct unfair background conditions for consent would this seem to be a worry for consent theory. But Rawlsians cannot, I suspect, intend to claim that such changes are impossible or wrong, given that their aim (in their nonideal theory, at least) is in part precisely to identify the practical steps that we ought to take in order to accomplish this correction.

A serious attack on consent theory must argue more directly that gen-uinely free, informed (etc.) personal consent is either not necessary or not sufficient for political obligation and political legitimacy. To show that consent is not necessary for political obligations, one should defend an

---

[38] John Rawls, *Justice as Fairness: A Restatement* (Cambridge, MA: Harvard University Press, 2001), 53. See also John Rawls, *Political Liberalism* (New York: Columbia University Press, 1993), 287.

alternative account of possible grounds for such obligations that would force the consent theorist to accept at least a pluralistic theory of political obligation and legitimacy.[39] Or one could, like Hume, try to undermine consent theory more completely by arguing that the alternative account defended in fact shows consent to be utterly superfluous to the generation of political obligations—so that even in those cases where consent might appear to bind us, there is another more basic ground of obligation already instantiated.[40]

I have tried over quite a few years to defend the view that none of the alternative accounts of political obligation and legitimacy yet proposed is successful.[41] Indeed, it seems to me that one of the strongest arguments in favor of consent theory is precisely the failure of all of its rivals to satisfy the reasonable ambitions of a theory of political obligation.[42] For those who find my arguments against these rivals unpersuasive, I am afraid I have nothing new to offer here. Instead, I would like to consider the other natural strategy for attacking consent theory, which is to argue that, regardless of how rival accounts might fare, consent theory itself cannot successfully defend the kind of political consent on which it concentrates as *sufficient* to ground political obligations.

One can, of course, pursue this strategy by defending a general, wide-ranging skepticism about the obligating force of free, informed (etc.) promises or consent, maintaining that there is simply no good reason to regard them as morally binding, as always morally binding, or as binding within anything but a just society. We might argue, in short, that consent is simply not a privileged source of special obligation, contrary to the apparent assumptions of consent theorists. We value the choice involved in promising or consenting, say, only because respecting our choices normally leads to our getting what we want. But our wants are often ill considered or immoral, and even where our wants are not thus criticizable, we often choose unwisely or wrongly. It will not do to reply (with

---

[39] Assuming, of course, as the principal participants in these debates do, that it is at least *possible* for persons to have political obligations.

[40] The second part of Hume's attack on consent theory was to argue that promises/consent in fact bind us only because of the utility of the practice of promising. We can legitimately, as a consequence, appeal directly to the utility of obedience to law (support for government, etc.) to ground our political obligations, with no need to take the intermediate step of attempting to ground those obligations in personal consent. Joseph Raz advances an argument similarly designed to relegate consent to an "auxiliary and derivative" role in his essay "Government by Consent," in Joseph Raz, *Ethics in the Public Domain: Essays in the Morality of Law and Politics* (Oxford: Oxford University Press, 1994), 366–69.

[41] Principally, in Simmons, *Moral Principles and Political Obligations*; in chapter 8 of Simmons, *On the Edge of Anarchy*; and in essays 1–8 of Simmons, *Justification and Legitimacy*.

[42] Since I also argue that no existing states are legitimate even by consent theory's standards, I should perhaps clarify the sense(s) in which I take alternative accounts of legitimacy and political obligation to "fail." Their failure does not consist in their inability to show that some existing states are in fact legitimate. It consists, instead, in their being unable either (a) to explain how particularized *political* obligations could arise, or (b) to explain how political obligations could arise in large-scale, pluralistic modern political societies.

Mill) that our individual choices should be respected because, after all, we know ourselves best. For our choices often adversely affect others, whose true wants we cannot consistently claim to know best. Why should even free, informed consent that issues from unwise choices or choices that adversely affect others be taken seriously as a ground of moral obligation or legitimacy?

The answer to such general skepticism about consent must, I think, be to reemphasize more persuasively the reasonably obvious advantages of the practice of promising/consent, both in consequentialist/mutual-advantage terms and in terms of the promotion of the value of autonomy. Emphasizing the latter, for instance, we could argue that we respect consent (and, through this, the choices on which consent is based) wherever doing so is necessary to respecting every person's right to be self-directing or self-governing, a right that is itself perhaps grounded (as many libertarians would have it) in special claims that we have to our own bodies and labor. Where consent is so defective that we are disinclined even to impute it to a self-governing agent—as in cases of coerced or seriously misinformed consent—or where consent fails to respect the equal entitlements of others to self-governance, we take the obligating and legitimating powers of consent to run out. But consent that is merely unwise or that merely adversely affects others (without violating their rights) is nonetheless binding and legitimating, being just an unfortunate aspect of a morally acceptable—indeed, a morally mandated—regime of universal self-government.

Whether or not such arguments are found persuasive, I think that a more promising approach to defeating consent theory is to defend a skeptical view not about consent generally, but more specifically about *political* consent. Even if promises and consent are perfectly respectable sources of obligation and perfectly respectable as legitimating acts in our everyday lives, the argument would go, consent to a state, a government, or a political society is another matter. Because of the nature of states and governments, even free, informed consent to their authority may neither legitimate them nor ground political obligations for consenters. I will consider two variants of this approach. On the first line of argument, political consent is alleged to be insufficient to bind us because what this consent must be consent *to* is too vague and open-ended to constitute the content of binding consent. On the second line of argument, which we might take to be the *real* point of the earlier Rawlsian objection, political consent cannot bind us to or legitimate that to which we consent, because even free, informed (etc.) consent can (and regularly does) issue in plainly illegitimate political outcomes.

Consider first, then, what political consent would have to be consent to. Since in order to count as undertaking political obligations (and as legitimating government) we would have to consent to the permanent authority over us of some state, government, or society, the substance of our consent would appear to have to be both objectionably vague and objectionably long-termed.[43] We must consent to a government's making and enforcing binding law. But while we might be perfectly content with the government and laws as they stand when we give our consent, we simply cannot reliably predict the changes that will occur over time. Similarly, we cannot reliably predict other significant changes that might occur in the composition or character of our political society, changes that might also make us deeply regret our consent to membership in that society.[44] Unwise choices to consent are one thing. But consent that purports to undertake utterly unspecific future obligations is another. It simply cannot bind us, since it can be no part of a self-governing life.[45] Similarly, consenting to a government's authority over us seems to be completely indefinite as to term, much like a contract in perpetuity; and such open-ended consent might also be regarded as objectionable on the grounds that it frustrates, rather than promotes, self-government (except, apparently, in the case of marriage).

It seems plausible to respond to such arguments, however, by maintaining that they underestimate the extent to which a consent theory of political obligation and legitimacy can just absorb the criticisms without any apparent weakening of the theory. If it is true that consent's binding force is lost or diminished as the content of the consent is more open-ended, the consent theorist can simply accept this fact as one more case in which consent is insufficient for obligation. Since consent theory already accepts other such limits to consent, accepting another will not seriously affect the theory's force, unless this limit cannot be motivated by the theory justifying the relevant obligations (which, in this case, it plainly can be), or unless accepting this limit will show that the ideal of government by consent thereby becomes unacceptable, unattractive, or impossible to achieve in practice. But nothing of this sort follows from worries about vague or open-ended consent. Perhaps the consent theorist will insist in response that genuine, binding political consent must be (or must be understood to be) relatively specific as to its content, or that in order to continue to bind and legitimate, political consent must be given regularly, rather than once and for all. The theorist could argue that, in fact, consent's binding (and legitimating) force diminishes over time; or she

---

[43] See Raz, "Government by Consent," 362–63.

[44] In a Nozickian utopia (a framework of consensual communities), those who consent to membership in a community will specify in advance that the community must compensate them for unacceptable changes in its structure (Nozick, *Anarchy, State, and Utopia*, 324). Nozick does not comment on the moral position of those who fail to include such provisions in their contractual undertakings.

[45] Raz, "Government by Consent," 364. Something like this is often taken to be the real substance of Jean-Jacques Rousseau's objections to representative government in *On the Social Contract* (1764), ed. Roger D. Masters, trans. Judith R. Masters (New York: St. Martin's Press, 1978), bk. 3, chap. 15. It is also what motivates Robert Paul Wolff's more wide-reaching critique of both representative and majoritarian democracy in Robert Paul Wolff, *In Defense of Anarchism* (New York: Harper & Row, 1970), 27–58.

could accept in her moral theory analogues of the contract law doctrines of "frustration of purposes and impossibility," which "allow relief from contractual obligations when circumstances turn out very differently from what the parties expected."[46] However the consent theorist opts to respond to this class of objections, though, it seems clear that her response need not involve anything that interestingly weakens the appeal of consent theory or that argues against its claim that political consent is sufficient for political obligation and legitimacy.

VI. The Illiberal Consensual Society

I now arrive at the second line of objection to consent theory, the one that strikes me as the most formidable: that if consent is accepted as sufficient for legitimacy, this commits us to accepting the possible legitimacy of political societies that are uncharitable, intolerant, bigoted, and, more generally, illiberal. Since illiberal regimes are palpably illegitimate, the argument goes, there must be fundamental defects in consent theory's standard of legitimacy.

Suppose, to begin, that a group of persons (without obligations that would preclude this) comes together on a piece of land to which they have managed to establish a valid collective claim (say, an unwanted territory purchased from some sovereign state). By unanimous consent, they create for themselves a set of political institutions that provide for lawmaking, law enforcement, and more generally for both internal and external sovereignty over their territory. All are excluded from membership or residence in the territory of the new polity except on condition of consent to the authority of its constitution, laws, and government. Since, according to most libertarians, genuinely free and informed, unanimous consent can legitimate any kind of arrangement that does not violate the rights of outsiders, let us assume that the consenters are perfectly free (subject to the one constraint set by others' rights) to frame their new polity's institutions and laws as they wish.[47] The laws could provide for an absolute monarch or dictator (who is free to prey upon the masses), for political participation for only a privileged few, for draconian censorship and invasion of privacy, or for a police state. The consenters could provide that a small minority control the vast majority of the society's wealth and resources, that all members be required to practice one state religion, or that no one be permitted to practice any religion. They could require regular gladiatorial games, provide that members of disliked racial or

---

[46] Kent Greenawalt, *Conflicts of Law and Morality* (New York: Oxford University Press, 1989), 92. See more generally Greenawalt's discussion of open-ended promises at 81–82.

[47] We can, if we wish, imagine this as the first stage of Nozick's utopia: "a place where people are at liberty to join together voluntarily to pursue and attempt to realize their own vision of the good life in the ideal community but where no one can *impose* his own utopian vision on others" (Nozick, *Anarchy, State, and Utopia*, 312).

ethnic groups be denied citizenship or even entry into the society, ban contraception and "unnatural" sex, and guarantee that no societal resources whatsoever be used to improve circumstances outside of the society (except where such neglect would violate outsiders' rights, as opposed to their needs or wants). Indeed, if a strong form of libertarianism is correct and all rights are alienable, then the laws could provide for human slavery, allowing slaves and masters to be selected by any means one can imagine. In all of these ways and more, the society arising from free, informed, unanimous consent could be despicable almost beyond description, yet plainly legitimate nonetheless according to consent theory's standard. Virtually the only categories of vice such a society could not in principle exhibit, one might say, would be those that involve violations of the rights of nonconsenting outsiders. Doesn't such a catalogue of possibilities constitute a virtual *reductio* of consent theory?

Surprisingly, perhaps, the answer seems to me to be no. Consent theorists can grant, of course, that imposing a liberal egalitarian regime on persons *without* their consent may typically be *less* wrong than would be imposing an intolerant, inegalitarian regime (because the former is likely to violate fewer rights and do less wrong than the latter). Thus, if we are considering only the question of the least-bad illegitimate polity to impose on a captive audience, liberal egalitarians might be right to favor what they favor. Libertarian consent theorists, of course, will favor more minimal political arrangements than those favored by liberal egalitarians, even where the question is only that of the least-bad illegitimate state to impose on the unwilling. But consent theorists with more robust moral theories than those generally embraced by libertarians could concede this much to the liberal egalitarian without in any way weakening their defense of consent standards for legitimacy and political obligation. What must be addressed more directly by the consent theorist, however, is the claim that the unattractive features of illiberal political societies obviously render them illegitimate.

What, then, is it about the ugly, illiberal, consensual society that is supposed to render it plainly illegitimate? In my view, a state or political society, like any other institutional arrangement, is legitimate if and only if it actually possesses the rights to do what it does (or, perhaps, the rights to do what it most centrally does). Territorial states, on this analysis, are legitimate if and only if they actually possess the rights to exclusively make and enforce law, to be obeyed by their subjects, to be free of various kinds of external interference, and to exercise jurisdiction and control over a geographical territory.[48] But there is no reason to suppose that simply by virtue of being ugly and illiberal the consensual state described above must lack the rights to do these things. After all, ugly and illiberal

---

[48] See my fuller discussion of these matters in A. John Simmons, "On the Territorial Rights of States," *Philosophical Issues* 11 (2001) (supplement to *Noûs*): esp. 300–306.

people have all sorts of rights to govern their own lives as they please. If the members of the illiberal society genuinely own the territory on which they conduct their business (and so are entitled to control over it), and if each member has freely alienated the rights that might give him valid grounds for complaint about being subjected to illiberal arrangements, then it is initially hard to see from what quarter complaints of illegitimacy might arise. However unattractive their society may be to us, it seems to have the rights it needs to be legitimate with respect to its subjects, and they seem to owe it political obligations grounded in their free consent; and that, of course, is precisely the kind of legitimacy with which we are here concerned.

VII. Objections and Replies

I can imagine three kinds of responses to the argument as I have presented it thus far. The first is that some rights simply cannot be alienated, so there must be some "internal" limit to the illiberal arrangements that could be legitimated even by free consent. The second is that the illiberal consensual society cannot be legitimate because it is *unjust*. The third, closely related to the second, is that while the members of the illiberal consensual society may have no reasonable grounds for complaint against each other (or against their state), other groups of persons (e.g., the members' children or outsiders) plainly do, and the grounds of their complaints are what delegitimate such societies. In responding to these objections, I will have to try in places to distinguish how a right-libertarian consent theorist would respond from how a more moderate consent theorist (like myself) should reply, so that we can appreciate both the force of these objections against a libertarian consent theory and what I take to be their true force.

I will begin with the charge that the creation of my imaginary illiberal consensual polity involved the alienation of rights that are in fact inalienable. I begin here, but perhaps contrary to first appearances, it is not really necessary for the consent theorist to remain here long or to say much in response to this line of argument. The libertarian consent theorist, of course, will strongly object to the very idea of inalienable rights, and for her the battle can be waged on that point. I am not convinced that the libertarian will lose that battle, but I will not try here to defend that view.[49] Suppose, instead, that my illiberal consensual polity cannot in fact be legitimated by consent, because some of the rights that would have to be alienated in order to legitimate it are actually inalienable. That result might affect the libertarian element of libertarian consent theory, but it is hard to see how it would affect the consent theory. Consent theory maintains that genuine, nondefective consent is both necessary and sufficient

---

[49] I discuss at some length the idea of inalienable moral/natural rights (along with my reasons for being skeptical about arguments for inalienability) in Simmons, *On the Edge of Anarchy*, chap. 5.

for political obligation and legitimacy. If only defective consent—for instance, "consent" that involves an attempt to alienate the inalienable—could (apparently) legitimate a particular polity (or kind of polity), then that polity is simply in principle illegitimate by consent theory's standards.[50] Indeed, if the liberal egalitarian (e.g., Rawlsian) critic of consent theory were to press this point harder, arguing that *all* illiberal societies could acquire the rights in which their legitimacy consists only by citizens' alienating the inalienable, then it might seem that he had done the consent theorist a favor—by bringing the consent theorist's standards of legitimacy into conformity with his own and depriving himself of the benefit of exploitable differences in the implications of the two views.

It seems unlikely, however, that the liberal egalitarian critic of consent theory will want to carry the argument to such extremes. For surely not all of the rights alienated in my imaginary consensual polity (that is, not all of the rights whose alienation contributed to the illiberality of the resulting polity) could be plausibly argued to be in principle inalienable. The rights to associate with whomever we please or to engage in consensual sexual relations of whatever sort and with whomever we please, for instance, seem to be rights that we normally take ourselves to be perfectly empowered to alienate, even for very long terms, as when we join a monastic order, enlist in the military, commit ourselves to a monogamous intimate relationship or marriage, and so on. If rights like these are in fact alienable, then there is no apparent reason why they could not be alienated *en masse* in the creation of an illiberal polity, a polity that will use the acquired rights to enact and enforce bigoted or puritanical policies. In short, there is no real possibility that liberal egalitarians will turn out to approve of everything that consent theory regards as legitimate.

And that, perhaps, may finally get us near the real point of the liberal egalitarian critique (the second possible response imagined above). It is not that people cannot make binding devil's bargains in their private lives, but rather that their doing so *en masse* cannot legitimate the resulting polity. Of course people are entitled to make private choices that flow from very unsavory motives, such as dislike of certain races, sexual preferences, or appearances. But polities, unlike our private relationships, are governed by principles of justice, and illiberal polities are illegitimate precisely because they are unjust. Political authorities are bound as a matter of justice to treat their subjects fairly and well, as equals and as equally inviolable. As Dworkin puts it, "No government is legitimate that

---

[50] Consent theory obviously must explain the idea of "defective" consent in ways that are not ad hoc or "cooked up" simply to generate certain results in arguments like these. What makes consent defective must be explained in terms of the same arguments that are used to explain why nondefective acts of consent should be regarded as binding and legitimating (see Raz, "Government by Consent," 362). If it is possible to argue for inalienability in these same terms (which I doubt), then acts of consent that involve attempts to alienate inalienable rights will also be properly described as defective.

does not show equal concern for the fate of all those citizens over whom it claims dominion and from whom it claims allegiance." [51] And the authorities of the consensual illiberal society cannot discharge the duty to treat all as equals if those subjects have agreed to arrangements that are degrading or that make them unequal.

Once again, of course, the libertarian consent theorist will simply reject the liberal egalitarian theory of justice that is alleged to have these implications, arguing that if one cannot point to clear wrongdoing in the process that creates the polity, one has no grounds for claiming that the resulting polity is unjust. But suppose that one finds it difficult to follow the libertarian this far, committed as one might be to a more moderate, left-libertarian or liberal egalitarian conception of social justice. Even in that event, I think, there is nothing to prevent one from nonetheless accepting consent theory's standards for legitimacy and political obligation.

A liberal egalitarian theory of justice and a consent theory of political legitimacy can be consistently conjoined if one accepts the distinction between what I have called "justification" and "legitimacy"—which I take to be two kinds of favorable evaluations of political institutions within quite different dimensions of evaluation.[52] General good qualities and virtues of a political society—such as benevolence or justice—are what is appealed to in *justifying* that society's existence, in showing why such a society is *a good thing*. But the society's *legitimacy* is a function of its specific interactions with particular subjects and consists (in part) in its having a particular set of rights over a subject. A state's legitimacy (or illegitimacy) with respect to me and its possession of other good (or bad) general characteristics are, in my view, simply independent variables, in the same way that a business's general good (or bad) qualities are independent of its right to have me as a client. States can be evaluated independently in either dimension, sometimes producing mixed evaluations (as when we refer to "benevolent dictatorships").

If this is correct, then even if the liberal egalitarian critic of consent theory is right—contrary to the claims of the libertarian—that consensual political societies can be unjust (simply because they are illiberal), it does not follow from this that such societies are also illegitimate, or that consent theory's standard of legitimacy is flawed. These conclusions about legitimacy seem to follow only to those who conflate two importantly independent dimensions of institutional evaluation: justification and legitimacy. All that in fact follows from the liberal egalitarian critique is that illiberal societies are (in a variety of ways) *bad*, that the world would be morally better without them (or, at least, that it would be morally better if they lacked those bad traits). Institutional legitimacy is a function of the

---

[51] Ronald Dworkin, *Sovereign Virtue* (Cambridge, MA: Harvard University Press, 2000), 1.

[52] The hasty and largely undefended claims that follow in this paragraph in the text are elaborated and defended more carefully and at much greater length in my essay "Justification and Legitimacy," included in Simmons, *Justification and Legitimacy*, 122-57.

rights arising from specific relations between those institutions and particular persons, considered one by one. And consent theory maintains, persuasively I contend, that a person's genuine, nondefective consent to arrangements simply removes for that person reasonable grounds for complaint about those arrangements, at least so far and so long as his consent specifies.

The reason many insist, as a condition of legitimacy, that political authorities must treat all persons as equals is that we normally lack the opportunity to decide for ourselves how we wish to be treated in the political realm (and being treated as equals at least preserves most of our private-life options). The members of modern political societies are a captive audience. And the liberal egalitarian (e.g., Rawlsian) theory of justice is precisely about the kinds of institutional coercion to which such a captive audience may reasonably be subjected when its members have no choice in the matter. But my imagined consensual illiberal society is not a captive audience; it is a body of persons that has freely chosen the coercion to which it is subject. There is no need to appeal to "second-best" standards of legitimacy for captive audiences. The second-best theory is simply about the best and the worst that illegitimate societies can be. Such a theory is morally interesting, but it is not a theory of legitimacy. And finally, of course, there is also a clear sense in which the government of a consensual illiberal society *does* treat its subjects as equals and as equally inviolable—precisely by taking seriously their free, nondefective choices about how they wish to live.

How might the liberal egalitarian critic of consent theory respond? Perhaps he would answer with the third response imagined above. What you say may seem well and good, he might allow, so long as we focus solely on the happy consenters who live out their lives in the despicable illiberal society of their dreams. But what about some other classes of persons who may not be made so happy by the structure of such a political society? These classes might include: (a) those who give their binding consent to illiberal government, but who later change their minds or find themselves with new personal preferences or commitments of a sort that will make continued citizenship in such a society oppressive; (b) those of subsequent generations who are born within the illiberal society's territories; (c) those who are excluded from illiberal societies, or those who are excluded except on condition of consent to illiberal arrangements and whose opportunities for membership in other societies are few, costly, or unattractive; and (d) those who need what the illiberal society possesses.

How we understand the moral situation of the persons in these various groups will differ depending on how strictly we are prepared to defend narrowly (right-) libertarian aspects of libertarian consent theory. For instance, if we accept the familiar libertarian position with respect to positive rights—namely, that there are no positive rights that do not arise from consent or from obligatory restitution—then it will be relatively easy to dismiss the complaints of most of these groups. Provided only that the illiberal consensual society is not responsible for the plights of these persons, they can be treated according to whatever policies the society has elected to adopt.

But again, even those who find such libertarian arguments unpersuasive need not be led by consideration of these unfortunate groups of persons to conclude that consent theory is defective. It is perfectly consistent to accept the consent theorist's standards of political obligation and legitimacy while also maintaining

(a) that while merely "changing one's mind" may not be enough to free one of obligations consensually undertaken, fundamental changes in circumstances may do so;

(b) that societies must provide their "captive," nonconsenting residents (e.g., the consenters' children) with a reasonable set of options, so that the choices they must make may be made adequately freely or willingly—for instance, the society could offer them a choice between significant assistance in relocation and a resident, nonmember status that is less burdened with objectionable obligations than is full membership;

(c) that persons may not be excluded from membership in any political society (and must be offered reasonable terms of entry) unless those persons have genuine and reasonable opportunities for membership elsewhere; and

(d) that the needs of those outside one's society may require one to give individual assistance (or to participate in collective assistance) to the needy, regardless of whether or not one has agreed (or one's society has agreed) to this. Consensually undertaken obligations are not the only obligations to which persons are subject, and consenters may not escape their unchosen moral responsibilities by agreeing with others to ignore those responsibilities.

VIII. Conclusion

These responses to the liberal egalitarian critique of consent theory are, I know, objectionably brief, but they should suffice at least to indicate why I believe that this third apparently promising objection to consent theory, like the other two, will not succeed. I have, of course, argued that libertarians are committed to consent theory, regardless of its virtues. But we can now see that libertarians should be enthusiastic about this implication of their views, embracing consent theory, with the rest of us, because it is true.

Philosophy and Law, University of Virginia

PREROGATIVES, RESTRICTIONS, AND RIGHTS*

By Eric Mack

I. Introduction

In this essay, I offer a defense of the most prominent component of the anticonsequentialism articulated in Robert Nozick's *Anarchy, State, and Utopia*.[1] This component is Nozick's affirmation of moral side constraints and the moral rights that are correlative to these side constraints. It is because of these side constraints and rights that the imposition by persons or groups of certain sacrifices upon others is morally impermissible even if the imposition of those sacrifices yields some (putatively) best outcome. These side constraints and rights prohibit persons and groups from advancing even the most alluring ends by means of imposing certain costs upon other individuals. Indeed, Nozick's opening sentence in *Anarchy, State, and Utopia* states, "Individuals have rights, and there are things no person or group may do to them (without violating their rights)."[2] Yet it is a common and fair comment about Nozick's seminal work that it provides little in the way of sustained justification for this opening statement. This essay provides one strand of that missing justification.

In order to introduce my argument, I need to situate it within the broad debate in moral theory between consequentialists and anticonsequentialists. More than that, I need to draw attention to a common progression within anticonsequentialist argumentation and to an important proposal that this progression should be halted at a point that is halfway between full consequentialism and full anticonsequentialism. More specifically, the proposal is that the progression of anticonsequentialist argumentation should be halted before it arrives at the anticonsequentialist component most prominent in Nozick, namely, the affirmation of moral side constraints and correlative moral rights. I shall examine and reject this proposal. My argument in defense of side constraints and rights is my

* A distant ancestor of this essay was written during the spring of 1997 when I was a Visiting Scholar at the Social Philosophy and Policy Center, Bowling Green State University. The draft of the present essay was composed during the tenure of a summer research grant from the Murphy Institute of Political Economy at Tulane University. I am very grateful to both institutions and to Ellen Frankel Paul and Mary Sirridge for their exceedingly helpful editorial advice.

[1] Robert Nozick, *Anarchy, State, and Utopia* (New York: Basic Books, 1974).

[2] Ibid., ix.

argument against the proposal to halt this progression before it arrives at the promised land of side constraints and rights.

By consequentialism, I mean the view that has the following two major components and two major implications. The first component is the claim that, at least for the most part, alternative social states can be ranked against one another and that everyone has reason to favor and to promote more highly ranked overall states over more lowly ranked states. The second component is the claim that rightness in action consists in the promotion of the best available overall state. In the final analysis, the promotion of the best available overall state is the only measure of rightness. The first major implication of consequentialism is that the individual ought to perform the action that yields the best available overall outcome whatever the costs *to herself* of performing the action. The second major implication is that the individual ought to perform the action that yields the best available overall outcome whatever the costs *to any other individual*.[3] According to consequentialism, it is right to sacrifice oneself for the overall good and it is right to sacrifice others for the overall good. It would be wrong for one to impose sacrifices upon oneself or upon others only if those sacrifices actually failed to promote the best available social state.

Naturally enough, anticonsequentialists object to both major implications. First, they object to the idea that just as it is rational for an individual to impose costs *on herself* whenever that will yield a better overall life for herself, it is rational for an individual to impose costs on herself whenever that will yield a (putatively) better overall social state.[4] Second, they object to the idea that one may impose costs *upon others* whenever doing so will yield the (putatively) best available overall social state. In this latter case, the anticonsequentialist insists that there are principles of justice or rights that one violates if one imposes certain costs on others — whether or not the imposition of those costs yields the (putatively) best overall social state. These principles and the moral side constraints or restrictions associated with them are "deontic" in the sense that the wrongfulness of actions that violate the principles or the associated side constraints or restrictions is not a matter of those actions failing to yield valuable consequences. Violations of these principles and associated side constraints or restrictions would be wrong even if the violations were to yield valuable results.

The common progression in anticonsequentialist argumentation is from a rejection of the first implication of consequentialism (the implication that it is always right for the individual to impose *on herself* whatever costs need to be imposed to engender the best overall outcome) to the

---

[3] Of course, the costs of promoting a given social state are factored into the determination of whether it is the best available state.

[4] When I am speaking in my own voice or in the voice of others who also reject the ranking of overall social states, I insert the cautionary "(putative)." When I am speaking in the voice of one who accepts such rankings, I omit this cautionary formula.

rejection of the second implication (that it is always right for the individual to impose *on others* whatever costs need to be imposed to engender the best overall outcome). Put more positively, the common progression is from affirming that it is at least permissible for the individual to decline to sacrifice herself for the sake of the (putatively) best outcome to affirming that it is impermissible for the individual to impose sacrifices on others for the sake of the (putatively) best outcome. This progression of argumentation is present within Nozick's basic critique of consequentialism, as it is present in the passages from John Rawls's *A Theory of Justice*[5] on which Nozick's critique is modeled. In a well-known passage from *Anarchy, State, and Utopia*, Nozick argues:

> Individually, we each sometimes choose to undergo some pain or sacrifice for a greater benefit or to avoid a greater harm. . . . Why not, *similarly*, hold that some persons have to bear some costs that benefit other persons more, for the sake of the overall social good? But there is no *social entity* with a good that undergoes some sacrifice for its own good. There are only individual people, with their own individual lives. Using one of these people for the benefit of others, uses him and benefits the others. Nothing more. . . . To use a person in this way does not sufficiently respect and take account of the fact that he is a separate person, that his is the only life he has. *He* does not get some overbalancing good from his sacrifice, and no one is entitled to force this upon him. . . . [Moral side constraints] reflect the fact that no moral balancing act can take place among us; there is no moral outweighing of one of our lives by others so as to lead to a greater overall *social* good. There is no justified sacrifice of some of us for others. This root idea, namely, that there are different individuals with separate lives and so no one may be sacrificed for others, underlies the existence of moral side constraints. . . .[6]

Nozick begins by rejecting the consequentialist endorsement of the individual's imposition of costs *upon herself* for the sake of the overall social good. He then moves on, not merely to reject the consequentialist endorsement of the individual's imposition of costs *upon others* for the sake of the overall good, but also to hold that (some) such impositions of costs on others are *wrong*; they impermissibly violate moral side constraints. Moreover, the strong suggestion in the passage is that the rejection of self-sacrifice for the (putative) overall good leads on to the condemnation of other-sacrifice for the (putative) overall good. The suggestion is that something underlies the rejection of self-sacrifice—perhaps it is the error of moral balancing; perhaps it is the error of putting anyone on the sacrificial

---

[5] John Rawls, *A Theory of Justice* (Cambridge, MA: Harvard University Press, 1971).
[6] Nozick, *Anarchy, State, and Utopia*, 32–33.

altar; perhaps it is the failure to take seriously the separateness of persons—
and this something also underlies the wrongfulness of imposing sacrifices
upon others. There is some rationale for the rejection of the demand that
one impose sacrifices upon oneself, and this rationale leads on to the
condemnation of one's imposition of sacrifices upon others.[7]

But should one follow this argumentative route all the way to moral
side constraints and correlative moral rights? In *The Rejection of Consequentialism* Samuel Scheffler takes the view that one should not.[8] Scheffler
holds that one may reject the first implication of consequentialism (that it
is always right for the individual to impose on herself whatever costs
need to be imposed to engender the best overall outcome) while not
rejecting the second implication of consequentialism (that it is always
right for the individual to impose on others whatever costs need to be
imposed to engender the best overall outcome). Put more positively, the
doctrine articulated in *The Rejection of Consequentialism* is that at least
sometimes the individual is allowed not to sacrifice herself on the altar
of the overall good, but she is always at least allowed to sacrifice herself
or others on that altar. In Scheffler's language, the individual has a
prerogative—albeit, we shall see, a modest prerogative—not to sacrifice
herself for the sake of the overall good, but the individual is not subject
to any moral *restrictions* that make it wrong for the individual to impose
sacrifices on herself or others for the sake of the overall good.[9] If we were
to travel the whole anticonsequentialist route laid out in the passage from
Anarchy, State, and Utopia, we would first arrive at a prerogative that
allows the individual not to impose costs upon herself for the sake of the
(putative) overall good, and then we would journey on to restrictions that

---

[7] There is substantial similarity of language and argumentation between the cited passage
from Nozick (and other associated passages in *Anarchy, State, and Utopia*) and passages in
sections 5 and 6 of *A Theory of Justice*. Rawls is *more* explicit than Nozick in maintaining that
the initial plausible norm is that the individual should advance as much as possible the
attainment of her own ends (cf. *A Theory of Justice*, 143). According to Rawls, this principle
of individual choice withstands the consequentialist attempt to argue that balancing costs
and benefits across individuals is just as rational as an individual balancing costs and
benefits within her own life. And the rejection of balancing across individuals leads on to the
affirmation of rights that preclude the imposition of (certain) costs on others:

> The reasoning which balances the gains and losses of different persons as if they were
> one person is excluded. *Therefore* in a just society the basic liberties are taken for
> granted and the rights secured by justice are not subject to political bargaining or to
> the calculus of social interests. (28, emphasis added)

Of course, this fully anticonsequentialist Rawls is only one of many different manifestations
of Rawls that appear in *A Theory of Justice* and elsewhere.

[8] Samuel Scheffler, *The Rejection of Consequentialism*, rev. ed. (Oxford: Oxford University
Press, 1994). The revised edition includes several subsequent essays; the essay "Prerogatives
without Restrictions" (167–92) is of particular relevance.

[9] For Scheffler, it is still always *permissible* for the individual to impose costs *on herself* to
promote the overall optimal outcome. But it is consistent with this idea that the individual
have a prerogative that also makes it *permissible* for her *not* to impose such optimizing costs
on herself.

preclude the individual from imposing costs on others for the sake of the (putative) overall good. But Scheffler's contention is that we should stop after the first leg of the journey. We should depart from consequentialism as far as adopting a prerogative, but not as far as adopting restrictions. The progression of anticonsequentialist argumentation should halt at this halfway point—long before it arrives at the anticonsequentialist component most prominent in Nozick.

Scheffler's position is that there is a rationale for the introduction of a prerogative into moral theory but not for the introduction of restrictions. There is a rationale for the introduction of the first component of anticonsequentialism but not for the second component—that is, not for the moral side constraints and rights component that is most prominent in Nozick. Because it accedes to the first anticonsequentialist objection but rebuffs the second, Scheffler's position is a "hybrid" of consequentialism and anticonsequentialism. Moreover, Scheffler explicitly rejects the suggestion—which I think is present in the common progression of anticonsequentialist argumentation—that the rationale for moving to the halfway point on the anticonsequentialist road is also (a major part of) the rationale for moving on to the final point on that road. He rejects the thought that the rationale for introducing a prerogative into moral theory is also a rationale for introducing restrictions into moral theory.[10] Scheffler challenges the proponent of full anticonsequentialism to show why a system of prerogatives without restrictions is unacceptable. More specifically, the challenge is to show that a system of prerogatives without restrictions is unacceptable because the rationale that supports the affirmation of the prerogative also supports the affirmation of restrictions. It is by meeting this challenge that I show why the progression of anticonsequentialist argument should not halt at the affirmation of a prerogative but, instead, should go on to the affirmation of restrictions. By showing that the argument should go on to the affirmation of restrictions, I provide what Nozick failed to provide: an explicit line of justification for side constraints and correlative rights.

Thus, the general plan of argument is this:

(1) Identify the rationale for the inclusion of a prerogative in morality.
(2) Show that the introduction of a bare prerogative—a prerogative not clothed with restrictions—fails to satisfy the rationale for the introduction of that prerogative.
(3) Show that only the further introduction of restrictions—restrictions against suppressions of the exercise of that prerogative—satisfies the rationale for the introduction of that prerogative.

---

[10] Scheffler calls the contention that the rationale for a prerogative is not also a rationale for restrictions the "independence thesis." See Scheffler, *The Rejection of Consequentialism*, 81–82. The independence thesis must be true for Scheffler's hybrid doctrine to be intellectually stable.

This general plan is complicated by the fact that prerogatives and their rationales come in different degrees of robustness. The more robust a prerogative is, the more fully it allows the individual to engage in personally rewarding action and to forgo personally costly service to the overall good. In the discussion that follows, we will encounter both the modest Schefflerian prerogative and the much more robust individualist prerogative. If my main argument is correct, the more robust an introduced prerogative is, the more robust will be the restrictions that will have to accompany this prerogative if the rationale for the prerogative is to be satisfied. Here, robustness in restrictions is a matter of the extent to which others are required not to interfere with an individual's personally rewarding actions.

As we shall see, Scheffler never attempts to specify the exact strength of his prerogative. Thus, I cannot specify the degree of robustness of the restrictions that must accompany the Schefflerian prerogative if the rationale for that prerogative is to be satisfied. This is no problem for me because I have no particular interest in specifying the robustness of the restrictions to which Scheffler should be committed in order for the rationale for his prerogative to be satisfied. Rather, I make use of Scheffler's framing of the question—Can it be shown that prerogatives without restrictions are unacceptable?—to arrive at the general conclusion that a given prerogative must be accompanied by restrictions against the suppression of the exercise of that prerogative. I then go on to consider the special case of the maximally robust prerogative and its accompanying restrictions. This is the case associated with the thorough rejection of the consequentialist belief in the authority of rankings of overall social states. This maximal prerogative is the prerogative that most fully sanctions the individual's pursuit of personally rewarding action and most fully rejects a requirement that the individual forgo such action for the sake of promoting the impersonally best outcome.

In Sections II and III of this essay, I examine Scheffler's prerogative, the rationale for that prerogative, and the reasons why the rationale is not satisfied unless the prerogative is accompanied by restrictions against the suppression of its exercise. In Sections IV and V, I examine the maximally robust individualist prerogative, the rationale for its introduction into morality, and the reasons why this rationale is not satisfied unless the individualist prerogative is accompanied by restrictions against suppression of its exercise. In Section VI, I recast some of the main conclusions about restrictions into the language of rights that are correlative to those restrictions. One further structural feature of this essay may be worth highlighting: In Section II, I intimate that a recognition of agent-relative values is crucial for the rationale for the Schefflerian prerogative. In Section IV, I argue that an affirmation of such values *and* a denial of agent-neutral values is crucial for the rationale for the individualist prerogative. I also say some things in favor of the claim that the affirmation of agent-relative values supports the rejection of agent-neutral values. Thus, if everything I argue for or gesture toward is correct, then even the very guarded departure from consequentialism associated with a modest prerogative like Scheffler's puts one on the road to the individualist prerogative, and that road is also the road to robust moral side constraints and correlative rights.

II. Scheffler's Prerogative and Its Rationale

Scheffler's whole discussion of the introduction of a prerogative into morality assumes that morality begins as fully consequentialist morality. We have some formula for ranking overall states of the world from impersonally best to impersonally worst, and the impersonally best state of the world summons everyone to do her bit in its promotion. Indeed, for Scheffler, it is a fixed and unshakeable idea that individuals and/or their representatives (e.g., the government) are always allowed to perform whatever action will promote the impersonally best outcome. That "one may always do what would lead to the best available outcome overall" is "the deeply plausible-sounding feature" of utilitarianism and of consequentialism in general. The moral theorist is simply "faced with the plausibility of the idea that it is always permissible to do what would have the best outcome overall." [11] Given Scheffler's assumptions, the only sort of rejection of consequentialism that has any chance of being accepted is a rejection of the consequentialist claim that each individual *must* always do what promotes the overall best outcome. Scheffler is prepared to allow the individual some dispensation from ceaseless self-dedication to the impersonally best.

Scheffler says that a plausible prerogative "would allow each agent to assign a certain proportionately greater weight to his own interests than to the interests of other people." Each agent would be "allowed to give M times more weight to his own interests than to the interests of anyone else." [12] An agent is allowed to refrain from performing an optimal action that benefits others if the overall benefit to others is less than the cost to the agent of performing the optimal action multiplied by M. Let us assume that M = 4 and that all of the lives involved have equal value. An agent— let us call her Rebekah—will be allowed not to donate her vital organs if this donation would save only three other lives. Of course, if Rebekah's organs would save five other lives, then this prerogative will not allow Rebekah to keep her organs. Many questions arise here that Scheffler does not address. How high does M have to be for commonsense morality to be satisfied? How high does M have to be for it to be rational for an individual to opt for sacrifice whenever the gains to society from her

[11] Ibid, 4.
[12] Ibid., 20 and 169.

sacrifice are M times her loss? Suppose that M is fairly high, for example, 158, so that *each* of us may opt out of the enterprise of promoting what is said to be the impersonally best outcome unless the benefit to others of that promotion is more than 158 times greater than one's personal cost of doing so. If, for each of us, our own concerns and commitments have this sort of weight, does it still make any sense to talk about the impersonally best outcome—albeit an impersonally best outcome that we are often excused from serving?

I have followed Scheffler in speaking as though the overall best outcome is the state of affairs in which the good is *maximized,* but it should be noted that Scheffler endorses the introduction of distribution-sensitivity into the ranking of overall states of affairs. On the one hand, he correctly holds that the introduction of distribution-sensitivity into the ranking of overall states of affairs is not itself a departure from consequentialism. One need not hold to an aggregative conception of the overall best in order to be a consequentialist. On the other hand, he fails to notice that this distribution-sensitivity makes it very difficult to see how one can specify the *magnitude* of the value difference between the best overall state of affairs and the state of affairs that will obtain if Rebekah performs her most personally rewarding action. Yet one needs to be able to specify this magnitude, along with the magnitude of the value difference for Rebekah between the two states of affairs, if a Schefflerian prerogative is to tell us whether Rebekah may decline to sacrifice her own concerns and commitments. For Rebekah may perform the nonoptimal action if and only if the magnitude of her gain from doing so (compared to her performing the optimal action) multiplied by M is greater than the magnitude of overall gain if the optimal action is performed (compared to Rebekah's most personally rewarding action).

Scheffler's prerogative makes it sometimes acceptable that Rebekah not perform the optimal action. However, even when it is acceptable for Rebekah to perform some more personally rewarding, nonoptimal action, it remains acceptable for her to perform the optimal action. Although it is sometimes permissible to depart from the optimal course of action, it is always permissible to adhere to the optimal course. This claim seems reasonable enough within the context of the sort of example we have just considered—an example in which Rebekah needs to choose how to deploy *her* personal resources. A prerogative that allows Rebekah to keep her organs—because M is high enough compared to the number of people who could be saved by transplanting those organs—does not *require* Rebekah to forgo evisceration. Yet Scheffler goes further than this. Quietly stepping beyond cases in which an agent may choose to produce the best overall outcome by devoting *her* resources to or sacrificing *herself* for that outcome, Scheffler concludes that the ascription of a prerogative to individuals does not at all limit the permissibility of agents' performing optimizing actions—even if an agent's optimizing action consumes *others'* resources or lives. Scheffler observes that it is in no way an implication of Rebekah's possessing a prerogative that Rebekah is under a restriction against imposing costs *on herself* for the sake of overall optimal outcomes. From this he seems to infer that the general introduction of prerogatives can in no way call for accompanying restrictions on anyone against *any* optimizing action.

Scheffler has other bases for his belief that morality does not include restrictions—in particular, restrictions that might forbid some optimal action. There is, of course, his fixed belief that optimizing actions are always permissible. In addition, there is his belief that the deontic character of restrictions renders them paradoxical. Scheffler's belief in the "paradox of deontology" requires a brief explanation. If individuals are subject to some deontic restriction—for example, the restriction against unprovoked killing of other individuals—then sometimes they will be required to abide by the restriction even if a result that is at least in some ways more attractive will be produced by violating the restriction. If individuals are subject to such a restriction, they may even be required not to engage in a certain sort of behavior in situations in which their engaging in this behavior would have the attractive result of minimizing how much of that very kind of behavior occurs. For instance, if Rebekah is subject to a deontic restriction against unprovoked killing, Rebekah may be required not to engage in an unprovoked killing of Joshua even if her unprovoked killing of Joshua would prevent Sebastian from engaging in the unprovoked killing of five other people. Advocates of deontic restrictions are well aware of this feature of such restrictions and are, on reflection, comfortable with it.[13] Scheffler, however, thinks that any putative deontic restriction against a kind of behavior must rest on the disvalue or objectionable character of the behavior (or its results). Hence, as he sees it, the claim that Rebekah ought to abide by the restriction against unprovoked killing even if her engaging in unprovoked killing would minimize the extent of unprovoked killing amounts to the paradoxical claim that Rebekah ought to find unprovoked killing objectionable, ought to be directed against unprovoked killing by its objectionable character, and yet ought to avoid doing what would minimize the extent of this objectionable activity. In Scheffler's eyes, compliance with the restriction seems paradoxically to serve or at least tolerate the disvalue or objectionable property that the restriction is supposed to oppose. (Advocates of deontic restrictions will say that Scheffler merely points to what is already well known: that a deontic restriction may require one to forgo producing an outcome that is at least in some ways more attractive than the outcome of abiding by the restriction.)[14]

---

[13] Nozick, *Anarchy, State, and Utopia*, 30–33.

[14] The "paradox of deontology" is entirely a product of ascribing to the advocate of deontic restrictions a conception of the ground for those restrictions—that some disvalue or objectionable property is to be minimized overall—which the advocate of restrictions rejects. See Eric Mack, "Moral Individualism: Agent-Relativity and Deontic Restraints," *Social Philosophy and Policy* 7, no. 1 (1989): 81–111, esp. 110–11.

Finally, in support of his combined acceptance of a prerogative and rejection of restrictions, Scheffler maintains that whereas there is a plausible rationale for the prerogative, there is no comparably plausible rationale for deontic restrictions. More pointedly, Scheffler maintains that the plausible rationale for the personal prerogative does not also serve as a rationale for accompanying deontic restrictions. This is the previously mentioned "independence thesis."

In order to assess Scheffler's introduction of his prerogative and his independence thesis, we need to know what this rationale is. This rationale is the accommodation within moral theory of the moral independence of the personal point of view. This rationale emerges from a recognition of the clash between the impersonal point of view and the personal point of view. To trace its emergence, let us start with the impersonal standpoint. This standpoint is the one that recognizes and takes direction from impersonal value—value that attaches to conditions or activities, or to certain distributions of valuable conditions or activities, in such a way that everyone has reason to promote the valuable conditions, activities, or distributions. (If there is no impersonal value to recognize and take direction from, there is no impersonal point of view; there is merely a mistaken belief in the existence of an impersonal point of view.)

A patch of sensorial pleasure is often thought to be impersonally valuable if anything is. It is just a good thing for such a condition to obtain. The universe is better for it. And each person, in principle, has reason to contribute to the existence of this condition—usually, in practice, by allowing the lowest-cost producer of the patch to "do his thing." Of course, if this patch of sensorial pleasure comes to exist, it will exist at a particular (mental) location, within a particular (lucky) receptacle—for example, within Joshua. The particular receptacle, Joshua, will almost certainly have a greater desire than others that this valuable patch of pleasure obtain and will be more motivated than others to promote it. Still, Joshua has, in principle, no more (and no less) reason to promote this pleasure than any other agent. Indeed, each has the *same* reason: its impersonal goodness. A slightly more extensive patch of pleasure experienced by Sebastian would, by hypothesis, be more impersonally valuable than the pleasure desired by Joshua. And every individual would, in principle, have a stronger reason—whatever his natural subjective preferences—to promote the more extensive patch of pleasure than he would have to promote the pleasure for which Joshua longs. If only one of the patches could be produced, it would be better overall for the larger patch to be produced; and, all things considered, each individual would have reason to contribute to that outcome. Joshua would have the same reason as everyone else for promoting the larger patch in Sebastian rather than the smaller patch in himself.

Of course, the choices that will have to be made between alternative outcomes will typically be more complicated than the choice between a lesser and a more extensive patch of sensorial pleasure. One will have an operative impersonal standpoint only if one has some formula for making these choices, that is, some formula for ranking alternative sets of impersonally valuable (and disvaluable) conditions and activities against one another, and hence for determining which overall outcome everyone has reason to promote.[15] If the impersonal point of view captures all of morality's directives, then we are each thoroughly subject to the claims of the impersonally best. Each of our lives should be morally dedicated to the best overall outcome.

Yet surely we are not each thoroughly subject to the claims of the impersonally best. Surely benefits that would accrue to others—to make the point sharply, benefits that would accrue to strangers—do not as thoroughly or unconditionally rationally direct us to incur costs for their promotion as do benefits that would accrue to ourselves (or to those within the ambit of our special concerns and commitments). The view that we are all thoroughly subject to the claims of the impersonally best seems to miss something essential. In this era's most renowned challenge to full-fledged consequentialism, this view is said to miss the separateness (and distinctiveness) of persons.[16] Invoking Rawls's basic criticism, Nozick says that this impersonalist perspective misses the fact that "there are different individuals with separate lives."[17]

For Scheffler, this sort of consideration is introduced by way of the idea of the independence of the personal point of view. Within each individual, "concerns and commitments are *naturally* generated from [that] person's point of view quite independently of the weight of those concerns in an impersonal ranking of overall states of affairs." "Each [personal] point of view constitutes . . . a locus relative to which harms and benefits can be assessed, and *are* typically assessed by the person who has the [relevant personal] point of view."[18] Each individual naturally ascribes value to or recognizes value in particular conditions or activities that stand in some special relationship to him or her. Joshua ascribes value to or recognizes value in the patch of pleasure that he would experience. Rebekah ascribes value to or recognizes value in her achievement of her career ambitions. Sebastian ascribes value to or recognizes value in his compliance with norms to which he has committed himself. And these ascriptions of value to or recognitions of value in particular conditions or

---

[15] Such a formula captures the commensurability of the various valuable (and disvaluable) conditions, activities, and so on. To the extent that such a formula is not available and the various values (and disvalues) are incommensurable, the impersonal standpoint becomes less operative. Some advocates of impersonal value seek to limit the tyranny of impersonal value over the lives of individuals by upholding the incommensurability of diverse impersonal values. See, e.g., John Finnis, *Natural Law and Natural Rights* (Oxford: Clarendon Press, 1980), esp. chaps. 3 and 4.

[16] Rawls, *A Theory of Justice*, 27.

[17] Nozick, *Anarchy, State, and Utopia*, 33.

[18] Scheffler, *The Rejection of Consequentialism*, 56.

activities occur independently of any consequentialist judgment that the valued conditions or activities would be part of the best overall state of affairs. One important piece of evidence for this independence is that the value a given individual ascribes to or recognizes in some particular condition or activity is not the value ascribed to it or recognized in it by the impersonal standpoint.[19] Joshua naturally ascribes value to his prospective patch of pleasure—and takes himself to have reason to promote that pleasure—even though the realization of that pleasure would preclude the realization of Sebastian's more extensive pleasure and, hence, would be disfavored by the impersonal calculus.

Although this pretty much exhausts what Scheffler says about the naturalness and the independence of the personal point of view, it hardly seems enough to draw the conclusion that moral theory ought to accommodate or reflect the existence of this standpoint. After all, many commentators have noticed that it is *natural* for individuals to have personal concerns and commitments that differ in their motivational direction or strength from the concerns or commitments they would have if they were purely impersonal in their point of view. These commentators have gone on with perfect consistency to *condemn* this natural feature of human beings and to urge its greatest possible suppression or transcendence. Many people have seen the "selfishness" of the personal point of view not as something that moral theory should accede to or even embrace but, rather, as something that moral theory should direct us to annihilate. Moreover, a moral theory that commands us to transcend our special regard for our own concerns and commitments cannot be said to fail to recognize the naturalness and independence of the personal point of view. Nor can we get to the conclusion that the personal standpoint is to be accommodated or reflected in moral theory from the assertion that "[t]o have an independent point of view is part of the nature of a person if anything is."[20] For one could accept this and with consistency sermonize against the rebelliousness of our nature and in favor of its being brought back under the authority of the impersonal.

What Scheffler needs, but does not explicitly endorse, is the proposition that the particular conditions and activities that are the objects of an individual's special concerns and commitments do indeed have value for that individual and provide the individual with reasons to favor those conditions or activities quite independently of any value they have or any reason they provide from the impersonal standpoint.[21] He needs to explicitly recognize that the objects of these concerns and commitments have agent-relative value and provide agent-relative reasons. Scheffler approaches this explicit recognition when he says that for each individ-

---

[19] Ibid., 57.

[20] Ibid., 58.

[21] Or at least *some* of the objects of a person's concerns and commitments have value. To avoid complexity, I omit this important qualification in the discussion that follows.

ual, "[h]is own projects and commitments have a distinctive *claim* on his attention."[22] And he comes even closer when he defends the idea "that personal projects and commitments can have . . . *moral weight* for an agent . . . independently of the weight those projects and commitments have in the impersonal calculus."[23] It is because personal projects and commitments have this sort of moral weight—for the agent whose projects and commitments they are—that it is a "decisive objection to consequentialism" that

> it requires each person always to *act as if* he had no further concern for his projects and plans once the impersonal assessment was in. It singles out the impersonal calculus as identifying the right course of action for the individual, no matter how his own projects and plans may have fared at the hands of that calculus. . . . [I]t requires that he devote energy to his projects in strict proportion to the weight from the impersonal standpoint of his doing so.[24]

In light of the moral significance of the personal point of view, a sensible moral theory will contain some element (or set of elements) that protects individuals from being morally under the impersonalist thumb. It will contain some element (or set of elements) that liberates individuals from the moral subjugation to the impersonalist calculus that would otherwise be their moral fate.

The rationale for the prerogative takes the form of liberation of the individual from moral subjugation to the impersonal standpoint. Still, the rationale for Scheffler's prerogative cannot be *total* liberation from the claims of the overall best. For Scheffler does believe in the impersonal standpoint, which means that he believes that to some considerable extent we all ought to be morally subject to it. All we can say is that, for Scheffler, the rationale for the prerogative is to liberate individuals from moral subjugation to the impersonal standpoint to some unspecified extent. Scheffler's claim is that the inclusion within morality of a prerogative that allows each individual to weigh gains and losses for herself M times as much as gains and losses for others will satisfy the rationale for that prerogative. However, given that we get neither a specification of the extent to which that rationale calls for individuals to be protected against subjugation to the impersonal standpoint nor a specification of M, how can we determine whether the inclusion in morality of a bare prerogative—a prerogative without accompanying restrictions—satisfies the rationale for that prerogative? The answer is that we can determine that the introduction of the prerogative—with whatever M it embodies—will fail to satisfy

22 Ibid., 57 (emphasis added).
23 Ibid., 61 (emphasis added).
24 Ibid., 57.

the rationale for the prerogative if there are two distinct dimensions along which an individual can be liberated from or subject to the impersonal standpoint and the introduction of the prerogative into morality liberates the individual along only one of those two dimensions. If the introduction of the prerogative simply does nothing to liberate the individual along the second dimension, then the mere introduction of the prerogative will leave the rationale for its introduction crucially unsatisfied. As we shall see, there are two distinct dimensions: An individual can be liberated from or subject to the impersonal standpoint with respect to whether she herself is required to devote herself to the production of impersonally best outcomes and with respect to whether others are allowed (or even required) to devote her to the production of impersonally best outcomes. If only the further inclusion in morality of deontic restrictions will liberate the individual along the second dimension, then we can conclude that prerogatives without accompanying restrictions are unacceptable.

III. The Schefflerian Prerogative without Restrictions Is Unacceptable

Suppose $M = 4$, so it is acceptable for Rebekah not to volunteer for evisceration even though the healthy organs that would be made available through her fatal dismemberment would save the equally valuable lives of three other individuals. Similarly, it is acceptable for Rebekah to spend n dollars on an expensive vacation for herself even though she might instead use that money to send three other people on much less expensive but, for them, equally satisfying vacations.[25] The inclusion within morality of a prerogative (with $M = 4$) frees Rebekah from moral subjugation to the impersonal standpoint in these circumstances in the sense that Rebekah is not morally required to choose these optimal courses of action.

But what does a morality that departs from full consequentialism only through its inclusion of such a prerogative say to *other agents* about how they should act with respect to Rebekah's exercise of her prerogative? What does such a hybrid morality say to other agents about their being allowed or even required to coerce Rebekah into donating her organs to save three other individuals or donating her vacation fund to send the three to Atlantic City? After all, as Scheffler repeatedly says, the introduction of a bare personal prerogative does not morally preclude any agent from choosing the optimal action. Such a hybrid morality will tell other agents that whenever the specific costs associated with suppressing Rebekah's exercise of her prerogative (i.e., with coercing her instead into

---

[25] I assume that these choices will not trigger whatever distribution-sensitivity is built into the operative theory of the overall good.

performing the optimal action) are low enough, the agent is morally allowed to suppress Rebekah's exercise of her prerogative.

Moreover, since the specific costs of some other agent suppressing Rebekah's exercise of her prerogative will often be low enough, some other agent will often be morally allowed to interfere with Rebekah to block her exercise of her prerogative. Furthermore, in almost all cases in which some other agent will be morally allowed to suppress Rebekah's exercise of her prerogative, that agent will also be morally required to suppress it. I contend that a morality with these implications thoroughly undermines the moral independence of the personal point of view vis-à-vis its teaching about what may or must be done to the individual *by others* in accordance with the impersonal standpoint. It subordinates the personal point of view not through teaching that the individual must direct herself to the impersonally best, but rather by teaching that others often may and often must direct her to the impersonally best. Such a hybrid morality does not satisfy the rationale for the inclusion of the personal prerogative in morality; along a crucial dimension, the inclusion of the bare prerogative leaves individuals morally subjugated to the impersonal standpoint. To sustain this conclusion, I will say a bit more in support of the multipart claim that it is the teaching of hybrid morality that (a) whenever the special costs of doing so are low enough, it will be allowable for some other agent to suppress Rebekah's exercise of her prerogative; (b) the costs will often be low enough; and (c) in almost all cases in which it is morally allowable for another agent to suppress an individual's exercise of her prerogative, it is also morally required for that agent to suppress that exercise.

If Joshua can coerce (or trick) Rebekah into donating her organs or vacation fund without too much additional cost—cost *in addition to* Rebekah's cost were she voluntarily to donate the organs or the vacation fund—then, under the circumstances, Joshua's so coercing (or tricking) Rebekah will almost certainly be his optimal action. Hence, the hybrid morality says that such suppressions of Rebekah's exercise of her prerogative would be morally allowable. Moreover, it is likely that the additional costs (if any)[26] of suppressing Rebekah's exercise of her prerogative will be low enough for the suppression to be morally allowable. For there are substantial impersonal gains to be had from directing Rebekah's organs or vacation fund to the three other individuals. There is a net gain to the world of two lives or two satisfying vacations. Hence, even some considerable additional costs—borne by Rebekah or Joshua or some other party—will be low enough for interference with Rebekah's exercise of her prerogative to be Joshua's optimal course of action.

---

[26] Joshua's coercing (or tricking) Rebekah into donation might be a *lower*-cost route to helping out the three other individuals than the voluntary route, for it might be quite costly to Rebekah to come to the voluntary decision to donate to the three others, and it might be quite costly to others to elicit this decision from Rebekah.

Here it is worth noting that the higher M is, the greater the potential impersonal gains from suppressing individuals in the exercise of their prerogatives; and, hence, the higher M is, the more readily a given cost associated with such suppression will be low enough for the suppression to be morally allowable. The more M is raised in an attempt to make the prerogative more robustly reflective of the moral independence of the personal point of view, the greater the social gain from coercing individuals (who would otherwise exercise their prerogative) into the performance of the relevant optimal actions and the less likely that any special costs associated with coercing individuals into performing the optimal actions will be too high to allow that coercion. *The more the prerogative is strengthened in an attempt to protect the moral independence of the personal standpoint, the more systematically the resulting hybrid morality will say that others are allowed to coercively block individuals from the exercise of that very prerogative.*

Furthermore, under a hybrid morality, any suppression of Rebekah's exercise of her prerogative that is allowable to another agent will be morally *required* of that agent unless abstention from the suppression would be allowed under *that* agent's prerogative—that is, unless the agent has a considerable personal stake in Rebekah's remaining alive or having a satisfying vacation. So friends of Rebekah and her trading partners will not be required to promote the impersonally low-cost transfer of her organs or her vacation fund to the other three individuals. But all who are not her friends or trading partners will be morally required to suppress Rebekah's exercise of her prerogative.

Suppose, however, that I have miscalculated in my account of the hybrid theory's teaching. Suppose that the hybrid theory does not *as pervasively* inform other agents that it is morally allowable and even morally required that they intervene against Rebekah as I have argued it does. Would this weaken the conclusion that the hybrid theory thoroughly fails to liberate Rebekah from the impersonal standpoint vis-à-vis its teaching about what may or must be done to her *by others*? The answer is no. For in every instance—however many there may be—in which according to correct hybrid calculations it is not allowable for Joshua to intervene to prevent Rebekah from exercising her prerogative and, hence, not required of Joshua that he intervene, intervention will fail to be allowable because of its *impersonal* costs. In every such instance, the case that Rebekah would have to make against the intervention being allowable would have to consist in showing that the additional impersonal costs of imposing the sacrifice upon her were too high. She would have to show that, due to these additional impersonal costs and contrary to initial appearances, the intervention would not really serve the overall good. This reveals that, whether or not in a particular instance hybrid morality proclaims that others may or even must suppress Rebekah's exercise of her prerogative, whether or not others may or even must so act is entirely a deliverance of the impersonal point of view. No matter how often it turns out—according to hybrid calculations more subtle than those I have offered—that others are to allow Rebekah to exercise her prerogative, these dispensations will still indicate that Rebekah's conduct is hostage to, not liberated from, the impersonal standpoint.[27]

The impersonal standpoint threatens the moral independence of the personal point of view in two ways. First, it threatens to require that Rebekah submit to its directives, sacrificing even her most important projects and commitments if that is the way the impersonalist calculus works out. Second, it threatens to morally allow or even to morally require that others submit Rebekah to its directives and impose on her the sacrifice of even her most important projects and commitments if that is the way the impersonalist calculus works out. Scheffler's tendency to ignore this second threat is revealed by the fact that when he speaks of how, in the case of a given individual, the directives of the impersonal standpoint undermine the personal point of view, he speaks entirely in terms of *that individual's adherence* to those directives; he does not speak or think at all of the undermining of the moral independence of the personal point of view vis-à-vis what may or must be done to that individual by *others in their adherence* to these directives. Since there are these two dimensions along which the personal point of view can be subjugated to or liberated from the impersonal standpoint, and since the prerogative only deals with one of these dimensions, and since the rationale for the prerogative is to liberate the personal standpoint from subordination to the impersonal standpoint, the introduction of the prerogative cannot by itself satisfy the rationale for its introduction.

Within a preliminary phase of his discussion of hybrid morality, Scheffler focuses on integrity rather than the moral independence of the personal point of view. At that point, he envisions the introduction of a prerogative into morality for the purpose of recognizing or protecting the importance or value of integrity.[28] At this stage of his discussion, Scheffler

---

[27] Scheffler discusses whether, within the hybrid view, *the government* may or even must often intervene to impose sacrifices on individuals that they have a prerogative not to impose on themselves (ibid., 33–35). If the moral mandate of the government is very different from that of individuals, *the government* may not always be allowed or even required to impose the sacrificial alternative on individuals. Scheffler thinks that the government *might* have a very different mandate because it *might* be that hybrid-minded individuals would establish a government that would advance their individual aims as long as that advancement did not "exceed the bounds of their prerogatives" (ibid., 35). It does not seem likely, however, that hybrid-minded individuals would agree only on a government that would be constrained in this way. The reason is that, if individuals would agree on such constraints on government, they would also agree on such constraints as part of their common morality. But then they would not be hybrid-minded.

[28] Here and in his subsequent discussion of the independence of the personal point of view, Scheffler is building upon but trying to contain the anticonsequentialist indications of Bernard Williams's essay "A Critique of Utilitarianism," in J. J. C. Smart and Bernard Williams, *Utilitarianism: For and Against* (Cambridge: Cambridge University Press, 1973), 77–150, esp. 108–18.

anticipates something like the objection I have developed here against a morality that includes a prerogative but no accompanying constraints. The objection he considers is that a morality that issues "a requirement that governments always do what would have the best outcome overall would clearly nullify the effects of the [integrity-recognizing] prerogative." [29] Scheffler counters this objection with the claim that even though hybrid morality does endorse this requirement, it does not undermine integrity (or at least does not undermine integrity in some especially unfortunate way). For a requirement upon the government to force individuals not to pursue their own concerns and commitments does not violate "the integrity of agents by virtue of what it *directly* requires them to do." [30] The core idea here seems to be that a morality will only threaten the integrity of an individual if it requires *that individual herself* to strictly follow the impersonalist calculus in her decisions about how she will act. A morality that allows the individual to give disproportionate weight to her own concerns and commitments in her decisions about how she will act will not undermine her integrity even if that morality also always requires the government to force the individual not to carry out her nonoptimal decisions.

Our concern here is not with the plausibility of this specific claim about integrity. Rather, it is with the plausibility of a parallel claim about the moral independence of the personal point of view that Scheffler might attempt to advance. Scheffler could counter the argument I have offered if he could plausibly maintain that a morality will only threaten the moral independence of the personal standpoint if it requires the individual herself ("directly") to strictly follow the impersonalist calculus in her decisions about how she will act. This would be to maintain that no matter how systematically the impersonalist component of hybrid morality demands that *others* prevent individuals from exercising their prerogative—a prerogative that has been introduced into morality in order to secure the moral independence of the personal point of view—this morality cannot be said to unduly subordinate individuals to the impersonal standpoint.

This counterclaim is not plausible. A morality that decrees in the name of the impersonally best that individuals may be or even must be systematically forced to forgo personally rewarding actions—even those rewarding actions that an individual herself is allowed to choose under the morality's prerogative—subordinates individuals to the impersonal standpoint. Its subordination of individuals to the impersonal standpoint is comparable to, albeit different in kind from, the subordination involved in morally requiring an individual herself to decide in favor of the optimal action. Furthermore, it is worth noting how little protection is provided to the individual by a morality that forswears directly requiring

---

[29] Scheffler, *The Rejection of Consequentialism*, 37.
[30] Ibid., 38 (emphasis added).

that individual to decide how she will act entirely on the basis of the impersonalist calculus.

Since any hybrid morality incorporates some personal prerogative, it is true of any hybrid morality that it does not always *directly* require individuals to forgo personally rewarding actions and to choose the impersonally optimal action; hybrid morality does not *directly* require this sacrifice as long as the sacrifice by the individual would be sufficiently great. It is easy to see, however, that this exclusion of direct requiring does not preclude highly intrusive interventions by others, for example, the government, to prevent an individual from exercising her prerogative. Suppose that Rebekah has two possible actions before her. One is personally rewarding action *p*, which she is morally allowed to perform under the prerogative. The other is impersonally optimal action *o*. Moreover, there is only one low-cost intervention on the part of the government that will bring it about that Rebekah performs *o* rather than *p*. This low-cost intervention works by causing a "decision" within Rebekah to perform *o* rather than *p*. A painless microinjection of some mind-controlling chemical causes Rebekah to "choose" *o* rather than *p*. The impersonalist component of hybrid morality requires the government to engage in this low-cost intervention. No prerogative that merely allows Rebekah not to decide directly on behalf of the optimal action will preclude the permissibility of this low-cost intervention. All that follows from Rebekah having such a prerogative is that, if she manages to decide herself on behalf of the more personally rewarding action and against the optimizing action, she will have acted permissibly. But this does not preclude its being permissible for others—for example, the government—to prevent her from so deciding. If it were true that the impersonally best outcome would be achieved by an enlightened despot microinjecting everyone else so as to make them each "choose" the optimal alternatives before them,[31] hybrid morality would morally require the despot to carry out the injection program. That hybrid morality would morally require such a program is a pointed indication of its failure to accommodate the moral independence of the personal point of view.

In the course of his rejection of restrictions, Scheffler presents the reasoning of someone who would disagree with him—in particular, someone who thinks that the very rationale for the inclusion of a prerogative in morality calls for the inclusion of restrictions. This advocate of restrictions maintains the following:

> Agent-centred [i.e., deontic] restrictions . . . serve to protect individuals from the demand that they organize their conduct in accordance

---

[31] On some specific theories of the good, e.g., ones that emphasize the goodness of autonomy, it might not be possible to optimize by injection. If one appeals to such a theory, one's rejection of interferences with persons' exercise of their prerogatives will be based upon the *impersonal* costliness of those interferences.

with some canon of impersonal optimality. They prevent individuals from becoming slaves of the impersonal standpoint, and in so doing they serve to insulate the personal point of view against external demands. For this reason they represent a rational response to the fact that individuals are naturally independent of the impersonal perspective.[32]

Unfortunately for Scheffler, this sounds exactly right. Any canon of impersonal optimality threatens the personal point of view in two distinct ways—along the two dimensions I have previously cited. It threatens by way of its demand that individuals themselves decide how they will act entirely by working through the impersonalist calculus, and it threatens by way of allowing or even requiring others to treat individuals in whatever ways yield the impersonally best overall outcome. Any such canon directs Rebekah to enslave herself—if the impersonal benefits of her enslavement are great enough. But it also directs others to enslave Rebekah—if her enslavement would be an impersonal improvement. What Rebekah needs in the first instance to be morally insulated from these external demands is a prerogative that allows her to give special weight to her own concerns and commitments in deciding how she will act. What Rebekah needs in the second instance to be morally insulated from these external demands is for others to be restricted in how they may treat her in the course of promoting the good. The restriction on others that seems to be the natural companion of a given prerogative is a restriction against suppressing Rebekah's exercise of that prerogative.

Why does Scheffler miss the obvious plausibility of the plea for restrictions that he himself articulates? He misses its plausibility because of his odd understanding of this plea. He takes the proposed restrictions not to be restrictions *against others* devoting Rebekah to impersonal optimality but, rather, restrictions *on Rebekah* against devoting herself to the impersonally best. He imagines that the proposed restrictions have the purpose of further protecting Rebekah against her *self*-enslavement to the impersonal standpoint. He takes the idea behind the plea to be that Rebekah will be somewhat protected against self-enslavement by a prerogative that allows her not to self-enslave, but she will be more protected against self-enslavement by a restriction that forbids self-enslavement. He then argues that there is no point to adding this prohibition to Rebekah's already ascribed prerogative. For this prerogative already provides all the protection Rebekah needs against impersonalist demands for her *self*-enslavement: "The *permission* not to produce the best states suffices to free individual agents from the demands of impersonal optimality, and thus to prevent them from becoming slaves of the impersonal standpoint."[33]

[32] Ibid., 94.
[33] Ibid., 94–95.

Amazingly, when he articulates this plea for restrictions, the possibility that the purpose of the restrictions is to morally insulate individuals from others acting under the authority of the impersonal standpoint is not even on Scheffler's radar screen.[34]

The rationale for the Schefflerian prerogative—to liberate individuals as occupants of their own personal standpoint from the demands of the impersonal standpoint—is not satisfied by the introduction into morality of a bare prerogative. Thus, some additional element that protects individuals from subordination to the impersonal standpoint needs to be included within morality. However, it might be suggested that this additional element need not be deontic restrictions against suppression of the exercise of the prerogative. A seemingly natural alternative candidate for inclusion would be a maxim calling for the minimization of acts of suppression against exercises of the prerogative. Such a maxim would be an alternative to deontic restrictions precisely because the maxim would *endorse* an agent's suppressing a given individual's exercise of her prerogative whenever that suppression would have the effect of minimizing the overall number of such suppressions. So, to complete my argument for the need to add accompanying restrictions in order for the rationale for the Schefflerian prerogative to be satisfied, I have to say why this minimizing maxim is not an appropriate candidate for the additional protective element.

The introduction of bare prerogatives leaves a crucial gap in the defense against the canons of impersonalism. This gap cannot be fortified with the minimizing maxim because the maxim is itself an impersonalist canon. The minimizing maxim reflects the ascription of impersonal disvalue to each suppression of an exercise of the prerogative. From this ascription we can infer that having fewer suppressions is always impersonally better overall than having more, and from this we can infer that, ceteris paribus, everyone ought to act so as to minimize these suppressions.[35] Thus, the minimizing maxim is not responsive to the specific threat at hand; it is not responsive to each person's exercise of her prerogative being subject to allowable (and even required) suppression by others

---

[34] At other times, Scheffler does consider restrictions that have the purpose of morally insulating the prerogative-holder from others' optimizing actions, but he dismisses this possibility on the grounds that such restrictions would, after all, make some optimizing actions impermissible and that such restrictions would "paradoxically" morally preclude acts that would minimize the number of violations of such restrictions.

[35] Within an overall impersonalist calculus, the disvalue of suppressions and the related value of preventing suppressions may only be two of *many* disvalues and values that will enter into a determination of whether the suppression of this particular exercise of Rebekah's prerogative is morally allowed or required. Even if, for the sake of argument, we permit the consequentialist or hybrid theorist to ascribe a high disvalue to such suppressions, there is every reason to expect that sometimes that theorist's calculations will allow or even require the suppression of Rebekah for the sake of impersonal gains that do not come in the form of other suppressions being prevented. The minimizing maxim, built as it is on ascribing impersonal disvalue to suppressions, allows its champion to say that sometimes the prevention of suppressions justifies suppression. It does not allow its champion to say that *only* the prevention of suppressions justifies suppression.

whenever that suppression serves the impersonally best outcome. The minimizing maxim does not fortify this gap in the defense against marauding impersonalism. Indeed, all the maxim does is refine the specification of when it will be impersonally best to engage in such suppression. The maxim tells us that, since any such act of suppression is an impersonally very bad thing, agents should only engage in an act of suppression when the impersonal gain from doing so is high—as it will be if the gain is the prevention of a greater number of suppressions.

Concern about one sort of threat to the moral independence of the personal point of view—a concern about self-subordination—leads the hybrid theorist to favor the inclusion in morality of a personal prerogative *for everyone*. Concern about another sort of threat to the moral independence of the personal point of view—a concern about subordination by others—supports the inclusion within morality of restrictions against subordination by others, restrictions that morally insulate *everyone* against certain forms or degrees of subordination. In contrast, the minimizing maxim does not insulate everyone. It only insulates those individuals whose subordination is not impersonally expeditious—under the refined specification of the expeditious.[36] Deontic restrictions constitute the dimension of morality that says that each individual possesses a moral immunity against such and such forms or degrees of subordination. I have suggested that the restriction that most appropriately accompanies a given personal prerogative is the restriction against preventing individuals from exercising that prerogative. A morality that forbids suppressions of exercises of its prerogative morally insulates everyone from subjugation; it morally liberates everyone. Some people may not abide by this restriction; *they* may wrongly subjugate others in the name of their personal ends or the impersonalist calculus. But that some people may act in this way hardly reveals a defect in the moral code that condemns such actions whenever they are performed.

IV. THE RATIONALE FOR THE INDIVIDUALIST PREROGATIVE

The argument that I have made points to a very general conclusion. To the extent that a prerogative is introduced into morality in order to accommodate the personal point of view, the rationale for the introduction of that prerogative will not be satisfied unless the prerogative is accompanied by restrictions against suppression of its exercise. Thus, it is always unacceptable for prerogatives that are introduced into morality in order to accommodate the personal point of view to be unaccompanied by restrictions. Indeed, an even stronger conclusion is indicated: The more robust the introduced prerogative is, the more robust the accompanying

---

[36] The real minimizing maxim at work throughout Scheffler's investigation is this: Minimize departures from consequentialism.

restrictions must be. The more readily the individual is allowed to choose personally rewarding, nonoptimal actions, the more extensively others will be required not to suppress actions of the individual, even if suppression would serve the overall good. A maximally robust prerogative would, it seems, need to be accompanied by maximal restrictions if the rationale for that maximal prerogative is to be satisfied.

A maximal prerogative—what I call the individualist prerogative—will always allow the individual to opt for her more personally rewarding course of action. It will always allow her to refuse to sacrifice her personal concerns and commitments on the altar of what is *described as* the impersonally best. This individualist prerogative is not based on the conviction that M is *very* high so that the multiplied weight of the individual's own concerns and commitments always overbalances the weight of the impersonally best. Rather, the individualist prerogative is based on combining an affirmation of the personal standpoint with a rejection of the impersonal standpoint. Since the impersonal standpoint is rejected, the individual needs no multiplication by M in order to be allowed to pursue her most rewarding path. With the rejection of the impersonal standpoint, we step outside of the framework in which we first affirm the impersonal standpoint and then think about how much dispensation from its demands is to be granted. We no longer think of the personal standpoint as a counterweight against the central and unquestioned weight and authority of the impersonal standpoint. This makes the case of the individualist prerogative somewhat special and deserving of some separate discussion.

My primary task for the remainder of this essay is to defend the claim that if it is rational to introduce the individualist prerogative into morality, then it is also rational to introduce restrictions against suppressions of its exercise. This claim, like the general conclusion it instantiates, is conditional. It is not part of the main task of this essay to justify the antecedent claim that the individualist prerogative ought to be introduced into morality. Nor is it part of the main task of this essay to back up further in order to vindicate the rationale for introducing the individualist prerogative. Nevertheless, the conditional claim is only of interest if there is some decent prospect of justifying the individualist prerogative and its rationale. So, just as I provided some enhancement for Scheffler's case for the rationale for his prerogative, in this section I will provide some persuasive remarks on behalf of the more controversial rationale for the individualist prerogative.

The affirmation of the personal standpoint conjoined with the dismissal of the impersonal standpoint comes down to the affirmation of agent-relative values and reasons for action conjoined with the dismissal of agent-neutral values and reasons for action. To rehearse these notions briefly, let us consider the contrasting agent-relativist and agent-neutralist understandings of the value of a patch of Rebekah's sensorial pleasure and of the reason for action associated with this value. On the agent-relativist understanding, this pleasure has value for Rebekah in virtue of its standing in some special value-conferring or value-grounding relationship to Rebekah, for example, its being desired by her or being enjoyed by her. Its being desired by Rebekah or its simply being *her* experienced pleasure is essential to its value—which is its value-for-Rebekah. This value-for-Rebekah provides her with agent-relative reason to bring about the pleasure, reason that need not be shared by anyone else. Of course, Rebekah's pleasure may also have agent-relative value for other individuals—for example, Mary, who deeply cares about Rebekah. If Rebekah's pleasure has value-for-Mary, then Mary also will have agent-relative reason to promote Rebekah's pleasure. But this reason will not derive simply from the pleasure's value-for-Rebekah. Nor will it be the same reason that Rebekah has to promote the pleasure. Nor will any third individual who does not himself stand in some special value-conferring or value-grounding relation to Rebekah's pleasure have reason to promote it.

Let us add to the picture another condition that is understood as having agent-relative value, namely, a larger (i.e., more extensive or more intensive) patch of Joshua's sensorial pleasure, which has value-for-Joshua and provides Joshua with reason to promote it. And let us assume that Rebekah and Joshua have no personal concern for or commitment to one another of the sort that might make the other's pleasure valuable for her or him. Suppose that only one of these pleasures can obtain. On the agent-relativist understanding of these values, which pleasure's occurrence is better? The answer is that the occurrence of Rebekah's pleasure is better, more valuable, relative to Rebekah and the occurrence of Joshua's pleasure is better, more valuable, relative to Joshua. And that is the end of the story. We cannot say of either pleasure that its occurrence is *overall best* (nor that the occurrences would have equal value). We cannot say that there is more *value* in the occurrence of Joshua's pleasure than in the occurrence of Rebekah's, even though we have stipulated that there will be more *pleasure* if Joshua's pleasure occurs. All there is in prospect is value-for-Rebekah or value-for-Joshua, and these two values are incommensurable in virtue of their agent-relativity. It is because of the agent-relativity of the value of these pleasures that, to paraphrase Nozick, no moral balancing act can take place among the pleasures of Rebekah and Joshua; there is no moral outweighing of one of their pleasures by the other so as to lead to the more valuable, indeed optimal, overall outcome. If all value is agent-relative, there is no single value metric in terms of which the gains to some individuals can be measured against the losses to others so as to assess trade-offs among individuals and to rank alternative trade-offs. If all value is agent-relative, then all the deliverances of the so-called impersonal standpoint are spurious.[37]

---

[37] Notice that the claim here is *not* the claim advanced in standard discussions of interpersonal comparisons of utility, namely, that the *magnitudes* of the gains and losses of different individuals cannot be compared.

What is the contrasting agent-neutralist understanding of the value of Rebekah's sensorial pleasure and the reason for its promotion? If this pleasure has agent-neutral value, then the value of the pleasure is not merely value for Rebekah (or for Mary), who stands in some special value-conferring or value-grounding relationship to the pleasure. Although Rebekah may be the site of the pleasure, and although her desire, anticipation, or experience of it may fulfill a condition of its having value, namely, that *someone* desire, anticipate, or experience it, the resulting value of the pleasure is not merely value-for-Rebekah. The pleasure has value *simpliciter*. This value provides Rebekah with reason to promote the pleasure, but it also provides everyone else with the same reason to promote the pleasure. For what *rationally* beckons Rebekah is simply the pleasure's agent-neutral value, and this agent-neutral value equally rationally beckons everyone. (If the pleasure has agent-neutral value, then it is valuable for everyone in the sense that it beckons everyone, not in the sense that it has value-for-Rebekah, value-for-Joshua, and so on.) Let us add to the picture another condition understood as having agent-neutral value, namely, a larger patch of Joshua's sensorial pleasure. On the agent-neutralist understanding, although Joshua is the site of this pleasure and we may say that the pleasure is agent-relative, the value of the pleasure is not. The pleasure just has value, period. It provides Joshua with reason to promote it, but it provides every other agent with the same reason to promote it. Each is equally rationally summoned to the production of this pleasure.

Suppose that only one of these pleasures can obtain. On the agent-neutralist understanding of these values, which pleasure's occurrence is better? The answer is simple. The occurrence of Joshua's larger pleasure is better overall. These two values are commensurable in virtue of their agent-neutrality. This commensurability allows us to assess the trade-off of Rebekah's pleasure for Joshua's; it allows us to rank the two alternative outcomes. Although both Rebekah and Joshua have some reason—the very same reason—to promote Rebekah's pleasure, both have stronger reason—the very same stronger reason—to promote Joshua's pleasure. All things considered, whichever of them is in a position to choose which pleasure will occur has reason to choose Joshua's pleasure. The impersonal standpoint is nothing but the faculty of recognizing agent-neutral values, combining them in accordance with some favored formula (for example, pure aggregation or distribution-sensitive aggregation), and taking direction from the all-things-considered reasons for action that arise from the recognition and combination of agent-neutral values.

The following seems to me to be the strongest case for the existence of agent-neutral values and reasons for promoting those values:

1. Some conditions (for example, the pleasure experienced by Rebekah) are valuable, and someone has reason, not merely nonrational motivation, to promote these conditions.

2. For something to be valuable is for it to be valuable *simpliciter*. For instance, if the pleasure experienced by Rebekah is valuable and not merely the object of Rebekah's affection, it must be a good thing for this pleasure to obtain. That goodness is not itself relative to Rebekah.

3. For something to be a reason is for it to be a reason *simpliciter*. If anyone (for example, Rebekah) has reason to promote some condition (such as Rebekah's pleasure) and not merely nonrational motivation to promote the condition, then there must be reason to promote the condition. Rebekah has reason to promote the pleasure if and only if there is reason to promote it for Rebekah to glom onto. That reason is not itself relative to Rebekah.[38]

4. To have value is to have agent-neutral value; to be a reason is to be an agent-neutral reason. (This is derived from 2, 3, and the meaning of agent-neutrality.)

5. There are some agent-neutral values and agent-neutral reasons. (This is derived from 1 and 4.)

This strongest case rests on the idea—expressed in 2 and 3 and summarized in 4—that value and reason *must* be agent-neutral. But this key agent-neutralist idea has to be rejected by anyone who proposes the inclusion of a personal prerogative in morality, because any proposal to include a personal prerogative in morality involves some affirmation of agent-relative values and reasons and, hence, an acknowledgment that value and reason need not be agent-neutral.

Of course, even if we assume that value and reason need not be agent-neutral and that some values and reasons are agent-relative, it does not follow that no values and no reasons are agent-neutral. Some things may have agent-neutral value even though it is not essential to something having value that the value be agent-neutral. Some agents may have agent-neutral reasons even though it is not essential to an agent's having reasons that she have agent-neutral reasons. More specifically, even if some conditions can and do have agent-relative value, this does not preclude some of those conditions from also having agent-neutral value. While Rebekah's pleasure can and does have value-for-Rebekah, this does not rule out this pleasure also having agent-neutral value that beckons everyone to its production. (Rebekah gets beckoned and rebeckoned.) Still, the rejection of the key agent-neutralist idea on the grounds that there are, indeed, agent-relative values and reasons throws a heavy bur-

---

[38] I take claims like 2 and 3 to be central to Thomas Nagel's position in Thomas Nagel, *The Possibility of Altruism* (Oxford: Oxford University Press, 1970). Nagel came to reject these claims in his more recent work, *The View from Nowhere* (Oxford: Oxford University Press, 1986), in which he seeks to affirm the existence of both agent-neutral and agent-relative values.

den of proof on those who would assert that there are also some agent-neutral values and reasons. Here are some reasons why.

Once one recognizes the existence of agent-relative values and reasons for action, it is difficult not to see agent-neutral values and reasons as much more mysterious. Indeed, the often-noted mysteriousness of the value or goodness of this or that condition seems specifically to be a feature of agent-neutral value or goodness. It seems quite unmysterious that, in virtue of her career being the object of her aspiration or the fulfillment of her talents, Rebekah's career as a pianist should have value-for-Rebekah and that she should have reason to advance that career. Being the object of one's aspirations or the fulfillment of one's talents seems to be the sort of relational feature of an object that can make the object valuable for the person who stands in that relation, which would make the object beckon to the person in that relation. By definition, however, no comparable sense can be made of the claim that Rebekah's career is a value that stands above and beyond its value-for-Rebekah and that beckons everyone to bring it about.

The standard and seemingly minimally contentious view about an agent's rationality in the pursuit of ends is that this rationality consists in an agent's effective pursuit of her own ends, utility, or welfare. The most serious challenge to this view of rationality in the pursuit of ends comes from the key agent-neutralist idea that values and reasons must be agent-neutral. For if value must be agent-neutral, there is nothing special for any given agent about her own ends, utility, or welfare. We have just noted, however, that this agent-neutralist idea has to be rejected by the advocate of *any* prerogative. So, given that morality should contain some sort of prerogative, the strongest challenge to the standard view has to be dismissed. In our thinking about rationality in the pursuit of ends, we should at least start with the minimally contentious view. If we start with this view, however, it is very difficult to make a plausible case for going beyond it to the view that an agent's rationality in the pursuit of ends consists in her effective pursuit of some combination of her own ends, utility, or welfare *and* the ends, utility, or welfare of others. Indeed, a reliable formula for coming up with a bad argument in moral philosophy is: Come up with an argument that moves from the rationality of each agent's pursuit of her own ends, utility, or welfare to the rationality of each agent's pursuit of others' ends, utility, or welfare. Mill's argument from each person's happiness being the good for that person, and hence providing that person with reason for its promotion, to everyone's happiness being the good for everyone, and hence providing everyone with reason to promote the aggregate good, is only the most notorious testimony to the reliability of this formula.[39]

---

[39] John Stuart Mill, *Utilitarianism* (1861; reprint, Indianapolis: Bobbs-Merrill, 1957), 44–45.

Many arguments in support of impersonal demands are readily deconstructed once there is a recognition of agent-relative values and reasons. For instance, Mill's argument can be seen as first establishing the value of each individual's happiness on the basis of that happiness being desired by the individual and then inferring, by way of a failure to distinguish between agent-relative and agent-neutral value, that each individual's happiness has agent-neutral value. Another well-known argument begins by pointing out that nothing could be more rational than Rebekah's choosing a smaller pain at the dentist's office today so as to avoid a larger pain at the dentist's office next week. It is suggested that what makes this choice rational is simply the greater badness of the larger pain. It is then pointed out that the same choice between a smaller pain and a larger pain is present when a larger pain located within Joshua can be prevented by a smaller pain within Rebekah. Given the account of the rationality of the intrapersonal trade-off of a larger pain for a smaller pain, the interpersonal trade-off must also be rational. The agent-relativist deconstruction of this argument challenges its account of the rationality of the intrapersonal choice. What really makes it rational for Rebekah to go to the dentist today and not wait until next week is that next week's pain will be more *bad-for-Rebekah* than today's pain will be *bad-for-Rebekah*.

Here is one final consideration against the affirmation of agent-neutral values, given the affirmation of agent-relative values. If both agent-relative and agent-neutral values are affirmed, then in making ends-oriented decisions about how to act, each agent will have to weigh the overall agent-relative value of her most personally rewarding action against the overall agent-neutral value of her most agent-neutrally valuable action. On what scale of values is this weighing supposed to take place? It is not merely that it would be difficult to know exactly (or even roughly) what M is. The problem is that there is the same sort of incommensurability between value-for-Rebekah and value *simpliciter* as there is between value-for-Rebekah and value-for-Joshua. Suppose that both agent-relative and agent-neutral value are affirmed and that action p ranks highest in terms of value-for-Rebekah and action o ranks highest in terms of value *simpliciter*. No amount of flawless deliberation will get Rebekah beyond the utterly unhelpful conclusion that p is better on the scale of value-for-Rebekah and o is better on the scale of agent-neutral value.

V. The Individualist Prerogative without Restrictions Is Unacceptable

The rationale for the individualist prerogative is the complete moral liberation of the personal point of view as it is realized in each individual. Moral liberation from what? As the personal standpoint replaces the impersonal standpoint, as the former becomes (relatively) more and more weighty, until one arrives at the special case in which the personal is affirmed and the impersonal is rejected, the immediate source of threat to the moral independence of the personal standpoint as it is realized in a given individual shifts from the impersonal standpoint to the personal standpoint as it is realized in other individuals. As the threat of moral subordination to the impersonal standpoint is preemptively checked, the threat to the individual of moral subordination to the personal standpoint as it is realized in other individuals comes to the fore.[40]

With the argument for the rationale for the individualist prerogative, we have arrived at the limiting case. The threat from the impersonal standpoint is entirely checked, so that all that is needed for insulation against subordination to the impersonal standpoint are reminders that this standpoint is spurious. At this point, the imminent threat to the moral independence of the personal point of view as it is realized in any given individual comes from the personal standpoint as it is realized in other individuals. "[T]he demand that [individuals] organize their conduct in accordance with some canon of impersonal optimality"[41] retreats before the dismissal of the impersonal standpoint. But this retreat invites the demand that the individual organize her conduct in accordance with one or another of the canons of *personal* optimality that others are now free to invoke. Thus, the primary function of the individualist prerogative and, I shall argue, its accompanying restrictions is to insulate each individual from moral subordination to the personal standpoint as it is realized in other individuals.

Let us start with the way in which the individualist prerogative insulates Rebekah from self-imposed subordination to the demands that proceed from the personal point of view as it is realized in other individuals. If Rebekah performs action *p*, she will experience a patch of sensorial pleasure, but if she performs a different action, Joshua will experience a greater pleasure. Previously, we have spoken of this alternative action as action *o*, the impersonally optimal action. However, informed as he is about the dismissal of the impersonal standpoint, Joshua does not call upon Rebekah to perform this alternative action in virtue of its impersonal optimality. Rather, he points out how beneficial this action would be for him. He points out that Rebekah can readily see how valuable-for-

---

[40] Scheffler never explicitly recognizes that as the personal standpoint becomes relatively weightier, its realization in others becomes more and more the source of the threat to Rebekah's moral independence. It is this substitution that underlies the problem identified by philosopher Shelly Kagan, namely, that in the exercise of their prerogative others will be allowed to harm Rebekah unless those others are also subject to restrictions. This problem leads Scheffler to consider including restrictions against "non-optimal harming" in his moral theory—but not, of course, restrictions against optimal harming. See Shelly Kagan, "Does Consequentialism Demand Too Much? Recent Work on the Limits of Obligation," *Philosophy and Public Affairs* 13, no. 3 (1984): 239–54; and Scheffler's "Prerogatives without Restrictions" (cited above in note 8).

[41] Scheffler, *The Rejection of Consequentialism*, 94.

Joshua this alternative action would be and how much reason Joshua has for favoring Rebekah's performance of it rather than action *p*. Joshua says:

> I'm not going to try to hoodwink you with fast and spurious talk about the alternative action being the impersonally optimal one. I'm simply pointing out that the outcome of the alternative action— formerly known as *o*—would be really really good for me, considerably more good for me than your performing *p* would be good for you. Surely you, Rebekah, cannot think that your good is somehow cosmically more important than my good. Surely you cannot think that your good is so much more important than my good that you should think it is better for your very small patch of sensorial pleasure to obtain than for my very large patch of sensorial pleasure to obtain.[42] If you appreciate the magnitude of the value of my much greater pleasure, you will decide to forgo your lesser pleasure so that my greater value will be realized.

Joshua here calls for Rebekah's self-imposed ("direct") subordination to Joshua's personal standpoint.

The individualist prerogative performs the not very arduous task of insulating Rebekah against this moral self-subordination. The good that Joshua invokes is genuine, and the individualist prerogative protects Rebekah from the call that she serve this genuine good by advising her to look to her own concerns and commitments, her own ends, utility, or good. The reasoning behind this prerogative allows Rebekah to deconstruct whatever appeal Joshua's proposal might seem to have. It allows her to point out that she does recognize the great value-for-Joshua that a large patch of experienced-by-Joshua pleasure would have; she does appreciate the magnitude of that value. However, that value provides reason for Joshua to promote the pleasure and not reason for Rebekah. In taking this stance, Rebekah is not holding that her good is somehow cosmically more important than Joshua's. She simply takes her pleasure to be more valuable-for-Rebekah than Joshua's pleasure would be, just as she recognizes that Joshua's pleasure would be more valuable-for-Joshua than Rebekah's pleasure would be. The reasons behind the prerogative also remind Rebekah that there is no genuine agent-neutral value attached to Joshua's pleasure for Joshua to invoke in support of Rebekah's self-imposed sacrifice.

---

[42] Whenever I have supposed a situation in which Rebekah's smaller pleasure and Joshua's greater pleasure cannot both obtain, I have also assumed away a philosophically very important and common feature of such situations, namely, that Joshua can *purchase* Rebekah's performance of the alternative action in an exchange that benefits both parties. A system of robust prerogatives and restrictions encourages discovery of and engagement in such mutually beneficial exchanges by eliminating the prospect of achieving gains through inducing or imposing sacrifices.

Consider now a morality that consists simply in this individualist prerogative. Following Scheffler's terminology, we can call this the "individualist hybrid." Under the individualist hybrid, each individual is entirely liberated from the moral demand that she voluntarily sacrifice her good for the good of other individuals and, as a reminder, is also entirely liberated from the moral demand that she sacrifice for the overall good. Would this hybrid morality satisfy the rationale for the adoption of the individualist prerogative? At the outset of the previous section, I noted the general conclusion that is indicated by our examination of Scheffler's advocacy of hybrid morality. To the extent that a prerogative is introduced into morality in order to accommodate the personal point of view, the rationale for the introduction of that prerogative will not be satisfied unless the prerogative is accompanied by restrictions against suppression of its exercise. I also mentioned that an even stronger conclusion is indicated. The more robust the introduced prerogative is, the more robust the accompanying restrictions must be. Since the individualist prerogative is maximally robust, one would expect that the rationale for its introduction will not be satisfied unless it is accompanied by maximally robust restrictions—maximally robust restrictions against suppressions of the exercise of the individualist prerogative.

The crucial move in arriving at these conclusions was the recognition that the moral independence of the personal point of view can be threatened in two different ways, along two different dimensions. It can be threatened if a morality calls upon the individual to submit herself sacrificially to external demands—the demands of an impersonal calculus *or* the demands of another's individual good. And it can be threatened if a morality allows or even requires others to submit her sacrificially to their impersonal *or* personal demands. Thus, a morality can suborn Rebekah's personal point of view both by way of what it requires *of Rebekah* and by way of what it allows to or even requires *of others* in their treatment of Rebekah. Since there are these two dimensions along which the personal point of view (as realized in any given individual) can be subjugated to impersonal demands *or* to the personal demands of other individuals, and since the prerogative only deals with the first of these dimensions, the introduction of a prerogative cannot by itself satisfy the rationale for its introduction.

We have seen that with the adoption of the rationale for the individualist prerogative, the source of the threat to the moral independence of the personal standpoint as it is realized in a given individual shifts: whereas the threat once came from the impersonal standpoint, it now comes from the personal standpoint as it is realized in other individuals. The individualist prerogative insulates the individual against the first form or dimension of this threat by insulating her against the demand that she impose sacrifices on herself. But the individualist hybrid leaves the individual vulnerable to the second form or dimension of this threat. There are now all those other individuals, each of whom has been fully liberated from any requirement that he ever forgo personally rewarding actions because of the moral weightiness of the good of others. The individualist prerogative tells each individual that it is morally allowable for him to choose his most personally rewarding action. The affirmation of agent-relative values and the rejection of agent-neutral values tells each individual that, as far as *end-oriented* rationality is concerned, it is rational for him to choose the most personally rewarding action. As far as *end-oriented* rationality is concerned, his choice to advance his most personally rewarding alternative is both permissible and right.

So consider the moral position that the individualist hybrid puts Rebekah in vis-à-vis these other individuals. Just as Scheffler's hybrid morality (almost) always calls upon other individuals or the government to suppress Rebekah's exercise of her prerogative *if* doing so will be impersonally rewarding, the individualist hybrid always calls upon each individual to suppress Rebekah's exercise of her prerogative *if* doing so will be personally rewarding for that individual. Just as Scheffler's hybrid morally subordinates the personal standpoint as it is realized in Rebekah to the impersonal standpoint, the individualist hybrid morally subordinates the personal standpoint as it is realized in Rebekah to the now marauding personal standpoints of every other individual.

Someone might offer the counterargument that the individualist hybrid does not subordinate the personal standpoint as it is realized in Rebekah because it does not require Rebekah *directly* to choose the sacrificial alternative; it merely endorses the imposition of this sacrifice upon her by other individuals. But such a counterargument would be no more plausible than the response proposed by Scheffler—and disposed of in Section IV—that his hybrid morality does not subordinate the personal standpoint because it does not require Rebekah *directly* to choose the sacrificial alternative. Surely if a morality is said to subordinate the individual to external demands if it requires the individual to submit herself to those demands, then it must also be said to subordinate the individual to those demands if it endorses others' submitting her to those demands. Just as the inclusion in morality of Scheffler's bare prerogative fails to satisfy the rationale for the inclusion of that prerogative, the inclusion of a bare individualist prerogative in morality fails to satisfy the rationale for the inclusion of this prerogative. Just as the inclusion of the Schefflerian prerogative is unacceptable unless it is accompanied by restrictions against the suppression of its exercise, the inclusion of the individualist prerogative is unacceptable unless it is accompanied by restrictions against the suppression of its exercise.

Recall here another point made in Section IV. The point was that a morality will properly be said to subordinate Rebekah to the impersonal standpoint if, according to the morality, the government may proceed to suppress Rebekah's exercise of her prerogative whenever such suppression would be the impersonally most rewarding course of action. A morality that endorses the suppression of Rebekah's exercise of her prerogative whenever that suppression would serve the impersonal standpoint subordinates Rebekah to that standpoint even if, in fact, it is rarely the case that suppression of her exercise of her prerogative will actually promote the impersonally best outcome. Rebekah is, morally speaking, enslaved to the impersonal standpoint if she may be treated as a slave whenever that serves the impersonal standpoint—even if, in fact, treating her as a slave rarely serves that standpoint. Similarly, a morality will properly be said to subordinate Rebekah to the personal standpoints of diverse other individuals if, according to the morality, each of those individuals may proceed to suppress Rebekah's exercise of her prerogative whenever that suppression would be the personally most rewarding course of action for that other individual. A morality that endorses the suppression of Rebekah's exercise of her prerogative whenever such suppression would serve the personal standpoint of another individual subordinates Rebekah to that individual's standpoint even if, in fact, it is rarely the case that suppression of her exercise of her prerogative will promote an outcome that is personally best for the other individual.

We can dispose even more quickly here than we did in Section IV of the suggestion that the prerogative need not be accompanied by *restrictions* because it can instead be accompanied by a maxim calling upon individuals to minimize suppressions of the exercise of the prerogative. For, as we saw previously, this sort of maxim—whether it is aimed at minimizing suppressions of the Schefflerian prerogative or at minimizing suppressions of the individualist prerogative—reflects the ideas that each act of suppression is agent-neutrally bad, that fewer suppressions are agent-neutrally better overall than more suppressions, and that individuals ought to be guided by such judgments about agent-neutral value. There is, however, no room for such ideas within a morality grounded in the acceptance of agent-relative values and the rejection of agent-neutral values. Given this rejection, if there are to be fundamental limits on how the individual may be treated by others, those limits must take the form of deontic restrictions.

VI. Rights

Do not concomitant restrictions diminish the prerogatives they accompany? More on point, do restrictions on Rebekah against suppressing others' exercise of their individualist prerogatives diminish Rebekah's individualist prerogative? After all, there are actions that would seem to be allowed to Rebekah by the individualist prerogative yet are forbidden to her by these restrictions. However, if the accompanying restrictions do diminish the individualist prerogative, then, in the end, that prerogative is not maximal. This is troublesome. For it suggests that a morality with only an individualist prerogative (i.e., the individualist hybrid) would better protect the moral independence of the personal standpoint along the first, self-imposed subordination dimension than would a morality with an individualist prerogative accompanied by restrictions. This would leave the advocate of a morality with the prerogative and accompanying restrictions in the very uncomfortable position of having to say that he favors that morality over the individualist hybrid because *overall*, across the self-imposed and other-imposed dimensions, it does a better job of protecting the moral independence of the personal standpoint. This would be uncomfortable because it seems to involve comparisons across incommensurable dimensions.

Fortunately, however, the restrictions do not diminish the prerogative they accompany. More precisely, there is a natural initial understanding of the individualist prerogative such that no conduct on Rebekah's part that is sanctioned by her individualist prerogative is forbidden by her being subject to a restriction against suppressing others' exercise of their individualist prerogative. What is this natural initial understanding of the individualist prerogative? It is that each individual may especially devote *herself* (e.g., her personal resources, talents, and energies) to the promotion of her own valued ends. For each individual, her prerogative operates upon or ranges over a certain discrete set of resources: to begin with, the various resources for purposive action that constitute her person.[43] For each individual, the individualist prerogative sanctions her devotion of the personal resources that fall within the ambit of her prerogative to her own valued ends. Since the personal resources that Rebekah's prerogative operates upon and the personal resources that Joshua's prerogative operates upon are distinct sets of resources, Rebekah's prerogative does not sanction her devotion of the resources that are within the ambit of Joshua's prerogative to the promotion of her own ends. This is why, given this natural initial understanding of the prerogative, Rebekah's being subject to a restriction against suppressing Joshua's exercise of his prerogative does not prohibit any conduct on Rebekah's part that is endorsed by her prerogative.

Why is this the "natural initial understanding" of the individualist prerogative? The answer to this question begins with recollecting that the introduction of any personal prerogative constitutes a departure from full consequentialism and, more specifically, from consequentialism's first implication: that each individual ought to devote *herself* to the promotion of the overall best. Any personal prerogative departure from this feature of full consequentialism is naturally understood as sanctioning each indi-

---

[43] I say "to begin with" to signal that in this essay we are proceeding as though the only resources for the promotion of personal or impersonal ends are persons themselves, i.e., their various capacities, parts, and energies. One might, however, investigate whether persons have prerogatives over the disposition of external resources and whether they are subject to restrictions against suppressing others' exercise of such prerogatives.

vidual's devotion of *herself*, at least to some extent, to her own most valued outcomes. Moreover, essential to the appeal of any proposed prerogative is the anticipation that under it *each* individual will be warranted in devoting herself, at least to some degree, to her personally most highly valued ends. A proposed prerogative will have this appeal only if it is understood as *not* also sanctioning each individual's devotion of *other* individuals to her valued ends—a devotion that would interfere with the other individuals' own exercise of the proposed prerogative.

That the natural initial understanding of any prerogative is that it specifies some degree to which each individual may devote *herself* to her own personal ends is confirmed by noticing that we implicitly understand Scheffler's prerogative in precisely this way. In presenting his prerogative, Scheffler repeatedly speaks of an agent's allocation of "energy and attention."[44] Under full consequentialism, "people ought to devote energy and attention to their projects and commitments in strict proportion to the weight from an impersonal standpoint of their doing so."[45] In contrast, the prerogative "would permit people to devote energy and attention to their projects and commitments out of proportion to the weight from an impersonal standpoint of their doing so."[46] *Whose* energy and attention? I think it is clear that we read all these passages as making claims about the agent's *own* energy and attention. Under full consequentialism, each agent may devote her *own* energy and attention to her personal projects and commitments only to the extent that this devotion of her energy and attention is impersonally best. Under Scheffler's prerogative, each agent may devote her *own* energy and attention to her personal projects and commitments to some greater extent. A condition of our finding the introduction of the Schefflerian prerogative plausible is our reading into it this identification of *whose* energy and attention the agent gets to devote to her personal ends. We presume that other people's energy and attention are not within the ambit of Rebekah's prerogative. For each agent, the prerogative operates over her own energy and attention and not over the energy or attention of others. And, of course, under (even) Scheffler's prerogative, it is not just an agent's own "energy and attention" that we understand the agent may especially devote to her personal ends. If Rebekah says, "Given that M = 4, I may retain my vital organs even though my evisceration would save three other lives," we do not expect Scheffler to say, "Well, I was talking about energy and attention, not bodily parts."

What, then, do the restrictions against suppressing exercises of the individualist prerogative add to a morality that already includes this prerogative? How do they block threats to the moral independence of the

---

[44] Ibid., 9 and 16.
[45] Ibid., 17.
[46] Ibid., 21.

personal point of view? The restrictions morally *prohibit* Rebekah from devoting Joshua—that is, his energy, attention, bodily parts, and so on—to the promotion of her personal ends. They say that, in the exercise of her prerogative, Rebekah *must not* treat Joshua as though he is within the scope of the operation of her prerogative. Correlative to these restrictions is a right of Joshua to his own person and, hence, a right against being treated as though he is within the ambit of the operation of Rebekah's prerogative. It is this right that secures the moral independence of each person vis-à-vis his possible treatment by other individuals. The inclusion of these restrictions and correlative rights within morality *also* serves to make explicit the originally implicit understanding of the scope of the operation of the prerogative. If Rebekah must not treat other individuals as grist for her mill, then the scope of the operation of her prerogative should not be reinterpreted so that everyone is grist for Rebekah's mill. Proposals to move to a more expansive understanding of the scope of the operation of the prerogative—that is, proposals to go beyond the initial natural understanding of the prerogative—are to be rejected because such an understanding of the prerogative would bring it into conflict with the rights of individuals, which secure their moral independence vis-à-vis others' possible treatment of them. The addition of rights makes explicit and stabilizes the natural initial understanding of the scope of the individualist prerogative by ascribing to each person rights over what falls within the operation of her prerogative, namely, her own person.

Throughout the core of this essay, I have spoken of restrictions against the suppression of the exercise of one's prerogative. If we speak of restrictions in this way, then the correlative rights would be rights against the suppression of the exercise of one's prerogative. It is important to notice that this is not a right to the exercise of one's prerogative. If Joshua is unable to carry out activities that would be personally rewarding and others do not step forward to enable him to carry them out, Joshua's right against the suppression of the exercise of his prerogative has not been violated. What actions by others *would* violate Joshua's right? The answer again points to rights over specified sets of resources.[47] Joshua's rights are violated by actions that block Joshua's chosen employment of what is within the scope of the operation of his prerogative, that is, his chosen employment of his energy, attention, bodily parts, and so on. It is the right of each individual over his own person that underlies the right of each against the suppression of exercises of his prerogative. It is because Joshua possesses this right, while each other individual possesses rights over himself, that others do not violate Joshua's rights when they decline to devote themselves to enabling Joshua to carry out his personally rewarding activities. It is also because Joshua possesses this moral self-ownership

---

[47] I defend the view that rights are fundamentally jurisdictional claims in Eric Mack, "In Defense of the Jurisdiction Theory of Rights," *The Journal of Ethics* 4, nos. 1–2 (2000): 71–98.

that others do violate his rights when they suppress his chosen devotion of himself to his personal concerns and commitments *and*, incidentally, when they suppress his chosen sacrificial devotion of himself to the good of others.

VII. CONCLUSION

Prerogatives without restrictions are unacceptable—at least if the rationale for the introduction of prerogatives into morality is recognition of the moral independence of the personal standpoint. For the insulation of the personal point of view as it is realized in each individual from moral subordination to external demands requires both that the individual have a prerogative not to enslave herself to those demands and that others be restricted from enslaving her to those demands. The rationale for the adoption of a prerogative will not be satisfied unless that prerogative is accompanied by restrictions that prohibit others from suppressing its exercise. The more robust the prerogative that is introduced into morality, the more robust its underlying rationale will be, and the more robust will be its accompanying restrictions. The most robust prerogative—the individualist prerogative—always allows the individual to decline to sacrifice herself for the good of others, and its accompanying restrictions are restrictions against interference with the individual's choices about the ends to which she will devote *herself*. The moral right that is correlative to these restrictions is the right of self-ownership. This is precisely the moral right that Nozick gestures toward in his affirmation of moral rights at the outset of *Anarchy, State, and Utopia* and that he presupposes in arguments throughout that work.[48] By showing why anticonsequentialist argumentation ought not to halt when it arrives at the individualist prerogative, but instead ought to go on to restrictions against the suppression of exercises of that prerogative, I have provided a sustained justification for this crucial moral right.

Philosophy, Tulane University

---

[48] For instance, this right is presupposed in his arguments against coerced redistribution; see Nozick, *Anarchy, State, and Utopia*, 172.

INDEX

NATURAL RIGHTS LIBERALISM
FROM LOCKE TO NOZICK